THE COMPLETE ESSAYS OF

J. V. CUNNINGHAM

We are deeply indebted to Timothy Steele for his assistance with this project and to J. V. Cunningham's family, especially his niece Roberta Collinsworth, for their permission to collect his work in this volume.

THE COMPLETE ESSAYS OF
J. V. CUNNINGHAM

INTRODUCTION BY

JAMES MATTHEW WILSON

CONTENTS

I

WOE OR WONDER:
THE EMOTIONAL EFFECT OF SHAKESPEAREAN TRAGEDY

II

TRADITION & POETIC STRUCTURE

III

IV

V

INTRODUCTION

BY JAMES MATTHEW WILSON

Counter-Revolution

To encounter the work of J. V. Cunningham (1911-1985) as a young writer and be transformed by it, as I certainly was, requires one already to have been, in some sense, disenchanted with the art of poetry. "There is less to be said about literature than has been said, and this book adds a little more," runs the first sentence of his *Collected Essays*, and Cunningham dedicated his career as a poet and critic to saying things within and about literature while also recognizing that probably less needed to be said. "Say to her that I gave you few but true words," he writes in one of his finest poems, the early "Elegy for a Cricket." "A book you can't put down before you've read it," he mockingly complains of his own *Doctor Drink* (1950). Cunningham gives us a clear sense that terseness, brevity, the readiness to fall silent as soon as what must be said has been said, was not just a disposition of the author's character but a personal test of his truthfulness—no, more, it was a union of the two, a way of living and, only within that life, a way of knowing and writing. Taciturnity was to him a morality.

To appreciate that morality, again, one had to have some awareness of what exaggerated, voluble, and voluminous things had been said in poetry's favor. We mean by this, first of all, not mere falsehoods, but rather the romantic wish to say "[v]ery nice things" about the art, as Cunningham puts it: but most of those things "are not true." A liberal humanism and romanticism rooted in the sentiments had long insisted that poetry was in essence "elevated thought, imagination, or feeling," and that, the more strongly one felt, the better a poet one was. To see that balloon punctured, to see the gas running out for the gas that it was, was, in the sense I intend, to be disenchanted. The puncturing had taken place already in the criticism of Cunningham's great mentor and colleague, Yvor Winters, but Cunningham's work continued it; to change metaphors, to read his work was to turn away from the drunken ecstasies of romanticism in favor of sober clarity, even though it may be only a clear-eyed anger at what had been done in poetry's name, what had been done to the obscuration of actual poems, of their history, and of their meaning.

In Cunningham's lifetime, romantic enthusiasm, including the mode of it found in the New Criticism, gradually disappeared from the classroom, though it persisted in various forms in the work of later poets. What succeeded romanticism was something worse, those various hermeneutical methods that came to be called postmodern literary theory or just "theory." "Theory" comprehended *methods* indeed, in the sense that they required no actual thought, but only the application of someone else's thought to literary texts. It was criticism by recipe, a machine for the endless production of scholarly articles.

In substance, "theory" meant, first, the dissociation of writing from speech and meaning, best known as the "deconstruction" practiced by Jacques Derrida. "Theory" meant, second, the dissociation of all writing from those distinctive spheres of experience or knowing called the aesthetic, literature, or humane learning, through the "genealogical" researches of Michel Foucault. Deconstruction stripped the text of meaning and left it helpless before the willful play of its critics, who could then force it to mean whatever their derivative cleverness proposed. Genealogy stripped works of literature of their prestige as ways of encountering reality or acquiring truth or wisdom, so that the mere text could be studied as a site of ideological contestation, at once a residue, image, and a tool of the will to power. Genealogy dissolved the literary text into its possible political uses, even as it dissolved politics into methods of social control; deconstruction simply dissolved it into the will of the literary theorist. Cunningham's fellow poet (and friend in what would become the unofficial Winters Circle at Stanford University), Helen Pinkerton, in one of her late epigrams, would liken these practices to rape:

> Abusing its otherness, its soul and wit,
> He rapes the text, claiming its benefit—
> And that, inscrutable, it asked for it.

To encounter Cunningham's work, in such an age, was to see that the romantics were overblown and self-absorbed but also that the theorists who replaced them were vacuous and guilty of rapine. Had too much not once been said in favor of poetry by mere sentimental good will, perhaps the perverse reaction of "theory" with its reduction of everything to ill will would not have occurred. In Cunningham's work could be found the sober vision necessary to appreciate literature as an enduring good, one that kept beneath the romantic winds and turned its back in disdain on the facile debunking of the theorist.

To encounter Cunningham, the laconic poet of short lyrics and epigrams, who wrote many poems but few coming to more than a slender bundle of lines; to encounter Cunningham the scholar and literary critic who denominated his essays as works of "classical Classical Philology"; to encounter poems and essays alike, was to discover a way of living that saw through the pretensions of the romantics and the willful depredations of the theorists. His work drew one to a clearer, more austere, more definite, more bracing, more hard-headed, and more modest understanding of poetry and the literary life. One did not even need to understand the meaning of Cunningham's poems—and his abstract style and unusual concerns, as he confessed, rendered some of them obscure. It was sufficient to experience the gripped restraint of the lines themselves to know that they stood against much haze and bluster in favor of a more classical and jaundiced kind of perception. So we find in this memorable and transparent epigram against latter-day romanticism:

> This *Humanist* whom no beliefs constrained
> Grew so broad-minded he was scatter-brained.

And so we find in this more cryptic, prototypical Cunningham verse that straddles the epigrammatic and the lyric mode:

> The dry soul rages. The unfeeling feel
> With the dry vehemence of the unreal.
> So I in the Idea of your arms, unwon,
> Am as the real in the unreal undone.

Cunningham's taut verse loosened the arms of the dreamed up Ideal woman of poetry to see the real thing, plain though she may be, with a "dry soul." His essays did the same. Deliberately and dryly academic in some ways, they were not academic in the sense of being at a remove from human experience. Cunningham showed a great respect for the possibilities that methods of careful scholarship opened. Much of his work takes for explicit subject one modest interpretative question or another in literary history, particularly those touching on the poetry of the English renaissance. In contrast with Winters, whose literary criticism was consistently polemical and vehement even at its most scholarly, Cunningham was more than willing simply to settle questions of fact. Despite the staid subject matter and academic method, however, Cunningham's essays constituted a wrestling with human experience: one which insisted the road to knowledge involves neither swollen rhetoric nor a nihilistic toying with meaning's elusiveness, but discipline, training, and a patience in going about the art of discovery. It might be best to say that his essays seek to overcome human experience, or rather, the way in which we allow our own experience to obscure the historical reality of literature's meaning. His aim was truth.

Cunningham's epigrammatic style in the poem often found its echo in the epigrammatic apothegms of the literary essays, formulations at once dry and wry. On a popular liberal humanist misinterpretation of Shakespeare, he observes, "we constructed the fact from our feeling." Revisiting the phenomenon later, he says that the one who appreciates "a work of art . . . in defiance of the known historical intention of the work . . . is not integrating in his experience the experience of the past . . . he is abusing the monuments of history to inform them with his own life." Of the literary text, which outlives us and stands outside of us, where we can see it and discuss it, he states with finality, "It is a thing external and eternal, a potentiality of experience waiting to be realized. It is the poem." Correcting another misinterpretation that occurs when imperceptive readers encounter Andrew Marvell's verse concerning "vegetable love," in "To His Coy Mistress," Cunningham sighs, "They envisage some monstrous and expanding cabbage."

Summing up the paradox on which the work of Chaucer and all poets depends, he observes, "He was an artist, and he worked by artifice, for he knew that realism is artifice." Speaking of modernist poetry in general, Cunningham considers another paradox: it depends on its readers' "customary expectation to be disappointed. The new is parasitic upon the old." In his diagnosis of Wallace Stevens's modernist metaphysics and method, he notes, "Stevens had a homemade machine for the endless production of poems." Opining on his own work, he says, more favorably, "verse is a professional activity, social and objective, and its methods and standards are those of craftsmanship." And, to leave off with this list: aware that truisms will often be startling in our day because the true and obvious goes so often obscured, he writes, "a good poem is the definitive statement in meter of something worth saying." To encounter passages such as these was to realize that, though much had been said about literature—too much in fact—the little that needed to be said had not properly been expressed. Cunningham did what he could to say that little in little at last.

To discover Cunningham's work, in sum, was to discover the poetry and criticism of a writer who was deliberately unfashionable, because fashion belonged to an age of charlatans. He was deliberately taciturn and plodding, because emotional logorrhea had already undone other minds and draped the truth beneath gaudy and falsifying glosses. To follow him on the path, however tentatively and with however many reservations, was to break bread with the modestly great; it was to learn the meaning and practice of poetry in an atmosphere of seriousness and near silence; it was to set out on pilgrimage in search of a more classical, more disciplined, more compelling and intelligent way of living, knowing, and writing in the world.

I have consistently made joint reference to his poems and his essays and this is not accidental. The attitude to be found in both is one and the same. His scholarship takes poetry for subject, but his poems often enough take scholarship for subject in turn. Among the last essays collected in this volume, we find Cunningham providing prose commentaries on his own verse. As he himself put it, "verse and prose are different dialects of a common language." His work in verse and prose were two ways of speaking within a single way of life; they were complementary means toward a single end. To encounter the fullness of Cunningham's language, to encounter the poet whole, we must also come to know the scholar. Academic though his essays' subjects often are, and as strictly historical as their claims most certainly are, they manage to become also more or less veiled expressions of his grappling with experience as a poet. The poet was inseparable from the critic, and the critic helps us better to appreciate the poet. The critic and the poet are one.

Drawing to a close his thoughts on the modernist literary revolution that had come to be represented by the mandarin authority of T. S. Eliot, Cunningham states plainly, "we need a counter-revolution." To read the epigrams and essays of Cunningham is to know the bliss of dawn of the counter-revolution.

Of Rage and Pedantry

Unfashionable indeed. Unromantic indeed. Intelligent indeed. Counter-revolutionary indeed.

Born in 1911, Cunningham was "a renegade Irish Catholic from the plains of Montana." Although he claimed to be "a Catholic by tradition, training, and deep feeling," the most obvious formative influences in his life were not that. Rather, as

Timothy Steele writes in his introduction to *The Poems of J. V. Cunningham* (1997), the great event of his life was the Black Tuesday stock market crash of 1929. Cunningham's father had died in a construction accident in 1926. With the Crash and the onset of the Great Depression, his family life was further disrupted. He spent the next two years "wandering through the Southwest, trying to eke out a living by freelance writing for trade journals of the day," Steele tells us.

In 1931, he wrote a letter to the already distinguished young poet and critic Yvor Winters. He soon came to Palo Alto, moved into a shed in the backyard of the Winters's family homestead, and enrolled at Stanford. As had also been the case with Winters, initiation into the scholarly discipline and methods, under the mentorship of William Dinsmore Briggs, opened up a whole new way of life. Cunningham earned his undergraduate and doctoral degrees at Stanford. After a series of short-term teaching posts, he joined the faculty of Brandeis University in 1953, where he taught for the rest of his life. His method of instruction combined both the attentive listening to the poem read aloud with the patient historical exegesis of its meaning. He considered such practices to stand athwart those of the New Critics, chiefly because of their concern with the facts of literary history and the sounding of the poem, and he would later state with some pride that his was among the best graduate programs in the country. Much like Winters before him, his own mentorship would aid the career of an impressive number of distinguished poets and writers. He died in 1985.

Few poets and critics could have taken for the founding principles of their work less auspicious materials than did Cunningham. Those principles were five in number. They emerge no doubt from his experience of penury during the Depression and the modest but unprecedented consolation that came from studying alongside the combative and "reactionary" poet-critic, Winters, and also from studying under the staid senior scholar, Briggs.

"All Choice Is Error," the title of one of his early poems declares, and Cunningham believed it. Freedom exists only in possibility; actuality determines being and therefore diminishes it. Everything that could be is, in time, reduced to history, that is to say, historical particularity or determined fact. That was the first principle. The second was rage. If every moment of one's life is nothing other than the further determination and diminution of that life, then this was just the opposite of what life seemed to promise. It promised purpose, aim, actualization, freedom, and fulfillment; it meets with calcification, frustration, and extinction. And so, the mind's only freedom in the human condition is a retrospective, ineffectual rage. Cunningham says just this in one of his epigrams: "dispassionate hate / Is my redemption though it come too late." The consolation of rage is to come to know, and in that sense master, the determined details of time. It is to know history, and so a third principle has only one name: pedantry. "I am a pedant," writes Cunningham, in his brief essay, "Graduate Training in English."

Wisdom sees things whole; wisdom uplifts the soul beyond itself, from the perception of individual truths to the contemplation of them within the transcendent unity of Truth, or so tradition says. There is no such thing as wisdom, Cunningham dryly asserts. Just as life breaks things down to determined acts, which is sad, history breaks all things down to determined details, which are facts. Life and history together are a collection of sad facts. All may rage at this, but it takes a pedant to resign oneself to knowing them and asking no more, to understanding them without mistaking understanding for transcendence.

Cunningham's species of pedantry had two chief facts in view: verse and tradition. To know verse is to know what poetry is and how it can be written. This, Cunningham holds—however uninspiring the idea may seem—is to say that poetry and verse are one. Both words mean nothing other than the making of propositions through "metrical composition." To know the tradition is to know what kinds of things poems have said, what they have meant, and, measuring that meaning against history and experience, to know what makes a good poem. A "good poem is the definitive statement in meter of something worth saying," concludes Cunningham. Verse is poetry; the tradition is the sum total of the different ways things worth saying have been said in poetry. Verse and tradition are the fourth and fifth principles that ground Cunningham's work.

The ordering of these principles is not accidental. They follow from one another in a determined and meaningful sequence. It could be the case, for instance, that Cunningham as a scholar was merely pedantic, and his dismay at the New Critics and those more egregious forms of romantic charlatanry upset him to the point of rage. This indeed is what John Williams gives us in his wonderful campus novel, *Stoner* (1965), in its title character, William Stoner, who is generally regarded to be based on Cunningham. Stoner, who has escaped from the dreary frustrations of farm life through the careful work of literary scholarship, reacts with a rare instance of rage when he encounters the graduate student Charles Walker. During his qualifying exams for the doctorate, Walker attempts to conceal his scholarly incompetence with smooth rhetoric. Stoner's anger follows from his seeing the goods of scholarship, of pedantry, ravaged. The pedantic soul rages.

In Cunningham's case, however, it is certainly more proper to say that pedantry follows rage rather than vice versa. Rage is the first available free response to the determinations of history, and pedantry follows from it. The raging soul "pedants." Pedantry becomes the consolation and calming of rage because only the careful and docile use of scholarly methods makes the mind adequate to the historical fact; it reduces the mind to what is. Let us, then, consider each of these principles individually and in order.

Being as Exclusion

Winters spoke in his great essay, "The Morality of Poetry" (found in *In Defense of Reason*), of the necessary "tragic attitude" of the poet or of anyone who would live well. We recognize our own finitude and put "by the claims of the world without the abandonment of self-control, without the loss of the ability to go on living, for the present, intelligently and well." This strengthening of the inner self, particularly of the mind, in the face of an external world beyond our control and sometimes arrayed against us, is the attitude most often found in Winters's poems and in the poems by others he championed. It is often described more or less rightly as a stoic attitude (to which point we shall return).

Winters hardly knew what to do with the radical mutation of his tragic idea that took place in the mind of Cunningham. In a poem we have already cited, "All Choice Is Error," Cunningham writes, after tracing the "sad initials" of a beloved he has carved in the bark of a "Gaunt tree,"

> All choice is error, the tragical mistake,
> And you are mine because I name you mine.
> Kiss, then, in pledge of the imponderables
> That tilt the balance of eternity

A leaf's weight up or down. Though we must part
While each dawn darkens on the fortunate wheel,
The moon will not soften our names cut here
Till every sheltering bird has fled the nest.
They know the wind brings rain, and rain and wind
Will smooth the outlines of our lettering
To the simplicity of epitaph.

The lover looks upon the inscribed initials as the fact of their love. The first full sentence of this stanza has a double valence: the beloved is his because of the fact of his naming her with the engraved initials; but this means that she is also his "tragical mistake," his "choice." Their love lives not as a spirit, elusive, non-material and enduring, but only in the lines cut in drying wood. The wooden fact is what makes the beloved "mine." It is their love. As time passes, the outline of initials will become weathered and fade. The fact of love that is the initials will be reduced to an epitaph, to a reminder of what is no more, but this reduction only follows from and furthers what was already the reduction of the spirit of love to the fact of the initials carved in the tree trunk.

Every action, the poem indicates, is a reduction. Every choice moves us from the freedom, but also the non-existence, of possibility or potential to the determined, fixed, reduced reality of the actual fact. The beloved is the lover's tragical mistake, because he chooses her. In choosing her he excludes all other possible loves, but were he to choose another, she would be no less a mistake, no less an occasion to exclude other possibilities. The error is exclusion, determination, but *every* choice entails these things. Cunningham's poem "Haecceity" states this judgment more bluntly:

Evil is any this or this
Pursued beyond hypothesis.

It is the scribbling of affection
On the blank pages of perfection.

Hypothesis is good, hypothesis is freedom. Actuality, "this absolute of fact," precisely because it is "act," is evil. All choice is a surrender of freedom and a diminution of possibility, which alone is "perfection."

In Winters's poem, "Inscription for a Graveyard," he ponders the freedom of the hearts of the living, which are so mutable as to dazzle us with their swarming variability. This contrasts with the dead who, in exchange for "choice" have "now certainty," the fixity of death and eternity. Cunningham's poem undermines this distinction between life as actual freedom and death as a state of final fixity. Every act of the living is a summoning from the non-existence, but also from the freedom, of "blank" potential to the fixed, determined fact of actual existence. Every act, far from a realization, is a diminishment, of our being. The difference between life and death is only in the degree of our fixity.

In "The Quest of the Opal," Cunningham's prose commentary on his early poems, he states that this idea was of "the greatest importance . . . at least for the author." As he explains it there, "choice implies exclusion, rejection, restriction, limitation. To choose *this* is not only to prefer one thing to something else, but rather to prefer it to everything else." In one sense, this will be familiar to all of us. To order the beef wellington for dinner generally entails forgoing the chicken parmesan; we can spend our afternoon either at a friend's birthday party or at the football game taking place simultaneously across town, but usually not both. How many human decisions are taken with fear and trembling merely because we know that by doing *this*, we will never get to do *that*.

In another sense, however, Cunningham's idea of action as reduction, determination, and exclusion will seem perverse. If Cunningham found his idea of great importance, perhaps I can be forgiven for claiming its antithesis is of even greater importance. I would, in fact, dare to say that it may be the most important discovery in the western philosophical tradition. Aristotle, in the first book of his *Physics*, engages the monism found in the thought of many of his pre-Socratic predecessors. "All things are one," some of those voices declared. The appearance of individuality, difference, and change was a mere illusion; to discover truth was to sink into the mystical oneness of being. Other voices said just the opposite: only change is real, and in the endless flux of things nothing is one. There is no "being" but only "becoming."

Aristotle replies by saying that such claims are not helpful beginnings to inquiry; they are indeed not even serious (*Physics* 185a). We can take for granted that a multiplicity of things exist, that they change—meaning come into and go out of being—as we can see with our own eyes. We can also take for granted that all things are in some sense one, but not in a sense that requires us to deny individuation and the change or movement of individual beings. Things are one in the sense that they can be referred to a common principle—and that principle is being, in which all things share. The challenge, then, argues Aristotle, is not to affirm either oneness or change, which are obvious, but to explain how change is possible within the oneness of the principle of being and vice versa.

Aristotle invents the field of physics in the course of explaining the principles of being that allow change to occur within it.

They are three: substance, potency, and actuality. A substance is an individual that exists or has being. All the substances in nature are subject to change, because to be "natural," for Aristotle, means to be changeable. Either a substance's material stays the same, but is changed to take on different form, as when clay is molded from a lump to a pot, or the form remains the same, while the matter is transformed, as in the animal that sustains its being by taking food into itself. As he unfolds the implication of this theory, Aristotle makes clear that all substances, insofar as they are at all, are somewhere in the process of moving from mere, passive potency to a fullness of activity or actuality, or from actuality back to potency. In this movement we see that some sub-stratum (substance) always remains the same while some aspect of it undergoes the change.

We come to understand the nature of substances when we discover the forms, that is to say, the active intellectual principles, that cause mere passive matter to be realized (brought into act) as this or that particular substance (or being). Things are real insofar as they have journeyed from potency to actuality, from passivity to activity. The apparently exclusive theses—either all being is one or all is continuous change—are finally reconciled in Aristotle's thought. Change is nothing other than the process by which the non-existent oneness of *material* potency comes into being as a multitude of actual, existing *formed* substances. To be in-formed is to be enacted, to be made actual; and, to become actualized, is therefore to enjoy a fullness of being. To attain form is to emerge from mere potential and to become more fully real, to become more substantial (a proper something rather than nothing)—and all beings seek by their nature to pursue this course. Beings seek to become more fully themselves by becoming actual. The more active we are, the more fully we exist.

Aristotle's discovery of a philosophically compelling account of change was in itself a monumental discovery that dismissed forever some of the mystical paradoxes of early Greek thought and its oriental sources. The principles of being, potency, and actuality made possible a further discovery, however, and this is the subject of Book II of Aristotle's *Physics*. There, Aristotle argues that we can come to understand the nature of change and the nature of changeable (or natural) being insofar as we understand the causes of that change. To come to a knowledge of causes is the definition of *science*; all scientific activity is the study of causes. They are four in number. Listed in order of least to greatest importance, they are: the material cause, the efficient cause, the formal cause, and the final cause.

Earlier philosophers, Aristotle observes, had held that the material cause—the stuff of which something is made—was the primary or even sole cause needed to understand a substance. A house is a house, because it is made of stone, was a classic instance. All beings are made of fire or of water, was another. In modern parlance, we sometimes hear that human beings are "just" their "genes."

But this is all preposterous. Matter is the passive stuff that has no real identity as a being until it has received form. The active principle of form is what causes this-or-that matter to become the kind of thing that it is; form is the essence, the nature, the actuating principle of a thing. Genes would not be genes had more fundamental parts not been formed into the gene. While genes are part of the human being, there would be no actual human being were those various genes not formed, essentially united, into the greater whole that is the human form. To speak of material causality to the exclusion of formal causality is to speak incoherently and arbitrarily. Incoherently, because one is still speaking about forms (matter without form would be nothing but passive potency to receive form; there would be nothing to say about it in itself). Arbitrarily, because one is electing to count some forms as real (stone) while excluding others from reality (houses).

The efficient cause is the particular agent that occasions the union of form and matter. An efficient cause is always itself actual, that is, an acting agent, and so is in this sense more important than the material cause, but it is less important than the formal cause, because form is the very essence of a thing; form is what makes a being actual by conferring *quiddity*, whatness, upon it. The most important of the causes, however, indeed the cause of causes, is the final cause, what is called the *telos*. The *telos* of a thing is the why, the for-sake-of which, the purpose and goal of a being. The formal cause acts; the *telos* is the end to be actualized and achieved, such that a being in a state of potency can become most fully itself, so that it can realize its potential and fulfill its nature as a particular kind of being, as a good. What a thing is for determines the form, as many of us know from the familiar axiom, "form follows function." Houses are made of stone, wood, and straw (material causes), and shaped in a particular way (formal cause), only because of the end they serve, which is as a shelter from the elements (final cause).

Aristotle's argument, as one would expect from its opening gestures, leads us to a particular vision of reality. We see that reality is one insofar as it all operates on shared principles. Those principles include the possibility of change. We see that change is generally (though not always) directed or purposeful; the natural is what occurs all or most of the time. We can understand the world because we can perceive those purposes, those goods, both when they are actualized and when they are frustrated. We can also perceive when things are *not* purposefully done, but only within the broader, indeed universal, context of nature as the realm where purposeful change (aimed at some good) occurs. Things in the world operate in such a way that they come into being by moving from the mere potential attainment of some end to actually becoming the kinds of beings who are insofar as they actualize their natural end. If becoming actual is for a form to realize its being, it is also the case that becoming actual is to fulfill one's end, one's *telos*, one's good. And here is the most important point for our purposes: to become some particular being is to become *more* rather than *less* real, *more* rather than *less* actual, and *more* rather than *less* good.

Cunningham's thesis holds just the opposite. He rejects the identification of fullness-of-being with being-in-act, and he rejects final causality, the good proper for a being to attain, as the primary way in which we know what something is. Potency alone is fullness, albeit nonexistent fullness. Actuality is not a fulfillment of being, but a diminishment and determination of it. The journey from potency to actuality is in fact a decline from boundless fullness and oneness of Being to a bounded (withered), fixed oneness of beings. Potency is goodness; actuality an evil. A "fact" after all means, by definition, not an active principle, but a thing done, an achieved reality that cannot be changed. Facts are facts. We know them because they have been "reduced," or impoverished to act; we know them not because of what they are for, but because of what they have been rendered.

In his chapter on Cunningham in his last book, *Forms of Discovery* (1967), Winters viewed the inverted physics of his friend and colleague as bizarre:

what we have here is a kind of mysticism of pure passivity (which would be unconsciousness), of retreat to the womb . . . I have known Cunningham for more than thirty years; during these years, he has tried, as he tells us, to realize various choices in poetic form as precisely as possible. Yet his being (his intelligence) has increased, not diminished, from choice to choice. Cunningham is fully aware that he is more intelligent now than he was fifty years ago.

We shall see that in one sense Cunningham did not think himself "more intelligent" than he once had been; that depends on what one means by intelligence. But, on the whole, this seems a reasonable and serious criticism of Cunningham's inverted Aristotle. To be passive or potent is not to be at all; if every action is a determination and an exclusion, it is also a further realization, a further coming into being. Form limits, to be sure, but form makes actual. The freedom of a blank page, the freedom of potential is no *actual* freedom, but mere indeterminacy; freedom is a form's realization of its *telos* as it moves out of potential and into act. One substance excludes from its being another, but only as formed substance does being become *this actual being* rather than nothing at all or the formless protoplasm of possibility. Furthermore, nearly all our movements from potency to act are purposeful movements toward the achievement of some end, which is the good of our action. Aristotle's arguments are compelling for many reasons, not least because their antithesis is unintelligible.

But Cunningham's position is not without a response to all this. Underlying it is Cunningham's general rejection of understanding reality in terms of either physics (the philosophy of changeable being) or especially metaphysics (the philosophy of being per se, including that which is eternal and unchanging, such as the classical ideas of logic and mathematics). For Cunningham, the only permanence is mere possibility. Everything actual is actual only insofar as it enters into time and becomes a fixed part of the past. That is to say, the true science of changeable being is not Aristotelian physics but rather the study of history. It follows from Cunningham's understanding of the nature of choice that he be a pure historicist.

Cunningham's first book, *Woe or Wonder: The Emotional Effect of Shakespearean Tragedy*, begins by signaling his concern with history as one that goes beyond intellectual and literary history as usually conceived in his day to include the more elusive phenomena of emotion: "the quality and structure of the emotional life varies from society to society, for there is a history of the emotions as well as a history of ideas." To study that history involves setting aside one's own feelings and indeed setting aside "the critic's total impression of the work," as a principle of interpretation. Cunningham thus rejects the New Critical "doctrine of organic form," which would hold that the parts of a work must be interpreted in light of the whole (as we see it) and where apparent contradictions or tensions must be reconciled by way of a theory of "irony" and polysemantic complexity—or by any other means of saving the unity of the work.

Cunningham's study of the emotions supposed (by their authors) to be educed by tragic dramas will not concern itself with such reconciliations. In his study, the plays discussed are often reduced to their individual parts, which will indeed be fragments, so that we can see the way in which the playwrights express the classical Donatan theory of tragedy as involving great characters, "actions fearful in the extreme, and the outcome" as "sad" and involving violent "deaths." All this was done, according to the theory, for the sake of the author making the audience to feel fear, which will be refined in definition as the feeling of "woe" and also the more complicated feeling of "wonder." (Among the valuable historical recoveries in these chapters is an idea of which we can make no more than mention here because Cunningham does so little with it: the recognition of wonder as a principle of philosophical inquiry, rhetorical effect, and poetic phenomenon. This provides the necessary basis for recovering the Aristotelian vision of poetry and philosophy as intimately connected means of knowing reality).

Cunningham's study in the history of emotion may simply be that—a study, and one which implies no larger doctrinal commitments. In the body of the main text, he gives none, except insofar as he alternately patronizes and rejects those who would construct "the fact from our feeling," rather than seeking to ascertain the text's original, author-intended meaning. In two appendixes however, Cunningham outlines the principles undergirding his historical study.

In the first, Cunningham implicitly critiques Allen Tate's foundational essay for the New Critical movement, "Miss Emily and the Bibliographer" (1940). Tate had argued that philological and historical literary criticism may have their place, but that place is strictly at the service of the aesthetic evaluation that follows from the theory of organic form. We may find it helpful to know the historical background of a poem, but what we really want to understand is the poem itself, as an organically unified, self-dependent generator of its own meaning or meanings. Tate had mocked the academic study of literature, because it perpetually remained at the level of "professional" historical research, and perpetually postponed the critical interpretation it claimed to serve—and did so because it implicitly judged such interpretation as amateurish. Tate thus has posited an "ancient quarrel between history and poetry." Cunningham says in fact there is no such quarrel. The distinction between the work of art "as artistic phenomenon and historical fact" is "a distinction which leads logically to the disappearance of the work of art itself." To appreciate the work of art as an artistic phenomenon requires actually understanding the work's meaning, and to understand that meaning not only requires historical study—it *is* historical study. In brief, "historical interpretation *is* aesthetic appreciation" (emphasis mine), the two are one.

By way of allusion to T. S. Eliot's "Tradition and the Individual Talent," Cunningham argues that, yes, we may "integrate" into our own experience "the monuments of the past," but in doing so we are not receiving them but digesting them: turning a substance not ourselves into part of ourselves. Eliot's famous "historical sense" is in fact the transmutation of historical texts into one's personal emotions; only historical interpretation seeks to perceive the work of art in itself and according to its intended meaning. In this observation, Cunningham continues the demolition of Eliot's critical theories begun years before in Winters's essay, "T. S. Eliot, or the Illusion of Reaction" (1943) and brought to a modest conclusion with another member of the Winters circle, Donald E. Stanford's chapter on Eliot in *Revolution and Convention in Modern Poetry* (1983).

Cunningham's literary historical theory has at least two consequences for the poet. First, as Cunningham argues in his poem "Lector Aere Perennior," "Poets survive on fame." Poets are not immortal, for, once deceased, their soul is gone. Do they survive in their work? No, because the text is but "a name / Wherewith no soul's arrayed." They survive in "fame," that is to say, in the admiration of their posthumous readers, whose enthusiasm "Breathes on the words they [the dead poets] made." Just like the initials carved in the tree, the poem is reduced to its text, but the text is too cramped as it were to contain immortality; the immortality lies in the readers who appreciate the poem. But, of course, the readers only appreciate the poem if they actually understand its meaning. Hence, historical interpretation is the only possible aesthetic appreciation where the poet in a meaningful sense survives. Everything else is digestion.

In one of Cunningham's best known poems, "To the Reader," we learn further how difficult, nay almost impossible, this immortality must be:

> Time will assuage.
> Time's verses bury
> Margin and page
> In commentary,
>
> For gloss demands
> A gloss annexed
> Till busy hands
> Blot out the text,
>
> And all's coherent.
> Search in this gloss
> No text inherent:
> The text was loss.
>
> The gain is gloss.

It is the ahistorical commentary of the New Critic that blots out the text, to be sure, but does not even the historical interpretation gradually put us at a remove from the text itself, until the "text was loss" and the "gain is gloss"?

In a later essay, "Plots and Errors: *Hamlet* and *King Lear*," Cunningham does affirm the possibility of holding onto text and gloss alike. There he writes, to articulate the problem,

> When we come to interpretations we do not simply interpret a text but rather attempt to order a massed experience of discussion, quotation, and concern that has a ghostly yet substantial existence distinct from the page . . . We write our own poems in the form of literary criticism, and what we divine are our own forms.

In the essay that follows, however, he addresses several romantic interpretations of Shakespeare's best-loved passages, dismissing them specifically as romantic, only to provide us with an interpretation of each passage that is rooted in the tradition Shakespeare knew and followed. The interpretations will not "satisfy" the modern reader, but they are the true interpretations nonetheless. We do not have to lose the text, but we generally do. Historical interpretation's gloss at least keeps the text visible.

In Cunningham's second and much shorter appendix, he makes explicit his rejection of a metaphysical interpretation of literature, one that presumes a work's meaning is self-dependent and ever-present and available to the reader of the text. Those who read literature this way generally tend "to be an uncritical Realist, a simple-minded believer in a realm of essences." They mistakenly assume "there is a stable and external reality corresponding to the idea of tragedy." They answer the question "What is tragedy?" as if it were a metaphysical question about a timeless essence. In fact, tragedy's essence is not a transcendent reality, but a product of history. Tragedy is what its writers and theorists make it to be, thus constituting the materials of a tradition. We have not to look to an idea outside of time for the definition of tragedy but only to the "historical evidence" of what the authors call "tragedy" and what they "intended" for the reader to recognize. The idea to be known is not beyond time but buried in time past and capable of being unburied only by study of the enduring artifacts of history. Such a radical historicism would be identical with the "genealogical" researches of Foucault, but for two details. Cunningham simply assumes that works of literature are things we desire to know and appreciate, and that we are capable of knowing them and appreciating them as long as we are willing to follow the trail of historical evidence. He assumes no transcendent stability of ideas or emotions, but only the availability of historical facts and the desire to grasp those facts for the sake of our enjoyment of poetry. Cunningham also affirms authorial intention as the lost idea to be reconstructed in the act of interpretation; Foucault sought to see through ideas and intentions to the vicissitudes of power that, he thought, subtended and directed them.

In the final fragment of his "Journal of John Cardan," Cunningham contrasts Aristotelian science with his own historical science. All "logical or nonhistorical systems" operate on the premises that causes determine effects, individual facts are instances of general truths, and that time is "reversible" in the sense that we can move from effects back to causes and then from causes to effects. In a word, we can have necessary or law-like knowledge of things. A "historical system" is just the antithesis.

We know the effects, that is to say the "specific fact," and can trace it back to its cause (this is again a mild form of Foucault's "genealogy"). The specific fact is really, simply itself; any generalizations are a "methodical device" in the scholar and not present in reality. Because facts are just themselves, and not instances of a universal or supra-historical essence, facts alter each other, they are radically contingent and even fortuitous. We can discern the facts and we can describe them, and where they come from within history, but we cannot argue our way from the facts to some mode of general knowledge. We can argue backward, from a fact to its cause, but we cannot argue the reverse, from a cause to its fact. Historical inquiry explains facts; it does not produce them. Historical knowledge is just that: historical.

Although he does not claim as much in the "Journal," Cunningham's previous arguments suggest that historical and logical knowledge are not really two distinct modes of reason. One is legitimate and delivers the fact, while the other is in some sense specious. Only in some sense, however. Some of Cunningham's most distinctive and difficult poems, not to say his best poems, celebrate logical deduction or are themselves works of logic. His epigram on detective stories depicts the scholar as "a mere conservative" who "By Aristotle's saws brings crimes to light." Like Dorothy Sayers before him, Cunningham appreciated that detective fiction was exemplary to demonstrate the "saws" or principles of plot structure that Aristotle offers in the *Poetics*. Those "saws" began as an argument from effects back to their cause; Aristotle was in that sense a historical thinker. In the literary tradition, including the Donatan tradition that Cunningham studied in his first prose book, those "saws" became causes (laws) whose effects were the tragedies of the Elizabethan stage.

Cunningham's poems operating on a logical basis are almost too many to name, but we should quote four, the first two of which appear in succession in his "Epigrams: A Journal." "History of Ideas" runs: "God is love. Then by conversion / Love is God, and sex conversion." "On the Calculus" is slightly longer but no less logical:

> From almost naught to almost all I flee,
> And *almost* has almost confounded me,
> Zero my limit, and infinity.

The epigram in general is, as the poet David Middleton has shown, the "ultimate poem of definition." By definition here we mean not the etymologies of the Oxford English Dictionary, which trace historical usage across time, but a logical deduction. Cunningham's "Meditation on Statistical Method" is an especially complex logical poem, chiefly because it relies on the reader to overcome its own leaps in logic. It begins by crying out, "Plato, despair!" Plato, like Aristotle after him, held that all intelligibles (ideas or forms) were universals that transcended their individual realizations (for Plato, they alone were being). The poem's title alludes to René Descartes's *Meditations on First Philosophy* (1641) and his *Discourse on Method* (1637), two of the founding texts of modern quantitative rationalism. While it is often held, and with good reason, that Descartes's understanding of mathematics is every bit as universal and ideal as Plato's, Cunningham suggests something else. Descartes's mathematicism is "Empiric," meaning grounded in the sensible particular, and relative, insofar as it is based on probabilities and averages (Descartes's sometime rival Blaise Pascal would be the real innovator of probability theory, but his understanding of number is based on Descartes's). In brief, the poem argues, the logical process of mathematics is not an ahistorical universal, as Plato holds, but is itself rooted in and bound by historical time.

One of his late epigrams makes a nearly identical argument in favor of modern historical or empirical mathematics and against classical universals. As Steele shows in his edition of Cunningham's poems, in "Cantor's Theorem: In an Infinite Class the Whole Is No Greater Than Some of Its Part," Cunningham refutes Euclid with the set theory of the Russo-German mathematician Georg Cantor (1845-1918):

> Euclid, alone, who looked in beauty's heart,
> Assumed the whole was greater than the part;
> But Cantor, with the infinite in control,
> Proved that the part was equal to the whole.

Once again, mathematics as a logical and ahistorical kind of reasoning is legitimated precisely by showing that it does not really open onto anything transcendent. It does not lead us beyond the finite to the universal, but rather shows us that even the infinite is nothing more than the sum of its parts. This is by implication not only a refutation of Euclid's geometry, but also of Plato's and Aristotle's understanding of the liberal arts, the sciences, as leading beyond finite things to the infinite reality of the Good or God, and of Christian theology's distinction between absolute infinity and relative infinity. Absolute infinity is God as Pure Act, Infinite Being eternally present; relative infinity is the term used to recognize the mere potency of adding number to number, on and on; it is a merely *potential* infinity.

Earlier we saw Cunningham reject Aristotelian physics precisely because he judged actuality as a diminishment of being, a reduction to mere historical fact. Here we see that he also rejects the idea of any reality that would transcend history. Mathematics is vindicated, if that is the word, by being shown to exist within the boundaries of time and finitude. It becomes one more fact within the historical set, rather than a way of knowing that exceeds history by being different in kind from it. Once again, Plato must despair, for it was in the *Republic* that Plato proposed mathematics as a liberal art, that is to say, an intellectual stepping stone from becoming to being, from appearance to reality. For Cunningham, there is no such escape; mathematics is one more historical fact.

When Cunningham turns to logical and ahistorical forms in his essays, he does so specifically to show that they are part of the historical data, the facts, that we will discuss under the heading of Tradition. "Logic and Lyric: Marvell, Dunbar, and Nashe" holds in contempt some of Eliot's pronouncements on Marvell's great poem, "To His Coy Mistress," which seeks to defend the poem by the power and variety of its "images." In the aftermath of the *imagiste* movement, nothing could vindicate a poem more completely than to speak well of its images. Behind such praise was the increasing—and impoverishing—suggestion that poetry in general should consist of nothing but images and emotions. The abstract and the intellectual are to be eschewed as "unpoetic." To the contrary, Cunningham argues, Marvell's poem scarcely contains any imagery at all: "A conceit is not an image. It is a piece of wit." He then proceeds to show that Marvell's poem is nothing other than "the exposition of a syllogism," in which each of the two premises and the conclusion are elaborated by a series of conceits. The poem is "not merely the subject of logical analysis" but is itself "logical in form." We may conclude then that Cunningham does have a place for logical reasoning.

It lies within the bounds of historical reasoning and is one fact among other facts therein. He was no dualist. Historical and logical reasoning were not two, alternative and equally legitimate ways of knowing; rather, logic is one of the facts contained within historical knowledge.

Cunningham, as a practitioner of what Winters celebrated, in *Forms of Discovery*, as "The Plain Style Reborn," naturally approved of a style intellectual and abstract against the merely suggestive poetry of images. Winters and Cunningham alike were both defenders of the use of abstract, logical, and conceptual language in poetry. Winters's defense was rooted in the premise that poetry is a way of knowing the fullness of reality and of mastering our experience: one of the ways we come to know, in fact the chief way, is by the abstract intellection of universals. In his poetry, Winters's use of abstract statements is limited and merely complementary of his often sensuous descriptions. Cunningham's far more extensive use of abstract and logical language in his poetry is less ambitious and indeed the inverse of Winters's; the austerity of such language simply allows us better to perceive the fact alone. It delimits connotations rather than multiplies them; as yet another Winters student, Wesley Trimpi, argued in his study of Ben Jonson, that is the essence of the plain style. In rejecting Aristotle's understanding of being as actuality, it followed that Cunningham must reject also Aristotle's science of causes. In lieu of a science of final causes, he settled for history as a gathering of facts.

"Rage, rage against the dying of the light"

One may find Cunningham's reasoning on being and history counter-intuitive and even perverse. The delight that he seems to show in correcting ahistorical observations about poetry, such as that of Eliot just cited, in his otherwise austere and restrained essays may lead one to suspect him of being superior or smug, his only pleasure the reduction of wholes to the sum of their parts—if not something less. In fact, Cunningham's first response is that of rage. We see it primarily in the poems rather than the essays and with good reason. In *Tradition and Poetic Structure*, Cunningham will compare poetry to a game of chess (an analogy to which we shall return). In chess, of course, one has an opponent. In the literary essay, in historical scholarship, one's "opponent" is the text which must be understood, but in the writing of poetry, the opponent is closer to hand: "The poet, too, has an opponent. His opponent is experience." In "The Quest of the Opal," trying to explain the obscurity of his own poems, he writes, "The appeal to immediacy of experience is always a recourse. It is always an apology and a defense of some thoughts and actions, for these are objectifications of the self, and only these need apology." The poems then are the place where we find Cunningham confronting—at the level of experience—the consequences of his understanding of actuality as exclusion and reality as a mere history of facts of which there is no transcendence.

How does he reply? In the same manner Dylan Thomas enjoined for his dying father: to rage. Rage appears in the early "Elegy for a Cricket," where the poet kills a noisy cricket with his shoe, only to wish it "go down to hellfire." There, the cricket may "find in that fire her whom I loved once," and so the poet begs,

> Say to her, if she ask what shoe you wear now,
> That I gave you my last, I have none other.

The beloved has, presumably, left him and broken his heart; there is probably no reversing this. She is dead and in hell; there is definitely no reversing it. The only thing to be done is to give voice to belated rage in "few but true words." There is nothing to be done, rather, but there may still be something to be said. We can raise a curse among the "fixed," the damned of hell.

Cunningham's understanding of reality renders impossible the very notion of a good action. Every action diminishes us, and is thus far an evil. But most of us expect reality to conform to Aristotle's theory: every action is an accumulation of being, a movement toward some purposeful end and that end is the action's good. Fullness of being and fullness of goodness are one. Cunningham holds that the opposite is the case; that which is is not itself a good thing (by definition *is* is not good), but rather, as we've said, a sad fact. The only free response one can give to the impoverishment of being is retrospective outrage. We can judge reality, but we cannot change it. We can become enraged. This is not action, but a posterior judgment, hence the title of Cunningham's second book of poems, *The Judge is Fury* (1947), which begins with an epigram:

> *Experience is defendant, and the jury*
> *Peers of tradition, and the judge is fury*

Generally, the experience Cunningham refers to is erotic love and its failings. We see this in "Ars Amoris," where present passion leads us to act, even though after the "ensuing, / And brief, commotion," love will end. The false belief that action will fulfill us leads to action, but the realization we have been fooled follows quickly upon the act, upon the loss of being. The first epigram, in "Epigrams: A Journal," begins, "Each that I loved is now my enemy / To whom I severally inscribe my journal." He cannot act against their past betrayal; he can merely write down what they have done to him. What have they done? They have "defrauded" him of his "vanity," and thus stripped him "like a grain of wheat to the white kernel." Whereas actions diminish us, rage is not action but a feeling in retrospect. It does not further diminish us, but merely protests against loss. The text is choice and therefore loss; the rage is gloss.

In the second epigram, he claims to understand his own history: "I think I know / Much of the circumstance in which I flow." But since, as he has noted already, all knowledge is retrospective and historical, "knowledge is not power." The only outlet for retrospective knowledge is rage: "The dry soul rages." Many of Cunningham's poems, including the late, most ambitious, but least satisfactory, *To What Strangers, What Welcome*, may be distilled into this epigram, another *ars poetica*, quoted in part above:

> Dark thoughts are my companions. I have wined
> With lewdness and with crudeness, and I find
> Love is my enemy, dispassionate hate
> Is my redemption though it come too late,
> Though I come to it with a broken head
> In the cat-house of the disheveled dead.

The ancient stoics, whom Cunningham in some ways resembled, held not that being's determinations were evil, but that the universe was a determined material whole whose outward events could not be altered. They held that those determined movements were the order of nature, of the cosmos, of fate—in a word, what must necessarily be. The only freedom of action existed in the human soul, specifically in the human soul's ability either to assent to the order of the cosmos or to rebel against it. To ascent was to be morally good; to dissent was to be evil.

Cunningham's experiential rage is the opposite response but of the same moral significance. Only in raging against the implacable determinations of history can we "redeem" the time and experience some scintilla of freedom. It is not a freedom that does anything, but that is just as well, because, as we have seen, all action, all choice, is error.

Winters, in his discussion of Cunningham in *Forms of Discovery*, also addresses what he called the "doctrine of hatred or anger." He describes it thus:

> The doctrine, briefly, and as nearly as I can understand it, is that hatred is the only cleansing emotion and the most moral of emotions . . . it is not without justification in experience. During the Romantic movement a great deal of sentimental nonsense was written about the isolation of the artist, and the nonsense usually verges on self-pity . . . The fact remains, however, that the artist, if he is really an artist, is really isolated, and his personal life in this respect is a hard one. There are few people with whom he can converse freely without giving offense or becoming angry. It is no accident that so many great writers have sooner or later retreated from society: they retreat because they are excluded. A first-rate poet differs from his contemporaries . . . not in being eccentric or less human, but in being more central, more human, more intelligent. But the difference in this respect between, let us say, a great poet and the most distinguished scholar is very great, and few scholars are distinguished . . . To the scholar in question, the poet is wrong-headed and eccentric, and the scholar will usually tell him so.

To be an artist is to be "more central" than the average man, and so to be isolated in general and provoked to anger on contact with the mediocrities who make up the thoughtless mass of society. To be a poet is also to be condescended to by the scholar, that professional mediocrity who takes one for a dilettante, and so also to be provoked. These may be real experiences. Indeed, they were the actual experiences of Yvor Winters, who vented his rage against the philistines in his youth and against the superficial academic romantics in his maturity. His rage was a weapon at the service of his genius. It was also his professional experience, for Winters, as a poet and scholar in the Stanford English Department, was treated as an "embarrassment" until very late in his career. However arrogant his posture may sound, Winters knew what he was describing.

But that same Winters was one of whom Cunningham wrote tacitly, in "The Quest of the Opal," as being among the "congenital romantics, however classical their creed." Winters proves too willing to digest Cunningham's poetry and make it part of his own poetic drama. That makes good poetry, but bad history. It is, as it were, New Critical interpretation, or Eliotic digestion, not historical interpretation. Were Winters to adapt Cunningham's plodding historicism, he would not fail to connect the doctrine of rage, the effect, with its proper cause. The cause is not Cunningham's being a romantic genius forever misunderstood, but rather his belief in the inverted physics we discussed above—those same ideas that Winters himself discussed and found implausible: the "important" idea that actuality is exclusion, that being is diminishment of freedom, and reality reducible to the carved bark of historical facts. Had Winters read more carefully, he would have judged that Cunningham's historicism is the cause and rage the effect.

"I am a Pedant."

To rage in perpetuity, however, is to flop from "cat-house" to "cat-house." Life would come to appear like an endless succession of visits to Las Vegas strip clubs, where the action of desire is met with disappointment, and disappointment ineffectually "overcome" only by rage. Cunningham describes just such an experience in *To What Strangers, What Welcome*;

> Her ass twitching as if it had the fits,
> Her gold crotch grinding, her athletic tits,
> One clock, the other counter clockwise twirling.
> It was enough to stop a man from girling.

What but the object of sexual desire rendered vulgar, fungible, mechanical, and gross could kill that desire? What but the shabby and disappointing display of history could diminish the desire for action to be good? What but the discovery of sad facts as all there is could allay the natural, ineffectual rage at fate? In brief, if rage is our experience and our only kind of freedom, it need not be final. We cannot act without loss and error, so we rage. We can diminish, if not extinguish, rage, if we can discover there is in fact less to be enraged about than we had previously expected. Cunningham's historicism already indicates that wholes are at most the sum of their parts and usually less than that (e.g. that a tragedy could really be a bundle of fragments that do not form a cohesive unity). One can, as it were, take into oneself the implications of this historicism only by a calm, disinterested view of things; such a view of things can come to us only through a patient and methodical study of the facts of history. In brief, the solution to rage is pedantry. The only endurable response to the sad facts of history is to come to know those facts for what they are—and nothing more—and having stated them, to say no more.

Initiation into the life of scholarship was for Cunningham, as it had been for Winters, a great blessing, but for different reasons. By exploring the archives of the tradition, Winters discovered the wisdom and discipline of the ancients; he discovered the justness of their thought and remolded his romantic disposition until it became something more classical: "Laurel, archaic, rude," as he put it in "On Teaching the Young." The life of learning opened not merely a larger but a more permanent world to him. In youth, he had, like a western American Walter Pater, understood life as a series of fragmentary, intense, and ecstatic sensations within the flux of material nature. At Stanford, he discovered that one's life may accumulate and grow into a greater whole, one that is more than the sum of its sensuous parts. To learn was in fact to grow beyond sensation and to grow in wisdom; the life of learning meant to cultivate the mind, and to live and act better in the world in consequence. In "For Howard Baker," one of his Stanford students, he concludes,

> Music and strength of art
> Beneath long winter rain
> Have played the living part,
> With the firm mind for gain.
>
> Nor is the mind in vain.

The poetic and scholarly life is the cultivation of a firm mind. It is no mere vanity but genuine fulfillment of our human nature. But that is not all, as he writes in "The Morality of Poetry":

Poetry, if pursued either by the poet or by the reader, in the manner which I have suggested, should offer a means of enriching one's awareness of human experience and of so rendering greater the possibility of intelligence in the course of future action; and it should offer likewise a means of inducing certain more or less constant habits of feeling, which should render greater the possibility of one's acting, in a future situation, in accordance with the findings of one's improved intelligence. It should, in other words, increase the intelligence and strengthen the moral temper; these effects should naturally be carried over into action, if, through constant discipline, they are made permanent acquisitions.

To gain wisdom is to become more "central," that is, to gain a more universal wisdom that comprehends human moral experience, that enables us to understand and to act better than did the untutored, savage men and women the young Winters encountered in the desert of the Southwest. Winters's literary theory is humanistic and, with its not insubstantial debt to the scholastic thought of Thomas Aquinas, it may even be called a species of Christian humanism. The contemplation of the form of a work of art leads to the reform and actualization of the mind; the mind has wisdom or intelligence as its intrinsic good and intelligent action as its useful good. Winters's poems suggest that many fail in this aim. The romantic destroys himself by giving into the mere impulse of emotion; the hard scrabble pioneers of the West often reduced themselves to their mere animal, sensuous natures. But the one who cultivates reason may realize the human *telos* within this world: a life of wise contemplation and intelligent action.

For Cunningham the rationale and *telos* of the scholarly life, if that be the word, are less traditional. Cunningham mocks Freudian psychology in several of his epigrams, including this one:

> I showed some devils of a moral kind
> To a good friend who had a Freudian mind.
> Doctor, there was no need for therapy.
> I should have had myself to comfort me.

It may well be, however, that "self-therapy" is a not entirely unsatisfactory way of describing the role of pedantry in his poetry and essays. To be a pedant is to silence one's passions and attend scrupulously to the facts, however unsatisfactory. Because all facts will be unsatisfactory, in Cunningham's scheme, pedantry becomes a way of reconciling oneself to the sad facts of history. It is a kind of psychological adjustment. It serves no greater purpose, but it is something one might do.

The philosopher Jacques Maritain once said, in discussing the relentless orientation of the artist to the thing to be made, "the ennui of living and willing ceases at the door of every workshop." For some, great sorrow can prove a distraction to work and leave one helpless with anxiety to get anything done; but, for most, work is a place apart that does not merely distract one from one's troubles but renders them, for the moment, irrelevant. Our subjective worries drop away as we give ourselves over wholly to the making of an object. Artistic work is a kind of self-forgetfulness and self-sacrifice for the sake of the work to be made. This account of artistry, also, is not wholly unsatisfactory to account for Cunningham's understanding of scholarly pedantry.

In Cunningham's case, however, there is something more at stake—and for both Cunningham the poet and the scholar. For the poet, there is the act of reification. He states near the end of "Poetry, Structure, and Tradition," that "Our experience" of a poem "derives from and refers to an object that stays steady and persists. The text remains." Further on, he concludes with lines we have read before, "it is the work itself. It is a thing external and eternal, a potentiality of experience waiting to be realized. It is the poem." In "The Quest of the Opal," as we have already noted, he will write, "Verse is a professional activity, social and objective, and its methods and standards are those of craftsmanship. It is a concern of the ordinary human self, and is on the whole within a man's power to do well or not." Poets may survive on fame and not in the text that makes them famous, but the text nonetheless remains the text. It is, again, "external and eternal." If reality is history and history consists of facts, then the poem is the way in which an engagement with experience can become an objective part of history. It becomes a new fact in the world and exists in itself. That is the only immortality for Cunningham (though a few poems, especially "Hymn in Adversity" and "Timor Dei," glance backward at a residual Catholic understanding of the immortal soul).

The reifying action of the poem becoming fact may be a form of pedantry, but naturally it is in the scholarship that pedantry comes to the fore. By coming to a solid, distinguished, and expert knowledge of some poems through a pedantic method of historical scholarship, Cunningham the scholar calms his experience of, and rage at, the sad facts of history and attains a disinterested view of them. He knows them for what they are.

The *Collected Essays*, in a manner of speaking, gives us the narrative of a gradual reconciliation of the poet with the world through the pedantry of scholarship. In *Woe and Wonder*, his dissertation book, Cunningham is nothing but the historical scholar—except for a few wry passages here and there—through to the end. Only in the appendixes, as we saw, does he suggest the principles of vision that guide his otherwise academic preoccupation with arriving at a correct historical knowledge of what Shakespeare and his contemporaries thought they meant by tragedy.

In *Tradition and Poetic Structure*, Cunningham allows his authority as a practicing poet to enter, however mildly, into his definitions of poetry and tradition. The individual studies are in method the same as in the first book, but we hear Cunningham opining more frequently about the deficiencies—the lack of pedantry—found in the New Critics and, in his essay on Wallace Stevens, what we really find is a contemporary's debunking of the modernist master in defense of the anti-modernist epigrammatic style that Cunningham favored. He is an accurate exegete of Stevens, but one with a superior alternative in mind nevertheless. In the essays collected in Part III, especially in "How Shall the Poem be Written," Cunningham speaks, for the first time, more as a poet with a strong formation in historical scholarship. If his knowledge is of history, it is at the service of defining problems for the contemporary poet.

So also does he speak in the miscellaneous studies collected in Part IV. Of special note are the essays "Lyric Style in the 1590s" and "In Shakespeare's Day," where Cunningham's attention to historical fact helps him to see minute differences in rhetorical structure, even within the work of John Donne, that would elude the attentive ear of most of us. It also leads him to make what may seem a superfluous apology. In his essay on Emily Dickinson, he begins:

I am a renegade Irish Catholic from the plains of
Montana, upper lower class, a onetime scholar in
Latin and in the English Renaissance. Consequently,
I speak without authority on a nineteenth-century
New England spinster, of the American governing
class, schooled in the feelings and expectations of re-
vivalistic Calvinism, and an admirer of Emily Brontë
and Elizabeth Barrett Browning.

Only if one is thoroughly convinced that reality is nothing
more than its sum total of ever-shifting historical facts will this
sort of disclosure seem necessary. But he was, and so it did.

In Part V, we find Cunningham's commentaries on his own
poems and poetic practice. The pedantic scholar and enraged
poet become one at last. Not even the poet's own work is spared
the scholar's pedantic treatment, and we realize, if we have not
already, that even in his most scholarly and disinterested essays,
the poet, trying to master his technique, was always present and
taking notes.

We might look at this as a narrative of progress and judge it
a well-earned maturation and a journey toward wisdom. That,
as we saw, is how Winters viewed the scholarly life; recall also
his confidence that, Cunningham's inversion of Aristotelian
physics notwithstanding, the younger poet had grown more in-
telligent across his fifty years of life rather than less so. Perhaps
Winters should have asked him. Cunningham himself objects to
being called wise. Indeed, he objects to the presumption of the
existence of wisdom in the first place. In "The Journal of John
Carden," he confesses,

When I began writing some years ago I had a shocking amount of assurance. I knew right and wrong, truth and error, and it all formed much of a system—what holes there were in it I knew could be worked out. But I feel quite differently now. It isn't that I've become anything so innocent as a sceptic or so crude as disillusioned; it is that I am left with limited insights, the plain implications of experience but restricted in generality, and cold assumptions whose systemic development unfolds as one lives them. These you might say constitute a group of points of whose location I am fairly assured; the curve that embraces them and the equation that generates the curve I trust are figurable. But there is all that paper that the curve will not enclose, if it be a closed curve, all those propositions that I used to make or that I now read in others' books but can make no sense of, can find nothing to refer them to.

Wisdom speaks of the whole. Wisdom enfolds reality, from understood first principles to the furthest out-workings of reason. Cunningham may once have thought he was wise or aimed at wisdom, but now he sees that all he has learned is a "group of points," a bunch of facts. Yes, he can trace a line from point to point and form a curve, the continuation of which leads on to facts he does not yet know but which are nonetheless "figurable." But a capacity for a few further inferences is not the same as the supposed comprehension of wisdom. That is because, on his account, there is no wisdom. There is knowledge of the fact or facts, and that knowledge will always be more or less fragmentary: a curve appearing here, leading a bit beyond itself, an inexplicable outlying point there. All we really know is the fact. To be a pedant is to be the one who does not go beyond the fact, but resigns himself to a fragmentary and restricted, but also a definite, knowledge. Pedantry is abiding *amid* the facts rather than a wise comprehension and transcendence of them. It has no *telos*. It does not fulfill human nature. It does not actualize the mind. The mind, to be sure, comes to know more than it once did, but its span remains narrow and its accumulation is not organic growth but a pedantic collection; its increase is not fulfillment. The mind does not ascend beyond the facts, but reconciles itself to them. It settles. It becomes almost one with them.

Cunningham, knowing that his acquisition of knowledge would perforce be limited, devoted himself to two sad facts, verse and tradition. With a description of these we shall conclude.

Verse

We mentioned at the opening Cunningham's deflation of the humanistic and romantic conceptions of poetry. In "Poetry, Structure, and Tradition," he clearly takes pleasure in mentally dissecting those who say "that poetry is difficult to define." Those who say this generally are not interested in what poetry is, but in what it does to them. Others wish to defend poetry and assign it a place of honor, but in so doing, they have "erected pretensions that no linguistic construction, no poem, could ever hope to satisfy." More defensible perhaps are those accounts of poetry derived from Plato and Aristotle, but these on the whole focus on plot so that we come to identify poetry as a general term for fiction (as does Sir Philip Sidney, quite directly, for instance). Cunningham refuses all this and in characteristic, memorable fashion:

I prefer with respect to poetry . . . the common or garden variety of definition. I mean by poetry what everyone means by it when he is not in an exalted mood, when he is not being a critic, a visionary, or a philosopher. I mean by poetry what a man means when he goes to the bookstore to buy a book of poems as a graduation gift, or when he is commissioned by a publisher to do an anthology of sixteenth century poems. Poetry is what looks like poetry, what sounds like poetry. It is metrical composition.

Poetry, in a word, is verse. All other accounts of poetry seek to mark some exemplary quality of this or that poem and take it for the definition of the whole. No doubt some poems give one the feelings its romantic apologists claim, but not all poems do. What do all poems have in common? Only, says Cunningham, that they are composed in meter.

Cunningham notes directly that his definition takes a different path than does Aristotle, and not just in his discounting the role of plot in some poems as insufficient to characterize the whole. Rather, as we saw above, Aristotelian science is a science of causes, and no cause is more important than the final cause. An Aristotelian definition marks off a species by what is distinctly exemplary about it, what is its particular virtue when it attains most fully to being, hence the definition of man as "rational animal." Not all men actually are rational, but all fully actualized men are.

A true Aristotelian definition of poetry, even if it departed from Aristotle's account in the *Poetics* (as it would have to, since Aristotle does not properly address the lyric or comedy and dismisses out of hand expository and didactic modes of poetry, which allows his later readers to make the otherwise unconvincing identity of poetry and fiction), would still need to be rooted in knowledge of the final cause. It would need to ask what poems are in terms of what they are *for*. Cunningham is not interested in the *telos*, but in the fact, "trivial" or "offensive" as it may seem. He desires merely "to mark off the territory and to describe the thing unmistakably." Verse is a fact. It is the fact to which he clings, despite the pretensions and ecstasies of the romantics. This Cunningham dramatizes in one of his best poems, "For My Contemporaries":

> How time reverses
> The proud in heart!
> I now make verses
> Who aimed at art.
>
> But I sleep well.
> Ambitious boys
> Whose big lines swell
> With spiritual noise,
>
> Despise me not,
> And be not queasy
> To praise somewhat:
> Verse is not easy.
>
> But rage who will.
> Time that procured me
> Good sense and skill
> Of madness cured me.

From Sidney forward, the distinction between "poetry" and "verse" had become a commonplace. There were many "versifiers" who did not attain to the level of poets and there were many poets who did not need, in Sidney's word, the "apparel" of meter and rhyme, which we call verse. Have at it, says Cunningham. Though I thought myself an artist, I'll settle for versifier. Indeed, I shall prefer it. I shall sleep well, for I will not be blown about by spiritual gas, but rather shall be disciplined by the "sense and skill" of a maker. While others stutter their formless private visions, he will make a work "external and eternal." He will be the more sane for being a plodding foot-counter. He may not be a prophet, but he will have the definite knowledge and vision of a pedant.

Recall the passage we quoted above, which is in fact Cunningham's gloss on this very poem; in contrast to a poet like Stevens, Cunningham has no desire to mystify or confuse: "Verse is a professional activity, social and objective, and its methods and standards are those of craftsmanship." For Winters, the discipline of poetry could be a practice of contemplation that led to growth in wisdom. For Cunningham, as we are abundantly prepared to see, even wisdom would be a bit "queasy." He is content with the steadying knowledge and practitioner's competence of the fact of verse-craft. He sleeps well in the fact. In answer to the question that is the title of his finest single essay, "How Shall the Poem Be Written?," says he: "in metrical language." In his hands, verse serves as what Aristotle would call a material cause. Poems are made of meter the way trees are made of wood. Cunningham is one of the few materialists of poetic theory in our history. As his comment about the "graduation present" indicates, however, most of us are materialists in this sense, we just have not risen to the level of theory. We become conscious of it, only when we hear a modernist free verse poem and cry out in disgust, "What?! A Poem?! It doesn't even scan!" Just so, replies Cunningham.

Tradition

Cunningham's essays have little to say about meter in itself, that is to say, verse as verse. His former student, Timothy Steele, would fill that absence by writing two important books on prosody that argue closely from Cunningham's principles. Cunningham himself offers a brief defense of syllabics as metrical, and complains of "parasitic" meters, in "How Shall the Poem Be Written?" Commenting on the emergence, in Elizabethan England, of iambic pentameter blank verse from the ungainly fourteener line, he observes (correctly), "a new meter is a new attitude."

In general, however, his attentions are to the rhetorical structures and linguistic usages that follow upon versification, in a word, to all the ways in which a poem may be written beyond its meter. This is what Cunningham means by tradition. A tradition, he says at the beginning of *Tradition and Poetic Structure*, "is a body of learning capable of being applied to the production of what are called original works. It is the method by which the sentences of a poem are discovered: it demarks the field of discovery and orders the succession of sentences. It is the potentiality of any work in the tradition." The rules of verse are equivalent to the rules of chess; the tradition is the historical experience of the whole game—the games played—of chess. Later in the same book, he goes further,

> A literary form exists only in what I call a tradition. I use that word in the sense in which we speak of the tradition of the hard-boiled detective story or say that Shakespeare's sonnets are in the tradition of the *Astrophel and Stella* sequence or, more generally, in the Petrarchan tradition. A tradition is the body of texts and interpretations current among a group of writers at a given time and place.

Poetry is verse, but tradition is all the things poets do with verse as they grapple with their opponent, experience, and try to say something worth saying about it. We may be tempted to say that meter is the material cause, but tradition the total body of formal causes, but this is not right. All the forms of tradition are *outside* the essence—the fact—of poetry. They are different things that poets have done with the fact.

Readers of the great philosopher of "tradition-based rationality," Alasdair MacIntyre, will recognize a kinship between this aspect of Cunningham and MacIntyre's thought. It is a fascinating coincidence that they were colleagues at Brandeis in the years just before MacIntyre published his great work on the theory of tradition and reason, *After Virtue* (1981). For Cunningham and MacIntyre alike, "tradition" is like a language, a condition of possibility. In both their works, tradition makes possible the perception, interpretation, expression, and understanding of our experience.

In my book, *The Fortunes of Poetry in an Age of Unmaking*, I argued that Cunningham's understanding of verse as poetry and tradition as what is done with poetry would benefit from revision with the help of MacIntyre's thought. Specifically, MacIntyre brought into modern moral theory the Aristotelian understanding of causality. For Aristotle, as we noted, all science is the science of causes with final causality predominating. MacIntyre shows that Aristotle's science of *Ethics* is no exception. *Ethics* is the science that defines the good life for man (his *telos* or final cause) and then discerns what qualities must be made present or cultivated if one is oneself to *become* such a person, that is to say, what virtues (formal qualities) and properties (external goods) are essential to a life well lived. What are people for? In the answer to that question lies the answer to another: What form shall our lives take?

Cunningham explicitly rejected that sort of reasoning: poetry is verse, that's a fact. All the various ends to which the matter-of-fact of poetry may be put are retained under the exogenous rubric of tradition. I argued that this is not satisfactory, not because it is "trivial," but because we recognize poetry *in itself* as comprehending other things, more things, than meter—even as meter is clearly of the essence of poetry, just as Cunningham says. While not all poems—perhaps no one poem—will attain perfectly to poetry's end, we see that all poems move toward some kind of end. We even see that some poems are "more poetic" than others. The end toward which all poems tend comprehends qualities of memory, metaphor, and meter; it deploys these qualities in various ways and proportions in the lyric, narrative, didactic, and dramatic modes. Such a formulation lacks the simplicity of Cunningham's definition, but it allows everything that is the poetic case to be included at least by way of analogy. It is not my intention to make my argument here, but merely to note the intriguing aspects of Cunningham's theory and to indicate that critical engagement with it may prove fruitful.

I am not at all satisfied with Cunningham's distinction between poetry and tradition. I am however wholly amazed and edified by what he does in his studies in tradition. His contrast between the classical lyric tradition of Statius and the modern sonnet; his defense of the logical form of the lyric; his demonstration that Chaucer was a more traditional poet than the scholars had claimed; his suggestions of how scholastic theology informs Shakespeare; his correction of the romantic fetish of "character" by reminding us of the classical preeminence of plot in dramatic form; and, finally, his demonstration that much modernist poetry is "parasitic" on tradition, seeking to upend it, but incapable of breaking free of it—all these studies in "classical Classical philology" are in fact expert lessons in craft and invention for the contemporary poet. Staid and academic though his chapters seem on first reading, they constitute in themselves apprenticeships with a master. They are an initiation into a way of life even for those of us who reject out of hand the idea of being-as-exclusion from which his work begins. If not all choice is error, then the discipline of reticence and craft, careful study and restrained and refined speech are indeed good choices to make.

1976

My first edition of Cunningham's *Collected Essays* is copyrighted 1976, the bicentennial of our country. Cunningham's rugged, taciturn style should remind us of his distinctive western American upbringing and education, though few of his poems make any direct reference to the region ("Montana Fifty Years Ago" does and is one of his finest poems). His poetry and essays alike should be celebrated as among the literary fruits of American culture, and the American West in particular, even if much of it was composed in the Eastern enclave of Brandeis, in Waltham, Massachusetts. They have greater claim to being a true expression of the western character than do the woozy poems of his contemporaries who initiated the so-called "San Francisco Renaissance." In Cunningham, we find expressed the sensibility of the far West and not merely the hallucinations of a certain period on Haight-Ashbury.

But I draw attention to the copyright year for another reason. It is the year after my own birth. My lifetime is a long time for Cunningham's great book to have gone without reprinting. Cunningham has become one of the great minor poets of the last century; his influence has shaped generations of poets, even when it has gone unrecognized. We are all fortunate that Swallow Press/Ohio University Press issued an annotated edition of the poems, in 1997, at the end of the last millennium. We are now equally fortunate that Wiseblood Books has brought back into print this strange monument, this collection of sad facts, this body of learning that makes no pretense to wisdom, by a man who slept well at night, not because all was right with the world, but because the fact of poetry was something worth doing and thinking about. This new Wiseblood edition of *The Collected Essays* gathers in its final pages those last essays and addresses Cunningham published after 1976 and does so for the first time. The *Collected* is now *Complete*. It is my hope that a new generation of readers and writers will find their eyes and minds clarified by a fresh encounter with the fact of Cunningham's achievement.

A COMMENCEMENT ADDRESS

June 11, 1978
Lawrence University
Appleton, Wisconsin

I have chosen on Commencement Day to speak of endings. And of these there are many sorts. Indeed, I imagine that a full account of the kinds of endings would be endless. There's "Well, that's over" and "We got through it," and their cousin "Thank God it's Friday." There are things that just quietly stop, and others that fizzle out. So I shall confine myself to three rather special forms of conclusion, and begin with perhaps the most notable.

There were three—one could think of others—special events in my life and in that of most of my contemporaries. They were public events, however much they may have affected private lives; they were sudden, of an overwhelming absoluteness in their happening, however much they may have been anticipated and in the aftermath dragged out. And each has fixed in memory irrelevant associated experiences that are attached as iron filings to the central magnet. For instance, you have all heard or read of where this one or that one was and what he was doing when he heard of the assassination of President Kennedy. Irrelevant details are fixed and structured in the central event.

I shall deal briefly with three; the assassination of President Kennedy occurred too late in my life to be of the same order: they are, the first Armistice Day, when I was 7; Black Tuesday, when I was 18; and Pearl Harbor, when I was 30.

In November 1918, I was staying with my Aunt Kate in Sheridan, Wyoming—my mother had gone East on family matters. I had the flu—it was the year of the epidemic—and several weeks of my life were blank to consciousness. I had begun to come to when the bells rang for the false Armistice, and was able to walk across the tracks with my Aunt on November 11th to watch the parade. I remember only at the head of the procession a young man leading a white goat and carrying a sign: "We got the Kaiser's goat." Emergence from illness, some sense of the momentous in the occasion, and that miserable goat.

Black Tuesday, October 29, 1929, was another matter. I had been working for over a year as an office boy and runner in what was at that time by far the largest brokerage house in Denver. The market had been erratic for some time, and then suddenly there was Black Thursday, followed by some recovery and stabilization, and then, five days later, Black Tuesday. The day had a finality, inarguable, absolute, though in fact the day seemed not to end. The ticker tape ran on past midnight Mountain Time, we slept a few hours in office chairs, and were back at work at 8 a.m.

Yet everyone had a conviction, not just a feeling and not just in retrospect, that things had come to an end. What followed was, as a friend of mine once described it, The Morning After—indeed, a morning after that lasted for ten years. A favorite cartoon of the time showed a squirrel asking a bum on a park bench why he hadn't put something away for a rainy day. "I did," the man said.

My final event in this kind was Pearl Harbor. Again there were, as in different ways there were for others, accompanying circumstances, fused into a whole by the suddenness, the magnitude of the event. I was coming out of a bout with the flu, though not of the serious 1918 sort; I was living in the country with my three-year-old daughter. A friend came by around noon and brought the news. That night, where the lights of San Francisco could usually be seen reflected against the clouds, there was total blackness, as there was in the immediate neighborhood. The only radio stations I could get were Tacoma and Salt Lake City, and both carried regular announcements that enemy planes were over San Francisco—of course, they were not. And the words of Lord Grey at the beginning of the First World War came into my mind: "The lights are going out all over Europe [and now all over America]. We shall not see them lit again in our time." Life, of course, went on, but it had also stopped.

Let us turn now to a different sort of endings. There are, for instance, the periods in human life, the traditional Ages of Man, which rest on biological fact and social custom, and custom varies. Middle age, for instance, in recent years has been spreading out. I mention, for the amusement of the young and perhaps the nostalgia of the old, the moment when in my life boyhood ended. When I was about eleven or twelve years old my mother bought me my first long trousers! I had graduated. There are also the various periods of history, though hardly so sharply defined as in the famous story of the Byzantine emperor who asked one morning when his valet woke him what day it was. "January 1, 476 A.D., Sire," was the answer, "It is the first day of the Middle Ages."

But there has developed in recent years—it began, I believe, in the 1890s—a sort of instant construction of historical periods based on an irrelevant mathematics. I mean, for example, that mourned-for period, recurrently discussed in newspaper and conversation, the recent Sixties. The Boston Globe had a long article about a month ago, "What did we do to deserve the 1970s?" We have passed from one historical period to another, and it happened on New Year's Eve.

First, the irrelevant mathematics. We are in the 1970s only as measured by the calendar the insurance company sends at Christmas, but not by the Jewish, the Islamic, or the Chinese calendars. And we mark off the calendar by decades, as if the decimal system—there are useful mathematical alternatives, duodecimal, for instance—as if the decimal system were the principle of the universe. And second, it is instant history. We cannot wait for the patient historian to organize into units the flow of time. We have the answer in our pockets.

To the best of my knowledge this sort of thing first appeared in the 1890s, with a self-conscious awareness that a century was coming to an end, and the unquestioned assumption that a century or a decade was not merely a way of dating, but in fact a substantial reality. An American poet, then 21, notes in his journal on December 31, 1900: "Well, it is some satisfaction to be still living in the nineteenth century—it's a rather cosy century and we've got used to it; but the change is coming—it must be pretty well on its way across the Atlantic at this time."

And Thomas Hardy in "The Darkling Thrush," which he first titled "The Century's End" and dated December 1900, memorializes the occasion:

> I leant upon a coppice gate
> When Frost was spectre-gray,
> And Winter's dregs made desolate
> The weakening eye of day.
> The tangled bine-stems scored the sky
> Like strings of broken lyres,
> And all mankind that haunted nigh
> Had sought their household fires.

The land's sharp features seemed to be
The Century's corpse outleant,
His crypt the cloudy canopy,
The wind his death-lament.
The ancient pulse of germ and birth
Was shrunken hard and dry,
And every spirit upon earth
Seemed fervourless as I.

At once a voice awoke among
The bleak twigs overhead
In a full-hearted evensong
Of joy illimited;
An aged thrush, frail, gaunt, and small,
In blast-beruffled plume,
Had chosen thus to fling his soul
Upon the growing gloom.

So little cause for carolings
Of such ecstatic sound
Was written on terrestial things
Afar or nigh around,
That I could think there trembled through
His happy good-night air
Some blessed Hope, where of he knew
And I was unaware.

It is a sort of secular apocalypse, intimating, if not the end of the world, at least the end of a world, and the death of Queen Victoria the following January 22nd seemed a verifying sign.

But the constructions of instant history, if one perceives what they represent and lives within it, are not only constructions but experiences, and hence realities. And if the constructions are ordered by irrelevant mathematics, in the ordering the mathematics becomes relevant. Indeed, literary historians in later years have recognized a special atmosphere characterizing the 90s which permeates the work of, not all, but a significant number of the writers of that time. It may all have been an illusion, but illusions are real.

Of subsequent decades, though we have gotten into the habit of reifying any of them, only two, are felt to have had, like the 90s, a describable atmosphere, to have been more than a convenient label, to have been, in fact, a principle at work in the lives of, at least, a good many groups of people. These are the 20s and the 60s, and the bounds of each were given by elements outside the bounds of irrelevant mathematics. The 20s began a few years after the Armistice, as the nation recovered from the dislocations of war, and ended with an abrupt finality on Black Tuesday.

The bounds of the 60s, at least as experienced at that time in the university, were given by the internal nature of the movement. For it was that recurrent American phenomenon, A Great Awakening, with transcontinental camp meetings, with prayer sessions called teach-ins, with the end of the world is at hand, either a nuclear or an environmental end, and with crowd psychology. It was an old-fashioned revival, but without Christianity, without a place to put and structure irrationalities. I said at the time that if St. Paul had come on any university campus he would have walked off with sixty-five percent of the students; forty percent of the faculty; and perhaps five percent of the administration. And it came to a climax, as with all revival movements, and then sheepishly collapsed, with a few firm converts left. So we have the 70s.

But endings need not be so public, so newsworthy. There are many little ones every day of our lives, and each gives shape of a sort to some fragment of experience. I shall illustrate a few of these shapes by reading a few poems—after all, poetry is my trade—but the process of shaping is not the peculiar province of poets. We are all artists of our experience, including the experience of imagining.

I begin with Edward Thomas, "The Owl."

Downhill I came, hungry, and yet not starved;
Cold, yet had heat within me that was proof
Against the North wind; tired, yet so that rest
Had seemed the sweetest thing under a roof.

Then at the inn I had food, fire, and rest,
Knowing how hungry, cold, and tired was I.
All of the night was quite barred out except
An owl's cry, a most melancholy cry.

Shaken out long and clear upon the hill,
No merry note, nor cause of merriment,
But one telling me plain what I escaped
And others could not, that night, as in I went.

And salted was my food, and my repose,
Salted and sobered, too, by the bird's voice
Speaking for all who lay under the stars,
Soldiers and poor, unable to rejoice.

Night, and journey's end, and the associated irrelevance of the owl's cry.

The second example gives simply the experience of an end, without beginning, and is, so to speak, secured by verbal repetition. Stevens, "The House Was Quiet and the World Was Calm"

The house was quiet and the world was calm.
The reader became the book; and summer night

Was like the conscious being of the book.
The house was quiet and the world was calm.

The words were spoken as if there was no book,
Except that the reader leaned above the page,

Wanted to lean, wanted much most to be
The scholar to whom his book is true, to whom

The summer night is like a perfection of thought.
The house was quiet because it had to be.

The quiet was part of the meaning, part of the mind:
The access of perfection to the page.

And the world was calm. The truth in a calm world,
In which there is no other meaning, itself

Is calm, itself is summer and night, itself
Is the reader leaning late and reading there.

The next poem will be familiar to many of you. It depicts a momentary lull, a kind of coffee break, and ends with well, I must get going.

Frost, "Stopping by Woods on a Snowy Evening"

Whose woods these are I think I know,
His house is in the village, though;
He will not see me stopping here
To watch his woods fill up with snow.

My little horse must think it queer
To stop without a farmhouse near
Between the woods and frozen lake
The darkest evening of the year.

He gives his harness bells a shake
To ask if there is some mistake.
The only other sound's the sweep
Of easy wind and downy flake.

The woods are lovely, dark, and deep,
But I have promises to keep,
And miles to go before I sleep,
And miles to go before I sleep.

I shall conclude with one of my own poems, a sequence of short poems, but I shall read only enough to illustrate the organizing endings. The speaker drives from the East Coast to the West, and some time later returns. It begins:

I drive Westward. Tumble and locoweed
Persist.

In the next, there is, as in "The Owl," a local ending; night, lodging, irrelevancy:

> And then the twilight harboring
> In a small park. The room is warm.

> Coming out of the mountains just below Ventura:

> And finally here: the surf breaking
> . . . and inevitably
> The last rim of sunset on the sea.

So ends the first ending, graced by a sunset. There follows the intimation of a valued experience, the rejection of that experience—an ending—, and the return across the continent in ten syllables:

> By desert, prairie, and this stone-walled road.

> Finally, the poem that began in Winter concludes

> in the last warmth
> Of a New England Fall.

And with an acceptance of the rejection of the Valued experience. These several endings form in Frost's words "A momentary stay against confusion."

INTRODUCTION

The Swallow Press Edition

There is less to be said about literature than has been said, and this book adds a little more. What it adds is, or was when first published, new, though it would take a lifetime of bibliographical search to be sure. And it has the merit and defect of brevity, with an occasional repetitiveness that may at times redeem the brevity.

I have excluded from this collection the articles and reviews published between the ages nineteen and twenty-three. They can be found in the periodicals (see Charles Gullans, *A Bibliography of the Published Works of J. V. Cunningham,* Los Angeles, 1973). These were apprentice pieces, written for money, in the honorable tradition of literary journalism, a calling graced—to name only old friends, two now dead—by Allen Tate, Yvor Winters, Philip Rahv, and Irving Howe. What I have retained is later, and in a narrower tradition: the tradition, to speak broadly, of classical Classical Philology.

Hence many of the essays are concerned with various aspects of form, including style, prosody, and the different kinds of fiction and forms of experience. And with the historical interpretation of texts: that is, with experiencing a text on its own terms. The spirit killeth, but the letter giveth life.

The two concerns tend to coincide, for forms are realized in circumstance. In fact, the essays themselves were in part determined by length and occasion, for, to note the overlooked obvious, length is a major principle of form, and often stipulated by occasion. "Woe or Wonder," for example, is a dissertation stripped to a monograph, which is to the scholarly "book" as the novelette is to the novel, with like advantages and disadvantages. Again, eleven of the pieces were public lectures. These are, by tradition and scheduling, from fifty to sixty minutes: that is, from five to six thousand words, for the public lecture voice speaks a hundred words a minute. Five others were read at special conferences and vary in length with the time allotted. I may add, one's colleagues do not always observe the limits. There are also three introductions to anthologies, a book review, and a brief biography, and in each case the context determined the form.

Forms may be given or discovered—this corresponds to the current distinction between closed and open form—and may be both. But if, to quote E. M. Forster, "All that is prearranged is false," one could not in good faith give a public lecture or read a paper at MLA. Or meet his classes, or cash his salary check.

Lecture, paper, and introduction are further determined by the anticipated audience. Topic and text are often given, and should, at any rate, be ones the audience is familiar with, or thinks it should be familiar with. There are also certain antecedent forms given in the tradition, not stipulated but available and comforting. For example, one may begin with "the state of the question." The point of departure, then, will be some classic statement of the position disputed, and the speaker will hope to transfer that classicality to his own statement. For, though the end of the paper as published will be to inform and persuade, the end as delivered is to impress. For this is the oratory of display, a kissing cousin of sophistic declamation, and what is said is said with voice and presence, and it is public.

The length of "The Quest of the Opal," on the other hand, was not given, and the occasion was private. Several friends were puzzled by some poems I had written, and so, "a heretic of paraphrase," I turned them into prose, as any Elizabethan schoolboy had learned to do with his texts. I continued the practice for a while, then put the notes away. Coming across them some years later, I sensed an inherent form. In this case, the length of the final piece was determined by the material and the felt form. Later I salvaged twelve unused paragraphs and called them "The Journal of John Cardan."

Verse and prose are different dialects of a common language, and to turn one into the other is to translate. If something is lost in translation, something is also gained. In fact, to experience the literature of the past, or even of an alien culture of one's own day, is in a sense to translate, though the translation need not be formulated. If formulated, it is historical interpretation. I have discussed the principles and claims of such interpretation in numerous passages, but, since the virtue and defect of my prose is brevity, I shall add a few more words, and a few more interpretations.

First, what it is not. It does not consist in ascertaining the spirit of an age, and then relating particular works to that construction. It was not an age of reason that produced poems in syllogistic form, but a common schooling in the Old Logic. Hence I am not concerned with such notions as Modernism, except insofar as the notion itself is operative in a work. I have, for instance, as a poet been urged "to confront the twentieth century." The phrase is instant history, a tangle of doctrinaire prescriptions, written in the halls of academe. It implies the necessity of that Modernism whose memorial services are now being held. If my poems are not of their times, they are nevertheless part of the evidence for what the times are.

Now what it is. Every utterance is historical, even this, but not every one calls for interpretation. To interpret is to answer the question, What did he mean by that? and this implies the perception of some difficulty, some relevant uncertainty or ignorance, together with an imputation of value; the question was worth asking. Sometimes the answer is gloss: it is in The Dictionary. But we do not always recognize that there is a question, or we accept a mistaken answer. To the many glosses scattered through these essays I add a few more.

There is the couplet from Donne's verse letter, written while the English expeditionary fleet was becalmed in the Channel:

> No use of lanterns, and in one place lay
> Feathers and dust, today and yesterday.

Commentators, who know that lanterns are lanterns, tell us they were hung out at night to keep the fleet together, and would not be needed in a calm. The explanation reassures us, but it is inapposite. For "lanterns" at that time also meant "ventilators" (O.E.D., *s.v.* 4), which would, of course, more obviously be of no use in a calm.

Sometimes a little more than gloss is needed. When Othello seconds his wife's request—it is their wedding night—to accompany him on the expedition to Cyprus:

> I therefore beg it not
> To please the palate of my appetite,
> Nor to comply with heat, the young affects
> In my defunct and proper satisfaction,
> But to be free and bounteous to her mind.

He disclaims lust as a motive. But he parenthetically affirms the satisfaction that belongs to marriage, and states also, what is of legal importance, that the marriage has been consummated:

"my defunct . . . satisfaction." Under *defungor* in Lewis and Short we read: "to have done with, acquit oneself of, discharge, perform, finish." The word is used in its basic Latin sense. There is, consequently, no need to emend, and read, as is commonly done:

> Nor to comply with heat—the young affects
> In me defunct—and proper satisfaction

which spoils the rhythm, and has been read as a confession of impotence.

To sum up:

> As woods whose change appears
> Still in their leaves throughout the sliding years,
> The first born dying, so the aged state
> Of words decay, and phrases born but late
> Like tender buds shoot up and freshly grow.
> Ourselves and all that's ours to death we owe.

And not words only, but forms of experience and the forms by which we construe it. We have dreams, but not dream visions. We think, but seldom syllogistically. The House of Hamlet and the House of Polonius were not nuclear families in the Bronx. Election is a safe and adequate pension, and damnation is to live remote from Manhattan or Cambridge, Mass. To re-experience with some immediacy and on their own terms these lost literary, academic, social, and religious forms is to possess the past. If we are concerned with experience in our own forms, we can write our own poems.

J. V. Cunningham

I

WOE OR WONDER

THE EMOTIONAL EFFECT OF SHAKESPEAREAN TRAGEDY

RIPENESS IS ALL

I am concerned here with understanding precisely what Shakespeare meant. It is true that "when we read Shakespeare's plays," as one scholar says, "we are always meeting our own experiences and are constantly surprised by some phrase which expresses what we thought to be our own secret or our own discovery."[1] But the danger is that the meaning we find may really be our own secret, our own discovery, rather than Shakespeare's, and the more precious and beguiling for being our own. The danger I have in mind can be illustrated by our attitude toward one of the most famous of Shakespearean phrases, "Ripeness is all." It is a favorite quotation of Mr. Eliot's. "It seems to me," he says in discussing the question of truth and belief in poetry, "to have profound emotional meaning, with, at least, no literal fallacy."[2] He does not specify what this meaning is, but I take it that it is something not strictly denotative though emotionally compelling.

The phrase, indeed, has seemed to many to represent a profound intuition into reality and to sum up the essence of Shakespearean, or even of human, tragedy. It speaks quite nearly to us. What it means to each will perhaps depend on his or her own experience and his or her own way of relating the texture of experience to the insights of literature. Yet all would agree that "Ripeness is all" gathers into a phrase something of the ultimate value of this life; it reassures us that maturity of experience is a final good, and that there is a fulness of feeling, an inner and emotional completion in life that is attainable and that will resolve our tragedies. Such at least seems to be the interpretation of a recent critic. "After repeated disaster," he says of Gloucester in *King Lear:*

he can assent, "And that's true too," to Edgar's "Ripeness is all." For man may ripen into fulness of being, which means, among other things, that one part of him does not rule all the rest and that one moment's mood does not close off all the perspectives available to him.[3]

In this way we discover in Shakespeare's phrase the secret morality of our own times. It is a meaning I can enter into quite as deeply as anyone, but it is not what Shakespeare meant.

Shakespeare meant something much more traditional. The phrase occurs in *King Lear.* In an earlier scene Edgar had prevented Gloucester from committing suicide, that act which consummates the sin of despair, and Gloucester had accepted the situation in the true spirit of Christian resignation:

> henceforth I'll bear
> Affliction till it do cry out itself
> "Enough, enough," and die.
>
> 4. 6. 75-77

But now Gloucester seems to relapse for a moment, saying:

> No further, sir; a man may rot even here.

And Edgar stiffens his resolution with these words:

> Men must endure
> Their going hence even as their coming hither:
> Ripeness is all.
>
> 5. 2. 9-11

The context is the desire for death. The conclusion is that as we were passive to the hour of our birth so we must be passive to the hour of our death. So far, surely, the speech is an affirmation of the spirit of resignation, and it would be reasonable to suppose that the summary clause at the end, "Ripeness is all," is but the final restatement of this attitude. It was certainly an available attitude. The experience of Christian resignation was dense with the history of the Western spirit, and that history was alive and present in Shakespeare's time; it spoke daily from the pulpit and in the private consolations of intimate friends. The theme, furthermore, was a favorite with Shakespeare. It had been fully explored in the Duke's great speech in *Measure for Measure:*

> Be absolute for death. Either death or life
> Will thereby be the sweeter. Reason thus with life:
> If I do lose thee I do lose a thing
> That none but fools would keep. A breath thou art,
> Servile to all the skyey influences
> That do this habitation where thou keep'st
> Hourly afflict. Merely thou art death's fool;
> For him thou labour'st by thy flight to shun,
> And yet runn'st toward him still. . . .
>   Yet in this life
> Lie hid moe thousand deaths; yet death we fear
> That makes these odds all even.
>   3. 1. 5-13, 39-41

But the finest expression, other than in the passage from *Lear,* is Hamlet's speech to Horatio as he goes to the catastrophe:

we defy augury: there's a special providence in the fall of a sparrow. If it be now, 'tis not to come; if it be not to come, it will be now; if it be not now, yet it will come: the readiness is all.

5. 2. 230-33

This is as much as to say that we must endure our going hence, be it when it may, since the hour of our death is in the care of Providence: *the readiness is all.*

It has been said that this is Stoic, and certainly "augury" hints toward Antiquity. But he who speaks of a special providence in the fall of a sparrow could trust an audience in the age of Elizabeth to think of Christian theology and the New Testament:

> And fear not them which kill the body, but are not able to kill the soul: but rather fear him which is able to destroy both body and soul in hell. Are not two sparrows sold for a farthing? *and one of them shall not fall on the ground without your Father.* But the very hairs of your head are all numbered. Fear ye not therefore, ye are of more value than many sparrows.

> Watch therefore: for ye know not what hour your Lord doth come. But know this, that if the goodman of the house had known in what watch the thief would come, he would have watched, and would not have suffered his house to be broken up. *Therefore be ye also ready:* for in such hour as ye think not the Son of man cometh.

Matt. 10:28-31; 24:42-44

It was not only Seneca and his sons who could urge men to meet death with equanimity. Bishop Latimer, the Protestant martyr, in a sermon preached before King Edward VI speaks the thought and almost the words of Hamlet:

> *Unusquisque enim certum tempus habet praedefinitum a Domino*: "For every man hath a certain time appointed him of God, and God hideth that same time from us." For some die in young age, some in old age, according as it pleaseth him. He hath not manifested to us the time because he would have us at all times ready; else if I knew the time, I would presume upon it, and so should be worse. But he would have us ready at all times, and therefore he hideth the time of our death from us. . . . But of that we may be sure, there shall not fall one hair from our head without his will; and we shall not die before the time that God hath appointed unto us: which is a comfortable thing, specially in time of sickness or wars. . . . There be some which say, when their friends are slain in battle, "Oh, if he had tarried at home, he should not have lost his life." These sayings are naught: for God hath appointed every man his time. To go to war in presumptuousness, without an ordinary calling, such going to war I allow not: but when thou art called, go in the name of the Lord; and be well assured in thy heart that thou canst not shorten thy life with well-doing.[4]

The similarity of the phrase in *Hamlet* to the one in *Lear* is so close that the first may be taken as the model and prototype of the other. But in *Lear* the phrase has been transmuted, and with it the idea and attitude. The deliberate and developed rhetoric of *Measure for Measure* has served its purpose to explore the area of experience, and has been put aside. The riddling logicality of Hamlet's speech has been simplified to the bare utterance of:

> Men must endure
> Their going hence even as their coming hither

and the concept of the arbitrariness of birth has been introduced to reinforce the arbitrariness of death. Finally, Hamlet's precise and traditional statement, "the readiness is all," has been transformed into a metaphor.

What does the metaphor mean? There is no need for conjecture; it had already by the time of *Lear* become trite with use, and with use in contexts closely related to this. In Thomas Wilson's *Art of Rhetoric* (1560) we read:

> Among fruit we see some apples are soon ripe and fall from the tree in the midst of summer; other be still green and tarry till winter, and hereupon are commonly called winter fruit: even so it is with man, some die young, some die old, and some die in their middle age.[5]

Shakespeare has Richard in *Richard II* comment on the death of John of Gaunt:

> The ripest fruit first falls, and so doth he:
> His time is spent
>
> 2. 1. 153-54

8

That is, as fruit falls in the order of ripeness, so a man dies when his time is spent, at his due moment in the cosmic process. Again, Touchstone's dry summary of life and time in *As You Like It*:

> And so, from hour to hour, we ripe and ripe,
> And then, from hour to hour, we rot and rot
>
> 2. 7. 26-27

does not mean that we ripen to maturity and then decline, but that we ripen toward death, and then quite simply and with no metaphors rot.

But death is not incidental to Shakespearean tragedy; it is rather the defining characteristic. Just as a Shakespearean comedy is a play that has a clown or two and ends in marriages, so a tragedy involves characters of high estate and concludes with violent deaths. The principle of its being is death, and when this is achieved the play is ended. In this sense, then, "Ripeness is all" is the structural principle of Shakespearean tragedy. Thus in *Richard III* the Cassandra-like chorus, the old Queen Margaret, enters alone as the play draws rapidly on to the final catastrophe and says:

> So now prosperity begins to mellow
> And drop into the rotten mouth of death
>
> 4. 4. 1-2

And in *Macbeth*, Malcolm says toward the close:

> Macbeth
> Is ripe for shaking, and the pow'rs above
> Put on their instruments.
>
> 4. 3. 237-39

9

In this passage the powers above, who are the agents of Providence, are associated with the ripened time. Providence is destiny, and in tragedy destiny is death.

By "Ripeness is all," then, Shakespeare means that the fruit will fall in its time, and man dies when God is ready. The phrase gathers into the simplest of sentences, the most final of linguistic patterns, a whole history of attempted formulations, and by the rhetorical device of a traditional metaphor transposes a state into a process. Furthermore, the metaphor shifts our point of view from a man's attitude toward death, from the "readiness" of Hamlet and the "Men must endure" of the first part of Edgar's speech, to the absoluteness of the external process of Providence on which the attitude depends.

But this is not what the phrase means to the uninstructed modern reader, and this poses a problem. The modern meaning is one that is dear to us and one that is rich and important in itself. It would be natural to ask, Need we give it up? I see no reason why we should give up the meaning: maturity of experience is certainly a good, and the phrase in a modern context is well enough fitted to convey this meaning. But it is our phrase now, and not Shakespeare's, and we should accept the responsibility for it. The difference in meaning is unmistakable: ours looks toward life and his toward death; ours finds its locus in modern psychology and his in Christian theology. If we are secure in our own feelings we will accept our own meanings as ours, and if we have any respect for the great we will penetrate and embrace Shakespeare's meaning as his. For our purpose in the study of literature, and particularly in the historical interpretation of texts, is not in the ordinary sense to further the understanding of ourselves. It is rather to enable us to see how we could think and feel otherwise than as we do. It is to erect a larger context of experience within which we may define and understand our own by attending to the disparity between it and the experience of others.

In fact, the problem that is here raised with respect to literature is really the problem of any human relationship: Shall we understand another on his terms or on ours? It is the problem of affection and truth, of appreciation and scholarship. Shakespeare has always been an object of affection and an object of study. Now, it is common experience that affection begins in misunderstanding. We see our own meanings in what we love and we misconstrue for our own purposes. But life will not leave us there, and not only because of external pressures. What concerns us is naturally an object of study. We sit across the room and trace the lineaments of experience on the face of concern, and we find it is not what we thought it was. We come to see that what Shakespeare is saying is not what we thought he was saying, and we come finally to appreciate it for what it is. Where before we had constructed the fact from our feeling, we now construct our feeling from the fact. The end of affection and concern is accuracy and truth, with an alteration but no diminution of feeling.

AUGHT OF WOE OR WONDER

Whatever emotion and whatever tragedy may be, it has always been said that tragedy, and especially the tragic catastrophe, evokes strong and specific emotions. The doctrine is common to Antiquity and the present day as well as to Shakespeare and the Renaissance. "In undertaking any piece of literature," Erasmus remarks in a little Renaissance treatise on how to teach, "it is advisable to show what kind of work it is, the nature of its subject-matter, and what especially is to be looked for in that kind of work. . . . In tragedy one looks especially for the emotional effects, which are quite strong, and then for the means by which these effects are excited."[1] The nature of the effects, however, alters from period to period as the nature of tragedy alters and as the quality and structure of the emotional life varies from society to society, for there is a history of the emotions as well as a history of ideas. The effects we are concerned with here are those of Shakespearean tragedy and those specifically intended by the author and supported by his tradition. The question is, What emotional effects did Shakespeare intend to be evoked by the catastrophe of his greater tragedies?

I

We are told explicitly at the end of *Hamlet* what the emotional effect of the tragic catastrophe is: it is one of fear, sorrow, and wonder. The point is made in two passages, the first of which reads:

I follow thee.
I am dead, Horatio. Wretched queen, adieu!
You that look pale and tremble at this chance,
That are but mutes or audience to this act,
Had I but time (as this fell sergeant, Death,
Is strict in his arrest) O, I could tell you—
But let it be. Horatio, I am dead;
Thou liv'st; report me and my cause aright
To the unsatisfied.

5. 2. 343-51

The scene is familiar to every reader: the King and Queen are dead, Laertes has uttered his last words. And now Hamlet, in a fashion conventional to the Elizabethan drama, addresses his remarks rapidly to one character after another—to the dying Laertes, to Horatio, to the Queen; and finally he turns to the other actors on the stage, to the "mutes" who serve as "audience to this act." These "look pale and tremble": it is their function to express the proper emotional attitude and so to convey that attitude directly to the larger audience who witness the play, for emotional effects are directly transferable; indeed, they are much more communicable than ideas.

The way in which this process was understood in Shakespeare's time is explained by his contemporary, Thomas Dekker, in the prologue to one of his plays:

That man give me whose breast filled by the Muses
With rapture into a second them infuses;
Can give the actor sorrow, rage, joy, passion,
Whilst he again by self-same agitation
Commands the hearers, sometimes drawing out tears,
Then smiles, and fills them both with hopes and fears.[2]

The dramatist derives emotions from his sources of inspiration, infuses them into the actor, who in turn communicates them to the audience. The scheme of thought here is Platonic. It is that which Socrates explains to the professional reciter of Homer in Plato's dialogue *Ion* under the figure of a magnetic chain of attraction (533C), and doubtless is borrowed from that model. The Muse inspires Homer as a magnet moves an iron ring, the reciter Ion is moved by Homer as another ring by the magnetized one, and the audience finally is moved by Ion, so that three rings hang like a chain from the magnet. Thus feeling runs directly from the sources of poetry to the audience through the medium of poet and actor, and the emotions which in this case Ion excites in his hearers—fear, sorrow, and wonder (535B-C)[3]—are curiously enough those which Shakespeare in *Hamlet* ascribes to the tragic catastrophe. They are also, of course, the emotional effects which Aristotle ascribes to Greek tragedy—pity and fear, certainly, and as we shall see, wonder, too.[4]

The particular emotion denominated in the first passage from *Hamlet* is the conventional tragic effect of fear or terror, for to "look pale and tremble" are the very marks and signs of this. Richard in *Richard III* queries Buckingham on his qualifications for the role of tragic villain:

> Come, cousin, can'st thou quake and change thy color . . .
> As if thou wert distraught and mad with terror?

And Buckingham reassures him:

> Tut. I can counterfeit the deep tragedian.
>
> 3. 5. 1, 4-5

The emotion of fear is evoked by "this chance," in men who are "mutes or audience to this act." What is the precise meaning of "this act" and "this chance," since it is with respect to these that the effect is predicated? *Act* in such contexts signifies the particular course of events under consideration. So the First Gentleman comments on the narration of those extraordinary events that untangle the knot of *The Winter's Tale:* "The dignity of this act was worth the audience of kings and princes, for by such was it acted." (5. 2. 86-88) And Prospero in the Tempest, referring to the whole business of his deposition and exile, says to Alonso: "Thy brother was a furtherer in this act." (5. 1. 73) But the closest parallel to the present passage is in the final speech in *Othello* where Lodovico, the representative of the Venetian state, closes the play thus:

> Myself will straight aboard, and to the state
> This heavy act with heavy heart relate.

This heavy act—that is, "The tragic loading of this bed," the deaths of Desdemona and Othello. There is here an exact correspondence between the quality of the events and the quality of the emotion they evoke, between the heaviness of act and the heaviness of heart. Similarly the emotion of fear or terror would naturally be provoked by such fearful and terrible events as the deaths of the King, Queen, and Laertes, and the imminent death of Hamlet himself.

"This chance" has a meaning similar to "this act." It is, furthermore, a notion and a term intimately associated with the central Elizabethan conception of tragedy, and especially of the tragic catastrophe. It concentrates in a word the two main aspects of that event, aspects that had long been fused in the Latin equivalent, *casus*. For that word may signify, as it does in the late medieval collections of tragic stories, the fall and death of a great figure which constitutes the catastrophe; and it may also signify the external cause of such a fall, the operation of that agency which to man seems Chance or Fortune, but which from a true and theological point of view is to be regarded as the unfolding of Divine Providence. Indeed, nothing really happens by Chance or Fortune with respect to an absolute God, but only with respect to secondary causes: *nihil est a casu vel fortuna respectu Dei, sed respectu ceterarum causarum.*[5] Hence the display on the stage of the operation of Chance, which is but the inscrutable ways of Divine Providence, strikes the witnesses with fear and terror when the case is notable, for it illuminates the disparity between the relative world of man and the absoluteness of the Eternal Cause.

The bare word, of course, though shot through with the larger meanings of that historic term, does not carry with it such a full and explicit theory as has just been sketched. Yet its use here does imply the prior existence of such a context. What the bare word means can be ascertained by glancing through a Shakespeare concordance: the meaning ranges from the relatively colorless significance of "ordinary happening or event," through the denomination of such events as make up a narrative (*Cymb.* 5. 5. 391), to the strictly philosophical significance of "Chance or Fortune." But the phrase, "this chance," has also a special and restricted meaning. It means the fall and death of notable persons and has in it an element of suddenness and surprise, of the apparently fortuitous.

For example, in the *Tragedy of Locrine* (about 1591), a bad but representative play, the chorus promises us:

17

> the sequel shall declare
> What tragic chances fall out in this war.
>
> 2 Prol., 16-17[6]

And fall they do, one after another. So also King Henry in *Henry VI* speaks of the dead slain in battle:

> How will the country for these woful chances
> Misthink the king, and not be satisfied!
>
> 2. 5. 107-08

But the best example is in *Macbeth,* where Macbeth speaks of the murder of Duncan after its accomplishment:

> Had I but died an hour before this chance,
> I had liv'd a blessed time.
>
> 2. 3. 96-97

That is, "My life had ended in the state of grace (*I had liv'd a blessed time*) if I had died before resolving to murder my King (*an hour before this chance*)," for the fall from the state of grace was coincident with the moral decision. "This chance," then, is the murder of Duncan, a notable fall. In the passage from *Hamlet* it is the tragic catastrophe. And the immediate emotional effect of this on the audience is said to be fear.

But fear is not the only effect ascribed to the catastrophe. In another passage the effects are designated as those of sorrow and astonishment, or woe and wonder. After the death of Hamlet, the young Fortinbras enters in the majesty of state, and as he enters asks:

Where is this sight?

Horatio answers him:

> What is it you would see?
> If aught of woe or wonder, cease your search.
>
> 5. 2. 373-74

The tableau of destruction remains on the stage:

> O proud Death,
> What feast is toward in thine eternal cell
> That thou so many princes at a shot
> So bloodily hast struck?
>
> 5. 2. 375-78

And Horatio, who was privy to it all, defines this sight as one of woe and wonder, *doloris et admirationis.* It is interesting to note that in the First Quarto, the mangled stage version of *Hamlet,* the passage reads:

> *Enter Fortinbrasse with his traine*
>
> FORTINBRASSE: Where is this bloody sight?
>
> HORATIO: If aught of woe or wonder you'ld behold
> Then looke upon this tragicke spectacle.

In both texts the spectacle is characterized by its proper effects. One of these is *woe* or sorrow, which is the ground of pity, as it was to the Watch who discovered the bodies of Romeo and Juliet:

> We see the ground on which these woes do lie,
> But the true ground of all these piteous woes
> We cannot without circumstance descry.
>
> 5. 3. 179-81

Hence pity is evoked by the woes of the catastrophe of *Romeo*, the tragic deaths, by what the chorus-character, Friar Laurence, had already called in the same scene "this lamentable chance." (146) Nevertheless, woe is not precisely pity. It is the more general term, of which pity is a species. It is the English equivalent of that *dolor sive tristitia* which in the medieval tradition of literary criticism is noted, rather than pity (*misericordia sive commiseratio*), as the subject and effect of tragedy,[7] and which in the medieval tradition of psychological analysis (which is substantially the Renaissance tradition) is treated at length along with fear as one of the basic and most powerful passions of the soul. The others are joy and hope (St. Thomas, *ST,* 1-2. 25. 4). Pity, then, denotes precisely the relationship of the spectator to the catastrophe; but the nature of the catastrophe itself is woeful.

The relationship of the terms is that expounded by Edgar in *Lear.* To Gloucester's question:

> Now, good sir, what are you?

he answers:

> A most poor man, made tame to fortune's blows,
> Who, by the art of known and feeling sorrows,
> Am pregnant to good pity.
>
> 4. 6. 224-27

If we may apply this passage to the general notion of trage-
dy, we may say that Edgar is the ideal spectator. He has attained
the moral effect of that excitation of feeling; he has been "made
tame" by participating in "fortune's blows," which are the mate-
rial of tragedy; he has penetrated into that experience consciously
and has realized its significance in feeling, and so has attained to
the habit of, the capacity for exercising, the virtue of pity.

The catastrophe is sorrowful and naturally begets pity. It is
also sudden, surprising, on a large scale, and involves great per-
sons; hence it evokes wonder. This is an emotion less discussed in
connection with tragedy than either fear or sorrow, and one that
the literary person today does not easily think of as an emotion,
but it is a commonplace in the Renaissance especially in con-
nection with the deaths of notable persons and with the effects
of drama and fiction. Dekker, for instance, with reference to the
death of Queen Elizabeth, speaks of "the sorrow and amaze-
ment that like an earthquake began to shake the distempered
body of this island (by reason of our late sovereign's departure)."
And Sidney characterizes tragedy as "stirring the affects of ad-
miration and commiseration."[8] *Admiration,* of course, is simply
the Latin term for "wonder," as *commiseration* is for "pity." The
emotion itself is that state of overpowering surprise, the shocked
limit of feeling, which represents either the extreme of joy or, as
in this case, the extreme of fear. Indeed, in the medieval tradition
of psychological analysis it is defined as a species of fear (*ST,* 1-2.
41. 4), and thus the relation of wonder to fear is similar to that of
pity to sorrow.

II

Fear, sorrow, and wonder are the explicit effects of the tragic catastrophe of *Hamlet,* or so at least it is here argued. But even if one grants that the effects are named in the particular passages cited, they are not spoken by the author in his own person. They are spoken by characters in a play. The remarks are in character, no doubt, and have some bearing on the delineation of character, but they can hardly be taken as expressing the author's intention with regard to the play as a whole, for drama by its very nature denies the author not only the right but even the possibility of speaking in his own person. Whatever a character thinks, says, or does must be taken only as an expression of character, and as an action in the sense that character and action are but aspects of each other. Hence Hamlet's and Horatio's remarks are elements in the total effect of the play, functionally related to all other elements, but not to be taken as explicit comments which furnish a guiding principle of order for the whole and consequently represent the author's intention.

But the assumptions that lie behind this point of view do not apply to Elizabethan drama though they do apply to a good many modern works. The principal assumption is that the work as a whole is an indissoluble unit that exists only in its total effect. This is one aspect of the doctrine of organic form. The assumption operates in this way among others: whatever is said in a play is construed in the light of the critic's total impression of the work, or more often of the character who speaks since the delineation of character is usually taken to be the primary end of fiction. Hence a speech is first read as contributing to the whole, either of the play or of the character, and then reinterpreted so as to conform to the whole that the critic has constructed.

Whatever is discordant with this must be reconciled, often by the invocation of "irony," a device as fertile as Stoic allegory for disposing of the difficulties which the original text puts in the way of an interpretation.

Now, if every speech of an effective character is dramatic, in the modern sense, then it never means what it says but is only an expression of what the critic thinks the character's character is. What this leads to in practice can be made clear by an example. A modern critic, and a scholar quite learned in Renaissance thought, sees in Iago's rejoinder to Roderigo's confession of moral helplessness (*Othello,* 1. 3. 319*ff.*) "a grand perversion of the theory that good is the end and purpose of reason."[9] Roderigo has confessed with a shameless determinism his love for Desdemona, even though she is Othello's wife:

> What should I do? I confess it is my shame to be so fond, but it is not in my virtue to amend it.

And Iago replies:

> Virtue, a fig! 'Tis in ourselves that we are thus or thus. Our bodies are our gardens, to the which our wills are gardeners; so that if we will plant nettles or sow lettuce, set hyssop and weed up thyme, supply it with one gender of herbs or distract it with many— either to have it sterile with idleness or manured with industry—why, the power and corrigible authority of this lies in our wills.

The critic notes, "This passage states the ethics, the infidelity, of selfishness."

Perhaps he is misled by "Virtue, a fig!" (the punctuation is mine), overlooking the fact that in the context ("it is not in my virtue to amend it") "virtue" has quite obviously the common Elizabethan meaning of "power," and that Iago is consequently by no means making light of that virtue which is the opposite of vice. For what does Iago say? He picks up Roderigo's assertion that it is not in his power not to be a sinning fool, to go kill himself for love, and maintains that we do have the power to make ourselves one thing or the other, good or evil, to control or not to control our bodies, our lower natures, and that this power is our will. This, so far as I can see, is a notorious commonplace of the Christian tradition, as well as of the Aristotelian. It is plain and hoary orthodoxy, and there is no perversion in it. Of course, a theologian might object that Iago's position is too Pelagian, that it makes no provision for the Grace of God, but the statement is brief and is not theological in context; in fact, you will hardly restrain a man from killing himself for love by suggesting that the Grace of God may prevent his accomplishing his purpose.

The second objection that could be made against the orthodoxy of this passage is that it is, perhaps, too voluntaristic, that nothing is said of reason. But this objection fails if we quote the whole passage, for Iago continues:

> If the balance of our lives had not one scale of reason
> to poise another of sensuality, the blood and baseness
> of our natures would conduct us to most prepost'rous
> conclusions. But we have reason to cool our raging
> motions, our carnal stings, our unbitted lusts; whereof
> I take this that you call love to be a sect or scion.

That is, Iago identifies the power and corrigible authority that lies in our wills with reason. Hence, it is evident that it is the medieval and Christian concept of the reasonable will which he opposes to the deterministic sensuality of Roderigo. Finally, no one, I trust, will maintain that Iago slanders in this instance true Love by designating Roderigo's infection as lust, which it is.

Yet on this latter passage the critic remarks: "Iago understands the warfare between reason and sensuality, but his ethics are totally inverted; reason works in him not good, as it should according to natural law, but evil, which he has chosen for his good." This, as a remark on Iago's character and actions in general, is aptly and accurately put. But the remark purports to be on this particular passage, and as such it is precisely wrong.

The passage is one of the finest statements, especially in its rhythm, of the traditional and orthodox view of the relation of the reasonable will to the sensitive soul; it has, then, its own absolute value as "thought," as the accomplished saying of something very much worth saying. It has also its function in the plot and its relation to Iago's character, but this function and relationship is rather "mechanical" (in fact, hierarchical) than "organic" (that is, monistic). Yet the passage serves the larger purposes of the plot without losing and altering its own quality as such. In the plot, it is an argument to persuade Roderigo from suicide, and is such an argument as a divine might use. But Iago's purpose in persuasion is not to save Roderigo's soul but to save his person and his purse for the benefit of Iago's own designs. The evil lies in the end, the intention; the means and the accidental effects are in themselves good, nor do they lose that quality in being used for an evil end. It is good to prevent a man from killing himself. The argument employed is orthodox and true, and no less true for the circumstances. The devil quotes Scripture to his purpose, but you need not for this reason take Scripture as an expression of the devil's character.

A Shakespearean speech, then, takes its point in part from it-self, especially if it goes beyond the bare gist of what is needed for the plot, and in part from its context, from who says it and under what circumstances. But the relation of context and speech is one that depends on relevant considerations, and relevance is con-strued in terms of what is appropriate. It is beside the point, then, in considering the last scene of *Hamlet*, that Hamlet occupies a privileged position among Shakespeare's heroes, that he is said to be of all those the most lovingly and sympathetically presented, so much so that many feel in this instance the author has been partial to his character. It is beside the point, even, that earlier in the play Hamlet has shown a critical interest in the discussion of drama. His remarks to the players are called forth by that sit-uation and are appropriate to it, though they are also interesting in themselves and go quite beyond what is needed for the action.

It is somewhat in point that Hamlet is the hero, and especial-ly that he is at the moment he speaks the sole surviving member of the royal family, and hence for that moment the head of the state; he has the right to speak authoritatively. Besides, he is dy-ing, and one's last words are commonly supposed to be truthful. But the real point is that his remarks are addressed to the stand-ers-by as to an audience. They are a comment on the reactions of an audience, and must be taken as expressing how an audience would and should react. His remarks simply put into words what the other actors on the stage are to express in gesture, and if the actual audience does not feel the like, the play has been a failure.

III

The character of Horatio, however, and the circumstances under which he speaks are, in this respect, a little more complicated. In the first place, he speaks at the request of Fortinbras. And what is the significance of Fortinbras? He is the principle of renewed order in the state. He is the indispensable character for concluding a Shakespearean play; for each play, with the notable exception of *Troilus and Cressida*, begins with disorder in the state and concludes only on the restoration of order. As the representative of order he is in virtue of his office conceived of as reason: for authority is order, and order is reason. This is common doctrine. He speaks the truth and the truth is spoken to him. Consequently, his presence is almost a necessary condition for Horatio's remarks.

But what is the position of Horatio himself? Horatio, as has often been noted, is a kind of chorus. He is a special character outside of the plot, except insofar as he is the confidant of and spokesman for Hamlet. But he is not the kind of chorus that is swayed now to this side and now to that as the tides of sympathy and fortune shift, as is the Greek chorus, or the chorus in Jonson's *Cataline*. Horatio is the well-tempered man. He is the man of whom Hamlet has said:

> Since my dear soul was mistress of her choice
> And could of men distinguish, her election
> Hath seal'd thee for herself. For thou hast been
> As one, in suff'ring all, that suffers nothing;
> A man that Fortune's buffets and rewards
> Hath ta'en with equal thanks; and blest are those
> Whose blood and judgment are so well commingled
> That they are not a pipe for Fortune's finger
> To sound what stop she please. Give me that man
> That is not passion's slave, and I will wear him
> In my heart's core, ay, in my heart of hearts, As I do thee.
>
> 3. 2. 68-79

This speech has its own function in the scene—it is the play scene—and it serves particularly as a contrast with the later bitter ragging of Rosencrantz and Guildenstern: "You would play upon me; you would seem to know my stops; you would pluck out the heart of my mystery . . . ," and so on (3. 2. 380*ff.*). It has its own function as a thought worthy of being expressed and not inappropriate to the circumstances. But it is also the speech that establishes in fairly full and explicit terms the relevance of Horatio to the play.

One of the key terms in the passage is "election." This is a technical term in the medieval tradition for the act of moral choice (*ST,* 1-2, 13, translating Aristotle's *proairesis*) with respect to choosing the means to an end. The end is happiness, or some aspect of it, and true friendship with a just man is the means:

> Horatio, thou art e'en as just a man
> As e'er my conversation cop'd withal.
>
> 3. 2. 59-60

Thus election chooses Horatio. But moral choice is a function of reason, of the soul, and is exercised as soon as one attains the "age of reason," but not before (*ST,* 1. 100. 2, and 1-2. 13. 2. *contra*). Finally, the metaphor of sealing derives from the common Aristotelian and scholastic figure of imposing a seal on wax, which represents the relationship of form and matter: the choice of means gives determinate form to the end desired (*ST,* 1-2. 13. 1. c., especially *ad fin.*). The meaning is illustrated in the following passage:

NESTOR: . . . It is suppos'd
>
> He that meets Hector issues from our choice;
>
> And choice, being mutual act of all our souls,
>
> Makes merit her election
>
> *Troilus*, 1. 3. 346-49

Choice is an act of the soul; the particular act of choosing this or this as means is "election." Sometimes the choice is erroneous, the will is carried away by the sensitive appetite (*ST,* 1-2. 77):

HECTOR: But value dwells not in particular will:
>
> It holds his estimate and dignity
>
> As well wherein 'tis precious of itself
>
> As in the prizer. Tis mad idolatry
>
> To make the service greater than the god;
>
> And the will dotes that is attributive
>
> To what infectiously itself affects
>
> Without some image of th' affected merit.

TROILUS: I take to-day a wife, and my election
>
> Is led on in the conduct of my will,
>
> My will enkindled by mine eyes and ears,
>
> Two traded pilots 'twixt the dangerous shores,
>
> Of will and judgment. How may I avoid,
>
> Although my will distaste what it elected,
>
> The wife I chose?
>
> *Troilus*, 2. 2. 53-67

Similarly in *Cymbeline*:

SECOND LORD: If it be a sin to make a true election,
>
> she is damn'd.
>
> 1.2.29-30

To return, Hamlet says that Horatio is the man whom Hamlet, when he came to the age of reason, selected by a reasonable choice as the fit co-respondent of his dear soul, which is in its essence reason. For Horatio is one who is open to all experience but who suffers by it no inner alteration of his reasonable form. He is impassive to all passions. He is indifferent to the external operations of fortune, for he is a man of perfected self-mastery, scaled by grace, in whom the irrational and the rational are in due relation, the one subordinated to the other; and thus the inner unalterable core of reasonable order is not subject to the irrational alterations produced by the impingement of external circumstances. Hence Horatio should be regarded as the ideal commentator, like the similar characters in Jonson's plays, Cordatus, Crites, and Horace: he is reason expressing reasonable judgment on the action.

The point perhaps calls for some elaboration. The ideal spokesman in Elizabethan literature is always spokesman by virtue of his reasonableness. He is never intended to be biographically identifiable with the author, though of course it would be impossible for authors so individual as Shakespeare and Jonson not to infuse some of their own qualities into a character. But the Elizabethan author had no intention of expressing his own personality, either in a character or in his work as a whole. In fact, he did not know that he had such a thing as a personality, for the concept of personality can hardly be said to have been formed. It was the reasonable soul that was the central psychological concept of the Renaissance, and a man was praiseworthy, as Horatio was, insofar as the reasonable soul spoke in him and was hearkened to. It is true that a man was considered to have certain individualizing properties derived from his sex, his time of life, and his position in society, but these were comprised in the concept of decorum. They were the differentiations of reasonableness in accordance with circumstance. Whatever traits he might have beyond these, as for instance, melancholy or foppery, were the result of a disturbance of reasonable balance and a deviation from the ideal norm, and they were vicious insofar as they deviated. All this is familiar to the student of the Renaissance, but the conclusion is that the character who is presented as conforming to the ideal norm is presented as a standard by which deviations from the norm may be charted, and when he speaks he speaks in the light of reason, and what he says represents the author's explicit intentions. For the author himself is reason.

IV

The question of under what circumstances Horatio speaks has now been answered in part. He speaks in reply to Fortinbras's request, and Fortinbras is the principle of reason and order in the state, who expounds and exacts the truth; and he himself is the reasonable commentator.

But the situation is more complicated than this. The situation at the end of *Hamlet* is the kind of final one which is customary in Shakespeare's plays. The loose ends, or most of them, are now tied up; the course of action is recapitulated and in part explained; and the representative of the state invites the principal remaining characters to "go hence, to have more talk of these sad things" (*Romeo,* 5. 3. 307), "where we may leisurely / Each one demand and answer to his part."(*The Winter's Tale,* 5. 3.152-53) But in *Hamlet* this basic situation is given a curious expansion and development.

We have already seen how Hamlet treats the cast on the stage as spectators of the catastrophe, and have quoted the passage in which he turns to Horatio, and, as it were, deputizes him. He lays on Horatio the charge "to tell my story," a charge which Horatio accepts when he proposes later to "speak to th' yet unknowing world / How these things came about." Indeed Fortinbras accepts the proposal: "Let us haste to hear it," he says, "And call the noblest to the audience." (5. 2. 360, 390, 397-98)

The lines are so familiar that the reader may not notice what is happening. It is implied in a series of ambiguities, as was implied more openly in Hamlet's speech, that the minor characters who remain on the stage are to be regarded as an audience. Such a notion is involved in Fortinbras's pun, to "call the noblest to the audience," for they shall attend the audience of the new king, and they shall be an audience to whom the events will be related. In like fashion, Horatio asks, before he begins his resumé of the plot, that orders be given that the bodies of the main characters in the catastrophe "High on a stage be placed to the view"; these bodies, then, which are to be placed on a ceremonial stage become by virtue of an obvious pun the characters who will act on a theatrical stage. For the difference between Hamlet's relation to his quasi-audience and Horatio's is this: the other characters are treated by Hamlet as spectators of the events which just took place on the stage; they are treated by Horatio as spectators or auditors of the events that he is about to recount or present. Horatio, who has been deputized by Hamlet to tell his story, is treated in the end almost as if he were the author of the play of *Hamlet*. The events which we have just seen on the stage are treated according to the usual dramatic convention as if they had just now really happened. They are reality, and the play about this reality will only begin when the play we have seen is over.

Thus Horatio, who is about to give an account of these events, is the imitator and expounder of the reality we have seen. It is in keeping with this curious sleight-of-hand that, in preparation for the play that will follow the final bare stage, Horatio presents the argument of the events in a kind of prologue:

> give order that these bodies
> High on a stage be placed to the view;
> And let me speak to th' yet unknowing world
> How these things came about. So shall you hear
> Of carnal, bloody, and unnatural acts;
> Of accidental judgments, casual slaughters;
> Of deaths put on by cunning and forc'd cause,
> And, in this upshot, purposes mistook
> Fall'n on th' inventors' heads. All this can I
> Truly deliver.
>
> 5. 2. 388-97

The passage is in effect a summary of the preceding action. It is in form an argument of the relation which is supposed to follow, and it has the stylistic qualities of the conventional argument. But what is more—it is the truth: "All this can I truly deliver," for I am the repository of Hamlet's trust, I am the reasonable man and hence the ideal spokesman, I am the intention of the author.

Consequently, Horatio's *Hamlet* is also Shakespeare's *Hamlet*. Each is constituted by the plot, by what happens. Each is concerned with "carnal, bloody, and unnatural acts," and these are, respectively, the adultery, murder, and incest which precede and lay the foundation for the play. The accidental judgment which leads to the casual slaughter is Hamlet's mistaking Polonius for the King, a judgment based upon misconstrued signs and hence not a true or substantial judgment. This is clear to anyone who is familiar with the scholastic discussion of manslaughter, or casual homicide. To employ the Latin terminology which Shakespeare uses in its anglicized form, this judgment *per accidens* leads to a slaughter which is *praeter intentionem*, and so casual, not causal (*ST, 2-2*. 64. 8).

Perhaps the idea here deserves a short digression. It appears again in an extraordinary passage in *The Winter's Tale*. Florizel says, in reply to the question, "Have you thought on a place whereto you'll go?" after marrying Perdita:

> Not any yet;
> But as th' unthought-on accident is guilty
> To what we wildly do, so we profess
> Ourselves to be the slaves of chance and flies
> Of every wind that blows.

> 4. 4. 548-52

The philosophy, no doubt, is too great for the occasion, but there is no reason to assume that it is not pertinent. Nevertheless, this is surely an odd passage, and the oddness lies in the comparison, in the *as* clause. For, to profess oneself the slave of chance and fly of every wind that blows is a common notion and fairly easy to understand; it is an indulgence often granted to young lovers by those whom their actions are not liable to hurt. But the notion is qualified by the preceding clause: we are the slaves of chance, Florizel says, in the sense in which the unthought-on accident is guilty to what we wildly do. What does this mean?

It depends on the distinction in casuistry that is drawn in Horatio's phrase above—that between causal and casual actions.

The distinction is especially clear in the discussions of actions which arise from drunkenness, or any similar slate of "wildly doing." For example, if a man gets drunk and in that state "unintentionally" kills another, he is not directly guilty of homicide spiritually, whatever he may be legally, for the result is beyond his intention. But he does not on this account get off spiritually easily. He is guilty of such a degree of irrational drunkenness as rendered the homicide possible, or even probable. The substance of his sin, then, lay in the choice by which he came into the condition of "wildly doing." The example is St. Thomas's. Hooker in the *Laws of Ecclesiastical Polity* deals with an analogous case:

> Finally, that which we do being evil, is notwithstanding by so much more pardonable, by how much the exigence of so doing or the difficulty of doing otherwise is greater; unless this necessity or difficulty have originally arisen from ourselves. It is no excuse therefore unto him, who being drunk committeth incest, and allegeth that his wits were not his own; inasmuch as himself might have chosen whether his wits should by that mean have been taken from him.
>
> 1.9.1[10]

In brief, then, the initial choice is intentional; the precise consequences may be accidental and the result of chance. Such is the scheme of thought that lies behind the *as* clause. The initial choice of going off with Perdita is within Florizel's power, and he will make it, for he has embraced the condition of "wildly doing":

> FLORIZEL: From my succession wipe me, father! I
>   Am heir to my affection.

CAMILLO: Be advis'd.

FLORIZEL: I am, and by my fancy. If my reason;
      Will thereto be obedient, I have reason;
      If not, my sense, better pleas'd with madness,
      Do bid it welcome.

CAMILLO: This is desperate, sir.

4. 4. 491-96

He is heir to his emotions; he is advised by imagination to which his reason must subscribe. Hence what follows, as particularly the place whereto they'll go, will be accidental and the result of chance. It will be, like the death of Polonius, casual.

But to return to Horatio's speech in *Hamlet*—the "deaths put on by cunning and forced cause" are, of course, the deaths of Rosencrantz and Guildenstern, and "this upshot" in which the intrigue with dramatic justice recoils on the intriguers is the final scene of the play.

There is obviously a point-for-point correspondence between the items of Horatio's list and the main events of the central plot of *Hamlet.* However, the items themselves are not particularized as in the traditional argument, but generalized.[11] No names are mentioned, no particular circumstances alluded to. And the generalization is pointed by the consistent use of the generalized plural: *acts, judgments, slaughters, deaths, purposes, inventors;* for, though some of these items may be considered to be proper plurals, it is significant that all are pluralized. The items listed are such classes of action as generally form the subject matter of tragedy. They do not precisely correspond to, but they are of the same nature as, the items in the Donatan tradition, or in, for example, Scaliger's list of the subject matters of tragedy: "The matters of tragedy are great and terrible, as commands of kings, slaughters, despair, suicides, exiles, bereavements, parricides, incests, conflagrations, battles, the putting out of eyes, weeping, wailing, bewailing, funerals, eulogies, and dirges." Nor are such lists simply to be found in critical treatises: they are the common property of the times. In his theological controversy with Bishop Jewel, Mr. Harding seizes the occasion of Jewel's mention of Sophocles to insert a summary description of tragedy. "A tragedy," he says, "setteth forth the overthrows of kingdoms, murder of noble personages, and other great troubles, and endeth in woful lamentations." And Jewel retorts with a full list of the terrible tragic events associated with the villainous Popes of Rome.[12]

In brief, Horatio promises his audience a tragedy. "So shall you hear," he says—and then follows a generalized list of items which every member of the audience recognized at once as equivalent to the single word—"tragedy." The implication is that *Hamlet* is a tragedy because it presents such tragic actions. Furthermore, the effects of tragedy that Shakespeare mentions in this scene—pity, fear, astonishment—arise from the nature of the tragic actions themselves, for these actions are, as Scaliger says, great and terrible, and they evoke a corresponding response. They are terrible in that they are great, and pitiable and wonderful for the same reason. Such an equation between the greatness of the persons and the action and the greatness of the tragic response is explicitly formulated in the final comment of Octavius, the representative of the state at the conclusion of *Antony and Cleopatra:*

> High events as these
> Strike those that make them; and their story is
> No less in pity than his glory which
> Brought them to be lamented.
>
> 5. 2. 363-66

37

A tragedy, then, is defined by the kind of actions it presents, and the effect of tragedy is the direct result of the presentation of such actions, though the validity of the effect may depend upon other considerations. The effect, moreover, is one of fear, sorrow, and wonder. This is no doubt a relatively crude aesthetic, but it is substantially Aristotle's, and it is Shakespeare's. It is also true.

THE DONATAN TRADITION

Fear, sorrow, and wonder are the emotions explicitly associated with tragedy, not only in *Hamlet,* but generally in the tradition of literary criticism of Shakespeare's day. The tradition is well known. It derives from a few timeworn texts which were repeated with the singlemindedness with which one recites the penny catechism.[1]

I

The basic text for the theory of tragedy comes from a schoolbook of the late classical period, Donatus on Terence:

> There are many differences between tragedy and comedy, but the principal difference is that in comedies the characters are of moderate estate, the difficulties that arise are slight, and the outcome of it all is joyful; but the marks of tragedy are precisely the opposite; the characters are great, the actions fearful in the extreme, and the outcome is sad and involves deaths. Again, in comedy all is disturbed at the beginning and tranquil at the close; in tragedy the order of progression is exactly reversed. The moral of tragedy is that life should be rejected; of comedy, that it should be embraced. And, finally, in comedy the story is always made-up; in tragedy, the story is commonly true and based on history.[2]

Tragedy and comedy are precise contraries; from this center the particular marks of distinction are evolved and disposed. Such a way of looking at things was quite congenial to the medieval mind, whose basic discipline was the logic of Aristotle and the principles of identity, contradiction, and the law of the excluded middle, and whose view of men was conditioned by the doctrine of Heaven and Hell, good and evil, grace and sin, and of the irreparable differences between them. There went along with this the clarity of definition and discrimination which this habit of mind encouraged. If the clarity broke down in practice, if in the hurly-burly of the stage comedy intruded on tragedy, this could only be ascribed, so long as the habit of mind persisted, to the imperfect nature of man, which it was the duty of thought and intention to remedy. Hence tragicomedy, for example, did not pose a practical problem since it was actually in existence, nor a problem of authority since it had the warrant of Plautus, but a logical problem, and almost an insuperable one, for the two elements were defined by their opposition.

The distinctions which Donatus establishes between the two forms are firmly held throughout the tradition. They are distinctions of 1) character, 2) order of progression in the plot, 3) source and kind of plot, 4) moral purpose, 5) kind of incident and the accompanying emotional effect, 6) kind of conclusion and the accompanying emotional effect, together with three additional principles stated in other texts than Donatus— 7) the nature of the subject matter, 8) the principle which accounts for the turn in the fortune of the characters, and 9) the nature of the style. Several of these imply each other, and a few corollary distinctions enter in the later tradition, but on the whole these principles, the first six of which are clearly stated in Donatus, sufficiently characterize the tradition and amply account for the nature of tragedy on the Elizabethan stage. Indeed, if these distinctions are taken seriously and regarded as principles of order by which the dramatist writes as he does rather than as rules external to the work, it will be seen that Elizabethan tragedy, including *Hamlet,* is in large part given merely by the acceptance of these principles. It follows that the historian of Elizabethan drama might more plausibly begin with the traditional definition than with the earliest examples of medieval drama. The latter are historical forerunners which only in small part account for the developed product; the definition is almost the Archetype itself, in which the seminal ideas, the principles of order, explicitly dwell.

The first distinction is that the tragic characters must be great, and this means of high rank. It is the modern feeling that this is an artificial stipulation, explicable only in light of the erroneous social ideas of our ancestors. But *The Death of a Salesman* is not a tragedy in the old sense, and so one might conjecture there is something else involved: there is involved a radical difference in the nature of the tragic effect. For the field of tragedy will be the state, since men of high rank are rulers of the state. Tragedy will then involve not private life and private feeling—this is the province of comedy—but public life and public feeling. But public feeling is different in kind from private.[3] A public calamity moves us in a different way than does a private one. The murder of John Doe is one thing; the assassination of Trotsky or of Admiral Darlan is another. Hence the tragic emotions in the older tradition will be predominantly communal and public, and we will find that a similar qualification is implied in the other principles of order which Donatus distinguishes.

The second distinction is that the direction of the action in tragedy is from order to disorder; in comedy the converse. How deeply this scheme had entered into Shakespeare's thought can be conjectured from the passage in *Lear* in which it forms the structural framework of the expression. Edgar soliloquizes on the heath:

> To be worst,
> The lowest and most dejected thing of fortune,
> Stands still in esperance, lives not in fear.
> The lamentable change is from the best;
> The worst returns to laughter.

4. 1. 2-6

The change appropriate to tragedy ("the lamentable change") is from the best; the change from the worst is comedy. Yet Shakespearean tragedy does not exhibit this progression in its simple form. The greater part of a Shakespearean tragedy does, it is true, consist of a progression toward deeper and deeper disorder, but a) the beginning is not tranquil since there is already some disorder (as in the opening scenes of *Romeo, Hamlet,* and *Othello*), and b) the end always involves (with the curious exception of *Troilus* whose literary form is still a matter of dispute) the restoration of order and tranquility. That is, the principle is clearly operative, but under certain limitations.

We can see, however, why the limitations are introduced: a) Since the play deals with disorder, it is simple craftsmanship to begin with at least the first motions of disorder, and if a traditional precept be needed, Horace is at hand with the admonition to begin in the middle of things, which Shakespeare himself invokes in the prologue to *Troilus*. b) As for the conclusion, the concept of order was of such importance to Shakespeare and his contemporaries, and politically of such importance, that we may assume that he neither cared to end a play in disorder (except for *Troilus*), nor perhaps would he have felt safe in so doing. But beyond this, order at the end of such harrowing experiences as constitute tragedy implies an intention to communicate to the spectators a commensurate order in feeling—by a tranquil close to dismiss them in calm of mind, all passion spent. But this calm of mind is correlative with order in the state: the aesthetic feeling is in part political in nature.[4]

The third distinction is that the plot of tragedy is commonly historical and true, not feigned. We can understand, then, the fusion of the historical chronicle play and tragedy in Elizabethan drama, for it has its critical justification in this tenet. But if tragedy is historical, it is not merely realistic as distinguished from being fanciful; it has rather the compelling absoluteness of accomplished fact. Hence its effect will be accompanied by the recognition that things could not be otherwise, since this is how in fact they were. It follows from this, as from the principles of high rank in personages and of concluding order in the state, that the emotional effects of tragedy will be of a kind consonant with these requirements. They will be more impersonal than personal. The experiences which the spectator will associate with these effects, the traces and memories which will give them substance, will be drawn not from the guarded and private world of his sensibility, but from the more communal world of his public self. The content of the effects will thus be different in kind from that which the uninstructed modern reader will experience, and a comparable difference in kind is implied in the next principle.

This, the fourth, is the moral purpose of tragedy. Donatus tells us that the lesson expressed in tragedy is the rejection of life (*fugienda vita*). Thus, in a Christian and political context tragedy will be regarded as a warning against pride and against trusting in worldly prosperity. Sidney, for example, maintains that tragedy "with stirring the affects of admiration and commisera-tion teacheth the uncertainty of this world and upon how weak foundations gilden roofs are builded";[5] and Jonson closes *Sejanus* with these massive reflections:

> Let this example move th' insolent man
> Not to grow proud and careless of the gods.
> It is an odious wisdom to blaspheme,
> Much more to slighten or deny their powers;
> For whom the morning saw so great and high,
> Thus low and little fore the even doth lie.

But if one takes into account the subsequent principles in Donatus' definition, the fifth, that the incidents of tragedy in-volve great fears, and the sixth, that the catastrophe involves deaths and is sorrowful (*exitus funesti*), it will be clear that resigna-tion to death in the Christian sense is the natural moral to such tragedy. It is, in fact, the moral of *Hamlet,* expressed by the hero as he goes to the catastrophe, disturbed by forebodings of the tragic issue:

> we defy augury; there's a special providence in the
> fall of a sparrow. If it be now, 'tis not to come; if it be
> not to come; it will be now; if it be not now, yet it will
> come: the readiness is all.
>
> 5. 2. 230-33

Such acquiescence, if we should take the Donatan moral se-riously, would constitute the catharsis of this kind of tragedy, the effect of the tragic effect. It would be one of logic and theolo-gy, whose instrument is teaching, and whose end is Christian resignation.

But what must be the nature of the emotional effects themselves if they are to conduce to such an end? They must be impersonal to a marked degree. For resignation is the subsumption, and almost the loss, of the individual under the general. One's own death cannot be a matter of frightened concern, since it is not peculiar but common, since it is inevitable and given. So Caesar:

> Of all the wonders that I yet have heard,
> It seems to me most strange that men should fear,
> Seeing that death, a necessary end,
> Will come when it will come.
>
> *Julius Caesar,* 2. 2. 34-37

And Gertrude to Hamlet:

> Thou know'st 'tis common. All that lives must die,
> Passing through nature to eternity.
>
> 1. 2. 72-73

Thus the emotional disturbance of tragic incident is resolved in resignation.

The process is traditional in Christianity. Thomas Aquinas, for example, tells us (*ST,* 1-2. 42. 2. ad 3) that death and other lapses of Nature have Universal Nature, or Eternal Law, as cause; but the nature of a particular being fights against such lapses as much as it can, and from this striving springs sorrow and anguish when death is seen as present, fear and terror when it looms in the future. These are the tragic emotions, and aroused by the tragic fact of death. Resignation in this tradition is nothing other than the acquiescence of Particular in Universal Nature. It is nothing other than an effective belief in logic, so that to perceive the subsumption of instance under rule is to be satisfied. If all men are mortal, then Hamlet, being a man, is also mortal.

But emotional effects that are ordered toward acquiescence, disturbances that are intended to subside, are different in kind from those that are exploitable and are intended to be enjoyed. The latter are sentimental and private; the former are in potency to the impersonal order of their envisaged end.

II

A tragedy is a succession of fearful incidents, enacted by persons of high rank, that progresses from initial calm into ever-deepening disaster, and concludes sadly in deaths. Fear and sorrow are its appropriate emotions, fear of the catastrophe and sorrow at its accomplishment. They are appropriate because they are the natural emotions with which men regard death in prospect and in fulfillment. They are, furthermore, emotions of a public and impersonal order.

The similarity of this definition to that of Aristotle's *Poetics* is obvious, and in all likelihood the tradition derives partly from Aristotle himself, if not from the *Poetics* (which seems to have been little known in Antiquity and to have been recovered in the West only in the thirteenth century), then from his lost dialogue *On Poets* and from his student Theophrastus and the Peripatetic School. From such sources the tradition descended to the Alexandrian and Roman scholars, and from them to the school texts of late Antiquity.[6] But the history is not important in this connection. What is important is that these notions entered into the texture of medieval thought and came to the Renaissance as commonplaces. Hence, I shall present now a few additional texts in which may be distinguished certain further and corollary principles of order, together with a text from the late Middle Ages and one from Shakespeare's day in which can be seen the consistency of the tradition and the liveliness of reapprehension with which it was entertained two thousand years after Aristotle.

Of equal importance with that of Donatus is the definition of Diomedes, a grammarian of the fourth century A.D.:

> Tragedy involves the full cycle of fortune turning to adversity in characters of the heroic age—this is Theophrastus' definition. . . . Comedy—we render the Greek definition—involves a full cycle in the fortune of private citizens, but never the danger of death. . . . The fortunes involved in comedy are those of little streets and unimportant households, not as in tragedy of princes and men of state. . . . The distinctions between comedy and tragedy are these: the characters of tragedy are semidivine, leaders of the state, kings; those of comedy are unimportant and private persons. The subjects of tragedy are woes, exiles, deaths; of comedy, love affairs and seductions. Finally, the movement of events in tragedy is almost always from happy circumstances to bitter deaths, accompanied at the end with the perception that the fortunes of the house involved have gone to ruin. Hence comedy and tragedy are by definition distinct: the one a full cycle of harmless incident, the other a reversal of great fortunes. Sorrow, then, is characteristic of tragedy.
>
> *Ars Grammatica,* 3[7]

To this may be added two passages from Isidore of Seville's encyclopedia, the *Britannica* of ten centuries. The first is from the section "On Poets":

> The tragic writers have attained considerable fame, principally for the plots of their plays, which are fashioned in the image of truth. . . . The comic writers deal with the lives of private citizens; the tragic, however, with affairs of state and the histories of kings. Similarly, the plots of tragedies deal with woful material; of comedies, with happy.
>
> *Etymologiae*, 8. 7. 5-6

The second passage is from the section "On Shows":

> Tragedians are those who recite to an audience a lamentable poem about historical events and the crimes of wicked princes.

As early as the tenth century this is contracted into the curt phrase: *tragoedia luctuosum carmen.* Tragedy is a lamentable tale, a woeful story. To these texts may be added the influential sentence from Boethius' *Consolation of Philosophy: "quid tragoediarum clamor aliud deflet nisi indiscreto ictu fortunam felicia regna vertentem?"* which Chaucer translates:

> What other thyng bywalen the cryinges of trage- dyes but oonly the dedes of Fortune that with unwar strook overturneth the realmes of great nobleye? (*Glose. Tragedye is to seyn a dite of a prosperite for a tyme, that endeth in wrecchidness.*)
>
> 2. Prose 2

together with Ovid's remark, "Tragedy is weightier in style than any other genre." (*Tristia,* 2. 381)

From these texts we may distinguish some additional principles of order. The seventh defines the range of subject matter: woes, exiles, slaughter, the crimes and villainies of princes, the ruin of a noble house, the downfall of kingdoms. The eighth defines the organization of the plot, which describes a period, a full circle, so that the tragic character may say at the end as Edmund says in *Lear:*

> The wheel is come full circle; I am here.
>
> 5. 3. 174

The principle of alteration, the power that turns the circle of prosperity, is Fortune, whose indiscriminate blow overturns prosperous kingdoms. The importance of this principle is well known and generally conceded. It accounts for the dominant conception of tragedy in the late Middle Ages and the Renaissance, that tragedy is the fall from prosperity of a character of high estate.

A classic example is Marlowe's *Edward II,* where in the final scene the Queen says to Mortimer:

> Now, Mortimer, begins our tragedy.
>
> 2591

And the nature of the tragedy is defined a few lines later by Mortimer himself:

> Base Fortune, now I see that in thy wheel
> There is a point to which when men aspire
> They tumble headlong down. That point I touched,
> And, seeing there was no place to mount up higher,

Why should I grieve at my declining fall?
Farewell, fair Queen, weep not for Mortimer
That scorns the world and, as a traveller,
Goes to discover countries yet unknown.

2627-34

The fall in this case is followed by Mortimer's death, and in general the tragic fall is consummated by death, so that the principle of Fortune and the principle of death are identified. Nevertheless, it is probably significant to ascertain upon which of the two emphasis is laid: here the emphasis is clearly on the fall; in Shakespeare it is clearly on death. Furthermore, the fall is generally sudden and absolute: note Chaucer's mistranslation as "unwar strook," or unforeseen, of *indiscreto ictu,* which means "a random stroke." This introduces the element of surprise, which will in part account for the addition of the effect of wonder, and which will obviously serve to transfer the effect of fear from the incidents that precede the catastrophe to the catastrophe itself.

The ninth is the principle of style: tragedy requires the weighty or high style, a requirement which is implied by the principle of decorum:

But to present a kingly troop withal,
Give me a stately-written tragedy,
Tragoedia cothurnata, fitting kings.
Containing matter, and not common things.

Spanish Tragedy, 4. 154-57

For only the high style in its aspect of gravity is fitted to deal with affairs of state, and only the high style in its aspect of forceful utterance, of passion and vividness, is fitted to deal with crimes and villainies, and to call forth the terror, the woe, and especially the wonder which it is the peculiar function of high rhetoric to produce.

These texts, with others which need not be cited here, were copied again and again throughout the Middle Ages, repeatedly glossed, and indeed became so trite and commonplace that they can scarcely be said to have a history, only a continued and recurrent existence. One example will suffice to illustrate the continuation. It is a passage from Lydgate's *Troy Book* (about 1420) in which he develops a remark by Guido delle Colonne to the effect that tragedies and comedies were said to have been first acted at Troy:

> And first also, I rede, that in Troye
> Wer song and rad lusty fresche comedies,
> And other dites, that called be tragedies.
> And to declare, schortly in sentence   845
> Of bothe two the final difference:
> A comedie hath in his gynning,
> At prime face, a maner compleyning,
> And afterward endeth in gladnes;
> And it the dedis only doth express   850
> Of swiche as ben in pouert plounged lowe;
> But tragidie, who so list to knowe,
> It begynneth in prosperite,
> And endeth euer in aduersity;
> And it also doth the conquest trete   855
> Of riche kynges and of lordys grete,
> Of mighty men and olde conquerou[ri]s,
> Whiche by fraude of Fortunys schowris
> Ben ouercast and whelmed from her glorie

Of a Theatyre stondynge in the princypale
paleys of Troye, declarenge the falle of
Pryncys and others.

And whilon thus was halwed the memorie   860
Of tragedies, as bokis make minde,
Whan thei wer rad or songyn, as I fynde,
In the theatre ther was a smal auter
Amyddes set, that was half circuler,
Whiche in-to the Est of custom was directe;   865
Up-on the whiche a pulpit was erecte,
And ther-in stod an aw[n]cien poete,
For to reherese by rhetorikes swete
The noble dedis, that wer historial,
Of kynges, princes for a memorial,   870
And of thes olde, worthi Emperours,
The grete emprises eke of conquerours,
And how thei gat in Martis high honour
The laurer grene for fyn of her labour,
The palm of knyghthod disservid by [old] date,   875
Or Parchas mad hem passyn in-to fate.
And after that, with chere and face pale,
With stile enclyned gan to turne his tale,
And for to synge, after al her loos,
Ful mortally the stroke of Antropos,   880
And telle also, for al her worthihede,
The sodeyn brekyng of her lives threde:
How pitiously thei made her mortal ende
Thorugh fals Fortune, that al the world will schende,
And how the fyn of al her worthines   885
Endid in sorwe and in highe tristesse,
By compassyng of fraude or fals tresoun,

By sodeyn mordre or vengaunce of poysoun,
Or conspirynge of fretyng fals envye,
How unwarly that thei dide dye;   890
And how her renoun and her highe fame
Was of hatrede sodeynly made lame;
And how her honour drowe un-to decline;
And the meschef of her unhappy fyne;
And how Fortune was to hem unswete—   895
AI this was tolde and rad of the poete,
And whil that he in the pulpet stood,
With dedly face al devoide of blood,
Singinge his dites, with muses al to-rent,
Amydde the theatre schrowdid in a tent,   900
Ther cam out men gastful of her cheris,
Disfigurid her facis with viseris,
Pleying by signes in the peples sight,
That the poete songon hath on hight;
So that ther was no maner discordaunce   905
Atwen his dites and her contenaunce:
For lik as he aloft[e] dide expresse
Wordes of Ioye or of heuynes,
Moving and cher, bynethe of hem pleying,
From point to point was alwey answering—   910
Now trist, now glad, now hevy, and [now] light,
And face chaunged with a sodeyn sight,
So craftily thei koude hem transfigure,
Conformyng hem to the chaunt[e]plure,
Now to synge and sodeinly to wepe,   915
So wel thei koude her observaunces kepe.[8]

Here are all the elements of the tradition, though jumbled together and in no particular order. The concept of tragedy is essentially determined, as it is in Donatus and Diomedes, by contrast with the concept of comedy. (845-46) Tragedy begins happily and ends in adversity (852*ff.*); the external principle of the reversal is Fortune (858-59; 884; 895); the characters are rich kings and great lords (856); tragedy is rhetorical (868), that is, in high style—"stile enclyned" (878)—and in verse (844); the subject matter is historical (869); the narrator clearly displays fear (877) and this is associated with the rhetorical manner and with the subject of death (878*ff.*); in fact, the terror which the narrator displays "with dedly face al devoide of blood" "as he tears the cat ("the muses al torente") in bombastic high style is mirrored in the pantomime of the dumb-show, and, in general, there is an exact correspondence between the fear, sorrow, emotional excitation ("meving"), and the joy of the text and of the illustrative action, together with a considerable range in the emotions called forth. (897-916) Furthermore, the catastrophe is piteous (883) and sorrowful (886); it is sudden (882), and is brought about by violence and deceit—fraud, false treason, sudden murder, the vengeance of poison, or the conspiracy of biting envy (887-89); in fact, the tragic catastrophe is precisely sudden and violent death. (880*ff.*).

But here are also most of the elements of Elizabethan tragedy, and some that, though corollaries to the principles enunciated in the earlier tradition, are not explicit there. For example: if Marlowe's *Tamburlaine* is a tragical discourse and its presentation a "tragic glass," as it is called on the title page and in the prologue to the original edition, this is because the play is in high style and as Lydgate here says:

54

> doth the conquest trete
> Of riche kynges and of lordys grete,
> Of mighty men and olde conquerou[ri]s.

The introduction of the notion of the "conspiringe of fre-tyng fals envye" as engineering the tragic catastrophe will help account—to choose one example among many—for the curious circumstance that the debate between Comedy and Tragedy in the Induction to the popular Elizabethan play of *Mucedorus* is conducted by Comedy and by Envy, who speaks for tragedy. It accounts also for many an Elizabethan play, particularly for the motivation of *Othello* and of Jonson's *Sejanus*. The concern for the honor and reputation of the protagonist after his tragic death is peculiarly relevant to the last scene of *Hamlet*. The "ven-gaunce of poysoun" is *Hamlet* again. Finally, the confusion of high style with bombast—"the muses al to-rente"— is markedly Elizabethan; the first we hear of Shakespeare in London is that— as Greene querulously complains—he thinks he can bombast out a blank verse with the best of them, even as Hamlet later thinks he can swing it as well as Laertes— "Nay, an thou'lt mouth, / I'll rant as well as thou." (5. 1. 306-07) In brief, if the words of the narrator were distributed among the actors of the dumb-show and the Globe were erected in Troy, Lydgate's play could be the *Spanish Tragedy* or *Hamlet*.

The persistence of a critical awareness of these principles may be illustrated from a single text, the Prologue to *Henry VIII*, usually said to be by Shakespeare and Fletcher. Who wrote the Prologue is unknown, but it does not matter:

I come no more to make you laugh. Things now
That bear a weighty and a serious brow,
Sad, high, and working, full of state and woe,
Such noble scenes as draw the eye to flow,
We now present. Those that can pity, here   5
May (if they think it well) let fall a tear:
The subject will deserve it. Such as give
Their money out of hope they may believe,
May here find truth too. Those that come to see
Only a show or two and so agree   10
The play may pass—if they be still and willing,
I'll undertake may see away their shilling
Richly in two short hours. Only they
That come to hear a merry bawdy play,
A noise of targets, or to see a fellow   15
In a long motley coat guarded with yellow,
Will be deceiv'd. For, gentle hearers, know,
To rank our chosen truth with such a show
As fool and fight is, beside forfeiting
Our own brains and the opinion that we bring   20
To make that only true we now intend,
Will leave us never an understanding friend.
Therefore, for goodness sake, as you are known
The first and happiest hearers of the town,
Be sad, as we would make ye. Think ye see   25
The very persons of our noble story
As they were living. Think you see them great,
And follow'd with the general throng, and sweat
Of thousand friends. Then, in a moment, see
How soon this mightiness meets misery.   30
And if you can be merry then, I'll say
A man may weep upon his wedding day.

The basis for discussion is again the sharp distinction of comedy from tragedy, which is expressed not only in the opening lines (1-2), but also is introduced with a certain truculence into the middle where the historical nature of tragedy is affirmed (13-22, but especially 17-21), and lies behind the turn of thought in the final lines: for it would be as proper to weep at the weddings which are the external signs that a comedy has been concluded:

> Our wooing doth not end like an old play:
> Jack hath not Gill. These ladies' courtesy
> Might well have made our sport a comedy.
>
> *Love's Labour's Lost*, 5. 2. 883-85

as to be merry at the deaths which conclude a tragedy. For tragedy is woeful. Its subjects are grave and of serious aspect (2); they are sad, lofty, and have a strong emotional effect ("working," 3); they are noble scenes which evoke tears and pity (3-7), being full of affairs of state and at the same time of woe, with the implication that the former qualifies the latter. Furthermore, the height of the persons and the richness of the emotional effect are, it is almost implied, proportional to each other; this is a notion which we shall find made explicit at the conclusion of *Antony and Cleopatra:*

> High events as these
> Strike those that make them; and their story is
> No less in pity than his glory which
> Brought them to be lamented.
>
> 5. 2. 363-66

In the final part of the Prologue the spectators are abjured to achieve the full emotional effect intended; they are to be as sad as the authors and actors wish them to be. (23-25) They can attain this end (the process is clearly described) by vividly realizing the events on the stage as if they were real, or, indeed, by imputing to them the reality which in fact they have because of the warrant of their historical truth (23-27); in this way the spectators are to achieve the emotional end of historical tragedy, woe or pity—"for sorrow is characteristic of tragedy," as Diomedes says. This effect culminates in the tragic catastrophe, the sudden and violent ("in a moment, see" 29) fall from mightiness to misery. (27-30)

III

So much for the tradition. But what does Shakespeare himself mean by tragedy? What does the term denote in his works, and with what notions is it associated in context? It denotes primarily violent death, and the notions with which it is associated are the principles of the Donatan tradition. I give now a number of representative passages from Shakespeare's works in which the term *tragedy* or one of its derivatives appears.

A. Talbot in *1 Henry VI*

Speak, Salisbury; at least, if thou canst speak.
How far'st thou, mirror of all martial men?
One of thy eyes and thy cheek's side struck off?
Accursed tower! Accursed fatal hand
That hath contriv'd this woful tragedy!

1. 4. 73-77

Tragedy is death in battle, the sudden and violent death of a notable person. It is woeful. It is brought about by circumstances ("Accursed tower!") and by a responsible agent ("Accursed fatal hand").

B. Gloucester in *2 Henry VI:*

> I know their complot is to have my life;
> And if my death might make this island happy
> And prove the period of their tyranny,
> I would expend it with all willingness.
> But mine is made the prologue to their play;
> For thousands more, that yet suspect no peril,
> Will not conclude their plotted tragedy.
>
> 3. 1. 147-53

Tragedy is the consequence of political intrigue; it involves the destiny of the state; and it concludes with unexpected deaths. But the point of the prophecy in this instance is that here not even holocausts, or tragedy on tragedy, will conclude the plot.

C. Warwick and Queen Margaret over the dead body of Gloucester in *2 Henry VI*—The Queen speaks:

> Then you belike suspect these noblemen
> As guilty of Duke Humphrey's timeless death?

And Warwick:

> Who finds the heifer dead, and bleeding fresh,
> And sees fast-by a butcher with an axe,

But will suspect 'twas he that made the slaughter?
Who finds the partridge in the puttock's nest
But may imagine how the bird was dead,
Although the kite soar with unbloodied beak?
Even so suspicious is this tragedy.

3. 2. 186-94

Tragedy is "timeless death"; that is, untimely, violent, as in *Titus Andronicus* (E, below).

D. Henry VI to Richard in the Tower, *3 Henry VI*:

Ah, kill me with thy weapon, not with words!
My breast can better brook thy dagger's point
Than can my ears that tragic history.

5. 6. 26-28

The tragic history is an account of the death of the young Prince Edward.

E. *Titus Andronicus*, 2. 3. 265: "timeless tragedy" means murder, untimely death.

F. *Titus Andronicus*, 4. 1. 45-60: tragedy is rape and murder.

G. *Richard III.* "Enter Queen with her hair about her ears, Rivers and Dorset after her":

QUEEN: Ah, who shall hinder me to wail and weep,
To chide my fortune, and torment myself?
I'll join with black despair against my soul
And to myself become an enemy.

DUCHESS OF YORK: What means this scene of rude impatience?

QUEEN: To make an act of tragic violence.
  Edward, my lord, thy son, our king, is dead!

2. 2. 34-40

The nature of the act of tragic violence is defined in the preceding speech as sin ("And to myself become an enemy"), and specifically as the sin of despair. The characteristic act of despair is suicide. The act of tragic violence, then, is suicide.

H. Hastings in *Richard III:*

But I shall laugh at this a twelvemonth hence,
That they which brought me in my master's hate,
I live to look upon their tragedy.
Well, Catesby, ere a fortnight make me older,
I'll send some packing that yet think not on't.

3. 2. 57-61

Tragedy is violent unexpected death.

I. *Richard III.* "Enter old Queen Margaret":

So now prosperity begins to mellow
And drop into the rotten mouth of death.
Here in these confines slyly have I lurk'd
To watch the waning of mine enemies.
A dire induction am I witness to,
And will to France, hoping the consequence
Will prove as bitter, black, and tragical.

4. 4. 1-7

The preliminaries are dire—that is, the tragic atmosphere is one of fear—and promise by the law of aesthetic congruity that the consequence will be bitter and black—that is, tragical. The principle of order that connects preliminaries and consequence is the waning of prosperity: the wheel of Fortune.

J.   *Midsummer Night's Dream:*

THESEUS: " . . . very tragical mirth."
          Merry and tragical? tedious and brief?
          That is hot ice and wondrous strange snow. . . .

PHILOSTRATE: And tragical, my noble lord, it is;
          For Pyramus therein doth kill himself. . . .

THESEUS: . . . Marry, if he that writ it had played
          Pyramus and hang'd himself in Thisby's garter,
          it would have been a fine tragedy.
                                        5. 1. 57-59, 66-67, 365-67

Tragedy and comedy are precise contraries. The distinguishing mark of tragedy is violent death, suicide.

K.   The Archbishop of Canterbury in *Henry* V, 1. 2. 105-06, speaks of "Edward the Black Prince," whose warlike spirit "on the French ground play'd a tragedy" by slaughtering the French army.

L.   *Othello,* 5. 2. 363: the representative of the state speaks of the dead bodies of Desdemona and Othello as "the tragic loading of this bed."

M.   *The Phoenix and Turtle,* 52: "the tragic scene" is the death of the phoenix and the dove.

N. Lucrece in the *Rape of Lucrece:*

"O comfort-killing Night, image of hell!
Dim register and notary of shame!
Black stage for tragedies and murthers fell!
Vast sin-concealing chaos! nurse of blame!
Blind muffled bawd! dark harbour for defame!
    Grim cave of death! whisp'ring conspirator
    With close-tongu'd treason and the ravisher!"

           764-70

This passage constitutes a congeries of the fundamental notions and attitudes associated with the concept of tragedy; its objective content is murder, death, whispering conspiracy, close-tongued treason, rape; it deals in sin—night, its symbol, is the image of Hell, where grace dies ("comfort-killing") and chaos spreads, for chaos is the issue of sin as order is of grace; tragedy is preoccupied with fame (cf. *Hamlet*, 5. 2. 355-60); its atmosphere is dim, vast (that is, "disordered"), black, blind (that is, "irrational"), dark, grim.

O. The lover in *A Lover's Complaint* is portrayed as a master of insincere rhetoric and capable of expressing all the external signs of the appropriate emotions:

To blush at speeches rank, to weep at woes,
Or to turn white and sound at tragic shows.

           307-08

The effect of tragedy is fear or terror.
    In brief, the tragic atmosphere and the anticipation of the tragic catastrophe is fearful; the catastrophe woeful. The process

by which the catastrophe comes about involves intrigue, hypocrisy, political conspiracy and treason, acts of sin, and is conducted by responsible agents. These are the connotations of *tragedy*. The denotation is violent, unexpected death—murder, death in battle, suicide. To these is added rape.

This denotation of *tragedy*, however, is not merely Shakespearean; it is generally Elizabethan, as indeed is well known. Death in *Soliman and Perseda*, speaking as a chorus at the beginning of the play, says: "And what are tragedies but acts of death?" (1. 1. 7). And, again, at the conclusion:

> Packe *Loue* and *Fortune*, play in comedies,
> For powerfull Death best fitteth Tragedies.[9]

In the Induction to *A Warning for Fair Women*, which was produced by Shakespeare's company, the characters are Tragedy, History, and Comedy. Tragedy is called "a common executioner," "murther's Beadle," "The common hangman unto Tyranny," and a little later it is remarked:

> Then we shall have a tragedy indeed;
> Pure purple buskin, blood and murther right.
> > Induction, 6, 19, 20, 61-62[10]

Finally, Fletcher in the preface to the *Faithful Shepherdess* distinguishes tragicomedy from tragedy "in respect it wants deaths, which is enough to make it no tragedy. . . ." Hence death is the essential mark (note the technical language of "in respect"), the defining characteristic.

The tragic fact is death. Even the most natural death has in it a radical violence, for it is a transition from this life to something by definition quite otherwise; and, however much it may be expected, it is in its moment of incidence sudden, for it comes as a thief in the night, you know not the day nor the hour. Hence the characteristics of suddenness and violence which are attached to death in tragedy may be viewed as only artistic heightenings of the essential character of death: the unnaturalness of the tragic event is only pointed and emphasized by the unnatural precipitancy of its accomplishment. If Elizabethan dramas often end in almost indiscriminate butchery, the intention, even if mistaken, is only to make them the more tragic.

That tragedy is death is a conception which will account for a puzzling feature in the history of Elizabethan drama: namely, that we have a number of interesting plays, particularly those traditionally associated with Shakespeare's name, *Arden of Feversham, A Warning for Fair Women,* and the *Yorkshire Tragedy,* in which recent and actual murders are dramatized. These were regarded as tragedies; indeed one of them has the extensive Induction which was quoted from above, in which Tragedy after an argument with History and Comedy introduces the play. Nevertheless, in these plays the usual notion that tragedy involves a notable reversal of prosperity and the fall of a person from high estate to low is little attended to, though not unnoticed, and at the same time the corollary notion that the chief characters should be of princely, or at least of noble, rank is deliberately violated. These are domestic tragedies. The characters involved are usually of what we would call the middle class—they are normally gentlemen. The situation is sordid, not splendid.

It is obvious that such a play, if the principle of decorum is to be observed, must forgo the high style appropriate to traditional tragedy. It must forgo at the same time the splendor and universality of great events; it must temper its effect to the meanness of its theme. The advantage which such tragedy claims for itself in exchange for the advantages of traditional tragedy is that of unadorned truth—truth in the literal historical sense, and unadorned in the sense of unrhetorical, or lacking the high style. So Tragedy in *A Warning for Fair Women* introduces the sordid story of murder with these remarks:

> My scene is London, native and your own.
> I sigh to think my subject too well-known.
> I am not feigned.
>
> 1. 86-88

"I am not feigned." Again, the author of *Arden of Feversham*, invoking the age-old commonplace of simple truth as opposed to artful feigning, a commonplace that derives from the early Christian defense of the unliterary character of the New Testament and from the older classical commonplace of nature and art, concludes the play with these words:

> Gentlemen, we hope you'll pardon this naked Tragedy,
> Wherein no filed points are foisted in
> To make it gracious to the ear or eye;
> For simple truth is gracious enough,
> And needs no other points of glosing stuff.
>
> Epilogue, 14-18[11]

A "naked tragedy" is unrhetorical, lacking in ornament, a tragedy in other than high style. Perhaps one should remark that the play does have a good deal of Kydian ornament in it, but this is beside the point, being only another lamentable example of the gap between profession and practice.

To conclude: if violent death is the distinguishing mark of tragedy, and this seems to be Shakespeare's understanding of the term, it follows 1) that domestic tragedy is a legitimate species since it has the defining characteristic and the associated property of historical truth; 2) that high tragedy will by logical implication involve the fall of princes since the violent death of a high character is such a fall, but that this theme is not logically primitive, but derived; 3) that the tragic attitude will be the attitude toward death; 4) that the tragic effects will be those appropriate to violent death: fear, sorrow, and perhaps wonder at the suddenness and violence; and 5) that the effect of tragedy is consequently not infinitely subtle but quite obvious. On this account the tragedy of *Hamlet* is the holocaust which concludes it, and the tragedy of Hamlet himself is his death.

WONDER

But is wonder a traditional effect of tragedy? Does it appear in the tradition so closely associated with tragic woe that Horatio's *aught of woe or wonder* could be taken as a designation of the tragic effect? Certainly it is not explicit, if present at all, in Donatus or Diomedes. Yet about twenty years before the publication of *Hamlet* Sir Philip Sidney had defined tragedy in the passage already quoted as "stirring the affects of admiration and commiseration."[1] The literal meaning of *admiration* in the Renaissance—it is the meaning of the Latin word *admiratio*—is "wonder." Hence Horatio's phrase is simply a translation from Latin to Germanic diction of Sidney's, with the substitution of the more general and more traditional notion of sorrow for the more special and more Aristotelian notion of pity. Of course, we need not picture Shakespeare as filching his phrase from Sidney, though this is not at all improbable. The question is rather, How did wonder, or admiration, come to be recognized as an effect proper to tragedy, and on what authority was it raised to an equal status with sorrow and fear? On what precedent did Sidney and Shakespeare speak? For surely neither intended to say anything novel on this subject.

I

The precedent is as old as Aristotle's *Poetics*.[2] It is true that in the famous definition of tragedy (1449b24-28) Aristotle speaks only of "incidents arousing pity and fear, wherewith to accomplish its catharsis of such emotions." There is, however, another emotion explicitly associated elsewhere in the *Poetics* with tragic incident and with the tragic catastrophe, and this is wonder or astonishment (*ekplexis, to thaumaston*).

Three principal texts bear on this point. The first occurs toward the end of the *Poetics,* in the comparison of tragedy and epic:

> The marvellous is certainly required in tragedy. Epic, however, offers more opening for the improbable, the chief factor in the marvellous, because in it the agents are not visibly before us. The scene of the pursuit of Hector would be ridiculous on the stage—the Greeks halting instead of pursuing him, and Achilles shaking his head to stop them; but in the poem the absurdity is overlooked. The marvellous, however, is a cause of pleasure, as is shown by the fact that we all tell a story with additions, in the belief we are doing our hearers a pleasure.
>
> 1460a 11-17[3]

The marvellous is certainly required in tragedy. Furthermore, from the example which Aristotle gives of telling a story with additions it is clear that the marvellous derives its value from the point of view of its effect on the audience: wonder, for like begets like.

The point is supported by a later passage, the second principal text, in which Aristotle is discussing the sort of criticisms one may make of the poet's art:

> As to the criticisms relating to the poet's art itself. Any impossibilities there may be in his descriptions of things are faults. But from another point of view they are justifiable, if they serve the end of poetry

itself—if (to assume what we have said of that end) they make the effect of either that very portion of the work or some other portion more astounding. The Pursuit of Hector is an instance in point.

1460b23*ff.*

That is, impossibilities can be defended on the grounds that they make some portion of the work more astounding. The astounding has therefore a kind of absolute value. As such, it is not merely permissible, but necessary. In fact, the implication of this passage, which occurs in the extended comparison of tragedy and epic, is that epic surpasses tragedy in this respect: you can get away with more of the marvellous in a narration than on the stage, for what seems marvellous when told may seem ridiculous when seen. What is presented on the stage and before our eyes cannot "fly from all humanity." Thus, the element of wonder, which rests upon the improbable, cannot bulk so large or be handled so indiscreetly as in straight narrative, but it cannot be dispensed with. So Aristotle arrives at his canon for the stage: "a likely impossibility is always preferable to an unconvincing possibility." (1460a26-27)

Furthermore, Aristotle posits here that wonder is an end—if it be not the end—of poetry, of which tragedy is a species. Now the end in the Aristotelian scheme is that toward which all things conspire and to which they are subordinated. It will be worth our while, then, to reconcile if possible this passage in which wonder is spoken of as the end of poetry with those others in which is implied that a specific kind of pleasure (involving pity and fear) is the end of tragedy (1448b18; 53a36; 53b11 and 12; 62a16; and 62b13). This passage will furnish the general solution; the third principal text, which will be noticed later, will furnish the specific solution applicable to tragedy.

71

The relationship of wonder and pleasure is that wonder is pleasurable. (1460a17) It is pleasurable in itself. It is pleasurable also in that it is the occasion and motive for learning, as is clear from the famous passage in the *Metaphysics:*

> For it is owing to their wonder that men both now be-
> gin and at first began to philosophize. . . . And a man
> who is puzzled and wonders thinks himself ignorant
> (whence even the lover of myth is in a sense a lover of
> Wisdom, for the myth is composed of wonders).
>
> 1. 2. 982b11-19

Furthermore, myth, which furnished the material for Greek trag-edy, is described as composed of wonders, and the lover of myth is a lover of Wisdom in that he, too, seeks to know.

Wonder is the occasion and motive for learning; learning is pleasurable: by this chain are wonder and pleasure connected. This is explained in the *Rhetoric*:

> Again, since learning and wondering are pleasant, it
> follows that such things as acts of imitation must be
> pleasant—for instance, painting, sculpture, poetry—
> and every product of skilful imitation; this latter, even
> if the object imitated is not itself pleasant; for it is not
> the object itself which here gives delight; the specta-
> tor draws inferences ("That is a so-and-so") and thus
> learns something fresh. Dramatic turns of fortune
> and hairbreadth escapes from perils are pleasant, be-
> cause we feel all such things are wonderful.
>
> 1. 11. 1371b4-12

Wonder and pleasure are the principal effects of art, and consequently of tragedy and the tragic catastrophe; they are its end. The two are correlative, for one is the motive for inference, the other its natural accompaniment. Furthermore, what we now call aesthetic experience is for Aristotle substantially the experience of inferring. This is clear from the passage just cited, and is reinforced by the well-known passage early in the *Poetics* in which Aristotle analyzes the general origin of poetry. He points out that men, and especially the young, are natural copycats and prone to make-believe. This is how they learn. Secondly, he says, "it is natural for all to delight in works of imitation":

> The truth of this second point is shown by experience: though the objects themselves may be painful to see, we delight to view the most realistic representations of them in art, the forms for example of the lowest animals and of dead bodies. The explanation is to be found in a further fact: to be learning something is the greatest of pleasures not only to the philosopher but also the rest of mankind, however small their capacity for it; the reason of the delight in seeing the picture is that one is at the same time learning—gathering the meaning of things, e.g. that the man there is so-and-so; for if one has not seen the thing before, one's pleasure will not be in the picture as an imitation of it, but will be due to the execution or colouring or some similar cause.
>
> 4. 1448b4-19

Wonder, then, is associated with pleasure as the end of poetry, and it is also posited as required in tragedy. But is it specifically associated, as it is in Hamlet, with the proper tragic effects of pity and fear? It is, as one would expect, since Aristotle tells us that through pity and fear tragedy attains its proper pleasure (1453b10-11), and pleasure involves wonder. The text, which is the third of the principal texts, reads:

> Tragedy, however, is an imitation not only of a complete action, but also of incidents arousing pity and fear. Such incidents have the very greatest effect on the mind when they occur unexpectedly and at the same time in consequence of one another; there is more of the marvellous in them then than if they happened of themselves or by mere chance. Even matters of chance seem most marvellous if there is an appearance of design as it were in them; as for instance the statue of Mitys at Argos killed the author of Mitys's death by falling down on him when a looker-on at a public spectacle; for incidents like that we think to be not without a meaning. A Plot, therefore, of this sort is necessarily finer than others.
>
> 9. 1452a1-11

It is implied again that wonder has an absolute value in itself. Furthermore, the degree of surprise, the amount of the marvellous, in the plot of a tragedy is the measure of the pity and fear it provokes, so that in the strict mathematical sense wonder is a function of pity and fear: $PF = W$.

Two further passages may be cited in this connection. In discussing the kinds of incidents which will produce the tragic pleasure of pity and fear, Aristotle remarks:

> A better situation [than the one previously dis-
> cussed] is for the deed to be done in ignorance, and
> the relationship [of the parties involved] discovered
> afterwards, since there is nothing odious in it, and
> the Discovery will serve to astound us.
>
> 14. 1454a2-4

And later, in analyzing the kinds of Discovery, he remarks:

> The best of all Discoveries, however, is that arising
> from the incidents themselves, when the great sur-
> prise comes about through a probable incident, like
> that in the *Oedipus* of Sophocles.
>
> 16. 1455a16-18

In brief, let wonders happen, but make them—at least at the mo-
ment of their happening—plausible and convincing. This can
best be accomplished by making the tragic incident unexpected,
and yet, as soon as it has happened, obviously logical and sup-
ported by the situation and the preceding action. The incident is
not what we expected, but what, as soon as we see it, we realize
that we should have expected. Something of this sort is involved
when we understand a person: he acts spontaneously at a cri-
sis in a way we would never have predicted, yet the moment the
thing has happened we know that we knew that was the sort of
person he was. The point will be clear if we contrast this with our
attitude toward the critical actions of those whom we do not un-
derstand: their actions simply puzzle us, and the measure of our
bewilderment is the measure of our lack of understanding.

There is no need to think all this original with Aristotle:
both rhetoric and poetic—the latter in Antiquity is only partially

distinguishable from the former—had already a long history by this time. Much of the evidence, it is true, has been lost, and much must be reconstructed by divining earlier features in later texts.[4] But it is clear from the remarks of the rhapsode Ion in Plato's dialogue that fear, pity, and wonder were the commonly recognized effects of the recitation of epic, and particularly of the striking passages: for the whole point of the dialogue, which is simple-mindedly ironic, is that what Ion says should represent common opinion:

> Ion: . . . When I speak of anything piteous, my eyes are filled with tears; when I mention anything fearful or terrible, my hair stands on end with fear and my heart throbs . . .
>
> Soc: And do you not know that you produce the same effects on many of the spectators?
>
> Ion: I know it right well, for when I look down from the platform I see them weeping and showing signs of terror and astonishment at my words.
>
> *Ion,* 535B-C[5]

Nevertheless, most of the subsequent history of the concept of wonder can be derived from the Aristotelian texts. Wonder is, first of all, the natural effect of a marvellous story, and hence of those myths which furnished the plots of ancient tragedy and epic, as well as of those extraordinary events which in later Hellenistic times, as earlier in Herodotus, are narrated in certain types of history and in the marvellous tale. Apuleius, for instance, in the first sentence of the *Metamorphoses* claims that his purpose is to evoke wonder: "I have told these stories," he says, "in this style that you may wonder (*ut mireris*)."

Wonder is, in the second place, the result of a surprising and unexpected turn in events, and is thus intimately involved in the tragic catastrophe and in its proper effect. Furthermore, since in tragedy the turn is toward the worse, the effect of surprise will be inwoven with sorrow or pity as well as astonishment, and the astonishment will take that form which is akin to fear. From this line of thought, though not necessarily from Aristotle, is derived the following passage from a little scrapbook of short treatises by the famous rhetorician Hermogenes of Tarsus, which goes under the title of *How to Speak Effectively*:

> Philippics, dialogue, comedy, tragedy, and the Socratic symposia weave the whole by a kind of double method. . . . The web and woof of tragedy are woe and wonder, as is to be seen both in the tragedies of tragic writers and in those of Homer whom Plato called the father of tragedy and the choregus.[6]

Thirdly, wonder is an end of poetry. This concept is generalized in the Neo-Platonist Plotinus, to whom wonder is an effect of beauty:

> This is the effect that Beauty must ever induce, wonderment and a pleasant astonishment, longing and love and a dread that is pleasurable.
>
> *Enneades,* 1. 6. 4[7]

However, the more restricted view, which we found in Aristotle, that wonder is along with pleasure the end of poetry is a commonplace in later Antiquity; it is chiefly associated with the name of Eratosthenes, the poet-scholar, friend and disciple of

Callimachus. We gain our knowledge of his position principally from the criticisms which Strabo levels against it in the *Geography*. "Eratosthenes," he says, "is wrong in his contention that the aim of every poet is to entertain, not to instruct." (1. 1. 10)[8] The argument is long and somewhat tedious. In brief, Strabo holds that the poet either pleases or instructs—pleases when what he says is false, instructs when what he says is true. (1. 2. 3, and 7-9) On this basis the ends of the various branches of composition are distinguished:

> Now the aim of history is truth, . . . the aim of rhetorical composition is vividness, as when Homer introduces men fighting; the aim of myth is to please and excite amazement.
>
> 1. 2. 17

The purpose of myth—that is, of a story—is pleasure and wonder.

Eratosthenes' distinction, as preserved by Strabo, appears also in the historian Polybius. He is criticizing one of his predecessors, Phylarchus, of whom he says:

> Leaving aside the ignoble and womanish character of such a treatment of his subject, let us consider how far it is proper or serviceable to history. A historical author should not try to thrill his readers by such exaggerated pictures, nor should he, like a tragic poet, try to imagine the probable utterances of his characters or reckon up all the consequences probably incidental to the occurrences with which he deals, but simply record what really happened and what

really was said, however commonplace. For the end of tragedy is not the same as that of history but quite the opposite. The tragic poet should amaze and charm his audience for the moment by the verisimilitude of the words he puts into his characters' mouths, but it is the task of the historian to instruct and convince for all time serious students by the truth of the facts and the speeches he narrates, since in the one case it is the probable that takes precedence, even if it be untrue, the purpose being to create illusion in spectators, in the other it is the truth, the purpose being to confer benefit on learners.

2. 56[9]

The passage is intellectually more respectable, of course, than that from Strabo. For Polybius, though he does not exclude—as no one should since literature is a part of life—general ethical judgments ("Leaving aside the ignoble and womanish character of such a treatment of his subject"), is nevertheless capable of discussing literature on its own terms and with reference to its own proper ends ("let us consider how far it is proper and serviceable to history"). The end of tragedy is to astonish and please—but not without qualifications, for he points out in the passage that follows this quotation that unless we know the causes of a catastrophe and the course of events which led up to it, it is impossible to feel due indignation or pity. In brief, the effect must be adequately motivated.

Plutarch in his essay on *How the Young Man Should Study Poetry* repeats the commonplace:

But when poetic art is divorced from the truth, then chiefly it employs variety and diversity. For it is the sudden changes that give to its stories the elements of the emotional, the surprising, and the unexpected, and these are attended by very great astonishment and enjoyment; but sameness is unemotional and prosaic.

7. 25[10]

In an earlier passage he applies Eratosthenes formulation of the end of poetry to a play by Aeschylus:

But it is patent to everybody that this is a mythical fabrication which has been created to please or astound the hearer.

7. 17

The following passage from the ancient *Life of Aeschylus* obviously springs from the same context of critical notions: Aeschylus has "few devices for drawing tears" and "uses the spectacle and plot more to strike by the marvellous than to effect (artistic) illusion."[11]

II

The marvellous is pleasurable. Thus wonder is an end of poetry, or it is with pleasure the end of poetry. Hence it would obviously be involved in the effect of any particular kind. It is, however, associated with the specific, rather than with the generic, effect of tragedy even in Aristotle, since the specific effects of pity and fear are most truly effective when they also involve wonder. Indeed, the marvellous is required in tragedy. Consequently, it becomes traditional to distinguish the purpose of fiction, especially of epic and tragedy, from that of history and of rhetoric on these grounds: fiction aims at wonder and pleasure; history at truth and instruction; rhetoric at vividness and persuasion. But, of course, these lines of distinction were not fixed and unalterable in Antiquity, since the subjects of the distinctions were not simple. Poetry and rhetoric had a great deal in common; fiction commonly involved history, and history fiction. Furthermore, from the time of Aristotle poetry was often identified with fiction, and the mythical was a characteristic property. Thus, the end of poetry was often said to be pleasure and instruction, as in Horace and Strabo, and its methods were usually rhetorical.

However, wonder is not only an effect of a story or of a subject matter, it is also an effect of language and of style. It is precisely the effect of characteristically poetic, or tragic, style, as opposed to the plain straightforward style proper to prose and to dialectic. For the fundamental distinction which prevails in Antiquity and informs the traditional theory of the three (or four) styles is the distinction in diction between the unornamented language native to prose and the unusual, figurative, ornamented language of poetry, and especially of tragedy. The distinction remained current even though poetry appropriated the language of prose, as in the later tragedians, and prose in the rhetorical tradition of Gorgias appropriated the language of poetry (Aristotle, *Rhet.* 3. 1. 1404a20-34; Strabo, 1. 2. 6). The point is made clear by Aristotle in the *Rhetoric*. The effect of poetic diction is wonder:

> People do not feel towards strangers as they do towards their own countrymen, and the same thing is true of their feeling for language. It is therefore well to give everyday speech an unfamiliar air: wonder

is a characteristic of things off the beaten track, and the wonderful is pleasant. In verse such effects are common, and there they are fitting: the persons and things there spoken of are comparatively remote from ordinary life. In prose passages they are far less often fitting because the subject-matter is less exalted.

3. 2. 1404b8-15[12]

The later theory on the subject derives partly from such passages as this, probably by way of Theophrastus' work on style, and partly no doubt from Sophistic theory as developed by Gorgias among others. (Diodorus, 12. 53; Gorgias, *Helena,* 9.) It seems to have been based, at least originally, upon a distinction between style which employs plain language and to the point, whose aim is merely truth, and whose concern is simply with content (*rem tene, verba secuntur*), and a style cultivated as such. The former uses proper expressions only; the latter intermingles figurative. Its aim is to move, to convince, to please; its concern is with the effect on the audience. The former is the style of dialectic and, in general, of philosophy; and the latter is the style of poetry and of rhetoric. So Theophrastus in a passage preserved in one of the later commentaries on Aristotle's logic:

> Language is divided into two types, according to the philosopher Theophrastus, the one having reference to the hearers, the other to the matter concerning which the speaker aims to convince his audience. To the division with reference to the hearers belong poetry and rhetoric. Therefore its function is to choose the more stately words, and not those which are common or vulgar, and to interweave them with each

other harmoniously, to the end that, by means of them and the effects which result from the employment of them, such as vividness, sweetness and other qualities of style, together with studied expansion and contraction, all employed at the suitable moment, the listener shall be charmed and astonished and, with respect to the intellectual persuasion, overmastered. The division looking to the matter will be the especial concern of the philosopher, refuting the false and setting forth the true.[13]

The effect of astonishment or wonder is the natural correlative of unusual diction, as it is of the unusual event. The proper word satisfies by its exactness; the unusual pleases or displeases by its startling effect. Upon this basis, which though obvious is not unimportant, together with the doctrine of the appropriateness of style to subject, rests the whole later theory of the kinds and characters of style in all its elaboration. Hence, the theorists will ascribe to any style which is noticeable as such the quality of wonder. That style which is elaborated for the purpose of charm or pleasure—the *genus floridum*—will evoke the kind of pleasant wonder that the marvellous story does, and will be appropriate to such subjects: for instance, the Milesian style of Apuleius, for the effect of wonder is ascribed in the passage cited above not only to the subject matter but also to the style. The high style, the forceful, the grand—the style of Demosthenes and of Aeschylus—will evoke that wonder which is akin to fear, and will be especially appropriate to tragedy. Yet wonder may be on a lesser scale than this: it corresponds to the displacement, large or small, that initiates internal movement: with respect to the intellect, inference, the processes of logic, and learning; with respect to the irrational part of the soul, feeling and emotion. Hence style can evoke emotion in the audience, and at the same time by the law of decorum the degree of unusual diction should be proportionate to the height and intensity of the feeling inherent in the subject matter. Again, to wonder at style is to regard it highly, to approve of it, to admire in the modern sense, but this attitude, though not unaccompanied by feeling, nevertheless implies no specific shade of emotional coloring.

This much may serve to introduce the following citations in which is exhibited the continuity in Antiquity of the Peripatetic and Sophistic tradition that wonder is an effect of style, and especially of the high style appropriate to tragedy. The treatise on style by Demetrius (probably first century A.D.) is clearly in this tradition. He cites a line of Homer in which a figurative shift in construction elevates the style, and contrasts this with the ordinary way of saying the same thing. "But everything ordinary is trivial," he says, "and so fails to attain wonder." (59-60) Again, to take a longer quotation:

> The sayings of Demades, too, possess power, although their expression sounds peculiar and unusual. Their power arises partly from their significance and partly from their allegorical form and lastly from their exaggerated character.
>
> This is an example: "Alexander is not dead, Athenians. If he were, the whole world would smell the corpse." The use of the word "smell" for "perceive" involves both allegory and exaggeration. The fact that the world perceived it signifies Alexander's strength, and at the same time the sentence has an

effect of astonishment which is due to a combination of three causes. Everything that astonishes is powerful, because it creates fear.

282-83[14]

The rhetorical concept of wonder is the subject of the famous treatise on elevated style (*On the Sublime*), which has been ascribed to Longinus. The subject is announced in the opening chapter. The author premises that the eminence and renown of great writers, both in prose and in verse, is derived from distinction in language. (1. 3) The effect of such distinction he conceives of in the traditional way—the doctrine is precisely that of the passage cited above from Theophrastus—as astonishment, which overpowers the hearer and puts him in a state of transport. This effect is differentiated from that of persuasion, and incidentally of pleasure, on the grounds that this is irresistible while persuasion for the most part involves voluntary assent, and secondly that this is a matter of detail and that of the work as a whole. (1.4)

In this way the differences which Eratosthenes, Polybius, and Strabo, among others, had established between the various kinds of literary works are here applied in the context of rhetorical theory to single out the special effect of certain details in a work. The analysis gets sometimes a little complicated. Thus, in discussing the kind of image in which out of an inspired passion the writer thinks he sees what he is describing and makes his hearer see it—a well-known rhetorical device in Antiquity—Longinus distinguishes between the purpose of such images in oratory and in the poets. In poetry the end is astonishment; in prose vividness; though both alike seek to stir up excitement. (15. 36) But the poetic image tends to be fabulous, exaggerated, and to go beyond what is believable, whereas the virtue of imagery in prose is always its reality and truth. (15. 40) Nevertheless, imagery in prose can exceed persuasion and attain astonishment, combining vigor and passion with argument and fact so that the hearer is not merely persuaded but actually enslaved, for the stronger effect of wonder will absorb the weaker of persuasion. (15. 41)[15]

The notion also appears, as we might expect, in the Latin authors. Cicero, for example, in the teacher-pupil dialogue on the *Classification of Oratory* associates wonder with ornate or figurative diction, and hence with the charming style (*genus suave*). He points out that style will be charming if something unusual, original, or novel is said—he is thinking of phrasing—"for anything wonderful pleases." (22) Again, a charming account is one that has causes of wonder, suspense, and emotional outcomes, along with interpolated emotional passages, dialogues, sorrow, anger, fear, joy, and desire. (32) Cicero is here speaking of those expositions of events which form part of a speech, but the description could easily apply to a play, and particularly to such as *The Winter's Tale* or to many of Beaumont and Fletcher. In another passage he says that in developing a subject in the decorative style we should take up those aspects that produce suspense, wonder, and delight. (58) Finally, he points out in an extended passage that in epideictic speeches, whose chief purpose is to please and entertain an audience, the speaker should make use of striking phrases, which have a great deal of charm; that is, he should use coined words, archaisms, and metaphors; should construct phrases such that one echoes another by similarity of rhythm and ending, thus giving doublets and a verbal rhythm, not sounding like verse yet satisfying the ear with an appropriate harmony. But the ornament should not be merely verbal; there should also be in the matter a good deal of what is wonderful and unexpected, things foreshadowed by portents, prodigies, and oracles, and what seems to the man to whom this happens to be the result of divine intervention or of fate. For the feeling of suspense in the audience, and wonder, and the unexpected outcome always give a certain pleasure in the hearing. (72-73)[16] What is described here is represented in Elizabethan times by Lyly's *Euphues,* and all its progeny in the Elizabethan drama. Wonder is an effect both of style and of subject.

The doctrine of Antiquity on wonder is summed up and transmitted to posterity by Quintilian:

> . . . those words are the most to be commended which express our thoughts best, and produce the impression which we desire on the minds of the judges. Such words undoubtedly must make a speech both worthy of admiration and productive of pleasure; but not of that kind of admiration with which we wonder at monsters; or of that kind of pleasure which is attended with unnatural gratification, but such as is compatible with true merit and worth.
>
> 8. *Pr.* 32-33

> It was the sublimity, magnificence, splendour, and dignity of his [Cicero's] eloquence, that drew forth that thunder of approbation. No such extraordinary commendation would have attended on the speaker, if his speech had been of an everyday character, and similar to ordinary speeches. I even believe that his audience were insensible of what they were doing, and that they gave their applause neither voluntarily nor with an exercise of judgment, but that, being

carried away by enthusiasm, and unconscious of the place in which they stood, they burst forth instinctively into such transports of delight.

But this grace of style may contribute in no small degree to the success of a cause; for those who listen with pleasure are both more attentive and more ready to believe; they are very frequently captivated with pleasure, and sometimes hurried away in admiration. Thus the glitter of a sword strikes something of terror into the eyes, and thunder storms themselves would not alarm us so much as they do if it were their force only, and not also their flame, that was dreaded. Cicero, accordingly, in one of his letters to Brutus, makes with good reason the following remark: *That eloquence which excites no wonder, I account as nothing.* Aristotle, also, thinks that to excite wonder should be one of our greatest objects.

8. 3. 3-6[17]

III

So much for Antiquity. It will be sufficient now to establish the continuity of the tradition in the Middle Ages, and later in the Renaissance. The effect of wonder will be a familiar notion to any Christian since it is frequently noted in the New Testament as the effect of the words and works of Christ:

And the disciples were astonished at his words.

Matt. 13:54

> And straightway the damsel arose and walked, for she was of the age of twelve years. And they were astonished with a great astonishment.
>
> *Mark 5:42*

Wonder, of course, is the natural effect of miracles, real or apparent. St. Augustine makes the point in the text which furnishes the standard definition for medieval theology: "I call a miracle anything great and difficult or unusual that happens beyond the expectation or ability of the man who wonders at it" (*De Utilitate Credendi,* 16. 34).[18] And St. Thomas, in turn, integrates the Augustinian definition with the Aristotelian. In the Summa he takes up the question, "Whether everything that God does outside of the natural order is miraculous?" He cites an authoritative text from St. Augustine: "When God does anything contrary to the course and custom of nature as we know it, we call it a miracle." For the term is indeed derived from the word for wonder, and wonder arises whenever an effect is manifest and its cause hidden, as Aristotle says in the *Metaphysics.* Consequently, what is wonderful to one man may not be wonderful to another, but a miracle is fully wonderful since it has a cause—namely, God—absolutely hidden from all. (*ST,* 1. 105. 7)

The marvellous event, and so the marvellous story, provokes wonder. The explicit recognition of this effect is common throughout the literature of the Middle Ages, and has behind it a tradition derived from Christian dogma. Thus the German *Niebelungenlied* of the twelfth century begins by promising us that now we will hear a wonder told, and so likewise in countless romances.

But with the recovery of the Aristotelian writings in the twelfth and thirteenth centuries, the concept of wonder as the end of poetry again enters firmly into the tradition under the authority of Aristotle and in association with most of the other elements in the tradition which were distinguished in the preceding sections of this essay. One of the most interesting texts is to be found in the works of St. Albert the Great, the teacher of Thomas Aquinas. It occurs in Albert's *Commentary on the Metaphysics of Aristotle;* I cite it at length:

> Ch. 6: *In which it is shown that philosophy is a speculative, not a practical, science.*
>
> That philosophy is speculative, not practical, is clear from the motive that first moved men to philosophize. For everyone who has philosophized, now or in the past, has been motivated only by wonder. Now, wonder is defined as a constriction and suspension of the heart caused by amazement at the sensible appearance of something so portentous, great, and unusual, that the heart suffers a systole. Hence wonder is something like fear in its effect on the heart. This effect of wonder, then, this constriction and systole of the heart, springs from an unfulfilled but felt desire to know the cause of that which appears portentous and unusual: so it was in the beginning when men, up to that time unskilled, began to philosophize—they marvelled at certain difficulties, which were, as a matter of fact, fairly easy to solve. The Pythagoreans, for example, were concerned with the theory of number, with even and odd numbers, with complete, increasing, and diminished number. Then men advanced bit by bit in learning and, becoming more proficient, raised graver questions whose causes were not easy to see: such as the changes of

the moon with respect to mansions, accessions, and eclipses, or questions about the sun and the stars. . . . In like fashion they advanced in Physics, and began to wonder about generation in general, asking whether the universe was created or given.

Now the man who is puzzled and wonders apparently does not know. Hence wonder is the movement of the man who does not know on his way to finding out, to get at the bottom of that at which he wonders and to determine its cause. A token in proof is that the famous Philomithes according to this way of looking at the matter is a Philosopher, for he constructed his stories out of wonderful events. I hold that Philomithes was a poet who loved to fashion stories: for *mithes*, with the first syllable long, is the word for stories, and *Philomithes,* then, means a lover of stories, if you make the penultimate syllable long. Thus Aristotle shows in that branch of logic which is called poetic that the poet fashions his story for the purpose of exciting wonder, and that the further effect of wonder is to excite inquiry. Such is the origin of philosophy, as Plato shows with respect to the stories of Phaeton and Deucalion. The single purpose of these stories is to excite one to wonder at the causes of the two deluges of fire and of water (which issued from the circuit of wandering stars), so that through wonder the cause would be looked for, and the truth discovered.

Hence poetry offers a method of philosophizing, just as do the other sciences of logic. But the other sciences or branches of logic offer a method of proving a proposition by reasoning, that is, by conclusive or probable argument; poetry, however, offers no method of proof but rather a method of wonder by which we are incited to inquiry. Therefore, though poetry is a subdivision of grammar with respect to prosody, with respect to its purpose it is one of the branches of logic.

To get back to the point: we define the man who wonders as one who is in suspense as to the cause, the knowledge of which would make him know instead of wonder.

In I Met. Tr. 2, ch, 6[19]

The poet Philomithes, of course, is a character that grew from a misreading of the Greek text in the passage in which Aristotle states that "the lover of myth (*philomuthos*) is in a sense a lover of Wisdom, for the myth is composed of wonders" (*Metaphysics,* 1. 2. 982b18-19). But he is a charming character, and he makes the point. The end of poetry is wonder, and the end of wonder is to excite inquiry; thus poetry is a branch of logic with respect to its purpose, and distinguished from other branches in that they offer methods of proof but poetry offers a method of motivation. Its physiological effect is similar to that of fear.

St. Thomas holds substantially the same position, and cites Aristotle in the *Poetics* to the same effect. He is discussing the causes of pleasure, and comes finally to the question, Does wonder cause pleasure? He first takes up the objections:

Apparently it doesn't 1) since wonder is a property of ignorance, and ignorance is not pleasurable, but rather knowledge. 2) Furthermore, wonder is the beginning of wisdom, being as it were a way of looking for the truth, as is said in the *Metaphysics,* 1, 2. But it is more pleasurable to contemplate what is already known than to inquire into the unknown, as Aristotle says in the *Ethics* X, 7. (1177a23*ff.*), since the latter offers difficulties and impediments, but the former does not, and pleasure arises from unimpeded operation. Therefore, wonder is not a cause of pleasure, but rather a hindrance. 3) Furthermore, everyone delights in what he is used to; hence, the operation of habits acquired through daily use is pleasurable. But what one is used to is not wonderful, as Augustine says (at the beginning of *In Joan.,* tr. 24). Therefore, wonder is precisely not a cause of pleasure.

But to the contrary is the text of Aristotle (*Rhet.* 1. 11. 1371a31): *wonder is a cause of pleasure.*

My position is that to attain anything one feels a want of is pleasurable; and the measure of anyone's desire for something he loves is the measure of his pleasure in attaining it. Indeed, in the very augmentation of desire there is an augmentation of pleasure, in that there arises a hope of what is loved, and desire itself is pleasurable in its aspect of hope. But wonder is a kind of desire for knowledge. The situation arises when one sees an effect and does not know its cause, or when the cause of the particular effect is one that exceeds his power of understanding. Hence, wonder is a cause of pleasure insofar as there is annexed the hope of attaining understanding of that which one wants to know.

For this reason, everything wonderful is pleasurable: for example, anything that is infrequent, as well as any representation of things, even of those that are not in themselves pleasant. For the soul delights in comparing one thing with another, since this is a proper and connatural activity of reason, as Aristotle says in his *Poetics*. (4. 1448b 13*ff.*) And for this reason even to be released from great danger is quite pleasurable, as is said in the *Rhetoric*. (1. 11. 1371b 1*ff.*)

As to the first objection, wonder is not pleasurable insofar as it involves ignorance, but insofar as it involves learning the cause, and learning something new: namely, that such-and-such is such-and-such, though we had not thought it was.

As to the second objection, there are two kinds of pleasure: acquiescence in the Good, and awareness of such acquiescence. With respect to the former, since it is a more complete experience to contemplate known truth than to inquire into the unknown, the contemplation of things known is in itself more pleasurable than inquiry into things unknown; nevertheless, it sometimes happens that, with respect to our awareness of experience, inquiry is more pleasurable in that it has more drive and springs from a greater desire. For desire is especially aroused by the awareness of ignorance, and consequently a man takes the greatest pleasure in those things which he discovers for himself or learns from the ground up.

As to the third objection, doing what we are used to is pleasurable insofar as it is in a way natural to us. Still, on the other hand, what is unusual can be pleasurable, either with respect to the process of learning, since our desire for knowledge is proportional to the marvellousness of the subject, or with respect to the actual doing, since the mind is strongly impelled by desire to that which is felt intensely because of its novelty. But an activity, the more full it is, the greater the pleasure it causes.

ST, 1-2.32.8[20]

Wonder is also a species of fear, as the Damascene teaches. To the objection that wonder and amazement (*admiratio et stupor*) are not species of fear, since fear refers only to evil, and wonder and amazement refer to the unusual, whether good or evil; and again, to the further objection that philosophers are moved by wonder to inquire into the truth, whereas fear does not move one to investigate but rather to run from the scene of investigation; St. Thomas answers that the authority of the Damascene and of Gregory of Nyassa is sufficient to establish the point. He then solves the objections by dividing the six traditional species of fear into three whose source is internal and three whose source is external—wonder (*admiratio*), which arises when one contemplates some great evil whose issue he cannot see; amazement (*stupor*), which arises when one contemplates some unaccustomed evil, for it will seem to be great because it is unaccustomed; shocked surprise (*agonia*), which arises from the unforeseen. Hence, to the former objection Thomas answers that only that wonder and amazement which arises from the contemplation of evil is a species of fear; to the latter objection he answers that a man who wonders does fear at the moment to give a judgment, fearing that he will fail, but that he looks into the matter in the future; the amazed man, however, fears both now and in the future; hence wonder is the beginning of philosophizing, but amazement an impediment to it. (*ST,* 1-2. 41. 4)

IV

Whatever appears in the scholastic philosophers and at the same time in Aristotle, as well as in Cicero and Quintilian, is likely to appear anywhere in Renaissance literature. It will be commonplace. Thus the rhetorical tradition is gathered up, assimilated, and integrated into a consistent structure in Pontanus's dialogue on poetry (*Actius,* about 1500). There the end of poetry is said to be "to speak well and appropriately so as to attain wonder," and this is later corrected by one of the speakers into the form, "to speak exceptionally well," so as to distinguish the poet from the orator who also must speak well and appropriately. The wonder referred to is conceived under two aspects: it is admiration, in the modern sense, for the eloquence of the poet himself, who from this source derives his fame and glory; at the same time, it is the emotion of wonder in the audience. The poet moves wonder not only by sublime words, but also by his subject matter, and since truth alone cannot guarantee this he shades truth with fiction and myth. Nor is wonder only the effect of the grave and serious; it is also the effect of the pleasant and delightful. And in speaking so sweetly, sublimely, and marvellously, the poet teaches others to speak well, so that every literary form derives from poetry.[21]

The same line of thought is developed in Fracastoro's dialogue *Navagero* (published 1555), in which the emphasis, however, is laid on the final remark, and poetry is distinguished from all other forms in that it is the master-art of eloquence. For, though poetry excites wonder, this is not its exclusive characteristic since wonder is also the effect of oratory and history: "Who can read Cicero himself without wonder?"[22]

The idea is common throughout the Renaissance. Minturno, who is in the same line of tradition as Pontanus and Fracastoro, begins his dialogue on the poet, *De Poeta* (1559), with the statement that "no one can be called a poet who does not excel in the power of arousing wonder." Minturno, however, goes beyond the rhetorical tradition, making a good deal of Aristotle's *Poetics* which had lately been translated, paraphrased, and expounded by a good many of his fellow countrymen. Thus he introduces the notions of wonder and pleasure in connection with tragedy:

> The poet does not deal with what does not please, nor does he move the emotions without delight. Rather, excited by the force of language and the weight of his ideas he rouses, attracts, and moves the audience tensely to the point of wonder—either through fear pity, or both.[23]

In fact, the idea of wonder is so commonplace in the Renaissance it would be surprising not to find it in Sidney or in Shakespeare. Hence, to establish the availability of the idea, I will only add to these citations and that from Sidney's *Defense* the following passages from Spenser:

A. Wonder is the effect of theological discourse, being, of course, the highest subject matter and hence affording by its very nature the highest eloquence; as such, however, it is an effect of subject, not style:

And that her sacred Booke, with blood ywritt,
That none could reade, except she did them teach,
She unto him disclosed every whitt,
And heavenly documents thereout did preach,
That weaker witt of man could never reach,
Of God, of grace, of justice, of free will,
That wonder was to heare her goodly speach:
For she was hable with her wordes to kill
And rayse againe to life the hart that she did thrill.

Faerie Queene, 1. 10. 19

Compare Milton's *Paradise Lost:* At Raphael's speech Adam,

with his consorted Eve,
The story heard attentive, and was filled
With admiration and deep muse, to hear
Of things so high and strange.

7. 50-53

B.   The palmer finds good Guyon, "slumbering fast, in senseles dreame":

Whom when the palmer saw, abasht he was
Through fear and wonder, that he nought could say.

FQ, 2. 8. 7.1-2

Fear and wonder is the effect of apparent unexpected death.

C. Ruth (that is, pity or woe) and wonder is the effect on the bystanders at a mortal combat:

> With that they both together fiercely met,
> As if that each ment other to devoure;
> And with their axes both so sorely bet,
> That neither plate nor mayle, whereas their power
> They felt, could once sustaine the hideous stowre,
> But rived were like rotton wood a sunder,
> Whitest through their rifts the ruddie bloud did showre,
> And fire did flash, like lightning after thunder,
> That fild the lookers on attonce with ruth and wonder.
>
> *FQ*, 4. 3. 15

"Attonce" means "both."

D. The following marvellous events quite properly provoke great wonder of a kind akin to fear, as do the prodigies of Nature:

> Then forth he brought his snowy Florimele,
> Whom Trompart had in keeping there beside,
> Covered from peoples gazement with a vele.
> Whom when discovered they had throughly eide,
> With great amazement they were stupefide;
> And said, that surely Florimell it was,
> Or if it were not Florimell so tride,
> That Florimell her selfe she then did pas.
> So feeble skill of perfect things the vulgar has.

Which when as Marinell beheld likewise,
He was therewith exceedingly dismayd;
Ne wist he what to thinke, or to devise,
But, like as one whom feends had made affrayd,
He long astonisht stood, ne ought he sayd,
Ne ought he did, but with fast fixed eies
He gazed still upon that snowy mayd;
Whom ever as he did the more avize,
The more to be true Florimell he did surmize.

As when two sunnes appeare in the azure skye,
Mounted in Phoebus charet fierie bright,
Both darting forth faire beames to each mans eye,
And both adorn'd with lampes of flaming light,
All that behold so strange prodigious sight,
Not knowing Natures worke, nor what to weene,
Are rapt with wonder and with rare affright:
So stood Sir Marinell, when he had scene
The semblant of this false by his faire beauties queene

FQ, 5.3.17-19

Then Artegall steps forth and says this "'is not (I wager) Fiorimell
at all'. . . For proofe whereof he bad them Florimell forth call."

Then did he set her by that snowy one,
Like the true saint beside the image set,
Of both their beauties to make paragone,
And triall, whether should the honor get.
Streight way so soone as both together met,
Th' enchanted damzell vanisht into nought:
Her snowy substance melted as with heat,
Ne of that goodly hew remayned ought,
But th' emptie girdle, which about her waste was wrought.

100

As when the daughter of Thaumantes faire
Hath in a watry cloud displayed wide
Her goodly bow, which paints the liquid ayre;
That all men wonder at her colours pride;
All suddenly, ere one can looke aside,
The glorious picture vanisheth away,
Ne any token doth thereof abide:
So did this ladies goodly forme decay,
And into nothing goe, ere one could it bewray.

Which when as all that present were beheld,
They stricken were with great astonishment,
And their faint harts with senseless horrour queld,
To see the thing, that seem'd so excellent,
So stolen from their fancies wonderment:
That what of it became none understood.
And Braggadochio selfe with dreriment
So daunted was, in his despeyring mood,
That like a lifeless corse immoveable he stood.

FQ, 5.3.24-26

E. "Calidore sees young Tristram slay / A proud discourteous knight":

Which when he saw, his hart was inly child
With great amazement, and his thought with wonder fild.

FQ, 6.2. *Argum.* and 4.8-9

F. In *The Ruines of Time:*

> Before mine eyes strange sights presented were,
> Like tragicke pageants seeming to appeare.
>
> 489-90

Then follows a series of visions in which a gold image, a stately tower, a pleasant paradise, a giant, a gold bridge over the sea, and two white bears successively fall to ruin:

> Much was I troubled in my heavie spright,
> At sight of these sad spectacles forepast,
> That all my senses were bereaved quight,
> And I in minde remained sore agast,
> Distraught twixt feare and pitie; when at last
> I heard a voyce, which loudly to me called,
> That with the sudden shrill I was appalled.
>
> "Behold," said it, "and by ensample see,
> That all is vanitie and griefe of minde,
> No other comfort in this world can be,
> But hope of heaven, and heart to God inclinde;
> For all the rest must needs be left behinde."
>
> 575-86

The effect of these tragic pageants is wonder ("That all my senses were bereaved quight") which suspends and mediates between fear and pity. The ultimate effect is to teach the rejection of this life.

Certainly the aesthetic effect of wonder was a notion easily available to Shakespeare. But if Horatio's *aught of woe or wonder* is to be taken as aesthetically significant, it must be shown not only that Shakespeare could have been but also that he was aware of the tradition. Does Shakespeare use the notion of wonder, and the synonymous *amazement, astonishment,* and *to be struck senseless,* in any other contexts than this one in *Hamlet?* He does. In fact, he uses almost the full range of meanings which are to be found in the tradition.

Wonder is the effect of such an incident, conventional to tragedy, as the appearance of the Ghost in *Hamlet* and the recognition of his likeness to the dead King:

> BERNARDO: Looks it not like the King? Mark it, Horatio.
>
> HORATIO: Most like. It harrows me with fear and wonder.
>
> 1. 1. 43-44

The appearance is regarded by Horatio (1.1. 113-25) as of the same nature as those signs and portents, those foreshadowings of tragic consequences, which preceded the death of Caesar. Indeed, such "precurse of fierce events," such "harbingers preceding still the fates / And prologue to the omen coming on" have precisely the same effect upon Casca in the play of *Julius Caesar:*

> CASCA: It is the part of men to fear and tremble
>
> When the most mighty gods by tokens send
>
> Such dreadful heralds to astonish us.

To which Cassius replies:

> CASSIUS: ... You look pale, and gaze
> And put on fear, and cast yourself in wonder,
> To see the strange impatience of the heavens.
>
> 1. 3. 54-56, 59-61

Wonder, then, is an emotion which is a kind of fear and is produced by striking and supernatural events. But, truly, one doesn't have to see the ghost in order to experience the effect: the Ghost in the closet scene is invisible to Hamlet's mother, yet the effect on her of Hamlet's apparently wild actions, his holding discourse with the incorporeal air, and the communicated effect of his manifest fear and wonder:

> Forth at your eyes your spirits wildly peep;
> And, as the sleeping soldiers in th' alarm,
> Your bedded hairs, like life in excrements,
> Start up and stand an end.

are characterized by the Ghost himself as an effect of amazement:

> But look, amazement on thy mother sits.
>
> 3. 4. 119-22, 112

Wonder is also an effect of the plot as a whole, and not merely of incident. Theseus and Hippolyta in *Midsummer Night's Dream* discuss the events of the same play, the plot of the criss-crossing lovers, from the point of view of literary criticism (the passage contains the famous remarks on "the poet's eye in a fine frenzy rolling"):

HIPPOLYTA: 'Tis strange, my Theseus, that these
　　lovers speak of.

THESEUS: More strange than true. . . .

HIPPOLYTA: But all the story of the night told over,
　　And all their minds transfigur'd so together,
　　More witnesseth than fancy's images
　　And grows to something of great constancy;
　　But howsoever, strange and admirable.

5. 1. 1-2, 23-27

The plot, whether true or not, is certainly strange and wonderful ("admirable").

Wonder, however, is especially the effect of the denouement of those plays which the literary historian calls romances, especially if they conclude with a marvellous and surprising turn of events, thus, in *The Winter's Tale* the "discovery" that Perdita is the King's daughter is described by the First Gentleman as "a little amazedness." He goes on:

> But the changes I perceived in the King and Camillo were very notes of admiration. They seem'd almost, with staring on one another, to tear the cases of their eyes. There was speech in their dumbness, language in their very gesture. They look'd as they had heard of a world ransom'd, or one destroyed. A notable passion of wonder appeared in them; but the wisest beholder that knew no more but seeing, could not say if th' importance were joy or sorrow; but in the extremity of the one it must needs be.
>
> 5. 2. 5-6,11-21

He, however, had been commanded out of the chamber, and did not have the full story; hence, so far as he was concerned, it was "a little amazedness," provoked mainly by the wonder of the King and Camillo. The Second Gentleman, who now enters, is better informed and tells us:

> Such a deal of wonder is broken out within this hour
> that balladmakers cannot be able to express it.
>
> 5. 2. 25-27

Wonder, then, is the effect of the surprising and the marvellous; it is an extremity of feeling, and hence may be either joy or sorrow, fear or rapture. It is, if not the actual effect of such plots as *The Winter's Tale,* at least the effect aimed at. Thus Paulina, the mistress of ceremonies in the following scene, remarks as she discloses Hermione standing like a statue:

> I like your silence; it the more shows off
> Your wonder.
>
> 5. 3. 21-22

And the disclosure certainly has such an effect on Perdita; witness the King's speech:

> O royal piece,
> There's magic in thy majesty, which has . . .
> From thy admiring daughter took the spirits,
> Standing like stone with thee!
>
> 5. 3. 38-39, 41-42

But there is more wonder still! Paulina warns her audience that they remain at their own risk:

Quit presently the chapel, or resolve you
For more amazement.

5. 3. 86-87

And when the King commands, "No foot shall stir," she speaks
to the statue:

'Tis time; descend; be stone no more; approach;
Strike all that look upon with marvel.

5. 3. 98-100

So, if the reader finds the events of the play improbable, that is
the point. They are intended to be improbable. The effect aimed
at is pleasurable wonder.

In comparable circumstances, at the denouement of the se-
rious plot of *Much Ado About Nothing,* when Hero appears alive,
the Friar says:

All this amazement can I qualify. . .
Meantime let wonder seem familiar.

5. 4. 67, 70

Wonder, then, is associated not only with extreme fear but
also with extreme joy, and is marked by silence and immobility, it
is the shocked limit of feeling. Hence, Descartes a few years later
chose wonder as the first, and indeed the principal, passion of the
soul (*Les Passions du Ame,* 2. 53; 69-78).

It is easy to understand that the marvellous is intended to be
wonderful, whether in fact the reader finds it so or not. But trag-
edy should not so fly from all probability. In what way, then, does
Shakespearean tragedy in general, and the tragic catastrophe in

particular, admit of the effect of wonder? I have already shown how certain conventional tragic incidents and certain conventional appurtenances of tragic atmosphere involve fear and wonder. But a tragedy is not merely a spectacle and a plot, it is also something written and spoken; it is in large measure a series of declamations. This is obviously true of Elizabethan tragedy and of Shakespearean.

In fact, the revolution in the English theater of the 1580s out of which came the great plays of the succeeding decades consisted largely in the introduction of an adequate rhetoric. Nashe, for example, characterizes the pre-Shakespearean *Hamlet* and related plays as "handfuls of tragical speeches." Again, it is Greene's dying complaint against the companies of actors that he has been "of them forsaked," "those puppets . . . that spake from our mouths, those antics garnished in our colors"—that is, in our colors of rhetoric. It is his complaint against Shakespeare himself that he "supposes he is as well able to bombast out a blank verse as the best of" Greene's companions.[24] Marlowe's *Tamburlaine, Parts I* and *II* are, according to his printer, "tragical discourses"; and Marlowe himself enunciated in the prologue to *Tamburlaine I*, in those lines which constitute the charter of the greater Elizabethan tragedies, the rhetorical principle of high style in tragedy and its concomitant effect of wonder or astonishment:

> From jigging veins of rhyming mother wits
> And such conceits as clownage keeps in pay,
> We'll lead you to the stately tent of war
> Where you shall hear the Scythian Tamburlaine
> Threatening the world with high astounding terms
> And scourging kingdoms with his conquering sword.
> View but his picture in this tragic glass,
> And then applaud his fortunes as you please.

Though these lines have often been quoted, they are worth noticing again, for they are packed with critical doctrine. They are a manifesto. The first two lines constitute an explicit rejection of the old theatrical tradition of the fourteener with its rhyme and its marked regularity of meter ("jigging veins"); of the uneducated, unartful writer ("mother wits"); and of the tradition of the irresponsible clown. In its stead is proposed the modulated and rhymeless line, and the wholly serious play. This play involves a high subject, *war*, and by implication and the enjoinment of decorum a *stately* style, a high and royal style. The effect will be largely one of language and of rhetoric, for there "you shall hear," and you shall hear what is grand, or even grandiose, a "threatening the world," expressed in "high astounding terms."

Let us dwell on this phrase. A *term* is not any word, but a word belonging to a special vocabulary; so we speak of logical terms, and philosophical terms, and in the field of rhetoric there is, for example, that specialized literary diction which the Scots called "aureate terms." And Chaucer says in the *Canterbury Tales:*

> Youre termes, youre colours, and youre figures—
> Keep hem in stoor til so be that ye endite
> Heigh style, as whan that men to kinges write.
>
> *Clerk's Prologue,* 16-18

Tamburlaine will speak, then, in a choice and sifted language, the diction of *high* style, whose effect is here defined as that of wonder or astonishment, the "astounding." This effect is supported by the kind of action involved, "scourging kingdoms with his conquering sword."

The manifesto concludes with the proposition that the work of literature should merely present the object and leave the question of judgment to the spectator. This last, it seems to me, is

Marlowe's one distinctive contribution to literary theory (I do not say that it is correct), and *Tamburlaine* is perhaps the only play of the period—perhaps the only play of Marlowe's—that clearly adheres to the doctrine. Yet it is only an extreme statement of a general trend in Elizabethan drama, the trend toward emancipating the story from the exemplum. However, it is the other ideas which are of concern here, and these ideas are the common critical property of the time. They enunciate the principle of high style, high characters, and high matters, to which Shakespeare gave allegiance, though a less thoroughgoing allegiance. The significance of this passage is that they are here expressed for the first time in Elizabethan drama, that they are expressed memorably, that the play to which these ideas are prologue is, if we leave aside Kyd and *The Spanish Tragedy,* the first notable application of the ideas, and, finally, that the play itself was a great success and had great influence on the course of Elizabethan drama.

The reader today is fairly unmoved by grand speeches, but the testimony of our fathers as to the overwhelming effect of the grand style is explicit and fairly unanimous. It should cause no surprise, then, to find that Shakespeare ascribes the quality of wonder to eloquence. He echoes Tamburlaine at the beginning of *1 Henry VI* (if the passage be indeed his); there the Dauphin, deeply impressed by Joan of Arc's long speech, exclaims seriously:

> Thou hast astonish'd me with thy high terms.
>
> 1. 2. 93

Again, in *Henry V* the Archbishop of Canterbury in delineating the ideal character of the King ascribes the same quality to the eloquence of theology and to the sweet style:

Hear him but reason in divinity,
And, all-admiring, with an inward wish
You would desire the King were made a prelate...
Turn him to any cause of policy,
The Gordian knot of it he will unloose,
Familiar as his garter; that, when he speaks,
The air a charter'd libertine, is still,
And the mute wonder lurketh in men's ears
To steal his sweet and honey'd sentences.

1. 1. 38-40, 45-50

But the point is clear enough in *Hamlet* itself, and in connection with "tragical speeches." In the graveyard scene, after Laertes' outburst of rhetoric, Hamlet discloses himself and answers rant with rant:

Nay, an thou'lt mouth,
I'll rant as well as thou....

What is he whose grief
Bears such an emphasis? whose phrase of sorrow
Conjures the wand'ring stars, and makes them stand
Like wonder-wounded hearers?

5. 1. 306-07, 277-80

The terms "emphasis" and "phrase" make quite clear that Hamlet refers to Laertes' style, which is at least intended to wound (that is, "to strike") the hearers with wonder.

Wonder in Shakespeare is the effect of tragic incident and tragic style, as well as of the marvellous turn in events. But this does not exhaust the complexity of the notion of wonder: one more strand at least remains to be unraveled. For the notion derives not only from the tradition of literary criticism, as the proper effect of marvellous events, and the tradition of rhetoric, as the proper effect of marvellous eloquence, but it derives also from the tradition of philosophy, in which wonder is the primary cause of learning.

Wonder, in this sense, is that which strikes our attention and provokes intensity of interest and intensity of curiosity. Hence it is obviously relevant to drama and fiction, for a story that does not interest us may as well not exist, as Mine Host will instruct us, who commented on the Monk's famous, but deadly, tragedies:

> Sire Monk, namoore of this, so God you blesse! . . .
> Nor certeinly, as that thise clerkes seyn,
> Where as a man may have noon audience,
> Noght helpeth it to tellen his sentence.
>
> VII 3978, 3990-92

It is especially relevant to the conclusions of Shakespearean plays, which are as persistently occupied with the explanation of "How these things came about" (*Hamlet,* 5. 2. 391) as are the conclusions of the modern detective story. For wonder, as the motive for acquiring knowledge, demands explanation and is satisfied by it. Now, to satisfy by explanation, though it may seem a misguided impulse to the modern reader who lives by the current maxim of "Never explain," was not unimportant to the Elizabethan: it is the chief concern of the dying Hamlet. He charges Horatio:

> report me and my cause aright
>   To the unsatisfied. . . .
> O good Horatio, what a wounded name

(Things standing thus unknown) shall live behind me!
If thou didst ever hold me in thy heart,
Absent thee from felicity awhile,
And in this harsh world draw thy breath in pain,
To tell my story.

5. 2. 350-51, 355-60

For this reason, to satisfy the unsatisfied as to Hamlet's motives and actions, Horatio soon summarizes the events of the play, but not for this reason only. The unexplained gives scope to the irrational; hence:

let this same be presently perform'd
Even while men's minds are wild, lest more mischance
On plots and errors happen.

5. 2. 404-06

There is, then, in the resolution of wonder a kind of *catharsis*, a further effect of the effect of the catastrophe, and one appropriate to Shakespearean drama. To understand is to acquiesce. The movement of the drama is from this point of view an increasing intensity of interest which culminates in the striking events of the climax. These astonish the spectator so that he stands for the moment stone still, but at the same time they demand explanation, and with the explanation his emotion subsides and order prevails, as on the stage at the close of the play order prevails in the state.

Certainly the philosophical notion of wonder enters into the explanation of the catastrophe. In the passage already cited from *Much Ado About Nothing*, the Friar hastens to remark on the marvel of the catastrophe:

All this amazement can I qualify,
When, after that the holy rites are ended,
I'll tell you largely of fair Hero's death.

5. 4. 67-69

First wonder, then explanation. So also in *As You Like It*, Hymen, who enters to conclude the comedy, speaks thus:

Peace ho! I bar confusion.
'Tis I must make conclusion
　　　Of these most strange events...
Whiles a wedlock hymn we sing,
Feed yourselves with questioning,
That reason wonder may diminish
How thus we met, and these things finish.

5. 4. 131-33, 143-46

And the general scheme is very well explained by Quince, as prologue to the "tragical mirth" that concludes *A Midsummer Night's Dream*:

Gentles, perchance you wonder at this show;
But wonder on, till truth make all things plain.

5. 1. 128-29

VI

To sum up: the primary effect of tragedy is sorrow or woe, of which pity is a species. The tragic atmosphere and the incidents leading to the catastrophe are fearful. This is the Donatan tradition in which the tragic fact is violent, unexpected death, and corresponds to the medieval tradition of psychology in which the anticipation of death is fearful and its accomplishment woeful. But since the catastrophe is unexpected, it will startle the audience, and so the emotion of fear which has accompanied the course of tragic incident will become attached in special measure to the catastrophe. But this will be that fear which results from external events, wonder, astonishment, or shocked surprise. Hence woe or wonder are the effects of the tragic spectacle. Horatio's phrase, then, as is Sidney's, is only a distillation of the tradition, and woe is even a more proper term than "pity," *wonder* than "fear."

In the preceding section, I have cited texts in which Shakespeare explicitly names wonder as an effect of tragic incident, of tragic style, and as the principal effect of the catastrophe of those nontragical plays which involve marvellous events, being the natural correlative of marvels and the motive for understanding them. But is wonder named in any other work of Shakespeare as an effect of the tragic catastrophe, or does it appear only in the one passage from *Hamlet?* Again, is it customary to name explicitly the intended effect at the end of other Elizabethan plays?

It will be expected that woe or pity will be the most commonly named, and in fact there are more texts than anyone wishes to look through. To cite one example, the anonymous *Tragedy of Locrine* is drenched with mournful complaints. These occur after each of the successive tragic catastrophes which constitute the play (1. 1. 227*ff*.; 3. 1. 16*ff*.; and especially 43*ff*.; 3. 6. 1*ff*.; 5.1. 1*ff*. and especially 16*ff*.), but most notably at the end. Here in Estrild's lament over the death of Locrine, the concept of lamentation and pity is explicitly associated with the concept of tragedy as involving both the fall and death of the great, and the lesson of the instability of this world-for here as in glass we plainly see that all our life is but as a tragedy, a confused chaos of mishaps:

Break, heart, with sobs and generous suspires!
Stream forth, you tears, from forth my watery eyes!
Help me to mourn for warlike Locrine's death!
Pour down your tears, you watery regions,
For mighty Locrine is bereft of life!
O fickle Fortune! O unstable world!
What else are all things that this globe contains
But a confused chaos of mishaps?
Wherein as in a glass we plainly see
That all our life is but as a tragedy,
Since mighty kings are subject to mishap.

5. 4. 111-21[25]

But the effect of wonder is common enough. In Greene's
Orlando Furioso the Emperor of Africa, who is the representative
of the state, replies after hearing an account of the action from
Orlando:

I stand amazed, deep overdrenched with joy,
To hear and see this unexpected end:
So will I rest content.

5. 2. 1425-27[26]

This is the kind of wonder we have already met at the end of
The Winter's Tale. Of like kind is the effect of the discovery in
Marston's *Malcontent* that Malevole is Altofont, the former and
legitimate Duke of Genoa:

MALEVOLE: Banish amazement; come, we four must stand
Full shock of fortune. Be not so wonder stricken. . . .

PIETRO: . . . Give leave to recollect
　　My thoughts dispersed in wild astonishment.

4.5

This is the principal catastrophe of the play, though there follows in the fifth act, amid masquing and comedy, a second reversal—the fall of Mendoza. Of a similar nature is the discovery of Andrugio at the end of Marston's *Antonio and Mellida:*

> We are amazed, our royal spirits numbed
> In stiff astonished wonder at thy prowess.

And, a little later, when Antonio rises from the coffin:

> Stand not amazed, great states!...
> Most wished spectators of my tragedy.[27]

There is a different, but not too dissimilar, kind in the 1610 *Mucedorus,* the version played before King James. Here Comedy and Envy in the Epilogue suddenly kneel before the majesty of James:

> ENVY: My power has lost her might; Envy's date's expired.
> 　　Yon splendent majesty hath felled my sting,
> 　　And I amazed am. *Fall down and quake.*

65-67[28]

But for wonder as the immediate effect of the catastrophe of a tragic, rather than of a comic or heroic, catastrophe, Shakespeare himself gives precedent. The catastrophe of Shakespeare's poem *The Rape of Lucrece* is Lucrece's suicide—at which:

117

> Stone-still, astonish'd with this deadly deed,
> Stood Collatine and all his lordly crew.
>
> 1730-31

This is the wonder that is a species of fear; but, as the shock subsides, woe and pity rise:

> About the mourning and congealed face
> Of that black blood a wat'ry rigoll goes,
> Which seems to weep upon the tainted place;
> And ever since, as pitying Lucrece's woes,
> Corrupted blood some watery token shows.
>
> 1744-48

The poem ends finally with Brutus' speech, which again provokes wonder:

> This said, he struck his hand upon his breast
> And kiss'd the fatal knife to end his vow;
> And to his protestation urg'd the rest,
> Who, wond'ring at him, did his words allow.
>
> 1842-45

Quite parallel to this is the conclusion of Jonson's *Sejanus*. Here signs and prodigies precede the fall of Sejanus:

> But now a fiery meteor in the form
> Of a great ball was seen to roll along
> The troubled air, where yet it hangs unperfect,
> The amazing wonder of the multitude!
>
> 5. 4. 48-51

The fall itself provokes wonder:

> MACRO: Wherefore, fathers,
>   Sit you amazed and silent.
>
>   5. 10. 246-47

But the final effect is a curious kind of terror, emotionally rather
subtle, for, though terror is not directly named, no one can miss
it: the more our pity is solicited in the subsequent speeches for
the attendant circumstances of Sejanus' fall, the more our terror
rises. The pity which these accounts summon is really a kind of
aghast terror at the mob and at the political corruption which
still persists and is not resolved with Sejanus' fall. The pity we
feel is certainly not pity for Sejanus himself, who had disclaimed
any such softness:

> When I do fear again, let me be struck
> With forked fire, and unpitied die.
>
>   5. 6. 75-76

to whom it had been denied by Macro:

> And no man take compassion of thy state.
>
>   5. 10. 242

and whose fall is described thus by Lepidus:

> And this man fall! Fall? Ay, without a look
> That durst appear his friend, or lend so much
> Of vain relief to his changed state as pity!
>
>   5. 10. 283-85

Finally Arruntius at the very end of the play sums it all up:

> Forbear, you things
> That stand upon the pinnacles of state
> To boast your slippery height: when you do fall
> You pash yourselves to pieces, ne'er to rise;
> And he who lends you pity is not wise.
>
> 5. 10. 458-62[29]

The immediate effect of the fall is wonder, but its final effect is a terror begotten by the detailing of the occasions for pity. But the pity is simply for the human state and the innocent bystanders; there can be no real pity for the fall of a thorough villain. And here is disclosed how fear or terror enters properly into the catastrophe of an Elizabethan play. We feel pity for the death of the good and for death itself, but the violent end of the wicked begets fear. Thus Shakespeare's Queen Margaret anticipates the fall of Richard III:

> But at hand, at hand
> Ensues his piteous and unpitied end.
>
> 4. 4. 73-74

and Richmond later comes from the field of battle:

> God and your arms be prais'd, victorious friends!
> The day is ours; the bloody dog is dead.
>
> 5. 5. 1-2

Contrast this with Bolingbroke's comment on Richard II, who was weak but not villainous:

Lords, I protest my soul is full of woe
That blood should sprinkle me to make me grow.
Come, mourn with me for what I do lament.

5. 6. 45-47

In like fashion the death of Macbeth is not mourned—he is spoken of as "this dead butcher and his fiendlike queen" (5. 8. 69)—though that of Siward's son is:

Your cause of sorrow
Must not be measur'd by his worth, for then
It hath no end.

5. 8. 44-46

Sorrow and pity are reserved for the deaths of the good, or for the human fact itself—even Richard III's end will be piteous, though unpitied. Hence, at the end of *Lear*, Albany, the representative of the state, says after the deaths of Lear and Cordelia:

Bear them from hence. Our present business
Is general woe.

5. 3. 318-19

But on the earlier reported deaths of Goneril and Regan, one of whom was his wife, he only says:

This judgement of the heavens, that makes us tremble,
Touches us not with pity.

5. 3. 231-32

Fear, then, is the effect of the violent death of the wicked as distinguished from that of the good, whose fall evokes sorrow and pity.

The striking effect of pity and sorrow is explicitly named at the end of two later Shakespearean tragedies. Octavian, the representative of the state, sums up *Antony and Cleopatra:*

> High events as these
> Strike those that make them; and their story is
> No less in pity than his glory which
> Brought them to be lamented.
>
> 5. 2. 363-66

The verb "strike" here denotes the effect of wonder—at least, this is its ordinary meaning. Aufidius utters similar sentiments at the end of *Coriolanus:*

> My rage is gone,
> And I am struck with sorrow. Take him up.
>
> 5. 6. 148-49

Again, to be struck is the effect of wonder. Consequently, these three plays at least—*Hamlet, Antony and Cleopatra, Coriolanus*—together with *The Rape of Lucrece,* are intended explicitly to evoke the emotional effect of woe and wonder.

From the later tradition I will quote only the following close parallel: The Cardinal in Middleton's *Women Beware Women* characterizes the catastrophe thus:

> The greatest sorrow and astonishment
> That ever struck the general peace of Florence
> Dwells in this hour.
>
> 5. 1. 240-42[30]

REASON PANDERS WILL

I

The emotional effect of the catastrophe, of course, is not equivalent to the experience of the work. It is a final element in that experience, enters into it, and in part determines it. But there is more to the experience of art than the emotional effect even of the whole, and certainly more than the effect of the conclusion. There is, among other things, the experience of the language of the work. There is, especially in the Renaissance, the intellectual experience of persistent sententious thought. And there is in the typical play the central intellectual experience of plotting, counter-plotting, and mistakes: the events of Hamlet are characterized by Horatio at the end of the play as "mischance" that "on plots and errors happen" (5. 2. 405-06). This is an experience of the same sort as that of a game of chess, and is like chess intense in its kind, for though it is intellectual it is not without emotion: otherwise it would not be experience. Nevertheless, the other aspects of a work are related to the effect of the conclusion, and not only as elements in the larger experience of the whole. They are related in this way: though the effect itself is largely a result of the bare fact, of what happens, it is not sufficient merely to attain an effect: the effect must be justified. We must acquiesce in the conclusion.

We acquiesce out of a feeling of inevitability: what will be will be. But what is the source of this feeling? A conclusion is inevitable *within the closed system of a work of art* when it satisfies a pattern or principle of order acceptable to the audience. Such patterns are of different kinds, some larger, some smaller. They may be external, as, for example, the full circuit of Fortune's wheel, the fulfillment of the retributive justice of God, or the progression from order to disorder, concluding sadly in deaths. The pattern may exhibit the causal sequence of realistic fiction, which consists in an exemplification of a syllogistic conclusion (more precisely, an enthymeme) made persuasive. For a causal sequence shows a probable course of action, and by probability we mean a conformity to some accepted commonplace about how men of a certain type will behave under certain conditions. This is persuasive when sharply and compellingly presented so that we do not explicitly recognize the syllogistic nature of the conclusion. We merely believe it, speak of it as if it were really determined, and hence inevitable. We say the conclusion was logical.

The pattern may, however, be internal and involve artistic foreshadowing and completion, suggestion and fulfillment. Artistic devices of this nature are usually referred to and grounded on the personality of the characters, and so exhibit that adjustment of feeling which comprises the ethics of sensibility. Or, and this is quite different, the pattern may be internal and involve the structure of character. In this case it will exhibit responsibility and moral choice, and will exemplify the ethics of character. Of this sort is the pattern or principle of order which is the subject of this essay. It is only one among many, but it will serve to illustrate the kinds of principles I have in mind and the relationship of these to the emotional effect of the conclusion.

The basic text for this principle of order in Renaissance tragedy is the definition of tragedy in Averroës' paraphrase of Aristotle's *Poetics*, which was current throughout the later Middle Ages and was probably more widely reprinted in the Renaissance than the work of any other commentator. The definition reads:

Tragedy is the imitative representation of a notable action, brought to completion by a voluntary decision, and having in it a certain force of generalization with respect to matters of some import, as distinguished from a particular proposition about some individual fact. By means of this imitative representation there is induced in the minds of the audience a rightness of feeling which springs from the pity and terror which the representation begets in them?[1]

The final effect of tragedy according to this definition is ethical: it results in an ordering of the irrational by means of a presentation which evokes specific emotional effects. The internal spring of the plot is a willed act, or moral choice. The final cause is right feeling, which is obviously the correlative of the ethical principle of right reason. This rightness of feeling comes through the tragic emotions, but apparently the effective cause of ordered feeling is the force of generalization in the plot. The universal here is an immanent power, not explicit or allegorical, and not singular or particular.[2]

Some of the greater tragedies of Shakespeare correspond well enough to this definition, which supplements the Donatan tradition with, among other principles, the principle of action involving moral choice. But choice in tragedy is usually a choice of evil, and hence the question in Renaissance terms is one of sin. How does a man sin? There are two main views in the Renaissance, the intellectualist view of the Aristotelian and Thomistic tradition, and the voluntarist view whose tradition is more complex. In the former the act of sin is primarily intellectual so that the process involves erroneous reasoning: action follows on reasoned deliberation as the conclusion of a syllogism follows on its premises. The will is considered to be subservient to reason and to embrace almost necessarily what reason proposes. Erroneous choice, then, from this position will be ascribed primarily to sophistry. Practical reason in the possession of the immutable principles of right action fails in the particular application, and so sins. In Duns Scotus' phrase, "We sin by paralogism." For the will never moves except "under the show of goodness," as St. Thomas says,[3] or, as Iago puts it in *Othello*:

> Divinity of hell!
> When devils will the blackest sins put on,
> They do suggest at first with heavenly shows,
> As I do now.

2. 3. 356-59

We may account for sin, then, by saying that it is the result of a logical confusion, a failure to discriminate between a good and the good. Thus in the case of Macbeth it will be granted that the kingship is a good, but it was not for Macbeth the good. The irrational part of the soul, the passions and perturbations, will affect man, so long as he remains man and is in the possession of his faculties, only to the extent that his reason may be sophisticated so that he accepts invalid for valid argument. For, "if the passions of the mind be strong," Hooker relates, "they easily sophisticate the understanding; they make it apt to believe upon very slender warrant, and to imagine infallible truth where scarcely any probable show appeareth." (*EP*, 5. Dedication) In brief, reason is not dethroned or suspended, but is perverted, commits an error in logic, and is actively enlisted on the side of false desire. The process is one of reasonable choice though the reasonableness be unreasonable. It is briefly summed up in a phrase in *Hamlet*, "reason panders will."

The phrase occurs in the closet scene. It is in its context the last and most violent in a series of illustrations of the perversion of the natural order of things. Hamlet says to his mother:

> Rebellious hell,
> If thou canst mutine in a matron's bones,
> To flaming youth let virtue be as wax
> And melt in her own fire. Proclaim no shame
> When the compulsive ardour gives the charge,
> Since frost itself as actively does burn,
> And reason panders will.
>
> 3. 4. 82-88

Rhetorically, this is a very curious passage. It is a series of adynata, of impossibilities. As such, it employs the tritest device of classical and Renaissance rhetoric. We are accustomed to sigh when we meet it. But these are adynata in an ethical context; they are impossibilities only to right reason and uncorrupted nature. To be sure, frost from the point of view of Renaissance science cannot burn as if it were active. But every observer of Renaissance and fallen man knew that lust not only could but regularly did break out, even in those in whom by age and station it was especially indecorous. And every Christian knew that man was inherently sinful, and that the state of sin was that in which reason pandered will. Yet he knew that these perversions of the due order were not right, and he would feel the moral horror that Hamlet, and Shakespeare, expresses by this rhetorical device: the horror that these impossibilities, repugnant to Reason and true Nature, should be not merely possible but actual and in our sense almost natural.

The phrase, then, expresses nothing new in the history of thought. The idea is at least as old as Aristotle; it is, in fact, a compendious statement of the Aristotelian analysis of the act of erroneous moral choice which had been taken up, developed, and rendered almost conventional by a long line of medieval and Renaissance philosophers. In this tradition when reason panders will the due and proper subordination of the irrational to the rational is overturned, and overturned the more grievously in that reason is not merely suspended or dethroned but is actively enlisted in the service of desire. The man who is swept away by emotion acts unreasonably and wrongly but not perversely; the man whose reason is bent to further his unreasonable desires is in that measure diabolical.

As idea, then, it was available and in a sense trite. It had already been employed by Shakespeare, most clearly in one passage which may be regarded as the direct ancestor of this. The passage is in the reply of Adonis to the arguments of Venus in *Venus and Adonis*, for it was the quaint device of the Elizabethans to believe in discourse of reason, and they would seem, if we may accept the testimony of their literature, even to have attempted seduction by the method of disputation, and by the same method to have repelled it. Such is the case with Comus and the Lady in Milton's poem. And as the Lady in *Comus* extricates herself from the designs of the villain by opposing true reason to false reasoning, true love to earthly lust:

> I had not thought to have unlockt my lips
> In this unhallowed air but that this juggler
> Would think to charm my judgement as mine eyes,
> Obtruding false rules pranked in reason's garb.
>
> 756-59

so Adonis answers Venus's arguments and defines in context the nature of sin:

> What have you urg'd that I cannot reprove?
> The path is smooth that leadeth on to danger.
> I hate not love, but your device in love,
> That lends embracements unto every stranger.
>   You do it for increase. O strange excuse,
>   When reason is the bawd to lust's abuse!
>
> 787-92

Here the idea is more fully and more analytically presented than in the phrase in *Hamlet*, though less fully and less analytically than in St. Thomas or Aristotle. To achieve the later phrase there remained only to subject this passage to the Shakespearean transmutation: to turn idea into intuition, to condense it to three words, and by the metaphorical panders, a violent and sensuous word, to exhibit reason and will as sinful and shabby figures in a disreputable world.

But though this was the orthodox view, resting on the long Aristotelian tradition, it was not the only view at that time. Erroneous action was often presented in Elizabethan drama as the result of the dethroning of reason. This latter possibility is allowed for in the Scholastic scheme, for it is an obvious fact of experience, but it is minimized. St. Thomas says, for example, that in cases of sudden and violent emotion, when reason cannot come to the opposition, mortal sin is not involved. But this is only a limiting case. For if the passion, say of love or anger, were in its origin voluntary the consequences would involve sin even though the passion took away the use of reason entirely. The critical point of decision is simply moved further back. Only if the cause were not voluntary but natural, as for example some bodily sickness, would the consequences be excused of sin. (*ST*, 1-2. 77. 7)

Nevertheless, interest in the limiting case grew in the Renaissance. The full history of this development is somewhat obscure but the principal lines are clear. In the first place, there was the development of a mechanistic psychology, the Galenic psychology of humors, with its emphasis on the involuntariness of strong passion; the most famous text in English is Burton's *Anatomy of Melancholy*. In the second place, there was the development of a voluntaristic metaphysics in the Franciscan school associated with the name of Duns Scotus, and the subsequent extension of this point of view to ethics. The issue of this movement was the predestinarianism of the Reformation with its emphasis on the helplessness of man, and particularly of his reason, and the corollary interest in Stoic Fate, which was supported by the prestige of Seneca's tragedies. Here, especially in the *Phaedra*, as also in Ovid's *Medea*, were classic exemplars of tragic characters swept, away by an overmastering passion: "I see the better course, and approve of it; I follow the worse."[4] It is curious that this view of human action which ascribes to the will, the faculty of inner motion in man, the ultimate control of his destiny should in practice have issued often in an extreme determinism. Perhaps this is a sign of the thoroughgoing rationalism of the period; the more the will was considered to be irresponsible to the dictates of reason and free to act arbitrarily, the more some principle of compulsion must be invoked to account for the irresponsible arbitrariness of the will.

But whatever the reasons, there are at least four sorts of compulsion to be found in Elizabethan drama. There is, first, the compulsion which is accounted for by a mechanistic physiology and psychology, a type that has been studied a good deal in recent years, notably by Hardin Craig. He points out, for example, that the sudden and apparently unmotivated jealousy of Leontes in *The Winter's Tale* is explainable in such terms.[5]

> Too hot, too hot!
> To mingle friendship far, is mingling bloods.
> I have tremor cordis on me; my heart dances,
> But not for joy; not joy.
>
> 1. 2. 108-11

I have tremor cordis on me. But Leontes's jealousy is conceived also as voluntaristic, as involving the primacy of feeling. This is explicit in the key line of the speech in which Leontes embraces his unjustified jealousy:

> Can thy dam—may't be?
> Affection! thy intention stabs the centre.
>
> 1. 2. 137-38

Affection denotes the passions, emotions, and feelings which are associated with the will in the moving faculty of the soul, as distinguished from the rational faculty to which the will is attached as the rational appetite. *Intention* denotes the directed movement of a faculty of the soul toward realizing a possibility. It is that which is required to raise the potentiality of knowledge to act, and it is also the movement by which the rational will tends toward and embraces the end of action proposed by reason.[6] The passage means, then, that affection directing its own movement penetrates to the knowledge of the fact which gives the grounds for being jealous, and at the same time embraces the decision to be jealous. Hence we may translate Leontes' speech into modern terms: "Feeling rather than reason hits the mark and furnishes the decision." This is explicit voluntarism.

The third type of compulsion is that exercised by the Stoic Fate, and operating often through the influence of the stars. The fourth is the theological compulsion of grace and predestination. The two are conjoined and offered as alternative explanations of the tragic action in Heywood's *A Woman Killed with Kindness*. The tragic villain speaks:

> I am a villain if I apprehend
> But such a thought! Then, to attempt the deed,
> Slave, thou art damn'd without redemption.—
> I'll drive away this passion with a song.
> A song! Ha, ha! A song! As if, fond man,
> Thy eyes could swim in laughter, when thy soul
> Lies drench'd and drowned in red tears of blood!
> I'll pray, and see if God within my heart
> Plant better thoughts. Why, prayers are meditations,
> And when I meditate (oh, God forgive me!)
> It is on her divine perfections.
> I will forget her; I will arm myself
> Not t'entertain a thought of love to her;
> And, when I come by chance into her presence,
> I'll hale these balls until my eye-strings crack,
> From being pull'd and drawn to look that way.
> *Enter, over the Stage, Frankford, his Wife, and Nick*
> O God, O God! With what a violence
> I'm hurried to mine own destruction!
>
> 2. 3. 1-18

And again:

> I will not; zounds! I will not. I may choose,
> And I will choose. Shall I be so misled,
> Or shall I purchase to my father's crest
> The motto of a villain? If I say
> I will not do it, what thing can enforce me?
> What can compel me? What sad destiny
> Hath such command upon my yielding thoughts?
> I will not;—ha! Some fury pricks me on;
> The swift fates drag me at their chariot wheel,
> And hurry me to mischief.
>
> 2. 3. 96-105

The tragic action follows. And since the first citation above is a soliloquy and the second an aside, they may be taken as representing the view of tragic motivation which the author himself proffers. This is one of sheer fatalism. The character attempts to distract his thoughts, as St. Thomas for example suggests he should (*ST*, 1-2. 77. 2: "Whether reason can be overcome by passion against its knowledge"), but the divine sensuality of love overpowers him. He attempts to exercise rational choice, but fury and Fate hurry him to mischief, and with him the other characters. He sees the better course and approves it, but follows the worse. Yet an alternative explanation, which could be regarded as the same explanation under another aspect, is given at the end of the play. Here the leading character, a good man, sums up the whole:

> God, that hath laid this cross upon our heads,
> Might (had He pleas'd) have made our cause of meeting
> On a more fair and more contented ground;
> But He that made us made us to this woe.[7]

133

For what seems to man to be a result of Fate or fury is but the concealed operation of the Providence of God.

The contrast between the intellectual and voluntarist positions can be made clear by comparing Sextus Tarquin's soliloquy before committing the rape in Heywood's play *The Rape of Lucrece* with the similar soliloquy in Shakespeare's poem of the same title. In the former, Tarquin enters Lucrece's bedchamber carrying a drawn sword and a lighted taper. He speaks:

> I am bound
> Upon a black adventure, on a deed
> That must wound virtue and make beauty bleed.
> Pause, Sextus, and, before thou runnst thyself
> Into this violent danger, weigh thy sin . . .
> Back! yet thy fame
> Is free from hazard and thy style from shame.
> O Fate! thou hast usurped such power o'er man
> That where thou pleadst thy will no mortal can. . .
> Forward still!
> To make thy lust live, all thy virtues kill.
>
> 4. 3[8]

Certainly reasonable deliberation in the sense of rational awareness is involved here as it was in the previous citation from *A Woman Killed with Kindness*. But it does not enter into the decision. The character in the grip of strong emotion must act contrary to the dictates of reason: Fate sweeps him on. He makes no attempt to justify his sin; the end is not presented under the show of goodness.

But in Shakespeare's poem, the poet himself explains the course of Tarquin's soliloquy:

Thus, graceless, holds he disputation
'Tween frozen conscience and hot burning will,
And with good thoughts makes dispensation,
Urging the worser sense for vantage still;
Which in a moment doth confound and kill
    All pure effects, and doth so far proceed
    That what is vile shows like a virtuous deed.

246-52

God for his own inscrutable reasons does not assist Tarquin on this occasion with his grace (*Thus, graceless*). Hence Tarquin must reach this moral decision on a human and ethical plane. And how is the process described? It is described in medieval terms as the holding of a disputation. In this disputation Tarquin urges the worser sense for vantage still; reason is actively enlisted in the service of desire. When the process reaches the point of decision it doth in a moment confound all pure effects, for Tarquin by the decision has sinned mortally. Consequently, the undoing—not of his character, really, in the modern sense, but of his moral principle—doth so far proceed that what is vile shows like a virtuous deed. He sins by paralogism under the show of goodness.

II

The act of decision in the intellectualist tradition has as a further characteristic mark that it is divided into two steps: the choice of the end (*intentio*) and the choice of means (*electio*). The steps are distinct, though the second is dependent on the first. (*ST*, 1-2. 8. 3) I shall now analyze two scenes in Shakespearean tragedy, one in *Othello* and one in *Macbeth*, each of which portrays an act of moral choice that leads to the catastrophe; and I shall conclude with a discussion of the whole scope of *Hamlet*.

The scene in *Othello* concerns the choice of the end, for there is here no serious question of means. Othello has it in his power to kill Desdemona at any time, and presuming his grounds are correct the killing is justified. "Cassio did top her," he says to Emilia:

> Oh, I were damn'd beneath all depth in hell
> But that I did proceed upon just grounds
> To this extremity.
>
> 5. 2. 136-39

As for the death of Cassio, Iago promises to take care of that. The only question, then, is the question of fact; for it is assumed in the play, and made more plausible by locating the action in Venice and Cyprus, that if Desdemona has been unfaithful she must die.

The action of the play, so far as it concerns the moral act, is roughly this: Iago plants in Othello's mind the idea that his wife may be unfaithful, and he does it so skillfully that he is not himself open to attack. The mere idea is sufficient to upset most men:

> Dangerous conceits are in their nature poisons
> Which at the first are scarce found to distaste,
> But with a little act upon the blood
> Burn like the mines of sulphur.
>
> 3. 3. 326-29

But Iago does more than plant the idea; he insinuates a number of fairly vivid and violent images; he raises an efficient head of passion. More than this, he brings to bear on the question a number of commonplaces which make the fact more credible: women are weak; most husbands are cuckolds. He shows that in this special situation infidelity is even more likely, for as Desdemona has deceived her father so she may deceive him. Besides, there is the fact of their disproportion in race, in age, and in social position. Any man would be almost convinced of his wife's infidelity after such insinuation.

But its effect on Othello is only to get him into a passion in which he may do anything. He may even, as he threatens, kill Iago. At this point Iago intervenes with an appeal to reason:

> Are you a man? have you a soul? or sense?[9]
>
> 3. 3. 374

That is, "Are you a man or beast? Have you a rational soul, since reason is the distinguishing characteristic of man? or merely sense, the sensitive soul, the distinguishing characteristic of animals?" He appeals to reason because he does not want to put Othello merely in a passion: there can be no directed action without a reasoned conclusion. And Othello answers this appeal by stating the disjunctive syllogism upon which the play turns:

> I think my wife be honest, and think she is not;
> I think that thou art just, and think thou art not.
> I'll have some proof.
>
> 3. 3. 384-86

But he has prefaced this with the statement, "Nay, Stay. Thou shouldst be honest." And it has been reiterated throughout the play, not without purpose, that Iago is honest. So when the disjunction is presented almost in technical form: Either Iago is honest or Desdemona is honest, the conclusion that: Iago is honest, therefore Desdemona is not, is almost guaranteed by the assumption that Iago is. Hence Othello goes on:

> Her name, that was as fresh
> As Dian's visage, is now begrim'd and black
> As mine own face.

Nevertheless, Othello's feeling is so strong he does not yet assent; he demands some proof. If he cannot see his wife strumpeted before his eyes, let him at least have some circumstantial sign. However, as Iago has confided to the audience (3. 3. 321-24), Othello, in the distraught state of mind in which he is prepared to assent to the syllogism proposed, will accept as proof the flimsiest trifle of a sign, a mere handkerchief which he saw really but a moment ago. When to this is added Iago's account of Cassio's remarks in his sleep, which is accepted substantially as testimony to a confession on Cassio's part, the cause is finished. Othello consents, "Patience, I say," Iago interposes, "your mind perhaps may change." "Never, Iago." (3. 3. 452-53) The choice is made and solemnly ratified by oath. The following scene (3. 4 together with 4. 1 and 2) supports the decision but is subsequent to it. The play moves on to the catastrophe.

No one cares to see such things happen. Nevertheless, we can acquiesce since we can see "How these things came about." A man "not easily jealous: is operated on by a skillful insinuator and becomes so "perplex'd in the extreme" that his passions easily sophisticate his understanding: "they make it apt to believe upon very slender warrant, and to imagine infallible truth where scarcely any probable show appeareth." Othello is perplexed both intellectually and emotionally, but primarily intellectually.

For, as Francis Bacon relates in the *Advancement of Learning*, there is a seducement that works by the subtlety of the illaqueation and another by the strength of the impression. The latter overmasters the reason by power of sense and imagination; the former works by perplexing the reason.[10] The process is described more fully in a sermon by Bishop Andrewes with reference to the fall of Eve:

> For this is not the least policy of the Devil, not to set upon her bluntly, but like a serpent slily and slowly to creep in her little by little, until he has espied some vantage. Therefore his order is: to bring her from questioning in talk to a doubt in opinion, and from that to an error in judgement, and so at last to a corrupt action in practice. And to corrupt her mind within, first he useth this order, to tickle her ears with curiosity, and by that to cause her to have a giddiness and swimming in the brain by fantastical imaginations and surmises; and then to make her secure and careless of the truth, and so at last maketh her somewhat inclinable to error and falsehood.[11]

But Othello's transition to jealousy and sin has not seemed plausible to every reader. It is not true to life, we are told, and the theatrical convention of the calumniator credited has been invented to solve the difficulty.[12] But the crediting of calumny is no mere convention of the theater; it is a fact of daily life. The truth is, the modern critic is concerned to defend the niceness of life, to maintain that successful hypocrisy is unlikely, that no one omits speaking up when he should, that no decent husband suspects his precious wife, and that if he does they just talk it over like civilized people. Anyway, no woman of character will sleep with a man's best friend.

Such critics make the optimistic assumption that men are not likely to go wrong unless there is sufficient cause. But this is modern, and not too well founded in fact. The general assumption of the Renaissance was that men were not likely to go right unless there was a supernatural cause. "Such is the propensity of all creatures unto evil," Bishop Jewel says, "and the readiness of all men to suspect, that the things which neither have been done, nor once meant to be done, yet may be easily both heard and credited for true."[13] The modern critic feels that women do not tend to be unfaithful; the Renaissance man, who was still smarting under Eve's transgression, felt that women were pretty likely to be unfaithful if they only had a chance. He would take Othello's remarks on cuckoldry as hardly exaggerated:

> 'Tis destiny unshunnable, like death.
> Even then this forked plague is fated to us
> When we do quicken.

3. 3. 275-77

Furthermore, the appeal of Desdemona's innocency is much greater for the reader than it was for Othello; the reader knows she is innocent, which is precisely what Othello does not know.

Anyone who is willing to believe in evil, and personally I do not find this difficult to do, will not find Othello's jealousy implausible. He may be worried, however, that it all seems to happen in so short a time, and he may wonder just how it is that Othello seems to be convinced that his wife is unfaithful—not how Iago persuades him, for that is clear enough, but by what process he comes to accept the proposition himself. I have held that the process is the traditional one of moral choice and intellectualist in character. For all his passion Othello is not swept away; he is presented with a disjunctive syllogism, draws what seems to him a proper conclusion, confirms the conclusion with a sign, and proceeds upon what he thinks are just grounds to this extremity. The process of choice itself takes place in a point of time and is properly represented as occurring within a single scene.

The restriction of the process of choice to a point of time and a single scene contributes to the feeling of implausibility. Our natural tendency, as can be seen in the novel, is to consider the process of choice as distributed through a number of scenes and as in large measure unconscious. We tend to find the condensed incredible and the diffused plausible. We regard decision as so implicated in the circumstances that condition it that neither can profitably be distinguished from the other. We can believe anything if only it be an indistinct compound of environment and heredity, and if we can be persuaded that it has evolved. For what is perhaps the greatest single difference between our habits of thought and those of the Middle Ages and Renaissance is located in the problem of continuity. We believe in the continuous. We believe that contraries shade off into each other. We believe a character is real when he is neither good nor bad but a middling gray. We disbelieve in, though we have not yet disproved, the law of the excluded middle. But the Renaissance believed firmly in Aristotelian logic: for them, B was either A or Not-A.

They also believed firmly in sin and repentance, each of which takes place in a point of time. Sin and grace were precise contraries that could not shade off into each other. Hence their view of the moral life was radically different from ours; it was essentially theological. Man's destiny hung on each decisive act, a life of grace could be cancelled by one mortal sin, and conversely the departing soul of an old and confirmed sinner could, though it was not likely, at the furthest margin of life repent of his sins and so pass joyously into the company of the elect. Such a view was held by both the great parties in the theological wars of the sixteenth century; it was proclaimed openly by those who emphasized man's free choice, but it was also maintained, if paradoxically maintained, by many of the fieriest proponents of predestination. For though a man be predestined to Hell, still he must willfully embrace that act by which he is eternally condemned, for the responsibility must be his and not the pre-destinating God's. So likewise, if he be predestined to Heaven, though he make an ungodly life his profession, still at the pre-destined moment he shall have grace to repent and his will must embrace that repentance. It is clear, then, that the restriction of the process of choice in Elizabethan drama to a single scene is not the result merely of foreshortening and condensation for dramatic purposes, but is a result of the Elizabethan view of the moral life. At the same time, of course, it is more dramatic.

The process of the decisive choice of evil can be seen more clearly, and this time with respect to the choice of means, in one scene in Macbeth.[14] It is the seventh of the first act. Macbeth enters and announces in a soliloquy that he has already fallen from the state of grace, that he has preferred the show of goodness in things temporal to the solid goodness of things eternal:

> If it were done when 'tis done, then 'twere well
> It were done quickly. If th' assassination
> Could trammel up the consequence, and catch,
> With his surcease, success; that but this blow
> Might be the be-all and the end-all here,
> But here, upon this bank and shoal of time,
> We'ld jump the life to come.
>
> 7. 1-7

His will has already moved to embrace the end, the kingship, but he is disturbed. He does not see how to accomplish it; he does not see how he can get away with the murder of Duncan:

> But in these cases
> We still have judgement here, that we but teach
> Bloody instructions, which, being taught, return
> To plague th' inventor.
>
> 1. 7. 7-10

Thus there is a consequent weakening of the will:

> I have no spur
> To prick the sides of my intent, but only
> Vaulting ambition, which o'erleaps itself
> And falls on th' other side.
>
> 1.7.25-28

Enter Lady Macbeth.

To understand what follows it will be well to recapitulate the requirements for a moral act. Reason must propose an end as good, and when the end is proposed the will moves naturally to embrace it. This has already happened in Macbeth, but it is not sufficient to constitute moral choice. The practical reason must discover means by which to accomplish the end (*consilium*), and not until the means are available is the choice finally made. There must follow sufficient emotion (*consensus*) so that the choice is actually put into operation (*usus*). This emotion precedes, accompanies, and follows the act of choice. It is the steam pressure that makes the engine move; there must be a certain excitement in the will to account for the step to choice and from choice to action. It is the office of rhetoric to supply this excitement; its function is to persuade. So Bacon defines it in a passage that has often been quoted but usually not properly understood: "The duty and office of rhetoric is to apply reason to imagination for the better moving of the will."[15] By apply here is meant "to put into practical contact with," so that if one were to use these words in a modern context he would rather say that imagination is applied to reason.

The traditional analysis, popularized and lacking the complication of multiplied distinctions, is expounded by the character of Tragedy himself in a play presented by Shakespeare's company (ca. 1598) a few years before *Hamlet*. *A Warning for Fair Women* begins with an argument between Tragedy, Comedy, and History. Later in the play, at the moment of moral choice, Tragedy steps forward and explains the process:

> Prevailing sin having by three degrees
> Made his ascension to forbidden deeds,
> At first, alluring their unwary minds
> To like what she proposed, then practising
> To draw them to consent; and, last of all,
> Ministering fit means and opportunity
> To execute what she approved good;
> Now she unveils their sight, and lets them see
> The horror of their foul immanity.
>
> 2. 865-741[16]

But to return to *Macbeth*. He has embraced the end, and now falters in resolution because he does not see how the end can be accomplished. There is required now fit means and opportunity to execute what he approved good, together with a concurrent

144

sustaining and heightening of resolution, the maintaining of an efficient head of passion. To fulfill this last requirement, the Ghost had appeared to Hamlet in the closet scene, and for the same reason Hamlet was made to observe Fortinbras and his army marching across "a plain in Denmark." For the same reason in this scene Lady Macbeth speaks in such shockingly violent terms:

> I have given suck, and know
> How tender 'tis to love the babe that milks me.
> I would, while it was smiling in my face,
> Have pluck'd my nipple from his boneless gums
> And dash'd the brains out, had I so sworn as you
> Have done to this.
>
> 1. 7. 54-59

So also, to Macbeth's assertion:

> I dare do all that may become a man.
> Who dares do more is none.

which is sound doctrine, implying the notion of decorum and the mean. Lady Macbeth answers with the old commonplace that Iago had used, of soul and sense, distinguishing man from beast through the characteristic of willed action:

> What beast was't then
> That made you break this enterprise to me?
> When you durst do it, then you were a man;
> And to be more than what you were, you would
> Be so much more the man.
>
> 1. 7. 46-51

This is obvious sophistry. It makes the will and not reason the distinguishing characteristic of man; it opposes rashness to timidity, excluding from consideration the reasonable mean of right courage. But it takes Macbeth in. His only question now is as to the means: "If we should fail?" Lady Macbeth outlines the way in which the murder can be accomplished and suspicion diverted. As soon as the means are proposed Macbeth assents and the moral choice is complete:

> I am settled and bend up
> Each corporal agent to this terrible feat.
>
> 1. 7. 79-80

This final decision of the soul, accompanied of course by disordered emotion, persists unaltered through the catastrophe.

But in *Hamlet* the process of moral choice extends throughout the play. The first half is concerned with the choice of end, which rests here as in *Othello* on a question of fact: did Claudius really kill the old King, Hamlet's father? or, what is the same question, is the Ghost a true ghost or a diabolical apparition? To resolve this question of fact Hamlet devises the play scene as an *experimentum crucis:* "If he but blench," Hamlet says in a soliloquy, "I know my course." (2. 2. 625-26) At the close of the play scene, when the King does blench, Hamlet turns to Horatio and says, "I'll take the ghost's word for a thousand pound! Didst perceive?" (3. 2. 297-98) The question of fact is now resolved and Hamlet embraces the end which the Ghost had proposed in an early scene of the play: "Revenge his foul and most unnatural murther." (1. 5. 25) The rest of the play concerns the choice of means, but the means in this case is not easy to find. The King cannot be killed at his prayers and so dispatched to Heaven: "Why, this is hire and salary, not revenge!" (3. 3. 79) He does kill him in the Queen's closet, or so he thinks, but it turns out to be only Polonius, that "wretched, rash, intruding fool." And so on to the close of the play. The proper means to accomplish the end is never discovered until it is too late, until Hamlet when he knows that he is dying stabs the King with the envenomed sword. It is too late, now, for a successful plot.

Hamlet, of course, is a touchy subject. I do not wish to imply that his character is equivalent to this analysis; he is something more and something other. He is an imitation of a person, and thus has an imputed reality. He has a name, which is a chief instrument of individualization. He is implicated in circumstances of some particularity. He does and says much that is not reducible to the central choice. He is presented in a specific body of writing. Nevertheless, a fictional character is not a given, a brute fact of existence. He is a construction, a fiction, and hence he must be constructed according to a scheme and must have a scheme to be intelligible. I am maintaining only that both the play and the character of Hamlet are in part constructed according to the scheme of moral choice as it was analyzed in the scholastic tradition.

It would follow that those who interpret Hamlet's character in terms of irresolution are in a way right, for here the process of choice is extended over the whole play. But they are wrong when they see in this a trait of character. Hamlet delays, not because he is irresolute, but because he is reasonable. His reason must be satisfied as to the end before his will moves to embrace it; his reason must discover the appropriate means before the moral choice can be ratified and action move on to the conclusion. He is irresolute because, as Hooker says, "the Will notwithstanding does not incline to have or do that which Reason teacheth to be good, unless the same do also teach it to be possible." (*EP*, 1. 7. 5) Hamlet could quote in his defense against his detractors, who perhaps like Coleridge are mightier with the pen than with the sword, the apology of the old counsellor in *The Winter's Tale*:

> if ever fearful
> To do a thing where I the issue doubted,
> Whereof the execution did cry out
> Against the non-performance, 'twas a fear
> That oft infects the wisest.
>
> 1. 2. 258-62

Yet in a sense the resolution of the plot is apprehended partly in terms of moral action. Everyone knows the famous line in Hamlet's soliloquy, "Thus conscience," that is, knowledge and awareness, "does make cowards of us all":

> And enterprises of great pith and moment
> With this regard their current turn awry
> And lose the name of action.
>
> 3. 1. 83, 86-88

and the later speech prompted by the sight of Fortinbras's exploits:

> What is a man,
> If his chief good and market of his time
> Be but to sleep and feed? A beast, no more.

Here again is the commonplace of soul or sense.

> Sure he that made us with such large discourse,
> Looking before and after, gave us not
> That capability and godlike reason
> To fust in us unus'd. Now, whether it be
> Bestial oblivion, or some craven scruple
> Of thinking too precisely on th' event,—

in which event, of course, means "outcome" or "upshot." The problem here involves a choice between no action, rational action with a view to consequences, and action at any cost. The contrast between the latter two resembles that between the chivalric rashness of Hotspur and the staid courage of Prince Hal. In this case it is solved in favor of Hotspur. Hamlet decides:

> Rightly to be great
> Is not to stir without great argument
> But greatly to find quarrel in a straw
> When honour's at the stake.

and concludes:

> O, from this time forth,
> My thoughts be bloody, or be nothing worth!
>   4. 4. 33-41, 53-56, 65-66

From this time forth his actions as well as his thoughts are as bloody as anyone could wish. To the earlier death of Polonius he adds the deaths of Rosencrantz and Guildenstern, of Laertes by accident, and the King by design. He acts now partly from "perfect conscience," in the ethical sense of that which incites or binds us either to do or not to do something, and partly in the rashness of honor. Reasonable action has proved inadequate in the circumstances, and is abandoned:

> Being thus benetted round with villanies,
> Or I could make a prologue to my brains,
> They had begun the play.

5. 2. 29-31

Deliberation is fatal; only rashness has a chance of success:

> Rashly—
> And prais'd be rashness for it; let us know,
> Our indiscretion sometime serves us well
> When our deep plots do pall; and that should learn us
> There's a divinity that shapes our ends,
> Rough-hew them how we will—

5. 2. 6-11

Man proposes, and God disposes. Indeed, Heaven is ordinant even in the accidental details. And so Hamlet gives up the human attempt to achieve justice by rational action, by the calculation of means, abandons himself to the tide of circumstance which is the Special Providence of God, and proceeds to the catastrophe despite his misgivings. He is resigned to destiny, which is God's will; "the readiness is all." The play whose plot had displayed the scheme of moral action ends with the renunciation of it.

APPENDIX I

The Ancient Quarrel Between History & Poetry

A work of art is the embodiment of an intention. To realize an intention in language is the function of the writer. To realize from language the intention of the author is the function of the reader or the critic, and his method is historical or philological interpretation. For Philology, in the older sense of the term, is concerned with the relationship of expression and intention; it revivifies the letter by ascertaining its spirit. And when Philology has accomplished this task, there remains not even the appreciation of the spirit, since the task cannot be accomplished without this.

This premise resolves the quarrel between the historical and the aesthetic approach to literature and to other branches of art. Everyone is familiar with the distinction, and apparently everyone agrees that there is a distinction. Even those who have defended the historical attitude against the onslaughts of the aesthetes have maintained the dualism of the two approaches. For they have held either that the historical is an independent discipline with its own rights to existence, or, more commonly, that though the historical is subordinate, it is a necessary handmaid to the aesthetic: we need historical knowledge to remove the hindrances to appreciation.

The two positions are, of course, compatible: one can hold that the discipline of literary history has independent validity and at the same time hold that it furnishes useful aids to literary appreciation. Furthermore, it is true enough that there is a body of knowledge associated with literature that is in itself worth knowing: not only literary history proper, but also history in the ordinary sense of the term, and indeed many other fields of learning. What is more, all these are useful; in fact, it is doubtful if there be any kind of knowledge that will not at some point or other prove useful in the study of literature. Furthermore, the ways of understanding and the habits of attention which are developed by some of these disciplines are of the greatest value, both in themselves and for the study of literature, and there is much to be said for the old argument that a thorough grounding in Anglo-Saxon and textual criticism form a good preparation for the study of the English essay or the poetry of T. S. Eliot. But the general habits formed in this way can be acquired without these disciplines; the information needed to understand a given work can be picked up from those who have it; and as to the associated learnings, the aesthetic critic can grant them validity and properly ignore them on the grounds that a man can only do so much and that his business is appreciation. Let the historian write history, let the aesthetic critic appreciate—or let the one man alternately do both.

Such is the common resolution of the problem, and the only argument is over the spoils: which shall have the greater prestige or make the more money. But the dualism is not only unnecessary, it is pernicious.

It rests apparently upon an empirical basis. We are told that works of art take on new color with each succeeding generation if not with each succeeding reader, that they are complexes of symbols that seem to offer an almost inexhaustible variety of interpretations. They are all things to all men and all ages. And the living greatness of a work of art is often thought to reside in this chameleon character. It is this, we are told, which distinguishes the major from the minor work, which marks the difference between *Hamlet* and *The Spanish Tragedy*, or the work of living interest from the work of mere historical interest.

But is this really the case? The difference is obviously in part one of merit, or of imputed merit. The case is not that the one is better because it is more living, but simply that it is more living because it is better. The argument, then, mistakes an effect for the cause, or is naïvely circular. There is, moreover, a second consideration which is usually unnoticed in these discussions. The work that is thought to be more alive and more universal usually turns out to be simply more familiar, for the familiar is that with which we feel we can take liberties. Donne, for instance, achieved universality by becoming fashionable, and so with Gerard Hopkins. Thus the contemplative spirit becomes fashion or custom.

But the position rests in truth, as a distinguished scholar tells us, not so much upon an empirical basis as upon an assumed distinction between the work of art "as artistic phenomenon and historical fact," a distinction which leads logically to the disappearance of the work of art itself. The distinction is made clear by Walter Curry in the following passage:

> But as historical fact it [the work of literature] must inevitably bear upon it, in both form and content, the stamp of historical associations which influenced its production and from which it emerged. Criticism, we may say, attempts to report faithfully upon the efficacy of an artistic construction as a stimulus of aesthetic experience; historical interpretation, on the other hand, is concerned with orienting the historical fact in relation to the historical events— traditional or otherwise— which urged the dramatist to create it. But wherever these scattered events originally focussed upon the drama have been forgotten, it is evident that criticism cannot exercise its function properly and completely without relying upon the findings of historical interpretation.[1]

Although in the last sentence the scholar suggests that historical interpretation is the handmaid of criticism or appreciation, the dualism he erects does not leave room even for this. For the distinguishing mark of literature, insofar as it is true art, he asserts, is its universality, and by this is meant that "as art-work it may be immediately possessed by the contemplative spirit of men in any age and under any circumstances; as a stimulus to aesthetic experience it is timeless, self-sufficient, and free."

From this account it is not at all evident how criticism and historical interpretation can have anything to do with each other. On the one hand, the historian is concerned with the origin of the stimulus, with what urged the writer to create it. On the other hand, criticism reports on the "timeless" response to the stimulus—any response, and the only question is: Does it get a response? So the multiplicity of wild and inconsistent interpretations of *Macbeth*, as Curry hastens to explain, testify to the virility of the Macbeth-stimulus, and not at all to the stupidity, confusion, and selfishness of the interpreters. But who is going to look at the stimulus itself? Here are ancestors and descendants, but where is the man? Who is going to look at *Macbeth*? And if the scholar himself looks very closely and very accurately at *Macbeth*, this only refutes his theory by his practice, for his practice exhibits that fusion of accuracy and feeling which we have defined as genuine historical interpretation.

But, according to the theory, appreciation is the actual response to the work of art, though usually it is the response of certain selected persons. For it is not held to be, except by some cultural anarchists, any response of any person, but rather that of what is generally called the man of sensibility who appreciates in the light of universal aesthetic values. Now, few will deny that there are men of sensibility and men of insensibility, that there are those who are capable of responding to works of art and those who should not be allowed to try, though there may be some dis-agreement as to who belongs in what category. But when we have settled on the elect, what have we? We have contemplative spirits who immediately possess the aesthetic experience, which is timeless, self-sufficient, and free. There is apparently a kind of Oversoul of Culture in which are absorbed all the aesthetic monuments of the past, which have put off the body of this death and the material clothing of their particular expressions, and in which the elect participate by a parody of the Beatific Vision.

The more cautious will bring this heaven down to earth, and will allow the work of art its material embodiment. But they will regard the historical nature of the work only as a hindrance to the universality of the artist's vision, or as an accident to be disengaged from the substance. They will maintain that histori-cal interpretation is necessary, but that its purpose is to remove the ignorance or misapprehensions which hinder our direct ap-preciation of the text.

On the contrary, the accidents are integral to the substance. Hindrances are not merely hindrances; they are in themselves important. They are the points at which we become conscious that the text cannot be understood on our own terms. We are reading another, not ourselves. This fact should provoke us to look with some skepticism on what is meant by the universal in the context of aesthetic appreciation. By the universal is usually meant that which concerns you; hence as a principle of aesthetic importance, it is the principle of selfishness and ignorance. For what you immediately understand you regard as essential; what you do not, as accidental.

However, we need not deny that the appreciation of a work of art on one's own terms and even in defiance of the known historical intention of the work is more valuable than a dry and desiccated antiquarianism. For the one has life and the other has not. And such appreciation is especially valuable to the man who would integrate in his own experience the monuments of the past. But the man who does this should remember that he is not integrating in his experience the experience of the past. By being unhistorical he has abjured that experience; he is abusing the monuments of history to inform them with his own life. At the best, if he is himself a competent artist and if the material is tractable, he may produce a new and different work, and this may in itself have value.

This is sometimes accomplished, for example, in the transcription and arrangement of old music, as in Bach's transcription of Vivaldi or Chavez's of Buxtehude. In literature the best and most obvious examples are to be found in the seventeenth and eighteenth-century adaptations of the classics. Today, it is usually done in critical essays for the reviews. But in such cases we are dealing with a new, though derived, work. The new work may throw some light upon its source, and an understanding of the source may be an important element in the understanding of the work. But the point is: an adaptation is an independent work and not primarily an interpretation.

On the other hand, translation and interpretation are essentially alike. For, although a translation is manifestly other than its original, nevertheless we can designate a translation as correct or incorrect, as more or less adequate to the original. Now, it is that understanding of the original which enables us to say that a given translation is more or less adequate, which is the aim of historical interpretation. Furthermore, this understanding of the original is the work of art. Hence, the work of interpretation consists precisely in the recovery, so far as is possible, of the original; that is, of the author's intentions as realized in the particular text under consideration.

For this is the way in which the genuinely sensitive man approaches a work of literature. It is a method that, as a matter of fact, does have close analogies with the method of religious surrender. It consists in yielding as completely as possible to the experience of the work, with the intention of formulating afterwards the alterations which this surrender has wrought. As such, it is not only unobjectionable but necessary, both in art and in life. It is the initial act of abandonment, of faith and sympathy, without which we will never penetrate any human experience.

But, unless it is protected by the constant awareness that the experience we are penetrating is that of another, such aesthetic surrender can only be an elaborate game by which we discover with surprise that the attitudes and preconceptions with which we view the object are really there, although in fact we put them there in a somnambulistic trance. Thus the aesthetic experience proves often enough to be only an affirmation of solipsism, and the aesthetic soul a parody of the Neo-Platonic God whose spirit infuses all things, which are but degradations of Itself. However, if the act of faith and sympathy with which we surrender ourselves to an object be one which involves a scrupulous responsibility toward the object in all its specificity, this is nothing other than historical interpretation.

It is in fact nothing other than morality, if it is not too out of fashion to connect morality with such pursuits as poetry and scholarship. For the understanding of an author in the scholarly sense involves the exercise under defined conditions of the two fundamental principles of morality in the Western tradition: 1) the principle of dignity, or of responsibility to the external fact, in the special form of respect for another person as revealed in his works; and 2) the principle of love, the exercise of sympathetic insight, or of imaginative transformation.

For (to sum up) the premise of historical interpretation is that a piece of writing is a historical document, and by this is meant that it is to be interpreted, understood, and experienced as nearly as possible in the way in which it was originally intended to be interpreted, understood, and experienced. Hence, in historical interpretation our allegiance is to the external, to the historical experience implicated in the system of signs which is the work under consideration.

For whatever be the case with the other arts, the arts of language consist of statements, and a statement means what it says. We look at what a work says to find out what it means, and the apprehension of its meaning is the work of art. Insofar as the meaning is not expressed in or not recoverable from the statements, the work is deficient. Furthermore, it is a simple principle of ethics, provable in daily conversation, that the meaning of a statement is not what anyone chances to attribute to it—how hurt we are when we are misconstrued—but what it was intended to convey. The intention is the intention of the author as expressed in the language which he used and qualified by the circumstances under which he expressed it. Hence every statement is a historical statement, and it is properly understood only by historical interpretation.

Thus, since a work of literature is precisely the apprehension of its proper meaning, the appreciation of literature resides in historical interpretation. There are not two approaches to the study of literature, but only one: historical interpretation is aesthetic appreciation. If the two are distinguishable, they are distinguishable only as aspects of one another. The historical is that act of respect by which we recognize otherness: to this the various historical disciplines are subsidiary. The aesthetic is that act of sympathy by which we realize the other and make it our own.

I add: There is a distinction to be made in the use of the term historical. In the wider sense, it denotes that interpretation which takes into account the time, place, and conditions of an utterance. But there is a fundamental difference in methodology between the literary approach to a text and the approach of the historian in the narrower sense of the term. The literary interpreter is interested solely in understanding what the text was intended to say, neither more nor less. The historian, in the narrower sense, is interested primarily in the reality supposed to lie behind the text. He is as interested in what the text does not say as in what it does. His method consists in breaking down the text, in destroying its literary finish in order to penetrate to the reality that the words conceal. In brief, the historian treats a text as evidence, the literary interpreter treats it as a composition whose surface is inviolate. The historian's allegiance is to the facts which the text enables him to conjecture, to infer, or to establish. The allegiance of the literary interpreter is to the text itself.

Perhaps a trivial example will make the distinction clear. The notorious seacoasts of Bohemia in *The Winter's Tale* are evidence to the historian of a certain casualness and vagueness about geographical matters on Shakespeare's part. To the literary interpreter this is irrelevant. Bohemia to him is precisely what it was to Shakespeare, a remote kingdom which may as well have a seacoast as not.

APPENDIX II

Tragedy as Essence

The humanist in areas that are of special concern to him, as in the case of tragedy, tends to be an uncritical Realist, a simple-minded believer in a realm of essences. Let us take the case of tragedy and see what this belief entails. The assumption that there is a stable and external reality corresponding to the idea of tragedy, the assumption, indeed, that there is an Idea of tragedy, and the subsequent inquiry into its definition always presupposes at least that there is a given and prior body of material associated with a common name in common use. Otherwise, one could never begin. Furthermore, the name itself, being a term in common use, has associated with it a group of notions whose content and relationship is only partly fixed and defined. A certain vagueness and slipperiness is part of their meaning. The process of investigation, then, consists in introducing a more explicit structure into the notions associated with the term and a more limited reference into the term itself. In this way the element of slipperiness and vagueness, if not eliminated, is considerably reduced. The term in its more closely defined sense is then reintroduced into the body of the material so that some items are excluded from consideration, while others are arrayed in degrees of importance on the basis of their approximation to the definition. *The Spanish Tragedy* is not really a tragedy but a melodrama, and *King Lear* is more tragic than *Richard III*.

The result of such investigation is a definition which cannot be regarded as merely arbitrary, as simply stipulated. It refers to reality and proposes to get to the heart of it. And the heart of it is an essence. But if what one arrives at by this process be an essence, in any of the normal senses of this term, we must suppose that the terms of ordinary language, or at least some of them, derive their content and reference from some source other than the historical process of usage, and that this source is to a sufficient extent controlled by a realm of essences. We must further suppose that the methods by which we clarify the definition of the word and thing is the reverse of that by which the word in the historical process of actual usage became corrupted by vagueness of content and slipperiness of reference, and we must assume that the process is reversible. These assumptions seem to me to entail a Platonism that is denied by my experience and by what historical knowledge I have of, for example, the notions of tragedy in various literatures and various times.

I should prefer to define such a notion as tragedy in terms of those principles of order that enter into the intention of a given work or given body of works insofar as the explicit recognition by the author of those principles as the principles of what he calls tragedy and their intended recognition by the reader is guaranteed by historical evidence. There may thus be a relationship between tragedies of various authors, groups, and periods so far as similar principles of order can be defined in different traditions. There is in this sense a continuity in the tradition of tragedy between Classical Antiquity and the English Renaissance. In this the chief mediating source was not Aristotle's *Poetics* but the definition of tragedy gathered by the grammarians of later Antiquity out of Classical theory and practice and transmitted to the writers of the Renaissance as a scheme to be realized. Consequently, it is possible to construct a history of tragedy from Aeschylus to John Ford that would be a genuine history without presupposing that any such entity as tragedy really exists except in the notions of tragedy that writers and readers have entertained.

II

Tradition & Structure

POETRY, STRUCTURE, & TRADITION

I

These chapters are about poetry, and particularly about the structure of individual poems and their relationship to a tradition. Consequently, I shall begin with some more general remarks on the nature of poetry, of structure, and of tradition.

To begin with the definition of poetry. It is said that poetry is difficult to define, and the difficulty would seem to be of two sorts. In the first place, there is in different definitions a difference in what is being defined. Poetry is regarded as a kind of literature, a quality of experience, a way of knowing. It is contrasted with verse, with prose, and with science. It is defined in such a way as to favor a special view of experience or to promote the writing or approval of a special kind of poem. The difficulty, then, lies in the fact that the object of definition is not constant. The hesitations, the scruples, the blurring in the act of definition result from this. There remains, however, a constant point, if not of reference at least of departure, in all these formulations, and this is poetry as it is ordinarily understood: the body of linguistic constructions that men usually refer to as poems.

The second difficulty springs from the need to defend and to praise poetry. Very nice things are said of it. In fact, it is felt that one has not only to define poetry but also in so doing to put it in a place of honor, to recover some of the prestige that once accrued to the Muses. A particularly happy definition, one is led to believe, might elicit a donation from some elderly recluse or from a foundation. But these claims for poetry, which invade the description and definition of it, this concern with a higher something, knowledge or feeling, while they might seem designed to improve its estate, have in fact weakened it. They have on the one hand erected pretensions that no linguistic construction, no poem, could ever hope to satisfy. The statements, in brief, are not true. Poets, for example, are not "the unacknowledged legislators of the world," and a good thing it is that they aren't. And the claims have, on the other hand, by qualifying the conception of poetry both limited the kinds of poetry that can be written and the audience that is prepared to receive it. They have exiled most of human experience from the poet's page, and he is left with an image and a mood:

> For all the history of grief
> An empty doorway and a maple leaf [1]

If one glances through the history of criticism it would appear that there are in general three definitions of poetry that have persisted throughout the tradition. The commonest is that which regards it as a quality of experience associated with a special selection and use of language, and the quality of experience is normally one that is thought to command prestige. A representative formulation is offered by one of the standard dictionaries, where poetry is characterized as: "The expression of beautiful or elevated thought, imagination, or feeling, in appropriate language, such language containing a rhythmical element and having usually a metrical form." [2] Of such a definition we may say that it appears to isolate and explore the activity and subject matter of poetry, but that in fact it introduces a principle of value which is prescriptive as to what kinds of poetry should be written or cherished. Furthermore, the principle which arrogates to poetry a higher kind of experience is pretentious. Finally, we may observe that such definitions are fairly reticent about meter, but firmer with respect to rhythm, which is usually regarded as primitive and emotional, and hence, no doubt, higher. Nevertheless, it is true that at different times certain attitudes toward the kinds of experience and certain associated selections of language have been comprised in the idea of poetry. Hence, as a method of defining, not poetry, but the poetry of a given tradition, this is an appropriate and useful method.

The second of the definitions that are commonly offered is usually ascribed to Aristotle in the *Poetics*. In that work Aristotle attempts to distinguish a kind of what he calls imitation which had been, he says, up to that time without a name. It is the kind of imitation in which an action is represented by means of language, and he cites as examples the Platonic dialogue and the mimes of Sophron. Of the same kind, with the exception that music as well as language is used as a means of imitation, are epic, comedy, and tragedy. For this more general kind he appropriates the name of poetry, a name which had been more customarily applied, as he points out, to compositions in meter.[3] Aristotle, of course, is simply developing and systematizing a notion already available in the tradition, the notion Socrates accepts in the *Phaedo* (61B) that a poet to be really a poet must employ fiction. It follows, then, that for poetry in this sense meter is not essential; it can be at most a contributory means appropriate to the end. For what is being defined is what we call fiction, and this may be, as it is in Plato's dialogues, in prose, or as in Homer and Sophocles, in verse. However, the use of a common term implies a common object of reference and so the question has arisen again and again since Aristotle's day whether a poem need be written in meter, and whether a poem that is not in some sense an imitation of an action, that is, fiction, is really a poem or rather something else—perhaps rhetoric. But fiction and metrical composition are simply two different things: a work may be both, or either, or neither.

However, though every composition in meter need not have a narrative structure, need not be fiction, it is pretty likely to have some sort of structure analogous to the narrative structure of fiction. If we use *fiction,* then, in a wider sense, if we generalize the notion to extend to the device, whatever it is, that orders the material of the poem in outline, we may regard a metrical composition as having a principle of fiction, and we may discuss what is the fiction of this particular poem, what kinds of fictions various poems exhibit, and perhaps what kinds of fictions are possible or practical in poetry. A fiction in this broader sense is a major principle of order in a work, and I shall discuss a number of such principles in the following chapters.

I prefer with respect to poetry the third, the common or garden variety of definition. I mean by poetry what everyone means by it when he is not in an exalted mood, when he is not being a critic, a visionary, or a philosopher. I mean by poetry what a man means when he goes to a bookstore to buy a book of poems as a graduation gift, or when he is commissioned by a publisher to do an anthology of sixteenth century poems. Poetry is what looks like poetry, what sounds like poetry. It is metrical composition.

To define a poem in this way will seem trivial to some and offensive to others. It will seem to depreciate the importance of poetry. It will seem to single out what is thought to be an accidental and to ignore the essential quality of poetry. It will be objected to, in addition, as affording no principle of value by which one could distinguish a good poem from a bad, for certainly that distinction will not lie solely or even largely in the meter. But all of these objections, where they are not motivated by a concern to advance the prestige and practice of a special kind of poetry or by the inveteracy of old habit now appalled, spring from a tacit and perhaps unconscious assumption about the nature and function of a definition. It is assumed that the definition is offered in the form and spirit of the Aristotelian tradition. It is assumed that a definition, in marking off an object from all other objects of the more general kind to which it belongs, purports to distinguish the peculiar virtue of the object, and in terms of the point of difference to offer a principle of judgment, a scale of values. And it is assumed that the point of difference is more important than, is important to the detriment of, the general class to which the object is assigned. But there is no need to assume this. The purpose of the definition is simply to mark off the territory and to describe the thing unmistakably.

How these assumptions tacitly operate can be seen in the traditional definition of man as a rational animal. This formulation was preferred to the alternatives, that man is a two-legged or a laughing animal, largely because it was felt that in his rationality lay his peculiar glory and claim to prestige, and that this was a worthy principle of evaluation that could be applied to the rating of particular men. There is not much glory in two-leggedness or laughter, and neither would offer an acceptable scale of values. Again, in the traditional definition, and in the views that grew out of it, the rationality of man was attended to the depreciation of his animality; the specific took precedence over the generic. But the tacit demands here made on a definition are demands of a different order than the requirements for clarity and accuracy of definition, and the alternative formulations might have served the latter purpose as well or better.

II

To begin, then, with the general class to which poems belong: a poem is a composition; that is, it is a system of propositions. I take *proposition* in a more general sense than is usual; a proposition is a determinate relationship of signs forming an element in a composition consisting of successive elements of this nature. Thus an algebraic equation is a proposition, and that equation subjected to a successive series of transformations would constitute a system of propositions. The syllogism in logic is of the same order, as is a piece of music insofar as the musical signs are grouped into elements, for example, into what are called phrases. Of the same order is a recorded game of chess, in which the elements, of course, are the distinct moves: P-K4, P-K4. But each of these differs from such things as an incident, a statue or picture, a football game or a horse race. We can formulate propositions about these; we can describe the incident, the picture, or the game, and the formulation refers to the object, but it is not the object. The poem, however, is the text; the equation is the equation; and the game of chess is the recorded series of moves. Whatever the source of the propositions and however the man who wrote them down may have arrived at them, once the formulation has been recorded the experience it refers to and the experience it directs are properly confined to the meanings of the terms and the meanings of their relationship and succession.

Consequently, there is an exact analogy between poetry and chess, since they are things of the same kind. The poet in writing a poem has a good many experiences that do not appear in the propositions he puts on paper, the completed poem. The player at chess has a good many experiences that do not appear in the moves he makes on the board, the moves that recorded in the standard notation constitute for him and for anyone who knows chess the game he played. This game is repeatable as the poem is repeatable, and the experiences that properly belong to it are the repeatable experiences. In fact, the game as played and the poem as written constitute a principle of order, a method, for discriminating the relevant from the irrelevant among one's immediate experiences as he plays or reads or writes, and among one's retrospective experiences as he sums up after the game or after the completion of the poem. To be repeatable and to be a method for discriminating relevant from irrelevant experiences are characteristics of all composition.

There is a further characteristic. The player at chess in making each move envisages a variety of alternative moves, and we in replaying the same game must do alike if we are to achieve the recorded experience. Similarly the text of a poem consists of what little is left, out of the wide-strewn wreckage of alternative phrases, lines, and possibilities of development. No one has read a poem who has not constructed and rejected as he read some of the alternative poems whose nonexistence gives timbre and resonance to the text.

There is also an inexact analogy between poetry and chess. It is slightly fanciful, but not untrue and not without its applications. The player at chess has an opponent. He makes his moves not only within the rules of the game and the limitation of the board and his pieces, but also within the possibilities afforded by his opponent's moves and by the potentiality of his future moves. The player is not free to erect what structure he pleases within the rules of the game. If he chooses to be whimsical, there are consequences that must be dealt with. If he moves his pieces merely to accomplish a pretty design, an apparent pattern, he moves to disaster. The poet, too, has an opponent. His opponent is experience. The nature and quality of the game the two of them play will depend not only on his own skill but also on the adroitness and resourcefulness of his opposing experience. If experience is simple, unseasoned, without depth, the poet may have an easy time of it but the game suffers; it lacks depth and interest. And if the opponent is dishonest, if he throws away a queen to extricate the poet from a difficult spot, the game will be shoddy and not worth the playing. There are poems that are praised for their order, simplicity, and charm that so far as I can see represent a victory over nothing at all. We must distinguish between the simplicity of a Capablanca against a Nimzowitsch,[4] of a master of chess against a master of chess, and the simplicity with which one defeats a friend when he negligently forgets to castle. But this is a digression.

To return: it is characteristic of a composition that it is re-peatable, that it is a method for discriminating the repeatable from the unique in experience, and that it is the specification of a range of possible compositions. There is a further characteristic which all compositions have. They all conform to the rules of the game, by which is stipulated beforehand what kinds of terms, of propositions and successions of propositions are admissible. For example, the rules of the traditional syllogism of the type *All men are mortal* are fairly simple and fairly easily stated. In brief, there will be three propositions and in this order: all items belonging to a certain general class have a certain property; this item be-longs to that general class; therefore, this item has that property. The rules are a method for inventing further syllogisms with the same structure. The rules of chess are more complex, but of the same order. The rules of poetry, or rather the rules of the various traditions of poetry, are of the same order, but even more com-plex. Nevertheless, they are describable, and to describe the rules of the game is to define a tradition. A tradition is all the ways a particular poem could have been written; it is the potentiality of realized structures, as the rules of chess contain all the games that may be played.

III

But a poem is not only a composition; it is a composition of a special sort. What distinguishes a poem from all other items in its general class is that the propositions are in meter, and hence if poetry has any peculiar province this issues from the fact that it is metrical. There are three possibilities. Since meter is an aspect of language it is possible that certain special meanings can be conveyed by meter that cannot be conveyed by unmetrical language, either different kinds of meaning or more or less refined versions of similar meanings. It is said, for example, that metrical language can deal more subtly and more accurately with feeling. Again, meter may have some special effect on those who use it. Poetry, for example, tends to be more memorable than prose and tends to support a greater extraordinariness of language. The third possibility is this: wherever one finds alternative forms in a language, the existence of a distinction in form tends to beget a distinction in function or purpose, and usually by an unnoticed historical process. In time, then, certain areas of experience will be assigned to metrical and others to unmetrical composition, and this is what has happened in the history of literature. Furthermore, the areas assigned to each medium shift and vary from time to time and place to place. It follows, then, that poetry of a given time and place will tend to deal with those areas of experience which convention and history have assigned to writing in meter. In brief, a poem is the sort of thing that poets write, and what they write is the sort of thing their society has come to regard as poetry. By their society here I mean the larger or smaller group at a given time and place who are concerned with the production and appreciation of poetry. What that society regards as poetry is what I mean by tradition. What it regards as poetry will furnish the rules of the game.

Consequently, though a tradition is historical in that it issues from a historical process, it is not in itself its history. It exists at each moment in completed form. For a tradition is rather, both in the terms in which it must be described and reconstituted by the literary historian and in the actual way in which it is attained and apprehended by a given writer at a given time, a context of notions, often jumbled and sometimes not too consistent with one another, together with the methods and attitudes by which these notions are grasped and applied. A tradition can be located in the body of texts and interpretations current among a given group of writers and readers. Such a description applies equally to the traditions in which Chaucer or Shakespeare wrote and to those which are now current: one must be learned as well as the other, and in the same way.

A tradition, however, is not simply a body of learning, it is a body of learning capable of being applied to the production of what are called original works. It is the method by which the sentences of a poem are discovered: it demarks the field of discovery and orders the succession of sentences. It is the potentiality of any work in the tradition.

Hence, the notions which constitute a tradition are not ideas merely, but principles of order. They are schemes which direct the production of works. For a principle of order is that which directs and determines the selection of the materials that enter into a work, and their succession and importance. Such principles may relate to language as such. Meter and rhyme are of this sort, and so is what we ordinarily call language. A poem in Latin is not a poem in English. But even within a given language there are many sublanguages, and there have been in all periods of the history of poetry special selections of language appropriated to poems, or to certain kinds of poems, or to certain groups of poets.

By selection of language I mean not merely a limited and special vocabulary (the aureate diction of the Scottish Chaucerians, for example) but also certain possibilities of phrasing allowed and others disallowed, certain syntactical patterns predominant and others seldom or never used. The language of Lyly's *Euphues* is an obvious and easily characterized sublanguage of this sort.

The principles of order may relate to literature as such, regarded as a separate activity and not as an imitation of life, and of this sort are the numerous literary conventions which both writers and historians have recognized. The conventions of the Petrarchan sonneteer are only partly to be found in the unliterary life of his times; to a considerable extent they exist rather in the experience of literature. The idea of tragedy in a given tradition, though not unrelated to life, is a literary idea. I shall discuss at length in a later essay a principle of order of this sort, the medieval literary convention of the dream vision.

Lastly, principles may be derived from sources external to literature, and may be of the sort that order the material of nonliterary experience. Of this nature are the methods of logic, and I shall subsequently discuss such principles at length, or notions proper to theology which I shall take up in connection with *The Phoenix and Turtle*. Principles of a similar nature are common in fiction, those principles, namely, which deal with how men generally act and feel, which have been appropriated by the science of psychology from the ancient art of rhetoric, together with those abstractions as to life and the universe, which belong as abstractions to the province of philosophy and in exemplification to the province of fiction. But all these, though they may be regarded as material or conclusions in other branches of endeavor, are for the man who writes primarily the methods by which he both finds what he has to say, and says it in succession and with appropriate emphasis and development.

Consequently, there is a sense in which a work of literature is nothing but an adjustment of a congeries of principles of order. In another sense, it is only a specification of the potentialities of a tradition. The specification is the structure of the poem. For the poem itself is a structure and it has a structure. By the structure of a poem, then, I mean the principles of order that determine it and their interrelationships with each other. It should be remarked that no poem could have only a single principle: meter, for example, is always an independent principle. However, to give a full description in every case of the principles that enter into a work would be difficult, certainly clumsy, and largely unnecessary. And so in the following essays I shall in practice discuss only one or two of the leading principles of order in a work and the tradition to which these are related.

IV

If a poem is a system of propositions, and if the propositions are discovered and ordered by a system of principles, then these principles are not extrinsic to the work; they are not merely possible ways of viewing the object, but are intrinsic to it. They are formative elements in the work itself and hence in the experience of the work.

Consequently, it will be relevant to ask at this point, How do we experience a poem? By what process do we apprehend it? And we will find that the question we are raising is really the question, Where and in what way does the poem or work of art exist? What is its mode and locus of existence?[5] It is obvious that the poem is not simply in the text, in the closed book. *Hamlet* as an experience, in fact, is neither in the text, nor, for that matter, on the stage. It can exist as an experience only in the experience of some person, some reader or member of the audience. But there are difficulties in this statement, and not merely the difficulty that the experience of each reader is different, and different at each separate reading, and that some of these experiences, no doubt, are quite far removed from others. There is another difficulty, and one whose resolution will perhaps resolve the difficulty which has just been stated. *Hamlet* is not in the immediate experience of a member of the audience as he is seeing or reading the play. If it were we could never think or speak of the play as a whole. We could only deal with this moment in my experience of the play, and we would have to treat our aesthetic experiences as Rochester treated his erotic, regarding each moment as absolute: "All my past life is mine no more. . . . The present moment's all my lot."

The play is rather the experience of having experienced the play. It is the result of a reconstruction in memory and a summing up in judgment after the play is over. The process is described by St. Augustine in one of those passages in the *Confessions* in which his extraordinary genius for introspection is given full scope. He is describing the act of reciting a Psalm:

I am about to repeat a Psalm that I know. Before I begin, my expectation is extended over the whole; but when I have begun, how much soever of it I shall separate off into the past, is extended along my memory; thus the life of this action of mine is divided between my memory as to what I have repeated, and expectation as to what I am going to repeat; but "consideration" is present with me, that through it what was future may be conveyed over so as to become past. Which the more it is done again and again, so much the more the expectation being shortened, is the memory enlarged; till the whole expectation be at length exhausted, when that whole action being ended shall have passed into memory.

11.38[6]

So I know a poem or play thoroughly when the beginning, middle, and end are comprehended in one synthetic act of recollection, and that synthetic act of recollection is the play.

That is, one leaves the theater or lays down his book, lights a cigarette, and held within the spell of the experience the experience grows steady; it seems to come together. This is the unity of the work. The process is not wholly intellectual, nor wholly describable in intellectual terms since it is an experience, yet experience never comes together except when ordered by some principles, implicit or explicit, and the principles are describable. Nor is it a matter of indifference what the principles are, for in consolidating the experience they alter it. The difference between the ordinary view of *Hamlet* and the one I shall later urge does not lie primarily in a difference in antecedent experiences, nor in a difference in experiences simultaneous with the experience of the text, since the text is a method of discriminating between the relevant and the irrelevant in those experiences. It does not lie primarily in the varying meaning that various readers impute to the words and constructions of the poem. It lies in the principles allowed and employed in constructing the final experience of the work.

The process is not peculiar to poetry. St. Augustine draws this moral himself in the passage which follows the one just quoted. He says:

> And this which takes place in the whole Psalm, the same takes place in each several portion of it, and each several syllable; the same holds in that larger action, whereof this Psalm may be a part; the same holds in the whole life of man, whereof all the actions of man are parts; the same holds through the whole age of the sons of men, whereof all the lives of men are parts.

It is the process by which each one of us sums up and unifies his life, so far as it can be unified. It is the process by which each constructs his personality. In this precise analogy may be located the moral, or as we now say the emotional or educational, importance of literature: it is an exercise in the recollection, the gathering up, of the elements of personality and in their ordering. And it is moreover true that the kinds of material which we notice, select, and emphasize in this process, together with the principles of order which we elicit from or impose on this material, are—in our society at least—largely derived from the art we favor.

But, though the process here described is not in general peculiar to poetry, there is a feature in the experience of poetry and of similar systems of propositions that is peculiar to it. It is that the object of experience in that case remains steady. In the case of our autobiography, for example, the experience does not remain steady unless we have formulated it and reduced it to a system of propositions. If we sit musing on our past the events shift with the transition of feeling. What was important a moment ago recedes and what was excluded as irrelevant grows large. Images and judgments waver and transform themselves into others, structures dissolve, as in our memory of a dream.

But it is different with a poem. Our experience there derives from and refers to an object that stays steady and persists. The text remains. Our experience is subject to verification and correction, and hence it has an element of externality in it. Furthermore, since it is the peculiar nature of a composition that the experiencing of the work may be repeated, and that we may be assured that this experience refers to the same work as did our previous experience, there is an element not only of externality in each experience, but also of stability, or of what may be called eternality. So in the cumulative re-experience of a given composition, except insofar as habituation ("That monster, custom, who all sense doth eat") deadens the impact, we may hope to come nearer and nearer to the norm of that experience which is ideally implicit in the work. It is the ideal implicit norm of, for example, *Hamlet* that enables us to say that we have seen *Hamlet* five times, though one of the performances was "hardly *Hamlet!*" The ideal implicit norm is the structure of the work; it is the congeries of principles of order that determines the work; it is the work itself. It is a thing external and eternal a potentiality of experience waiting to be realized. It is the poem.

CLASSICAL & MEDIEVAL

Statius on Sleep

There are different kinds of poems. There is, for example, a poem by Statius, the lovely invocation to sleep, which has captured the fancy of many critics, especially the English. They like it so well they call it almost a sonnet, and they would excise three lines in the middle of the poem to make it more sonnet-like. But the poem is not a sonnet and the lines should not be excised, for to do so is to convert a poem of one kind into a poem of another. The poem reads:

> Crimine quo merui, iuuenis placidissime diuum,
> quoue errore miser, donis ut solus egerem,
> Somne, tuis? Tacet omne pecus uolucresque feraeque
> et simulant fessos curuata cacumina somnos,
> nec trucibus fluuiis idem sonus, occidit horror
> aequoris et terris maria adclinata quiescunt.
> Septima iam rediens Phoebe mihi respicit aegras
> stare genas; totidem Oetaeae Paphiaeque reuisunt
> lampades et totiens nostros Tithonia questus
> praeterit et gelido spargit miserata flagello.
> Unde ego sufficiam? non si mihi lumina mille,
> quae sacer alterna tantum statione tenebat
> Argus et hand umquam uigilabat corpore toto.
> At nunc heu! si aliquis longa sub nocte puellae
> brachia nexa tenens ultro te, Somne, repellit,
> indo veni, nec te totas infundere pennas
> luminibus compello meis—hoc turba precatur
> laetior—: extreme me tango cacumine virgae,
> sufficit, aut leuiter suspense poplite transi.[1]

I have translated this as literally as possible, taking care at the same time to represent those formal aspects of the poem which will come under discussion so that the reader whose English is better than his Latin may be at ease in the argument:

> What was my crime, youthful most gentle god,
> What folly was it that I alone should lack,
> Sweet Sleep, thy gifts? All herds, birds, beasts are still,
> The curved mountains seem wearily asleep,
> Streams rage with muted noise, the sea-wave falls,
> And the still-nodding deep rests on the shore.
> Seven times now returning Phoebe sees
> My sick eyes stare, and so the morning star
> And evening, so Tithonia glides by
> My tears, sprinkling sad dew from her cool whip.
> How, then, may I endure? Not though were mine
> The thousand eyes wherewith good Argus kept
> But shifting watch, nor all his flesh awake.
> But now, alas! If this long night some lover
> In his girl's arms should willingly repel thee,
> Thence come, sweet Sleep! Nor with all thy power
> Pour through my eyes—so may they ask, the many,
> More happy—: touch me with thy wand's last tip,
> Enough, or lightly pass with hovering step.

The conventional opinion of this poem is based on Mackail's comments. "Perhaps the finest, certainly the most remarkable," he says of Statius's occasional verses, "is the short poem (one might almost call it a sonnet) addressed to Sleep." He then quotes the text and remarks:

Were the three lines beginning *Unde ego sufficiam* struck out—and one might almost fancy them to have been inserted later by an unhappy second thought—the remainder of this poem would be as perfect as it is unique. The famous sonnet of Wordsworth on the same subject must at once occur to an English reader; but the poem in its manner, especially in the dying cadence of the last two lines, recalls even more strongly some of the finest sonnets of Keats.[2]

This judgment has been accepted, extended, and hardened by English critics and literary historians. Tyrrell says: "This beautiful and pathetic little poem seems to have (more than any other ancient poem except, perhaps, the *Sirmio* of Catullus) the effect of a sonnet." Slater speaks of Statius's "short poem on sleep, which is admitted to be a masterpiece," paraphrases Mackail's comments, and quotes Fyfe's translation of the poem in the form of a sonnet (published 1903), remarking that the translator "has excised what Mackail considers a blemish in the original, the allusion to Argus of the thousand eyes." Garrod in *The Oxford Book of Latin Verse* quotes Fyfe's translation in the appendix, "Translations and Imitations," and follows it with six sonnets to sleep by Sidney, Daniel, Drummond, Wordsworth, Keats, and Hartley Coleridge. E. E. Sikes preserves the comparison with the English sonnet—the poem "is deservedly famous and may well take rank with the sonnets to Sleep by Wordsworth and Keats"—but translates the poem himself in three six-line stanzas and defends the Argus passage. In this he is a lone dissenter. Mozley in the introduction to the Loeb translation comments: "Best known of all the *Silvae,* probably, is the little sonnet-like poem addressed to the god Sleep." Duff quotes Mackail's "one might almost call it a sonnet," and adds that "if certain mythological lines are dropped, it can be reduced to the requisite proportions." He then prints his own early translation (published 1906) of the poem in the form of a sonnet. Finally, Philip Schuyler Allen says in introducing an English rendering by Howard Mumford Jones: "the translation has been designedly cast into a form suited to display to English readers the virtues of its original: a verse scheme after Sir Philip Sidney's hexameter sonnet."[3]

It is time now to examine Mackail's judgment. One must admit there is a nice sensitiveness in the comparison between the "dying cadence" in Statius's last lines and a similar effect in the last lines of some of Keats's sonnets, though not particularly, as the later critics have assumed, of the sonnet *To Sleep*. But the close of the sonnet *On the Sea:*

> Sit ye near some old cavern's mouth, and brood
> Until ye start, as if the sea-nymphs quired!

and especially of the sonnet *On a Leander Gem:*

> see how his body dips
> Dead-heavy; arms and shoulders gleam awhile:
> He's gone: up bubbles all his amorous breath![4]

have a close similarity of effect to the close of Statius's poem. The similarity, however, is not mysterious; it is not the result of some affinity of spirit that can only be intuited by the literary tact of the critic. It resides in, and wholly in, the use of precisely the same technical devices by both poets, with such differences only as are required by the difference in language and in poetic tradition. In both the Leander sonnet and Statius's poem there is a kind of semidramatic colloquialness ("He's gone" and "sufficit") and the use of a more specialized statement for the direct statement it implies ("up bubbles all his amorous breath," which implies "He is drowned," and "leviter suspense poplite transi," which implies "May I be even the least bit asleep.").

But these similarities only support and limit the kind of similarity Mackail points to. This is the similarity in the movement of the verse. One may ask, What determines the movement of a verse line? It is determined by the metrical principles of the line itself, and by the relation of syntactical units to the ends of lines. In these terms there is a distinction between two traditions of verse movement, and this will ultimately turn out to be a distinction between two kinds of poetry. To one of these traditions both the passage from Statius and those from Keats belong.

It will be well to make this distinction clear by citing two other passages, both in English. The first is the invocation at the beginning of Gascoigne's *The Steele Glas,* the earliest non-dramatic poem of any length in blank verse; the second is Milton's invocation at the beginning of *Paradise Lost.* That the one is universally conceded to be better than the other is for the present beside the point—we are interested in making a distinction:

> The Nightingale, whose happy noble hart,
> No dole can daunt, nor fearful force affright,
> Whose chereful voice, doth comfort saddest wights,
> When she hir self, hath little cause to sing. . . .

> Of Mans First Disobedience, and the Fruit
> Of that Forbidden Tree, whose mortal tast
> Brought Death into the World, and all our woe.[5]

The differences are obvious. The meter of the one, though not without certain discreet variations, displays and enforces in every line the simple metrical pattern. Every line conforms strictly to type: a regular alternation of unaccented and accented syllables with a pause after the fourth syllable.[6] The lines in the second passage also conform to a metrical type, but they conform in a different sense. They conform in the sense that the type can be inferred from a collection of lines; it is implicit in them. In the first passage the type is apparent and, as it were, explicit in any single line. Milton, as he himself says, observes "apt Numbers" and "fit quantity of Syllables";[7] that is, his metrical practice is based on the concept of decorum, or the reasonable adherence to an implicit norm. Gascoigne's practice is based on the concept of law, or the rational adherence to an explicit norm.

The passages differ also with respect to the relation of syntax to the metrical structure. In Gascoigne each line is end-stopped, and the internal pause occurs at precisely the same point in each line. The thought is apprehended in units of alternately four and six syllables. But it is a principle of Milton's prosody that the sense should be "variously drawn out from one Verse into another," that the thought should be apprehended in units that cut across the metrical structure. The difference is not simply one of merit or skill, a question of monotony and variety; it is a difference in kind. For the first passage, though not distinguished, is not without merit. What it needs is rhyme, and for two reasons. Rhyme would sustain the verse line, which tends as it is to disappoint the ear, and would impart, if not a singing quality, at least a kind of conviction to the rhetoric—for example:

> The nightingale whose happy noble heart
> No dole can daunt, no fearful force can start

Secondly, since conformity to an external pattern is the guiding principle in this tradition of poetry, the articulation of rhyme in a fixed stanza would impose on the poem that order and articulation of thought, the lack of which is here more offensive than is the apparent monotony of the verse line. For the poem is conceived in couplets, but not written in couplets.

Clearly the method of Milton is that of Keats and of Statius. The metrical line in each, though it conforms to the patterns of their respective traditions, yet exhibits considerable variety in the permissible substitution of feet, in the placing of the pause, and in the playing of accent against quantity in the quantitative meter[8] and of quantity against accent in the accentual meter. In each the syntactical structure of thought deviates from and plays against the verse line. These formal elements carry with them a disposition of feeling which is inherent in the method and which is of the same general nature in each poem. But the agreement between the close of the Leander sonnet and the close of Statius's poem is much more particular; it is almost coincidental:

> see how his body dips
> Dead-heavy; arms and shoulders gleam awhile:
> He's gone: up bubbles all his amorous breath!

> hoc turba precatur
> laetior—: extremo me tange cacumine virgae,
> sufficit, aut leviter suspense poplite transi.

> so may they ask, the many,
> More happy—: touch me with thy wand's last tip,
> Enough, or lightly pass with hovering step.

The types of syntactical structure and their placing relative to the metrical line are almost identical in the two passages. There could hardly be found for one ignorant of Latin a better illustration of the formal effect of Statius's lines than this passage from Keats.

Thus far I have approved of Mackail's remarks, and have even extended them. There remain now the two propositions, that the poem is sonnet-like and that the Argus passage should be excised. It is clear what Mackail and his successors have in mind. If you excise the three lines on Argus the poem falls into two parts of ten and six lines, which is close enough to the proportions of a sonnet. Furthermore, you may consider that the four lines (7-10) which precede the Argus passage (11-13) and which relate with four mythological references how the poet has been sleepless for a full week could be reduced to two lines at the most and could at the same time be improved by being disencumbered of mythological adornment.[9] What the modern reader fails to see, it may be remarked in passing, is that myth for the Latin poet is a field of poetic details parallel to and comparable with the field of natural landscape, as is illustrated in this poem. However, in this way a poem is begotten that corresponds precisely to the eight and six lines of the sonnet. Moreover, the octave can be conceived to present the situation, and the sestet the reflection upon the situation, and thus the poem could be said to exhibit perhaps the commonest type of internal form to be found in the sonnet. But this is not Statius's poem; it is one the critic has written himself in a form familiar to him.

The form of the original can be studied by comparing it with the famous sonnet by Wordsworth on the same subject to which Mackail and his successors allude:

A flock of sheep that leisurely pass by,
One after one; the sound of rain, and bees
Murmuring; the fall of rivers, winds and seas,
Smooth fields, white sheets of water, and pure sky;
I have thought of all by turns, and yet do lie
Sleepless! and soon the small birds' melodies
Must hear, first uttered from my orchard trees;
And the first cuckoo's melancholy cry.
Even thus last night, and two nights more, I lay,
And could not win thee, Sleep, by any stealth:
So do not let me wear to-night away:
Without Thee what is all the morning's wealth?
Come, blessed barrier between day and day,
Dear mother of fresh thoughts and joyous health![10]

The resemblance of the two poems is quite close—the parallels in the third and fifth lines are particularly striking. This similarity in subject will consequently afford a surer basis than might otherwise have been for the comparison of formal qualities.

The sonnet has in common with Statius those elements that have already been discussed, a complex meter and the run-over line. In fact, if the run-over lines are scrutinized more closely they will be seen to be both of a special type: in both the phrase halts early in the subsequent line:

> the sound of rain, and bees
> Murmuring . . .

> I have thought of all by turns, and yet do lie
> Sleepless . . .

>   donis ut solus egerem,
> Somne, tuis?

In the first and third instances, at least, and less obviously in the second, the grammatical construction could be considered completed at the end of the line: "the sound of rain, and bees" and "donis ut solus egerem" are phrases sufficient in themselves. Yet the additional word or phrase at the beginning of the next line is by no means otiose: what it does is to extend the construction from one recognized syntactical pattern to another so that the addition, though it is not required, nevertheless affords when it has been made that effect of inevitability which arises from a completed pattern. Hence the resolution of the latter carries with it the special effect that it is the resolution of a pattern which emerged out of a former one.

In these respects, then, the poems are similar. But the respects in which they differ are more numerous, more obvious, and more important. The most obvious is that Wordsworth's poem is a sonnet, a fixed form, whereas Statius's could have been of any length. There was nothing in the ancient poet's tradition that prescribed the exact number of lines. In fact, it is a characteristic of Latin antiquity that even poems with a fixed refrain have an irregular number of verses between the refrains: for example, Vergil's Eighth Eclogue and Catullus lxii. Consequently, the particular length of this poem could only have been determined by chance, as Coleridge tells us the length of *Kubla Khan* was determined, or, as seems rather to be the case here, by what may be called an internal necessity: that is, the length was determined by the law of decorum or tact, by the fitness and aptness of the external form to the internal form of what was to be said. But the law of the sonnet is law in the strict sense: it is fixed, eternal, and given. It has the characteristics of Jehovah's pronouncements.

Thus the form of a sonnet does not emerge like the more modern God and take shape in the process of writing; it is an Idea and prior to the specific poem. The case is not that the poet has an inspiration in the sense of having a subject that moves him to write and that the poem turns out when he is finished to be a sonnet of exactly fourteen lines. If this were so, there would be few sonnets. The case is quite otherwise: he who would write a sonnet must begin with the idea of the form, and one can almost say, for paradox is sometimes an instrument of truth, that he hopes it will turn out to have a subject.

Of course, it is possible, and I have done it myself, for a poet relatively late in the process of writing to expand or reduce to the compass of a sonnet what was originally conceived as a Poem, say, in quatrains, though scarcely one in blank verse. He may even begin scribbling lines, poetically exploring some subject with no defined notion of its ultimate form apart from the meter, and even that may be changed at an early stage in the process of composition. Finally, when a certain number of lines and approximate formulations are scattered on the page, pages, or backs of envelopes, he may suddenly realize that the whole can best be redacted in the form of a sonnet. But at what point was the poem as it finally exists in the text first conceived? It was conceived when its potential realization was envisioned, when the poet saw that it would make a sonnet. But the kind of form which is envisioned alters essentially both the experience of writing and the final text so that a distinction in kinds of form is a distinction in kinds of experience and in kinds of poetry; in the one the external form is fixed and given in the tradition; in the other the external form presents at least the illusion of being a free determination.

191

But a sonnet is not only a poem of a given length; it is also a poem that conforms to one of a very few patterns, and patterns that are for the most part established in the tradition. The pattern of Wordsworth's sonnet is the familiar one in which two units of expression of four lines each comprise the first major division, and three units of two lines each comprise the second. Furthermore, the divisions are marked by an obvious device of external form, the arrangement of rhymes, and the divisions of thought correspond point for point with the external divisions. An outline of the rhyme-scheme and an outline of the thought of the poem would coincide. Even the relation of the two major divisions is an accepted one; the first is an exposition of the situation, the second a reflection on it.

But Statius's poem falls into two, or three, divisions, and the uncertainty on this point is characteristic of his kind of poetry. The first division comprises the first ten lines, in which are presented, as in Wordsworth's poem, the fact of the poet's sleeplessness and the contrast with the peace and quiet of external nature. But the passage is not subdivided into equal parts. The opening question, "Why do I alone lack sleep?" occupies two and one-third lines. The illustration of the uniqueness of the poet's experience by contrast with the due and proper rest after exertion which external nature enjoys is expressed in three and two-thirds lines. And the return to his own situation, the complaint that he has been sleepless for a full week so that the gods pitied him, is expressed in four lines. Here is no point for point correspondence of the internal to the external form, no units of expression that bear a simple mathematical ratio, one to the other.

So it is with the rest of the poem, whether the Argus passage is taken as a separate major division or as a part of the concluding section of nine lines. The passage itself occupies three lines:

"I could not endure to lie thus open-eyed"—an aspect of sleeplessness—"even though I had the thousand eyes of Argus and could open and close ones by turn." Then in two lines: "But, taking the situation as it is, if there are those who can sleep, being happy in love, and will not since they would enjoy their love"—and now in one-third of a line: "transfer their rights in sleep to me." The paraphrase may be halted at this point since the second point of difference between the two poems is now sufficiently clear; the one conforms to an established pattern, the other establishes its own.

There is a third point of difference. If the above paraphrase is compared with the actual text, it will be found that little of what is made, and must be made, explicit in the paraphrase is explicit in the poem. It is true that the opening proposition is relatively explicit, yet it is given a rhetorical treatment that removes it from the bluntness of plain statement. The poet does not say directly that he alone has been sleepless; rather he asks why he alone has lacked thy gifts, Sleep. And the whole is framed in a rhetorical question as to the causes why sleep has been denied him, which by the gravity of the causes suggested (*crimen, error*) implies the gravity of the effect. Thus something else is said by indirection than could have been said in the same compass by direct statement, and this something else requires the active participation of the reader in finding it out. The reader must actively assist in constructing the poem.

For example, Statius does not say as one translator has him say:

But my sad eyes their nightly vigil keep.

He does not say that he has been sleepless a full week, though this is clearly what he means. He says:

Septima iam rediens Phoebe mihi respicit aegras
stare genas; totidem Oetaeae Paphiaeque reuisunt
lampades et totiens nostros Tithonia questus
praeterit et gelido spargit miserata flagello.

Seven times now returning Phoebe sees
My sick eyes stare, and so the morning star
And evening, so Tithonia glides by
My tears, sprinkling sad dew from her cool whip.

Is this nothing but rhetorical amplification? It is that, of course, but with a purpose. The sad plight of the poet is essential to the poem, and there is required a certain bulk of language to give it due importance. Such is the primary function of amplification. But the passage in its precise wording has further purposes. The succession of the moon, the morning star, and then the evening star, and finally dawn again indicates by its very succession the continuity and duration of time. It is the implying of a process by a kind of poetic imitation of the process.

There are other types of implication in the poem. In the last line of this passage the poet says that Tithonia sprinkles from her cool whip. There seemed no way of excluding the word dew from the translation; English style will hardly permit the omission. In the original, however, the reader is not told what the dawn goddess sprinkles but must himself complete the inference from the material furnished by the poet, and the completion of the inference is an integral part of the experience of the poem. Furthermore, in the same line there is involved another process of completing the inference, the process that has come to be called fusion in modern criticism. For Tithonia who sprinkles dew also takes pity on the poet. But to take pity on someone is to shed a tear for him, and that tears are the dew of the eyes has been established by generations of poets.[11] Consequently, the reader must not only elicit both dew and tears from a passage that makes no mention of either; he must also through a feeling for literary tradition fuse or identify the image of dew and of tears.

Of the four kinds of poetic implication which have been analyzed so far—implication by rhetorical figure, by a kind of imitation of a process, implication in the proper logical sense, and implication by fusion—the two latter may be discussed a little more fully. Why is it that the poet cannot sleep? Is it, as Vollmer conjectures, because the poem was written during a spell of illness? Certainly insomnia accompanies some illnesses, and from another poem we learn that the poet was once quite ill.[12] But when we ask why the poet asserts that he cannot sleep, we must answer in terms of the particular poem. He cannot sleep in this poem because he is that conventional figure, the unhappy lover. For this reason Tithonia, rising from the bed of her senile husband, pities his condition; and for the same reason he begs of Sleep that if some happy lover willingly gives up his sleep, since being happy in love he could sleep if he would, some portion of that rejected sleep should be transferred to him. But the request is strictly qualified. He disclaims any petition for full or contented sleep, for it would be impious of the unhappy lover to pray for what is not his due. In the ancient erotic tradition sleeplessness is an inseparable accident of the unrequited lover; hence he asks only for the least bit of sleep. Thus the reader construes what is said in the poem in the light of the literary tradition, and infers what the situation of the poet is. The process is similar to, though not quite the same as, the construction of a hypothesis that saves the phenomena. It is different in that a poem is a closed system, and that tradition furnishes the lines of construction.

Implication by fusion will account for the Argus passage. The poet asks only for a little sleep, in fact, only for so much as Argus had who could close some of his thousand eyes while the others kept vigil. In this lies the function of the passage which Mackail would excise; it is the turning point in the poem, the hinge upon which the whole swings. It announces for the first time the conceptual basis of the poem, for this is not the contrast between no sleep and full sleep, but between a lack of sleep and the least degree of it. The Argus passage, then, foreshadows the final prayer, and being held in memory fuses with the last lines. The reader sees at that moment that the poet wishes to be Argus with respect to sleep.

To sum up, the paraphrasable meaning of Statius's poem is implicit in the text rather than explicit. But in Wordsworth's sonnet, on the contrary, the paraphrasable meaning is quite explicit. "I have thought of all by turns," he says, and by *all* he means the images of external nature which constitute the opening lines, "and yet do lie Sleepless." The poet himself gives in explicit statement the paraphrasable content of the octave; the wording of a paraphrase would be the wording of the text. This is clear also in the sestet:

> Even thus last night, and two nights more, I lay,
> And could not win thee, Sleep! . . .
> So do not let me wear to-night away.

The fourth and final point of difference between the two poems emerges from what has already been said. The conceptual basis of Statius' poem is not the contrast between sleeplessness and its logical contrary, but between degrees of sleeplessness. But Wordsworth's sonnet takes no note of such humanistic quibbling.

The contrast there is plainly between one state and its logical opposite: the poet is either A or Not-A with respect to sleep, and there is in the text no middle ground.

In the course of this chapter six characteristics of one kind of poetry have been discriminated and opposed to six characteristics of another kind. The one employs a complex and modulated meter; the other an obvious meter conforming to a simple mathematical scheme. The one plays the syntactical structure against the metrical line; the other shows a marked coincidence of the two. In the one tradition the length of the poem tends to be a free determination; in the other it tends to be fixed and given. The outline of thought in the one tends not to correspond to the units of the external form; in the other it tends to correspond. The paraphrasable meaning of the one is largely implicit and to be inferred from the text; with the other it is explicit. Finally, the conceptual basis of the first kind of poetry will tend to be one of continuity and degree; in the second kind it will tend to be one of discontinuity, identity, and contradiction. The first kind is exemplified by the poetry of Horace, Vergil, and Statius, by Milton's *Lycidas* and most of his sonnets, and by a great deal of more modern poetry. The second kind is exemplified in most medieval and Tudor lyric. The first may be called the classical method, the second the medieval, and the history of the English lyric may be construed in terms of the transition from the second to the first.

MY FIRES & FEARS ARE MET

Sappho, Longinus, & the Rhetorical Tradition

I shall deal in this lecture with Sappho's Second Ode, as it used to be called.[1] It is probably only the beginning of a longer poem, the rest of which has been lost. But we have evidence that what remains was independently famous in Antiquity, and the passage can be dealt with as such. As in the previous lectures on Dickinson I alluded to legend and dealt with text, so also with Sappho, who is the very prototype of legend in that kind, I will disregard the legend and regard the text. It reads in my translation—I note as an aside: the meter of the translation is strophic, basically syllabic, three nines and a five, with the nines tending toward iamb-anapest-anapest-unaccented syllable, and with two stresses in the fives—and now the poem:

> He is, I should say, on a level
> With deity, the man who sits over
> Against you, and attends to the nearby
> Sweetness of your voice
>
> And charm of your laughter. I tell you
> It frightens the quick heart in my breast.
> For, soon as I look at you, there is
> No voice left to me,
>
> My tongue has been fractured, a thin fire
> Instantly runs underneath my skin,
> My eyes cannot see anything, and
> My ears re-echo.

I am in a cold sweat, a trembling
Seizes me all over, and, pallid
As range grass, I think I am almost
On the point of death.

What follows may constitute another line—scholars have not set-
tled the matter—but if so, the continuation is not dear. I shall
deal only with the sixteen lines.

The situation in the poem is social and erotic, the speaker is
observer. There are three parts (perhaps four, if you include the
final disputed line): first, an assertion of value, of remove from or-
dinariness; second, a delineation of the occasion: it is sometimes
taken to be a wedding feast. The more general human occasion
can be delimited by two quotations from Burton's *Anatomy of
Melancholy,* that pedantic mine of humanity: "And to say truth,
with a lascivious object who is not moved, to see others dally,
kiss, dance?"; and again: "men are mad, stupefied many times
at the first sight of beauty, amazed. . . . "[2] The third part is the
concomitants of extremity of feeling, and, if there is a fourth, it is
comment. Longinus deals only with the third part, the concomi-
tants; he describes the procedures involved and offers gloss, gloss
that seems to derive from a tradition of interpretation. I mean by
gloss a description of a text that applies to some texts but not to
this. I shall begin with a current gloss.

A poem must be read in some context, and one currently fa-
vored is to read the poem in the context of Sappho writing it. I
give three brief excerpts from the commentary of three eminent
scholars:

. . . Sappho mercilessly depicts the failure of her senses and her body—how she is brought to the brink of death.

Sappho speaks of her sensations as dispassionately as if she were an interested bystander . . .

We cannot and need not believe that such pieces were written in the very moment of passion, but they imply only a short interval of recollection from its first onslaught, and indicate that it is still at work in Sappho's whole being.[3]

This is biographical criticism with a lack of biographical detail to relate it to. This is the legend of the poet as poet.

I shall now read the poem in the context in which it has come down to us. The poem is preserved as an example in an ancient handbook on composition, probably late First Century A.D., Longinus *On the Sublime,* though we do not know the name of the author, and "the sublime" is generally, and rightly, regarded as a mistranslation. It is a rhetorical treatise, largely occupied with the figures of speech, with Art and Nature, with Pathos and Ethos. It is in the form of an epistle, which permits the digressions for which the work is famous, the set pieces on the *Iliad* and *Odyssey,* on Demosthenes and Cicero, the occasional cross-classification which the overlapping categories of rhetoric demand, and the interpolated dialogue toward the end. It thus affords the unsystematic within the systematic. Now, rhetoric is a productive, not a descriptive, science, descriptive only in the service of production. Hence I shall conclude this lecture with a contemporary poem conceived and written within the tradition in which

Longinus places Sappho's. That tradition defines the provinces of experience, the shapes, forms, figures of utterance, the learnable procedures by which a certain linguistic effect can be recognized, and produced, given experience and the gift of gab.

What is the particular effect he is concerned with here? It is not in our sense the sublime; it is that wonder or astonishment, that open-mouthed reaction to eloquence, stipulated from the earliest Sophistic as the potential consequence of deviation from the ordinary. So Theophrastus: the end of the deviations of poetry and rhetoric is that by these means

> together with studied expansion and contraction, all employed at the suitable moment, the listener shall be charmed and astonished and, with respect to intellectual persuasion, overmastered.[4]

So, too, Longinus. The heights of utterance that ensure immortality to poet and prose writer effect not persuasion but transport (*ékstasis*); they take us out of ourselves. The extraordinary shatters us, and dominates the persuasive and pleasant. His subject, then, is High Style in its aspect of the Striking.

The main part of the treatise is ordered under five rubrics; first Thought, then Pathos (strong feeling) and Ethos. These, though they somewhat correspond to our Thought, Feeling and Character, designate at the same time segregable passages that deal with one or the other. This was well understood in the Renaissance. Thus the "To be or not to be" soliloquy, which begins by proposing a subject for disputation: "that is the question," *haec quaestio est,*—for *question* is the technical term for the subject of a disputation—is a passage of Thought, not Passion or Character. For, has the Heir Designate to the throne ever personally experienced "the proud man's contumely," "The law's delay," or "the spurns / That patient merit of the unworthy takes"? On the other hand, "O what a rogue and peasant slave am I" is a Pathos, a passion, up to "About, my brains." At that point it becomes Thought. And *Richard III*'s opening soliloquy, "I am determined to prove a villain," is Ethos, or Character.[5]

The following sections in Longinus deal with the Figures of Thought and Speech; with Diction; and finally with Rhythm or Prosodic-syntactic Combination. Our text is cited in the section (Chapter 10) that marks the transition from Pathos to Figures of Thought; amplification, how to get wordage—one of the traditional Figures of Thought—is treated in the following section and distinguished explicitly from the procedure described in this, which is how to shrink it. The particular topic, then, is contraction, but the instances cited are also ones whose province is Pathos (strong feeling): Erotic Fear, The Terror of a Storm at Sea, The Castaway, and Alarm, all instances of fear. These are Topoi, kinds of passages that can be produced and inserted in due place in a work of larger scope. The Sappho passage, then, is a Pathos, a Passion, that exemplifies one of the methods of contraction. It also exemplifies, as Longinus points out, and we shall see, one of the methods of Prosodic-syntactic Combination.

What is the nature of the Pathos in Sappho's poem? And what rhetorical procedure is used to develop it? Longinus in introducing the poem says:

> Now since there are certain elements which naturally are found in association with all subjects of discourse and which co-exist with them, we find that the selection of the most telling of the elements thus contained and the ability to form subsequent combinations of

them with one another and make as it were a single body out of them, would necessarily be a cause of sublimity.[6]

The procedure described is a descendant of the Aristotelian doctrine of properties: "An attribute necessarily resulting from the notion of a thing, but not entering into the definition thereof."[7] It is also Epicurean. In rhetoric it appears as *the signs of.* For example, in a treatise long attributed to Cicero are listed the signs of a bad conscience: "blushed, paled, faltered, spoke uncertainly, collapsed, or made some offer."[8] Except for the final one, the bribe, these are the signs of organic disturbance that Sappho lists. We tend when we think of poetry not to think of such an explicit, even logical, way of proceeding, since we associate such ways with other disciplines, with Psychology, perhaps, or Sociology. But the rhetoric of signs or of associated elements has a long history.

We find the elements, the general details, associated with Spring Love at the conclusion of one of Horace's odes: it is an Ethos, a way of life:

> nunc et campus et areae
> lenesque sub noctem susurri
>   composita repetantur hora,
>
> nunc et latentis proditor intimo
> gratus puellae risus ab angulo
>   pignusque dereptum lacertis
>   aut digito male pertinaci.

Now through the parks
Soft whisperings toward nightfall
Visit again at the trysting hour;

Now from her bower comes the charmed laugh,
Betrayer of the hiding girl;
Now from her arm the forfeit
Plundered, her fingers resisting not.[9]

The details are fitted into the strophe, not line by line but phrase by phrase, the soft whisperings, the charmed laugh, and the detail that finishes it, "her fingers resisting not." But there is also binding repetition, *now, now, now.*

Skelton in "Upon a Dead Man's Head" uses the procedure in the form of *the signs of* in a Pathos on Death, beginning with the traditional syllogism, all men are mortal, and interpolating exhortation and comment:

Your ugly token
My mind hath broken
From worldly lust:
For I have discust
We are but dust,
And die we must.
It is general
To be mortal:
I have well espied
No man may him hide
From Death hollow-eyed,
With sinews wydered,
With bones shydered,

With worm-eaten maw,
And his ghastly jaw
Gasping aside,
Naked of hide,
Neither flesh nor fell.
Then, by my counsel,
Look that ye spell
Well this gospel:
For whereso we dwell
Death will us quell,
And with us mell.[10]

The passage is held together by consecutive rhyming, as many as may be, by anaphora (*with-with, our-our*), and the details are given, a line each, in serial order. They are stacked one on the other in equal units, like the storage cubes you may buy in a furniture store.

Shakespeare also uses *the signs of,* but now in prose, in an Ethos on Old Age. The Chief Justice says to Falstaff:

Do you set down your name in the scroll of youth, that are written down old with all the characters of age? Have you not a moist eye? A dry head? A yellow cheek? A white beard? A decreasing leg? An increasing belly? Is not your voice broken? Your wind short? Your chin double? Your wit single? And every part about you blasted with antiquity?[11]

The passage is stylistically held together by the question form, by *a, a* and *your, your,* by the use of opposites twice (*increasing, decreasing, single, double*), and brought to finality by a sentence a good deal longer than the preceding ones. But the details are given one by one with no mortar between them.

And Pope, to conclude our examples, on the model of Martial, makes a poem out of the elements of the good life, an Ethos, though the good life of the eighteenth-century gentry; the necessary premise is inherited land. There is a minimum of comment, and some rhetorical repetition to hold the thing together, and hence it is allied to, but not quite, the method in the Sappho poem.

> Happy the man, whose wish and care
>   A few paternal acres bound,
> Content to breathe his native air,
>   In his own ground.
>
> Whose herds with milk, whose fields with bread,
>   Whose flocks supply him with attire,
> Whose trees in summer yield him shade,
>   In winter fire.
>
> Blest, who can unconcern'dly find
>   Hours, days, and years slide soft away,
> In health of body, peace of mind,
>   Quiet by day,
>
> Sound sleep by night; study and ease
>   Together mix'd; sweet recreation;
> And innocence, which most does please,
>   With meditation.

Thus let me live, unseen, unknown,
   Thus unlamented let me die,
Steal from the world, and not a stone
   Tell where I lie.[12]

There is a similar passage among the Sapphic fragments, the lines on the Evening Star "that brings back all the bright dawn disperses, that brings the sheep, brings the goat, brings the child to the mother."[13] These are the minimal details of a pastoral economy made single by the climactic nature of the final item and by the repetitions of anaphora.

Telling detail and its combination "to make as it were a single body" "would necessarily be a cause of a" special literary effect, for, as Longinus says in the passage dealing with Sappho:

> the first procedure wins over the hearer by the choice of the ideas to be expressed, and the last does so by the compact fitting together of what has been chosen. Thus, for example, Sappho always takes the emotions in the madness of love from the phenomena accompanying it and from the reality itself. Where does she show her excellence? When she shows her skill in choosing the most preeminent of these and those of the most surpassing force and in combining them together.

He then quotes the poem. We have in this passage, however, also an interpretation. The province of experience the poem deals with, he tells us, is erotic insanity, the madness of love. This I think is gloss, in the sense I have defined, a reading proper to some texts, but not to this. And in the remarks following the quotation of the poem he offers further gloss:

> Do you not marvel how at the same moment she seeks in vain her soul and her body, her hearing and her tongue, her sight and her color, all of which have ceased to be her own, and in contrary fashion, is at once chilled and burned, irrational and sensible— for either she fears or is all but dead—so that there may be seen in her not one passion, but a concourse of passions? All things happen to lovers in this way; but the choosing of the extremes and combination of them together is what has made the preeminence here.

There are two further glosses in this passage, though they are related: that the experience is *ekstasis,* ecstasy in the old sense, and that it is *enthousiasmos,* enthusiasm in the old, the Methodist, sense.

That the passage in Sappho's poem consists of *the signs of* is confirmed by Plutarch, whose interpretations are also those of Longinus. When the young man in the *Life of Demetrius,* desperately in love with his stepmother, tries to starve himself to death, the physician diagnoses the situation as "love, not sickness," for, I quote North's Plutarch, "he commonly perceived those signs in him, which Sappho writeth to be in lovers (to wit, that his words and speech did fail him . . and so on, until "he became like a man in an ecstasy or trance, and white as a kercher."[14]

Plutarch and Longinus agree in construing the experience as emotional illness and, alternatively, as ecstasy, as that being out of oneself that was earlier said to be the consequence of the

Striking High Style. For what else has Longinus in mind when he says, "soul, body, speech, sight, all these she feels the want of, as someone else's, as things lost." Certainly the speaker in Plutarch's dialogue on love so construes it: "divine possession," "supernatural agitation," "a greater ecstasy than that of the Pythian oracle or Cybelan cultist."[15] But, though "This is the very ecstasy of love" has a long tradition in Western poetry, it is not depicted here; the speaker does not go out of herself. It may be only a step from this to *enthousiasmos,* but it is a step. Erotic insanity, ecstasy, enthusiasm, all three are related in this tradition, and are experiences of prize in the First Century. They are read into our text, I should think, chiefly on the basis of the last line, "I think I am almost / On the point of death," and the suggestion of theophany in the opening lines.

It will be amusing to digress for a moment and note that in one of the most charming treatments of ecstasy in English poetry, in Marvell's "The Garden," a sexual partner is explicitly denied:

> Here at the fountain's sliding foot,
> Or at some fruit-tree's mossy root,
> Casting the body's vest aside,
> My soul into the boughs does glide:
> There, like a bird, it sits and sings,
> Then whets and combs its silver wings,
> And, till prepared for longer flight,
> Waves in its plumes the various light.

Such was that happy garden-state,
While man there walked without a mate.
After a place so pure and sweet
What other help could yet be meet!
But 'twas beyond a mortal's share
To wander solitary there:
Two paradises 'twere in one,
To live in paradise alone.[16]

The third gloss has been generally and rightly rejected, that the passage is generated by the procedure of paired terms, speech-hearing, and indeed of contradictories, hot-cold. You can find the elements in the passage, or, as with soul-body, read them in, but they are not paired off. They are paired off in the famous Sapphic epithet *glukapikron:*

Love strikes me again, that makes the legs give way,
That sweet-bitter, not-to-be-fought-with shape.[17]

but this is but one element in a couplet that also has concomitant detail ("that makes the legs give way"), judgment ("not-to-be-fought-with"), and personification ("shape"). So, too, in Catullus:

I hate and love her. If you ask me why
I don't know, but I feel it and am torn.[18]

there are opposites, but only once, expanded by the social context of colloquial address and comment. In later tradition, however, the procedure flourishes. It is the *I freeze, I fry* of medieval and Renaissance poetry Hence we may take this gloss, as we may take the two previous ones, as reflecting the concerns of the First and subsequent centuries, the concerns, for example, of John Gower in the Prologue to Book One of the *Confessio Amantis,* and of Shakespeare in *Romeo and Juliet.* The Prologue:

> Est amor egra salus, vexata quies, pius error,
> Bellica pax, vulnus dulce, suave malum.

Love is health that is a sickness, a stillness without quiet, a truancy that is faithful, a peace that is all war, a refreshing wound, a sweet evil.

And Romeo:

> Here's much to do with hate, but more with love.
> Why then, o brawling love, o loving hate,
> O any thing of nothing first create!
> O heavy lightness, serious vanity,
> Misshapen chaos of well-seeming forms,
> Feather of lead, bright smoke, cold fire, sick health,
> Still-waking sleep, that is not what it is!
> This love feel I, that feel no love in this.[19]

I should like now to gather up the multiple traditions I have been distinguishing in a single text, and then return to Sappho. There is a Renaissance text that employs in the same Pathos as Sappho's explicit contradictories, medical analysis, depiction of distraction, but instead of contraction uses amplification, not in the sense of touching all points, but in Longinus's special sense of "new starts and places of rest and at each new step fresh grandeurs." It begins:

Thou dost not know my sufferings, what I feel,

There follows a summary alliterative phrase, contradictories, a passage ordered by the lore on the location of passion, liver, heart, blood, with the last amplified by an extended metaphor:

> My fires and fears are met; I burn and freeze,
> My liver's one great coal, my heart shrunk up
> With all the fibres, and the mass of blood
> Within me is a standing lake of fire,
> Curled with the cold wind of my gelid sighs,
> That drive a drift of sleet through all my body,
> And shoot a February through my veins.

There is return to opposites:

> Until I see him, I am drunk with thirst,
> And surfeited with hunger of his presence.

Distraction:

> I know not where I am, or no, or speak

And then the something added when it seemed all over, the extra, the epiphoneme:

> Or whether thou dost hear me.

It is a speech from Ben Jonson's *The New Inn*,[20] and it has everything.

The province is Sappho's, the method is not. The province? Not sex, not jealousy, not ritual, but fear, and fear of that special sort that does not evoke the crouch, the arm thrown up, the fear rather that is wonder, amazement, astonishment. The context is erotic, the emotion is fear: "My fires and fears are met." And Sappho's method? What that is Longinus tells us, and, indeed, in a way uncharacteristic of him tells us again and again. It consists in the limitation of phrased detail to the most eminent, the most striking, and the binding of these together by juxtaposition only into prosodic-syntactic completeness.

> He is, I should say, on a level
> With deity, the man who sits over
> Against you, and attends to the nearby
> Sweetness of your voice
>
> And charm of your laughter. I tell you
> It frightens the quick heart in my breast.
> For, soon as I look at you, there is
> No voice left to me,
>
> My tongue has been fractured, a thin fire
> Instantly runs underneath my skin.
> My eyes cannot see anything, and
> My ears re-echo.
>
> I am in a cold sweat, a trembling
> Seizes me all over, and, pallid
> As range grass, I think I am almost
> On the point of death.

There are here in eleven lines ten of the most striking of the signs of fear. Lucretius in a similar passage on fear and terror, though now in hexameters, has seven of them, with the addition of the "legs give way" we found in another passage of Sappho's.[21]

How does one write such a passage? Well, one might read Darwin on *Expression of the Emotions in Man and Animals* and choose salient and relevant points; a process of leaving out, of contraction. The following is a small portion of Darwin's account:

> Fear is often preceded by astonishment. . . . The heart beats quickly and violently, so that it palpitates or knocks against the ribs . . . the skin instantly becomes pale as during incipient faintness. This paleness of the surface, however, is probably in large part, or is exclusively, due to the vaso-motor center being affected in such a manner as to cause the contraction of the small arteries of the skin. That the skin is much affected under the sense of great fear, we see in the marvellous manner in which perspiration immediately exudes from it. . . . there is a death-like pallor . . .[22]

The result would be an illustration of William James' theory of the emotions: "the bodily changes follow directly the perception of the exciting fact, and . . . our feeling of the same changes as they occur *is* the emotion."[23] And we would bring the passage to a close with a detail that, though the preceding details were hugger-mugger, with no inherent principle of order, had in it a certain finality: "I think I am almost / On the point of death."

To sum up, there is in Sappho sufficient detail to suggest selection, not of representative instances but of a few of the many phrases that come to mind. This is contraction, and has the resonance of what is not said. Furthermore, the details are salient, they are seized; they are not generated analytically as, for instance, by paired terms. Again, they are struck out of the inner nature of such experience; in this passage they are the accompanying organic disturbances, as Longinus notes, so that the passion, the Pathos, is, as it were, a meeting of the particularities of passion. Hence the details are generic, not individual. The procedure is Ideal in the old sense, narrowed to relevance and tending toward the extreme case.[24]

But the passage also attains completeness and coherence, together with the effect of wonder, Longinus tells us, by the prosodic-syntactic combination of the phrases. He makes two points: a) that the phrases follow in serial order with nothing inserted between them, no mortar, no amplification or development, no speculation on the vaso-motor center; and b) that, each in its right place, they support one another like stones in a New England dry wall. The expression is metaphorical, and difficult to explain otherwise, yet clear. The specifications are: the phrases shall come in a certain range of shapes and sizes, roughhewn, with none just rocks and none boulders. They shall be of a kind, except for the finality of the last, and find their place in the prosodic structure where they fit in, neither disposed by that structure nor violating it. There will be no subordination, nor will they be bound by such verbal figures as anaphora, "bedded as they are in the sound masonry of their own mutual relation."[25] There will be no verbal repetition and no structuring of the phrases in relation to each other, both of which we found in Horace and Pope. And in contrast to Sir Philip Sidney's method in treating the same material:

My muse, what ails this ardor?
Mine eyes be dim, my limbs shake,
My voice is hoarse, my throat scorched,
My tongue to this my roof cleaves,
My fancy amazed, my thought dulled,
My heart doth ache, my life faints,
My soul begins to take leave.[26]

there will be little coincidence of syntactic units and line units. Here, as we remarked earlier, unit is stacked on unit.

Longinus, after discussing Sappho, cites further instances of the Topos, the commonplace, of fear that employ the same procedures. "In the same way," he says,

Homer, in his description of storms, chooses the most grievous of the accompanying circumstances . . . What does Homer do? I will quote one passage out of many:

He fell on them as when a wave falls on a swift ship—
Violent, made great by the wind, with the storm-clouds
above it—
And the whole ship is buried in spray, and the dread
blast of the wind
Roars in the sail, and the sailors quake in their hearts
In terror: for they scud on at but a space out-from-
under death . . .

Homer does not circumscribe the danger to a single occasion, but paints a picture of men continually being all but brought to death again and again at every new wave.

217

And for the element of finality:

> Further he has taken prepositions, which are not naturally compounded with one another, and compelled them to unite contrary to their nature—out-from-under death—and thus tormented the verse in the semblance of the torment of terror arising in it; and by this contortion and compression of the verse he has with superlative skill caught the likeness of the terror and all but modelled in speech the peculiar quality of the danger: scud onward out-from-under death.

There follows an unidentified passage from Archilochus, and Demosthenes's account of the alarm at Athens on the news from Elatea. "Let me recount," he says, "some small but essential details." It was night, a messenger came to the selectmen, Elatea had been taken. They were sitting at dinner, instantly arose from the table, cleared the shops on the plaza of people; others sent for the officers and the bell ringer. The alarm spread through the city.[27] These details, being grounded in circumstance, have not the ideality of Sappho's, yet with adjustment of circumstances would characterize alarm at other times and places. This, rhetoricians would call a finite, a limited by circumstance, the other an infinite, an unlimited cause. In fact, the passages in this chapter are arranged in descending order from the generic treatment of fear as such in Sappho, through the details of a storm that would beget fear, down to the particularities of the alarm at Athens.

These, then, are describable, teachable, learnable, reproducible procedures. Let us put theory into practice. I am for personal reasons concerned with the quality of life on the plains of Montana some fifty years ago. I could research and produce an article or book on the subject, based on old newspapers, letters and journals, recollections of the still living, and first-hand acquaintance with the scene, and I could write a treatise on how to do this. Similarly, for a book of old photographs with accompanying letterpress, for a work of fiction in which that life should be background, accompaniment, or some aspect of it, the blizzards for instance, a central event in the story itself. But if I should be instructed by Longinus, and attempt to do it in a short passage, preferably in verse, how would I go about it? What would I produce?

I would produce an Ethos, a way of life, not a Pathos, and one implicated in circumstances, limited, not unlimited; let us not meet Homer and Sappho on their own grounds. We read, remember, and muse; let come to mind the elements innate to that life, and jot them down helter-skelter over a cup of black coffee down the highway, some simply enumerated, some phrased as they come to us. Men homesteaded, women were few, and those often mail-order housekeepers. People came who had TB or feared it. They built houses as in the Midwest, with front door and parlor though they were not used, read at the kitchen table by kerosene lamp, grew wheat, killed rabbits and rattlesnakes, dug root cellars and wells of alkaline water. So detail comes, and now selection, contraction, and fitting them in, neither schematically nor shaggily, to an antecedent prosodic structure. Keep the items in mind, the phrases and metrical patterns on your tongue, and set them down in a relatively short, a detachable passage that could be a complete short poem. It will need a last detail of a certain finality, and perhaps a concluding line.

Gaunt kept house with her child for the old man,
Met at the train, dust-driven as the sink
She came to, the child white as the alkali.
To the West distant mountains, the Big Lake
To the Northeast. Dead trees and almost dead
In the front yard, the front door locked and nailed,
A handpump in the sink. Outside, a land
Of gophers, cottontails, and rattlesnakes,
In good years of alfalfa, oats, and wheat.
Root cellar, blacksmith shop, milk house, and barn,
Granary, corral. An old *World Almanac*
To thumb at night, the child coughing, the lamp smoked,
The chores done. So he came to her one night,
To the front room, now bedroom, and moved in.
Nothing was said, nothing was ever said.
And then the child died, and she disappeared.
This was Montana fifty years ago.[28]

LOGIC & LYRIC

Marvell, Dunbar, & Nashe

The discussion in "Classical and Medieval: Statius on Sleep" raises the question, May the principal structure of a poem be of a logical rather than an alogical sort? For example, to confine ourselves to the Old Logic, May a lyric be solely or predominantly the exposition of a syllogism? and may the propositions of the lyric, one by one, be of the sort to be found in a logical syllogism?

The incautious romantic will deny the possibility, and with a repugnance of feeling that would preclude any further discussion. For logic and lyric are generally regarded as opposites, if not as contradictory terms. "It is a commonplace," says a recent writer on logic, "that poetry and logic have nothing to do with each other, that they are even opposed to one another."[1] You will find this explicitly stated, sometimes with the substitution of "science" for "logic," in most of the school handbooks on the study of literature, in most of the introductions to poetry. "The peculiar quality of poetry," we read in one of these,

> can be distinguished from that of prose if one thinks
> of the creative mind as normally expressing itself in
> a variety of literary forms ranged along a graduated
> scale between the two contrasted extremes of scien-
> tific exposition and lyrical verse.

And, a little later:

> [Poetry] strives for a conviction begotten of the emotions rather than of reason.

Consequently, we are told:

> The approach of poetry is indirect. It proceeds by means of suggestion, implication, reflection. Its method is largely symbolical. It is more interested in connotations than in denotations.[2]

This is common doctrine. Poetry is in some way concerned with emotion rather than reason, and its method is imaginative, indirect, implicit rather than explicit, symbolic rather than discursive, concerned with what its terms suggest rather than with what they state. The kind of poetry which most fully possesses and exhibits these concerns, methods, and qualities is generally thought to be the lyric, and hence it, of all poetry, is regarded as the most antithetical to reason, logic, and science.

This was not always the case. In the eighth century, for example, a scholiast of the school of Alcuin regarded not only grammar and rhetoric but dialectic or logic also as the disciplines that nourish and form a poet. In the medieval and renaissance traditions of commentary on Aristotle's logic, poetic is sometimes regarded as a part, a subdivision, of logic—as, indeed, I consider it myself. As late as the eighteenth century, David Hume writes in an essay, *Of the Standard of Taste:*

> Besides, every kind of composition, even the most poetical, is nothing but a chain of propositions and reasonings; not always indeed the justest and most exact, but still plausible and specious, however disguised by the coloring of the imagination.

And even today the writer on logic whom I quoted earlier asserts, in denial of the commonplace: "Every poem, except in rare extreme cases, contains judgments and implicit propositions, and thus becomes subject to logical analysis."[3]

But may the chain of propositions and reasonings be not merely plausible and specious but even sufficiently just and exact? May the poem be not merely subject to logical analysis but logical in form? May, to return to our point, the subject and structure of a poem be conceived and expressed syllogistically? Anyone at all acquainted with modern criticism and the poems that are currently in fashion will think in this connection of Marvell's *To His Coy Mistress*. The apparent structure of that poem is an argumentative syllogism, explicitly stated. "Had we but world enough, and time," the poet says,

> This coyness, lady, were no crime;…

> But at my back I always hear
> Time's winged chariot hurrying near;…

> Now, therefore…
>   let us sport us while we may.

If we had all the time and space in the world we could delay consummation. But we do not. Therefore. The structure is formal. The poet offers to the lady a practical syllogism, and if she assents to it the appropriate consequence, he hopes, will follow:

Had we but world enough, and time,
This coyness, Lady, were no crime;
We would sit down and think which way
To walk and pass our long love's day.
Thou by the Indian Ganges side
Shouldst rubies find: I by the tide
Of Humber would complain. I would
Love you ten years before the Flood,
And you should, if you please, refuse
Till the conversion of the Jews.
My vegetable love should grow
Vaster than empires, and more slow;
An hundred years should go to praise
Thine eyes and on thy forehead gaze;
Two hundred to adore each breast;
But thirty thousand to the rest;
An age at least to every part,
And the last age should show your heart;
For, Lady, you deserve this state,
Nor would I love at lower rate.

      But at my back I always hear
Time's winged chariot hurrying near;
And yonder all before us lie
Deserts of vast eternity.
Thy beauty shall no more be found,
Nor in thy marble vault shall sound
My echoing song: then worms shall try
That long preserved virginity,
And your quaint honor turn to dust,
And into ashes all my lust:
The grave's a fine and private place,

But none, I think, do there embrace.
Now, therefore, while the youthful hue
Sits on thy skin like morning dew,
And while thy willing soul transpires
At every pore with instant fires,
　　　　Now let us sport us while we may,
And now, like amorous birds of prey,
Rather at once our time devour
Than languish in his slow-chapt power.
Let us roll all our strength and all
Our sweetness up into one ball,
And tear our pleasures with rough strife
Thorough the iron gates of life:
Thus, though we cannot make our sun
Stand still, yet we will make him run.[4]

The logical nature of the argument here has been generally recognized, though often with a certain timidity. Mr. Eliot hazards: "The three strophes of Marvell's poem have something like a syllogistic relation to each other." And in a recent scholarly work we read: "The dialectic of the poem lies not only or chiefly in the formal demonstration explicit in its three stanzas, but in all the contrasts evoked by its images and in the play between the immediately sensed and the intellectually apprehended."[5] That is, the logic is recognized, but minimized, and our attention is quickly distracted to something more reputable in a poem, the images or the characteristic tension of metaphysical poetry. For Mr. Eliot the more important element in this case is a principle of order common in modern poetry and often employed in his own poems. He points out that the theme of Marvell's poem is "one of the great traditional commonplaces of European literature . . .

the theme of . . . *Gather ye rosebuds,* of *Go, lovely rose.*" He continues: "Where the wit of Marvell renews the theme is in the variety and order of the images." The dominant principle of order in the poem, then, is an implicit one rather than the explicit principle of the syllogism, and implicit in the succession of images.

Mr. Eliot explains the implicit principle of order in this fashion:

> In the first of the three paragraphs Marvell plays with a fancy that begins by pleasing and leads to astonishment. . . . We notice the high speed, the succession of concentrated images, each magnifying the original fancy. When this process has been carried to the end and summed up, the poem turns suddenly with that surprise which has been one of the most important means of poetic effect since Homer:
>
> > But at my back I always hear
> > Time's winged chariot hurrying near,
> > And yonder all before us lie
> > Deserts of vast eternity.
>
> A whole civilization resides in these lines:
>
> > Pallida Mors aequo pulsat pede pauperum tabernas
> > Regumque turres . . .
>
> A modern poet, had he reached the height, would very likely have closed on this moral reflection.

What is meant by this last observation becomes clear a little later where it is said that the wit of the poem "forms the crescendo and diminuendo of a scale of great imaginative power."[6] The structure of the poem, then, is this: it consists of a succession of images increasing in imaginative power to the sudden turn and surprise of the image of time, and then decreasing to the conclusion.

But is there any sudden turn and surprise in the image of time? and does the poem consist of a succession of images? This talk of images is a little odd since there seem to be relatively few in the poem if one means by image what people usually do—a descriptive phrase that invites the reader to project a sensory construction. The looming imminence of Time's winged chariot is, no doubt, an image, though not a full-blown one since there is nothing in the phrasing that properly invites any elaboration of sensory detail. But when Mr. Eliot refers to "successive images" and cites "my *vegetable* love," with *vegetable* italicized, and "Till the conversion of the Jews," one suspects that he is provoking images where they do not textually exist. There is about as much of an image in "Till the conversion of the Jews" as there would be in "till the cows come home," and it would be a psychiatrically sensitive reader who would immediately visualize the lowing herd winding slowly o'er the lea. But "my *vegetable* love" will make the point. I have no doubt that Mr. Eliot and subsequent readers do find an image here. They envisage some monstrous and expanding cabbage, but they do so in mere ignorance. *Vegetable* is no vegetable but an abstract and philosophical term, known as such to every educated man of Marvell's day. Its context is the doctrine of the three souls: the rational, which in man subsumes the other two; the sensitive, which men and animals have in common and which is the principle of motion and perception; and, finally, the lowest of the three, the vegetable soul, which is the only one that plants possess, and which is the principle of generation and corruption, of augmentation and decay. Marvell says, then, my love, denied the exercise of sense, but possessing the power of augmentation, will increase "Vaster than empires." It is an intellectual image, and hence no image at all but a conceit. For if one calls any sort of particularity or detail in a poem an image, the use of the wrong word will invite the reader to misconstrue his experience in terms of images, to invent sensory constructions and to project them on the poem.

A conceit is not an image. It is a piece of wit. It is in the tradition in which Marvell was writing, among other possibilities, the discovery of a proposition referring to one field of experience in terms of an intellectual structure derived from another field, and often enough a field of learning, as is the case in "my vegetable love." This tradition, though it goes back to the poetry of John Donne, and years before that, was current in Marvell's day. The fashionable poetry at the time he was writing this poem, the poetry comparable to that of Eliot or of Auden in the forties and fifties, was the poetry of John Cleveland, and the fashionable manner was generally known as Clevelandizing. It consisted in the invention of a series of witty hyperbolical conceits, sometimes interspersed with images, and containing a certain amount of roughage in the form of conventional erotic statements:

> Thy beauty shall no more be found,
> Nor in thy marble vault shall sound
> My echoing song.

It was commonly expressed in the octosyllabic couplet. Cleveland, for example, writes *Upon Phillis Walking in a Morning before Sun-rising:*

The trees, like yeomen of the guard,
Serving her more for pomp than ward.

The comparison here does not invite visualization. It would be
inappropriate to summon up the colors and serried ranks of the
guard. The comparison is made solely with respect to the idea:
the trees like the guard serve more for pomp than ward. Again:

The flowers, called out of their beds,
Start and raise up their drowsy heads,
And he that for their color seeks
May see it vaulting to her cheeks,
Where roses mix—no civil war
Divides her York and Lancaster.[7]

One does not here picture in panorama the Wars of the Roses.
One sees rather the aptness and the wit of York and Lancaster,
the white rose and the red, reconciled in her cheeks, or one re-
jects it as forced and farfetched. This is a matter of taste.

But if the poem is not a succession of images, does it exhibit
that other principle which Mr. Eliot ascribes to it, the turn and
surprise which he finds in the abrupt introduction of time's char-
iot and which forms a sort of fulcrum on which the poem turns.
Subsequent critics have certainly felt that it has. In a current text-
book we read:

The poem begins as a conventional love poem in
which the lover tries to persuade his mistress to give
in to his entreaties. But with the introduction of
the image of the chariot in 1. 21, the poet becomes

obsessed by the terrible onrush of time, and the love theme becomes scarcely more than an illustration of the effect which time has upon human life.

And the leading scholar in the field, a man who is generally quite unhappy with Mr. Eliot's criticism, nevertheless says:

> the poet sees the whole world of space and time as the setting for two lovers. But wit cannot sustain the pretense that youth and beauty and love are immortal, and with a quick change of tone—like Catullus' *nobis cum semel occidit brevis lux* or Horace's *sed Timor et Minae*—the theme of time and death is developed with serious and soaring directness.[8]

These, I believe, are not so much accounts of the poem as accounts of Mr. Eliot's reading of the poem. Let us question the fact. Does the idea of time and death come as any surprise in this context? The poem began, "Had we but world enough, and time." That is, it began with an explicit condition contrary to fact, which by all grammatical rules amounts to the assertion that we do not have world enough and time. There is no surprise whatever when the proposition is explicitly made in line 21. It would rather have been surprising if it had not been made. Indeed, the only question we have in this respect, after we have read the first line, is, How many couplets will the poet expend on the ornamental reiteration of the initial proposition before he comes to the expected *but*. The only turn in the poem is the turn which the structure of the syllogism had led us to await.

Mr. Eliot compares the turn and surprise which he finds in this poem to a similar turn in an ode of Horace's, and the scholars seem to corroborate the comparison. This is the fourth ode of the first book:

Solvitur acris hiems grata vice veris et Favoni,
    trahuntque siccas machinae carinas

The poem begins with a picture of spring and proceeds by a succession of images, images of the external world and mythological images:

> Sharp winter relaxes with the welcome change to Spring and the west wind, and the cables haul the dry keels of ships. The herd no longer takes pleasure in its stalls or the farmer in his fire, and the pastures no longer whiten with hoar frost. Cytherean Venus leads her dancers beneath the overhanging moon, and the beautiful graces and nymphs strike the ground with alternate foot, while blazing Vulcan visits the grim forges of the Cyclops. Now is the time to wind your bright hair with green myrtle or with the flowers that the thawed earth yields. Now is the time to sacrifice to Faunus in the shadowed woods, whether it be a lamb he asks or a kid:

> Pallida mors aequo pulsat pede pauperum tabernas regumque turres.

> Pallid death with indifferent foot strikes the poor man's hut and the palaces of kings. Now, fortunate Sestius, the brief sum of life forbids our opening a long account with hope. Night will soon hem you in, and the fabled ghosts, and Pluto's meagre house.[9]

Death occurs in this poem with that suddenness and lack of preparation with which it sometimes occurs in life. The structure of the poem is an imitation of the structure of such experiences in life. And as we draw from such experiences often a generalization, so Horace from the sudden realization of the abruptness and impartiality of death, reflects:

vitae summa brevis spem nos vetat incohare longam.

The brief sum of life forbids our opening a long account with hope.

But the proposition is subsequent to the experience; it does not rule and direct the poem from the outset. And the experience in Horace *is* surprising and furnishes the fulcrum on which the poem turns. It has, in fact, the characteristics which are ascribed to Marvell's poem but which Marvell's poem does not have. The two are two distinct kinds of poetry, located in distinct and almost antithetical traditions; both are valuable and valid methods, but one is not to be construed in terms of the other.

In brief, the general structure of Marvell's poem is syllogistic, and it is located in the renaissance tradition of formal logic and of rhetoric. The structure exists in its own right and as a kind of expandable filing system. It is a way of disposing of, of making a place for, elements of a different order: in this case, Clevelandizing conceits and erotic propositions in the tradition of Jonson and Herrick. These reiterate the propositions of the syllogism. They do not develop the syllogism, and they are not required by the syllogism; they are free and extra. There could be more or less of them since there is nothing in the structure that determines the number of interpolated couplets. It is a matter of tact, and a matter of the appetite of the writer and the reader.

The notion of a structure as a kind of expandable filing system may deserve a few sentences. The narrative structure of a Shakespearean play can be regarded as a structure of this order. It exists in its own right, of course, but it is also a method for disposing various kinds of material of other orders, a set speech or passion here, an interpolated comic routine in another place. The structure offers a series of hooks upon which different things can be hung. Whether the totality will then form a whole, a unity, is a question of interpretation and a question of value. It is a question, for example, of what sort of unity is demanded, and whether there are various sorts.

In Marvell's poem, only the general structure is syllogistic; the detail and development are of another order, and critics have been diligent in assigning the poetic quality of the whole to the nonsyllogistic elements. Is it possible, then, to write a lyric that will be wholly or almost wholly syllogistic? It is. There is such a lyric in *The Oxford Book of English Verse,* a lyric of somewhat lesser repute than Marvell's, but still universally praised and universally conceded to possess the true lyrical power. It is Dunbar's *Lament for the Makaris.*

The structure of Dunbar's poem is the structure of the traditional syllogism with which everyone is acquainted: "All men are mortal, I am a man"; together with a concluding practical syllogism, "What must be, must be accepted, but I must die." The syllogism is developed in two ways, both characteristic methods in the logical tradition of the later Middle Ages. It begins with the immediate induction from experience of the leading principle, the major premise:

> I that in heill wes and gladnes,
> Am trublit now with gret seiknes,
> And feblit with infermite;
>> *Timor mortis conturbat me.*

The experience, then, is the sudden alteration from health to illness, and this yields the generalization:

> Our plesance heir is all vane glory,
> This fals warld is bot transitory,
> The flesche is brukle, the Fend is sle:
>> *Timor mortis conturbat me.*

The premise, then, is: this false world is but transitory; and it is presently expressed in more restricted terms:

> The stait of man dois change and vary,
> Now sound, now seik, now blith, now sary,
> Now dansand mery, now like to dee:
>> *Timor mortis conturbat me.*

The syllogism is now developed by another form of induction, and this development accounts for the remainder of the poem, except for the last stanza. It is developed through induction by simple enumeration in support and explication of the major premise, but with this special feature, that the induction proceeds by a hierarchical method. Nothing could be more characteristic of medieval logic. The argument is: if everything sublunary changes and varies, is mortal, then every estate of man is mortal, and the poet enumerates the estates:

On to the ded gois all Estatis,
Princis, Prelotis, and Potestatis,
Baith riche and pur of al degre:
    Timor mortis conturbat me.

He takis the campion in the stour,
The capitane closit in the tour,
The lady in bour full of bewte:
    Timor mortis conturbat me.

He sparis no lord for his piscence,
Na clerk for his intelligence;
His awfull strak may no man fie:
    Timor mortis conturbat me.

Art, magicianis, and astrologgis,
Rhetoris, logicianis, and theologgis,
Thame helpis no conclusionis sle:
    Timor mortis conturbat me.

In medicyne the most practicianis,
Lechis, surrigianis, and phisicianis,
Thame self fra ded may not supple:
    Timor mortis conturbat me.

If all estates must die, then poets too must die. And now Dunbar proceeds by a simple enumeration, a roll call, of poets:

He has done petuously devour
The noble Chaucer, of makaris flour,
The Monk of Bcry, and Gower, all thre:
    Timor mortis conturbat me.

> The gude Syr Hew of Eglintoun,
> And eik Heryot, and Wyntoun,
> He has tane out of this cuntre:
> > *Timor mortis conturbat me.*

He continues to enumerate poet after poet whom death has taken, until he comes finally to his friendly enemy, the poet, Kennedy, and to himself:

> Gud Maister Walter Kennedy
> In point of dede lyis veraly,
> Gret reuth it wer that so suld be:
> > *Timor mortis conturbat me.*

> Sen he has all my brether tane,
> He wil nocht lat me lif alane,
> Of forse I man his nyxt pray be:
> > *Timor mortis conturbat me.*

Therefore, I must die, concludes the syllogism. And now follows the practical syllogism, the act of resignation:

> Sen for the deid remeid is none,
> Best is that we for dede dispone,
> Eftir our deid that lif may we.
> > *Timor mortis conturbat me.*[10]

Almost every proposition in the poem is strictly controlled by the syllogistic structure. The exceptions are the refrain and a certain number of affective phrases and affective sentences: "He has done petuously devour / The noble Chaucer" and "Gret reuth it wer that so suld be." These direct the feeling of the poem. Yet though the poem is so completely determined by logical method and logical structure it has seemed, and justly, to generations of readers to be a moving poem and properly poetical.

I shall conclude with another poem of the same sort, a lyric of even greater renown in modern criticism. This is the song from *Summer's Last Will and Testament* by Thomas Nashe, "Adieu, farewell, earth's bliss!" It too has a refrain, though in English, a response from the Litany of Saints, which was customarily recited through the streets of London in time of plague. The poem, like Dunbar's, consists of a series of discrete, self-enclosed stanzas, in which each line is end-stopped. The structure of the poem is, like Dunbar's and Marvell's, a practical syllogism explicitly propounded, though not quite so formally as in the preceding poem. It opens with the rejection of earthly happiness. The argument is, to begin with the suppressed premise: true happiness is certain, but the world is uncertain; therefore wordly happiness is not true happiness. The world is uncertain since it is subject to the certainty of death and change. Nor can the goods of this world buy continued life, nor the art of medicine procure it: the plague increases. What is best in this life—and here we have the structure of the next three stanzas—beauty, prowess, and wit, all fade:

> Haste therefore each degree
> To welcome destiny.

For the world after death is certain, and its happiness true happiness:

Adieu, farewell, earth's bliss!
This world uncertain is:
Fond are life's lustful joys,
Death proves them all but toys.
None from his darts can fly;
I am sick, I must die—
    Lord, have mercy on us.

Rich men, trust not in wealth,
Gold cannot buy you health:
Physic himself must fade;
All things to end are made;
The plague full swift goes by;
I am sick, I must die—
    Lord, have mercy on us.

Beauty is but a flower
Which wrinkles will devour;
Brightness falls from the air;
Queens have died young and fair;
Dust hath closed Helen's eye;
I am sick, I must die—
    Lord, have mercy on us.

Strength stoops unto the grave,
Worms feed on Hector brave;
Swords may not fight with fate;
Earth still holds ope her gate;
Come, come! the bells do cry—
I am sick, I must die—
    Lord, have mercy on us.

Wit with his wantoness
Tasteth death's bitterness;
Hell's executioner
Hath no ears for to hear
What vain art can reply;
I am sick, I must die—
    Lord, have mercy on us.

Haste therefore each degree
To welcome destiny;
Heaven is our heritage;
Earth but a player's stage;
Mount we unto the sky;
I am sick, I must die—
    Lord, have mercy on us.[11]

The poem is a series of fairly literal propositions, some exactly in logical form: "This world uncertain is, All things to end are made, Queens have died young and fair, Haste therefore each degree." They are such propositions as might have been translated from the *Summa Contra Gentiles* of Thomas Aquinas, and they are located in that general tradition. St. Thomas, for instance, discusses the following questions: That human happiness does not consist in carnal pleasures; that man's happiness does not consist in glory; that man's happiness does not consist in wealth; that happiness does not consist in worldly power; that happiness does not consist in the practice of art; that man's ultimate happiness is not in this life, "for if there is ultimate happiness in this life, it will certainly be lost, at least by death."[12] But these are the propositions of Nashe's lyric, some literally, some more figuratively put.

Of the propositions in the poem, perhaps the most figurative is "Strength stoops unto the grave," which yet is fairly literal, as we see the suggestion of an aged figure bent over more and more until he is almost prone. And there are, of course, affective elements in the poem, as in "death's bitterness" and "Hell's executioner." But the special distinction of the poem and the source of an unusual quality of feeling perhaps lies in the meter as much as in anything else. The six-syllable line glides from a regular iambic pattern into a triple movement—accented, unaccented, accented—and back again as if both were its mode of being and neither had precedence over the other.

> Beauty is but a flower
> Which wrinkles will devour;
> Brightness falls from the air;
> Queens have died young and fair.

The poem in this respect belongs to a curious episode in the history of English meter; for this phenomenon appears only to my knowledge in the songs written within a fairly short period, of perhaps ten or twenty years, in the 1590s and early 1600s. Of a similar sort is Shakespeare's:

> Come away, come away, death,
>   And in sad cypress let me be laid;
> Fly away, fly away, breath;
>   I am slain by a fair cruel maid.

But the special distinction of the poem has usually been found in the line, "Brightness falls from the air." This is certainly a proposition of a different order from those we have discussed, and one that has excited the sensibilities of innumerable modern readers. It is a line in the symbolist tradition. One remembers how Stephen Dedalus in A *Portrait of the Artist as a Young Man* recalls the line, though at first in an altered form:

> She had passed through the dusk. And therefore the air was silent save for one soft hiss that fell. And therefore the tongues about him had ceased their babble. Darkness was falling.
>
> *Darkness falls from the air.*

> A trembling joy, lambent as a faint light, played like a fairy host around him. But why? Her passage through the darkening air or the verse with its black vowels and its opening sound, rich and lutelike?
>
> He walked away slowly towards the deeper shadows at the end of the colonnade, beating the stone softly with his stick to hide his revery from the students whom he had left: and allowed his mind to summon back to itself the age of Dowland and Byrd and Nashe.
>
> Eyes, opening from the darkness of desire, eyes that dimmed the breaking east. What was their languid grace but the softness of chambering? And what was their shimmer but the shimmer of the scum that mantled the cesspool of the court of a slobbering Stuart. And he tasted in the language of memory ambered wines, dying fallings of sweet airs, the proud pavan. . . .

The images he had summoned gave him no pleasure. They were secret and enflaming but her image was not entangled by them. . . .

Yes; and it was not darkness that fell from the air. It was brightness.

Brightness falls from the air.

He had not even remembered rightly Nashe's line. All the images it had awakened were false.[13]

But all the images it had awakened were false for still another reason. The line as Joyce quotes it is certainly an evocative line, a line in the symbolist tradition, and hence apt and fitted to entangle itself in revery. But it seems out of place in the poem. It is so much a line in the symbolist tradition that the historical scholar grows wary and suspicious. He turns to the text. He looks in the great modern edition of Nashe, the edition of McKerrow, and he finds that the editor records with a sigh: "It is to be hoped that Nashe meant 'ayre,' but I cannot help strongly suspecting that the true reading is 'hayre' which gives a more obvious, but far inferior, sense."[14] So we have the alternatives: "Brightness falls from the air" or "Brightness falls from the hair." But the latter is a literal account of the effect of age and death. The proposition so read is of the same order as all the other propositions in the poem, of the same order as "Queens have died young and fair." There is no doubt, then, as to the correct reading. In fact, the symbolist line, however good, is a bad line in context since it is out of keeping. And so the poem loses its last claim to modernity. It becomes a Renaissance poem. It returns to the park of logic from the forest of revery. The experience of the poem is the experience of syllogistic thinking with its consequences for feeling, attitude, and action. It is a mode of experience that the Renaissance practiced and cherished, and expressed with power, dignity, and precision. It is a poetical experience and a logical one, and it is both at once.[15]

CONVENTION AS STRUCTURE

The Prologue to the *Canterbury Tales*

A literary convention is obviously a principle of order in poetry. I shall maintain in this chapter, against the consensus of scholarly opinion, that Chaucer derives the structure of the Prologue to the *Canterbury Tales* from one of the most common of the literary conventions of his time.

The Prologue is the only one of Chaucer's major works for which there is said to be no model, no genuine antecedents in the tradition. The *Book of the Duchess,* the *House of Fame,* the *Parliament of Fowls,* and the Prologue to the *Legend of Good Women,* for example, all belong to the well-recognized tradition of the dream vision, whose history and peculiar features have been described at length in a number of standard monographs. The antecedents of the *Troilus* are well known, and Chaucer himself assigns it to the medieval category of tragedy. The shorter complaints belong to a common literary type. But the most familiar of Chaucer's works and the one generally thought to be the best seems, as a whole, to be without literary predecessors, though there are, of course, sources for particular aspects and details. This circumstance has been construed by the literary historians in Chaucer's favor. They have seen in it the triumph of originality over convention and of realism over artifice. They have pictured Chaucer going directly to reality and reporting what he found. And so the defect of literary history becomes the glory of literary criticism.

The state of the question is summarized by one scholar: "For the *Prologue,* as for the general device of the Canterbury pilgrimage, no real model has been found." Another remarks: "There had never before . . . been the like of that singularly *modern* thing—to use our most complacent term of approbation—the Prologue." And a third: "no source for" the Prologue, "the most distinctive of Chaucer's works, has ever been discovered,"[1] The features which scholarship has particularly distinguished as unprecedented are the series of portraits in the Prologue and the device of a journey, and especially of a pilgrimage, as the frame for a series of stories. For example, the scholar continues in the passage just alluded to, "No such series of descriptions [of characters] is to be found in any work of ancient or medieval literature which could have come to Chaucer's attention."[2] It is recognized, of course, that "individual sketches of knights or priests or peasants are common enough," that the "allegorical writings of the age, both sacred and secular, abound in personified types . . . some of which Chaucer clearly imitates." But the general conclusion is that "in none of his predecessors has there been found a gallery of portraits like that in the *Prologue,* and there is very little that is comparable in later English poetry except in Chaucer's avowed imitators."[3]

For the second feature—the general idea of a frame story—it is agreed that no particular model need be sought. Chaucer had already used it in the *Legend of Good Women,* and the idea was common in the tradition. For the device of a journey, and especially of a pilgrimage, there is a distant analogue in Boccaccio's *Decameron* and a closer one in a contemporary Italian work in which the tales are actually told by a single figure in the course of a journey. But the difficulty here has been that, though Chaucer could have been acquainted with these works, we have no evidence that he was. Furthermore, what has seemed to modern scholarship the special merit of Chaucer's device—the interplay of personalities on the journey—is only rudimentary in these possible models. The conclusion has been, as a recent writer on the subject puts it: "There is really no necessity to search for the 'source' of Chaucer's pilgrimage. It would, indeed, have been strange had there been no reflections in imaginative literature of the common medieval custom of going on a journey with a party of travellers."[4] This is the general opinion. "For his particular device of a group of persons on a pilgrimage to Canterbury on horseback," we are told in the standard work, "he needed only to draw on life about him. . . . Thus the device of a pilgrimage as a narrative framework was repeatedly presented to him in actual life, and he was at liberty to adopt it for his literary purpose with whatever degree of realism he found convenient."[5]

It is noteworthy that this flight to reality on the part of eminent scholars is always subsequent to a search for an antecedent of the motif and a failure to find it. This is almost too obviously making a virtue of necessity and suggests that perhaps the search for antecedents has been misconducted. It has been a search for the prior appearance of the particular motif. And when this search fails, it has been felt that the only alternative is the recourse to reality. But the alternative is as unsatisfactory as the original undertaking, for it does not explain what it pretends to explain.

The pilgrimage was undoubtedly a common occurrence in Chaucer's day, and he had in all likelihood seen a good many groups of pilgrims among whom were to be found close analogues to the characters in the Prologue. Scholars have been concerned to establish that he lived in Greenwich on the Canterbury road, where he could have seen groups of pilgrims passing before his window, perhaps while he was writing the *Canterbury Tales*. Kittredge is willing to wager he had undertaken a Canterbury pilgrimage himself.[6] The argument is that what he found day after day in real life he needed no literary precedent to invent.

But this is not so. It is not the direct observation of murders and of the process of detection that leads to the construction of a detective story. Nor was it the perception of violent death in high places that prompted the Elizabethan dramatist to compose a tragedy. What a writer finds in real life is to a large extent what his literary tradition enables him to see and to handle.

It may be conceded that experience is sometimes obtrusively at odds with tradition. We can see that it is, for we can see how tradition has been modified to render it more supple to experience. But the one term is always tradition, not unalterable but never abandoned, as, of course, the other term is always experience. The one is form, method, a way of apprehending; the other is matter, realization, and what is apprehended. What we should be concerned with, then, is to discover, if possible, a literary form extant in Chaucer's tradition of which the Prologue to the *Canterbury Tales* is a realization. It must be a form that will account not only for particular motifs, for the device of the journey or the series of portraits, but also for the other elements of the work and for their order and succession.

A literary form exists only in what I call a tradition. I use that word in the sense in which we speak of the tradition of the hard-boiled detective story or say that Shakespeare's sonnets are in the tradition of the *Astrophel and Stella* sequence or, more generally, in the Petrarchan tradition. A tradition is the body of texts and interpretations current among a group of writers at a given time and place. The description of literary traditions is a principal subject of literary history, and the nature of a tradition can be reconstructed only by the methods of literary history. If one were to construct, for example, the tradition of a number of contemporary poets in America, it could be described in terms of the poetry of Eliot, of Pound, Hopkins, Auden, and some fragments of Donne and Marvell, together with the associated body of commentary, the "new criticism." When a poet in this tradition undertakes what he has learned to distinguish as a metaphysical poem, the principles that determine the realization of what he regards as a particular literary form—the appropriate subject, devices, and structure—are principles located in that tradition.

It follows from this that a literary form is not simply an external principle of classification of literary works, as is the Dewey Decimal System in the public library, nor is it an Idea. It is rather a principal operative in the production of works. It is a scheme of experience recognized in the tradition and derived from prior works and from the descriptions of those works extant in the tradition. It is, moreover, a scheme that directs the discovery of material and detail and that orders the disposition of the whole. If a literary form is an Idea, it is an idea only in the sense that it is the idea that the writer and reader have of the form. Thus a literary form may vary somewhat from work to work, since it is only a summary description of those elements of the tradition that entered into the conception and realization as into the appreciation by a qualified reader of the particular work.

I come now to my thesis, which may as well be stated clearly and simply at the start. The literary form to which the Prologue to the *Canterbury Tales* belongs and of which it is a special realization is the form of the dream-vision prologue in the tradition of the *Romance of the Rose* and of the associated French and English poems of the subsequent century and a half. This is certainly to find the answer in the most obvious place, to find it, like the purloined letter, in plain sight. For if one were to look for the source of anything in Chaucer, the first place an experienced scholar would look is in the *Romance of the Rose* and its tradition. The *Romance,* it has been said, "probably exerted on Chaucer a more lasting and more important influence than any other work in the vernacular literature of either France or England."[7] There are throughout Chaucer innumerable borrowings in detail from that work, and four of Chaucer's most extended poems are clearly in the form of the dream vision: one of them, indeed, is explicitly a prologue framing a series of tales, as is the masterwork of Chaucer's contemporary and friend, John Gower. If one asks why the similarity of the *Canterbury* Prologue to this well-known type has not been seen before, the answer lies in the method by which the form has been described in the scholarship on the subject. It has been described in terms of particular motifs, but the motifs have not been generalized and regarded as functional in a structure. One scholar, for example, enumerates "the regular features of the love-vision": "the introductory device of reading a book, the discussion of sleeplessness and dreams, the setting on May-day or in the spring-time, the vision itself, the guide (who in many poems takes the form of a helpful animal), the personified abstractions, Love, Fortune, Nature, and the like."[8] There is only one element in this description that is also to be found in the *Canterbury* Prologue, and that is the setting in spring, an element which is common to many other literary forms in the Middle Ages.

But if we describe the *Canterbury* Prologue in terms of the scheme of experience which orders it, in terms of its elements and their succession, we will find a striking similarity to—in fact, an identity with—the scheme of the dream vision. The Prologue can be described accurately enough in this fashion: at a certain time of the year—and the season is then described—the author comes to a place, to the Tabard Inn in Southwark. He there meets a company, who are then depicted, one after the other in panel fashion. After a brief digression, one of the company, not described so far (our host, Harry Bailly), is singled out as a master of ceremonies and proposes the device that orders the remainder of the poem, the telling of tales on the journey.

I shall now describe in the same fashion the opening of the *Romance of the Rose* and of a number of English poems in the same tradition. The *Romance* begins with some expository remarks on the truth of dreams, illustrated by the dream related in this book whose name is the *Romance of the Rose* and whose subject is an autobiographical account—for everything fell out just as this dream relates—containing the art of love. After a brief prayer and praise of the lady, the dream begins. It is May, and there is an extended description of the season. The author walks out into the fields, crosses a stream, and comes to a garden inclosed by a wall. He then describes, one after the other, a series of allegorical portraits painted on the wall, ten in number. He wants to enter the garden but can find no way in. Walking around the wall, he comes finally to a wicket gate and pounds on it. The porter Idleness, "whose hair was as yellow of hue as any basin newly scoured," opens the door and leads him into the garden, which is described at length. He finds Sir Mirth dancing and singing there in company and depicts the company in a series of set portraits, fifteen in number. He then walks in the garden, followed by the God of Love with his arrows ready. The garden is leisurely described, including the well where Narcissus died, which leads to the interpolated tale of Narcissus. In the well he sees a rose bush full of roses; there is one bud in especial which he has a great longing to pluck. At this point the God of Love, who has been stalking him, looses an arrow, and the author is committed to the sentimental enterprise which directs the remainder of the poem.

These are the elements and their order: after the preliminary matter and the dream, at a given time of the year—and there is a description of the season—the author comes to a place where he sees a number of allegorical characters painted on a wall and describes them; a guide then appears and leads him to another place, where he sees a company in action, though the characters are personifications, and describes them in the same manner. There follows a framed tale, and then one of the characters initiates the action which leads to the remainder of the poem. This character is not strictly a master of ceremonies, but he might in another poem and in other hands develop into one. The form is clearly not too unlike the form of the *Canterbury* Prologue, particularly if we collapse into one movement the two instances of an author's coming to a place and substitute for allegorical characters and personifications realistic portraits of representative members of society.

In other poems of this tradition the dream-vision prologue appears now as a separable and independent form, now as an element and sometimes a repeatable element in a work of larger scope, and most commonly as an introduction to a poem that continues now in one way, now in another. It is so used in the *Confessio Amantis.* In this poem, after a discursive and sententious preface, similar to, but more extensive than, the one in the *Romance of the Rose,* the author comes to his *matere.* He walks out in May and comes to a wood, where he begins to complain of his woe and falls into a swoon. On recovering, he utters a prayer to Cupid and Venus, whereupon he sees both of them come by. The King of Love, as he passes throws an arrow through his heart, but the Queen pauses and speaks to him. On hearing what he has to say, she proposes the device: he shall confess to her priest, Genius. The essential structure of the Romance is here preserved, though in summary fashion. The nature description is quite brief, as are the descriptions of the characters. A swoon supplants the dream, and the interpolated prayer, an element in the opening of the *Romance,* occasions the appearance of the figures. Nevertheless, the author goes out at a certain time of the year and comes to a place where he sees figures riding by, one of whom proposes the device that directs the remainder of the poem.

The scheme of the vision is repeated, this time without the dream, in the course of one of the tales that form the bulk of Gower's work. This is the tale of Rosiphelee.[9] Before dawn on a May morning she walks out in a park through which runs a great river. She bids her women withdraw. She sees the flowers blooming, hears the birds singing, and sees all the animals, male paired with the female. As she looks around, she sees a company of ladies riding by, whose dress is then described. She wonders who they are and then sees a woman on a horse, who is described at length. She questions her about the company of ladies and receives the answer which changes the course of her life. Here is the typical nature description, the character who comes to a place where he sees a company, and, finally, the master of ceremonies, who disposes the particular device of this poem. And in this case it is no dream.

So much for Gower. Chaucer himself had written, if we allow the accepted chronology of his work, four dream visions by the time he undertook the Prologue to the *Canterbury Tales;* indeed, while he was engaged in the composition of the *Tales,* he rewrote with considerable thoroughness the last of these, the Prologue to the *Legend.* The earliest, the *Book of the Duchess,* begins with preliminary matter on the melancholy and sleeplessness of the author, who reads a book to pass the time, the tale of Ceyx and Alcyone. At one point in the tale Alcyone prays to Juno for sleep and a dream, and the author decides to try the same method, whereupon he falls asleep and dreams. It is a May morning, with birds singing. He finds himself in a room with glass windows and full of pictures depicting the whole story of Troy and the whole *Romance of the Rose,* both text and gloss. He hears the sound of hunters, rises, takes his horse, and comes to a field, where he overtakes a great company of hunters. He inquires of one of them, "Who is hunting here?" and is told the Emperor Octavian. He follows the chase. When the hunt ends, he walks from a tree and follows a whelp into a field full of flowers, where he becomes aware of a man in black. This is the figure that introduces the device of the poem.

The *House of Fame* is a poem in the same tradition. It begins with preliminary matter similar to that in the *Romance* and the *Book of the Duchess,* a poem on dreams and an invocation. It continues with the dream. Exactly on the tenth of December— there is in this case no description of the season—the author falls asleep and in a dream finds himself in a temple made of glass. There are many images there, finely wrought portraits, among them one of Venus, "naked fleeting in a sea," of Cupid, and of Vulcan, "that in his face was full brown." As the dreamer walks about, he sees on the wall the story of the *Aeneid,* portrayed in a series of panels. These are described at length, one after the other—"There saw I," "There saw I"—in a manner and in a position in the scheme of the poem analogous to the portraits on the wall in the *Romance* or the portraits of the pilgrims at the Tabard. The author then leaves the temple, finds himself in a barren desert, looks up to heaven in prayer, and becomes aware of an eagle larger than any he has ever seen. The eagle is the figure who disposes the device which accounts for the remainder of the poem.

I come now to the Prologue to the *Legend of Good Women.* The later of the two versions is more relevant to our purpose, since it is closer in form to the scheme of the *Canterbury* Prologue, though the differences between the versions are not sufficient to call for separate treatment. The poem begins with preliminary matter, in this case of exceptional distinction, and then the poet late in the month of May falls asleep and dreams. He finds himself in a field—"With floures sote embrouded was it al"—where "The smale foules, of the seson fayn" sing a hymn to St. Valentine. There appear the God of Love and his Queen, Alceste, whose dress in particular is described at some length. Behind the god the author sees nineteen ladies in royal dress, and after them an extraordinary number of women. There follows the action which leads to the device: the King and especially the Queen as masters of ceremonies impose on the author the task of writing a series of tales of true lovers as penance for his heresy in love.

The underlying scheme of the dream-vision prologue should now be clear. If we set aside the preliminary matter as not relevant to the form of the *Canterbury* Prologue and begin, as it does, after the dream, we will find the following elements in this order. The poem is set at a given time of the year, generally in May, but perhaps exactly on the tenth of December, or sometime in the latter part of April, as the astrology of the *Canterbury* Prologue indicates. The time of the year leads in many cases to a description of the season, which may be brief or leisurely, simple or, as in the case of the *Canterbury* Prologue, ornate, with elements drawn from the introductory nature descriptions of other literary forms. The author, usually as the dreamer, is a character in his own poem, though when the scheme is used in a narrative, as in the tale of Rosiphelee, the principal character takes the place of the author. He comes to a place, usually a field, but sometimes a chamber or temple of glass, and in one case the Tabard in Southwark. He sees there a company, or occasionally one or two persons, and sometimes some birds who are treated as characters. Or he sees a number of portraits depicted on a wall, or incidents in a famous story, and then, after another journey, comes to a company. These may be described at length, one after another, in panel fashion, or they may, especially if the material is common in the tradition, be briefly and summarily denominated. At this point, or after another journey, or, as in the case of the *Canterbury* Prologue, after a brief digression, one of the company or another character who is now met—the man in black or Harry Bailly— initiates the action of the poem. This may consist, as in the Prologue to the *Legend* and the Prologue to the *Canterbury Tales,* in proposing the relation of a series of tales.

But the *Canterbury Tales* extend beyond the Prologue. Is there any precedent in the tradition for the particular way in which Chaucer proceeds to develop the poem? Of course, there is precedent in the *Legend* and in Gower for the framed tales, but I have in mind something more definite and limited than this. I have in mind the problem of the principles of order in the work as a whole, of which the idea of the frame story is only one. I have in mind a very restricted question: Is there in the tradition or in those realizations of the tradition that Chaucer had already accomplished any scheme of development from the dream-vision prologue that is similar to the development in the *Canterbury Tales*?

The whole problem of the construction of the *Canterbury Tales* is a vexed and difficult one. The work as it has come down to us consists of a number of fragments, each disjoined from the others and each consisting of several tales and of the prologues to and links between the tales. The general Prologue, for instance, is followed by three tales with the links between them and breaks off abruptly, shortly after the beginning of a fourth tale. This section is usually called the "A Fragment." I will concern myself only with this.

It is clear from the state of the manuscripts, then, that the project was never one that was complete in design though incomplete in execution. The design itself was in a fluid state. The general outlines of the framework were perhaps clear: it would involve a pilgrimage, and the completion of the journey would coincide with the completion of the design. The characters of most of the pilgrims, at least, were determined. There was to be a leader of the party, the Host, whose word was law. Each pilgrim was to tell a given number of tales, and the tales he told were to accord with his rank and nature according to the ancient principles of decorum. But within what was already determined there was much that was indeterminate, especially the principle or congeries of principles that would determine the succession of speakers and tales.

What principles had Chaucer? He begins with the principle of lots which could have served to order the whole, but he uses it only to determine the first speaker. Again, the principle of lots, whether by chance, by Providence guiding chance, or by the manipulation of the Host, serves to pick out the man of highest rank in the company as the first to speak. This again would have served as a sufficient principle; the order of precedence in society could have determined the order of precedence in the telling of tales, and the Host, who was a proper man to be a marshal in a hall, could easily have settled the questions of etiquette. But this principle breaks down immediately after the Knight's tale. The Host calls on the Monk, who would probably be considered next in social rank, to relate something that will fit in with the Knight's tale. But the Miller, who is a churl and will abide no man for courtesy, cries out in Pilate's voice, "I know a noble tale with which I will repay the Knight's." His tale, of course, is just the opposite: it is an ignoble tale of churls and obscenity rather than a noble tale of princes and high love.

Is there any precedent for this in the tradition? There is, in the scheme of experience of a dream vision which Chaucer wrote some years before this, the *Parliament of Fowls*.[10] In that poem, after the customary preliminary matter, the author falls asleep and dreams. A guide leads him to a spring scene, a garden full of birds and trees, where he sees Cupid and Will, his daughter, and many other allegorical figures and a temple of brass with more figures inside it and the story of many famous lovers painted on the wall. He walks forth again from this place and comes on the figure who disposes the device that orders the rest of the poem. This is Nature, who is holding a parliament of birds on St. Valentine's Day. The birds are then summarily described. Nature opens the parliament and stipulates that the birds shall speak in order of rank; and so they do until suddenly the lower orders break out, crying. "Have don, and lat us wende! . . . Whan shal youre cursede pietying have an ende?" The subject has been high courtly love, and now the vulgar point of view is urged by a vigorous churlish personality amid a certain amount of general uproar. Obviously, the scheme of progression at the beginning of the *Canterbury Tales* is similar in these general respects to the scheme of the *Parliament of Fowls*. It is not only the form of the Prologue that derives from the dream vision, but from the particular scheme of a particular dream vision that Chaucer had written some time before derives the underlying principle of order of the A Fragment as a whole. In both, the master of ceremonies, by stipulation and by lot, appoints the highest in rank to speak first. The discourse is on high courtly love. It is interrupted by the lower orders of society who urge a vulgar point of view, and there follows strife among the churls. This is developed in the A Fragment by a new principle, the principle of retaliation. The Miller tells a tale about a carpenter, and the Reeve, who had been a carpenter, answers with a tale about a miller. The Cook offers to go on in this vein, begins, and the fragment breaks off. It is open to question whether or not in this instance the form of the dream vision itself broke down, whether or not it was inadequate to handle the material which Chaucer wished to explore by its means. But it does not seem to me open to question that the form of the Prologue and indeed of the A Fragment is, if we understand by a "literary form" the method by which material is discovered and ordered, the form of the dream vision in whose terms Chaucer himself had learned to feel and think through many years of love and apprenticeship.

The identity of the literary form of the Prologue to the *Canterbury Tales* with the conventional form of the dream-vision prologue can be regarded as established. It may be felt, however, that the distinctive feature of the *Canterbury* Prologue—the series of portraits—has not adequately been accounted for. No one, I trust, will ask one to account for the greatness of Chaucer's portraits, for his peculiar skill in writing. If such matters can be explained, certainly they lie outside the scope and method of this chapter. The question is rather, I should say, Is the technique of portraiture in the dream-vision convention of the same kind as Chaucer's technique in the Prologue? It is. The model in the tradition—and the model to which Chaucer recurred here—is the double series of portraits at the opening of the *Romance of the Rose,* the portraits that occupy the same place in the scheme of that poem as Chaucer's do in the scheme of his.[11]

I would distinguish several points of similarity of technique in the portraits themselves and two further points in their connection with the remainder of the poem. The portraits are given in succession in both poems, without transition or with the most summary form of transition: "And next was peynted Covetise,"

"Eide was paynted after this," "And alderlast of everychon / Was peynted Povert al aloon," "And next hir wente, on hir other side," "Love hadde with hym a bacheler." Chaucer's technique is similar: "With hym there was his sone, a yong squier, / A lovyere and a lusty bacheler," "A Monk ther was." There are a number of such portraits, a group of ten and of fifteen in the *Romance* and twenty-one in the Prologue, plus the five guildmen who are treated as a unit and several others who are just named. The portraits are of varying length, but they vary roughly within the same range: in the *Romance* they run from four to ninety-six lines, averaging around thirty-two; in the Prologue they run from nine to sixty-two lines, averaging around thirty-one. The peculiar coincidence in the averages, of course, is of no significance. The portraits in each are introduced by brief critical remarks in which the terms derive from the medieval arts of poetry. The second series in the *Romance* begins (I quote the medieval translation of the poem which is often ascribed to Chaucer):

> Then gan I loken ofte sithe
> The shap, the bodies, and the cheres,
> The countenaunce and the maneres
> Of alle the folk that daunced there,
> And I shal telle you what they were.[12]

Chaucer begins with an explicit remark, "Me thynketh it accordaunt to resoun," that is, *secundum rationem,* in accordance with the law of the kind. He begins the Complaint of Mars with a similar remark, indicating an awareness of the requirements of a literary kind:

> The ordre of compleynt requireth shylfully.

He proceeds:

> Me thynketh it accordaunt to resoun
> To telle you al the condicioun
> Of ech of hem, so as it semed me,
> And which they weren, and of what degree,
> And eek in what array that they were inne.

These are the principal technical correspondences. But one might observe further that the method in both poems is one that allows not only objective presentation and analysis but also author's comment and that the portraits in both contain a good deal of sharp realistic detail of the same type. For example, of Hate:

> Hir heed ywrithen was, iwis,
> Full grimly with a greet towayle.

Avarice is clad

> Al in an old torn courtepy
> As she were all with doggis torn.[13]

There are two further points that concern the relation of the portraits to the remainder of the poem. The first is that at least some of the characters described act and interact as the poem goes on—this is obvious in the *Canterbury Tales* but is also true in some measure of the *Romance*. The second is that the author who describes these characters as an external observer becomes involved in action with them.

In brief, the technical features of the portraits in the *Canterbury* Prologue have exact analogues in the portraits of the *Romance*. There are in each a number of portraits of moderate length, containing realistic detail, introduced by critical remarks, described by the author in his own person, and presented one after another with the minimum of transition, as in the description of a panel of portraits on a wall. If a composition instructor were to assign the portraits in the *Romance* as a model for imitation and stipulate that the method there exhibited be applied to a range of figures from contemporary society, his better students would produce a series of characters not too unlike the series in the Prologue. And if he should extend his assignment to the whole scheme of the opening portion of the *Romance* and of the associated poems in the tradition, the result could well be the Prologue to the *Canterbury Tales*.

In these terms the development of Chaucer's career becomes intelligible. We must give up the naive conclusion of literary criticism and literary scholarship that in his earlier work Chaucer had yielded "with docility to medieval schematism" and then suddenly broke "with all such rigid notions of order." We can no longer say, as a recent writer on the subject does, that "one of the most astonishing things about the *Canterbury Tales* is that Chaucer, a courtly artist, steeped in French, Latin, and Italian models, chose as a framework a direct departure from them. He did not have to go to sleep and dream in order to get started . . ."[14] For Chaucer did not simply go to reality; he apprehended reality by the means he had learned and cultivated. He was original and traditional at the same time, and his originality lay in the application to fresh material of the old method—new wine in the old bottle. He brought to life a tradition that had grown, perhaps, too contrived, though the Prologue to the *Legend* is an exquisite thing of its kind. But he brought it to life within the framework of the tradition. He was an artist, and he worked by artifice for he knew that realism is artifice.

IDEA AS STRUCTURE

The Phoenix & Turtle

I am concerned in this chapter with another of the principles of order that determine the structure and detail of a poem. This is the use of some field or system of ideas in the writer's tradition which serves as a scheme or paradigm by which material of another order is apprehended and expounded. I have already appropriated in an earlier essay the term "conceit" for this procedure. Here I shall show how the material of courtly love in Shakespeare's *The Phoenix and Turtle* is treated in terms of scholastic theology.

I

The characteristic feature of scholasticism for our purpose is its terminology. The whole system, in fact, may be said to be implicit in the definition of its terms, as in our own times the systems of clinical psychology are implicit in such terms as "regression," "libido," "flight from reality," and "inferiority complex." Consequently, if we find that Shakespeare uses such a scholastic term as "essence" in its technical sense and in a technical context, we may presume not only that he was acquainted with scholastic notions but also that he was capable of thinking and feeling in those terms.

"Essence" occurs three times in Shakespeare. It appears in a well-known passage in *Measure for Measure*:

> Merciful heaven,
> Thou rather with thy sharp and sulphurous bolt
> Split'st the unwedgeable and gnarled oak
> Than the soft myrtle. But man, proud man,
> Drest in a little brief authority,
> Most ignorant of what he's most assur'd
> (His glassy essence), like an angry ape,
> Plays such fantastic tricks before high heaven
> As make the angels weep.
>
> 2.2.114-22

This is the scholastic notion in a scholastic context: man's essence is his intellectual soul, which is an image of God, and hence is "glassy" for it mirrors God. "Glassy" is used in this sense in *Hamlet:*

> There is a willow grows aslant a brook,
> That shows his hoar leaves in the glassy stream.
>
> 4. 7. 168-69

and in *1 Henry VI:*

> As plays the sun upon the glassy streams,
> Twinkling another counterfeited beam.
>
> 5. 3. 62-63

The full context of the notion here involved is given in the following passage from Ralegh's *History of the World:*

But man, to cover his own ignorance in the least things . . . that is ignorant of the essence of his own soul, and which the wisest of the naturalists, (if Aristotle be he) could never so much as define, but by the action and effect, telling us what it works, (which all men know as well as he,) but not what it is, which neither he, nor anyone else, doth know, but God that created it; (*for though I were perfect, yet I know not my soul,* saith Job;)—man, I say, that is but an idiot in the next cause of his own life, and in the cause of all the actions of his life, will, notwithstanding, examine the art of God in creating the world.[1]

"Glassy essence" is, of course, a sharp poetic phrase. But there is no need to fuse the denotation of the adjective "glassy" with connotations which are not exacted by the noun it qualifies in order to render it poetic. "Brittleness," "clarity," and "pellucidness" may be charming notions but they are inaccurate in context and beside the point. It is not irrelevance that makes a phrase poetic. Shakespeare's is poetic in that it initiates a moment's reflection and invites the energy of a linguistic inference by which one sees that the phrase means "image of God" through the ascending aspect of imaging rather than through the more customary descending aspect of being imaged.

"Essence" is also used technically in Valentine's speech about Silvia in the *Two Gentlemen of Verona:*

And why not death rather than living torment?
To die is to be banish'd from myself;
And Silvia is myself. Banish'd from her
Is self from self—a deadly banishment!

What light is light, if Silvia be not seen?
What joy is joy, if Silvia be not by?
Unless it be to think that she is by
And feed upon the shadow of perfection.
Except I be by Silvia in the night,
There is no music in the nightingale.
Unless I look on Silvia in the day,
There is no day for me to look upon.
She is my essence, and I leave to be
If I be not by her fair influence
Foster'd, illumin'd, cherish'd, kept alive.

3. 1. 170-84

The speech begins on a relatively human level, for the assertion that Silvia is myself and the question, "What light is light, if Silvia be not seen?" may both be taken sufficiently metaphorically. Nevertheless, Silvia is designated as perfection, for to imagine her present when she is absent is to feed upon the shadow, the image, of perfection. If she were here one would be in the presence of perfection. However, when a Christian of Elizabeth's time comes right down to it, there is only one true perfection, God, and only one set of terms in which to discuss it, the theological language of the Schools. And it is precisely in these terms that Valentine speaks. His language and thought are those, for example, of Hooker, except that Silvia is substituted for God:

> God hath his influence into the very essence of all things, without which influence of Deity supporting them their utter annihilation could not choose but follow. Of him all things have both received their first being and their continuance to be that which they are. All things are therefore partakers of God,

they are his offspring, his influence is in them. . . . Otherwise, how should the same wisdom be that which supporteth, beareth up, and sustaineth all. . . .

So that all things which God hath made are in that respect the offspring of God, they are *in him* as effects in their highest cause, he likewise actually is *in them,* the assistance and influence of his Deity is *their life.*

5. 56.5[2]

Silvia, consequently, is regarded as perfection, as Love in the absolute sense, as the ultimate principle of the lover's being, as that by which he is fostered, illumined, cherished, sustained. She is God. She is immanent and transcendent, and the lover's relation to her is that of scholastic creature to scholastic Creator. Apart from the blasphemy involved, there is only one difficulty in the passage: this resides in the proposition, "She is my essence." The proposition is technically incorrect with regard to the relation of creature and Creator in the scholastic system, *for* it is manifestly false to say that the soul is of the substance of God. Although the soul is a simple form in its essence, it is not its own being but is a being by participation.

Therefore, it is not pure act like God (*ST,* 1.90.1.c. and ad 2).[3] For man is made to the image and likeness of God, but "the preposition *to* signifies only a certain approach, as of something at a distance." (*ST,* 1. 93. 1)[4]

Valentine's relation to Silvia, it is true, conforms in general to the centuries-old scheme of courtly love; the lover is to the beloved as vassal to lord, of if the scheme be construed in Neo-Platonic terms, as it often was, as shadow to substance or as image to archetype. But the commonest and most available source of

Neo-Platonic ideas in the sixteenth century was the scholastic doctrine of the Christian God, who is only protected from utter Neo-Platonism by an unceasing vigilance in qualification. If one abandons the qualification, locates the infinite Idea in the finite beloved, maintains the theological language of the Schools regarding God's immanence and ceaseless providence and yet ascribes all reality to the Idea to the extent that the lover's essence is the Idea, he arrives at this passage. It is worldly Neo-Platonism, precipitated out of the latent Neo-Platonism of Christian dogma. However, there remain two difficulties for anyone familiar with these schemes of thought: 1) the analogical relationship of the derived and Underived is contradicted by the predication of identity of essence, and 2) the identity of essence takes the special form that the essence of the derived *is* the Underived.

II

The difficulties can be understood and their source located in the light of the third passage in Shakespeare in which "essence" occurs. The passage is found in his "poetical essay" on "the former subject, viz., the Turtle and Phoenix," one of a group of poems on this theme "by the best and chiefest of our modern writers"[5] which was appended to Robert Chester's *Loves Martyr* (1601). The poem represents a memorial service for The Phoenix and Turtle, the beloved and lover, and is divided into three parts. In the first part the poet appoints "the bird of loudest Jay" as Herald, the swan as Celebrant, and the "treble-dated crow" as one of the mourners, and interposes an interdict against the presence of certain others. There follows the anthem, with which we will be concerned, in which is stated the relationship of the lovers:

So they lov'd as love in twain
Had the essence but in one.

Reason concludes the poem by pronouncing a threne over the
urn where their cinders lie, to the effect that Beauty and Truth,
Love and Constancy, in their ideal forms are now dead:

Leaving no posterity:
'Twas not their infirmity,
It was married chastity.

There are a number of problems here, some integral to the
text and some only associated with it, but nevertheless trouble-
some. The characters in the poem, for example, are birds, and
the ordinary Elizabethan expectation would be that they repre-
sent persons in the situation the poem derives from and refers
to, but who they are is unknown, and the situation can only be
inferred from the text. It is apparently a poem with a key, and
the key has been lost. Read with a certain literal-mindedness,
and this is generally a good way to read poetry, it would appear
to commemorate the more or less simultaneous deaths of a mar-
ried couple who had taken and kept vows of marital chastity, and
hence in all likelihood were Recusants.[6] But Time and Chance
have destroyed or mislaid the evidence, with the consequence
that the uncertainty of reference imputes, illegitimately perhaps,
a kind of uncertainty to the poem as a whole.

And a similar uncertainty arises from the literary context of
the poem. It is one of a series of poems, signed by Vatum Chorus,
Ignoto, Shakespeare, Marston, Chapman, and Jonson, and ded-
icated to the recently knighted Sir John Salusbury of Lleweni.
What is clear from the text is that the poems were severally

271

written on a theme propounded to the poets and do not refer to a common situation. Both Marston and Jonson make this clear. In Shakespeare's, the first of the poems on the theme, the birds die without issue. Marston in the poem that follows Shakespeare's begins with a direct comment: "O 'twas a movin epicedium!" and then proceeds by inquiring, "can blackest Fate consume / So rare creation? No . . . Then look. For see what glorious issue . . . now springs from yonder flame." In brief, his poem is on a different situation, has another reference: in this case there is posterity. Jonson in his turn begins: "We must sing too? What subject shall we choose?" That is, clearly it is a command performance. And characteristically he asserts that there could not be

> A beauty of that merit that should take

> Our Muse up by commission. No, we bring
> Our own true fire. Now our thought takes wing,
> And now an Epode to deep ears we sing.[7]

And he copies out a poem he had had around the house for some time.[8] But beyond this it is difficult to go, though there is enough partial evidence available on the literary situation in 1601 so that a patient and divining spirit may some day make it all clear, particularly if he finds more evidence.

We are concerned, however, only with the central part of the poem, which states clearly, technically, and reiteratively the relationship of the lovers, and here there is no uncertainty:

> Here the anthem doth commence:
> Love and constancy is dead,
> Phoenix and the turtle fled
> In a mutual flame from hence.

So they lov'd as love in twain
Had the essence but in one;
Two distincts, division none:
Number there in love was slain.

Hearts remote, yet not asunder;
Distance, and no space was seen
'Twixt this turtle and his queen;
But in them it were a wonder.

So between them love did shine
That the turtle saw his right
Flaming in the phoenix's sight:
Either was the other's mine.

Property was thus appalled,
That the self was not the same;
Single nature's double name
Neither two nor one was called.

Reason, in itself confounded,
Saw division grow together,
To themselves yet either neither,
Simple were so well compounded;

That it cried, How true a twain
Seemeth this concordant one!
Love hath reason, reason none,
If what parts can so remain.

Here is stated in exact, technical, scholastic language the relationship of the lovers. They are Love and Constancy, Beauty and Truth, Phoenix and Turtle. The nature of their love was such that love in each had the essence (the defining principle by which anything that is, is what it is) only in one. Obviously, then, the effect of their love was unitive. But in what way? in terms of what scheme of ideas is this union conceived? Let us examine the possibilities. It is not unlike, of course, the Neo-Platonic union, in which the soul, being reduced to the trace of the One which constitutes its resemblance to it, is absorbed, submerged, and lost in the presence of the One. There is no more distance, no doubleness; the two fuse in one.[9]

But the language here is Latin and has passed, as had the doctrine of Plotinus, through the disputations of the Schoolmen: *essence, distincts, division, property, single nature's double name, simple, compounded.* Furthermore, the chief point of Shakespeare's poem is lost in the Plotinan formulation: for the central part of the poem consists wholly in the reiteration—line after line as if the poet would have you understand even to exhaustion—of the paradox that though identical the two are distinct; they are both truly one and truly two. Thus, for example, in the Plotinan union there is no interval between the two—"And no space was seen"—but the contrary clement of the paradox—"distance"—is lacking.

The language and the ideas of the poem, then, are technical and scholastic. But is this the scholastic doctrine of love? Is the scheme of thought here of the same order as the material of the poem? The doctrine of Thomas Aquinas on this point is sufficiently representative of the scholastic position. Love, he tells us (he is quoting the Neo-Platonist, the Pseudo-Dionysius), is a unitive force. The manner of this union, the way in which the beloved can be said to be in the lover, can be comprehended by an analogy. For just as when someone understands something there is a certain notion of the thing in the man who understands, so when someone loves something there is a certain impress, so to speak, of what is loved in the feeling of the lover, and with reference to this one can say that what is loved is in the lover as what is understood is in him who understands. (*ST,* 1. 37. 1) But union in this sense by no means amounts to absolute identification; it is not possible to say according to this account that she is my essence.

St. Thomas in another place distinguishes a three-fold sense in which union is related to love. There is the union which is the cause of love, and this is a genuine and substantial union with respect to one's love of himself; it is a union based on similitude with respect to one's love of others. Secondly, there is that union which is essentially love itself, and which involves a certain conformation of feeling toward the object, (see *ST,* 1-2, 28. 5) If this is the love of friendship, the nature of the relationship is similar to the substantial union spoken of above, for the lover loves the other as himself; if it is the love of desire, he loves the other as something that belongs to him. There is, finally, a third kind of union which is an effect of love, and that is that union of the parties involved which the lover seeks of the loved. This union is in accordance with the demands of love, for, as Aristotle says in the *Politics* (2. 4. 1262b11, "Aristophanes said that lovers desire from being two to become one," but since "the result of this would be to destroy either one of them or both," they seek a suitable and proper union, namely to live and speak together and to be joined in other ways of this nature. (*ST,* 1-2. 28. 1 ad 2)

From this much it is clear how carefully St. Thomas distinguishes and how painstakingly he points out that the effect of union in love, together with those other related effects which he goes on to discuss—a mutual inherence of one in the other, an ecstatic going out of oneself, and a zealousness in appropriating the good which one loves (1-2. 28. 2-4)—only take place in a certain sense. The love of desire, it is true, does not rest with attaining any external or surface enjoyment of what it loves, but seeks to possess it absolutely, penetrating as if to the very heart of the beloved. (1-2. 28. 2) But it is only *as if.* For human love admits of no real identification. Though we desire it, if it were attained, one or both would be destroyed.

In Shakespeare's poem, however, the lover is identified with the beloved; the beloved is his essence; they become one and yet neither is annihilated. The lovers are of course destroyed in that they have passed in a mutual flame from this life, but clearly they have only passed into the real life of Ideas from the unreal life of materiality.

It might be suspected, looking back on the passage in the *Two Gentlemen of Verona,* that the relation implied here is that of the Beatific Vision, in which our love of God and God's love for us finds its ultimate fulfillment. If this were so it would certainly offer us what we are looking for. It would offer us a model or paradigm by means of which the relationship of the lovers in this poem is constructed and construed. But though the doctrine of the Beatific Vision be thorny and difficult to understand, nevertheless one thing is clear: even in that last eternal embrace, in which, no longer through a glass darkly, we see the essence of God face to face (*ST,* 1. 12. 1: "We shall see Him as He is." 1 John 3: 2), there is no absolute identification of essence. St. Thomas makes this clear in the following passage, which I translate paraphrastically in order to render it as easy as possible to the uninitiated (italics mine):

Since some form is required in any cognition by which the object can be cognized or seen, there is required for the cognition of separated substances nothing less than the separated substance itself which is conjoined to our intellect as the form, being both the object and the means of understanding. In fact, whether this apply or not to other separated substances, it behooves us to accept that mode of understanding as applying to the vision of God through His essence, because in no other way could we be conducted to the divine essence. *But this explanation is not to be taken in the sense that the divine essence is really the form of our intellect, or that there results an absolute unity from the fusion of the divine essence and our intellect,* as is the case with form and matter in natural, as distinguished from supernatural, things. Rather, there is a proportion of the divine essence to our intellect on the analogy of form to matter. For, whenever there are two things in the same receptacle, of which one is more perfect than the other, they maintain a proportionate relationship of the more perfect to the less perfect, like that of form to matter.

3. 92. 1. c. sub fin.

III

But anything is forgiven a lover, the reader may exclaim at this point, even the grossest hyperbole. Perhaps this is so; our present business, however, is simply with interpreting a text. Now, if anything be clear in the history of the lyric, it is that *The Phoenix and Turtle,* whatever its merits, is not a gracious and charming trifle, and could not have been intended as such. One half of the poem consists of a grimly reiterated paradox, stated with the minimum of decoration and the maximum of technical exactitude. The inference is that the poet was trying to say something precisely, and this lays on us the obligation, if we wish to read the poem at all, of trying to find out precisely what he was saying.

The doctrine of the poem is not sanctioned by the scholastic doctrine of human love, nor indeed, so far as I know, by the facts of nature. It is not sanctioned by the doctrine of the Beatific Vision. Is there a source in the tradition from which is derived the structure of thought and the technical terms by which it is displayed? There is, in fact, only one model in the tradition for the notion that distinct persons may have only one essence, and that is the doctrine of the Trinity. Not, of course, the Incarnation, for the two Natures (or Essences) of Christ are distinct. (*ST,* 3. 2) The relation of lover and beloved in Shakespeare's poem is that of the Persons of the Trinity, and the technical language employed is that of scholastic discussion on the subject. With this clue, all the difficulties of the expository part of the poem are resolved, and if it still remains difficult to understand, it is no more difficult than the Trinity.

The principal point of the doctrine of the Trinity in this connection is summed up in Hooker's *Laws of Ecclesiastical Polity:*

> The Persons of the Godhead, by reason of the unity of their substance, do as necessarily remain one within another, as they are of necessity to be distinguished one from another. . . . And sith they all are but one God in number, one indivisible essence or substance, their distinction cannot possibly admit separation. . . . Again, sith all things accordingly love their offspring as themselves are more or less

contained in it, he which is thus the only-begotten, must needs be in this degree the only-beloved of the Father. He therefore which is in the Father by eternal derivation of being and life from him, must needs be in him through an eternal affection of love.

5. 56. 2-3

The Father and Son are distinct persons, yet one essence. Furthermore, as the learned Doctors tells us, the Son proceeds from the Father by way of the intellect in that he is the Father's understanding of Himself; and the Holy Ghost proceeds from both by way of the will in that He is the mutual love of both. But when anyone understands and loves himself, he is in himself not only through the identity of the subject, but also in the way in which what is understood is in the one who understands, and what is loved is in the lover. Thus the Holy Ghost, who proceeds from the reciprocal relation of the Father and Son, is a distinct person, but is at the same time the bond between Them, inasmuch as He is Love (*ST*, 1. 37. 1. c and ad 3):

> So they lov'd as love in twain
> Had the essence but in one.

In the next line—"Two distincts, division none"—the terminology is obviously scholastic, and its context is the doctrine of the Trinity. "To avoid the Arian heresy," St. Thomas says, "we must avoid the terms *diversity* and *difference* so as not to take away the unity of essence; we can, however, use the term *distinction* . . . So also to avoid taking away the simplicity of the divine essence we must avoid the terms *separation* and *division,* which apply to parts of a whole. . . . (*ST,* 1. 31. 2.)

"Number there in love was slain," for plurality is always the consequence of a division, as St. Thomas points out; but the division of a continuum from which springs number, which is a species of quantity, is found only in material things. But number in this sense cannot be applied to God. When numerical terms are used they signify only the things of which they are said, and so we may say one essence, signifying only the essence undivided, and many persons, signifying only those persons and the undividedness of each. (*ST,* 1. 30. 3) "Hearts remote, yet not asunder" repeats the central paradox. "Distance, and no space was seen"; the Son is co-eternal with the Father in order of time (1. 42. 2) and hence in order of space. (1. 42. 1., and see 1. 81. ad 3.) "But in them [and in God!] it were a wonder."

The next stanzas are based on the scholastic distinction of *proprium* and *alienum:* what is proper is what belongs to the one, but not to the other; what is alien is what belongs to the other, but not to the one. The terms are contraries, and exclude each other. But in the Trinity the relations which constitute the three Persons are their several Properties. Though property is the same as person, yet in the Father and the Son, as there is one essence in the two persons, so also there is one property in the two persons. (*ST,* 1. 40. 1.) So also in *The Phoenix and Turtle:* love so shone between them (and Love is the relationship of the Father and the Son in the Holy Ghost—1. 37. 2) that the one saw what belonged to him ("his right": *suum proprium*) in the sight of the other; but the other's sight was the instrument by which the second saw reciprocally what belonged to him in the sight of the first. Each was the other's "mine": *meum.* No wonder "Property was thus appalled": for "property" is the personification of *proprium.*

"Single nature's double name": Each of the Persons of the Trinity has His proper name, yet they are all of one nature, one essence (1. 13; 1. 33. 2; 1. 34. 1-2; 1. 36. 1; and especially 1. 39. 2-7), and the name *God* stands of itself for the common nature—hence, "Neither two nor one was called."

"Reason, in itself confounded,"—for reason is the principle of distinction and its method is division—"Saw division grow together"; each of the two was distinct ("To themselves"), yet neither one of them was one or the other ("yet either neither"). And the last line of this stanza repeats again the same paradox, and again by one of the common scholastic dichotomies: "Simple were so well compounded." Any separated substance is simple; thus the Phoenix and the Turtle are simples, but are so compounded as to form a simple. Hence, at the final recapitulation of the paradox, Reason confesses its inadequacy to deal with the mystery of love: "Love has reason, reason none / If what parts" can remain unparted ("can so remain").

The relation of the Phoenix to the Turtle is now clear. It is conceived and expressed in terms of the scholastic doctrine of the Trinity, which forms in this sense the principle of order of the poem. The Phoenix and Turtle are distinct persons, yet one in love, on the analogy of the Father and the Son in the Holy Ghost. If the reader does not immediately understand this mystery, the point of the poem is that it is a mystery at which Reason is confounded and confesses that true Reason is above it and is Love.[10]

PLOTS & ERRORS

Hamlet & *King Lear*

We read some works, even literary ones, coldly for what they are, as we read a menu or a casual novel. But not works of prestige. These we approach differently, under one of two kinds of context. Some we read possessively; they are the favorites of a group, whether socially broad or narrow. They are Works of Fashion. We come to them, either initially or in time, with a prepared attitude and verify that attitude in rehearsing the text. There is, for example, within the academic community that consistent and repetitive attitude toward the more popular works of Chaucer which may be called the Chuckle School of Criticism, or "Good old Chaucer." There is, more narrowly, the attitude toward Statius's *To Sleep* illustrated in an earlier essay, or the dominance of the Eliot gloss in our experience of Marvell's *To His Coy Mistress.* In each case there is a possessiveness of the group toward the text and a limitation of the experience of the text to the form of the prevailing gloss. It is a fixed point from which raids are made on the detail of the work.

But with such texts as *Hamlet* and *King Lear,* though antecedent glosses do in part direct our experience, as it is only human they should, there is something else involved. These are texts of a special sort in our society. They are not simply works of prestige: they are Scripture. They are much more than works; they are iron magnets for innumerable filings. And they must, in our society at least, be serious, if not solemn; they must engage our humanity. When we come to interpretations we do not simply interpret a text but rather attempt to order a massed experience of discussion, quotation, and concern that has a ghostly yet substantial existence distinct from the page. This constitutes a field, comparable to, or almost of the same kind as, the field out of which in one of the current modes of composition a poem is precipitated. There is involved a process of divination and emotional accommodation. The result must come together; it must satisfy. In the case of Scripture it must satisfy by attaining a unity ordered by the modes of our own emotional life and by alluding to those deeper concerns set loose by the autonomy of religion: human destiny, the human heart, tragedy and the plight of modern man. We write our own poems in the form of literary criticism, and what we divine are our own forms.

Consequently, for many years we have tended to regard the greater Shakespearean tragedies as primarily concerned with the psychological or spiritual nature and development of the main character, to regard character, routinely said to be indistinguishable from action, as the guiding principle of order that directs the construction of the plays. In this way we get rid of the action. Bradley, for example, says of *Hamlet,* "the whole story turns upon the peculiar nature of the hero." And Allardyce Nicoll, to choose one more example among many, speaks of "that which forms the very core of the tragedy, the mental and spiritual Hamlet."[1] Again, almost everyone assumes that the spiritual development of Lear is the principle of that play, and that all that is not directly concerned with Lear is nevertheless related. The story of Gloucester, it is said, repeats the design of the main plot; it forms a second, a sub- or echo-plot, and in the repetition emphasizes, intensifies, and even universalizes the significance of the main plot, the development of Lear's character. Hence we regard the political and local circumstances of the story as of little consequence; it is a universal and a domestic tragedy. Finally we view the internal method of construction according to the familiar

284

analysis of high school lore: it consists of the initial exposition, followed by the rising action which culminates in the emotional climax or crisis, and then falls away to the resolution. It is a curve of feeling which rises and falls, and the only problem is to locate the point of highest tension, whether in the storm scenes on the heath or later in the reconciliation with Cordelia.

Such ways of viewing experience and its reflections in fiction are familiar to us: they are common in the modern novel. But they are not necessarily the principles of all fiction. Indeed, for our present purposes we may distinguish broadly two kinds of fiction, corresponding roughly to the two kinds of lyric previously distinguished.[2] The one exhibits—to use our commonplace—artificial or mechanical form; the other aims at organic form. The former is found in Roman comedy, in Jonson, in many of the comedies and some of the greater tragedies of Shakespeare. It is differentiated by having as a major principle of order a plot in the old sense, a contrivance, a sequence of actions moved by scheming and mistakes. The latter would appear uncontrived. In it character is indeed indistinguishable from action, action from character, and in fact the parts subsist only in the impression of the whole. In the former things are brought about. In the latter they happen. Toward the end of Henry James' *Ambassadors,* for example, the principal character remarks: "I don't think there is anything I have done in such a calculated way as you describe. Everything has come as a sort of indistinguishable part of everything else."[3] This is not the sort of thing that Davos or Mosca, Iago or Edmund, or indeed Claudius or Laertes could with any accuracy say.

For what is missing in the modern accounts of Shakespearean tragedy is precisely the plot of the play, the series of intrigues and mistakes by which the situation as initially expounded comes to the catastrophe. For this reason the modern critic has always had special difficulties with *King Lear.* He wonders at the disappearance of the Fool, as if the Fool had some bearing on the issue of the action, And he finds that the play falls off after the storm scenes. It falls off after the storm scenes because the poet has action to deal with, a story to tell, a plot to unfold, and the modern critic is not interested in this. He would like to leave out the plot.

He would like to leave it out because in the modern view it is a good thing to be rid of. Mark Twain threatened to shoot anyone attempting to find a plot in his narrative of Huckleberry Finn. André Gide resolved in his *Journal of "The Counterfeiters"* "to avoid the artificiality of a 'plot'." And E. M. Forster commenting on that novel, apparently with approval, described Gide's attitude in these terms: "As for plot—to pot with plot, break it up, boil it down. Let there be those 'formidable erosions of contour' of which Nietzsche speaks. All that is prearranged is false." Sherwood Anderson: "The plot notion did seem to me to poison all storytelling. What was wanted, I thought, was form, not plot." Elizabeth Bowen asked: "What about the idea that plot should be ingenious, complicated—a display of ingenuity remarkable enough to command attention?" gives no answer, and passes on. The distinguished poet and critic, Edwin Muir, said: "It was Thackeray who first made a clear break with the plot both as a literary and a popular convention" so that in *Vanity Fair* "All the plot that remains is the series of incidents which widen and diversify the picture, and set the characters in different relations . . . What we ask [of the incidents] is that they should arise as naturally as possible, that the plot should not appear to be a plot."/ And again: "There is no external framework, no merely mechanical plot; all is character, and all is at the same time action." "This spontaneous and progressive logic is the real distinguishing feature of the dramatic novel."[4]

But "spontaneous and progressive logic" is not a characteristic of Shakespearean tragedy, and indeed was not a notion available at that time. I suggest a return from the concerns of modern fiction and modern life to the commonplaces of Shakespeare's own tradition, commonplaces that fit his work with a remarkably unsubtle obviousness. If this method of interpretation seems not to enrich our experience of the works but rather to limit and simplify that experience, I can only confess that this is my intention. Interpretation, I feel, should sharpen and define, subtract, not add. One does not make progress in this field; the trick is to go back, to recover.

If in the process of recovery we ask what traditions were available to Shakespeare, from what sources could he draw those structures and schemes of language, person, scene, and action which he used, and in what context would his audience perceive and feel them, we shall find that with respect to the theater there were, among others, three important traditions. The first, which will not concern us here, is the tradition of pageantry and court entertainment, of hermits, allegorical and supernatural characters, of special scenery, dance, song, and "the study of magnificence."[5] It is a tradition relevant to many of Shakespeare's comedies, and one that receives its final realization in the masques of Jonson.

The second is the tradition of show business, of the professional actor and the popular stage. It is a tradition of juggling, tumbling, comic beatings, of Tom o' Bedlam and "Exit, pursued by a bear," of fencing matches and vaudeville skits. In this tradition a narrative is only partly useful for its own sake; it is at the same time a device for disposing and arranging a series of theatrical routines, just as the story of the modern musical play is largely an occasion for songs, dances, comedy acts, and what not. It forms, as was earlier maintained, a sort of expandable filing system. Hence the story or plot of an Elizabethan play has in this sense a double function. It is presented for its own sake, and at the same time it forms a sort of framework or outline allowing a number of independent acts or routines. It is a way of plotting out, of arranging, a wide variety of theatrical material—comic scenes, songs, and exhibitions of odd characters, such as Osric in *Hamlet* or Clove and Orange in Jonson's *Every Man Out of His Humour:*

> MITIS: What be these two, signior?
>
> CORDATUS: Marry, a couple, sir, that are mere strangers to the whole scope of our play; only come to walk a turn or two in this scene of Paul's, by chance.
>
> 3. 1. 6-19

It allows for soliloquies or passions, and scenes of the same sort, such as the scenes on the heath, expressing the feeling attached to the story. It leaves room, as Jonson says in discussing unity of action, "for digression and art."[6] The critical rule that pertains to these is not that they should blend together and be integrated into a single and organic effect, that they should exhibit some kind of qualitative progression. It is rather the rule of decorum, the negative rule that they should be not inappropriate.

Plot in this sense, then, is a method for disposing and arranging the heterogeneous material of the play. And the difference in aesthetic effect between two plays with approximately the same quantity of plot but with greater and less digression and episode will be, as Coleridge noted of *Hamlet* and *Macbeth:* "the one proceeds with the utmost slowness, the other with a crowded and breathless rapidity."[7] Or, to put it less perceptively: the one in a school text I have at hand runs to fifty pages, the other to thirty.

The third tradition is academic, the tradition of literary criticism and analysis employed in the reading and discussion of Roman comedy in the schools. We shall find that Shakespeare constructs the plots of *Hamlet* and *King Lear* consciously and deliberately according to the rubrics of this tradition. The basic texts are the classics of ancient rhetoric and Donatus on Terence, and the general context is elementary school learning, rehearsed and repeated with the single-mindedness of a Freudian interpreter. We could assume that Shakespeare knew this tradition, knew it by heart, even without the work of the many scholars who in recent years have firmly established the fact,[8] for it was the tradition of prestige in his time. But how well he understood and how easily he handled the basic terms and distinctions of that tradition can be illustrated by the exegesis of a phrase in Polonius' speech about the players in which the councilor displays his familiarity with current literary and dramatic terms:

> The best actors in the world, either for tragedy, comedy, history, pastoral, pastoral-comical, historical-pastoral, tragical-historical, tragical-comical-historical-pastoral; scene individable, or poem unlimited.
>
> 2. 2. 415-18

The enumeration of dramatic genres begins like the enumeration in a patent for a company of players, and then introduces that contamination of genres which was being currently discussed and explicitly practiced, as in Guarini's *Il Pastor Fido* (1590), a pastoral tragicomedy, or in the comical satires of Jonson. The last two phrases in the enumeration, culminating in the quadrate contamination of "tragical-comical-historical-pastoral," are not in the text of 1604 (the second quarto) but appear for the first time in the folio text of 1623. They may represent an addition, gagging up the passage. However, the phrases we are specially concerned with are "scene individable" and "poem unlimited." The commentators do not know what is meant, and have settled on the guess that it is a reference "to dramas that observe the unities of time and place and also those that give no heed to such limitation."[9] It is a distant guess. A better guess and a more obvious one would be that "scene individable" refers to the question, which was receiving some attention at the time, of whether the acts of a play should be divided into scenes. Muretus in his notes to Terence (1550), which were incorporated in the later editions of that author, comments, "As to dividing the acts of a play into scenes, designating scene one, scene two, and so on, how skillfully and intelligently it is done is, I think, questionable. For my own part I take it that this distinction comes from the teachers of literature and not from the poets"; and he advises a friend whose tragedy he had read "to remove entirely the useless and superfluous and dreamed up by teachers division of acts into scenes."[10] Jonson may well have had such comment in mind in the following passage from *Every Man Out of His Humour* (1599, published 1600), in which Shakespeare was a principal actor:

MITIS: Does he observe all the laws of comedy in it?

CORDATUS: What laws mean you?

MITIS: Why, the equal division of it into acts and scenes, according to the Terentian manner. . . .

CORDATUS: O no, these are too nice observations.

Induction, 235-42

But there is no need to guess what "poem unlimited" means. All that is needed is an elementary Elizabethan education, a familiarity with the basic distinctions of Cicero and Quintilian, and a willingness to countenance the persistent Renaissance habit of using rhetorical concepts in the discussion of poetry. Let us translate the phrase, as an Elizabethan would naturally do, into Latin: *poema infinitum.* Of course. He had learned from rhetoric that there are two kinds of topics one could write or speak on: *quaestiones esse aut infinitas aut finitas.*[11] They are unlimited or limited; either general, without reference to persons, time, or place, or they are implicated in circumstance. "Should men marry?" is unlimited; "Should Antony marry Octavia?" is limited. An unlimited poem, then, is an expository poem on a general topic, such as *De Rerum Natura* or John Davies's *Nosce Teipsum* (1599).

The concepts of this tradition enter into the structure of Shakespeare's drama in various ways. The principle of social rank, for example, that tragedy involves heads of state and comedy the affairs of the citizen class, is retained and modified. It serves, to use our own terms, to distinguish domestic from true tragedy, and romantic from realistic comedy. One of the most interesting consequences of this principle in Shakespearean comedy is the implicit stipulation that romantic love is only possible to the wellborn, so that to introduce this element into the citizen comedy of the *Merry Wives of Windsor* the author must introduce a wellborn lover, a Mr. Fenton who is a courtier and so of necessity a Throckmorton, a Knyvett, or a Blount.

There is another principle relating to comedy that Shakespeare sometimes scrupulously observes and sometimes deliberately violates. It seems to have had a fascination for him. This is the stipulation that comedy should be *sine periculo vitae,* "without the threat of death." The action in one of his earliest comedies, the *Comedy of Errors,* is deliberately set in the frame of a violation of this law. Indeed, the observance of the law in *The Merry Wives of Windsor* is sufficient to distinguish that play absolutely in kind from *Much Ado About Nothing* and *Measure for Measure.* The knot of error in *Much Ado* is tied by a supposed death, and *Measure for Measure* exploits to the full the tragic attitudes of fear and resignation to death: "Be absolute for death." The former is simply comedy; the latter are tragicomedy in the form in which it was being developed at this time in practice and theory. For "he who composes tragicomedy," says Guarini, "takes from tragedy its great persons but not its great action . . . its danger but not its death."[12]

In brief, Cicero and Donatus, Quintilian and Diomedes furnish Shakespeare and his interpreter with the relevant notions. Consequently, when Viola exclaims in *Twelfth Night:*

> O Time, thou must untangle this, not I;
> It is too hard a knot for me t'untie!
>
> 2. 2. 41-42

we recognize the allusion to the Donatan tradition of analysis, and we perceive that the plot of *Twelfth Night* is constructed precisely according to that tradition. In general Donatus describes the structure of Terence's comedies in terms of the error that furnishes the problem of the play, and the plots and errors that complicate and lead to the tying of the knot whose resolution yields the catastrophe. He comments, for example, on *Andria* 2.4: "This scene ties the knot of error of the play, and the difficulty proper to comedy; it also sets in motion the schemes." On 2. 6: "This scene contains the plots of both characters, by which each marvellously takes, and is taken, in." On 5. 4: "And here the error of the play is wholly revealed." Again, on *Hecyra,* 4. 4: "In this scene is the final error before the catastrophe."[13] So in *Twelfth Night,* after the situation is expounded in a series of scenes, the plot begins with the initial error, an error like that in the *Silent Woman,* "error personae"[14]: Olivia falls in love with the disguised Viola, thinking her a man, and there follow later the subsequent errors springing from the twinness of Sebastian. Immediately after the initial error the first plot begins, Maria against Malvolio. This is a separate plot that has its own issue and has no bearing on the catastrophe. The next plot, however, does. Sir Toby and Fabian's practice on Sir Andrew, leading to the duels, precipitates the catastrophe. In brief, the action of the play develops simply and solely through plots and errors; they constitute the engine that runs the show.

Likewise in *Hamlet,* when Horatio after the catastrophe of that play proposes to "speak to th' yet unknowing world / How these things came about" and goes on after Fortinbras' assent to say:

> But let this same be presently perform'd,
> Even while men's minds are wild, lest more mischance
> On plots and errors happen.
>
> 5. 2. 404-06

one who knows that tradition understands the terms and perceives that it is being authoritatively stated that the catastrophe resulted from a series of plots and errors. As it does. It would not particularly bother him that the mechanisms of comedy are employed in tragedy, for he would know with Jonson and many others who wrote on the subject that "the parts of a comedy are the same with a tragedy."[15]

The action of *Hamlet,* the busy part of the play, begins with Hamlet's assumption of madness, an alteration that amounts to a disguise. The subsequent scenes are produced by the plots of the King and Polonius through Rosencrantz and Guildenstern, Ophelia, and the Queen to find out "The very cause of Hamlet's lunacy," and of Hamlet against the King to discover his guilt. This movement culminates in the killing by error of Polonius as an accidental consequence of his plot to use the Queen in discovering Hamlet's secret. Hamlet is immediately packed off to England—this is the King's plot; and Rosencrantz and Guild-enstern "go to't" by a plotted error:

> O 'tis most sweet
> When in one line two crafts directly meet.
>
> 3. 4. 209-10

In the final scene of the play the carefully contrived scheme to murder Hamlet, as it were accidentally, goes awry:

> purposes mistook
> Fall'n on th 'inventors' heads.

In error the foils are exchanged; in error the Queen drinks the poisoned cup.

This is a plot of intrigue, a tale of "mischance that on plots and errors happen," enriched by scenes and speeches of comedy, passion, satire, hung on the framework of the plot and not inappropriate to the whole. To our modern question, What is Hamlet's tragic flaw? or, In what way are we to construe his final death as issuing out of the depths of his personality? we answer: His tragic flaw is Claudius and Laertes. He was cold-bloodedly murdered by means of a contrived diabolical plot. One need not assume, therefore, that he was in our current jargon "murder-prone."

Lear, too, is a play of mischance that on plots and errors happen. There is in it also the spiritual story of Lear and the spiritual story of Gloucester, of course, but neither of these nor both together furnish the structure of the whole. It is not these that bring about the catastrophe.

The action begins with the first plot at the end of the scene of state that opens the play. Goneril and Regan, fearful of the threat to their new eminence from the King's character and his very kingness, as also from his hundred knights who with their retainers constitute a sizable army, begin to scheme:

> If our father carry authority with such dispositions as
> he bears, this last surrender of his will but offend us.
>
> 1. 1. 308-10

Regan says, "We shall further think on't," but Goneril fiercely replies, "We must do something, and in the heat." What she proposes to do becomes clear in a later scene. The second strand of the play is now introduced with the soliloquy of Edmund, who expounds his plot:

> Legitimate Edgar, I must have your land...
> Well, my legitimate, if this letter speed
> And my invention thrive, Edmund the base
> Shall top the legitimate.
>
> 1. 2. 16, 19-21

And with the entrance, first of Gloucester, then of Edgar, he immediately puts it into execution. The next scene shows Goneril's plot in operation: Lear is to be treated with such disrespect, offensive to the name of King as well as father, that, given his character which she knows, he will leave in a huff. "And let his knights have colder looks among you," she tells little Oswald:

> What grows of it, no matter; advise your fellows so:
> I would breed from hence occasions, and I shall,
> That I may speak; I'll write straight to my sister
> To hold my very course.
>
> 1. 3. 23-26

The difficulty between Lear and Goneril is not the spontaneous consequence of differing temperaments, nor is it the result of the offensive and riotous senility of an old man. These are merely Goneril's allegations, and have no standing against the claim of duty to a King and father. Rather, the difficulty between Lear and Goneril is coldly and explicitly provoked. It is the consequence of a plot.

The next scene shows Kent in disguise taking service with Lear, and Oswald furthering Goneril's plot, though he is tripped up for his pains in a comic routine. Up to this point, from the conclusion of the exposition, all has been plots on the part of Goneril and Edmund, and in the case of Kent's disguise an error. There follows an interlude, the Fool's routine with Lear, which, however important it may be to our feeling about the play, is irrelevant to the plot. Its primary purpose is to drive home the wrongness of Lear's initial mistake, and to display some wit. The plot resumes with the entrance of Goneril who has, as she planned, bred occasions to insult Lear. He hurries off in a rage to the other daughter, and she sends Oswald with a message urging Regan to a similar course of action. This plot comes to a head when

Lear, rejected by Regan, goes out into the storm. Meanwhile, Edmund's plot against Edgar has been successful; Edgar flees, is proclaimed, and assumes the disguise of Tom o' Bedlam. Kent in the storm discloses his political plot against the Dukes, the alliance with France which culminates in the battle. But this leads to the furtherance of Edmund's second plot, the plot against Gloucester, who has been approached by Kent's party and confides this to Edmund. By revealing the intrigue to Cornwall he destroys his father and attains his title and lands. This is the culmination of his original plot.

Gloucester is blinded, Cornwall slain, the French Army landed at Dover, Goneril and Regan vie for Edmund's favor, and Albany comes to the side of the good. Oswald, carrying a letter from Goneril to Edmund, runs across Gloucester, is slain by the disguised Edgar, and the crucial error of the plot occurs—Edgar finds on Oswald's body Goneril's letter. This leads to the unloosing of the knot of the play. For, with the defeat of Cordelia, Edmund is at the height of his power. He plots by way of the Captain the death of Cordelia and Lear. Meanwhile, Albany has been shown Goneril's letter and has consented to Edgar's scheme of a trial by combat. In the quarrel for pre-eminence between Albany and Edmund, Regan openly espouses Edmund; it is a marriage ceremony:

> Witness the world, that I create thee here
> My lord and master.

5. 3. 77-78

And Albany, on the evidence of the letter that went astray, forbids the banns:

> For your claim, fair sister,
> I bar it in the interest of my wife;
> 'Tis she is sub-contracted to this lord,
> And I, her husband, contradict your banns.
>
> 5. 3. 84-87

Regan has been poisoned by Goneril, and is led off. The trial by combat ensues, with Edgar triumphant and Edmund mortally wounded. Goneril is exposed, exits, and commits suicide. The death of Gloucester is announced, and then on the repentance of Edmund, who discloses his plot against Lear and Cordelia, his orders are recalled. But it is too late. Cordelia is dead and Lear soon dies. This is hardly the story of the psychological development of Lear and Gloucester.

We have left out much, and much that conduces to the richness and deep feeling of the play—the scenes on the heath, the mighty passions of Lear corresponding to the soliloquies of Hamlet, the regeneration of Lear and Gloucester—but we have left out none of the action, nothing that is necessary to the plot. In *Lear,* this is the plot of Goneril and Regan against Lear, of Edmund against Edgar and Gloucester, of Kent against the Dukes, of Goneril against Regan, of Edmund against Lear and Cordelia, and the counteraction stemming from the errors of Edgar's disguise and the letter gone astray.

Nor is there in the modern sense a double plot in the play, though there is in a Renaissance sense. A prominent Italian critic, for example, writing in the 1540s says:

> I call that plot double which has in its action diverse kinds of persons of the same station in life, as two lovers of different character, two old men of varied

nature . . . and other such things, as they may be seen in the *Andria* and in the other plots of the same poet, where it is clear that these like persons of unlike habits make the knot and solution of the plot very pleasing. And I believe that if this should be well imitated in tragedy by a good poet, and the knot so arranged that its solution will not bring confusion, double structure in tragedy will be no less pleasing (always remembering the reverence due to Aristotle) than it is in comedy. . . . [16]

Obviously, in these terms *King Lear* has a double plot, for Lear and Gloucester are two old men, though in this case of similar rather than of varied nature; Edgar and Edmund, and Cordelia on the one hand and Goneril and Regan on the other yield further doublings. But this is not what the modern critic has in mind when he speaks of the main and sub- or echo-plot of that play. Rather, a plot in this tradition consists of several lines of action, separately developed at the beginning, but impinging on each other to form the complication, and each necessary to the final solution or catastrophe. It follows in this tradition that a line of action necessary to the complication and solution does not constitute a separate or sub-plot but is an integral part of the plot itself. There is, consequently, on this view no double, no main and sub-plot, in *King Lear,* for Edmund and Edgar are the principal agents in the catastrophe.

The method and intention of such doubling in Renaissance drama is illuminated by a later critic, Guarini. "It now remains to defend this grafting in of subordinate stories," he says, and we recall that Shakespeare grafted the Gloucester story from Sidney's *Arcadia* onto the old story of Lear:

In order to do this I shall consider four agents indispensable to the plot of the *Andria* . . . : Pamphilus the first, Glycerium the second, Philumena the third, and Charinus the fourth . . . the principal subject is nothing else than the love of Pamphilus and Glycerium, not interrupted by that of Charinus, but greatly aided. And if that love alone had been represented, with the pregnancy of Glycerium and the displeasure of Simo, the father of Pamphilus, how insipid the story would have been! A young man fallen under the displeasure of the father because he had married a woman of no standing, who at last, when she is discovered to be a free woman, is given to him as his wife—what is there in that to make a plot? The plot might indeed have been pathetic and have displayed character, but there would have been no activity, which is the strength of the dramatic art. How would the plot have come to a crisis? From the indignation of the father and the love of the son strong feelings could have resulted, but not intrigues.[17]

The author's exclamation, "What is there in that to make a plot?" is clearly applicable to the plot of *Lear* as it is ordinarily summarized for us. An old man acts foolishly, estranges the child who loves him, is brutally rejected by his other children, goes into a feverish delirium, is finally reconciled to the good child, and then by a trick of fate she is killed and he dies brokenhearted. The story is repeated about another old man. One could say with our Renaissance author: "The plot might indeed have been pathetic and displayed character, but there would have been no activity, which is the strength of the dramatic art. How would the plot have come to a crisis? . . . strong feelings could have resulted, but not intrigues."

TRADITION & MODERNITY

Wallace Stevens

I have defined tradition in such a way that every poem necessarily has a tradition, but this is not the common meaning of the term. For we distinguish between what is traditional and what is not, and in the latter case the principle is a negative one. This is a concern for tradition that is a modern concern, and provoked by something so simple as a sense of alienation from the past, a feeling for history as distinct. It is motivated by the persuasion that tradition has been lost and is only recoverable in novelty. From this arises a corollary concern with modernity in poetry, for which the poetry of Wallace Stevens will serve as an illustration. He himself writes in the poem entitled *Of Modern Poetry*:

> The poem of the mind in the act of finding
> What will suffice. It has not always had
> To find: the scene was set; it repeated what
> Was in the script.
>   Then the theatre was changed
> To something else. Its past was a souvenir. (239)[1]

To be modern in this sense is not the same thing as to be contemporary, to be living and writing in our time, or to have lived and written within our normal life span. There are many contemporary poets who are not modern. The modern poet writes the new poetry, as it was called some years ago. His poetry is modern in that it is different from the old, the traditional, the expected; it is new. This is the sense in which *modern* has always been used in these contexts: the modern poets in Roman antiquity were Calvus and Catullus who wrote in new and untraditional poetic forms, in forms borrowed from another language and regarded by the traditionalists of the times as effete and decadent; whose subjects were novel and daring; and whose attitudes were in conscious distinction from those of the old morality. Again, the *moderni,* the modern thinkers in the late Middle Ages, were those who advocated and embraced the new logic of that time and whose attitudes were thought to be dangerous to the established order; it was later said that they caused the Reformation.

The modern poet, then, is modern only in the light of tradition, only as distinguished from the old. His forms, his models, his subjects, and his attitudes are different from and in opposition to the customary and expected forms, models, subjects, and attitudes of his own youth and of his readers. Consequently to be modern depends on a tradition to be different from, upon the firm existence of customary expectations to be disappointed. The new is parasitic upon the old. But when, the new has itself become the old, it has lost its quality of newness and modernity and must shift for itself.

This is the situation with respect to what is still called modern poetry; it is rapidly becoming the old and the traditional. There appeared some years ago a number of articles in the leading conventional journals of this country in defense of modern poetry. Had the poetry still needed defense, the articles would never have been accepted by the editors of those journals. But modern poetry is, in fact, in secure possession of the field, and its heroes are aged men with a long public career behind them. Wallace Stevens, in fact, died in 1955 at the age of seventy-six after a public career of forty years. Yet the attitude of modernity still persists. These poets still represent to the young writer of today the new, the adventurous, the advance guard, the untried. Their names are still sacred to the initiate.

For it is the condition of modernity in art that it appeal to the initiate, that it provoke the opposition of the ordinary reader who has the customary and old expectations which it is the purpose of modern art to foil. Hence it lives in an attitude of defense; is close and secret, not open and hearty; has its private ritual and its air of priesthood—*odi profanum vulgus et arceo*, "I despise the uninitiated crowd, and I keep them at a distance." It is obscure, and its obscurities are largely calculated; it is intended to be impenetrable to the vulgar. More than this, it is intended to exasperate them.

There is something of this in all art that is genuine. For the genuine in art is that which attains distinction, and the distinguished is uncommon and not accessible to the many. It is different, it must be different, and as such provokes the hostility of the many, and provokes it the more in that its difference is a claim to distinction, to prestige, and to exclusion. This claim is diminished by time. Wordsworth is now regarded as quite traditional, quite stuffy and conventional. For the particular qualities of difference in an older body of poetry that has been absorbed into the tradition become part of that tradition, and so something that the reader actually need not see since he does not know it is different. He may then in his early years and through his school days develop a set of social responses to the received body of poetry; he may enjoy that poetry without effort, be pleased by his conditioned responses, and think of himself as a lover and judge of poetry. When the audience for poetry becomes satisfied with a customary response to a customary poem, when, they demand of the poet that he write to their expectations, when distinction is lost in commonness, there is need for the modern in art, for a poetry that is consciously different, even if it often mistakes difference for distinction. The poet must exasperate his reader, or succumb to him.

Such was the situation out of which Stevens wrote, at least as it seemed to him and to those of his contemporaries who have become the aged fathers of modern poetry. They sought to appear different, and hence distinguished, and they succeeded perhaps too well. The first thing that strikes the reader of Wallace Stevens, and the quality for which he was for a long time best known, is the piquant, brilliant, and odd surface of his poems. They are full of nonsense cries, full of virtuoso lines, such as:

> Chieftan Iffucan of Azcan in caftan
> Of tan with henna hackles, halt![2] (75)

which unexpectedly make grammar and sense if you read them slowly with closed ears. They are thronged with exotic place-names, but not the customary ones of late romantic poetry; instead of "Quinquereme of Nineveh from distant Ophir" there is "a woman of Lhassa," there is Yucatan. Rare birds fly, "the green toucan," and tropical fruits abound, especially the pineapple. Odd characters appear—Crispin, Redwood Roamer, Babroulbadour, black Sly, Nanzia Nunzio—and are addressed in various languages—my semblables, Nino, ephebi, o iuventes, o filii. And they wear strange hats.

A good deal of this, of course, is simply the unexpected in place of the expected; a new and different collection of proper names, for example, instead of the old collection, but used largely for the same purpose while seeming to deny this by being designedly different:

> Canaries in the morning, orchestras
> In the afternoon, balloons at night. That is
> A difference, at least, from nightingales,
> Jehovah, and the great sea-worm.(142)

The process is common in Stevens, and can be seen neatly in one of his most engaging stanzas. The theme of the stanza is the traditional one of Tom Nashe's:

> Brightness falls from the hair,
> Queens have died young and fair.

But instead of Helen and Iseult there are references to the beauties in Utamaro's drawings and to the eighteenth-century belles of Bath:

> Is it for nothing, then, that old Chinese
> Sat tittivating by their mountain pools
> Or in the Yangtse studied out their beards?
> I shall not play the flat historic scale.
> You know how Utamaro's beauties sought
> The end of love in their all-speaking braids.
> You know the mountainous coiffures of Bath.
> Alas! Have all the barbers lived in vain
> That not one curl in nature has survived? (14)

A woman's hair is here used as a synecdoche for her beauty. Have all those who have cared for and cherished her hair, have all the barbers, lived in vain, that though much has survived in art, none has survived in nature? The poet concludes then, expressing the sense of the couplet of a Shakespearean sonnet:

> This thought is as a death, which cannot choose
> But weep to have that which it fears to lose.

in the more specialized terms of his synecdoche, but almost as movingly:

305

Why, without pity on these studious ghosts,
Do you come dripping in your hair from sleep? (14)

Much of this is rather amusing, and even, as we say now, intriguing. Sometimes, indeed, it is much more than that, as in the stanza just quoted which is poetry of a rare though too precious kind. But Wallace Stevens had a public career in poetry for forty years, and forty years is a little too long for this sort of pepper to retain its sharpness and piquancy. We have to ask, then, What is the motive and purpose in this?

It is usually said that these aspects of Stevens' work derive from a study of the French poets of the latter nineteenth century, the Symbolists and Parnassians, and this explanation no doubt is true enough. But it is not a sufficient explanation. The prestige of that poetry was not so high in Stevens' youth as to serve as a motive, though it might be sufficient now. The motive is rather a more human one. It is disdain—disdain of the society and of the literary tradition in which he grew up, of himself as a part of that society, and of his readers so far as they belonged to it. He sought, he tells us:

when all is said, to drive away
The shadow of his fellows from the skies,
And, from their stale intelligence released,
To make a new intelligence prevail. (37)

How did he go about it? He celebrated the rankest trivia in the choicest diction. He was a master of the traditional splendors of poetry and refused to exercise his mastery in the traditional way; he displayed it in the perverse, the odd:

he humbly served
Grotesque apprenticeship to chance event. (39)

He became "a clown" though "an aspiring clown." In his own summary, in the passage that immediately follows the lines quoted above, he explains:

Hence the reverberations in the words
Of his first central hymns, the celebrants
Of rankest trivia, tests of the strength
Of his aesthetic, his philosophy,
The more invidious, the more desired:
The florist asking aid from cabbages,
The rich man going bare, the paladin
Afraid, the blind man as astronomer,
The appointed power unwielded from disdain. (37)

He possessed "the appointed power"—the Miltonic and Scriptural phrasing is blasphemous in this context, and deliberately so—but would not wield it from disdain. The question then is, Why should he have felt such disdain? The answer can be collected from various of his poems but is given full and detailed exposition in the one from which I have just quoted. This is *The Comedian as the Letter C,* the showpiece and longest poem in his first book. The poem is sufficiently complex to have several centers of concern. I shall interpret it, however, in terms of our question, and we shall find that this will turn out to be a primary concern of the poem.

The poem consists of six sections, each of a little under a hundred lines of blank verse. It is in form and subject a poem that depicts the growth of a poet's mind, and though the main character is given the fictitious name of Crispin, he may be taken as an aspect of the author, a mask for Wallace Stevens the poet, so that the poem in effect is autobiographical. It belongs, then, to that literary form of which the model and prototype is Wordsworth's *Prelude*. It is not a wholly easy poem to read, partly because much of it is written in Stevens' fastidious and disdainful manner, partly because its structure is not adequately adjusted to its theme. The hero of the poem makes a sea voyage to a strange and exotic country, in this case Yucatan, and back to his own land. The motive for the voyage is explicitly given late in the poem in the passage already quoted:

> What was the purpose of his pilgrimage,
> Whatever shape it took in Crispin's mind,
> If not, when all is said, to drive away
> The shadow of his fellows from the skies,
> And, from their stale intelligence released,
> To make a new intelligence prevail? (37)

His voyage is a rejection of his society as banal and trite, of its intelligence as stale, and his quest is the quest of a new intelligence. His problem was the problem that every teacher of freshman composition sets his better students, the problem of striking through routine phrasing and syntax to the genuine, the honest, the possibly distinguished.

The hero is portrayed as having been before this trip a man who was master of his environment, but he was a little man, "the Socrates of snails," "this nincompated pedagogue," and the environment itself was trivial; it was a land "of simple salad-beds, of honest quilts." It was, in fact, to quote Stevens' own summary of his early environment in an essay of later date, "the comfortable

American state of life of the 'eighties, the 'nineties, and the first ten years of the present century."[3] It was the time and place when the sun

> shone
> With bland complaisance on pale parasols,
> Beetled, in chapels, on the chaste bouquets. (29)

It was that middle class culture of business, public chastity, and official Christianity which we often call, with some historical injustice, Victorianism. In this world Crispin wrote the conventional poetry of the times. He was one

> that saw
> The stride of vanishing autumn in a park
> By way of decorous melancholy . . .
> That wrote his couplet yearly to the spring,
> As dissertation of profound delight.

However, he found that

> He could not be content with counterfeit. (31, 39)

It was this dissatisfaction with the conventional—in society and in poetry—"That first drove Crispin to his wandering." He alludes to it as "The drenching of stale lives," a life of "ruses" that was shattered by the experience of his voyage.

He found the sea overwhelming; he "was washed away by magnitude." "Here was no help before reality." It was not so much that he was cut off from the snug land; he was cut off from his old self:

> What counted was mythology of self,
> Blotched out beyond unblotching.

and hence from his environment. He was destitute and bare:

> The salt hung on his spirit like a frost,
> The dead brine melted in him like a dew
> Of winter, until nothing of himself
> Remained, except some starker, barer self
> In a starker, barer world. (28, 29)

From this experience he came to Yucatan. The poetasters of that land, like the poetasters at home, in spite of the vividness of experience around them

> In spite of hawk and falcon, green toucan
> And jay. (30)

still wrote conventional verses about the nightingale, as if their environment were uncivilized. But Crispin's conversion at sea—for it was obviously a conversion—had enlarged him, made him complicated

> and difficult and strange
> In all desires. (31)

until he could reduce his tension only by writing an original and personal poetry, different and unconventional.

The experience at sea is now reinforced by another experience in Yucatan, of the same elemental, overwhelming sort:

one
>Of many proclamations of the kind,
>Proclaiming something harsher than he learned

from the commonplace realism of home:

>From hearing signboards whimper in cold nights.

It was rather "the span / Of force, the quintessential fact,"

>The thing that makes him envious in a phrase.

It was the experience that altered and reinvigorated his poetry, the source from which he drew that distinction of style that marks off his published work from the sentimental verses he had printed in the college magazine some twenty years before. The experience was of the type of a religious experience:

>His mind was free
>And more than free, elate, intent, profound
>And studious of a self possessing him,
>That was not in him in the crusty town
>From which he sailed. (32-33)

The poetry he now wrote issued from this context. It was conditioned by the kind of dissatisfaction that drove Crispin to his wandering, by such an experience as Crispin's on the voyage and in Yucatan, and by its results. This dissatisfaction lies behind a good many of Steven's poems, which deal, if one looks beneath the distracting surface, simply with the opposition between the aridities of middle-class convention and the vivid alertness of the unconventional, as in *Disillusionment of Ten O'Clock.* Some repeat in smaller compass and with other properties the subject of *The Comedian:* as *The Doctor of Geneva.* In others he attempts to deal directly with the experience of the sea, but this was a religious experience without the content of traditional religion. In fact, it had no content at all beyond the intuition of a bare reality behind conventional appearance, and hence was an unfertile subject for poetry since it was unproductive of detail. He treated it in one of his best short poems, *The Snow Man,* but when he had stated it, there was nothing more to be done with it, except to say it over again in another place. This he has repeatedly done, though with a prodigality of invention in phrasing that is astounding.

Most of what is interesting in Stevens issues from this problem. It can be put in various terms. It is the problem of traditional religion and modern life, of imagination and reality, but it can be best put for Stevens in the terms in which it is explicitly put in *The Comedian.* The problem is the relationship of a man and his environment, and the reconciliation of these two in poetry and thus in life. The two terms of this relationship are really Wordsworth's two terms: the one, what the eye and ear half create; the other, what they perceive. The reconciliation in Wordsworth is in a religious type of experience:

> With what strange utterance did the loud dry wind
> Blow through my ear! the sky seemed not a sky
> Of earth—and with what motion moved the clouds!
>
> Dust as we are, the immortal spirit grows
> Like harmony in music; there is a dark
> Inscrutable workmanship that reconciles
> Discordant elements, makes them cling together
> In one society.[3]

The reconciliation in Stevens is sought in poetry, in

> those
> True reconcilings, dark, pacific words,
> And the adroiter harmonies of their fall. (144)

For poetry is the supreme fiction of which religion is a manifestation:

> Poetry
>
> Exceeding music must take the place
> Of empty heaven and its hymns,
>
> Ourselves in poetry must take their place. (167)

What Crispin is seeking is such a reconciliation, a oneness between himself and his environment. He began in the illusion that he was the intelligence of his soil, but the experience of reality overwhelmed him, and he came to believe that his soil was his intelligence. At this extreme he wrote poems in which a person is described by his surroundings. But he perceived that this too was sentimental, and so he settled for the ordinary reality of daily life, married, had four daughters, and prospered. However, he did not give up poetry entirely; he recorded his adventures in the poem, and hoped that the reader would take it as he willed: as a summary

> strident in itself
> But muted, mused, and perfectly revolved
> In those portentous accents, syllables,
> And sounds of music coming to accord

Upon his lap, like their inherent sphere,
Seraphic proclamations of the pure
Delivered with a deluging onwardness. (45)

Such is Stevens' account of the source of his distinctive style and distinctive subjects. But he owed more than he acknowledged to the old and the traditional. He owed "the appointed power" which was "unwielded from disdain."

That he once had the appointed power is clear in his greatest poem, and one of his earliest, *Sunday Morning.* The poem is traditional in meter—it is in eight equal stanzas of blank verse—and has as its subject a deep emotional attachment to traditional Christianity and a rejection of Christianity in favor of the clear and felt apprehension of sensory detail in this life, together with an attempt to preserve in the new setting the emotional aspects of the old values.

The poem depicts a woman having late breakfast on a Sunday morning, when of course she should have been at church. She is for the moment at one with her surroundings, which are vivid, sensory, familiar, and peaceful. All this serves to dissipate the traditional awe of Christian feeling, but the old feeling breaks through:

She dreams a little, and she feels the dark
Encroachment of that old catastrophe,
As a calm darkens among water-lights. (67)

Her mood "is like wide water, without sound," and in that mood she passes over the seas to the contemplation of the Resurrection. The remainder of the poem consists of the poet's comment and argument on her situation, on two short utterances she delivers out of her musing, and finally on the revelation that comes to her in a voice.

The poet asserts that Christianity is a religion of the dead and the unreal. In this living world of the sun, in these vivid and sensory surroundings, there is that which can assume the values of heaven:

> Divinity must live within herself:
> Passions of rain, or moods in falling snow;
> Grievings in loneliness, or unsubdued
> Elations when the forest blooms; gusty
> Emotions on wet roads on autumn nights;
> All pleasures and all pains, remembering
> The bough of summer and the winter branch.
> These are the measures destined for her soul. (67)

The truly divine is the human and personal in this world: it consists in the association of feeling with the perception of natural landscape, in human pleasure and pain, in change, as in the change of seasons.

He then argues that the absolute God of religion was originally inhuman, but that the Incarnation by mingling our blood with His, by mingling the relative and human with the Absolute, satisfied man's innate desires for a human and unabsolute Absolute. Certainly, if "the earth" should "Seem all of paradise that we shall know," we would be much more at home in our environment:

> The sky will be much friendlier then than now . . .
> Not this dividing and indifferent blue. (68)

At this point the woman speaks in her musing, and says that she could acquiesce in this world, that she could find an earthly paradise, a contentment, in the perception of Nature, in the feel of reality, except that the objects of her perception change and disappear. Nature is an impermanent paradise. The poet, however, answers that no myth of a religious afterworld has been or ever will be as permanent as the stable recurrences of Nature:

> There is not any haunt of prophecy,
> Nor any old chimera of the grave,
> Neither the golden underground, nor isle
> Melodious, where spirits gat them home,
> Nor visionary south, nor cloudy palm
> Remote on heaven's hill, that has endured
> As April's green endures; or will endure
> Like her remembrance of awakened birds,
> Or her desire for June and evening, tipped
> By the consummation of the swallow's wings.

The woman speaks again, and says:

> "But in contentment I still feel
> The need of some imperishable bliss." (68)

There remains the desire for the eternal happiness of tradition. The lines that comment on this present some difficulties to interpretation until it is seen that the poet in his answer proceeds by developing the woman's position. Yes, he says, we feel that only in death is there fulfillment of our illusions and our desires Even though death be in fact the obliteration of all human experience, yet it is attractive to us; it has the fatal attractiveness of the willow in old poetry for the lovelorn maiden. Though she has lovers who bring her gifts—that is, the earth and its beauty—she disregards the lovers and, tasting of the gifts, strays impassioned toward death.

Yet the paradise she would achieve in death is nothing but an eternal duplicate of this world, and lacking even the principle of change, leads only to ennui. Therefore, the poet creates a secular myth, a religion of his irreligion. The central ceremony is a chant, a poem to the sun,

> Not as a god, but as a god might be. (70)

It is an undivine fiction that preserves the emotions of the old religion but attaches them to a poetry in which the sensory objects of a natural landscape enter into a union in celebration of the mortality of men:

> And whence they came and whither they shall go
> The dew upon their feet shall manifest. (70)

The biblical phrasing creates a blasphemous religion of mortality.

The poem now concludes with a revelation. Out of the woman's mood a voice cries to her, saying that the place of the Resurrection is merely the place where a man died and not a persisting way of entry into a spiritual world. The poet continues:

> We live in an old chaos of the sun,
> Or old dependency of day and night,
> Or island solitude, unsponsored, free,
> Of that wide water, inescapable.
> Deer walk upon our mountains, and the quail

Whistle about us their spontaneous cries;
Sweet berries ripen in the wilderness;
And, in the isolation of the sky,
At evening, casual flocks of pigeons make
Ambiguous undulations as they sink,
Downward to darkness, on extended wings. (70)

We live, in fact, in a universe suggested by natural science, whose principle is change, an island without religious sponsor, free of the specific Christian experience. It is a sensory world, it has its delights, its disorder, and it is mortal.

The poem is an argument against the traditional Christianity of Stevens' youth, and especially against the doctrine and expectation of immortality, in favor of an earthly and mortal existence that in the felt apprehension of sensory detail can attain a vivid oneness with its surroundings and a religious sense of union comparable to the traditional feeling. The former is undeniably traditional, and much of the deep feeling of the poem is derived from the exposition in sustained and traditional rhetoric of the position which is being denied. In this sense it is parasitic on what it rejects. But the positive argument is almost as traditional in the history of English poetry and in the literary situation of Stevens' youth: it is, with the important difference of a hundred years and of the denial of immortality, Wordsworthian in idea, in detail, in feeling, and in rhetoric. Passages comparable to the appositive enumeration of details of natural landscape associated with human feeling, as in:

Passions of rain, or moods in falling snow;
Grievings in loneliness, or unsubdued
Elations when the forest blooms. (67)

are scattered throughout Wordsworth's poetry, especially through the blank verse. I have already quoted a short passage, let me quote another:

> What want we? have we not perpetual streams,
> Warm woods, and sunny hills, and fresh green fields,
> And mountains not less green, and flocks and herds,
> And thickets full of songsters, and the voice
> Of lordly birds, an unexpected sound
> Heard now and then from morn to latest eve,
> Admonishing the man who walks below
> Of solitude and silence in the sky?

The movement of the verse is Stevens', the syntax, and the relation of syntax to the line-ends. The kind of detail is the same. And the idea, if one reads it out of the specific context of Wordsworth's system, is Stevens' idea; for the passage in isolation says, What does man need, what need he desire, more than a live appreciation of the detail of natural landscape, for the world beyond, the birds admonish us—or, Nature tells us—is a world of solitude and silence. This is not precisely what Wordsworth would have endorsed, but certainly what a young man who was drenched in Wordsworth could make of it. And as he read on in the poem—it is *The Recluse*—he would come to the rhetoric of one of his greatest stanzas and the theme of his greatest poem: he would read in Wordsworth:

> Paradise, and groves
> Elysian, Fortunate fields,—like those of old
> Sought on the Atlantic Main—why should they be
> A history only of departed things,

Or a mere fiction of what never was?
For the discerning intellect of Man,
When wedded to this goodly universe
In love and holy passion, shall find these
The simple produce of the common day.[4]

and he would write:

There is not any haunt of prophecy,
Nor any old chimera of the grave. (68)

The central concern of Stevens' poetry, the concern that underlay Crispin's voyage and the poet's meditative argument with the woman in *Sunday Morning*, as well as most of the more or less curious divergencies of his career, is a concern to be at peace with his surroundings, with this world, and with himself. He requires for this an experience of the togetherness of himself and Nature, an interpenetration of himself and his environment, along with some intuition of permanence in the experience of absoluteness, though this be illusory and transitory, something to satisfy the deeply engrained longings of his religious feeling. Now, there is an experience depicted from time to time in the romantic tradition—it is common in Wordsworth—and one that has perhaps occurred to each of us in his day, a human experience of absoluteness, when we and our surroundings are not merely related but one, when "joy is its own security." It is a fortuitous experience; it cannot be willed into being, or contrived at need. It is a transitory experience; it cannot be stayed in its going or found when it is gone. Yet though fortuitous and transitory, it has in its moment of being all the persuasion of permanence; it seems—and perhaps in its way it is—a fulfillment of the Absolute:

It is and it
Is not and, therefore, is. In the instant of speech,
The breadth of an accelerando moves,
Captives the being, widens—and was there. (440)

Stevens attempted to will it into being. He constructed a se-
ries of secular myths, like the one in *Sunday Morning*, that affirm
the traditional religious feeling of the nobility and unity of expe-
rience, but the myths remain unconvincing and arbitrary, and
conclude in grotesqueries that betray the poet's own lack of belief
in his invention, as in *A Primitive Like an Orb,* in which he evokes:

A giant, on the horizon, glistening,

And in bright excellence adorned, crested
With every prodigal, familiar fire,
And unfamiliar escapades; whirroos
And scintillant sizzlings such as children like,
Vested in the serious folds of majesty. (442)

For, as he asks in an earlier poem:

But if
It is the absolute why must it be
This immemorial grandiose, why not
A cockle-shell, a trivial emblem great
With its final force, a thing invincible
In more than phrase?[5]

He has attempted to contrive it by a doctrine of metaphor
and resemblances, which is precisely Wordsworth's doctrine of
affinities. He has sought to present in a poem any set of objects

and to affirm a resemblance and togetherness between them, but all the reader can see is the objects and the affirmation, as in *Three Academic Pieces*, where a pineapple on a table becomes:

> 1. The hut stands by itself beneath the palms.
> 2. Out of their bottle the green genii come.
> 3. A vine has climbed the other side of the wall. . . .

> These casual exfoliations are
> Of the tropic of resemblance.[6]

But there is a poem in *Transport to Summer*, one of the perfect poems, as far as my judgment goes, in his later work, that achieves and communicates this experience. It is a short poem in couplets entitled *The House Was Quiet and the World Was Calm*. There is no fiddle-dee-dee here. The setting is ordinary, not exotic. It is about a man reading alone, late at night. The phrasing is exact and almost unnoticeable. The style is bare, less rich than *Sunday Morning*, but with this advantage over that poem, that none of its effect is drawn from forbidden sources, from what is rejected. The meter is a loosened iambic pentameter, but loosened firmly and as a matter of course, almost as if it were speech becoming meter rather than meter violated. It has in fact the stability of a new metrical form attained out of the inveterate violation of the old. If is both modern and traditional:

> The house was quiet and the world was calm.
> The reader became the book; and summer night

> Was like the conscious being of the book.
> The house was quiet and the world was calm.

The words were spoken as if there was no book,
Except that the reader leaned above the page,

Wanted to lean, wanted much most to be
The scholar to whom his book is true, to whom

The summer night is like the perfection of thought.
The house was quiet because it had to be.

The quiet was part of the meaning, part of the mind:
The access of perfection to the page.

And the world was calm. The truth in a calm world,
In which there is no other meaning, itself

Is calm, itself is summer and night, itself
Is the reader leaning late and reading there. (358-59)

III

THE PROBLEM OF FORM

I shall stipulate that there is a problem of form in the poetry of our day, but I shall treat *form*, for the moment, as an undefined term, and I shall not until later specify the nature of some of the problems. I am, at the outset, interested in pointing to certain generalities, and to certain broad, simpleminded, pervasive attitudes and dualisms, of which the problem in poetry is to a large extent only a localization. These will give in outline the larger context of the problem.

To begin with, it is apparent that in our society we have too many choices. When we ask the young what they are going to do when they grow up, we should not be surprised or amused that the answers are whimsical and bewildered. The young poet today has a large and not too discriminated anthology of forms to realize: only illiterate ignorance or having made the pilgrimage to Gambier or to Los Altos will reduce the scope of options to manageable size—and even then there will be a hankering for further options. On the other hand, the young poet 250 years ago had it easy in this respect. He wrote octosyllabic or decasyllabic couplets, and the rhetoric and areas of experience of each were fairly delimited. For recreation he wrote a song in quatrains, and once or twice in a lifetime a Pindaric ode.

We come now to those attitudes and dualisms that make the problem of particular forms peculiarly our problem. We are a democratic society and give a positive value to informality, though some of the ladies still like to dress up. We will have nothing to do with the formal language and figured rhetoric of the *Arcadia,* for that is the language and rhetoric of a hierarchical and authoritarian society in which ceremony and formality were demanded by and accorded to the governing class. Instead, we praise, especially in poetry, what we call the accents of real speech—that is, of uncalculated and casual utterance, and sometimes even of vulgar impropriety. Now, if this attitude is a concomitant of the Democratic Revolution, the value we give to antiformality, to the deliberate violation of form and decorum, is a concomitant of its sibling, the Romantic Revolution. The measured, or formal, the contrived, the artificial are, we feel, insincere; they are perversions of the central value of our life, genuineness of feeling. "At least I was honest," we say with moral benediction as we leave wife and child for the sentimental empyrean.

If informality and antiformality are positive values, then the problem of form is how to get rid of it. But to get rid of it we must keep it; we must have something to get rid of. To do this we need a method, and we have found it in our dualisms of science and art, of intellectual and emotional, of regularity and irregularity, of norm and variation. We have been convinced, without inquiry or indeed adequate knowledge, that the regularities of ancient scientific law, of Newton's laws of motion, are regularities of matter, not of spirit, and hence are inimical to human significance. And so we embrace the broad, pervasive, simpleminded, and scarcely scrutinized proposition that regularity is meaningless and irregularity is meaningful—to the subversion of Form. For one needs only so much regularity as will validate irregularity. But Form is regularity.

So we come to definition. The customary distinctions of form and matter, or form and content, are in the discussion of writing at least only usable on the most rudimentary level. For it is apparent to any poet who sets out to write a sonnet that the form of the sonnet is the content, and its content the form. This is not a profundity, but the end of the discussion. I shall define form, then, without a contrasting term. It is that which remains the same when everything else is changed. This is not at all, I may say, a Platonic position. It is rather a mathematical and, as it should be, linguistic notion: $a^2 - b^2 = (a-|-b) (a - b)$ through all the potentialities of a and b. The form of the simple declarative sentence in English is in each of its realizations.

It follows, then, that form is discoverable by the act of substitution. It is what has alternative realizations. And the generality or particularity of a form lies in the range or restriction of alternatives. It follows, also, that the form precedes its realization, even in the first instance, and that unique form, or organic form in the sense of unique form, is a contradiction in terms. For it is the essence of form to be repetitive, and the repetitive is form. It follows, further, that there may be in a given utterance simultaneously a number of forms, so that the common literary question, What is the form of this work? can only be answered by a tacit disregard of all the forms other than the one we are momently concerned with.

It is time for illustration. Donne has a little epigram on Hero and Leander:

> Both robbed of air, we both lie in one ground,
> Both whom one fire had burnt, one water drowned.

What are the forms of this poem? First, both lines are decasyllabic in normal iambic pattern. Second, they rhyme. Third, it is phrased in units of four and six syllables in chiasmic order. Fourth, there are three "both's" and three "one's" in overlapping order. Fifth, the whole story of the lovers is apprehended, summarized, and enclosed in the simple scheme or form of the four elements. Finally, it is recognizably an epigram. Now Sir Philip

Sidney, a few years earlier, in one of the *Arcadia* poems has the following lines:

> Man oft is plagued with air, is burnt with fire,
> In water drowned, in earth his burial is?[1]

The lines are decasyllabic in normal iambic pattern. The adjacent lines do not rhyme, for the form of the poem is terza rima, an alternative form. It is phrased in units of six and four in chiasmic order. The first line repeats "with," the second "in." Man, not Hero and Leander, is apprehended in the scheme of the four elements, and in both cases the order of the elements is not formally predetermined. Finally, it is not an epigram, but part of an eclogue.

I have illustrated in these examples and in this analysis something of the variety of what may be distinguished as form: literary kind, conceptual distinctions, and all the rhetorical figures of like ending, equal members, chiasmus, and the various modes of verbal repetition. That some of the forms of Sidney's lines are repeated in Donne's, with the substitution of Hero and Leander for man, shows they have alternate realizations, and that so many operate simultaneously shows, not that a literary work has form, but that it is a convergence of forms, and forms of disparate orders. It is the coincidence of forms that locks in the poem.

Indeed, it is the inherent coincidence of forms in poetry, in metrical writing, that gives it its place and its power—a claim for poetry perhaps more accurate and certainly more modest than is customary. For this is the poet's *Poetics:* prose is written in sentences; poetry in sentences and lines. It is encoded not only in grammar, but also simultaneously in meter, for meter is the principle or set of principles, whatever they may be, that determines the line. And as we perceive of each sentence that it is grammatical or not, so the repetitive perception that this line is metrical or that it is not, that it exemplifies the rules or that it does not, is the metrical experience. It is the ground bass of all poetry.

And here in naked reduction is the problem of form in the poetry of our day. It is before all a problem of meter. We have lost the repetitive harmony of the old tradition, and we have not established a new. We have written to vary or violate the old line, for regularity we feel is meaningless and irregularity meaningful. But a generation of poets, acting on the principles and practice of significant variation, have at last nothing to vary from. The last variation is regularity.

THE PROBLEM OF STYLE

This is a book intended to ask questions, though most of the authors represented have given answers. But the answers are sometimes different, and often enough to different questions. For different answers: Aristotle, as Cicero points out, does not distinguish between the two figures of thought, metaphor and metonymy (by which a word associated with the expected word is used instead of it); to Roman Jakobson they are polar opposites. And for different questions: anyone who has taken a course in English composition knows about clichés, how awful they are and how he should avoid them. He will be amused at Frank Sullivan's "Cliche Expert." Yet the late Milman Parry, as Denys Page explains, showed that the *Iliad* and the *Odyssey* are composed very largely of formulaic phrases, that is, of clichés, yet for twenty-five centuries they have been justly regarded as summits of the Western tradition. And Walter Raleigh quietly points out that clichés are part of our public civilization, not to be lightly set aside. And so an answer becomes a question.

The initial question is, Is there such a thing as style? To the believer in organic form there cannot be. He will hold, with Benedetto Croce, that how a thing is expressed is indistinguishable from the expression, that a difference in manner is a difference in meaning. And so anyone who wishes to consider style must premise that something may be said in different ways and that the ways may be compared. He may even hold, what is something else again, that manner is a potentiality looking for and limiting a meaning, that style precedes any realized expression. For him, then, style is an absolute.

But if there is such a thing as style, what sort of a thing is it? Is it a Platonic Idea, as Cicero holds, an "unsurpassable ideal which seldom appears throughout a whole work but does shine forth at some times and in some places, more frequently in some speakers, more rarely perhaps in others," and so, like the Sublime of Longinus, that striking distinction in speech that bowls one over? Or is it a neutral concept, so that everything has style, though one may contrast various styles and find this good and that bad? Or good and bad for this purpose or that, and so invoke the criterion of decorum, of appropriateness. It is curious that Aristotle, the interminable definer, does not define style, but proceeds at once to characterize the qualities of good style, and then of bad.

And if there is such a thing as style, what sorts of things have it? The notion was first applied to speech, and particularly to written composition. In recent centuries it has been applied to art and artifacts, and defined, as Meyer Schapiro defines it, as "the constant form . . . in the art of an individual or group." Other historians seek to divine in these constant forms the inner forms of a personality or civilization as represented in their art, artifacts, and sometimes literature. But is a linguistic composition an artifact in the sense that a Pueblo Indian pot is? Or only by metaphor? And if style is a form of form, is not the inner form of the cultural historian a contradiction, since form is external? But if it is a contradiction, is it a purposeful and useful one enabling the historian to intuit or posit some pervasive principle, some formal cause, that will account for and supplant in value the observable external forms? Some spirit of the age, perhaps, or some oscillating or developing principle of the human spirit or of human history.

Again, is style rather a process, as Robert Louis Stevenson and Raleigh suggest, so that the realization of the design transforms the design? And, if it is a process, can language be regarded as material the speaker shapes as the potter shapes clay? If so, then the result is form, of which style may be taken as a species; it is then both process and shape. But the material itself may have its own inherent style, as Stanley S. Newman shows of a language. Then the style of a particular work, if linguistic, will be only a sublanguage, a dialect so to speak, of the larger language, and describable by the methods of linguistics. And does it then have itself a history, as languages have?

Finally, does it have an opposite? And is that opposite thought or matter, or bad style, or lack of style? Such are the questions that definition raises.

After definition comes division: Are there kinds of style? Certainly actual speech and speech in writing differ, for writing abstracts part of a speech situation and records it in repeatable form. It is possible to abstract more than conventional writing does, as James Sledd shows in his phonetic transcriptions, and, indeed, some linguists are now attempting to record intonation and gesture by a system of signs. Nevertheless, an actual utterance is not repeatable except by disc or tape. But is not this, too, an abstraction? And if it is, is it an abstraction of the same order as writing?

Another distinction is between styles that are unnoticeable and those that are noticeable. The first, according to Aristotle, gives clarity, the second weight. And from this comes the Ciceronian distinction between low, middle, and high style, and all the ancient and traditional lore of the figures of speech. For language, at least as abstracted in writing, is noticeable in detail either in its components or in its arrangement. The diction may be unusual, let us say that sort characterized as poetic, or, though not in itself unusual, unusually used. The various describable ways in which words may be unusually used comprise the tropes or figures of thought of traditional rhetoric, of which metaphor and metonymy are most commonly discussed. Yet these discussions are not always conducted with proper tact. If you are thinking of bridge cables as "swinging places where birds alight," you may translate this by metonymy into "The agile precincts of the lark's return."[1] This is figurative since the retranslation requires inference. But if there is a certain slant of light, winter afternoons, that

> When it goes 'tis like the distance
> On the look of death,[2]

"look" is not figurative for "face" since it is precisely the look that is being referred to. So, too, the Ancient Mariner's "At one stride comes the dark" is not metaphorical, for we all are making great strides these days. But the famous Gorgianic figure, that vultures are "living graves," is metaphorical, whether a good or, as Aristotle and Longinus think, a bad metaphor.

What is noticeable in arrangement is either unusual syntax, such as inversion or asyndeton (omission of connectives), or obtrusive repetition. The lack of conjunctions in "I came, I saw, I conquered" is not usual in speech and hence is noticeable. The figures of repetition, though they occasionally occur by chance in casual utterance, have generally the appearance of design and attract attention: "We have nothing to fear but fear itself." Since repetition is form, it gives to an utterance a form other than and concurrent with grammatical form, and hence tends, as verse does, to make a saying memorable. Since opposites imply each other, antithesis is a form of repetition: "Good is what we can do with evil." Finally, repetition is rhythm,[3] for "it is number that limits all things," and to number is to count, to note repetition, either exact or approximate. And since numerical recurrence can be anticipated, its completion gives finality, as in metrical lines which consist of speech-segments of equal length.

The transfer from verse to prose of the figures of arrangement marks the beginning of the history of style in the Western tradition as a conscious subject of discussion, as something to be taught and to be learned. The event can be plausibly dated 427 B.C., if truth may be tied to particular occasions. "This year the Leontines," writes an ancient annalist, "dispatched ambassadors to Athens":

> The leader of the embassy was Gorgias the rhetorician, who in eloquence far surpassed all his contemporaries. He was the first man to devise rules of rhetoric and so far excelled all other men in the instruction offered by the sophists that he received from his pupils a fee of one hundred minas. Now when Gorgias had arrived in Athens and been introduced to the people in assembly, he discoursed to them upon the subject of the alliance, and by the novelty of his speech he filled the Athenians, who are by nature clever and fond of dialectic, with wonder. For he was the first to use the rather unusual and carefully devised structures of speech, such as antithesis, sentences with equal members or balanced clauses or similar endings, and the like, all of which at that time was enthusiastically received because the device was exotic, but is now looked upon as laboured and to be ridiculed when employed too frequently and tediously.[4]

The effect of such speech, by all the testimony of Antiquity, and indeed of the Middle Ages and Renaissance, is astonishment, open-mouthed wonder at the gift of gab. But if it fails it seems frigid, bombastic, artificial. It is both offensive and impersuasive. And so the problem arises of hedging against failure, employing the art that conceals art, or alternatively, of developing an unrhetorical plain style whose "careful negligence" may yet permit distinction.

Such are some of the themes of *The Problem of Style* and their attendant questions. You may write the answers in the margin.

HOW SHALL THE POEM BE WRITTEN?

How shall the poem be written? I answer, In metrical language. In most periods of English literature this was a sufficient answer. One could explain meter but need not. It was learned as one learns his language, and indeed it was a language; it was, in a sense I shall later define, a dialect. But it is not now a sufficient answer. For metrical theory, description, and practice are a shambles.

The principal causes of this in metrical practice are the wide diversity of metrical forms and systems, and, in particular, the prevalence of what I shall call parasitic meter, the characteristic meter of our time. In theory and description it is partly a consequence of phonetic ignorance, even in high places—assonance is illustrated by "In Xanadu did Kubla Khan / A stately . . . "—conjoined with that mystique of sensitivity that was encouraged by the New Criticism. We read: "The richness and variety of sounds and rhythms heard in reading a poem of the highest order . . . is and always will remain indescribable." The sounds and rhythms of poems good and bad, as well as of lectures and conversation, are no more and no less than the sounds and rhythms of English, or of one of the varieties of English, and these are describable.

But it is also a consequence of that same mystique achieving insights in commentary by the application of the doctrine of norm and variation. One posits a metrical norm, and then searches for the significance of this and that deviation. For example:

> Rhythm . . . can . . . express the most delicate feelings and moods. No words can adequately paraphrase the effect of hopeless, absolute despair conveyed by

the final line of the stanzas of Keats's *La Belle Dame Sans Merci*:

> O what can ail thee, Knight-at-arms,
>   Alone and palely loitering?
> The sedge has withered from the lake,
>   And no birds sing!

> The final line is half the length of the preceding three. We have been prepared to find the final line rhythmically symmetrical with the others. Compelled by the rhythmic vacancy, our defeated expectation produces a desolation of spirit no other poetic device could produce.

Now, in the first place, if you are reading that in print, you can see the line is shorter; but even heard without text the rhyme tells you it is over. There is no vacancy, no defeated expectation to express what the poem literally says: "And no birds sing!" And what of the desolation of:

> A man is swimming in the lake
>   With no clothes on.

which has an identical stress contour.

Another remarks about Chaucer's "Woodring upon this word, quaking for drede": "the double inversion, at the start of the line and again after the caesura, gives the two participial verbs a special quiver." The quiver, of course, is begotten by the literal sense, "quaking for dread." Again, on Yeats's "Speech after long silence, it is right," we are instructed: "the fact that the reader must hurry over the two unaccented syllables of *after* before he can rest on the accent of *long* makes the emphasis on *long* greater than it would otherwise be; and this heavy emphasis on *long* fortifies the meaning of the word." It is a long *long*. But you don't hurry over anything or rest on anything; you speak English:

> Beer after sweet sherry, it is wrong.

Finally, "The heavy pause after *silence* . . . is dramatically right." A pause is silence.

Meter on this view has no inherent rights, but in its betrayals and its phonetic allegories is significant.

Nevertheless, it is clear from what is being published as poetry, approved of and commented on, that there is not only uncertainty with respect to the old tradition but also a widely felt need for some system of meter other than the traditional, and that none has been agreed on and established. There seem to be two conditions: the new meter will avoid both structural rhyme and the characteristic stress patterns of the old. The motive is rebellion, now become a habit, which is sufficient to destroy but not to establish.

This is the inconclusive issue of that revolution in the arts, poetry among the rest, which began in the first decade of this century, culminated in the twenties, and achieved almost universal cultural acceptance in the forties. I myself came into it in the late twenties, the latest possible moment to be touched by the original impulse. Soon afterward—let us date it by Eliot's tenure of the Charles Eliot Norton professorship at Harvard in 1933-34—what had been the advance guard had become practically the whole army. Everyone felt special in belonging to a club to which everyone belonged.

There is, as you know, a natural progression in time in such matters, from personal impulse to communication to and within a group, conversion of outsiders, institutionalization of the coterie spirit, and finally the establishment of sacred texts, *The Waste Land* and *Ulysses*, and orthodox commentary, Brooks and Warren, and the fixed formulas of The Creed whose repetition aids identification with the institution, but identification no longer with a cohesive group in ferment. Such is the natural history of revolution. In the beginning the slogans, the aims, do not especially matter; what is important is the revolutionary spirit, the destruction of the past. The revolutionaries are united in destruction, however different their explicit goals. In the end only the slogans matter, and the revolutionary stance. But the life has gone out of it. And so we ask: In the debris of revolution how shall the poem be written?

What are our metrical languages? Of the untraditional there is that heterogeneity of procedures, often on no discernible principles, that we call free verse, from the scriptural line of Whitman to the letters falling down the page in organic form as they spell "rain." Much of this is based on writing, on print. The lineation is determined by stipulation and whimsy, by the placing on the page, with no phonetic principle unless in reading and reciting it one gives a phonetic signal at the arbitrary line ends. But such signals, unless they coincide with idiomatic ones, are affected pronunciation.

Early free verse, however, and much still written, has a discernible principle. I call it grammatical meter: a line may end at any terminal juncture, any completed grammatical unit. If the line is short, as in much Imagistic verse, the sentence is, in effect, diagrammed; one might call it parsing meter. Some charming things were done in it; for example, Stevens' *Disillusionment of Ten O'Clock*:

The houses are haunted
By white night-gowns.
None are green,
Or purple with green rings,
Or green with yellow rings,
Or yellow with blue rings.
None of them are strange,
With socks of lace
And beaded ceintures.
People are not going
To dream of baboons and periwinkles.
Only, here and there, an old sailor,
Drunk and asleep in his boots,
Catches tigers
In red weather.

There was a moment in history for this sort of thing, and some nice things are still done in it, notations that might have been journal entries, but it is not properly a meter, which requires, as I shall later maintain, an independent and concurrent metrical principle. It is rather a form of punctuation that may display or distort by emphases the grammatical principle.

Some early free verse was intended to be an accentual meter, determined only by count of stress. But the problem with accentual meters in modern English is to determine which syllables are prosodically accented. As you know, there is one, and only one, primary stress in each phrase, and the others have varying degrees of stress determined partly by the grammatical function and partly by the internal stress contour of the word. In the old Germanic tradition prosodic stresses were pointed by structural alliteration:

In a somer seson when softe was the sunne

supported by the repetitiveness of formulas, and limited by the two and two phrasing of the lines. But we have no viable formulas, would be appalled by consistent structural alliteration, and would feel hemmed in by two and two phrasing. Yet without such support the meter remains wavering and ambiguous. It will not do. There is more to be said for a syllabic meter, determined by count of syllables only. It is, like the accentual, an old tradition in English; it accounts for the decasyllabic line of Wyatt and Donne:

So, if I dream I have you, I have you.[1]

and sometimes of Sidney:

If you hear that they seem my heart to move[2]

"observing only number (with some regard to the accent)," as Sidney himself describes it. In the modern tradition it has these rules: the syllabification is that of ordinary educated speech, not of careful enunciation, and elision is optional. Final unaccented syllables count. And there is a negative principle, testifying to the power of traditional meter, that no succession of lines should establish the expectation of a repetitive stress pattern. Consequently, verses of seven or of nine syllables are best. It is an interesting, though probably limited, meter. It can handle the ordinariness of experience, as in *Monday Morning:*

The flattery has been infrequent
And somewhat grudging. There is junk mail
And no letter. The weather cloudy
With more snow. Fortuitous meeting,
The rustle of flirtation, the look—
Self-esteem sustained by any excuse,
By any misconstruction? No. No.
It is now a January world,
An after-Christmas waiting. For what?
Not for this snow, this silence. There is
No resonance in the universe.
I must buy something extra today
And clutter up my house and my life.[3]

I should like now to seem to digress. Literary judgments, in general, are hand-me-downs. Or they are acts of belonging. In a time in which metrical experiment is thought to be in itself a good, the Renaissance experiment in classical prosody is universally condemned, even by those ignorant of classical prosody. Yet it was more rationally conducted, and was, perhaps, no greater a failure, than the metrical experiments of this century. The poetry of prestige at that time was Classical Latin, and only Latin prosody had been adequately described. Latin poetry had been written, was still being written, both in rhymed accentual-syllabic and in classical quantitative meters. Why not English? Furthermore, Latin was then pronounced with the sounds of English. The classical tunes were learned in childhood, and in one's native phonemic system. The problem would seem to be simple: to substitute English words and syntax for Latin. It had to be tried; it didn't work. It did not work primarily, I should think, because one does not hear in English length by position, which is essential to the classical system; it is not a perception relevant to our language habits. And because at the same time, in the 1580s and 1590s, there appeared a poetry in the native tradition to challenge "the comparison / Of all that insolent Greece or haughty Rome / Sent forth, or since did from their ashes come." And because the native tradition developed a rhymeless measure, blank verse, and an internal structuring of the line with alternative varieties of modulation, analogous to the potentialities of a quantitive prosody. So it wasn't needed.

In like fashion the current experimental procedures may not really be needed. For why have generations of poets set out to destroy the iambic pentameter and its predecessor, the iambic octosyllable? Partly because it was the fashion, but also because traditional meter carried with it the rhetoric, subjects, attitudes, and values the revolution was directed against, the linguistic and social notions of correctness. But that rhetoric, those subjects, and those values have been lost.

I turn now to traditional and its bastard issue, parasitic meter. On the traditional I shall make only a few points; they are the points on which I have something to say.

First, it is a meter by law. One rejects the textbook distinction between the metrical norm and the rhythm of a line, defined as the actual stress-contour, as a fiction, and a harmful fiction. Meter is perceived in the actual stress-contour, or the line is perceived as unmetrical, or the perceiver doesn't perceive meter at all. Donne's decasyllabic line:

So, if I dream I have you, I have you.

is by the laws of traditional meter unmetrical; that is what Jonson was referring to when he said "Donne should be hanged for not keeping of the accent."

346

Second. Traditional meter consists in the repetition of one or more of the figures of diction, the *schemata verborum* of ancient rhetoric: homoioteleuton, or rhyme, like ending; isocolon, or equality, usually syllabic equality, of units; cursus, the repetition of one of a group of syllabic patterns, long and short, or stressed and unstressed. Nor is this surprising, for rhetoric, as Aristotle says, borrowed the figures from poetry. Since it is repetitive it may be thought monotonous; since it is rhetorical it may be thought artificial. To these charges we shall return in a moment.

Third. Of these the dominant principle in English poetry since the Norman Conquest has been rhyme. In the first edition of *The Oxford Book of English Verse* (1900), there are 883 selections; 16 are unrhymed, or minimally rhymed. Furthermore, rhyme is a sufficient principle, with the ancillary principle that the rhyming syllables be not so hidden or remote that the rhyme is unperceived:

> I might as well give you my opinion of these two
>   sorts of sin as long as, in a way, against
>   each other we are pitting them,
> And that is, don't bother your head about sins
>   of commission because, however sinful, they
>   must at least be fun or else you wouldn't be
>   committing them.

It determines the line. It tells you where the line ends. It does not determine the length and internal modulation of the line.

Off-rhyme, if used systematically as in some of Wilfred Owen, is a form of rhyme, and could be exploited much more than it has been, as in the following quatrain where *demand* answers *mend,* and *face fuss:*

Prue loved her man: to clean, to mend,
To have a child for his sake, fuss
Over him, and on demand
Sleep with him with averted face.[4]

But in current practice off-rhyme is usually parasitic on the tradition of rhymed verse; it is an act of naughtiness, answering the plea of the girl in the old song, "Oh, violate me in the vilest way you know."

Fourth. The basic English measure is the iambic octosyllable. Instead of "The curfew tolls the knell of parting day," read:

The curfew tolls the knell of day,
The herd wind slowly o'er the lea,
The ploughman homeward plods his way,
And leaves the world to night and me.

And so on through the poem.

It follows that if you wish to say something in verse that when read aloud to an audience will be immediately apprehended and responded to as an utterance, write it in octosyllabic couplets:

An Oedipean Mom and Dad
Made Junior Freud feel pretty bad,
And when they died he was so vexed
He never after hetrosexed.[5]

And if you are looking for novelty within the scope of standard meter, there are possibilities in octosyllabic blank verse, of which there are almost no instances in English:

The night is still. The unfailing surf
In passion and subsidence moves
As at a distance. The glass walls,
And redwood, are my utmost being.
And is there there in the last shadow,
There in the final privacies
Of unaccosted grace,—is there,
Gracing the tedium to death,
An intimation? Something much
Like love, like loneliness adrowse
In states more primitive than peace,
In the warm wonder of winter sun.[6]

Fifth. Modes of recitation sometimes affect meter, for a mode of recitation is a dialect. I mean by a dialect a sublanguage, a system of enunciation, of grammar, and, in metrical speech, of lineation, as also of idiom and vocabulary, used by a particular group in specified social situations. Of the common modes associated with the recitation of poetry two are distinctly dialects. The first is the scanning in unison which we learned in grade school:

> *This* is the *for*est prim*ev*al, the *mur*muring *pines*
> and the *hem*locks.

Or:

> Of *man's* first *diso*bed*ience and* the *fruit*

This is the experiential basis for what I shall call the fiction of a metrical norm. And notice, the whole phonetic structure of

349

scanning aloud is unEnglish. If you spoke that way in any other situation you would probably not be understood, and certainly would be regarded as very odd. The second is the children's chant:

Jóhnny ís a stínkér.

The chant has a definite tune, and the form imposes accents on syllables that would be unaccented in ordinary speech, on "is" and "ker." The tune demands its four heavy beats, its Germanic heritage. Contrast the mnemonic rhyme:

Thirty days hath September,
April, June, and November

with its accents on "hath" and "and," with "The payments will be due in September, April, June, and November."

The other modes I shall enumerate are distinct from one another but all clearly forms of ordinary English. There is the elocutionary and expressive, and its cousin the rhetorical and declamatory; there is the voice of the public lecture, and the slowed-down enunciation of reading aloud. There is also semichant, favored by some poets, which blurs the distinction between grades of more than minimal accent, and in this respect is like the scanning mode. There is, finally, on the one hand, considered conversation, and, on the other, humdrum casual utterance. This latter is often taken to be the exemplar of real speech, though most of it is ritual, the noises of sociability. Furthermore, casual utterance in some places reduces the number of syllables, and at times gives minimal instead of tertiary, secondary instead of primary accent, and so this mode of recitation has metrical consequences.

The descriptive problems raised by different modes of recitation can be avoided by regarding a meter, not as a schematic diagram of scansions, but as a collection of syllabic-syntactic types; any one fulfills the law. Any line of the type, "A rosy garland and a weary head," is an iambic pentameter; for example, "The raving beauty or the common scold." And, indeed, this is the way we perceive meter when we read without hesitation or analysis, that is, poetically. We do not hear diagrams.

I turn now to the two charges against traditional meter: that it is monotonous and artificial. Monotonous, of course, is a value judgment. But is monotony necessarily monotonous? Is it monotonous to have coffee every morning, or is it necessary? Should other activities be substituted for the essential elements in the sexual act to relieve the boredom of how often a week?

However, there is a legitimate objection to standard meter that is somewhat akin to this, and one that is not usually explicitly stated. It is that the line is overdetermined, particularly when rhymed. For syllable count, stress pattern, rhyme, each would sufficiently determine the line. And if the line consists, as very often it does, of complete grammatical units, that would reinforce the determination. But it may be urged on the contrary that rigor in poetry as in science is an instrument of discovery.

Again, traditional meter is felt to be artificial, which, of course, is why it is used, and to exclude the natural rhythms of real speech. It is said again and again, as if it were true, that people do not talk in iambic pentameters. But they do; not always, but often enough. Some months ago I sat in the sun and wrote down these lines at random. They are segments of real speech:

I'll have the special and a glass of milk.
The order will be ready when you come.
We ought to be in Cleveland in an hour.
I haven't anything to say to you.
Goddamn it, what in hell is going on?
I'll think it over and I'll let you know.
Oh, go to hell! Who do you think you are?
She does her exercises every day.
How often shall I see you in a lifetime?

But perhaps more often people talk in the octosyllabic line, in iambic tetrameters:

I love her and I always will.
Young poets are a dime a dozen.
I'll be there anytime you say.
He doesn't love me anymore.
For Christ's sake, will you stop that noise?
I didn't ask you what you thought.
I've had a headache for two days.
Darling, I'd rather not tonight.
What's playing at the Paramount?
I put five dollars on the nose.
Some people do, some people don't.
Is there a doctor in the house?
We live in Massachusetts now.
Who do you think you are? The Pope?

If the ear for iambic pentameter and tetrameter has not been completely destroyed in our society, you will have heard each of these lines as simultaneously a completed grammatical segment and one of the various types of recognizable iambic lines. For as prose is written in sentences, without significant lineation, so poetry is written in sentences and lines. It is encoded not only in grammar, but also at the same time in meter, for meter is the principle or set of principles, whatever they may be, that determines the line. Consequently, grammar and prosody are separate and concurrent principles of the same order. And as we perceive of each sentence, without stopping to analyse it, that it is grammatical or not, so the repetitive perception that this line is metrical or that it is not, that it exemplifies the rules of its meter or that it does not, is the metrical experience. It follows that metrical analysis is irrelevant to poetry; metrical perception is of the essence. You do not have to explain the iambic pentameter; you do have to recognize it.

It follows, also, that the notion of norm and variation is not relevant to traditional meter. There are alternative patterns, each of which satisfies the metrical requirements, some more common, some less. You may begin "To be or not" or "Whether 'tis nobler"; the choice is metrically indifferent. An absolutely consistent preference of one to the other would constitute another meter. Furthermore, the theoretical iambic norm of modern prosodists, described as an alternation of minimal and maximal stresses, is a very uncommon pattern. Since there is only one maximal stress to a phrase, the line must be phrased in two-syllable units, "The man, the maid, the bed, the child," or "I came, I saw, I won." The monotony of the theoretical norm is grammatical.

But norm and variation is relevant to, is, in fact, the generating principle of parasitic meter. The term is descriptive and pejorative. Such meter presupposes a meter by law which it uses, alludes to, traduces, returns to. To perceive it one must have firmly in mind the prior tradition from which it departs and to which it returns. The *locus classicus* is Eliot's "the most interesting verse which has yet been written in our language has been done by taking a very simple form, like the iambic pentameter, and constantly withdrawing from it, or taking no form at all, and constantly approximating to a very simple one. It is this contrast between fixity and flux, this unperceived evasion of monotony, which is the very life of verse."

Meter may be parasitic in various ways. One finds a fairly simple form of it, supported by rhyme, in *Lycidas* and *Dover Beach*: the lines are either iambic pentameter or fragments, and usually conventional half-lines, of iambic pentameter. In general, the lines of a poem in parasitic meter will be partly in standard meter, at times parts of what would be a standard line, or they are felt to be equivalent in some aspect of sound or feeling to a standard line, or they exhibit some marked variation of a standard line, or some other principle of meter is used intermittently and supported and given authority by the presence and recurrence of standard lines. If it seems from this account that meter can be parasitic in many and devious ways, this is true, for the only consistent principle is that it depart from and return to a norm. It is the nature of parasitism that it may feed in different ways, that it may be irresponsible since it always has the responsible thing it feeds on to sustain it and keep it alive.

I shall conclude with some illustrations. Yeats in an eight-line poem produces three deviants of the iambic pentameter line by the transformation of a legitimate syllabic-syntactic pattern:

> Speech after long silence; it is right,
> All other lovers being estranged or dead,
> Unfriendly lamplight hid under its shade,
> The curtains drawn upon unfriendly night,

That we descant and yet again descant
Upon the supreme theme of Art and Song;
Bodily decrepitude is wisdom; young
We loved each other and were ignorant.

"Speech after lengthy silence" is transformed to "long silence" by substituting a monosyllabic for a disyllabic adjective; similarly "hidden by its shade" is transformed to "hid under its shade," and "the highest theme" to "the supreme theme."

Again, in many of Tate's poems most of the lines are fugitives from the iambic pentameter. It is, as he says, "a little like the man who either avoids or steps upon all the cracks in the sidewalk." In *The Wolves* he stepped upon five cracks out of twenty-seven.

In Stevens' *Hibiscus on the Sleeping Shores* nine of the fifteen lines are iambic pentameter, and the presence and recurrence of these supports the whole:

I say now, Fernando, that on that day
The mind roamed as a moth roams,
Among the blooms beyond the open sand;

And that whatever noise the motion of the waves
Made on the sea-weeds and the covered stones
Disturbed not even the most idle ear.

Then it was that that monstered moth
Which had lain folded against the blue
And the colored purple of the lazy sea,

And which had drowsed along the bony shores,
Shut to the blather that the water made,
Rose up besprent and sought the flaming red

Dabbled with yellow pollen—red as red
As the flag above the old cafe—
And roamed there all the stupid afternoon.

But it was Eliot, perhaps, who most exploited parasitic meter. In *The Love Song of J. Alfred Prufrock* and *Portrait of a Lady* rhyme is the dominant principle: about five-sixths of the lines in each. A secondary principle is iambic pentameter, its observance and avoidance: about two-fifths of the lines observe, the rest avoid in different ways. And *Prufrock*, especially, is supported by a good deal of rhetorical repetition, 27 out of 131 lines: "In the room the women come and go," "And would it have been worth it, after all?" Now *Prufrock* may be parasitic partly by accident of composition. The poem would seem to be in inception an anthology of relevant passages from the poet's notebook—fragments written now in this meter, now in that, but often enough in pentameter—rather than a planned departure from and return to a norm. But within particular passages there is sometimes a planned departure. The *Portrait,* on the other hand, seems planned.

But the nature of parasitic meter can be more clearly seen in what is perhaps the best passage in Eliot's *Gerontion*:

After such knowledge, what forgiveness? Think now
History has many cunning passages, contrived corridors
And issues, deceives with whispering ambitions,
Guides us by vanities. Think now
She gives when our attention is distracted
And what she gives, gives with such supple confusions
That the giving famishes the craving. Gives too late
What's not believed in, or if still believed,
In memory only, reconsidered passion. Gives too soon

Into weak hands, what's thought can be dispensed with
Till the refusal propagates a fear. Think
Neither fear nor courage saves us.

Let us go through some of this, line by line. "After such knowledge, what forgiveness? Think now" is a normal iambic pentameter with feminine ending. It has a slightly odd movement, but that has nothing to do with the metrical principle. The next line consists of a complete clause forming a normal iambic pentameter, but with the appositive phrase "contrived corridors" tacked on extra. "And issues, deceives with whispering ambitions" has an unusual variation in the second foot. "Guides us by vanities. Think now" contains an easily recognized part of a normal line, with the repetition of "Think now" added. We return in the next line and the line following to blank verse, with an unusual variation in the last foot of the latter. "That the giving famishes the craving. Gives too late"; this will not fit a standard pattern. The complete clause, however, could be taken as a headless pentameter, and the added phrase is supported by the repetition of "gives." The next line returns to normal. Finally, "In memory only, reconsidered passion. Gives too soon" is a standard line with the repetitive "Gives too soon" added. And so on.

An inductive examination of these poems, with no antecedent knowledge of English metrical tradition, would yield no metrical principle. This would not be true of Chaucer, Shakespeare, Milton, Wordsworth, or, in Antiquity, of Homer or Vergil.

We have lost the repetitive harmony of the old tradition, and we have not established a new. We have written to vary or violate the old line, for regularity we feel is meaningless and irregularity meaningful. But several generations of poets, acting on the principles and practice of significant variation, have at last nothing to vary from. The last variation is regularity.[7]

357

GRADUATE TRAINING IN ENGLISH

A university is an institution of learning. The undergraduate acquires learning; the faculty contribute to learning. The graduate student is in transition from acquiring to contributing.

To contribute to learning one must know something, and to know something means there is much one does not know. One specializes because one must, and because it is human: curiosity aggrandizes its object. One becomes a professional.

If the university is regarded as a way of life, the life of an institutionalized leisure class pursuing the semispiritual exercises of culture, then matters are different. For this is the life of the amateur.

Such, in brief, is the conflict between the creative soul in the university and the pedant. I am a pedant. Some of the contributors to this symposium are, no doubt, creative souls: for them, their servants will do their scholarship for them.

If I read books I should know how books are made and where to find them. If I read Shakespeare I should know it may not be Shakespeare. We call the one bibliography, the other textual criticism. If I read a language I should know the language, whether it be of Tudor London or contemporary Western American. We call this philology. If what I read has any real reference I should know something of the referent. We call this history. If the referent is, in part, as it is in *Lycidas,* prior literature I should know that. We call this literary history. These are the disciplines of graduate study, together with the literary disciplines of undergraduate study.

---

* This piece was originally part of "A Symposium: Graduate Training in the Humanities," a special section, by nine contributors, of a *Carleton Miscellany* issue.

It is true, many graduate instructors are dull and pedantic. And many graduate students in the humanities are dull and not even pedantic. They are fugitives from the worlds of business and the exact sciences, who come to graduate school to raskolnikov.

IV

IDEAL FICTION

The Clerk's Tale

My subject is Ideal Fiction, my instance *The Clerk's Tale.* The problems of *The Clerk's Tale* are in part problems of the subject matter, the relationship of the sexes in marriage, and these were problems to Chaucer and his audience as they are to us. But they are also in part problems of literary kind, for those exemplified in *The Clerk's Tale* are now in disfavor. In rejecting the kind we impute the fault to the instance.

I shall begin with Horace. It is difficult to make material in the public domain one's own. And yet it is better to rehandle the Trojan War in five acts than to produce something novel and so far unsaid. Hence, when Chaucer undertook to render Petrarch's prose tale in English rhyme royal, he did not, on the one hand, do it routinely or prepare a word-for-word crib, nor, on the other, in rivalry with Petrarch leap into difficulties by ignoring his own limitations and the limitations of the particular literary kind, the *lex operis.*[1] And there is our difficulty. For we do not recognize, and would not admit as valid if we did, that literary kind. What is it? and what is its law?

I shall, to begin with, premise that any work is a simultaneity of literary kinds, and shall in this instance deal with three. First, *The Clerk's Tale* is one of those fictions, common until fiction changed its nature in the nineteenth century, conducted by a Manipulator, in this case an authoritarian monarch, like the Duke in *Measure for Measure*, who has the power to manipulate. Another common form, of course, is the Practical Joker, like Claudio and his associates in *Much Ado About Nothing* who

363

engineer the extreme case: a couple who hate each other fall in love with each other. Officially, at least aesthetically, we are repelled by this, or explain it away as with Beatrice and Benedick, partly out of democratic and romantic feeling, and partly out of the conviction that contrivance is inimical to art. Yet art is contrivance, and the manipulator, God knows, is a common figure in what we call real life. We need not like him, but need not dislike the story because of him.

This brings us to the second, the principal form. Current theory permits us only two major ones, the fiction of ordinariness and probability, or fairy tale, fantasy, allegory, the terms by which we apologize for deviation from real life, as if real life itself were not a fiction. We read in Forster: "The other novelists say 'Here is something that could occur in your lives,' the fantasist says 'Here is something that could not occur.'" But *The Clerk's Tale* is in between; it is possible; it could occur, but not in your lives. And so we watch and do not identify. The story is distanced. It is Ideal Fiction.

The essence of Ideal Fiction is that it presents the extreme case, but yet a case. It is something that once happened to people with such names as we have, living in a nameable place. As extreme, however, it is in the literary sense improbable, improbable by definition: "Yet sometimes it shall fall on a day / That falls not afterward within a thousand years."[2] And this provokes two observations. First, the improbable is interesting. Your wife says, "God, another day," and you turn off your hearing aid. She says, "The damnedest thing happened today, I never would have believed it," and you are eager attention. Secondly, the improbable is also probable.[3] Several years ago I hailed a cab at 58th and Park Avenue, said "Grand Central Station," and the cabbie said, "How do you get there, buddy?"

But the Fiction of the Extreme Case, though consonant with medieval habits of thought and feeling, is not peculiarly medieval. It is also modern, though repugnant to our official ideas. It is true we are not so partial to notable images of virtues and vices, partly because we are routinely in revolt against what we take to be Sunday School morality, against the idea of extreme good and extreme evil. We will not accept More's or Shakespeare's Richard III, though we constructed such a character ourselves in Hitler and in Stalin. But the extreme case in our society deals rather with the little things and little people, with comedians, professors, cowboys, and not with the big things, death and supposed death, chiefs of state, their spouses and heirs. It flourishes particularly in oral literature; it is the point of many a joke.

There is the extreme case of W. C. Fields' "Who put water in my water?" as also the current story of the professor who taped his lectures, which were heard by fifty lonely tape recorders on fifty chairs. Or there is that classic of the two homosexuals on a street corner. A blonde walks by, wind blowing against her dress, and one says to the other, "Sometimes makes you wish you were a lesbian, doesn't it?" Or even more classic, the poker player hand to end the poker game in Eugene Manlove Rhodes's *The Trusty Knaves*. The slickers are setting the tenderfoot up for the kill, so our cowboy heroes sit in. In the climactic hand one cowboy calls the other, who lays down Ace, King; Queen, Jack, and ten of spades. He then lays down Ace, King, Queen, Jack, and ten of spades. "Well, well! It's a tie. We'll have to divide the pot."

What is notable in each case is the invention. There is nothing so simple as exaggeration: that yields a different sort of story, The Tall Tale or The Boast. Rather, the invention involves opposites, or what are taken to be opposites, whisky and water, man and machine. Or it finds that statement or that choice to which

nothing, but the point involved is relevant. So in Sidney's epi-
sode of Argalus and Parthenia, the hopeless and constant lover,
offered an exact replica of his love—indeed it is Parthenia herself,
unidentified—courteously declines. "It is only happiness I refuse,
since of the only happiness I could and can desire I am refused."
He is in love with her identity. Invention has found the extreme
case, and found it with a special flourish; the thing clicks, and
one thinks, What else? There is an apt ingenuity, a striking pro-
priety. This, too, is a quality now officially in disfavor; it falls
under suspicion of contrivance. Yet, here again, in nonaesthetic
matters we still sometimes appreciate the apt invention. There is
a useful allowance horse running at Aqueduct named Brooklyn
Bridge. He is by Swaps out of Conniver. What else?

The ideality of invention in *The Clerk's Tale* is a matter of
detail, of the premise, and of the conduct of the story. Of detail:
"She was not idle until she slept," for Nature requires that idle-
ness. Of premise: Walter is solicited by his subjects to marry, to
provide for the succession. To this the wealth and rank of the
mother-to-be is irrelevant, and so excluded in the choice, exclud-
ed by their opposites: "the poorest of the poor, the lowliest of the
low." The invention is controlled by the form, by the *lex operis*. In
the larger conduct of the story there is appropriateness in the se-
quence. The first trial is the supposed death of the daughter, the
second of the heir apparent, the third the rejection of the mar-
riage itself, and in the joyful catastrophe the supposed bride is
the restored daughter. Who else? In one scene of discovery all is
reversed. And the trials themselves are not the incidentals but the
essentials of marriage, children and the marriage itself. A mod-
ern Walter would leave faucets dripping.

In one scene of discovery. Here we have the third of our lit-
erary kinds, for *The Clerk's Tale* is both the *historia,* the story, of
rhetorical tradition, "an account of exploits actually performed,

but removed in time from the recollection of our age," and a narrative based on persons, displaying "particular traits of character, such as austerity and gentleness," or patience in marriage, and showing "the vicissitudes of life, reversal of fortune, unexpected disaster, sudden joy, and a happy outcome."[4] In such narrative character is narrowed to relevance, and the elements of action are extremes, high and low, joy and disaster, and they are not gradual but sudden. They invite the extreme case.

It follows, then, that in Ideal Fiction the characters are flat. But it is a fiction of our fiction that people are really round. The truth is we are not usually real life characters in real life. We are flat, and so are those we know. We are only round occasionally to others in a sympathetic moment, to ourselves in introspection, and now and again as a demand on others in the grim game of interpersonal relations: "I want to be treated as a person." We usually see others as truck drivers or neighbors, bore or blonde. And we are flat to ourselves when working efficiently, when we are most ourselves. When I write a poem I am a poet; I am narrowed to relevance.

Nor was the extreme case in Chaucer's world as extreme as one might think. In that Christianity which has been almost liquidated in my lifetime, each of us is an extreme case, destined for Heaven or for Hell. There is no individualistic Limbo in which we as real characters can hide. We are flat, flatly saved, or flatly damned. The ultimate world is ideal, and the ultimate our ultimate concern.

THE RENAISSANCE IN ENGLAND

In dealing with the past, as in dealing with our own autobiography, we parcel it out in periods. And these need not be merely arbitrary. What is arbitrary is that we mark off a period in light of some aspect of the times that interests us; in light of other aspects we would mark it off differently. For some, at least, of the authors in this book there was such a thing as the Renaissance in England. It was an event in the history of literature and or learning.

The time is the hundred and some years after Columbus's discovery of America, from the youth of Thomas More to the publication of Shakespeare's collected plays in 1623. It is the time of the diffusion of printing, the exploitation of gunpowder, the exploration of the New World. It is the time of the Reformation and of an increasing nationalism in Western Europe: Christianity became regional, and theology an instrument of international affairs.

The place is England, a small northern country on the edge of the great world of that time, and with about the same secondary importance in the international scene of its day as Great Britain has in the larger scene of today. But it was not, at the start, Great Britain. Scotland until 1603 was an independent kingdom and after 1603 still had an independent government under a common monarch. Moreover, in the preceding century it was often hostile and for the most part allied with France: Mary, Queen of Scots, for example, was for a time Queen of France. Nor was England itself a country unified and homogeneous. The North was remote, unruly border country, poor, feudal, and

* This essay was originally the Introduction for an anthology edited by J. V. Cunningham, *The Renaissance in England,* a collection of ninety-four selections from forty-some authors or sources.

feuding. It was the world of the border ballads, of the Percys and the Dacres. Wales, to the west, was at the beginning of this period still thoroughly Celtic, a region where Owen Glendowers still called "spirits from the vasty deep," though toward the end it had been sufficiently assimilated to the central culture of England. Ireland was an outpost in uneasy subjection, and the relationship of English and Irish was precisely that of the English and the American Indian. We are concerned, in brief, with London and with central, southern, and eastern England.

And with very few people. There were fewer, indeed, in the 1490s than there had been a century and a half earlier, as a consequence of the Black Death and the subsequent recurrent plagues. However, from this time on the population was on the increase. We do not have, of course, any precise figures since there was nothing like the modern census, but we can make informed guesses. The population in 1490 was about equal to the present population of Connecticut; in 1623, to that of Florida. The striking increase was in the population of London: from the size of Portland, Maine, to almost the size of Portland, Oregon, in a hundred and some years.

At the beginning of this period the literary models in English were Chaucer, Gower, and Lydgate in verse; there were none in prose. The only prose work of general reputation in the world of letters, Thomas More's *Utopia* (1516), was written in Latin. At the end of this period there were for models the achievements of Shakespeare and Jonson, Beaumont and Fletcher, Sidney and Spenser, Bacon and Donne. There was a literature that, as Jonson said of Shakespeare in the commendatory poem to the first collected edition, could challenge comparison with "all that insolent Greece or haughty Rome sent forth." At the beginning is Leonard Cox's simple assumption that "logic"—the old

Aristotelian logic—"is a plain and sure way to instruct a man of the truth of anything," and the lore of the four elements; at the end, William Gilbert's conception of the earth as a giant lodestone, and William Harvey's demonstration of the circulation of the blood.

This, then, was the Renaissance in England. For the Renaissance is a notion properly applicable to the world of letters and of learning. It denotes, of course, a rebirth and referred originally to a revival of interest in the literature of Antiquity and its associated learning after, so it was thought, the monkish barbarism of the intervening centuries. The idea was then extended to the Early Modern rebirth of a special kind of intellectual excitement. So, at least, some of the authors in this book themselves thought. Thomas Campian writes in 1602:

> Learning first flourished in Greece, from thence it was derived unto the Romans. . . . Learning, after the declining of the Roman Empire and the pollution of their language through the conquest of the barbarians, lay most pitifully deformed till the time of Erasmus, Reuchlin, Sir Thomas More, and other learned men of that age, who brought the Latin tongue again to light, redeeming it with much labor out of the hands of the illiterate monks and friars.[1]

Francis Bacon a few years later saw the literary and intellectual history of the immediate past in much the same terms, only more explicitly developed, and with dispraise for both parties, as befitted the rhetorician of the New Learning of modern science:

Martin Luther, conducted no doubt by a higher providence, but in discourse of reason finding what a province he had undertaken against the bishop of Rome and the degenerate traditions of the church and finding his own solitude being no ways aided by the opinions of his own time, was enforced to awake all antiquity, and to call former times to his succours to make a party against the present time. So that the ancient authors, both in divinity and in humanity, which had long time slept in libraries, began generally to be read and revolved. This by consequence did draw on a necessity of a more exquisite travail in the languages original, wherein those authors did write, for the better understanding of those authors, and the better advantage of pressing and applying their words. And thereof grew again a delight in their manner of style and phrase, and an admiration of that kind of writing; which was much furthered and precipitated by the enmity and opposition that the propounders of those primitive but seeming new opinions had against the schoolmen; who were generally of the contrary part, and whose writings were altogether in a different style and form; taking liberty to coin and frame new terms of art to express their own sense, and to avoid circuit of speech, without regard to the pureness, pleasantness, and, as I may call it, lawfulness of the phrase or word. And again, because the great labour that then was with the people (of whom the Pharisees were wont to say, *Execrabilis ista turba, quae non novit legen*), for the winning and persuading of them, there grew of necessity in chief price and request eloquence and variety of discourse, as the fittest and forciblest access into the capacity of the vulgar sort: so that these four causes concurring, the admiration of ancient authors, the hate of the schoolmen, the exact study of languages, and the efficacy of preaching, did bring in an affectionate study of eloquence and copy of speech, which then began to flourish. This grew speedily to an excess; for men began to hunt more after words than matter; more after the choiceness of the phrase, and the round and clean composition of the sentence, and the sweet falling of the clauses, and the varying and illustration of their words with tropes and figures, than after the weight of matter, worth of subject, soundness of argument, life of invention, or depth of judgment. Then grew the flowing and watery vein of Osorius, the Portugal bishop, to be in price. Then did Sturmius spend such infinite and curious pains upon Cicero the Orator, and Hermogenes the Rhetorician, besides his own books of Periods and Imitation, and the like. Then did Car of Cambridge, and Ascham with their lectures and writings almost deify Cicero and Demosthenes, and allure all young men that were studious unto that delicate and polished kind of learning. Then did Erasmus take occasion to make the scoffing Echo: *Decern annos consumpsi in legendo Cicerone;* and the Echo answered in Greek, *"Ove, Asine."* Then grew the learning of the schoolmen to be utterly despised as barbarous. In sum, the whole inclination and bent of those times was rather towards copy than weight.[2]

For Campian and Bacon, then, there is a clearly distin-
guished period in the history of literature and of learning
beginning around 1500—Erasmus (1465-1536), Reuchlin (1455-
1522), More (1478-1535), Luther (1483-1546)—and extending to
their own day. The initiators were Northern: German, Dutch,
English. Nothing is said of Italy. The culture opposed and dis-
placed is that of the Old Church, the scholasticism of monks and
friars. The New Learning is associated with the Reformation.

What did it involve? It involved, first of all, a revolution in
style, a rebirth, as they saw it, of the Latin language itself. Not
that Latin had ceased to be used in the Middle Ages: there is
more medieval Latin in print in a large university library than
a man could, or would, read in a lifetime. It was, in fact, the
only language of learning and remained the principal language
of learning until the nineteenth century. But medieval Latin had
shed the idiomatic quirks of the language of Plautus and the
stately period of the language of Cicero. It had become a kind
of Basic Latin, a clear, dry, precise medium that welcomed and
harbored all the technical words, "terms of art," of the medieval
sciences. And so the revolution in style was inevitably a revolu-
tion in learning, and, since learning was in large part divinity, it
was associated with the revolution in religion.

It was first a revolution in Latin and then a revolution in
the vernacular. And though the re-realization of classical models
and classical experience was only part of the story in the vernac-
ular literatures, it was part of the story. Something of Vergil's
descent into Hell had long before been assimilated in the me-
dieval tradition, and is realized again in Thomas Sackville's
Induction (1563). But the worlds of ancient dialogue and Horatian
satire are first naturalized in English in the early sixteenth cen-
tury by More and by Thomas Wyatt. And the subjective erotic

world of Propertius and Ovid is recaptured first by Donne in the Valedictions and Elegies of the 1590s. Indeed, the great stylistic achievement of the period, apart from the inimitable style of the later Shakespeare, the plain style of Jonson, and of Donne at his best, is consciously modeled on the classical plain style. It is a consequence of the Renaissance.

The Structure of Society

There were, to be simple about it, but no more simple than the views of the time warrant, two kinds of people in Renaissance England: those that mattered and those that did not. The latter were "the multitude, wherein be contained the base and vulgar inhabitants not advanced to any honor or dignity," as Sir Thomas Elyot puts it in *The Governor*. They were, for instance, the vulgar countrywomen at Dame Elinor's alehouse, figures of fun; the artisan, William Waring, doing ecclesiastical penance; the London rioters on Evil May Day; the gossipy servingmen in *A Yorkshire Tragedy*; or Annis Herd, the supposed witch. They were all minor figures, not of much account in that society.

The group that mattered is fairly easy to define. They were those who lived on the unearned income from inherited land. These were the men "of ancient honor and name," however recently acquired. To fall from this class, to lose one's patrimony and dissipate one's inheritance, as the Yorkshire gentleman did, is the final ruin. It is a disgrace not only to oneself but also to one's ancestors and posterity. It is for this reason that he kills his children in *A Yorkshire Tragedy*:

My lands showed like a full moon about me, but now the moon's in the last quarter, waning, waning. And I am mad to think that moon was mine, mine and my father's and my forefathers'—generations, generations. Down goes the house of us, down, down it sinks. Now is the name a beggar; begs in me that name which hundreds of years has made this shire famous. In me and my posterity runs out. . . .

My eldest beggar! Thou shalt not live to ask an usurer bread, to cry at a great man's gate or follow "good your honor" by a coach; no, nor your brother. 'Tis charity to brain you.

The gulf between the two estates was regarded as absolute, though in practice it was not quite. It is the distinction still preserved in the armed forces between the enlisted men and the commissioned officers. The one is governed, the other is the governing class. There were, however, two distinct views on the structure of the governing class, views that are clearly formulated by Fulke Greville in his account of the Queen's intervention in the quarrel between Sir Philip Sidney and the Earl of Oxford in 1579:

The Queen, who saw that by the loss or disgrace of either she could gain nothing, presently undertakes Sir Philip, and (like an excellent monarch) lays before him the difference in degree between earls and gentlemen, the respect inferiors owed to their superiors, and the necessity in princes to maintain their own creations as degrees descending between the people's licentiousness and the anointed sovereignty of crowns: how the gentleman's neglect of the nobility taught the peasant to insult both.[3]

The motivating fear in the Queen's position is fear of "the people's licentiousness," of the insulting peasant. If not structured and controlled by order and degree the irrational lower classes would destroy all order. For, says Elyot, when man "hath destroyed that wherewith he doth participate by the order of creation, he himself of necessity must then perish, whereof ensueth universal dissolution." "Imagine," says the character, Thomas More, addressing the London rioters in *Evil May Day:*

> that you sit kings in your desires,
> Authority quite silenced by your brawl,
> And you in ruff of your opinions clothed,
> What had you got? I'll tell you: you had taught
> How insolence and strong hand should prevail,
> How order should be quelled, and by this pattern
> Not one of you should live an aged man:
> For other ruffians, as their fancies wrought,
> With self-same hand, self reasons, and self right,
> Would shark on you, and men, like ravenous fishes,
> Would feed on one another.[4]

It was a plausible fear. There was no police force, no standing army. The London riot is put down by the presence of noblemen and their retainers, and by the eloquence of Thomas More. There was poverty, grievance, and there were too many rootless men, such as those described by Hythloday in More's *Utopia* and interviewed by Thomas Harman. To deal with this potentially disruptive situation, the means of order were, in the Queen's view, the reverence attached to "the annointed sovereignty of crowns" and the hierarchical stepping down by degrees of power and respect, inviting and compelling awe from inferior to superior. It was a congenial way of thinking, for the universe itself was so ordered, from the lowest element to the highest sphere, as was the celestial society that rose by degrees through all the orders of angels to God.

On the other hand, Sidney's view that there are really only the two classes, ordered by the relationship of master and servant, is perhaps more accurate of his society than the elaborate hierarchical structure that the Queen and Sir Thomas Elyot expound, though both apply. This is Greville's account of Sidney's position:

> Whereunto Sir Philip, with such reverence as became him replied: first, that place was never intended for privilege to wrong: witness herself, who how sovereign soever she were by throne, birth, education and nature, yet was she content to cast her own affections into the same moulds her subjects did, and govern all her rights by their laws. Again, he besought Her Majesty to consider that, although he were a great lord by birth, alliance and grace, yet he was no lord over him: and therefore the difference of degrees between free men could not challenge any other homage than precedency. And by her father's act (to make a princely wisdom become the more familiar) he did instance the government of King Henry the Eighth, who gave the gentry free and safe appeal to his feet against the oppression of the grandees, and found it wisdom by stronger corporation in number to keep down the greater in power, inferring else that if they should unite, the overgrown might be tempted by still coveting more to fall (as the angels did) by affecting equality with their maker.[5]

The motivating fear in Sidney's position is the fear of great magnates, of such "grandees" as had in the preceding century caused the feudal chaos of the Wars of the Roses. Those that matter are the "free men," and, among these, difference in degree is only a matter of ceremony. The particular relationship among the free men is of the same sort as the general relationship between the two classes of the commonweal; it is that of master and servant. All, for example, are servants of the crown. But Oxford, though a great lord, is not to be lord over Sidney, unless there had been, as there was not, some specific feudal obligation on Sidney's part to Oxford. And what obligations do exist do not inhere in the prerogative of degree but are under and by the law. Nor was this doctrine merely of theoretical interest. Mary, Queen of Scots, like the Princes in Sidney's *Arcadia* (1593, Book 5) claimed as a "prince absolute" not to be answerable to the law of England. The claim was disallowed, though the point was not settled.

This, then, is a world quite different from ours. In our world it is not the wealthy or the great officers of state and their associates who make the principal contributions to literature and learning. We have, at the most, an occasional man of letters somewhere in the government, an Assistant Secretary of State or a scientific adviser to the President. And we have no millionaire poets. But in the world of Renaissance England, literature and learning were produced by and for the wealthy and governing class. A simple enumeration will make this clear.

The highest officer of state in England, in dignity if not necessarily in power, was the Lord Chancellor (or, with lesser prerogatives, the Lord Keeper of the Great Seal). He took precedence. Two of the most important of our authors were Lords Chancellor, Thomas More and Francis Bacon, and Bacon's father had been Lord Keeper. John Donne, until the disgrace of his clandestine marriage, had been secretary to Sir Thomas Egerton, the Lord Keeper.

The next highest officer of state was the Lord Treasurer. Thomas Sackville, cousin to Queen Elizabeth, created Earl of Dorset by James I, was Lord Treasurer. Sir Philip Sidney was the son of a Lord Deputy of Ireland, and the nephew of the Earls of Warwick and of Leicester. At the time of his early death he was Governor of Flushing. Sir Walter Ralegh, of course, was for a long time one of the Queen's favorites, Captain of the Guard, Lord Lieutenant of Cornwall, Lord Warden of the Stannaries, and Governor of Jersey. Sir Fulke Greville, later Lord Brooke, "neither sought for nor obtained any great place or preferment in court during all the time of his attendance, neither did he need it, for he came thither backed with a plentiful fortune, which, as himself was wont to say, was the better held together by a single life, wherein he lived and died a constant courtier of the ladies." Yet he became eventually Chancellor of the Exchequer and a Privy Councillor.

Sir Thomas Wyatt, who was in a position to pursue in vain one of Henry VIII's mistresses, was Ambassador to the court of Charles V, as was also Sir Thomas Elyot. John Skelton and John Palsgrave were tutors, and Gilbert and Harvey were physicians to royalty. John Heywood was court entertainer and servant to three sovereigns, Henry VIII, Edward VI, and Mary. Richard Hooker's great work was commissioned by the government. Even Shakespeare, who had legitimate pretensions to gentility, which his success confirmed, was first the Lord Chamberlain's servant and then the King's servant, and wore the King's livery on a state occasion. The popular drama of his day could not exist except by the favor of the great. Even Ben Jonson, the stepson of a master bricklayer, becomes in legal documents "gentleman" and received for many years a handsome pension from the King. And Edmund Spenser wrote almost solely for court preferment: the *Prothalamium* celebrates the betrothal of the Earl of Worcester's daughters, and has as a kind of climax a fulsome compliment to the Earl of Essex. George Gascoigne's *Woodmanship* is a begging poem to Lord Grey of Wilton, Lord Deputy of Ireland, who was also Spenser's patron.

But it is not only a literature by and for the governing class, it is also a literature in which class distinctions are literary distinctions. Tragedy, for example, is concerned only with the governing class, and usually with heads of states, with Lear, with Claudius and Hamlet, with Julius Caesar. The death of a salesman was not tragic. Even those few plays which modern historians of literature distinguish as "domestic tragedies," that is, as not primarily political, are nevertheless concerned with men of ancient honor and means, as in *A Yorkshire Tragedy*.

This will seem strange to us, but what is even more strange is that there were class distinctions in matters of sex and of love. Whoring and lust may be expected in the lower class. It is whoring and lust in the upper class, or between nobility and the citizen's wife, that is particularly the object of satiric vehemence in Wyatt, Greville, and Jonson. The worst is the corruption of the best. So it is "my lord" Stallion and his "court-bred filly," "stretched upon the rack of lust," who are the special objects of invective. And, conversely, the whole area of what we call romantic love is the prerogative only of the upper class. It is an experience open to Lady Hungerford and Darrell of Littlecote, to Lady Rich and Sir Philip Sidney, to Argalus and Parthenia and Shakespeare's Viola and Orsino. In them it may be destructive or amusing; it may even be ridiculous to the calm sight of those not in love, as in Jonson's *Lovers Made Men*; but it is proper. In their servants it is comic and ridiculous, with the ridiculousness of impropriety:

Much ado there was, God wot;
He would love and she would not.

There are, furthermore, class distinctions in style. By and large, in the drama the one class speaks in verse, the other in prose. This is quite clear in the early Shakespeare, and in *A Midsummer Night's Dream* there are even further refinements. The heads of state speak a dignified blank verse, the wellborn lovers blank verse and couplets; the rude mechanicals speak rudely in prose; and the extra-human characters have their class distinction: they may use lyric measures. But there are distinctions also in prose. The sustained sentence, the aureate diction, the verbal figures of repetition are proper to, are required by, the heroic world of the *Arcadia*, and furnished for a century afterward the model for courtly speech. There was a consonance between elevation in rank and an elevated style. On the contrary, the lower-class character in the *Arcadia* (1590) speaks like Mrs. Quickly:

> Oh the good old woman, well may the bones rest of the good old woman! She called me to her into her house. I remember full well it stood in the lane as you go to the barber's shop, all the town knew her, there was great loss of her. She called me to her, and taking first a sup of wine to comfort her heart—it was of the same wine that comes out of Candia which we pay so dear for nowadays, and in that good world was very good cheap—she called me to her, "Minion," said she—indeed I was a pretty one those days though I say it—"I see a number of lads that love you."
>
> 2. 14

In brief, it was not a democratic society.

Shakespeare in the sixty-sixth sonnet, enumerating the up-side-downness of things in this world, how captive Good is in the service of Captain Ill, speaks of "art made tongue-tied by authority." It is an odd statement, and odd in its context, even if properly understood. For it is not, of course, as it is often taken to be, a reference to literary and dramatic censorship. His "art" is not our art. It referred, rather, to give a rough translation, to the world of learning. And what is complained of in the phrase is that the constant repetition of the old basic texts prevented the formulation of new propositions. It is as if he had been reading Bacon, or had been listening to Ben Jonson: "I know nothing can conduce more to letters than to examine the writings of the Ancients, and not to rest in their sole authority, or take all upon trust from them . . . For to all the observations of the Ancients, we have our own experience."

There was in Renaissance England what we may call the Old Learning and the New. The New Learning developed slowly and comes into prominence only toward the end of our period. It comprised a hodgepodge of recent concerns and developments: in mathematics and science, in various interests associated with the new classical philology, grammar, for example, and antiquarian research, all with a much clearer history on the continent than in England. But there were accomplishments: Gilbert's specula-tions, Harvey's demonstration, Bacon's intuition. There was the cold sociological interviewing of Thomas Harman. There were interesting developments in the common law, represented by Sir Edward Coke's *Reports* (1600-1615). There was the new histo-ry: Bacon's *Henry VII* (1622) and Lord Herbert's *Henry VIII;* the profound learning of John Selden; and the new antiquarian and topographical discovery of England, of which William Camden's *Britannia* (1586) and John Stow's *Survey of London* (1598) are best known. But, for the most part, the Old Learning was still dominant.

It was, essentially, the learning of the Middle Ages, and formed the matrix and texture of most of the thought and literature of the time. To understand that, we must relearn it, at least in outline. It was the common possession of everyone of the least education. It was an elementary learning, consisting largely of a series of clear and simple distinctions. There are the three souls, the four elements, the three grammatical genders, the seven deadly sins. These were learned as one learns the Catechism, and repeated again and again as one recites the Catechism. Indeed, the Catechism itself was a good part of the learning, for theology was still the principal science, as judicial astrology was still the principal experimental, that is, predictive, science.

Nor was this learning only a school matter. It was matter for well-bred conversation in the houses of the upper class. An Elizabethan musician, onetime "servant and scholar" to John Heywood, tells in his autobiography of the conversation in the household of a woman who had been to court:

> I took pleasure many times to talk and discourse of such things as she by experience had had some knowledge of: as sometimes, of religions, she would argue in matters of controversy in religion; sometimes of profane matters; sometimes she would touch matters of the country, with the good husbandry and housewifery thereof . . . sometimes we should enter into talk of humors, the which of them four, bearing chiefest rule in man, should instinct incline and

provoke him to follow those effects whereunto they were inclined. Then should we sometimes wade into communication and talk of the planets and the celestial signs with the constellations, and what their operations and workings were, and what effects they wrought in all things that were subject to them.[6]

It is only to be expected, then, that this system of elementary distinctions should appear everywhere in the literature of the times as allusion, as material, and as structural principle. A simple example of the latter is afforded by Donne's little epigram on Hero and Leander:

> Both robbed of air, we both lie in one ground,
> Both whom one fire had burnt, one water drowned.

The whole story of the lovers is apprehended, summarized, and enclosed in the simple scheme of the four elements, in phrases of four and six syllables, in iambic pentameter, and rhymed. It is neat, ingenious, and absolute in its own way. But it must not be thought that this is anything peculiar to Donne. Sidney, some years earlier, in one of the *Arcadia* poems, has the following two lines:

> Man oft is plagued with air, is burnt with fire,
> In water drowned, in earth his burial is.[7]

The two lines do not rhyme—the form is terza rima, not couplets—but otherwise the correspondences technically and in the structural use of the four elements are exact.

The elementary distinctions of this learning were so securely the possession of everyone who counted that a writer could jump from one to another without transition or strain. This is what Donne does in his witty conjugations. You will find in the fifth stanza of *A Valediction: of my Name in the Window* the doctrine of the three souls: the rational, by which one understands; the sensitive, in common with animals, by which one perceives; the vegetable, in common with plants, the principle of growth and decay:

> as all my souls be
> Imparadised in you—in whom alone
> I understand and grow and see—

He passes in the next stanza to the theological doctrine of the resurrection of the body:

> Till my return, repair
> And recompact my scattered body so.

And then the principle of judicial astrology, the influence of the stars:

> As all the virtuous powers which are
> Fixed in the stars are said to flow
> Into such characters as graved be
> When these stars have supremacy.

The modern reader who needs notes and patient explanation may think of Donne as ranging in such passages through various fields of learning. To Donne it was, for the exercise of wit, a single field with interchangeable parts. They were all of a piece.

What is new in these passages from Donne is not the learning or the use of learning, though it is a little more on display than was customary. What is new is literary. The monumental quality of Donne's epigram suggests the revived classical tradition of Sannazaro rather than the brutal doggerel tradition of John Heywood. And the world of the *Valediction* is the revived world of Latin erotic elegy, of Propertius and Ovid, where "thy melted maid, / Corrupted by the lover's gold, and page," lays "His letter at thy pillow."[8]

Death, Religion, & Love

People in different times and places are alike and different. If we stress the difference we make them seem unintelligible. If we stress the similarities we encourage ourselves to understand them too readily, and so to misunderstand them. All men are concerned with death and love, and hence with religion, but not all have the same concern.

The Englishman of this period was more at home with death than we are. He lived with it, and sometimes for it. He said much about it, but there is not much to be said about what was said: it is all so simple and direct. There was a preoccupation with the fact of death; not with the subtlety of decay, as in Thomas Mann's *Death in Venice*, but with the bareness of the whitened skull. It was a preoccupation directed to the calm acceptance of death. The principal art of life, in fact, was the art of dying well. John Skelton's *Upon a Dead Man's Head* is a meditation on a skull, and a meditation in medieval form. It begins with the traditional syllogism, "All men are mortal," in inverted order: the conclusion, "Die we must," followed by the explicit major premise, "It is general to be mortal." The signs of death are then enumerated, and we conclude with a prayer. Again, in one of Heywood's epigrams a prisoner, awaiting hanging and quartering, pauses as he searches for worms in his hand, and meditates: in doing this I am only showing myself an enemy to the worm and a friend to the crow who will eat me as I hang on the gibbet. To speak here of acceptance of death is understatement. And so, again and again, sometimes with the assurance of salvation, "When Thou hast done that Thou hast Donne," the simple fact of death is looked at and embraced.

The attitude, of course, is Christian, as was the society. The essence of Christianity was still the incomprehensible mystery of God, the Trinity, and the historical fact that God became man, the Incarnation, so classically stated by Hooker. "The strength of our faith is tried by those things wherein our wits and capacities are not strong." But there were variations in Christianity, some of which are important for our purposes. For a principal fact of England at this time is the change in religion, or rather the successive changes under four monarchs: Henry VIII, Edward VI, Mary, and Elizabeth. The two poles were Rome and Geneva, the Old Religion and the Reformed, with differences of doctrine, of feeling, and with political differences. For religion was politics, and politics religion, and neither was the less sincere for that. Of our authors four were executed for treason, and in each case religion and the question of the succession of the crown were involved: More, the Lady Jane, Chidiock Tichbourne, and finally Ralegh, though in his case as pretext rather than fact.

Between Rome and Geneva or Germany there was more than a difference in politics, or the differences in doctrine clearly stated, for example, in the *Examination of Lady Jane Grey*; there were also differences in feeling. They are apparent in the attitudes of the Lady Jane and Abbott Fecknam. They are apparent in two poems, each of the highest quality, that illustrate as well as anything the emotional difference between Calvinism and Catholicism. As feeling it can only be experienced. But one can say that in Greville's *Down in the Depths* the firm conviction of absolute corruption and the equal conviction of divine election ("Even there appears this saving God of mine") march doggedly through the stanzas with an unsocial and impressive solemnity. It is an experience of simultaneous corruption and salvation; it is not a prayer. Jonson's *To Heaven,* on the other hand, is a prayer, an act of perfect contrition:

> Yet dare I not complain, or wish for death
> With holy Paul, lest it be thought the breath
> Of discontent, or that these prayers be
> For weariness of life, not love of thee.

But Rome and Geneva were not the only possibilities. We can see in Donne's *Satire: On Religion* (the *Third Satire*, line 43 to the end) the possibilities open in the 1590s to a young man in his twenties, of good family, whose patrimony has been partially dissipated. He is ambitious for service in the State, partly for itself and partly to repair his fortunes, but he is also by family, training, and temperament a Roman Catholic. As such he would be debarred from preferment. He enumerates in the satire five positions, each of which he scornfully rejects, phrasing his scorn in similes identifying the quest for the True Church with that of true love. "Seek true religion. O where?" One man seeks her at Rome because he knows she was there a thousand years ago. But this is to worship her old clothes. Another at Geneva. For this Donne has even greater contempt. The passion for Calvinism is compared to a "lecherous humor" for coarse country wenches, "contemptuous yet unhandsome." The next possibility is that true religion is to be found in the English Church. It is good that Donne's *Satires* were not printed in his lifetime; he could not quite have been hanged for what he says. The English Church, he tells us, has changed like fashions in clothes. Whatever some preachers ("vile ambitious bawds") and some laws bid us accept at the moment we are to take as perfect. We are, in fact, to take our religion as a ward in that society must take whatever wife his guardian offers, or pay the forfeit. We must accept the current religion, or pay the fines for recusancy. These three positions, Rome, Geneva, and Canterbury, we may call regional. The next two are philosophical. The skeptic argues from the diversity of churches that there is no true church; his opposite maintains on the same grounds that one is as good as another, and so any one will do.

Donne's own position, which he now proceeds to sketch out, is a curious one but sufficiently clear. He is sure there is a True Church, and only one True Church, and he seems pretty sure that it is not one of the five already enumerated. The problem is to find it. There will be required, first of all, a patient searching of tradition, for though truth and falsehood are near twins, truth is a little older. Secondly, consider that Rome, Geneva, and Canterbury on any point may all be wrong. The example he gives is that the adoration, condemnation, and depreciation of images "may all be bad." Finally, "doubt wisely," for truth is to be found, as Polonius knew, by indirections and "assays of bias." But it is a wise doubting as a means to truth, which can be found and, once found, held to, not a wise doubting as a way of life. For we must find the True Church before old age, "death's twilight" "for none can work in that night." In brief he does not know the

True Church, but is certain he will find it in due time by patient and supple inquiry, and he is certain it will not be a church stipulated by the State. What good will it do at the last judgment, he asks, to plead that Philip of Spain or the Pope, Henry VIII or the Puritan Martin Marprelate, taught you your doctrines? The final source of power is God and not the State.

So we come to love. There are several traditions in the depiction of love, and it may be helpful to name them and to make some simple distinctions. There is, of course, love as an Idea, the exemplar being that heavenly love that Spenser hymned, of which the lady of courtly love is sometimes a parody. Then there is the tradition of Christian preaching, of Juvenal's satires and Martial's epigrams, and this is still with us. It is ugly, realistic in detail, brutal with either a vehement or an urbane brutality. Campian's *Epigram*, "Kate can fancy only beardless husbands," illustrates the urbane. Again, there is the tradition of Latin erotic poetry, of Catullus, Tibullus, Propertius, and Ovid. To put it too briefly, for the tradition comprises a wide range of themes and sentiments, it is frankly sexual, however musingly subjective. For this reason it seems realistic to us. Jonson's "You have a husband is the just excuse / Of all that can be done him," gives the essence of the matter, and Donne's *Elegy* and Campian's *It Fell on a Summer's Day* illustrate it. Finally, there is the tradition of courtly love, or perhaps one should say of love at Court. This seems to us artificial in comparison with Donne's world, and in this we are right and wrong. It is artificial, but it is an artificiality that had been lived and experienced by a society through many generations, whereas Donne's world was a recreation from literary Antiquity, though, perhaps, a recreation that had contemporary validity. The society was a society of people who thought themselves important, and were, and who often had superfluous leisure. How they occupied this Campian tells us in *Now Winter Nights Enlarge*: "Though love and all his pleasures are but toys, / They shorten tedious nights." So courtly love may involve an evening's unserious pastime, a ritual flirtation, the sentimental occupation of years, or it may be the ornate setting of vulgar adultery. But its locale is the Court where it helps pass the time. It helps pass the time as befitted the atmosphere, with formality, compliment, ceremony, with precedent and by rules. Sidney's *Astrophil and Stella* and Ralegh's *The Ocean to Cynthia* illustrate the tradition.

Astrophil and Stella is the earliest sonnet sequence in English, and raises the problem of that literary form, and the allied problem of love at Court. The poet depicts in a sonnet at the beginning of the sequence the slow progress on his part of the relationship, by stages from liking through loving, to an absolute submission to the tyranny of love at a time when he had already lost the opportunity for legitimate fulfillment. His reason argues sophistically against reason in favor of passion, and he sends this clear delineation of the act of mortal sin as a compliment to the lady. (This is curious hyperbole for an earnest Christian.) Then realizing the shame of enduring such tyranny, he meets the lady and tells her, "Go to, unkind, I love you not," though he doesn't mean it. She in turn takes the first step in the dance of love, the look, and admits the lover to a chaste relationship. Then the attempted kiss, the banishment, the denial, the poems in absence, and finally the resolution: that she should authorize him to accept, as in her service, an office of state. This, plausibly, would be the governorship of Flushing, which he accepted in 1585, the year before his death.

The problem of the sonnet sequence is usually conceived in terms of the question, Is this fiction? or memoir? and is sometimes solved by denying there is a problem. The poems "should be read as poems," that is, without locating the field of experience they refer to. But this is to destroy them as poems. To return: By fiction is meant that the situation is invented; the structure, at least in part, planned out in advance; and the work as a whole responsible to the truth of human nature but not to fact. As memoir, on the other hand, the poems are evidence, their genesis private, and the reader eavesdrops. If only the two terms, fiction and memoir, were available and applicable, one would have to say that the sequence is memoir. For this is not the way Sidney thought of fiction or wrote it.

We know from his critical treatise, *Defence of Poesy*, his conception of fiction, and we know from the *Arcadia* how he wrote it. Fiction was, first of all, ideal, presenting notable images of virtue and vice. What this means we can see in the episode of Argalus and Parthenia. (1. 5 and 7) The hopeless and constant lover, offered an exact replica of his love—indeed, it is Parthenia herself, unidentified—courteously declines: "It is only happiness I refuse, since of the only happiness I could and can desire I am refused." He is in love with her identity. This is a notable image of the virtue of constancy. But the images need not be only of virtue and vice. If there is a hunt, let it be the ideal hunt, as one might write an account today of the ideal summer vacation. If one thinks of representing a young girl in love, let it be not this girl or that but the essence of a young girl in love, and then one writes Jonson's *A Nymph's Passion*.

Fiction is also an imitation of an action, that is, an interconnected series of external events of a certain size—something more than a stolen kiss or a disturbance of feeling, something with a plot in the old sense. Something with such striking and notable events as the disfigurement and the cure of Parthenia.

The cure, one may remark on the side, is marvellous but not supernatural or impossible, though it was undoubtedly beyond the competence of any physician of the time. It is, in fact, an early instance of science fiction. The plot should also have, as almost necessary ingredients, a final reversal of fortune, usually as in this episode simultaneous with a recognition of identity. *Astrophil and Stella* may be, though I think not, ideal, but there is in it no imitation of an action, no striking event, no reversal of fortune, and no recognition. It is not fiction.

The poems, then, are memoir in that they record an experience in the game of love. But they are not memoir in the sense that the poet attempts to come to terms with that experience, or to delineate it for a reader or for himself. The poems are not private, though intended for a very limited audience, and are not written to be overheard, but are rhetorically addressed to an audience. It is a very small audience of those in the know. The poems are, in fact, actions in the game of love, and their locale is the Court. They are for the most part compliments to the lady, apologies, explanations, entreaties: their aim is to persuade.

The context of such poems is, interestingly enough, clearly pictured in the *Arcadia* (3.1) as a moment in the larger structure of the story of Pamela and Musidorus. Pamela at one point pities Musidorus in his love despair and shows her pity by a look. He, presuming, offers to kiss her, and is summarily banished. It is a situation from *Astrophil and Stella*. And then we have this depiction of the lover as poet:

> Then began he only so far to wish his own good, as
> that Pamela might pardon him the fault, though not
> the punishment: and the uttermost height he aspired
> unto, was that after his death she might yet pity his

error and know that it proceeded of love, and not of boldness. That conceit found such friendship in his thoughts, that at last he yielded, since he was banished her presence, to seek some means by writing to show his sorrow, and testify his repentance. Therefore getting him the necessary instruments of writing, he thought best to counterfeit his hand (fearing that already as she knew his, she would cast it away as soon as she saw it) and to put it in verse, hoping that would draw her on to read the more, choosing the elegiac as fittest for mourning. But never pen did more quakingly perform his office; never was paper more double moistened with ink and tears; never words more slowly married together, and never the Muses more tired than now, with changes and re-changes of his devices: fearing how to end, before he had resolved how to begin, mistrusting each word, condemning each sentence. This word was not significant; that word was too plain; this would not be conceived; the other would be ill conceived; here sorrow was not enough expressed, there he seemed too much for his own sake to be sorry; this sentence rather showed art than passion, that sentence rather foolishly passionate than forcibly moving. At last, marring with mending, and putting out better than he left, he made an end of it; being ended, was divers times ready to tear it, till his reason assuring him, the more he studied the worse it grew, he folded it up, devoutly invoking good acceptation unto it; and watching his time, when they were all gone one day to dinner, saving Mopsa, to the other lodge, stole up into Pamela's chamber, and in her standish (which first he kissed, and craved of it a safe and friend-ly keeping) left it there to be seen at her next using her ink (himself returning again to be true prisoner to desperate sorrow) leaving her standish upon her beds-head, to give her the more occasion to mark it: which also fell out.

3.1

It is in such a context, with just a shade of the comic about it, that *Astrophil and Stella* was written and is to be read.

But there can be nothing comic about it, except, perhaps, to an unconcerned modern observer, if the lady is the Queen. The cruel mistress to whose moods the lover is completely subject, who has power of life and death over him, may in other instances be an emotional reality or a courtly fiction; in the case of the Queen and her favorites it was the plain fact. "First of all, you must consider with whom you have to deal, "Sir Edward Dyer wrote to Sir Christopher Hatton on a crisis in his relationship with Elizabeth, "and what we be towards her; who, though she do descend very much in her sex as a woman, yet we may not forget her place, and the nature of it as our Sovereign." And so the offending lover did not despair in the solitariness of the woods but in the solitariness of the Tower. There, probably in 1592, Ralegh wrote the incomplete draft of the poems of the eleventh book of *The Ocean to Cynthia*.

The Revolution in Style

There is toward the end of this period a consciousness of achievement, especially in literature. This first appears in the 1590s, and indeed would not have been warranted before that decade. It was the decade of the *Faerie Queene,* of the first half of Shakespeare's work, of the first edition of Bacon's *Essays,* of Donne's most memorable poetry, and of Jonson's first great plays. There was a suddenness about the achievement that seems to call for an explanation.

But history is not a predictive science. It thinks up reasons for what has already happened, or is thought to have happened. It is what we can make of what remains of the past. And what *we* can make of it will depend on the nature of the remains and on our own concerns. If the remains are primarily literary, and our concerns are literary, we will look for a literary answer, though it may be only a partial answer.

Let us say, then, that the achievement of the 1590s, and of the subsequent decades, is partly a consequence of a revolution in style. For only then was there at hand an adequate instrument in poetry and in the drama. The importance of this is often overlooked. Literature, however, is not written with ideas, experiences, emotions, but with a pen, with language. And not with any language, but with a particular system of inclusions and exclusions; one writes with a style, and in poetry with a meter also, which is an aspect of style. And so a new style, a new meter, is a new attitude, a new form, new subject matter, so far unexpressed detail. Styles are innovated, and imitated, and imitation establishes a tradition.

The new styles that permitted the achievements of Elizabethan literature were innovated in the 1580s and perfected in the 1590s. This is clearest in the drama. The earlier dramas had been

397

written, with the exception of one in blank verse (1562) in which Thomas Sackville had a hand, in mediums that would have precluded *Richard III* and all that followed. One of John Heywood's plays, for instance, printed in 1533, begins with this speech:

> God speed you, masters, every one,
> Wot ye not whither my wife is gone?
> I pray God the devil take her,
> For all that Idol can not make her
> But she will go a-gadding, very much
> Like Antony pig with an old witch
> Which leadeth her about hither and thither,
> But, by our lady, I wot not whither.

This is, of course, verse in the old Germanic tradition, a four-beat accentual meter held together by rhyme instead of alliteration. It can express simple truth and simple vulgarities, but there are many things that cannot be said in this style. Another Medium is illustrated by the opening of *Cambises, King of Persia* (1570):

> My Council, grave and sapient, with lords of legal train
> Attentive ears towards me bend, and mark what shall be sain.

This is the grave fourteener of the mid-sixteenth century, rhymed in couplets. It yielded a few impressive short poems, but nothing in drama. With such instruments not even Shakespeare could have been Shakespeare. He could at best have written in the octosyllabic tradition the verses inscribed on his tomb:

> Good friend, for Jesus sake forbear
> To dig the dust enclosed here!

Sometime in the late 1580s a new voice is heard on the London stage. The innovation was blank verse. It was not wholly new, of course, it had been used in some translations from the Latin, by Gascoigne in *The Steele Glas* (1576), in a play acted at the Third University of England, the Inns of Court. But it suddenly took on. We do not know who established the fashion, or how he hit on the new instrument. Some say Kyd, some Marlowe, and it may have been someone else. But it made the difference between Heywood and Shakespeare. This is the voice:

> When the eternal substance of my soul
> Did live imprisoned in my wanton flesh,
> Each in their function serving other's need,
> I was a courtier in the Spanish court.
> My name was Don Andrea.

From this, the opening of Kyd's *Spanish Tragedy,* to *Hamlet* is simply a matter of time and genius. The means are available.

And the innovation derives from the attempt to realize in English some of the qualities of the poetry of Classical Antiquity. For the most simple and obvious difference between that poetry and the poetry of this time is that the one was unrhymed and the other rhymed. This is not just a difference in effect; it is a difference in what can be said. A word to be rhymed immediately suggests its rhymes, and at the same time rules out all expressions that are not potentially rhymable. It is a notable instance of a system of inclusions and exclusions. Furthermore, unrhymed verse involves not merely a freedom from limitations. It will have its own limitations, and one of these is that, in a tradition in which rhymed verse is common, the avoidance of rhyme is a positive principle of selection.

The heroic line of blank verse was developed originally in nondramatic poetry, and with rhyme. It is, ultimately, Chaucer's line. But something had happened to Chaucer's line in the centuries after his death, partly, no doubt, because the language had changed. At all events, it is clear that at the court of Henry VIII there was no commonly agreed-upon metrical tradition, particularly for the heroic line. It was a situation similar to our own, except that the possibilities of metrical confusion have multiplied since that time. And it is a serious situation for the history of poetry, more serious than the reader may think. For, as prose is written in syntax, in phrases, clauses, sentences, so poetry has a second principle of organization concurrent with that of grammar: it is written in lines. The meter of a poem determines the line. And as an uncertainty in grammar would make it difficult to write good prose, so an uncertainty in meter makes it difficult to write good poetry.

It would be a patient and delicate task to explore the whole problem in the early sixteenth century, but a brief analysis will show the nature of the problem. Wyatt more often than not writes the traditional heroic line as Chaucer had established it:

> But as for me, alas, I may no more.

But he also writes a line simply of ten syllables, sometimes counting the final unaccented syllable:

> In this also see you be not idle:

or of nine syllables, unless "laughter" is trisyllabic:

> It is but love; turn it to laughter.

or a ten-syllable line organized by the four-beat tune of the Germanic tradition:

From under the stall, without lands or fees.

This last was the principal problem, for the Germanic and the Chaucerian traditions cannot live together; the heavy four beat chant which we learned in our childhood ("Jóhnny ís a stínkér") drives out the grace and subtlety of the traditional meter. To write with both tunes in mind is to produce the baffling rhythms of Heywood's epigrams. To slip from one to the other, as Sir Thomas Elyot does, is metrical chaos:

The poet fashioneth by some pleasant mean
The speech of children, tender and unsure,
Pulling their eares from wordes unclean,
Giving to them precepts that are pure,
Rebuking envy and wrath if it dure.
Things well done he can by example commend;
The needy and sick he doth also his cure
To recomfort, if aught he can amend.

So it was that the poets of the next several generations undertook to discipline the syntax of poetry to the firm iambic line, the "drumming decasyllabon." They simplified the rules: they imposed special limitations. The ten-syllable line would be phrased in units of four and six syllables, in a limited number of syntactical patterns, and often enough the accented syllables in each phrase would be bound together and pointed by some rhetorical device, usually by alliteration and syntactical repetition:

The life is long that loathsomely doth last,
The doleful days draw slowly to their date.

It is a style that can handle obvious subjects, uncomplicated feelings, eternal truths, and simple sin. It is the style in which one writes from the Tower on the eve of execution. It is, furthermore, at its best an impressive style, as in Tichbourne's *Elegy*, and one that even Donne recurred to when he had an obvious subject and direct feelings about it. His *A Hymn: To God the Father* is clearly in this style: let us call it the moral style. The poem is phrased for the most part in units of four and six syllables in normal iambic pattern, and the phrasing is underlined by rhetorical repetition:

Wilt thou forgive that sin where I begun,
Which was my sin though it were done before?
Wilt thou forgive

It is an impressive but not a sufficient style; it excludes too much. It cannot handle ordinary life. It cannot rise and fall. And so there developed in the 1580s, out of a good deal of experimenting in prose and verse, several new styles: the ornate style of Spenser, and the new plain style, modeled on the plain style of Latin Antiquity. In this the innovator was Sidney. It is not his consistent style; he is often ornate; he writes sometimes in the moral style. But there are many passages in *Astrophil and Stella* in a fully accomplished plain style:

Dear, therefore be not jealous over me
If you hear that they seem my heart to move;
Not them, O no, but you in them I love.

It was there. It needed only to be recognized and imitated. It was recognized and imitated by Campian and Donne, and perfected by Jonson.

Campian (1591?):

> Whither thus hastes my little book so fast?
> To Paul's Churchyard. What? in those cells to stand
> With one leaf like a rider's cloak put up
> To catch a termer?

Donne (1597) on a calm at sea:

> No use of lanterns, and in one place lay
> Feathers and dust, today and yesterday.

or:

> What are we then? How little more, alas,
> Is man now than before he was. He was
> Nothing. For us, we are for nothing fit;
> Chance or ourselves still disproportion it.

Jonson (1616):

> Think,
> All beauty doth not last until the autumn.
> You grow old while I tell you this.

It became the central style of English poetry.

J.V. Cunningham and his dog, Bruce, in 1959.
Black Hills, South Dakota. Mt. Rushmore is in the background.
Photo courtesy of Roberta Collinsworth.

Pencil sketch of J. V. Cunningham, 1931
Private collection, used by permission

LYRIC STYLE IN THE 1590s

Wordsworth in the Preface to the *Lyrical Ballads* speaks of the formal engagement an author makes in the act of writing verse that "he will gratify certain known habits of association . . . that certain classes of ideas and expressions will be found in his book . . . that others will be carefully excluded." Now, the inclusion and exclusion of certain classes of ideas and expressions, and in verse of certain meters and metrical practices, constitutes a style. And in any literary situation certain attitudes and experiences, "certain known habits of association," are available to a particular style, and the exploration of other attitudes and experiences requires a new and different style, for a style is itself a principle of selection and order. This is what Wordsworth implies when he says in the sentence that follows: "This exponent or symbol held forth by metrical language must in different eras of literature have excited very different expectations; for example, . . . in the age of Shakespeare and Beaumont and Fletcher, and that of Donne and Cowley. . . ." What we are concerned with here is the discrimination of certain kinds, or traditions, or styles of metrical language in a given literary situation, the 1590s in England, and the indication, so far as our clumsy means permit, of the exponent or symbol that these hold forth.

The age of Shakespeare and Beaumont and Fletcher is the age of Donne; the age of Cowley is something else again. For Shakespeare and Donne, if we restrict ourselves to the evidence, appear on the literary scene at about the same time, around 1592, and Fletcher died five or six years before Donne. But the chronological dislocation that Wordsworth endorses still persists; it has distorted literary history, and consequently the interpretation of the relevant texts. In The Pelican Guide to English Literature, for example, the works of the 1590s are distributed through the first three volumes: Spenser in volume I, Shakespeare and Jonson the dramatist in volume II, Donne and Jonson the poet in volume III, and there are only seven volumes for the whole of English literature from Chaucer to the present day.

Let us imagine, then, a young man, probably of good family and possibly a younger son—Campian or Wotton or Davies or Donne—who comes to London around 1590s. He has, perhaps, a small patrimony, has had a thorough grammar school education, a year or two at Oxford or Cambridge, and has now entered the Third University of England, one of the Inns of Court. He is, in brief, Lorenzo, Jr., alias Edward Knowell, of Ben Jonson's *Every Man in His Humour*.[1] And, indeed, that character is quite possibly modeled on Donne, for not only did Jonson later write a dialogue on poetry in which Donne was the principal speaker, but also Donne's *First Satire* furnishes the "invention" of the play: a scholarly young man of good family, interested in poetry, is invited by a friend and goes out on the town to observe and describe the follies of various social types. Our poet, then, is something of a wit, and is ambitious. He will write some toys in verse, partly to display his wit, and partly in the hope he will be noticed by someone in power, some official of the state who might further his ambitions—Lord Essex, let us say, or Sir Thomas Egerton. What will he write, and in what way will he write it? What styles were available? What styles could he reject?

There were notably two. The first is the one commonly associated with the Elizabethan lyric, what C. S. Lewis has called the Golden. It is, he says, a "poetry which is, so to speak, innocent or ingenuous. In a Golden Age the right thing to do is obvious; 'good is as visible as green.' . . . Men have at last learned how to write; for a few years nothing more is needed than to play out again and again the strong simple music of the uncontorted line and to load one's poem with all that is naturally delightful—with flowers and swans, with ladies' hair, hands, lips, breasts, and eyes, with silver and gold, woods and waters, the stars, the moon, and the sun."[2] It is a style I would prefer to call the sweet or pleasant style, *dulce . . . orationis genus et solutum et fluens, sententiis argutum, verbis sonans,* "sweet, fluent, and copious, with bright conceits and sounding phrases,"[3] the style of epideictic oratory. Its exemplar in its octosyllabic form is *The Passionate Shepherd to His Love.*

> Come live with me and be my love,
> And we will all the pleasures prove
> That valleys, groves, hills and fields,
> Woods, or steepy mountains yields.

It is a poetry in which one sits

> By shallow rivers to whose falls
> Melodious birds sing madrigals.

Indeed, *The Passionate Shepherd* attains the perfection of which the sweet style is capable, for that style aims at a harmonious arrangement of elements that have already a preestablished harmony. It is really an abstract style, like a Navaho rug, dependent on design, and its triumphs are quite impersonal. Such a poem is written by no man but by a tradition.

But more basic and native at this time is another style, what Lewis calls the Drab and I, the moral style. It is the style of *The Nymph's Reply to the Shepherd,* ascribed quite plausibly to Ralegh:

> Time drives the flocks from field to fold
> When rivers rage and rocks grow cold
> And Philomel becometh dumb.
> The rest complains of cares to come.

It is relentlessly iambic; the line is organized in two distinct halves, with two four-syllable phrases bound into internal unity by structural alliteration of stressed syllables, or, for variation, the flat music of

> And Philomel becometh dumb.

It is a central, a limited, and an impressive style:

> But could youth last and love still breed,
> Had joys no date and age no need.

The *locus classicus* in decasyllabic form, of course, is:

> O eyes! no eyes, but fountains fraught with tears;
> O life! no life, but lively form of death;
> O world; no world, but mass of public wrongs,
> Confused and filled with murder and misdeeds![4]

In poulter's measure it is the style of Father Southwell's *The Burning Babe,* for the old habit of vision goes comfortably with it. It is the way in which one writes in the Tower on the eve of execution, "Even such is time that takes in trust," or Tichbourne's *Elegy* (1586):

I sought my death and found it in my womb,
I looked for life and saw it was a shade,
I trod the earth and knew it was my tomb,
And now I die, and now I was but made.
My glass is full, and now my glass is run,
And now I live, and now my life is done.

Tichbourne's *Elegy* belongs to a particular literary kind, what I call the moral poem, which is the exemplar and pattern of the moral style. It is a small but sturdy genre that flourished in the late middle ages, and continued to thrive until the last decade of the sixteenth century: Chaucer's "Flee fro the press, and dwelle with sothfastnesse," and Dunbar's "Be mirry, man, and tak nocht far in mynd," are examples of the style. It consists of a sequence in serial order of sententiae, maxims, proverbs, or propositions of a similar kind, usually one to a line, sometimes two, and occasionally a single sententia over two lines, commonly in decasyllables and in an extended stanza, often in ballade form. The decasyllable is normally phrased in fours and sixes in iambic pattern, though sometimes in reverse order of six and four, and the phrases are bound by alliteration of stressed syllables:

The life is long that loathsomely doth last,
The doleful days draw slowly to their date,
The present pangs and painful plagues forpast
Yield grief aye green to stablish this estate,
So that I feel in this great storm and strife
The death is sweet that endeth such a life.

Thus line is piled on line in unvarying units. When successful, as in Tichbourne's *Elegy*, the moral poem expresses a cumulative

413

experience of serious insistence. For it is moral, in the simple, old-fashioned meaning of that term.

Hence the exponent or symbol of this particular and quite limited tradition is easy to describe: a heavy-handed seriousness, a scorn of urbanity, a deliberate rejection of that delicacy which would discriminate shades of white and of black. It is a morally ruthless, secure, and overpowering style. And so Sidney in the *Astrophil* series, as he accumulates compliments, exploits sentiment, and dallies with the potentialities of adultery, is ever vigilant against the stable four and six structure and the firm advancing beat of the "drumming decasyllabon":

> Dear, therefore be not jealous over me
> If you hear that they seem my heart to move.
> Not them, oh no, but you in them I love.

In contrast, when he expresses the old morality in those sonnets that are often appended by editors at the end of *Astrophil,* he does it in the moral style:

> Band of all evils, cradle of causeless care,
> Thou web of will whose end is never wrought,
> Desire, desire! I have too dearly bought
> With price of mangled mind thy worthless ware.

And:

> Then farewell world, thy uttermost I see.
> Eternal love, maintain thy life in me.

By the end of the decade the moral style had lost for the most part its productive vigor; only Matheo and Bobadilla of *Every Man in His Humour* in 1598 think the "O eyes! no eyes" passage "simply the best that ever you heard. Yet on an apt occasion, with an obvious subject and direct feelings about it, those who grew up with the style can return to it, as Donne did in *A Hymn to God the Father,* with verbal repetition instead of structural alliteration:

> Wilt thou forgive that sin where I begun,
> Which was my sin though it were done before?
> Wilt thou forgive those sins through which I run
> And do run still though still I do deplore?

It is a poem from an earlier age.

The sweet and the moral, then, were available to the young man in 1590s; they were styles he could accept or reject, and those we are concerned with here for the most part rejected them. And the new style? It is said to be "metaphysical," and to have been innovated by Donne. Now much has been said of this style, and much that has been said is untrue. It is said to be colloquial, which it is not, except in rare passages of dialogue, as in the *First Satire.* But "colloquial" is not really a descriptive term in current criticism but a term of praise, like "subtle" and "complex," and like those terms in need of definition. By "colloquial," I take it, one means that in the sort of situation sketched or implied in the poem what is said is what could be said somewhat casually by one person to another without seeming to be affected, or indeed insane. One has only to visualize the situations in Donne's lyrics and try acting them out to have unappeasable doubts about his colloquiality:

> I wonder, by my troth, what thou and I
> Did till we loved?

This could possibly be said musingly, though hardly in reply to some remark of the partner. But what will the lady make of:

> Were we not weaned till then?
> But sucked on country pleasures childishly?
> Or snorted we in the seven sleepers' den?

No, the style is not really colloquial, for these are not dialogues. They are in part written in the familiar style of the familiar letter, as perhaps here, and in a variety of different styles. For the genuinely colloquial in the lyric you will do better with Sidney who sometimes writes a shorter poem in dialogue form:

> Take me to thee and thee to me.
> No, no, no, no, my dear, let be.

The truth is, the work of Donne that would be available to his circle at this time does not offer a consistent model of style. His answer to the *Passionate Shepherd,* for example, opens in the pleasant style:

> And we will some new pleasures prove
> Of golden sands and crystal brooks,

proceeds by way of a light line to a Petrarchan hyperbole:

> There will the river whispering run,
> Warmed by thy eyes more than the sun.

then to a Gorgianic figure of the "living sepulcher" type:

416

When thou wilt swim in that live bath,

developed now by the qualification of philosophic exactness:

Each fish which every channel hath

and ending with a juxtaposition of grammatical words which one may call colloquial but which defies the enunciation of common speech:

Will amorously to thee swim,
Gladder to catch thee than thou him.

Actually, this is probably an attempt to do what Latin permits and English resists. A little further on we get rather simple bad writing, the jammed-up line:

Let coarse, bold hands from slimy nest
The bedded fish in banks out-wrest,

And the poem concludes with an easy, and pleasing enough, urbanity:

That fish that is not catched thereby,
Alas, is wiser far than I.

This is not a style but a heterogeneity of styles.

A similar stylistic uncertainty can be seen in a much better poem, *The Calm*, written in 1597 during the Islands expedition, and one of the poems we have reason to believe would have been available as a model in this decade. It begins:

> Our storm is past, and that storm's tyrannous rage
> A stupid calm, but nothing it, doth swage.

The couplet is troubled by a tight idiomatic qualification, "but nothing it, which is not needed by the rationale of the poem; it is a metaphysical side-reflection, an operation on a term. There follows an allusion to an obscure fable. Then in a few lines:

> As steady as I can wish that my thoughts were,
> Smooth as thy mistress' glass, or what shines there,
> The sea is now.

This is random ingenuity. The young Donne is an improvisatory genius, an extemporal wit, a better-born Thomas Nashe. As Samuel Butler the elder put it: "Dr. Donne's writings are like Voluntary or Prelude, in which a man is not tied to any particular design of Air, but may change his Key or mode at pleasure. So his compositions seem to have been written without any particular scope," that is, end in view.

Yet he does in another sense have an end in view. His motive is clear and explicit; it is the desire for novelty:

> And we will some new pleasures prove.

Now, the charm of *The Passionate Shepherd* lies precisely in its lack of novelty; it is the almost accidental issue of an apparently stable tradition. Again, the force and weight of *The Nymph's Reply* is grounded on the age-old wisdom of her sentences. Novelty, however, is no positive principle; it stipulates only a something else. It is a principle of rejection rather than of selection. The author of *The Bait* will go neither Marlowe's way nor Ralegh's; but if he goes he must go some way, and we may ask, Where does he find it? In the detail of style, as we have seen, he goes uncertainly. And as for the invention? His shepherd is not a shepherd but a fisherman, and that is the clue. For at the end of the last century Sannazaro sought to treat the pastoral convention under a novel guise, and wrote his Latin piscatory eclogues. That is, Donne goes for his invention to that vast, once living though now dead, body of contemporary literature, the current Latin poetry of the Renaissance. And not only in this instance. The whole body of his early work, with the partial exception, and it is partial only, of the *Songs and Sonnets,* is an attempt to realize in English the contemporary forms of occasional poetry in Latin, and especially those that admitted the particularities of sexual or of disreputable experience, and the details of everyday life. He writes epigrams, not in the tradition of Heywood, but in that of Martial, and satires on the model of Horace. He uses the verse letter as the humanist poets used it. He naturalizes the subjective-erotic elegy of Propertius and Ovid, and writes an heroical epistle whose subject is lesbianism; as, also, an epithalamium which, if you compare it with Spenser's, is clearly the epithalamium of a Latinist.

But Donne was not alone in turning his interests to the erotic experience of Latin elegy and the realistic social description of satire and epigram. It is an interest that suddenly appears, and at precisely this time, in several other men of his own age, and one somewhat older, at the Inns of Court as he was. The older poet was Thomas Campian, whose elegies and epigrams in Latin were printed in 1595, but whose *Observations in the Art of English Poesy,* containing fully realized English epigrams in the Latin mode, and one elegy, may be the hook entered in the Stationers Register on October 12, 1591.[5] If the text entered in 1591 was

419

substantially the text printed in 1602, Campian may have given the hint, though to Ben Jonson, some years later, Donne is the innovator:

> Whose every work of thy most early wit
> Came forth example, and remains so yet.

But to realize new genres, to explore hitherto unexploited areas of experience, involves the problem of style. Neither the pleasant nor the moral style would do; the material was inherently repugnant to them. What was needed was the English equivalent of the Classical plain style in Latin. This John Davies, among others, attempted to supply in his *Epigrams,* datable about 1594. It is a plain style, but it is the plainest of plain styles, the *genus humile* rather than the *genus tenue.* However, it can handle the sights and sounds and characters and place names of the streets of London, directly and without disguise:

> See yonder melancholy gentleman
> Which hoodwinked with his hat alone doth sit,
> Think what he thinks, and tell me if you can
> What great affairs trouble his little wit.
> He thinks not of the war 'twixt France and Spain . . .
> But he doth seriously bethink him whether
> Of the gulled people he be more esteemed
> For his long cloak or his great black feather,
> By which each gull is now a gallant deemed.
> Or of a journey he deliberates
> To Paris Garden, Cockpit, or the play,
> Or how to steal a dog he meditates,
> Or what he shall unto his mistress say.

Here is no alliterative phrasing, or phrasing by fours and sixes. Here is nothing that is naturally delightful. It is a prosaic style; it has, in fact, the characteristics of good workaday prose, in which what interest there is is in what is being talked of. But it is workaday prose in metrical form at a time when there was little workaday prose in literary prose. It can handle any subject so long as it can be handled in its proper terms and without adornment. It is the flat style. It aims at an unassuming lack of distinction, and with appropriate material has its own rightness, as in Hoskyns's epitaph *On a Man for Doing Nothing:*

> Here lies the man was born and cried,
> Told threescore years, fell sick, and died.

But the difficulty with the flat style, of course, is that it is flat. This is what Jonson had in mind when he told Sir John Harington that his epigrams "were narrations and not epigrams," or said of Owen's that they were "bare narrations." That is, to translate the remarks into our English, Harington's epigrams and Owen's are unadorned exposition, without distinction of style. So Shakespeare in an experiment in the flat style and its attendant attitudes and subjects seeks to relieve or transform the flatness by introducing some verbal figures that might be thought congruent with the style:

> When my love swears that she is made of truth
> I do believe her though I know she lies,
> That she might think me some untutored youth
> Unlearned in the world's false subtleties.

So far all is flat, except for the slight rhetorical touch of "untutored," "unlearned." But now he introduces more pointedness:

> Thus vainly thinking that she thinks me young,
> Although she knows my days are past the best,
> Simply I credit her false-speaking tongue;
> On both sides thus is simple truth suppressed.

And concludes with an epigrammatic pun:

> Therefore I lie with her and she with me,
> And in our faults by lies we flattered be.

By such means, by a sparse use of the elementary verbal figures, together with a tightness of metrical form, there was developed what I call the English plain style. The chief technical difference between this and the Classical plain style, which I shall next discuss, is the bareness of its diction and the regular coincidence of grammatical and metrical units, whereas in the classical style, especially when written in decasyllabic couplets, the lines are often run over, or, as Jonson says, "broken like hexameters." Small masterpieces of the English plain style are Hoskyns's *Absence* and Aytoun's *Upon Love:*

> I loved thee once, I'll love no more,
> Thine be the grief as is the blame,
> Thou art not what thou wast before,
> What reason I should be the same?
> He who can love unloved again
> Hath better store of love than brain.
> God send me love my debts to pay,
> While unthrifts fool their love away.

Styles are noticeable or unnoticeable. The sweet and the moral are noticeable; the flat is unnoticeable but undistinguished. What is needed is a noticeably unnoticeable style, the style of Cicero's Attic orator, *Nam orationis subtilitas imitabalis illa videtur esse existimanti, sed nihil est experienti minus,* "a directness of speech that seems to one judging easily imitable, to one trying it nothing less so."[6] Such a style first appears in this particular literary situation scattered here and there in Sidney's *Astrophil and Stella,* as in the passage quoted earlier:

> Dear, therefore be not jealous over me
> If you hear that they seem my heart to move.
> Not them, oh no, but you in them I love.

If Campian's *The Writer to His Book* was written by 1591 there was a fully realized model in blank verse available to the poets we are concerned with:

> Whither thus hastes my little book so fast?
> To Paul's Churchyard. What? in those cells to stand
> With one leaf like a rider's cloak put up
> To catch a termer?

How close this is to Jonson:

> Nor have my title-leaf on posts or walls
> Or in cleft sticks advanced to make calls
> For termers.

It is the style of Donne's early poetry at its best. A style that can handle circumstantiality and detail, can accommodate in poetry what we think of as the material of prose, and yet without modulation of manner can strike through to the heart of human feeling. In Donne's early poetry it appears intermittently, amid a debris of other incongruous and indecorous manners, but when it appears it is absolute, unrevisably right. It appears in the verse letter, *The Calm,* to which we alluded earlier, in the couplet Jonson pointed out to Drummond of Hawthornden:

> No use of lanterns, and in one place lay
> Feathers and dust, today and yesterday.

a kind of exact and minute particularity almost unknown to the poetry of the preceding decades. Or:

> Whether a rotten state, and hope of gain,
> Or to disuse me from the queasy pain
> Of being beloved, and loving, or the thirst
> Of honor or fair death out pushed me first,
> I lose my end.

Or again:

> What are we then? How little more, alas,
> Is man now than before he was. He was
> Nothing. For us, we are for nothing lit:
> Chance or ourselves still disproportion it.

Where did Donne get this style? Possibly from Sidney, possibly from Campian, but certainly from the effort to realize in English the forms of Latin poetry, and their appropriate styles. There remained only for a Ben Jonson to recognize it, perfect it, and establish it, and in the forms that Donne had pioneered: epigram, elegy, satire, verse letter, epithalamium, and in the same tradition of Latin learning. The relationship of Jonson and Donne is that of Horace to Lucillius, perfector to inventor.

WITH THAT FACILITY

False Starts & Revisions in *Love's Labour's Lost*

The title page of the earliest extant edition of *Love's Labour's Lost,* the First Quarto of 1598, describes the play as "A Pleasant Conceited Comedie."[1] This is, of course, an advertisement, a blurb, and indeed we know from various allusions that title pages were struck off separately and displayed "at the recognised 'posts' throughout the town" "to catch a termer."[2] But an advertisement tells us something: it tells us what a seller thinks will be attractive to a buyer, and what it says of a product may sometimes be so. It is, I think, so in this instance. What is it a prospective buyer would anticipate who was interested in a pleasant conceited comedy? The description is not uncommon on the title pages of that time, though not routine. We have "The Old Wives Tale, a pleasant conceited Comedie . . . " in 1595; "A Pleasant Conceited Historic, called The taming of a shrew" in 1594; and the earliest text of *Romeo and Juliet,* the Bad Quarto of 1597, is "An Excellent conceited Tragedie. . . ." The term "conceit," of course, was also used to describe the striking hijinks of a comic character; the First Quarto of *1 Henry IV,* for example, promises on the title page not only the Battle of Shrewsbury but also "the humorous conceits of Sir John Falstaffe."[3] But when applied to a play as a whole, whether comedy, tragedy, or history, though it is peculiarly appropriate to comedy, "conceited" indicates that the work will be especially rhetorical in style, full of witty and ingenious turns of thought and speech.

It is interesting that whatever reputation Shakespeare had in the literary and theatrical world of London up to 1598, so far as we can recover it from the records of the time, was not a reputation for creation of character or contrivance of plot but precisely for qualities of style, and particularly for pleasant, conceited writing. The evidence is, considering the scantiness of records of this sort, surprisingly full. The first clear reference linking Shakespeare and the stage is, of course, the allusion by Greene in a pamphlet of 1592 to Shakespeare as player turned playwright; an antic, Greene says, "garnisht in our colours," that is, ornamented in those colors of rhetoric, those figures of speech, which the writer gives to the actor, and yet he now thinks "he is as well able to bombast out a blanke verse as the best of" the professional playwrights:[4] that is, to fill out "the spacious volubilitie of a drumming decasillabon,"[5] no doubt with "farre-fetcht phraise,"[6] for bombast, of course, is the foam rubber of the time, the material used to pad out fashionable clothing. Shakespeare, a mere actor, has picked up Greene's style and meter, the new style and meter that made possible the glories of the late Elizabethan stage. Chettle in a subsequent apology for Greene's attack, also of 1592, speaks particularly of Shakespeare's "facetious grace in writting, that aproues his Art"; that is, to translate the compliment into modern idiom, the witty and ingenious charm of style that ratifies his skill. For Barnfield in 1598 it is Shakespeare's "hony-flowing Vaine," his mastery of the sweet style, that pleases the world and praise obtains. In the well-known catalogues of Francis Meres, also of 1598, Shakespeare is listed with his peers, Sidney, Spenser, and others, as one by whom "The English tongue is mightiliy enriched, and gorgeouslie inuested in rare ornaments and resplendent abiliments"; again, "the Muses would speak with *Shakespeares* fine filed phrase, if they would speake English"; and, finally, "the sweete wittie soule of *Quid* Hues in mellifluous & hony-tongued *Shakespeare.*"[7]

428

One would expect, then, from the promise of the title page and from the reputation of the author, that *Love's Labour's Lost* would be a work replete with witty, charming, ingenious turns of thought and speech, that it would be a display of the rhetoric of the sweet, the pleasant style, the *genus amoenum* of Antiquity. And so it is.

It is, in fact, so much of a display that when the reader or viewer comes to the middle of the last scene, he will be suddenly delighted and relieved. For there the hero of the play renounces his rhetoric:

> O neuer will I trust to speaches pend,
> Nor to the motion of a Schoole-boyes tongue:
> Nor neuer come in vizard to my friend,
> Nor woo in rime like a blind harpers songue.
> Taffata phrases, silken tearmes precise,
> Three pilde Hiberboles, spruce affection:
> Figures pedanticall, these sommer flies,
> Haue blowne me full of maggot ostentation.
> I do forsweare them.
>
> 5. 2. 402-10

The modern lover, whose eloquence is confined to reciting what he takes to be the story of his life and who demands of love the illusions of sincerity, feels now at home. He applauds as Berowne goes on:

> and I here protest
> By this white Gloue (how white the
> hand God knowes)
> Hencefoorth my wooing minde shalbe exprest
> In russet yeas, and honest kersie noes.

429

And does not notice that Berowne, in renouncing rhetoric, re-
nounces it rhetorically, crowding in one phrase the figures of
exclamation, asseveration, and one of the varieties of verbal rep-
etition. He cannot renounce it, for to speak in russet and kersey
would be inappropriate to his rank in society and to Rosaline's,
and inappropriate to courtly love. For russet and kersey are cheap
cloths, the dress of the lowborn, and one woos only the lowborn
in russet yeas and honest kersey noes. Thus when Don Armado
of the fantastic phrase woos Jacquenetta the country wench, he
says with absolute russet simplicity:

"Maide."

To which Jacquenetta replies in kersey:

"Man."

But the play deals chiefly with love at court and courtly love, and
both demand witty invention and figurative language. For, as an
elder contemporary of Shakespeare's tells us: "But as it hath bene
always reputed a great fault to vse figuratiue speaches foolish-
ly and indiscretly, so it is esteemed no lesse an imperfection in
mans vtterance, to haue none vse of figures at all, specially in our
writing and speaches publike, making them but as our ordinary
talke. . . ." To make the point clear he uses the very analogy that
the hero used above, and that Francis Meres used in the passage
alluded to earlier where he spoke of the English tongue "gor-
geouslie inuested in rare ornaments and resplendent abiliments":

And as we see in these great Madames of honour, be
they for personage or otherwise neuer so comely and
bewtifull, yet if they want their courtly habilements

or at leastwise such other apparell as custome and ciuilitie haue ordained to couer their naked bodies, would be halfe ashamed or greatly out of countenaunce to be seen in that sort, and perchance do then thinke themselves more amiable in euery mans eye, when they be in their richest attire, suppose of silkes or tyssewes & costly embroideries, then when they go in cloth or in any other plaine and simple apparell. Even so cannot our vulgar Poesie shew it selfe either gallant or gorgious, if any lymme be left naked and bare and not clad in his kindly clothes and coulours, such as may conuey them some what out of sight, that is from the common course of ordinary speach and capacitie of the vulgar judgement.

Style, then, is an ornament, and a needed ornament, but it must also be fitting and proper. And what is fitting and proper to love at court? Or, to quote our author again, "In what forme of poesie the amorous affections and allurements were uttered." He answers: "And because loue is of all other humane affections the most puissant and passionate . . . it requireth a forme of poesie variable, inconstant, affected, curious, and most witty of any others. . . ."[8] "Variable," "inconstant," "affected," "curious," and "most witty"—the terms need explanation since, except perhaps for the last, they do not at all mean what the modern reader would take them to mean. It must be "variable," that is, there should be a copious variety of phrases, a flow and outpouring of eloquence, such as we shall see later in Berowne's display, making the worse appear the better cause. It should be "inconstant"; the style should not keep a single tenor, but rise and fall, with a mingling of styles. The violation of these two requirements in his own sonnets is the theme of Shakespeare's seventy-sixth sonnet:

431

> Why is my verse so barren of new pride?
> So far from variation or quicke change?

The style should also be "affected"; that is, it should show feeling. It should be "curious," or carefully, highly, finely wrought, and "most witty," with many turns and conceits of speech and thought.

It is an old theory of style, though out of fashion in our day, and clearly relevant to *Love's Labour's Lost*. The play as a whole is an illustration of the qualities of style of amorous poesy, as also at times of the foolish and indiscreet use of figurative speeches. The theory was simple: it distinguished between the naked thought nakedly expressed and the same thought decently or even gorgeously appareled. The problem in practice was to achieve, first, an ability to clothe any thought in rich and varied costume, to have "a mint of phrases in his braine" (1. 1. 166); and then to exercise discretion in choosing just what was suited to this speaker, addressing this person, on this occasion. The prior problem, of course, though usually subsequent in attainment, was to find the thought. They called this "invention," borrowing the Latin word for finding, and they especially prized an invention that was apt and peculiarly fitted to the speaker audience, and circumstances.

Such was the theory and practice of composition in Shakespeare's day. That he wrote explicitly by it, at least at times, is clear from several passages in this play. These are passages where, with some uncertainty but also with a good deal of plausibility, we can see Shakespeare at work.

But perhaps we should dwell for a moment on this point, for the desire to find genius at work has sometimes dispensed with scrutiny of the evidence. There have been those, and there still are, who would like to see in, for example, the earliest printed texts of *Romeo and Juliet* and *Hamlet,* the Bad Quartos as they are called in modern scholarship, Shakespearean first drafts, or the inferior work of a Shakespearean predecessor, or, most commonly, some mingling of both early draft and other work. The critic can then show by comparison how the prior effort has been transformed into a Shakespearean masterpiece. But if the current view of most textual critics is correct, the process is the other way around, and the evidence is no evidence for Shakespeare at work. It is not that a prior effort has been transformed by Shakespeare, but that Shakespeare has been mercilessly transformed and corrupted by others. For there is fairly general agreement that the Bad Quartos are reconstructions from memory of the authentic text. Why it was done, and by whom, are subjects for conjecture and imaginative fiction. But surely the "To be or not to be" soliloquy in its first published form would require a more than Shakespearean genius to transform it into the form we know. It reads:

> To be, or not to be, I there's the point,
> To Die, to sleepe, is that all? I all:
> No, to sleepe, to dreame, I mary there it goes,
> For in that dreame of death, when wee awake,
> And borne before an euerlasting Judge,
> From whence no passenger euer retur'nd,
> The vndiscouered country, at whose sight
> The happly smile, and the accursed damn'd.

And so on, for fourteen more lines.

There is in this portion something that does tend to support the view that this version represents an effort to remember and record the received text:

To Die, to sleepe, is that all? I all:
No, to sleepe, to dreame, I mary there it goes.

The man who is trying to remember the speech is dictating to a secretary who writes down all, including "No, that's not the way it goes," and "Yes, yes, that's the way it goes."

But the texts we will deal with and the evidence for revision are of a different kind, for we will be concerned with passages where the earliest editions preserve in the same text alternate versions of the same speech. It is not a situation peculiar to *Love's Labour's Lost;* there are other instances. In *Othello,* for one, there is a passage (2. 1. 77-83) whose significance for the textual history of the play has not been appraised. There are two early editions, the Quarto of 1622, and the Folio of 1623. The passage reads in the Quarto:

> —great *Iove Othello* guard,
> And swell his saile with thine owne powerfull breath,
> That he may blesse this Bay with his tall shippe,
> And swiftly come to *Desdemona's* armes.
> > *Enter* Desdemona, Iago, Emillia, *and* Roderigo.
> Give renewed fire,
> To our extincted spirits.
> And bring all Cypresse comfort,—O behold
> The riches of the ship is come ashore.

In the Folio:

> Great Iove, *Othello* guard,
> And swell his Saile with thine owne powreful breath,
> That he may blesse this Bay with his tall Ship,

Make loues quicke pants in *Desdemonaes* Armes,
Give renew'd fire to our extincted Spirits.
        Enter Desdemona, Iago, Roderigo, and Aemilia.
Oh, behold,
The Riches of the Ship is come on shore:

The texts are substantially identical up to line 80. There the author wrote "And swiftly come to Desdemona's arms" bringing the sentence and the speech to a close. Then, for whatever reasons, and I think we can see plausible reasons, he crossed out "And swiftly come," interlined "Make loues quicke pants" and swung the sentence over the line-end, making more vivid Othello's private life and acknowledging his public role.

What is textually interesting here is that one needs both Quarto and Folio to recover what Shakespeare wrote and what he rejected; that is, there must have been a manuscript ultimately common to both texts in which both first draft and revision indistinguishably stood. It would in this respect be like the copy for Romeo's last speech in the Good Quarto of 1599. The relevant portion reads:

     Ah deare *Iuliet*
why art thou yet so faire? I will beleeue,
Shall I beleeue that vnsubstantiall death is amorous,
And that the leane abhorred monster keepes
Thee here in the darke to be his parramour?
For feare of that I still will staie with thee,
And never from this pallat of dym night.
Depart againe, come lye thou in my arme,
Heer's to thy health, where ere thou tumblest in.
O true Appothecarie!

435

Thy drugs are quicke. Thus with a kiss I die.
Depart againe, here, here, will I remaine,
With wormes that are thy Chamber-maides: O here
Will I set up my everlasting rest:
And shake the yoke of inauspicious starres,
From this world wearied flesh, eyes looke your last:
Armes take your last embrace: And lips, O you
The doores of breath, seale with a righteous kisse
A dateless bargaine to ingrossing death:
Come bitter conduct, come vnsauory guide,
Thou desperate Pilot, now at once run on
The dashing Rocks, thy seasick weary barke:
Heeres to my Love. O true Appothecary:
Thy drugs are quicke. Thus with a kisse I die.

There are two false starts in the passage, both loving-
ly preserved by the printer, and both, of course, cancelled by
the subsequent revision. And we can, given the evidence, see
why. This is Romeo's great aria, and so the declarative "I will
believe" is immediately altered to the heightened form of a rhe-
torical question. What follows is adequate, but not sufficiently
extended, not copious enough, and not sufficiently elevated; in-
deed, with "where ere thou tumblest in" it falls to vulgarity. And
so Shakespeare picks up "Depart againe," getting thirteen lines
for four, introducing a Gorgianic figure of the vultures-are-living
sepulchres type ("With wormes that are thy Chamber-maides"),
figures of verbal repetition ("here, here," "O here"), apostrophe,
personification ("Come bitter conduct"), periphrasis ("And lips,
O you / The doores of breath")—a speech variable, inconstant,
affected, curious, and in an Elizabethan sense most witty.

The passages in *Love's Labour's Lost* are similar to the *Romeo*
passage. We have the first draft and the revision, and we can see

what was done to it. In each case the revised version immediately follows the first draft, and in two cases repeats with slight variation the opening line of the first draft. An eighteenth-century editor who first noted one of these passages (4. 3. 291*ff.*) explained convincingly what had happened in that instance: "penned in haste, found weak in some places, and its reasoning disjointed, it had instant correction; but wanting the proper mark of correction by rasure or otherwise, printers took what they found."[9]

There are three such passages, two of which have been noticed by previous commentators. But the third is the simplest, and we will begin with that. It reads in the earliest extant edition, 1598 (the Pedant, Holofernes, is speaking):

> PEDA. Sir, you shall present before her the Nine Worthies. Sir *Holofernes,* as concerning some entertainement of time, some show in the posterior of this day, to be rended by our assistants the Kinges commaund, and this most gallant illustrate and learned Gentleman, before the Princesse: I say none so fit as to present the nine Worthies.
>
> 5. 1. 124-30

There is a minor point to be noted in this passage before we come to the major one. The passage is reprinted in the first collected edition of Shakespeare's plays, 1623, with one correction: "rendered" for "rended." This could be right, for certainly the Pedant intended to say "rendered." But it is more likely that Shakespeare intended him to mistake the word and say "rended" instead. For the rendering of the Nine Worthies, when we come to it a little later, is certainly "rended," limb from limb. It is a habit of Shakespeare's comic characters to say the unselfconsciously obvious thing, to "mistake the word"[10] to their own derogation. For instance, the clown in *Love's Labour's Lost* says of a letter, "Sir the contempts thereof are as touching me." (1. 1. 191)

We come now to the major point. The Pedant, of course, is Holofernes, and so he would seem in the second sentence to be addressing himself. This is obviously wrong. One could perhaps justify it by some exquisite psychological construction but such subtlety would be out of place in a broadly comic speech. Besides, the Pedant is not entitled to be called "Sir," and Elizabethans were very finicky on such details. On the other hand, Nathaniel, the Curate, is entitled to "Sir" by virtue of his office, and editors usually correct "Holofernes" to "Nathaniel," so that the first sentence is addressed in direct reply to Armado, the second to Sir Nathaniel. But this is clumsy. Furthermore, both sentences say exactly the same thing, the first straightforwardly, the second in the Pedant's own style. The first is the naked thought; the second is clothed in figures pedantical.

The traces of what happened are clear on the printed page. Shakespeare wrote the speech prefix "Peda." and put down in a straightforward sentence what he wanted him to say. When, perhaps after a warm beer, he started over, writing the speech prefix "Holofernes," and recast what he wanted him to say in pedantical style. Either he neglected to mark the first sentence for deletion or the printer missed the mark. In the second sentence the printer corrected "Holofernes Sir" to the more plausible "Sir Holofernes." If this reconstruction is correct the passage should begin:

> HOLOFERNES: Sir, as concerning some
>   entertainment

And how does Shakespeare go about recasting the original sentence? First, he turns it into a suspended, a periodic, sentence, sending out an extended flanker movement before bringing up the main clause. This tends to elevation of style, and recognizes the social gulf between Armado, who is addressed, and the Pedant. Second, the notion in "you shall present" is expanded into two phrases, the second employing the phrase he had a moment before collected for his own phrase-book from Armado's jeweled speech: "The *posterior* of the day, most generous sir, is liable, congruent, and measurable for the after noone: the worde is well culd, chose, sweete, & apt I do assure you sir, I do assure." And finally, he finds a Latinate, an aureate term, "illustrate," to go with the other two complimentary epithets by which Armado is addressed. It is like "peregrinate," earlier in the scene, which Sir Nathaniel wrote down in his notebook for future use, "A most singuler and choyce Epithat."

The second passage comes toward the end of the last scene of the play. The princess has imposed a year's penance on the king, at the end of which he may claim her in marriage. After this, in the earliest edition, Berowne says to Rosaline, "And what to me my Loue? and what to me?" And she replies:

> You must be purged to, your sinnes are rackt.
> You are attaint with faultes and periurie:
> Therefore if you my fauour meane to get,
> A tweluemonth shall you spende and neuer rest,
> But seeke the weery beddes of people sicke.
>
> 5. 2. 827-32

Whereupon Dumaine says to Katherine, almost echoing the words of Berowne, "But what to me my Loue? but what to me?" And after she has put him off for a year, and Maria has put Longaville off for the same period, Berowne again addresses Rosaline, and she again imposes the same sentence on him, but with a significant addition:

> Oft haue I heard of you my Lord *Berowne,*
> Before I saw you: and the worldes large tongue
> Proclaymes you for a man repleat with mockes,
> Full of comparisons and wounding floutes:
> Which you on all estetes will execute,
> That lie within the mercie of your wit:
> To weede this wormewood from your fructfull braine,
> And therewithal to winne me, yf you please,
> Without the which I am not to be won:
> You shall this tweluemonth terme from day to day,
> Visite the speachless sicke, and still conuerse,
> With groning wretches; and your taske shall be,
> With all the fierce endeuour of your wit,
> To enforce the pained impotent to smile.
>
> 5. 2. 851-63

It is generally agreed that here too the printer set up an unrevised version followed by the revised version. In writing this final scene Shakespeare knew that by all laws of precedence the king's exchange with the princess must come first. He then went on with Berowne and Rosaline, who perhaps interested him as they interest us, but soon saw that by all the laws of interest these two must come last. So he started over, gave Berowne's speech to Dumaine with the change of "And" to "But," and after taking care of the other lovers returned to the hero and heroine. He must have seen that Rosaline's original speech was not only much too short for the purpose but also pretty flat in the writing.

Furthermore, the penance imposed on the hero had no special ingenuity to it, no exact fitting of the punishment to the crime. What he needs, then, is a notion, a gimmick, an invention, and this will yield the detail to amplify the passage and give it the requisite bulk. He keeps, then, only the idea of "purged" and develops it in the line "To weede this wormewood from your fructfull braine."

And for penance? Berowne's sin has been wit. He has been

> a man repleat with mockes,
> Full of comparisons and wounding floutes:
> Which you on all estetes will execute,
> That lie within the mercie of your wit.

And so the original idea of sentencing him to tending the sick for twelve months is given an apt and decorous twist:

> You shall this tweluemonth terme from day to day,
> Visite the speachless sicke, and still conuerse,
> With groaning wretches: and your taske shall be,
> With all the fierce endeuour of your wit,
> To enforce the pained impotent to smile.

The description of Berowne as a wit and the description of his penitential expense of that wit furnish the material for amplification.

In the first passage we found Shakespeare writing down what he wanted to say, and then saying it as he wanted to say it. The problem is one of clothing the thought. In the second passage the proper management of the ending led him to cancel the lines, and the flatness of style and of the climactic idea forced him to develop new lines and an ingenious twist of the old idea. It was a question of invention.

The third passage is the most extensive, and the one in which the reconstruction of the process of composition is the most conjectural. This is the first draft:

> Haue at you then affections men at armes,
> Consider what you first did sweare vnto:
> To fast, to study, and to see no woman:
> Flat treason gainst the kingly state of youth.
> Say, Can you fast? your stomacks are too young:
> And abstinence ingenders maladies.
> And where that you haue vowd to Studie (Lordes)
> In that each of you haue forsworne his Booke.
> Can you still dreame and poare and thereon looke.
> For when would you my Lord, or you, or you,
> Haue found the ground of Studies excellence,
> Without the beautie of a womans face?
> From womens eyes this doctrine I deriue,
> They are the Ground, the Bookes, the Achadems,
> From whence doth spring the true *Promethean* fire.
> Why vniuersall plodding poysons vp
> The nimble spirites in the arteries,
> As motion and long during action tyres
> The sinnowy vigour of the trauayler.
> Now for not looking on a womans face,
> You haue in that forsworne the vse of eyes:
> And studie too, the causer of your vow.
> For where is any Authour in the worlde,
> Teaches such beautie as a womans eye:
> Learning is but an adiunct to our selfe,
> And where we are, our Learning likewise is.
> Then when our selues we see in Ladies eyes,
> With our selues.
> Do we not likewise see our learning there?
>
>   4. 3. 290-317

There is no question of invention here. Berowne has already used at the beginning of the play (1. 1. 59*ff.*) the line of argument by which he will make the worse appear the better cause, and used it in a similar context. It is an extemporal display of wit, like the display of a fencing master: "Com'on then" in the earlier passage, and "Haue at you then" here. And it employs the same commonplace of the vanity of learning: "continuall plodders" in the first act, and "vniuersall plodding" here. It is a display in the tradition of Nashe, and perhaps of Tarleton: "but giue me the man whose extemporall veine in any humour will excell our greatest Artmaisters deliberate thoughts; whose inuentions, quicker than his eye, will challenge the prowdest Rhetoritian to the contention of like perfection with like expedition."[11]

There are some indications at the beginning and end of this first draft that Shakespeare was getting down something to say, as he did in the Holofernes passage. The line, "In that each of you haue forsworne his Booke," lacks metrical and rhetorical shape; it is a line that belongs to another style, a consequence of rhetorically unsuccessful exactness. In the next line he overcorrects by introducing rhyme in a line that is too easily and obviously shaped: "Can you still dreame and poare and thereon looke." There is a similar unsuccessful exactness at the end of the passage where he is trying out a new line of argument. Here the separate line "With our selues" has puzzled editors, and they have tended simply to omit it. But the argument is drawn from metaphysics—it is a development of the proposition "Learning is but an adiunct to our selfe"—and Shakespeare is trying to get it down exactly. He wrote, "Then when our selues we see in Ladies eyes, with our selues do we not likewise see our learning there?" He moved from verse to the exactness of prose; it was more reason than rhyme. But since metrical composition involves a habit of forming sentences simultaneously grammatical and metrical, the last ten syllables come in a syntactical unit metrically acceptable, and the printer set it up as verse. At this point Shakespeare abandons the thought, and the first start, and starts over again:

> O we haue made a Vow to studie, Lordes,
> And in that Vow we haue forsworne our Bookes:
> For when would you (my Leedge) or you, or you?
> In leaden contemplation haue found out
> Such fierie Numbers as the prompting eyes,
> Of beautis tutors haue inritcht you with:
> Other slow Artes intirely keepe the braine:
> And therefore finding barraine practizers,
> Scarce shew a haruest of their heauie toyle.
> But Loue first learned in a ladies eyes,
> Liues not alone emured in the braine:
> But with the motion of all elamentes,
> Courses as swift as thought in euery power,
> And giues to euery power a double power,
> Aboue their functions and their offices.
> It addes a precious seeing to the eye:
> A Louers eyes will gaze an Eagle blinde.
> A Louers eare will heare the lowest sound,
> When the suspitious head of theft is stopt.
> Loues feeling is more soft and sensible,
> Then are the tender homes of Cockled Snayles.
> Loues tongue proues daintie, *Bachus* grosse in taste,
> For Valoure, is not Loue a *Hercules?*
> Still clyming trees in the *Hesperides.*
> Subtil as *Sphinx,* as sweete and musicall,
> As bright *Appolos* Lute, strung with his haire.

And when Loue speakes, the voyce of all the Goddes,
Make heauen drowsie with the harmonie.
Neuer durst Poet touch a pen to write,
Vntill his Incke were tempred with Loues sighes:
O then his lines would rauish sauage eares,
And plant in Tyrants milde humilitie.
From womens eyes this doctrine I deriue,
They sparcle still the right promethean fier,
They are the bookes, the Arts, the Achademes,
That shew, containe, and nourish all the worlde.
Els none at all in ought proues excellent.
Then fooles you were, these women to forsweare:
Or keeping what is sworne, you will proue fooles,
For Wisedomes sake, a worde that all men loue:
Or for Loues sake, a worde that loues all men.
Or for Mens sake, the authour of these Women:
Or Womens sake, by whom we Men are Men.
Let vs once loose our othes to finde our selues,
Or els we loose our selues, to keep our othes:
It is Religion to be thus forsworne.
For Charitie it selfe fulfilles the Law:
And who can seuer Loue from Charitie.

4. 3. 318-65

Shakespeare had two problems, a problem of order and of amplification; the speech had to have size and to move. He had begun in the earlier wit display by dividing his subjects; he will take up the three vows in order. But the line of argument is that the second vow, "to study," entails rejection of the third vow, to see no woman," and hence part three of the speech, which is clearly indicated by the transitional "now for not looking on a womans face," must in effect simply repeat in other words the content of part two. He needs, then, a new principle of order, and suddenly finds it. He fuses the two vows, treats them together as inherently they demand to be treated, and fuses at the same time much of the detail of the draft. The notion of women as teachers becomes "beauty's tutors" who teach love poetry. The earlier "vniuersall plodding" suggests "leaden contemplation," as also the distinction of "Other slow arts." Out of the same sentence, dropping the inapt simile of the traveler, he picks up the physiological notion of "The nimble spirites in the arteries," which perform in Elizabethan science the functions of our modern "nervous system"; this is now identified with love, which "Courses as swift as thought in euery power" and increases each faculty. He proceeds to amplify, as the textbooks suggest he should, by division. The five senses are faculties, and so he enumerates four of them.

And why not five? Partly because the fifth would complete a pattern and might bring the fluent facility to a stop, and partly because he has suddenly found another principle of order that will keep the eloquence flowing. He will now move from new material to new material by clear and simple associative links. "Love's tongue proues daintie, *Bachus* grosse in taste" suggests a richer field of amplification, mythological comparisons, culminating in "the voyce of all the Goddes." This suggests poetry and the effects of music. When this flags, he has at hand the salvaged lines on the true Promethean fire, and brings the argument to a conclusion, summarizing in a pointed couplet:

Then fooles you were, these women to forsweare:
Or keeping what is sworne, you will proue fooles.

But the impetus persists; he is not willing to quit. The pointed couplet with its repetitions suggests a passage of verbal repetition: for, as a contemporary says, "the eares of men are not onlie delighted with store & exchange of divers words, but feele greate delight in repeticion of the same. . . ."[12] And now he finally concludes with what is really conclusive, and plucked out of nowhere, a Scriptual text: "For Charitie it selfe fulfilles the Law."

One sympathizes with the judgment of his colleague, Ben Jonson: "Hee . . . had an excellent Phantsie; brave notions, and gentle expressions: wherein hee flow'd with that facility, that sometimes it was necessary he should be stop'd. . . . His wit was in his owne power; would the rule of it had been so too."[13]

IN SHAKESPEARE'S DAY

There is Shakespeare experienced and Shakespeare explained. I remember as a boy reading the plays without introduction or notes in individual volumes bound in an imitation leather that smelled awful. It was an almost uncued experience, and I think I can remember something of the freshness and distance of that reading. Now, if the purpose of dramatic art, in Shakespeare's day and in ours, is "to hold the mirror up to nature," there must be a communicable constant, open to boy and scholar; else it would not be the mirror and it would not be nature. But if what is shown there—and there are other mirrors—are the features of virtue and images of scorn, these vary throughout our own world; they have changed in my own society in my lifetime. And if they are shown implicated in "the age and body of the time," abstracted in brief chronicle, some sense of the time must be intuited or acquired. Otherwise, the given is not given and the "form" the poet impresses on the time, as a seal on wax, is for us impressed on water.

Much of the given—mirror, nature, time—is given in the text if we will believe it, including the theory of drama just abstracted from *Hamlet*. If we will believe it. But we departmentalize art, especially canonized art, confine it to aesthetic patterns, and process the experience. We are told why the family warns Ophelia not to get involved with Hamlet, but we take the warnings as characterizing the warners and not as the facts of high political life at the time. We read as "character" what Aristotle calls "thought." But to be told is one thing, to perceive is another, for

* This essay was originally the Introduction for an anthology edited by J. V. Cunningham, *In Shakespeare's Day*, a collection of over a hundred selections.

that involves the persuasion of actuality. And so one needs not only the text but some such book as this, a book to browse in, thumb through, perhaps to read. A book of evidence, not of conclusions. A book of implicit answers looking for questions.

If it is not quite clear what to look for, it is partly because looking is thwarted by premature clarity. Begin, first, with simple, unfocused curiosity, and then with absorption there will come an ambience, an unreferred feel for the time, acquaintance seeking familiarity. Go with a German tourist to the Court of Queen Elizabeth and observe government by ceremony and magnificence, then cross the Thames by water taxi and see *Julius Caesar* at the Globe. Soon you will find that your experience of a play, of *Hamlet*, is invaded by a certain literalness. There were traveling players who turned up at provincial courts, pirates were not storybook, and the "same strict and most observant watch" of the first scene was an experience of 1599. On the other hand, the ghost does not wear "the ghost suit" and the "ghost bodice" listed in another company's theatrical inventory of 1598, but appears in "complete steel" and in his dressing gown, "in his habit as he lived." And so the texture of your experience of the play little by little becomes dense.

So far small detail, now for the large. The next step is cross-reference, and first on disguise. We regard it as a story element, something that happens in fiction, as in the source for *Measure for Measure*. For, if the best kind of plot, as Aristotle says, involves "discovery," a change in unknown to known, happening between those characters who happiness or unhappiness forms the catastrophe of the drama," then disguise and mistaken identity are obvious means. It is the disguise of Viola that ties the knot of *Twelfth Night*, and in the revelation of her identity and sex that unloosens it. But disguise also happened in real life. There is Moll Cutpurse, "a notorious baggage that used to go in men's apparel and challenged the field of divers gallants," and there is the disguise of make-believe in the game of courtly sex, as with the French king and his bride.

Again, at the end of *King Lear* Regan is murdered, Goneril commits suicide, Cordelia is executed, Edmund is killed in trial by combat, Gloucester's death is reported, and Lear himself "is gone indeed." But in the sources for the story, France and Cordelia are victorious, Lear is restored to the throne, and the principles, except Albany and Cornwall, are alive. The change deeply distressed Dr. Jonson. Yet, "the movement of events in tragedy," according to Diomedes, "is almost always from happy circumstances to bitter deaths, accompanied at the end with the perception that the fortunes of the house involved have gone to ruin." The House of Lear is destroyed, as was the House of Hamlet, and succeeded by the House of Gloucester. The story is seen in a "tragic glass." Nevertheless, *The Tragedy of Cymbeline* has a happy ending.

This suggests the need for negative capabilities, for a parsimony with generalizations and with the value judgements, both useful and necessary, but not idly to be employed. To start a sentence "Tragedy is" or "The Elizabethans thought" is to preclude the claims of variety and the hesitations of ignorance. The Elizabethans thought many, and sometimes, contradictory, things, though it is true they did not think some things we do. However, Marlowe was thought to be an atheist, "daring God out of heaven with that atheist Tamburlain." We read both "Bloodshed by bloodshed still is nourished" and "for empire and greatness it importeth most that a nation do profess arms as their principal honor, study, and occupation." The first points to Macbeth, the second to Henry V and, perhaps,

Fortinbras. Plays were divided into five acts on Horace's author-ity, Gloucester is blinded on stage despite Horace. So also with the value judgments. To compare the Shakespearean passage with Plutarch's description of Cleopatra and ascribe the differ-ences to Shakespeare's genius is to be on a race after it is official, and to miss the race.

Finally, each of us has his own interests, his own competen-cies, and one or other of these may be relevant to Shakespeare. I am an old hand with the iambic pentameter and the perception of style, and am interested also in realizing the literary situation as it was when Shakespeare entered it. So I look at the testimony. The first reference to him in that connection is as a player turned poet, one of "those antics garnished in our colors," that is, in our livery (players are the poet's servants", but also in our colors of rhetoric, our figures of speech, our new style. And this jack-of-all-trades "supposed he is as well able to bombast out a blanke verse as the best of" the new poets. Perhaps by writing bombast, but that meaning is a little later and derived from such passages as this. The metaphor here is new. Bombast was the foam rub-ber of the time with which you padded out the fashionable parts of the body. Now the obvious way to stuff out a blank verse line is with disyllabic possessives and adjectives, epithets that adorn, with the accent on the first syllable: "O tiger's heart wrapped in a woman's hide." (*1 Henry VI*, 1. 4. 137) or "From jigging veins of rhyming mother wits." (Prologue to *1 Tamburlaine*). It is to write "a bombast circumstance / Horribly stuffed with epiphets of war." (*Othello*, 1. 1. 13-14) This yields what Nashe calls "the spacious volubility of a drumming decasyllablon."

Enough: These are instances. Let not "my anticipation pre-vent your discovery."

THE HEART OF HIS MYSTERY

Fulke Greville comments on what I am about to do:

> Yet not asham'd these Verbalists still are,
> From youth, till age and study dimme their eyes,
> To engage the Grammar rules in civill warre,
> For some small sentence that they patronize.[1]

I shall begin with a "small sentence" and observe that a classic in time becomes a palimpsest, where interpretation blots the text, both in the local context and in the large. The task, then, becomes one of subtraction and recovery. My example is trivial, if anything is trivial that has been read, rephrased, written out, set, proofread, and glanced at in the study in edition after edition since Pope's, where it first appeared.

You will recall that the Ghost at his first meeting with Hamlet says: "But that I am forbid / To tell the secrets of my prison house / I could a tale unfold" that, among other phenomena, would make "each particular hair to stand an end / Like quills upon the fearful [or F, fretful] porpentine." (1. 5. 13-15, 19-20) And at the second meeting the Queen observes this phenomenon in Hamlet and likewise describes it by similes: "And, as the sleeping soldiers in th' alarm, / Your bedded hair . . . / Starts up, and stands an end." Vivid enough. But she also uses a parallel simile, "Your bedded hair, like life in excrements, / Starts up. . . ." (3. 4. 120-22) The usual gloss (I have seen only one deviation[2]) equates "excrements" with hairs—a piece of scientific lore, that hair is excremental, with presumably the meaning "like life in hairs," "as if it had life in it." But so understood it is no simile. To recover the

453

comparison one needs another piece of scientific lore. Your hair starts up as flies and such-like do from a pile of manure in spontaneous generation. A simile, and vivid enough.

Now to less trivial matters. I should like to pluck the mystery out of Hamlet's "you would pluck out the heart of my mystery" (3. 2. 382) and erase even more of time's palimpsest. There is no note on the passage in the many editions I have looked at—it is taken to be self-evident—yet the phrase has become central in the interpretation of the play, which for most consists in the interpretation of Hamlet's character, on the premise formulated by A. C. Bradley "that the whole story turns on the peculiar character of the hero."[3] We look, in Dover Wilson's *What Happens in Hamlet* and find in the Index under "Hamlet" the subheading, "his mystery." Harley Granville-Barker in the final pages of his Preface writes: "Here, for me, is the master-clue to Hamlet's 'mystery.' . . . He does not pluck out the heart of it himself. Neither are we meant to. For his trouble is rooted in the fact that it is a mystery."[4] Another critic says: Hamlet is "the greatest riddle of all—a mystery, he warns Rosencrantz and Guildenstern, from which he will not have the heart plucked out." And this is later generalized to "the haunting mystery of life itself that Hamlet's speeches point to,"[5] giving, as it were, the moral of the play. But you are all familiar with this, and with its premise: "In a play's world, each part implies the other parts, and each lives, each means, with the life and meaning of the rest," a descendant—to show my bias I will say a bastard descendant—of organic form. That is, the passage functions not in its local context but rather in a solution in which are suspended phrases, images, aspects of character, some actions, soliloquies, the interpretive tradition, the personal concerns of the critic, together with some principle or, perhaps, intuition of unity, all subsumed under what we call character in discussing fiction, as distinguished from experiencing it. But in its local context our passage is something else.

The King's response to the play has confirmed his guilt. "I'll take the ghost's word for a thousand pound! Didst perceive?" "Very well, my lord." "Upon the talk of the poisoning." I note in passing that in the renaissance tradition, in that rhetorical age, it is the word, "the talk of poisoning," and not the action in pantomime, that strikes the heart. It is Hamlet's speeches to his mother that strike her. To return: He then calls for music, "the recorders," and enter Rosencrantz and Guildenstern to report the King's "distemper" and to summon Hamlet to his mother's sitting room, as had been planned. He asks: "Have you any further trade with us?" *Trade,* a common figure for business. They have. They try to find out, as they had been instructed, what Hamlet is up to—in brief, *his* business. In reply he mingles, as in the ultimate sources of the play, "craft and candor."[6] For candor, he "lacks advancement"; he is only heir designate to the throne. He then takes them aside, borrowing one of the musician's recorders, and asks Guildenstern: "Will you play upon this pipe?" He replies he cannot; in effect, though not in these words, he doesn't know how: he doesn't have the trade, he is not competent in the mystery, the skill, the occupation of recorder playing. Yet, says Hamlet, you would play me, as indeed they were trying to, as one might play a recorder, to learn my occupation, my business, my mystery, to find out what essentially it is that I do. For there are two mysteries in Shakespeare's language, one from *mysterium,* whose provenance is theological, though also used more generally in our sense of the mysterious. The other is from ministerium and is a common word, as is *quality,* for craft, skill, trade, occupation. There is, for instance, the mystery of being a bawd, about which there is in the other sense no mystery. In brief, the

455

Hamlet of this passage corresponds to the Hamlet of Belleforest, who "pretending extreme madness" yet "spoke so aptly."[7] What he says is precisely responsive to the immediate situation, to the local context. In context, if you take the phrase as the commentators take it, he is saying to Guildenstern: "You are trying to find out why I have not already killed the King," or "You are trying to use me as a resource person to gather material for the definitive MLA paper on the mystery of my character."

There is a similar mildly figurative use of the synonym *quality* in Portia's "The quality of mercy is not strained" (*Mer. Ven.* 4. 1. 184), in which "quality" is rarely glossed by editors, though Dover Wilson gives "trait, human characteristic." That is, he glosses "quality" by "mercy." "Strained," however, is normally glossed, and usually as aphetic for "constrained," in direct answer to Shylock's "On what compulsion must I" be merciful? But an aphetic form of "*con*strained" seems odd, of "restrained" common, and I take "restrain" in the legal sense. Portia, recognizing that mercy cannot be compelled, turns the question upside down and says: There is no legal injunction, no restraint, against mercy being one's occupation, against "the quality of mercy." "It droppeth," and so on.

But to return to *mystery*. In *Henry VIII* "our travelled gallants" have returned from France fully Frenchified, and the Lord Chamberlain asks: "Is't possible the spells of France should juggle / Men unto such strange mysteries?" (1. 3. 1-2), into acting like foreigners, for *strange,* as you know, means "foreign," and *mysteries* are what they do.

Finally, in this sort, a passage in *Lear:* "And take upon's the mystery of things / As if we were God's spies." (5. 3. 16-17) Johnson's note is sufficiently close, though in the final clause *mystery* in the modern sense misleads him: 'As if we were angels

456

commissioned to survey and report the lives of men, and were subsequently endowed with the power of prying into the original motives of action and the mysteries of conduct." But now that *Lear* has displaced *Hamlet* as a source of literary religious texts, academic unitarianism, we find such notes as these: 'i.e. contemplate the wonder of existence as if with divine insight, seek eternal rather than temporal truths"; or, "profess to read the riddle of existence, as if endowed with divine omniscence."[8] We are back to the mystery at the heart of things.

What Lear says he and Cordelia will do in prison is presumptuous, as he indicates, but it is much less presumptuous than this. He says that in prison they will "tell old tales, and laugh / At gilded butterflies," that is, affected courtiers, "and hear poor rogues / Talk of court news; and we'll talk with them too, / Who loses and who wins, who's in, who's out"—then our passage, followed by "and we'll wear out, / In a walled prison, packs and sects of great ones / That ebb and flow by the moon." (5. 3. 12-19) The context is clearly court news, and great ones are the politically powerful, as in Bacon's *Of Great Place,* or Macbeth on Duncan: "So clear in his great office" (1. 7. not "so blameless," as glossed, but so distinguished a king, as in *viri clarissimi,* or perhaps *personae clarissimae.* Or Claudius on Hamlet: "Madness in great ones must not unwatched go" (3. 1. 196), or Hamlet himself: "Rightly to be great." (4. 4. 53) He is not talking—the Hamlet legend again—of "true nobility of soul," as Kittredge and others would have it, but of being the true prince. Lear and Cordelia, then, will take it upon themselves to relate court doings, to write John Chamberlain's letters to Dudley Carleton, as if they really knew, "As if we were God's spies."

In the preceding I may or may not have plucked the mystery out of some phrases, yet there still remains the question of why men act as they do, and, more narrowly, how Shakespeare perceived this, and, more narrowly still, how some of his characters perceived it. First, sometimes they do not know. "Why yet I live to say 'This thing's to do,'" says Hamlet, "I do not know." (4. 4. 44, 43) And Aufidius on Coriolanus gives three explanations—pride, defect of judgment, or a natural moral habit (what Hamlet calls "nature's livery"): "nature / Not to be other than one thing," "commanding peace / Even with the same austerity and garb [habit] / As he controlled the war;" concluding "but one of these— / As he has spices of them all—not all, / For I dare so far free him. . . ." (*Cor.* 4. 7. 36-47) He does not know which is the determining factor. Ignorance, I may add, is not mystery, or we would all be mysterious. Finally, Hamlet, in a passage that is not in the Folio, categorizes how men go wrong. He is not speaking of himself, but of men. It is a condensed monograph, which rhetoricians would have called thought, διάνοια, not character, ʼέθος:

> This heavy-headed revel east and west
> Makes us traduced and tax'd of other nations:
> They clepe us drunkards, and with swinish phrase
> Soil our addition: and indeed it takes
> From our achievements, though perform'd at height,
> The pith and marrow of our attribute.
> So, oft it chances in particular men,
> That for some vicious mole of nature in them,
> As in their birth—wherein they are not guilty,
> Since nature cannot choose his origin—
> By the o'ergrowth of some complexion,
> Oft breaking down the pales and forts of reason,
> Or by some habit that too much o'er-leavens

The form of plausive manners, that these men,
Carrying, I say, the stamp of one defect,
Being nature's livery, or fortune's star,—
Their virtues else, be they as pure as grace,
As infinite as man may undergo,
Shall in the general censure take corruption
From that particular fault: the dram of eale
Doth all the noble substance of a doubt
To his own scandal.

1. 4. 17-38

The Danes as a nation have soiled "their addition, "their title of honor, by drunkenness. So men, individually, may carry "the stamp of one defect, "impressing its form on the soul. This may be "some vicious mole of nature in them, / As in their birth"—he begins with an exception, "wherein they are not guilty." He is thinking not of inborn moral habit, that comes later, but of status, for instance bastardy, as with Don John or Edmund. Next, it may be a consequence of an imbalance of humors, or, again, of a dominant moral habit, in the Aristotelian sense: "some habit that too much o'er-leavens / The form of plausive manners." "Carrying, I say, the stamp of one defect," and then he throws in extra both natural habit, "nature's livery," and the external determinations of Fortune and "skyey influences," here identified: "fortune's star." To what end? The commentators say "The dram of evil" will "damn a man's whole reputation." I say, and I think Shakespeare said, will damn his immortal soul:

Their virtues else, be they as pure as grace,
As infinite as man may undergo,

459

The associations are theological, as also with "corruption" in the next line:

> Shall in the general censure take corruption
> From that particular fault.

On a national fault he spoke of reputation. On the particular faults of particular men he speaks of damnation: they shall in the General Censure, *iudicium generale,* the Last Judgment, take corruption. For the contrary case: Psalm 16:10: "For thou wilt not leave my soul in hell; neither wilt thou suffer thine Holy One to see corruption." To return: It takes just one mortal sin: "The dram of evil / Doth all the noble substance of ['em]," the immortal soul, "do out"—in our language "do in"—"To his [its] own scandal" (*Ham.*, 1. 4, 36-38),[9] to its moral ruination. For "scandal," though it had our current meaning at the time, had also a special meaning, technical and theological. It is by word or deed to be the occasion of moral or spiritual ruination to someone else. So St. Thomas.[10] And Hooker: "Men are scandalized when they are moved, led, and provoked unto sin."[11] But in this case the noble substance is done in, not to someone else's but to its own moral ruination. So in conclusion, for myself, and for you, I say out of context, "Angels and ministers of grace defend us," and God have mercy on our souls.

I add: The question of damnation is recurrent in *Hamlet* and, of course, implied in the moral problem of revenge, especially in a dynastic context. The principal references are Laertes: "To hell allegiance, vows to the blackest devil"—feudal allegiance and religious commitment—"I dare damnation." (4. 5. 131, 133) Hamlet resolves to kill the king when he is clearly engaged in an act of mortal sin "that his soul may be as damned and black / As

hell, whereto he goes." (3. 3. 94-95) And does: "Here, thou in-
cestuous, murd'rous, damned Dane"—the order of adjectives is
climactic—"Drink off this potion." (5. 2. 336-37)

SORTING OUT

The Case of Dickinson

I

I am a renegade Irish Catholic from the plains of Montana, upper lower class, a onetime scholar in Latin and in the English Renaissance. Consequently, I speak without authority on a nineteenth-century New England spinster, of the American governing class, schooled in the feelings and expectations of revivalistic Calvinism, and an admirer of Emily Brontë and Elizabeth Barrett Browning. That I have anything new to say seems unlikely at this date in Dickinson studies; even a new untruth—but we shall see. I shall at least be novel in what is not said.

My topic is sorting out. This is, of course, an element in all experience; we do it as we enter a room, we do it consciously at the laundromat. We do it as occasion and need require, and as motive directs. The particular occasion is this essay. The larger occasion is the publication in 1955 of an authoritative diplomatic text of the poems, and in 1958 of the letters, so that there has been, as it were, a starting over in Dickinson studies. It is a starting over that, despite much hard work and more publication, is still somewhat in confusion.

We have no authoritative normalized text. The more or less firm canon of better poems, established in the twenties and thirties, is no longer firm; poems of merit and poems that attract attention are mingled in the anthologies. The kinds of poems and the kinds of experience their abstractions allude to are incompletely and sometimes erroneously discriminated. There are, of course, reasons for this inherent in the situation. We have almost 1,800 items in the collected poems, all of them short, one after the other, with no apparent principle of order. It is easier to hold in mind and sort out the plays of Shakespeare or the novels of George Eliot, for they have scope and structure. So we come to motive. My motive is exasperation. I have become entangled with this woman, and I must get her in hand or get out.

But explicit sorting is a final stage. There is always an antecedent and implicit sorting given in the history of the text, of the commentary, and of our own involvement with them, and most unnoticeable of all, in the attitudes we bring to the task. In what cues our attention, our concerns precede us, and these may well have been handed us on the sly.

I should like, then, to deal briefly with two attitudes and one presupposition that affect the reconsideration of Dickinson; and, first, our attitude toward the striking. We tend to reject the striking phrase. The Gorgianic sobriquet for vultures, "living sepulchres," has been praised by some and rejected by most in the long history of sophistic rhetoric. We are uneasy with the striking, and tend to rephrase the matter harmlessly, to say in response to "The soul has bandaged moments," (512)[1] "Don't you mean we sometimes feel hurt?" But we can be cued to prefer the striking, and then not only the notable but every deviation from the ordinary or from propriety has inherent value. The off-rhymes, the wayward lineation, the colloquialisms, the bad grammar, indeed the pidgin English, that distressed the original editors and their public in the 1890s are now praised as triumphs over correctness.

But to return to matters of substance. Dickinson is sometimes striking in thought:

> It might be lonelier
> Without the loneliness. (405)

where the personification of a state of mind becomes a companion; more often in diction. And she achieves the effect commonly by a single device, by what rhetoricians call metonymy and I call the device of the proximate or neighboring word. "Bandaged," for instance, is in the neighborhood of "hurt." The device may be extended to the idea and the detail of a whole poem, especially if sufficiently short. In *A clock stopped, not the mantel's* (287) death is figured as a stopped clock, for to die is to quit time. And the detail is likewise neighboring: "Geneva's farthest skill / Can't put the puppet bowing," for the Swiss are famous for clockwork and "utmost" is "farthest." Then, "The figures . . . quivered out of decimals / Into degreeless noon," though duodecimals would be more correct; and "This pendulum of snow," this person cold in death.

The unusual has its virtues as has the usual. The proximate word may be striking, and so both memorable and satisfying to the occasional desire for novelty. It may also suggest a further and converging meaning. The stillness when she dies "Was like the stillness in the air / Between the heaves of storm," (465) "heaves" instead of "gusts," as with a horse or with the dying. It may, however, be only an alternative, an elegant variation: "Would not the jest / Have crawled too far!" (338) instead of the harmless "gone too far." Or, as we shall later see, it may suggest irrelevant frayed meanings. Finally, sometimes the apparently proximate word is not the proximate but proper; in "the distance / On the look of death," (258) "look" is more proper than "face."

In the poem, *A clock stopped,* the unusual is only novelty, the inferences from clock to person being immediately apparent, unless one judges that the analogy permits and protects the unexpected implication of the conclusion:

The Shopman importunes it,
While cool, concernless No
Nods from the gilded pointers,
Nods from the seconds slim;
Decades of arrogance between
The dial life and Him.

The Shopman can only be God, whose solicitation to immortal life the dead coolly, concernlessly rejects, superior through eternity. Nevertheless, contrast this relentless metonymy with the dry, unassaulting style of:

The last night that she lived,
It was a common night
Except the dying, this to us
Made Nature different. (1100)

I turn now to our attitude toward the finished. We think we approve of it, and sometimes we do, but in confrontation we often disapprove, for the finished has a precluding effect. It seems to shut us out. It invites only our admiration, not our participation; there is nothing to finish. So the mass and mess of the collected poems, with many items literally unfinished and most not subjected to finality, has advantaged her reputation, as has the diplomatic text, presenting as accurately as typography permits the authoritative copy with its eccentric lineation and its plentiful dashes, sometimes for punctuation, more often the squiggles of a nervous tic: poetry neither adorned nor nude and bare, but in disheveled undress, so that even the finished looks unfinished.

But what is the finished? It is, of course, the complete. The beginning will be a given, but the end must be an apparent end. Furthermore, no word, phrase, aspect shall challenge alteration;

the choices have been made and are not to be reopened. It is, however private its origin, public in expression, in idiom common. It must be correct, though not necessarily of a schoolmarm's correctness. There must be no sense of strain, but an accomplished easiness. The ingenious and the virtuoso, though locked tight in completeness, are not the finished. In brief, it must give an unanalyzed conviction of just-rightness, and it must be something somewhat better than good.

Hence formality is an indispensable element in the finished. Symmetrical pattern, exact meter and rhyme lay claim to it; they are by nature clinchers. It follows that if there is a taste for the unfinished, inexactness may become in itself a virtue, or it may suggest the value of the open as opposed to the closed, freedom instead of constraint, or finally the variations may be linked with other aspects and found significant. So it is thought to be with Dickinson, but it is not so. In one poem, *Because I could not stop for death* (712), she rhymes "me" and "immortality," "away" and "civility," "ring" and "sun," "chill" and "tulle," "ground" and "ground," "day" and "eternity." Yet in another, *There's a certain slant of light* (258), the rhymes are "afternoons" and "tunes," "scar" and "are," "despair" and "air," "breath" and "death." It is clear that in the economy of the poem there is no difference between the two sets. In her phonetic world identical, full, vowel with vowel, and terminal consonantal rhyme, including rhyming of cognate consonants, have the same status. There is no difference between them, and hence no significance in the difference; there is not even the piquancy of inexactness. Only in the larger economy of the English language and of poetic tradition are the variations noticeable.

The case is similar with some instances of inexact meter. She writes for the most part in the traditional measures of the hymn

467

book, and of much of the poetry in English, in common (8686) and short (6686) meters, and it is in these that the inexactitude occurs. The lines are regularly iambic—except, of course, that there are some poems in the trochaic analogue— but, especially in the first and third lines, the nonrhyming lines, a 6 or a 7 may replace the schematic 8, or a 7 or an 8 the schematic 6. In brief, under certain restrictions, trimeter and tetrameter, like full and off-rhyme, are prosodic equivalents whose phonetic difference has no aesthetic significance.

This is puzzling but, I think, explicable. One finds in her letters again and again passages in these meters incorporated in prose, and sometimes several bridged by prose links. She apparently went around the house with scraps of paper in her pocket on which she jotted metrical snatches to be later salvaged for poem or letter (or both), or to be thrown away. She had a habit of phrasing incomplete fragments of quatrains in common or short meter—it was a way of talking to herself—so that, unless she directed her attention to the matter, the choice of which form was accidental.

The situation can be further defined by contrast with her practice in other meters, particularly in tetrameter and what is called common particular meter on the one hand, and in iambic pentameter on the other. I find sixteen poems in iambic tetrameter, two in trochaic tetrameter catalectic. They are all unfailingly exact in meter except for one line, the last line in one poem: it is iambic trimeter. Again, in the 886886 stanza common particular meter, the situation is similar. Of thirty-four poems twenty-nine are exact, two begin with three eights, three conclude with a quatrain, but these exceptions are otherwise exact.

The contrast is clear, yet there is no difference in the kind and quality of poem between those in the four measures discussed or those in exact and in inexact meter. Common particular, for instance, is suited to the light as are the others, and to the plangent:

> These are the days when birds come back,
> A very few, a bird or two,
> To take a backward look.
>
> These are the days when skies resume
> The old, old sophistries of June,
> A blue and gold mistake.
>
> Oh; fraud that cannot cheat the bee,
> Almost thy plausibility
> Induces my belief,
>
> Till ranks of seed their witness bear,
> And softly through the altered air
> Hurries a timid leaf.
>
> Oh, sacrament of summer days,
> Oh, last communion in the haze,
> Permit a child to join,
>
> Thy sacred emblems to partake,
> Thy consecrated bread to take,
> And thine immortal wine! (130)

This is the central style and manner of women's poetry, a particular genre, from Emily Brontë through Christina Rosetti and Alice Meynell to Louise Bogan. Yet she writes it also in inexact meter:

As imperceptively as grief
The summer lapsed away,
Too imperceptible at last
To seem like perfidy (1540)

which begins in common and continues in short meter.

Iambic pentameter, however, is another matter. In this she is in effect, though not, I think, in explicit intention, experimental in our more recent sense. The experimental, though it borrows prestige from science, is not experiment, except that when genuine it is risk. To be experimental is to undertake the formally deviant, hoping to elicit a kind of thing not hitherto said. The experimental is exploratory in unforeseen contingency, and when it succeeds it is no longer experimental. One can be experimental, then, not only with respect to the tradition as a whole, but also with respect to the norm of one's own work, and it is in this sense that Dickinson is experimental in pentameter.

I find at most thirty poems containing that measure. In some she essays uncharacteristic styles; for instance, the poetic:

Unto guessed crests my moaning fancy leads me (295)

or:

And shade is all that devastates the stillness (1441)

or an idiomatic simplicity:

I cannot see my soul but know 'tis there (1262)

or:

I know some lonely houses off the road. (289)

In others she tries out the traditionally eloquent:

Next time to stay!
Next time, the things to see
By ear unheard,
unscrutinized by eye (160)

or:

'Tis compound vision, light enabling light,
The finite furnished with the infinite,
Convex and concave witness back toward time,
And forward toward the God of him. (906)

The last line is tetrameter, and in it the eloquent falls on its face. In brief, if she begins with pentameter she does not sustain it—there are two exceptions, both of four lines; in other poems pentameter comes and goes, a mixed meter in the general tradition of the English Pindaric. What's more, and this is curious, the nine-syllable iambic line—"Safe in their alabaster chambers"—which in most English poetry is an alternative tetrameter, seems rather to be for Dickinson, both in the line quoted and elsewhere, equivalent to the pentameter:

Safe in their alabaster chambers,
Untouched by morning and untouched by noon,
Sleep the meek members of the resurrection,
Rafter of satin and roof of stone. (216)

The middle lines are conventional pentameters—conventional is not a value judgment—in conventional high style, but in the fourth the meter breaks down, or is thrown away: it is a swinging four-beat line. In the three efforts she made at a second stanza she continues in the four-beat line, her all-out cadence:

> Light laughs the breeze in her castle above them,
> Babbles the bee in a stolid ear

In this case when pentameter broke down she had nowhere to go. Perhaps because the claimed enthusiasm of the cadence concealed a lack of belief.

In brief, there was a different and more varied poet, though not necessarily a better one, hidden in iambic pentameter that never quite got out.

II

But the ordering, interpretation, and evaluation of the poems has been from the first publication more openly dominated by presuppositions of biographical relevance: by the legend of Emily on the one hand, and by the responsible attempt on the other to locate the reference of the poems, and to order at least some of them by a reconstructed history of the poet's emotional life. This last, if it could be done, would give us a partial whole instead of splintered fragments and brief realizations. It would, in effect, arrange some poems in the form of a sequence.

But biography, as historical discipline, and literary interpretation have, though at times concurrent, ultimately divergent ends. History would destroy the text to attain the fact. Interpretation takes the poet at his word; it seeks only to realize the text, and to this end asks, What area of experience is here

referred to? What kind of poem is this? We have already in pass-
ing distinguished one kind, what Ruskin calls the poem of willful
fancy: *A clock stopped, not the mantel's.* Such "cheating of the fan-
cy" pleases, he says, because it "involves no real expectation that
it will be believed." Hence, such poems are not biographically
relevant, except insofar as one's poems are events in his life. And
so it is amusing that one of the best known of these, *I taste a liquor
never brewed* (214), has been until quite recently read as a self-por-
trait of Legendary Emily, that "Debauchee of dew," that "little
tippler / Leaning against the sun." But it seems more likely that
the speaker is not Emily at all, but a hummingbird; that the poem
is, as many similar nature poems are, a riddle; and we have long
missed the answer, not knowing *Guess Who?* was being asked.

Other poems, and a few of the best, are general: I call them
thoughts. They are definitions concerned with "The difference
between despair / And fear," (305) or gnomic conclusions on life
and pain:

> The heart asks blessing first;
> And then excuse from pain;
> And then those little anodynes
> That deaden suffering;
>
> And then to go to sleep;
> And then if it should be
> The will of its Inquisitor
> The privilege to die. (536)

To read these with particularity of reference, though indeed
they may apply to her life as perhaps to ours, is to misread, to
take an impersonal poem as a personal one. It is the difference

between "Women are bitches" and "My wife is a bitch." So, too, in *My life closed twice* (1732), to be concerned with the identity of the two the poet lost by death, to attempt to narrow the reference by biographical constructs, is to give a false particularity and to distort the text:

> My life closed twice before its close;
> It yet remains to see
> If immortality unveil
> A third event to me
>
> So huge, so hopeless to conceive,
> As these that twice befell:
> Parting is all we know of heaven,
> And all we need of hell.

The subject is immortality considered as parting; the literary form, a gnomic epigram concluded with the antithesis of Heaven and Hell, and structured internally by two to make ready and three to go, a structure given in childhood, not elicited from experience. If she had had only one such loss, or many, she still needed two for the poem.

But even this poem, of course, is not a mathematical theorem; it is not so general as to be of all time. The concern with personal immortality, and especially the open-endedness of the feeling, is of Dickinson's time and place, and peculiarly a Dickinson concern. It is relevant, then, to ask how the poem fits in to locate it in time and place, and in that biography in which the events are her poems.

III

We know of that biography that she lived in a Christian family, in a religious town, in a time of revivals. We know from her own statements that she was once converted, or almost, and that she immediately fell away. At fifteen she writes a friend: "I have had the same feelings myself Dear A. I was almost persuaded to be a Christian—and I can say I never enjoyed such perfect peace and happiness as the short time in which I felt I had found my savior. But . . . One by one my old habits returned to me and I cared less for religion than ever. . . . I feel I shall never be happy without I love Christ." (L: I, 27)[2] To such an experience a later poem alludes:

> If I'm lost now, that I was found
> Shall still my transport be,
> That once on me those jasper gates
> Blazed open suddenly. . .
>
> I'm banished now, you know it.
> How foreign that can be
> You'll know, sir, when the Savior's face
> Turns so away from you. (256)

She has lost salvation.

What, then, can we say of her attitude toward the orthodox religion of her youth and her time? The question has naturally been discussed in the commentary, but the form of the question has stipulated a kind of answer, however qualified, that misrepresents the evidence. The question implies an answer, but the evidence gives many answers. In fact, her attitudes cover the full range of possibilities, now this, now that, including, as We shall see, those current attractions, Taylorism and Perfectionism. Nor is there any clear sequence of development, no unfolding religious change, except that we may presume faith was given in childhood and only later became subject to diversity.

At one extreme there is a marching evangelical fervor, feeling in excess of belief:

> Given in marriage unto Thee,
> O Thou Celestial Host!
> Bride of the Father and the Son,
> Bride of the Holy Ghost! (817)

There is pious effusion, a little dialogue with Jesus:

> "Unto Me?" I do not know you;
> Where may be your house?
> "I am Jesus, late of Judea, Now of Paradise." (964)

But seldom simple belief and never the simple simple belief of a Herbert or a Jonson, as in Jonson's *To Heaven:*

> As Thou art all, so be Thou all to me,
> First, midst, and last, converted one, and three,
> My faith, my hope, my love, and in this state
> My judge, my witness, and my advocate.

And yet at times God is a living presence; she stays home, for God is her visitor. (674)

On the other hand, there are four lines of flippant doggerel on Faith versus Science, in favor of Science. (185) And there is irreverence; the mediation of the Son for the Father is compared to that of John Alden for Myles Standish. (357) And more than irreverence. She apologizes to the Heavenly Father "For Thine own duplicity." (1461) There are also complaints against God, perhaps in the spirit of Job:

> Of course I prayed, and did God care?
> He cared as much as on the air
> A bird had stamped her foot. (376)

Of this we may say it is still Christianity, though perhaps not commendably pious; but is it Christianity to assert, in the verses already cited, that life is a Spanish Inquisition, and the Inquisitor is God, of whom one asks only the privilege, or if you will the luxury, of dying, with the implication that death is final?

Hence, in other poems she professes substitute religions. In one, a religion of Nature, of the garden: "Some keep the Sabbath going to church; / I keep it . . . / With a bobolink for a chorister." (324) In another, the human consciousness is God; if they differ

> they do
> As syllable from sound (632)

as specification from ground. Indeed, the poet represents herself as acting as a predestinating god:

> The soul selects her own society,
> Then shuts the door;
> To her divine majority
> Present no more. (303)

For *majority* is "election," a neighboring word, and hers is divine.

So in "that religion / That doubts as fervently as it believes," (1144) disbelief and threatened belief recur. To lose one's faith is more than loss of an estate, for "estates can be / Replenished, faith cannot." (377) And yet we need it:

> Infinitude, hadst thou no face
> That I might look on Thee? (564)

Those who died in the past knew where they went:

> They went to God's Right Hand.
> That Hand is amputated now,
> And God cannot be found.

As a consequence we are trivialized:

> The abdication of belief
> Makes the behavior small.
> Better an ignis fatuus
> Than no illume at all. (1551)

And so at times she expresses not this or that note in the gamut of possibilities, but rather the dissonant chord of mixed feelings. She writes to her cousins toward the end of her life: "When we think of the lone effort to live, and its bleak reward, the mind turns to the myth 'for His mercy endureth forever,' with confiding revulsion." (*L*: III, 711)

Yet even this does not exhaust the range of possibilities. There is also Satanism: " . . . though in that last day, the Jesus Christ you love, remark he does not know me there is a darker spirit will not disown his child." An internalized Satanism of the divided self, as in the loaded gun poem. (754)

In brief, the poems that express her attitudes toward religion do not support one another, do not converge on an attitude. They must be sorted out. They must be taken one by one, and, indeed, sometimes the variants within a poem must be taken one by one. On the critical point of Immortality, for instance, there is a poem, extant in two copies, with alternate lines. In one, the attar of the rose, though roses decay, will make summer in the lady's dresser drawer when she lies "In ceaseless rosemary," immortality affirmed; in the other, "In spiceless sepulchre," immortality denied. (675)

IV

Is this simply whimsical whirlygig? Or spiritual crisis? It is, in fact, a prolongation of that adolescent crisis, already referred to, of incomplete conversion, in a context of emotional Christianity yet open to all the destructive anti-Christianity of nineteenth-century thought: "The Bible is an antique volume / Written by faded men / At the suggestion of Holy Spectres." (1545) It is a tale of Election, of Salvation and Perdition; of the rebirth of a Second Baptism; of Celestial Marriage to God, to someone, or simply in itself, by which one becomes a spiritual wife, "Sealed to eternity," and at the same time puts on maturity and puts away the child. It is a tale in which fantasies of dying are spiritual exercises, for death is the premise of immortality. It is also a tale of the failure to break through, to give up the world and self-will, to achieve election, with the subsequent conviction of being lost, of perdition, but it is not a perdition of hellfire. It is the perdition of death as final, or of the horror of stopless life. So one gives up hope, that last stage before conversion, gives up the enterprise and with it the fear. But it is not a tale, so far as the chronological evidence permits inference, of moving through successive positions to a final conclusion; rather, these are elements in a matrix of experience, reexperienced again and again in whole and in part, and concluded only by the poet's death.

Let us look into it:

> Soul, wilt thou toss again?
> By just such a hazard
> Hundreds have lost indeed,
> But tens have won an all. (139)

Election is at hazard, angels and devils witnessing, the odds ten to one against ever winning, favorable odds for a Calvinist. But notice: one may choose to play; one may provoke conversion; the attempt is a willed activity, and a repeatable one. It follows by emotional proximity that, if one can venture at will on conversion, one can succeed by willed assertion. One can succeed since the power of election has passed from God to man, or, perhaps, woman.

"Mine," she says, "by the right of the white election!" (528) What is mine? Clearly salvation, for white is the color of salvation, and, indeed, in one instance of perdition, "And that white sustenance, / Despair" (640), and hence of immortality: "Mine by the grave's repeal!" "Mine long as ages steal!" But there are two curious aspects to this poem, both contained in the line: "Mine here in vision and in veto!" It is salvation and immortality attained here, in this life, and hence Perfectionism:

> Eternity obtained in time,
> Reversed divinity! (800)

And it is election at the discretion of the elect, "in vision and in veto," and hence Taylorism; indeed, the phrase is a translation of

Taylor's maxim: "Certainty with the power to the contrary." In brief, God proposes, and man disposes.

But these poems are not doctrinal in reference; they refer to experiences, the decision to try again, the assertion of accomplishment. At this remove from Christianity they are experiences available to most of us only by imaginative empathy, and to that end the experience in prose, avowedly autobiographical with its claim to fact, may restore a legitimate vividness and a sense of actuality. We have such an account by John Humphrey Noyes, the founder of the Oneida Community, twenty years older than Dickinson but of the same region and social origins. He grew up in Brattleboro, in the Connecticut Valley, within fifty miles of Amherst. His father, as was Dickinson's, had been a Congressman. The religious setting for both was New England Congregationalism and revivalism. He writes— the date of the experience is 1834:

> The first results of the act of faith which I have described—[*it was:* If I pass through the form of dying, yet in fact I shall never die]—were delightful. I passed one night in unspeakable happiness. I felt I had burst through the shroud of death into the heavenly places. But I soon found that the spiritual transition which I had made had placed me in new relations to evil spirits as well as good, that I had entered a region where the powers of darkness were to be encountered face to face as I had never encountered them before.
>
> In the course of the following day a strange, murky spiritual atmosphere began to gather around me. . . . The multitude of involuntary thoughts which fermented in my mind finally settled into a

strong impression that I was about to part with flesh and blood either by ordinary death or by an instantaneous change. Nor was it merely an impression that seemed to summon me away. Ere long I began actually to feel a suffocating pressure on my lungs. This was not the effect of physical disease, for my organs of respiration were healthy before and afterward. Nor was it the effect of excitement, for I had no fear of death and was entirely calm in heart. I put my room in decent order, and lay down to die. The pressure increased till my breathing stopped, and my soul seemed to turn inward for its flight. At this crisis, when I had resigned myself wholly to the consciousness of dying, the pressure was instantly removed, and I arose with the joy of victory in my heart. To my imagination the transaction was as if I had been enclosed in a net, and dragged down to the very borders of Hades, and then in the last agony had burst the net and returned to life. This transaction was repeated several times.

After this I went through a protracted process of involuntary thought and feeling, which I can describe by no better name than a spiritual crucifixion. All the events of Christ's death were vividly realized in my feelings. I went through them not as a spectator, but as a victim. At length came the resurrection, and for a time I was released from suffering. . . .

After the spiritual crucifixion which has been described I received a baptism of that spirit which has since manifested itself extensively in the form of Millerism.[3]

And now Dickinson; it is an experience of the same ilk, though the outcome is opposite:

> Just lost when I was saved,
> Just felt the world go by,
> Just girt me for the onset with Eternity
> When breath blew back and on the other side
> I heard recede the disappointed tide! (160)

In the hazard of election, at the point of salvation she is lost. Is she sealed to Perdition? At the point of giving up the world, literally in some sort of spiritual suicide, breath returned—had she been holding it?—and the overwhelming tide missed its appointment. So far this is report of experience; she concludes with comment and anticipation. She has come back with intuitions of the novel and awful secrets of Revelation, and resolves next time to stay, to attain immortality. We have already seen that she claims to have done so. But the nature and structure of the experience are more fully detailed in another poem.

"Title divine is mine," she says (1072), and certainly the title she claims is divine, "Empress of Calvary." She is the bride of Christ, of suffering and Redemption. It is "Acute degree," that is, by the device of the proximate word, high rank. But she is "The wife without the sign," "Royal, all but the crown." Now *sign, seal, crown* are technical terms in the theology of Revelation. She is without "an appearance or occurrence indicative of the divine presence, and authenticating a message or messenger." And she lacks the crown of life: "Be thou faithful unto death, and I will give thee a crown of life." (Rev. 2:10) In brief, she is self-elected. She has, in fact, become married without the ordinary accompaniments of earthly marriage:

Betrothed without the swoon
God sends us women when you hold
Garnet to garnet, gold to gold.

She has been "Born, bridalled, shrouded in a day, /
Trivictory!" Reborn, as depicted in other poems, by a sec-
ond baptism: "except a man be born again, he cannot see the
kingdom of God." (John 3:3) She has been bridalled, and the
heavenly bridal suggests the earthly:

"My husband," women say,
Stroking the melody.
Is this the way?

Is this experience of mine, she asks, of the same kind as ordinary
marriage? Nor is the transition surprising, for as we all know, as
John Humphrey Noyes knew, "Religious love is very near neigh-
bor to sexual love. . . . The next thing a man wants, after he has
found the salvation of his soul, is to find his Eve and his Paradise,"
and to find them in terms of the theology of Revelation. So
"There came a day at summer's full" when "Each was to each
the sealed church," each was the saved and the source of salva-
tion to the other, bound by exchange of crucifixes, which I take
figuratively:

Sufficient troth that we shall rise,
Deposed at length the grave,
To that new marriage justified
Through Calvaries of love. (322)

The marriage is new; that is, the marriages of this world are can-
celled. The two are spiritual spouses, "sealed to eternity" not
through the mediation of the Son, but through each other's private

love and suffering—a strange doctrine of Justification! We do not know what other person was involved: the name, as elsewhere in Dickinson, may be N. What was involved, however, is clear.

Hence in another poem she asserts, "I'm wife." (199) There is here no theological reference, and indeed no other person: "I'm wife. Stop there!" This is spiritual marriage, that curious phenomenon of nineteenth-century revivalism, in a special form, and deprived of spouse. Noyes will again instruct us as to the nature of the experience. He writes to Abagail Merwin, an early disciple and early defector:

> Let it be distinctly understood at the outset, that I intend no interference with any earthly engagement. . . . At length in the midst of another series of sufferings at Prospect I saw you again clothed in white robes, and by the word of the Lord you were given to me. . . . I know now that my love for you is the gift of God, pure and free, above all jealousy and above all fear. I can say of you to my Father: "She was thine, and thou gavest her to me; all mine are thine, and thine are mine." Nothing can shake my assurance that in a coming time you will be my joy and crown—"a diadem of glory from the land of the Lord."

"Born, bridalled, shrouded in a day, / Tri-victory!" The experience, I think, is simultaneous, not successive—in another poem (473) she is "Baptized this day a bride"—and the crucial element is "shrouded." Attempted conversion involves, in Dickinson it is willfully provoked by, a fantasy of dying, what Noyes calls "the consciousness of dying." The poems that issue from this spiritual exercise are among her most impressive. In one she heard a fly buzz when she died:

and then it was
There interposed a fly
With blue, uncertain, stumbling buzz
Between the light and me,
And then the windows failed, and then
I could not see to see. (465)

In another she presides at her own funeral:

I felt a funeral in my brain,
And mourners to and fro
Kept treading, treading, till it seemed
That sense was breaking through.

And when they all were seated
A service, like a drum,
Kept beating, beating, till I thought
My mind was going numb.

And then I heard them lift a box
And creak across my soul
With those same boots of lead again,
Then Space began to toll

As all the Heavens were a bell
And Being but an ear,
And I and Silence some strange race
Wrecked, solitary here.

And then a plank in reason broke
And I dropped down and down,
And hit a world at every plunge,
And finished knowing then. (280)

Toward the close the experience expands into that of a double divided self; on the one hand, the total engrossment of being in the universe; on the other, personal identity and Silence, nonbeing, alienated and outcast. Lost. And to be lost is to lose all. So she passes out; it is a psychotic episode.

In other poems she gives up the enterprise, gives up hope, the preparatory stage, and with it the fear:

> When I hoped, I feared.
> Since I hoped I dared
> Everywhere alone
> As a church remain. (1181)

"As a church"? This is a peculiarly Dickinson idiom, as in "I wish I was a hay!" Thus, to remain a church, everywhere alone, is to be one of a Church Triumphant whose membership is one. Personal religion with a vengeance? Or the necessity of despair?

So she can finally view the consequences with acceptance, even with spiritual snobbery:

> The missing All prevented me
> From missing minor things.
> If nothing larger than a world's
> Departure from a hinge,
> Or sun's extinction, be observed,
> 'Twas not so large that I
> Could lift my forehead from my work
> For curiosity. (985)

Only loss of salvation justifies such hyperbole.

V

Some of the poems that have been cited are good, some indifferent, and some really bad, but all in the service of understanding and realization. Let us conclude, then, by bringing our inquiries to bear on a poem universally acknowledged to be of her best. We find, not the fallacy of willful fancy, but Ruskin's other pathetic fallacy, "shadows hold their breath." The odd-numbered lines vary from six to eight syllables with no significance in the variation. In kind, it is a report of a repetitive and involuntary experience, "None may teach it any"; it is not to be argued with; a nature experience yet theological in form, "heavenly hurt"; it is the intimation that one is sealed to Perdition: "'Tis the Seal, Despair!'":

> There's a certain slant of light,
> Winter afternoons,
> That oppresses like the heft
> Of cathedral tunes.
>
> Heavenly hurt it gives us;
> We can find no scar,
> But internal difference
> Where the meanings are.
>
> None may teach it any;
> 'Tis the Seal, Despair!
> An imperial affliction
> Sent us of the air.
>
> When it comes, the landscape listens,
> Shadows hold their breath;
> When it goes, 'tis like the distance
> On the look of death. (258)

LYRIC & LEGEND: DICKINSON

I

"I Had a Terror Since September"

I shall deal in these lectures with a woman who wrote lyric poetry, Emily Dickinson, and became legend, indeed in her lifetime. I will suggest that the poems may be read, and are better read, without the legend, that what should concern us is not the construct but the experiential referent of the poem, the experience delineated and delimited. To this some knowledge of time and place, and of tradition, is relevant, and I shall read them in the context in which they have come down to us: in this case, the biographical. But legend cannot be disregarded, for it is there. And in the case of the lyric poet it operates with a special simplicity.

The lyric poem—I quote current dictionaries—has "the character of a song-like outpouring of the poet's own thoughts and feelings," or, again, is "characterized by" or indulges "in a spontaneous, ardent expression of feeling." And the essential equipment for the lyric poet, especially in the nineteenth century, is a secret sorrow, a hopeless love, and a broken heart. Of this his poems are the spontaneous and ardent expressions. Howells, who when young was an aspiring poet, says of Bayard Taylor's poetry: It was graced for us by the pathetic romance of his early love. . . . We who were hoping to have our hearts broken, or already had them so. . . ."[1] A lady poet will also find useful a stern father, like Elizabeth Barrett's. A recent summary of Emily Dickinson's life, as others have done before, gives her the full equipment, both "stern father" and "hopeless love," and in those words.[2] But these and the secret sorrow are no discovery of scholarship; we have a note to her from her sister-in-law, who also

wrote poetry: "If you have suffered this past summer I am sorry
. . . *I* Emily bear a sorrow that I never uncover—If a nightingale
sings with her breast against a thorn, why not *we?*"[3] This is the
basic legend, the legend of Philomel, with the nastiness left out,
an archetypal form waiting for personification. It precedes the
person, and in literary interpretation it precedes the text.

But Dickinson herself gives a different account of the sources
of her poetry, though, no doubt, an incomplete one. In a famous
letter to Colonel Higginson she writes: "I had a terror—since
September—I could tell to none—and so I sing, as the Boy does
by the Burying Ground—because I am afraid."[4] This has gener-
ally been taken as referring, so powerful is legend, to a traumatic
experience of thwarted love in the previous September, for which
there is no evidence.[5] But she writes in one poem that when blos-
soms come back, "if blossoms do," and the robins begin:

> I always had a fear
> I did not tell, it was their last
> Experiment last year.[6] (#1080)

It is a terror rather of a New England winter—she is writing in
April—of absence and death. In the same year she writes her
cousins: "I noticed that Robert Browning had made another
poem, and was astonished"—Mrs. Browning had died the previ-
ous year—"till I remembered that I, myself, in my smaller way,
sang off charnel steps." And ten years earlier she writes her ab-
sent brother: "Your room looks lonely enough . . . whenever I
pass thro' I find I 'gin to whistle, as we read that little boys are
wont to do in the graveyard."[7]

Later in the "Terror in September" letter she says:

When a little Girl, I had a friend, who taught me Immortality—but venturing too near, himself—he never returned —Soon after, my Tutor, died—and for several years, my Lexicon—was my only companion—Then I found one more—but he was not contented I be his scholar—so he left the land.

First, a footnote on "my Lexicon." There has been much turning the pages of the 1846 Webster's, and her bibliography has a special listing, "Emily Dickinson's Dictionary." But she does not mean she spent her days and nights reading a dictionary. She means she occupied her time with reading and writing, making oblique reference to a sentence in the article that occasioned this correspondence:

> The statue is not more surely included in the block of marble than is all conceivable splendor of utterance in "Worcester's Unabridged."[8]

As to the three persons alluded to, they have been confidently, and sometimes variously, identified on insufficient evidence, though the one who "left the land" is plausibly her friend, Samuel Bowles, who had recently sailed for Europe. But what she is really telling Higginson—he wouldn't identify the particular persons anyway—is that she has been formed by the experience of death and absence, by cherished loss, and perhaps, we may conjecture, by retrospective importance. "To disappear enhances." (#1209)

In the next letter she amplifies:

My dying Tutor told me he would like to live till I
had been a poet, but Death was much of Mob as
I could master—then—And when far afterward—a
sudden light on Orchards, or a new fashion in the
mind troubled my attention—I felt a palsy, here—the
Verses just relieve—[9]

In time she somewhat mastered that mob, the fear of death—for
others as well as for herself—and now, when some intimation in
Nature recalls it, some "certain slant of light/Winter afternoons"
that "When it goes is like the distance/On the look of death"
(#258), putting it into verse relieves it, if only just barely. Or, as
she says in a poem, probably on the death of a friend in the Civil
War earlier in this same year, "Seems it don't shriek so under
rule." (#426)

Her editor notes that "In one way or another she has drawn
death into the texture of some five or six hundred poems."[10] I
have discussed elsewhere, though briefly, the association in some
poems of dying and religious conversion. In this lecture I shall
deal with another aspect of the death experience, and in more
detail with conversion.

There was in her society, as there was in the Irish work-
ing-class society of my boyhood, a special role that is, so far as
I know, no longer available, and that was the role of keeper of
the death watch. It was one of the roles of Sam Lawson, Mrs.
Stowe's dialect character in her classic of New England Life,
Oldtown Folks:

But the more particular delight of Sam's heart was in
funerals. He would walk miles on hearing the news
of a dangerous illness, and sit roosting on the fence

of the premises, delighted to gossip over the particulars, but ready to come down at any moment to do any of the odd turns which sickness in a family makes necessary; and when the last earthly scene was over, Sam was more than ready to render those final offices from which the more nervous and fastidious shrink, but in which he took almost a professional pride.[11]

But it is a role that perhaps was more often assumed by women, as it was in my society.

Hawthorne in the *American Notebooks* sets down an idea for a possible story:

> A change from a gay young girl to an old woman; the melancholy events, the effects of which have clustered around her character, and gradually imbued it with their influences till she becomes a lover of sick-chambers, taking pleasure in receiving dying breaths and in laying out the dead; also having her mind full of funeral reminiscences; and possessing more acquaintances beneath the burial turf than above it.[12]

The concern here is both in the role and in how one comes to it. And one might, if one had the fancy, as I do not, develop this story, beginning with an early teen-age experience of Dickinson's, an account of which has been accidentally preserved. It is contained in a letter to a schoolgirl friend, written at fifteen, two years after the event. The friend kept the letter, along with others which we shall allude to, and over forty-five years later made them available to Dickinson's editor. Otherwise we would know nothing about the event, but we could conjecture parallel ones. It is an account of the death of a young girl of fifteen:

> She was too lovely for earth and she was transplanted from earth to heaven. I visited her often in sickness and watched over her bed. But at length Reason fled and the physician forbid any but the nurse to go into her room. Then it seemed to me I should die too if I could not be permitted to watch over her or even to look at her face. At length the doctor said she must die and allowed me to look at her a moment through the open door. I took off my shoes and stole softly to the sick room.
>
> There she lay mild and beautiful as in health and her pale features lit up with an unearthly smile. I looked as long as friends would permit and when they told me I must look no longer I let them lead me away. I shed no tears for my heart was too full to weep . . . .

She then fell into a depression, was shipped off to an aunt's home in Boston, "stayed a month so that [her] health improved so that [her] spirits were better."[13]

But death was an open experience in that society, and not as at present "an unfashionable subject," as E.M. Forster calls it.[14] It was the subject of much of its literature, and people kept the death watch, not only in fiction, but in life. I quote the testimony of a Mrs. C—from the life of Dickinson's friend, Samuel Bowles:

> Once, as I was going home after watching all night by Mrs. Farrar's death-bed, I met him returning in the early morning from the office. . . . I told him the lesson I had gained by watching the peaceful close

of such a beautiful and unselfish life; and he took my hand, looked earnestly in my face, and said, "C—, will you come and stay with me at the last?" I said, "Do you mean it?" He said, "Certainly I do,"—and I promised.[15]

When he lay dying, another woman, a Mrs. B—, "whom he had once asked to be with him at the last," was sent for, and came. So Dickinson, in a mannered and unfinished poem:

> Promise this, when you be dying
> Some shall summon me . . . . (#148)

It will be hers to close the eyes in death, not with coins but kisses, and so on, though we may doubt whether, at the time this was written down, around 1862, she would have been able to come if asked.

In another poem she describes the experience with more coherence. It is one of those poems, written within a period of a few years before and after 1860, which employ forms of verbal repetition. In this case they enhance the sentiment without intruding sentimentality.

> I should not dare to leave my friend
> Because, because if he should die
> While I was gone, and I, too late,
> Should reach the heart that wanted me;
>
> If I should disappoint the eyes
> That hunted, hunted so to see,
> And could not bear to shut until
> They noticed me, they noticed me;

If I should stab the patient faith
So sure I'd come, so sure I'd come,
It listening, listening, went to sleep
Telling my tardy name,

My heart would wish it broke before,
Since breaking then, since breaking then,
Were useless as next morning's sun
Where midnight frosts had lain. (#205)

It is a quiet, unexceptional poem, except perhaps for "stab" in "stab the patient faith," and gets the experience. One is there as the dying's link to life.

It is within this context of the social act of dying that such a poem as this is to be read:

I've seen a dying eye
Run round and round a room
In search of something, as it seemed;
Then cloudier become;

And then obscure with fog;
And then be soldered down,
Without disclosing what it be
'Twere blessed to have seen. (#547)[16]

Another poem presents the value of the experience to the sitter:

As by the dead we love to sit,
Become so wondrous dear,

that is, death enhances.

As for the lost we grapple,
Though all the rest are here,

In broken mathematics
We estimate our prize,
Vast, in its fading ratio,
To our penurious eyes! (#88)

The ratio becomes vast, N to infinity. There is, I notice in an aside, a surprising amount of scientific reference in the poems, used casually, surprising until we remember that, though Amherst College in her earlier years was principally a preparatory school for Calvinist seminaries, under President Hitchcock, a scientist of international reputation, it became known largely for science.

But the poem that most fully realizes the experience of the death watch is "The last night that she lived." It is well known, and one of her best, though perhaps there are some slight flaws, as in the inversion of "shivered scarce." The poem says, it was an ordinary night "Except the dying," but this heightened acutely our perceptions. That "she must finish quite"—there is no hint at this point of infinity—while others lived provoked a zealous solicitude for her that itself almost partook of the infinite. There is then a fusion of the crowded death scene and the feelings of those present: "Too jostled were our souls to speak," the death, and then the problem of immortality and salvation:

And then an awful leisure was
Our faith to regulate.

It is the essence of the experience:

The last night that she lived,
It was a common night,
Except the dying; this to us
Made nature different.

We noticed smallest things,
Things overlooked before,
By this great light upon our minds
Italicized, as 'twere.

That others could exist
While she must finish quite,
A jealousy for her arose
So nearly infinite.

We waited while she passed;
It was a narrow time;
Too jostled were our souls to speak;
At length the notice came.

She mentioned, and forgot;
Then lightly as a reed
Bent to the water, shivered scarce,
Consented, and was dead.

Consented, and was dead. It was a good death.

And we, we placed the hair,
And drew the head erect;
And then an awful leisure was
Our faith to regulate. (#1100)

Except for the one we have referred to, and her mother's, we do not know how many death scenes she witnessed, but she must have witnessed many vicariously in the Victorian novel, and many vicariously in the lives of her community and her correspondents, and the experience was important to her. She says in one poem—I paraphrase; the poem is in one of her mannered styles—that to feel bereavement in the deaths of those we have never seen establishes a vital kinsmanship between our souls and theirs. From the premise that strangers do not mourn for strangers, she argues that these become by mourning for them immortal friends whom Death saw first, and this news paralyzes us. Though they were vital, that is, alive, only to our thought, in dying they bear away such presence it is as if our own souls suddenly absconded. (#645)

Consequently, the more detailed the news the better. "To know just how he suffered," she says in another poem, "would be dear"

> To know if any human eyes were near
> To whom he could intrust his wavering gaze
> Until it settled firm on Paradise.

Was he patient? Partly content? Was the experience what he thought it would be? Was it a pleasant day, with sunshine? What was his last thought—"his furthest mind" is her phrase of—home, God, or what the distant will say at the news? Then, "was he confident until /Ill fluttered out in everlasting well"? Afraid or tranquil? That is, in the technical language of the time, did he have "a hope?" (#622)

Though there is what seems to us a morbid concern with detail in this tradition, the central concern, especially in the earlier part of the century, was: Did his manner of dying give evidence of election? We have, for example, an abridged version, thirteen printed pages long, of a letter on the death of Professor Fiske, Mrs. Jackson's father (Dickinson, herself, late in life, alludes to president Humphrey's prayer on Professor Fiske's death). It was written to a distant relative, and no doubt intended to be circulated. I quote the account of the last words:

> Dr. Macgowan, wishing to ascertain whether he still retained a recollection of those precious truths which had so greatly comforted him during his illness, asked him if he still had peace of mind. He appeared to understand the question, and replied, *"Yes, I have peace."* "Are you able to lift up your thoughts to the Lord?" He said, distinctly, though slowly—*"Yes–I joy–in the Lord–of my salvation."* This . . . was uttered, a word at a time, and yet the thought was brought out very distinctly.[17]

It is in such a context, I think, that we must read a letter Dickinson wrote when she was about twenty. It is the first known of her appeals to the eminent outsider. She writes Edward Everett Hale at Worcester about the death some nine, ten months before of a friend, and former law-student of her father's. "I have often hoped to know," she says, "if his last hours were cheerful, and if he was willing to die." She then recounts her relationship with the man to establish her right to ask, and concludes: "He often talked of God, but I do not Know certainly if he was his Father in Heaven . . . I should love to know certainly, that he was today in Heaven." The letter is limited to this concern. Had she seen the death notice in one of the Worcester papers, she might have been reassured earlier. It reads: "he died peacefully, calmly, and hopefully . . ."[18]

If death was a preoccupation of the time all England and much of America kept a death watch over Little Nell—so, too, was conversion. The terms of that experience have little resonance now: Sovereignty, Total Depravity, Election, it is hard for most of us to realize, even when we know, how deep and pervasive these concerns were in that society, and yet at mid-century how threatened, crumbling almost instantly in some groups, like the one-hoss shay. Perhaps a brief speech by Mrs. Stowe's Sam Lawson in *Oldtown Folks* will give the context life.

> "Wal," said Sam . . . , "Parson Simpson's a smart man; but, I tell ye, it's kind o' discouragin'. Why, he said our state and condition by nature was just like this. We was clear down in a well fifty feet deep, and the sides all round nothing but ice; but we was under immediate obligations to get out, 'cause we was free voluntary agents. But nobody ever had got out, and nobody would, unless the Lord reached down and took 'em. And whether he would or not nobody could tell; it was all sovereignty. He said there wa'nt one in a hundred,—not one in a thousand,—not one in ten thousand,—that would be saved. Lord massy, says I to myself, if that's so they're any of 'em welcome to my chance. And so I kind o' ris up and come out . . ."

In a later passage in the novel the narrator, commenting on his and his companions' teenage experiences in this realm, says: "it may seem to some impossible . . . our minds should have striven with such subjects, but let it be remembered that these

501

problems are to every human individual a part of an unknown tragedy in which he has to play the role either of the conqueror or the victim." And Mrs. Stowe continues:

> A ritualistic church, which places all souls under the guardianship of a priesthood, of course shuts all these doors of discussion so far as the individual is concerned. "The Church" is a great ship, where you have only to buy your ticket and pay for it, and the rest is none of your concern. But the New England system, as taught at this time, put on every human being the necessity of crossing the shoreless ocean alone on his own raft; and many a New England child of ten or twelve years, or even younger, has trembled at the possibilities of final election or reprobation.[19]

It is this final concern that preoccupies the death watch.

Now it is interesting that the first four poems quoted in Higginson's article that introduced Dickinson's work to the public[20] deal with this subject. It is true he uses the first two, linking her name with the popular poets of the time, Celia Thaxter and Jean Ingelow, who wrote of the sea and lived by the sea, to show the imaginative power of "this secluded woman in her inland village," but he knows that at least the third and fourth deal with "the mightier storms and shipwrecks of the soul." The poems, except perhaps one, are not to our taste; they are of their time.

The first, "Glee! the great storm is over!" depicts, if not rafts on a shoreless ocean, men on a vessel at sea:

> Four have recovered the land;
> Forty gone down together
> Into the boiling sand.

In this context "the boiling sand" is rather vivid.

> Ring for the scant salvation! (#619)

The odds here are much better than Parson Simpson's, one to eleven, but still unfavorable.

The second, which has maintained its popularity, ends with a train, not a ship, but it is the same conceit as that of Mrs. Stowe's great ship, "where you have only to buy your ticket and pay for it":

> I never saw a moor,
> I never saw the sea;
> Yet know I how the heather looks,
> And what a billow be.
>
> I never spoke with God,
> Nor visited in heaven;
> Yet certain am I of the spot
> As if the checks were given. (#1052)

As if the conductor had taken up my ticket, punched out the seat check, destination Heaven, and put it in the slot at the top of my seat. The speaker is confident.

The third poem shows the soul at a game of chance, tossing for election or reprobation:

> By just such a hazard
> Hundreds have lost, indeed,
> But tens have won an all. (#139)

One to eleven. Curiously, this is not Calvinistic; the soul can venture at will, and again and again, with breathless angels—the universe is concerned—lingering "to record thee," and "Imps in eager caucus" raffling "for my soul."

In the fourth we have a more orthodox single game of chance. It is a little mixed up and not a good poem, but important for our argument. Let us segregate the elements. "As poor as I/Have ventured all upon a throw," and all is salvation. "Have gained" "the Victory." Have likewise hesitated to throw, hesitated "this side the victory." And if I gain, let the news come slow, "For heaven is a different thing/Conjectured and waked sudden in." Next:

> And if indeed I fail,
> At least to know the worst is sweet!
> Defeat means nothing but defeat,
> No drearier can befall. (#172)

Now, the terrestrial counterpart of the celestial finality of election is the conversion experience, in which, in the revivalistic religion which had become in that day almost the official religion of the country, there was "a climactic emotional experience, some special 'baptism of the Spirit,' some inward unmistakable sign that pardon was extended and a crown of glory laid up for him in heaven."[21]

We have a good deal of evidence for Dickinson's experience of failed conversion: for the early and middle teens, the letters to the schoolgirl friend to whom she described the death watch, but also for the year at Mt. Holyoke, and for her early twenties when conversion became a problem between her and her close friend and future sister-in-law, Susan Gilbert. In brief, in her early teens

504

she had felt she had had the experience but soon realized she had been deceived, and could not give up the world. It was what was called a soft conversion. A few years later she writes a friend about the revival of the past winter:

> I attended none of the meetings last winter. I felt that I was so easily excited that I might again be deceived and I dared not trust myself. Many conversed with me seriously and affectionately and I was almost inclined to yield to the claims of He who is greater than I. How ungrateful I am to live along day by day upon Christ's bounty and still be in a state of enmity to him and his cause.[22]

Note that in this tradition, though conversion is a private and spiritual experience, it is also public and social; the community strives to bring it about, and it must be demonstrable.

Soft conversion is the subject of this poem:

> If I'm lost now, that I was saved
> Shall still my transport be,
> That once on me those jasper gates

The wall of Heaven in *Revelations* (21:18) are of jasper, why not the gates?

> Blazed open suddenly.

Angels touched her "Almost as if they cared." But now she is banished:

How foreign that can be
You'll know, sir, when the Savior's face
Turns so away from you. (#256)

And failed conversion is the subject of this:

Except the Heaven had come so near,
So seemed to choose my door,
The distance would not haunt me so;
I had not hoped before.

But just to hear the grace depart

And she means Grace—

I never thought to see
Afflicts me with a double loss:
'Tis lost, and lost to me. (#472)

By twenty-three there had been a development. She writes to
Sue Gilbert:

Sue—you can go or stay. There is but one alterna-
tive. We differ often lately, and this must be the last
. . .

Sue—I have lived by this. It is the lingering emblem
of the Heaven I once dreamed, and though if this is
taken, I shall remain alone, and though in that last
day, the Jesus Christ you love, remark he does not
know me—there is a darker spirit, will not disown
his child.[23]

Satanism as an alternative.

About eight years later she recalls that earlier time in a poem sent to Sue. It is headed, "Dear Sue," and concludes with a note, "Dear Sue—you see I remember—Emily." It is not a good poem, though it is one of the ones she sent to Higginson in the early stages of their correspondence. But it is important in the history of commentary. The accepted view is that it commemorates the anniversary of the death of the law student whom she wrote to Hale about. It begins:

> Your riches taught me poverty,
> Myself a millionaire
> In little wealths, as girls can boast,
> Till, broad as Buenos Ayre
>
> You drifted your dominions,
> A different Peru. (#299)

The commentators have found here, and I think rightly, verbal echoes of a passage in Sir Thomas Browne's *Religio Medici:*

> I was not born unto riches, neither is it I think
> my Star to be wealthy . . . I have not Peru
> in my desires, but a competence, and ability
> to perform those good works to which he hath inclined
> my nature. He is rich who hath enough to be
> charitable.[24]

Now, the good works Browne speaks of are datable deeds, but this sense hardly fits the poem. However, an ordinary sense of good works, and a common one at this time, is the theological one, good works as distinguished from faith as a prerequisite, or sufficient, or insufficient for salvation. I take it, the speaker is rich in such good works as girls can boast of, but the riches of the conversion and presumed election of the addressee taught her the worthlessness of them. Good New England doctrine.

> And I esteemed all poverty
> For life's estate with you.

> Of mines I little know, myself,
> But just the names of gems,
> The colors of the commonest;
> And scarce of diadems

> So much that, did I meet the queen,
> Her glory I should know;
> But this must be a different wealth,
> To miss it beggars so.

I esteemed all else to be poverty compared with life's estate with you. In the passage quoted earlier she said, "Sue—I have lived by this," by our relationship. "It is the lingering emblem of the Heaven I once dreamed." I believe this is what she means here.

That the addressee is a woman is suggested, though not demonstrated, by "the queen." But the distinction between the wealth of this world and a different wealth can only be the distinction between natural and supernatural riches.

> I'm sure 'tis India all day
> To those who look on you,

I'm sure it is daily wealth to live in your presence.

> To have a smile for mine each day,
> How better than a gem.

The speaker will derive a kind of spiritual-emotional wealth from the association.

> At least, it solaces to know
> That there exists a gold,

a priceless spiritual condition,

> Although I prove it just in time
> Its distance to behold!

though it is denied me.

> Its far, far treasure to surmise,
> And estimate the pearl
> That slipped my simple fingers through
> While just a girl at school.

Since the gold and the gem are here of supernatural value, the pearl, perhaps of great price, that slipped through her fingers is plausibly the experience of conversion. And the final note, "See Sue—I remember" suggests she is referring, not to an amorous confidence, but to a shared experience.

The consequence of failed conversion is despair, which is both a state of feeling and, technically, the state of reprobation, as the initiator and consequence of success is hope, which is also technical, "to have a hope." The antecedent experience involves differing emotions, but primarily fear: "When I hoped, I feared."

(#1181) But despair is not just a negative state; it can be positive, as in Satan's speech in *Paradise Lost*:

> What reinforcement we may gain from hope;
> If not, what resolution from despair. (1.190-1)

Hence Dickinson speaks of:

> confident despair
> Advancing on celestial lists
> With faint terrestrial power. (#522)

Despair may be a stage in the process of conversion, as in this account cited by William James:

> All I felt was "I am undone," and God cannot help it, although he loves me . . . Still, my doom was sealed. I was lost to a certainty, and being naturally of a brave disposition I did not quail under it, but deep sorrow for the past, mixed with regret for what I had lost, took hold upon me, and my soul thrilled within me to think it was all over.

You will remember Dickinson's "At least to know the worst is sweet!" In another case it is the final stage:

> My life, for the success of which you send good wishes, will be what it is able to be. I ask nothing from it, I expect nothing from it. For long years now I exist, think, and act, and am worth what I am worth, only through the despair which is my sole strength and sole foundation.[25]

The context here is not specifically religious; it is the summary of a life, as is Dr. Holmes' description of Dudley Venner's state, the father of the rattlesnake girl, in *Elsie Venner,* published in 1861. He speaks of "the long struggle"

> between hope and fear, so long in conflict that despair itself would have been like an anodyne, and he would have slept upon some final catastrophe with the heavy sleep of a bankrupt after his failure is proclaimed.[26]

But failed conversion is the ultimate pattern of the experience.

In Dickinson's incantatory poem, "When I hoped, I feared," the earliest version of which was written down around 1862, the context is religious, though a strange religion. The speaker dares

> Everywhere alone
> As a church remain.

Now *The* Church is, properly, "the whole number of the Elect,"[27] but in this case, *"a* church," it has a membership of one:

> When I hoped I feared.
> Since I hoped I dared
> Everywhere alone
> As a church remain.
> Spectre cannot harm,
> Serpent cannot charm;
> He deposes doom
> Who hath suffered him. (#1181)

II

"He Never Saw Me in This Life"

In the previous lecture I dealt with three separate topics: with the legend, usually of thwarted love, with the death watch and the cherishing of the dead, and with election and the experience of conversion, or failed conversion. Each of these may be, and has been, regarded as traumatic, but they were also the ordinary, the normal, trauma both of romance and of society. Hence the poems that embody them express not merely a personal but also a communal experience. In this and the following lecture you will perceive how these several concerns come together, cross and merge in a lattice of lived and conceived experience; how, for instance, sexual love is religious conversion, and may be had for the dead. But before coming to this I should like, as a preliminary, to sanitize somewhat Dickinson biography.

She died at Amherst at the age of fifty-five in the house she was born in, and this in simple allegory frames her life. Though she was in constitution and temperament one of those rare spirits of mid-century Romance and should have died young, with an undisclosed and perhaps unacknowledged love, she in fact outlived by some years the average life-expectancy of her generation. The principal facts are: she was never married; she wrote poetry but did not publish; and she became a recluse, though she attracted more attention in seclusion than she would have in society. When she was born, Longfellow was twenty-four; when she died, Robinson was sixteen. Within five years of her death, in 1890, the first posthumous selection of her poems was published, and in her phrase "fame belonged to" her,[1] with an intermission in the first two or three decades of this century.

Around this "simple and stern" life,[2] as she herself once characterized it, much has gathered. To deal briefly with some minor matters, what we may call ancillary legends. She is commonly said to have written in the meters of the hymn book, and the Puritan association is usually noted, as also the brown sheepskin binding of her father's copy, with his name in gold on the cover.[3] That she wrote in those meters is true, and misleading. Much of English and American poetry, especially shorter poems, was written in iambic tetrameter and trimeter, occasionally trochaic, in rhymed quatrains and the Lady of Shallot stanza, with no suggestion of the hymn book, as is much of mine. She used dashes indiscriminately for punctuation, and much has been made of this, indeed a whole book. But she did not prepare her poems for publication; facsimile manuscripts of the period show dash and squiggle in common use; it is said of the first printed translations of de Toqueville in mid-century: "the use of the dash instead of the comma or semi-colon . . . was almost a hobby with both translators";[4] and anyone who has read blue-books knows this unsystematic form of punctuation. Again, it has been reiterated that she never saw the sea. Higginson, as we noted in the first lecture, started this, commenting on:

> I never saw a moor;
> I never saw the sea . . .

But the poem is not memoir; it is about potentiality of imagination to establish reality. She did not spend her whole life within thirty-six miles of Billings, Montana. She had "been upon the top of the State House in Boston,"[5] had visited Washington, returning by way of New York, had lived about fourteen months in Cambridgeport, and she writes in a poem on hope as a bird, which is dated earlier:

513

I've heard it in the chillest land,
       And on the strangest sea . . . . (#254)

Perhaps she never actually saw the open sea, but if one sentence is memoir, why not the other?

Finally, Johnson and his colleagues in preparing the standard edition of the poems found—the dating is based largely but not wholly on handwriting—that a very large number of poems were written down, and in most cases probably written, within a very few years. These are also the years to which the basic traumatic experience has been assigned, though in the earliest printed form it was dated some years earlier. So we get the rubric, The Poet at Work:

> By 1862 the creative drive must have been almost frightening; during that year she transcribed into packets [these are little gatherings of a few folded sheets] no fewer than three hundred and sixty-six poems . . . .[6]

Three hundred and sixty-six spontaneous orgasms. Certainly a poet of my scant production should not contract for such an output. Nevertheless, all the poems that are dated in the years 1859 through 1862, put together, come only to a little over 30,000 words, about 1-1/5 Hamlets, and only the first six of the sixty-four chapters of *David Copperfield*. It is true many of the poems Johnson assigns to these years express anguish and loss, with a claimed intensity of feeling, but is also true that many others are compliments, or sunsets, or describe a bird on the walk, praise old books, or tell what she sees from her bedroom window. For the presumed traumatic experience there is no contemporary external testimony—the letters addressed to Master I leave aside till the next lecture—and what little testimony there is points differently.

In this year, 1862, Samuel Bowles, a keen and level-headed observer, intimate with the families, in writing to the Austin Dickinsons speaks of "Emily's considerate attentions and full words." Later, "When next you write, tell Emily to give me one of her little gems"—obviously a poem—"How does she do this summer!" Exclamation mark, not question mark. Perhaps this can be glossed by a remark of hers late in life: "Drunkards of Summer are quite as frequent as Drunkards of Wine, and the Bee that comes Home sober is the Butt of the Clover." And the next spring, "to the Queen Recluse my especial sympathy—that she has 'overcome the world.'—Is it really true that they sing 'Old Hundred' and 'Aleluia' perpetually, in heaven—ask her . . . " Finally, about a month later, "I have been in a savage turbulent state for some time—indulging in a sort of disgust at everything and everybody—I guess a good deal as Emily feels,— . . . ."[7] This is a woman whose poetry and talk are recognized, a woman of considerate attentions, who can be joshed about her most special interest. A woman who has attained rank by seclusion, the motive being, perhaps, a disgust with the world, the secular counterpart of that overcoming the world which was an essential element in the conversion experience. And as for Bowles', and possibly Dickinson's, "savage, turbulent state," he was at the same time the busy and successful editor of one of the most influential newspapers in the country.

Now to major matters, and first that she never married and became a recluse. Neither was extraordinary. Mrs. Stowe's *Oldtown Folks*, as was the New England she knew, was crowded with spinsters. Of the ten who are snowbound in Whittier's poem four were unmarried women who, in fact, remained unmarried. And though her sister's "Kisses were very very sweet," as Joseph Lyman said, who was more or less engaged to her—ultimately less—of Emily he says (the quotations are from letters of late 1856 and 1858) she "is platonic—She never stood entranced in long embraces mixed with kisses sweeter, sweeter than anything on Earth." The quotation is from Tennyson's *Maud*. And elsewhere, that she would probably never marry, though she would make a most true and devoted wife.[8] So she became an old maid, with her quirks and quiddities and special invariable dress, as was conventional for the old maid of her time and place.

As for becoming a recluse, it was an accepted role in that society, as was that of the female poet, though both were noticeable. Of the twenty-four village types described and exhorted in Dr. Holland's *Letters to the Joneses* (New York, 1863), an early work of sociological analysis, one is Miss Felicia Hemans Jones, the aspiring poetess, and one is Mr. Diogenes Jones, the recluse. It was also, we should note, a possible role. The family was prominent and prosperous, and "the small circle so long occupying the old family mansion" was, as the Springfield obituary notes, "for a long generation overlooked by death, and one passing in and out there thought of old-fashioned times, when parents and children grew up and passed their maturity together, in lives of singular uneventfulness, unmarked by sad or joyous crises."[9] Need or disruption did not force her to teach school, to keep a boarding house, or work in the mills. And she was unfitted by temperament for "the traditional line of maiden sisters," the characterization is Samuel Bowles', "to take care of the children, while the woe is laid on, the mother is passing, and the joy ripened."[10] On the few occasions of this sort that we have record of her sister went. And she had no independent income. So the exotic travel or the social crusading of the fearsome British and American spinsters of the day was not open to her, even if she had had the appetite and the constitution.

But it was not wholly a recluse life; she was not cloistered, or homesteading in western Wyoming. She had a full and busy society to be withdrawn from. There was the small family circle, her brother's family and the Newman cousins next door, her sister-in-law's active social life, her father's often distinguished guests, the Commencement teas, the visits of the Cambridge cousins, and, what we have lost, giving resonance and texture to daily life, the hired help, with whom there would be no competition, but also with whom there could be human consolation. Toward the end of her life when she was told, "Mr. Lord is very sick"—Judge Lord is the only man we have evidence she was in love with—"I grasped at a passing chair . . . Meanwhile Tom—[this is Tom Kelley of the hired help]—had come, and I ran to his Blue Jacket and let my Heart break there—that was the warmest place. 'He will be better. Don't cry Miss Emily. I could not see you cry.'"[11]

Finally, she might have published and lived the public role of poet or author. Many did, and it has often been asked why she did not. There are two favorite answers, both of them of the traumatic sort. First, that the editorial changes in her few published poems appalled her. The only direct evidence for this is not. After "The Snake" was printed in the *Springfield Republican,* she wrote Higginson:

> Lest you meet my Snake and suppose I deceive it was robbed of me—defeated too of the third line by the punctuation . . . I had told you I did not print—I feared you might think me ostensible.[12]

That is, think me a fake. She is concerned with her reputation for veracity, and while at it corrects the punctuation. The truth is, it was not Dickinson but the later scholarly and poetic worlds that were appalled when, her reputation established, it was revealed how her earlier publications had been edited. And a word on that. Editors edit, especially in the nineteenth century, and especially if authors don't. George Washington, who is surely as sacred as Dickinson, refers to a small sum of money "as but a flea-bite at present." When published in mid-century it reads: "totally inadequate to our demands at this time."[13] Her work could not have been published in the Nineties without editing, though the actual editing could have been more judicious.

The other answer is, as a recent biographer puts it, that when she received Higginson's reply to her first letter, asking if her verse was alive, "the result was disastrous."[14] We do not have his letters of that time, but from hers we may infer that he raised some objections, and in his next letter gave praise, to which she responded:

> The "hand you stretch me in the Dark," I put mine
> in, and turn away— I have no Saxon now.[15]

that is, I am speechless, or perhaps, in context, I have no prose, for she continues with this poem:

> As if I asked a common Alms,
> And in my wondering hand
> A stranger pressed a Kingdom,
> And I, bewildered, stand.

As if I asked the Orient
Had it for me a morn,
And it should lift its purple dikes
And shatter me with dawn. (#323)

Higginson has had a hard time of it ever since he was instrumental in establishing her reputation, and those who bet the poetic sweepstakes after the result has been declared official feel that had this unknown sent them a few poems through the mail they would have instantly arranged with the Harvard Press for a variorum edition, and one that would preserve her quirks of grammar, lineation, and punctuation.

But all this is unnecessary. It is true that the mid-nineteenth century was the first time in Western history when women wrote and published on a large scale. (Only one woman, for example, is represented in the standard anthology of Renaissance poetry and that is because she was "Sidney's sister, Pembroke's mother.") And so publication was thinkable and possible. But it was as normal for women in that society not to publish as it was to publish. Emerson's first wife, Whittier's beloved sister, the first Mrs. Lowell, the first Mrs. Higginson, all wrote poetry and did not publish, though in several cases a memorial selection of their verse was published after their death, as Dickinson's sister-in-law thought of doing for her.

The attitude is expressed in *Miss Gilbert's Career,* a novel by Dr. Josiah Holland, Dickinson's special friend, published in 1860. In this, Miss Gilbert's father, a doctor, reads in the local newspaper:

We trust that we shall be deemed guilty of no in-
delicate breath of confidence, in giving publicity to
a statement that by some means has found its way
out of the private circle to which it was originally
communicated, to the effect that a young lady, *not a
hundred miles from the neighboring village of Crampton–*

(Where, by the way, the Gilberts lived)

the highly accomplished daughter of a distinguished
physician—is now busily engaged upon a work of
fiction. The fair authoress, we are assured, has not
exhausted the delicious term of "sweet-sixteen."

And so on. When the doctor questions his daughter about this
and she answers that she intends to publish, he says, "I did not
know but you would do it for your own improvement. It would
be a very fine diversion, you know, in case you take up German
and Hebrew, and the higher mathematics, this winter." In brief,
it is respectable to write the "Poetry of the Portfolio"[16] as a gen-
teel occupation like embroidery. When Miss Gilbert reads the
completed work to a somewhat older woman, who is presented
as a wholly admirable character, and speaks of publication, the
woman answers:

To me, the idea of making my name public prop-
erty—of permitting it to go abroad as an author,
subject to criticism, and to unjust and frivolous judg-
ments—the thought of being talked about in private
parlors and public places, and of coining my heart's
best emotions and my sweetest imaginations into
words which the world can use as a glass by which it
may read my life, is terrible.[17]

520

Dickinson's attitude toward publishing has the benediction of Dr. Holland, and the fears of Miss Gilbert's friend have been realized in her case.

She may have thought of publication but anything overt in that kind seems to have come from the outside. The two Valentines published anonymously when she was nineteen and twenty-two are introduced by editorial notes similar to the notice of Miss Gilbert's activities; the young lady poet or romancer was local news.[18] Again, at thirty-one her sister-in-law seems to have undertaken a campaign to get her published. There is the exchange of notes the year before on "Safe in their alabaster chambers," with her reservations: "Could I make you and Austin—proud—sometime—a great way off—'twould give me taller feet." "a great way off." And her sister-in-law's note when the poem appeared: *Has girl read Republican?* It takes as long to start our fleet as the Burnside." At this time General Burnside had been experiencing long delays in getting his campaign started in North Carolina. In brief, it is explicitly a campaign. Indeed, her writing Higginson and sending some poems a month and a half later may have been part of the campaign, for we have a letter of about this time from Bowles to Sue Dickinson: "What a fatality there is in your errands for me . . . Higginson has not been done in photograph—So all said . . . ."[19] But within a few months she comes to a final decision: "If fame belonged to me, I could not escape her—if she did not, the longest day would pass me on the Chase, and the Approbation of my Dog would forsake me then—My Barefoot Rank is better." In brief, she will not compete, and for the same reason that graduate students put off the dissertation—for fear of being found out. Fourteen years later she writes Higginson: "Mrs. Jackson . . . asked me to write for" the No Name Series. "I said I was incapable."[20] Non-publication and seclusion are parallel developments.

But, though unpublished, she already had, long before her death, fame of a sort; of a sort, in fact, that has ever since qualified the experiencing of her work. She must have been aware of it, and this awareness, I conjecture, prompted her remark in a letter to Higginson written in June, 1869: "My life has been too simple and stern to embarrass any." Higginson in the letter she is replying to does express a certain embarrassment, but not an embarrassment that the simplicity and sternness of a life would obviate. He wrote that sometimes he takes out her letters and verses, and, when he feels their strange power, it is not strange that he finds it hard to write, and that long months pass. If only he could meet her and know that she was real. As it is, he feels always timid lest what he writes should be badly aimed. It helps some to know an "actual uncle" of hers and a lady who once knew her.[21] The embarrassment is delicate and touching. But her reply is not responsive to this. It is responsive to a sort of legendary fame that must have been in oral tradition, where legend originates, in that part of the Connecticut Valley, and which gets into print in less than a decade. The evidence has been in the record for many years, but has not to my knowledge been construed.

To begin at the end, with the two obituary notices on record. One in a Northampton paper says, briefly, she died at her brother's home, which is not so; she died in the family mansion next door; that she had lived for many years a retired life; and then, at greater length, the item of interest:

> She was supposed by many of her friends to have been the author of the Saxe Holm stories . . . though she denied the fact during her life. Mrs. Helen Hunt Jackson, to whom the authorship of them has also

been assigned, said that she did not write them. The two were intimate friends in early life and it is possible that the stories were the joint work of each, so that each could with truth deny that she had written them.[22]

The fact is, Mrs. Jackson, and Mrs. Jackson alone, wrote the Saxe Holm stories, as also the anonymous *Mercy Philbrick's Choice* to which we will come shortly. But it is clear that many in the community thought that Dickinson was a published and successful author, an equal of the author of *Ramona*. This is fairly high rank in that literary situation. In the early 1920s I read *Ramona* two or three times, long before I ever heard of Dickinson.

The other notice, in the *Springfield Republican*, written by her sister-in-law, is more detailed, and gives the official family version, a version that is confirmed by other evidence. It is, though somewhat overwritten, the best brief biography I have seen. I quote: "Her talk and her writings were like no one's else, and although she never published a line, now and then some enthusiastic literary friend would turn love to larceny, and cause a few verses surreptitiously obtained to be printed." And then, again at length, was she a successful and published author?

> She withstood even the fascinations of Mrs. Helen Jackson, who earnestly sought her cooperation in a novel of the "No Name" series, although one little poem somehow strayed into the volume of verse which appeared in that series. Her pages would ill have fitted even so attractive a story as "Mercy Philbrick's Choice," unwilling though a large part of the literary public were to believe that she had no part in it.[23]

It is interesting that the conclusion is based on disparity in style, and not flatly asserted on family authority.

The Saxe Holm stories were published serially and in book form between 1871 and 1884, *Mercy Philbrick's Choice* in 1876. There was much speculation about the identity of the author—that was one reason for the common practice of anonymous and pseudonymous publication—but the general opinion was that both had been written by Helen Hunt Jackson, as in fact they were, though perhaps, some thought, with a collaborator. The most interesting of the speculations appeared in the *Springfield Republican,* July 25, 1878, on the publication in book form of the *Stories, Second Series.* It is a long article, headed: "Saxe Holm Evolved. Her Genius and Helen Hunt's. The Idea of Their Identity Dispelled. Suppose We Look for 'Saxe Holm' in Amherst?" It is a painstaking piece of detective work, and it is sad that the conclusions are not so.

> All these lead us to the conclusion that the author may be a person long shut out from the world and living in a world of her own . . . We may imagine her to be a member of one of those "sleepy and digni-fied" New England families whom she has so vividly described; of timid nature . . . devoted to literature and flowers. We cannot refrain, also, from picturing her robed in white, like Draxy Miller [a Saxe Holm character], whether it be a mourning for a friend, a religious notion . . . or, perchance, the result of some decree of fate. . . .[24]

There it is, full blown, in public print, eight years before her death. Two other Springfield papers in the following week identify her as Miss Emily Dickinson, and the *Republican* in an editorial issues a denial: "We happen to *know* that no person by the name of Dickinson is in any way responsible for the Saxe Holm stories."[25]

Three years later Mrs. Todd, the future editor of Dickinson, moved to Amherst with her husband, the new professor of astronomy. She writes home: "I must tell you about the *character* of Amherst. She is a sister of Mr. Dickinson and seems to be the climax of all the family oddity." Mrs. Todd notes in her journal: "His sister Emily is called in Amherst 'the myth' . . . One inevitably thinks of Miss Havisham." You remember young Pip's first visit to Miss Havisham's in *Great Expectations*: "She was dressed in rich materials . . . all of white."

> "Do you know what I touch here?" she said, laying her hands, one upon the other, on her left side. . . .
>
> "Your heart."
>
> "Broken!"
>
> She uttered the word with an eager look and with strong emphasis, and with a weird smile that had a kind of boast in it.

Mrs. Todd continues in the journal: "It is hinted that Dr. Holland loved her very much and she him, but that her father who was a stern old New England lawyer and politician saw nothing particularly promising or remarkable in the shy, half-educated boy, and would not listen to her marrying him."[26] The stern father and the broken heart. The story in one form or other has been read in the poems, and so we come again to Lyric and Life.

Dickinson in her fourth letter to Higginson says: "When I state myself as the Representative of the Verse—it does not mean me—but a supposed person."[27] The *I* is not personal. In the long history of Dickinson commentary few have believed her, particularly with respect to the poems touching on love and marriage. The remark has no limiting context in the letter, but among the not too many poems she had already sent there is one that perhaps calls for such a statement.

There came a day at summer's full
Entirely for me;
I thought that such were for the saints,
Where revelations be.

The sun, as common, went abroad,
The flowers, accustomed, blew,
As if no soul the solstice passed
That maketh all things new.

The time was scarce profaned by speech;
The symbol of a word
Was needless, as at sacrament
The wardrobe of our Lord.

Each was to each the sealed church,
Permitted to commune this time,
Lest we too awkward show
At supper of the Lamb.

The hours slid fast, as hours will,
Clutched tight by greedy hands;
So faces on two decks look back,
Bound to opposing lands.

And so, when all the time had leaked,
Without external sound,
Each bound the other's crucifix,
We gave no other bond.

Sufficient troth that we shall rise—
Deposed, at length, the grave—
To that new marriage, justified
Through Calvaries of Love! (#322)

The first gloss in print on this poem is the title "Renunciation," supplied probably by her sister-in-law who sent the poem to *Scribner's Magazine,* where it was first published in August, 1890. This locates the poem in the romantic tradition of thwarted love. The classic comment is George Whicher's:

> What do the poems tell us? They recur again and again to a momentous interview between two star-crossed lovers, a meeting pictured most completely and movingly, with a solemn procession of religious images, in "There came a day at summer's full."[28]

Let us look at the poem. It was an ordinary day, about the time of the summer solstice, except that in her cliché and ours it was *"her* day," the sort one thought reserved for the saints in heaven. The experience was regenerative: "As if no soul the solstice passed/ That maketh all things new," with its allusion to *Revelations,* 21, 4-5:

and there shall be no more death, neither sorrow nor crying, neither shall there be any more pain: for the former things are passed away.

And he that sat upon the throne said, Behold, I make all things new.

It was a wordless time, speech being as unnecessary as the Real Presence to the Eucharist. Each was "to each the Sealed church," "the whole number of the Elect," to the other, permitted, perhaps by God or Fate, to have this one earthly communion ("Permitted to commune this time"), lest they should be awkward with each other when they "are called unto the marriage supper of the Lamb." *Revelations,* 19.5.

We come, then to the cliche of "ships that pass in the night," which would seem to ratify that "this time" is this one time. Finally, "when all the time had leaked," as sands in an hourglass:

> Each bound the other's crucifix,
> We gave no other bond.
>
> Sufficient troth that we shall rise—
> Deposed, at length, the grave—
> To that new marriage, justified
> Through Calvaries of Love.

The holy suffering of love will validate the new marriage, the spiritual marriage, in heaven. Now in some forms of spiritual marriage, the new marriage entails a rejection of the earthly spouse, and so when Dickinson quotes the last stanza in a letter of consolation on the death of his wife to the Reverend Dwight, early

January, 1862, she modifies that line to "To that *new* fondness, justified" and italicizes "new." In brief, there is no renunciation here; rather it is anticipation, and anticipation with confidence.

A similar experience is explicit in another poem:

> 'Twas a long parting, but the time
> For interview had come
> Before the judgement-seat of God,
> The last and second time
>
> These fleshless lovers met,
> A heaven in a gaze,
> A heaven of heavens the privilege
> Of one another's eyes.
>
> No lifetime set on them,
> Apparelled as the new Unborn,
> except they had beheld,
> Born everlasting now.
>
> Was bridal e'er like this?
> A paradise the host,
> And cherubim and seraphim
> The most familiar guest. (#625)

They had met once long ago, and now meet again in Heaven, "The last and second time"; indeed the privilege of seeing each other is itself Heaven. They bring with them none of their life experiences, except the experience of having met. There ensues a spiritual marriage, with angels as guests.

Let us come now to another poem that depicts a lover's call, and keep in the back of our minds the two lines, "The last and second time/ These fleshless lovers met." It begins, "Again his voice is at the door"; (#663) it is a recurring visit. She says she feels again the sense of rank and importance, as she hears him ask "For such a one as me," for one who might have been thought unimportant. What follows curiously anticipates, for the poem is dated about 1862, the detail of Higginson's first visit in 1870. He relates:

> After a little delay, I heard an extremely faint and pattering footstep like that of a child, in the hall, and in glided, almost noiselessly, a plain, shy little person, the face without a single good feature . . . She came toward me with two day-lillies, which she put in a childlike way into my hand, saying softly, under her breath, "These are my introduction."[29]

In the earlier poem she writes, "I take a flower as I go/ My face to justify," that is, to redeem. "I cross the hall with mingled steps"— an extraordinary phrase—"I silent pass the door"

> And look on all this world *contains,*
> *Just his face*

The last four words are underlined in the manuscript. They talk "in careless and in toss," each shyly sounding the depths of the other's feelings. They then take a walk, leaving the dog behind. A romantic moon follows them a little way, and finally they are alone, "Alone—if *Angels* are alone / *First time* they *try* the sky!" She is metaphorically in Heaven, and possibly with some sense of literalness.

She concludes she would give the purple in her vein to live that hour again, but the man must himself count it, drop by drop. So far we have the intense experience of romantic love, concluded with appropriate hyperbole. But there is a shocker in the poem, which I left out so that it could shock you. She says she takes a flower to justify her face, and why? Because

> He never saw me in this life,
> I might surprise his eye.

"He never saw me in this life," yet his voice has been more than once "at the door," and is recognized. By implication he has seen her in the other life, where, presumably, her plainness was not apparent, where perhaps they were "fleshless lovers." The poem depicts, then, a recurrent fantasy of visitation by a spectral lover. But a special form of fantasy.

It is not daydreaming with its shifting and transforming images and situations, as in *Kubla Khan.* Nor is it the steady, progressive imagination by which at several times I have built over bourbon and beer at bedtime an imaginary house in a real place, once in Wyoming, once on the California coast, taking up on Tuesday precisely where the builder left off on Monday, the novelist's imagination. Rather, in this case, though the form of the experience is inveterate, "Again his voice is at the door," each particular one is isolated and begins anew, "He never saw me in this life," and the particular details may vary.

In the next lecture I shall deal more fully with marriage and spiritual marriage. Today, I shall conclude with a comment by one of the spinsters in *Oldtown Folks,* like Dickinson one of the Brahmin class of New England and eccentric in dress: "You never know what you may find in the odd corners of an old maid's heart, when you fairly look into them."[30]

III

The Vision Pondered Long

We concluded last time with some strange goings-on, but no
stranger than much in that society. For those were the days
of Millerism and the Second Advent, of the Finney reviv-
als and Mormonism, of spiritualism, mesmerism, phrenology,
Swedenborgianism, Free Love and spiritual wifery. But let us
deal now, in contrast, with the ordinary world and earthly mar-
riage before returning to the extraordinary. Of the poems on
marriage one begins:

> She rose to his requirements, dropped
> The playthings of her life

She put away girlhood—

> To take the honorable work
> Of woman, and a wife.

If as time went on she missed the fulfillment of the first anticipa-
tions, if the romance, "the gold, in using" wore away, it remained
unmentioned, as there is in the sea both pearl and weed, but
where is known only to the sea. (#732) An observation applica-
ble to many marriages of the time, and perhaps to some of ours.

But a poem that begins, "I gave myself to him," or, an al-
ternative line in the manuscript, "I gave him all myself" (#580)
presents problems for the searcher for real life. We know she nev-
er married, and one commentator in desperation finds that the
he is God.[1] There is, of course, another poem in which she is the
bride of God. But here it is a problem of pronouns. If the text

read *She gave herself*, instead of I gave, the poem would be of the same order as the preceding one. And, in fact, Dickinson sometimes juggles pronouns.

A poem signed "Emily" and sent to Sue begins "I showed her heights she never saw," but the copy among her own manuscripts reads, "He showed me heights." (#446) One could, without justification, construct a story: he showed me, then I showed her, but there is a different explanation. She writes in another poem, "Going to him! Happy letter!" "Tell him the page I didn't write. / Tell him I only said the syntax / And left the verb and the pronoun out." "Tell him . . . you wished you had eyes in your pages / So you could see what moved them so." "Tell him— no, you may quibble there / For it would split his heart to know it." "And night finished before we finished." The other version reads, "Going to her! happy letter" and "day finished before we finished." (#494) Each version expresses a precious emotional attachment, this is the syntax, the structure of the experience, but the particular referent may vary, the verb and the pronoun, and indeed also the noun, "day" and "night." Each copy is signed "Emily," and each, we are told, has been folded as if enclosed in an envelope, but the poem itself concludes, "But if he ask," with the variant "she," "where you are hid / Until tomorrow . . . / Gesture, coquette, and shake your head!" In the poem the letter is not delivered. The poem itself acts out a potentiality of expression.

So one may enact in a poem, not a particular marriage with its names, date, and place, but marriage itself with its potential disappointments, as if particular:

> I gave myself to him,
> And took himself for pay.
> The solemn contract of a life
> Was ratified this way.

The wealth might disappoint;
Myself a poorer prove
Than this great purchaser suspect;
The daily own of love

Depreciate the vision;
But, till the merchant buy,
Still fable in the isles of spice
The subtle cargoes lie.

At least, 'tis mutual risk;
Some found it mutual gain;
Sweet debt of life, each night to owe,
Insolvent every noon. (#580)

It is a poem of earthly marriage—"The solemn contract of a life . . . ratified," "the daily own of love"—not of symbolic or spiritual marriage, and hence not autobiographical. The bride speaks. She anticipates she may disappoint the groom, but no one knows the outcome ahead of time, and at least the risk is mutual. Perhaps the gain will be mutual, too: to discharge night by night the debt of life in complete giving.

Finally, in this kind, there is a poem in which the prospective bride speaks, again in the first person, "My worthiness is all my doubt, / His merit all my fear," an attitude more common in that day, but possible in ours. The poem concludes with a semi-identification of election and human love, and the groom is a sort of god:

So I, the undivine abode
Of his elect content

and consecrates the secular by a religious analogy, *as if:*

Conform my soul, as 'twere a church,
Unto her sacrament. (#751)

That the view of marriage in these poems conforms to some of the realities of marriage in her society is suggested by de Tocqueville's analysis of American marriage a generation earlier. He notes that in America there was "strictly speaking, no adolescence." Hence maturity and marriage coincide. That "long before an American girl arrives at the marriageable age . . . she already thinks for herself, speaks with freedom, and acts on her own impulse." "Yet in America the independence of woman is irrecoverably lost in the bonds of matrimony . . . It may be said she has learned by the use of her independence to surrender it without a struggle . . . She has been taught beforehand what is expected of her and voluntarily and freely enters upon this engagement. She supports her new condition with courage because she chose it."[2] The Dickinson poems, except in part for the last, are, so to speak, dramatized metrical translations of De Tocqueville. Hence they are, in the older sense, ideal, not as opposed to real, but ideal as expressing the normative form of experience. She speaks, not for herself, but for the community. The last poem, however, concludes by associating marriage and the experience of election, and this will lead us back to the extraordinary, in fact, ultimately to erotic Calvinism.

We come now to "Ourselves were wed one summer, dear," which Mr. Johnson has misinterpreted in the light of her biography. He says:

In 1862 she wrote a very enigmatic poem. One cannot say surely that the person therein designated is in fact Sue, yet the nature of their relationship at the time strongly suggests the probability, the more so because their relationship is the sole one that gives the poem meaning.

> Ourselves were wed one summer, dear;
> Your vision was in June,
> And when your little lifetime failed,
> I wearied, too, of mine,
>
> And overtaken in the dark
> Where you had put me down
> By someone carrying a light,
> I, too, received the sign.
>
> 'Tis true, our futures different lay;
> Your cottage faced the sun,
> While oceans and the North must be
> On every side of mine.
>
> 'Tis true, your garden led the bloom,
> For mine in frosts was sown,
> And yet one summer we were Queens,
> But you were crowned in June. (#631)

You and I were once in close accord, she is saying. I always thought that the way you saw things was the best possible way to see them, and when anything troubled you, I was so close to you that I felt it too. Deserted by you, someone else has brought me the light which has given me the right to happiness which you had claimed. I realize our lives had to be lived differently. Certainty and warmth lay ahead for you; uncertainty and isolation are my lot. Although these differences must be acknowledged, we did once share the same feeling . . . But your fate was always to be in the sun.[3]

I read a different poem. We two were married one summer; your marriage, or vision, was in June. But when you died young, "When your little lifetime failed"—if she is writing English I can't see how the line can mean anything else, and Sue outlived her by many years—I wearied, too, of my own life. And when in that emotional darkness there came one with spiritual illumination, "I, too, received the sign." That is, "an appearance or occurrence indicative of the divine presence, and authenticating a message or messenger."[4] Our futures, however, were opposite: yours in the sun of salvation, mine bleak and Northern. The garden of your emotional or spiritual life blossomed first, "For mine in frosts was sown." Yet one summer we were both Queens, though I was, by implication, Queen of Despair.

I turn now to some of the notions and forms of experience associated with marriage in Dickinson's time. There was, for one, a widespread belief at that time—it is still around though in lessened form—in the predestined person, the belief, to quote Mrs. Stowe,

that somewhere in this world, unknown to him, and as yet unknowing him, lives the woman that is to be his earthly fate,—to affect for good or evil, his destiny

. . . Such is the ideal image of *somebody,* who must ex-
ist *somewhere,* and is to be found *sometime,* and when
found is to be ours.

In a later passage, this predestined woman, though still not yet
disclosed, was, the narrator says, "in large part the unperceived
spring and motive of all I did."[5]

This is Dickinson's version:

Somewhere upon the general earth
Itself exist today
The magic, passive but extant,
That consecrated me.

Indifferent seasons doubtless play
Where I, for right to be,
Would pawn each atom that I am
But immortality,

Reserving that but just to prove
Another date of thee.
Oh, God of width, do not for us
Curtail eternity! (#1231)

These are the elements in the poem.

1. Somewhere, in some unspecified place—general in this sense
seems to have been a New Englandism. Dickens was struck by
the word when he was introduced by his host at a reception
in Worcester to his "general friends."[6] And Mrs. Stowe's Sam
Lawson, when a group starts out to hunt the missing children,
calls a halt for planning, saying "It's no use tearin' round gen'lly."[7]

2. Of indeterminate sex, "Itself," and this seems unusual. In another poem the figure is male:

> I know that he exists
> Somewhere in silence. (#338)

3. The figure possesses a consecrating magic. Consecration in this tradition is not willed, not a decision, and not just a notion; it is an experience, something that happens, and, it may be, under apparently accidental circumstances. The hero of Dr. Holland's verse-novel, *Kathrina,* in his mid-teens accompanies his mother on a visit, remains outside, unties a pet lamb that gets away from him and bounds up the mountain to the very top, the boy following. He finally secures the lamb, and looks down on the Connecticut Valley, "palpitant/ With a divine elixir."

> And there alone, upon the mountain top,
> Kneeling beside the lamb, I bowed my head
> Beneath the chrismal light, and felt my soul
> Baptized and set apart to poetry.[8]

In the Dickinson poem it is consecration to love, to an engrossed concern for the other.

4. The figure, though actually existing—"passive but extant"—does not actively perform the consecration. Yet in other poems he does:

> He put the belt around my life;
> I heard the buckle snap . . .
> Henceforth, a dedicated sort,
> A member of the cloud. (#273)

Dedicated, indeed, if we remember *Rev.* 10.1, "And I saw another mighty angel come down from heaven, clothed with a cloud," and 11.12, "And I heard a great voice from heaven saying unto them, Come up hither. And they ascended up to heaven in a cloud; and their enemies beheld them." Another text, 14.1, "And I looked, and, lo, a Lamb stood on the Mount Sion, and with him an hundred forty and four thousand, having his Father's name written in their foreheads," will furnish the context for another poem of active consecration:

> He found my being, set it up,
> Adjusted it to place,
> Then carved his name upon it. . . . (#603)

He then bade my being be faithful to the East in his absence, that is, to dawn and resurrection, and he would come again, "That time to take it home," whether man or God, or indistinguishably either.

5. Finally, giving all, reserving only immortality "to prove/ Another date of thee," as the "that time" in the poem just referred to, and "permitted to commune *this* time" in "There came a day," discussed in the previous lecture, suggests the theme of second meeting in heaven, and perhaps of spiritual marriage, for as Noyes points out, the popular Swedenborgianism of the time involved "the sentimentalism of predestined mating."[9]

But what if the predestined person does not come, what if one never "meets his fate"? Hawthorne has in *The American Notebooks* an idea for "A story, the hero of which is to be represented as naturally capable of strong and deep passion, and looking forward to the time when he shall feel passionate love, which is to be the great event of his existence. But it so chances that he never falls in love. . . ."[10]

She deals with this in one of the better-known poems, "I know that he exists / Somewhere in silence." He's just teasing me by not showing up:

> But should the glee glaze
> In death's stiff stare
> Would not the fun
> Look too expensive? (#338)

In another poem she depicts the experience of waiting for epiphany:

> If you were coming in the fall
> I'd brush the summer by . . .
> As housewives do a fly.

If in a year, if "only centuries delayed,"

> If certain when this life was out
> That yours and mine should be
I could handle it. But this complete uncertainty "of the length / Of this that is between,"

> Goads me like the goblin bee
> That will not state its sting. (#511)

If these poems are autobiographical, and if the dates assigned by the editor are approximately correct, she was still waiting to meet her fate years after the day the commentators have had her meet it.

Now, in the tradition of revivalism, with some infusions of Swedenborgianism, sexual and social experience is often expressed in terms of, and sometimes identified with, religious terminology and experience. Mrs. Stowe writes: "In such an hour Esther saw that she was beloved!—beloved by a poet soul,—one of that rare order to whom the love of woman is a religion! —a baptism!—a consecration!"[11] And this perception is coincident with her religious conversion. In such a context marriage in heaven would simply be the examplar of marriage, though in actual practice there were some odd goings on.

For instance, the old woman in Sarah Orne Jewett's *The Courting of Sister Wisby* relates the story of Deacon Brimblecom. He was, she says,

> Very pious accordin' to his lights in his early years. He lived way back in the country then, and there come a rovin' preacher along, and set everybody up that way by the ears. I've heard the old folks talk it over, but I forget most of his doctrine, except some of his followers was persuaded they could dwell among the angels while yet on airth, and this Deacon . . . felt sure he was called by the voice of a spirit bride. So he left a good, deservin' wife he had, an' four children, and built him another house over to the other side of the land he'd had from his father. They didn't take much pains with the buildin' because they expected to be translated before long, and then the spirit brides and them folks was goin' to appear and divide up the airth amongst 'em, and the world's folks and onbelievers was goin' to serve 'em or be sent to torments . . . Some on 'em went crazy, but the deacon

held on to what wits he had, an' by an' by the spirit bride didn't turn out to be much of a housekeeper an' he had always been used to good livin' so he sneaked home again . . . and then his poor wife died, and he had a spirit bride in good earnest.[12]

"They expected to be translated before long." Dickinson in a letter in her teens, describing a wedding she attended, says, "It seemed to me translation, not any earthly thing." And Mrs. Stowe remarks, "In the creed of most storytellers marriage is equal to translation." That is, a removal to heaven without a natural death, as in the case of Elijah: "And it came to pass as they still went on and talked, that, behold, a chariot of fire and horses of fire, and parted them both asunder; and Elijah went up by a whirlwind into heaven."[13] Well, it actually happened to Dickinson, or, perhaps, to a "supposed person."

> It was a quiet way.
> He asked if I was his.
> I made no answer of the tongue,
> But answer of the eyes.

This is that "telegraphy of the eyes" of the sentimental novel. And now what?

> And then he bore me on
> Before this mortal noise

(I confess I do not know what the "mortal noise" is.)

> With swiftness, as of chariots,
> And distance, as of wheels.

This world did drop away,
As acres from the feet
Of one that leaneth from balloon
Upon an ether street. (#1053)

Let us stop at this point and quote from the *Springfield Republican* of October 6, 1860:

> Precisely at 3 p.m., when the sky was clear and the face of nature warm and beautiful, the balloon of Mr. Spencer of Winstead, Ct., which had been inflated in front of the Mansion House, was cut loose from its moorings, and in the presence of thousands of spectators rose rapidly . . . In less than ten minutes from leaving the earth, the balloon was invisible to the sea of upturned faces that gazed heavenward. It almost seemed like the translation of the prophet Elijah.[14]

And then the article quotes the two stanzas of the Dickinson poem, beginning "And then he bore me on." The poem itself continues:

> The gulf behind was not,
> The continents were new,
> Eternity it was before
> Eternity was due.
>
> No seasons were to us,
> It was not night nor morn,
> But sunrise stopped upon the place
> And fastened it in dawn.

It is not an extraordinary poem, but it is an extraordinary experience.

Part of the experience is repeated in another poem:

> Our journey had advanced,
> Our feet were almost come
> To that odd fork in being's road,
> Eternity by term.

I doubt that the alternative at the fork is nothingness, though it could be; it is more likely a choice between remaining in time or turning to eternity.

> Our pace took sudden awe,
> Our feet reluctant led,
> Before were cities, but, between,
> The forest of the dead.

> Retreat was out of hope.
> Behind, a sealed route,
> Eternity's white flag before,
> And God at every gate. (#615)

Spiritual marriage is clearly implied, but not stated, in "It was a quiet way." In other poems it is stated, and takes a number of different forms. In one it is marriage to God in the tradition of the commentary on the *Song of Songs*.

> Given in marriage unto thee,
> Oh, thou celestial host!
> Bride of the Father and the Son,
> Bride of the Holy Ghost!

Other betrothal shall dissolve,
Wedlock of will decay;
Only the keeper of this ring

With an alternate reading, "this seal."

Conquer mortality. (#817)

Such marriage cancels all other involvements, is unwilled, and
ensures immortality. It is, in brief, a conversion experience.

In another poem the speaker lives with someone who is
dead, denied marriage.

I live with him, I see his face,
I go no more away
For visitor, or sundown;
Death's single privacy

The only one forestalling mine,
And that by right that he
Presents a claim invisible,
No wedlock granted me.
I live with him, I hear his voice,
I stand alive today
To witness to the certainty
Of immortality

Taught me by Time, the lower way:
Conviction every day
That life like this is stopless,
Be judgment what it may. (#463)

I live with him, I see his face, I hear his voice. I no longer have to go away when a visitor comes or at sunset. But the man is dead, and—the statement has a curious exactness in the phrasing—it is the invisible claim of death's bachelor seclusion, "Death's single privacy," that prevents our marriage. So I live with him in imagination, and bear witness to immortality, for such a way of living could not end, neither in Heaven nor in Hell: "Be judgment what it may."

Mrs. Jackson has expressed the experience in prose. We read in *Mercy Philbrick's Choice*:

> Slowly the whole allegiance of her [Mercy's] heart transformed itself to the dead man's memory; slowly her grief for his loss deepened, and yet with the deepened grief came a certain new and holy joy. It surely could not be impossible for him to know in heaven that she was his on earth? As confidently as if she had been wedded to him here, she looked forward to the reunion with him there, and found in her secret consciousness of this eternal bond a hidden rapture, such as has been the stay of many a widowed heart.[15]

Similarly, in Whittier's poem "The Sisters," at the intimation in a kind of vision of the death of her sister's betrothed in a wild storm off Annisquam, the speaker says:

> The love that I hid from myself away
> Shall crown me now in the light of day . . .
>
> Sacred to thee am I henceforth,
> Thou in heaven and I on earth! . . .

> But now my soul with his soul I wed,
> Thine the living, and mine the dead.[16]

This distinction between earthly and heavenly marriage is one of the elements the Mormons adopted from the revivalistic tradition:

> People, according to Mormon technology, are *married* for a time, but *sealed* for eternity . . . It is these wives, who, married to one man and sealed to another, are the "spiritual wives" of those to whom they are sealed.[17]

So Dickinson: "If I may have it when it's dead, / I'll be contented so / . . . Think of it, lover, I and thee / Permitted face to face to be / After a life—a death we'll say." (#577)

We come now to poems without partners. One begins flatly:

> I'm wife; I've finished that,
> That other state;
> I'm Czar, I'm woman now;
> It's safer so.

She muses, "How odd the girl's life looks," perhaps as earth looks to those in heaven, with the association of marriage with heaven:

> But why compare?
> I'm wife, Stop there! (#199)

The poem asserts the speaker has assumed maturity, has passed what John Noyes called spiritual puberty, has grown up and can no longer say as she did some years earlier, "I so love to be a child."[18]

Hence she has a baptism of the spirit, a secular conversion experience; "I am ashamed, I hide. / What right have I to be a bride, / So late a dowerless girl?" "Meek let it be, too proud for pride, / Baptized this day a bride." (#473) In another poem it is explicitly Second Baptism, without the marriage association: "I'm ceded, I've stopped being theirs."

> The name they dropped upon my face
> With water in the country church
> Is finished using now,
> And they can put it with my dolls,
> My childhood, and the string of spools.

The first time I was baptized "without the choice . . . Crowned, crowing on my father's breast, / A half unconscious queen"; this time "consciously of Grace" "With will to choose or to reject." So "Called to my full," "adequate, erect," "Existence's whole arc filled up," "I choose just a crown." (#508) This is willed maturity.

But to return to marriage, of a sort. The speaker in another poem will be married by dawn, "A wife at daybreak I shall be," "At midnight I am but a maid." There will be a symbolic transition from the midnight of maidenhood "Unto the East and Victory." She hears them call as "Angels bustle in the hall," and "my Future climbs the stair." When in my youth a woman spoke of her Future, she meant her predestined mate. So Dickinson writes, in an early letter, of her sister, "Vinnie . . . went to meet Tomorrow a few minutes ago."[19] In the next couplet the speaker is about to put off childhood, and then:

Eternity, I'm coming, Sir.
Savior, I've seen the face before. (#461)

In the two other manuscript copies of the poem, it is "Master" instead of "Savior," with presumably no variation in reference. This is, then, a spiritual marriage, involving Eternity, the Savior or Master, perhaps an anticipated marriage with God. But then there is the surprise ending, "I've seen the face before," a person, and at the very least a second meeting. But the next to last line in the earliest copy originally read, "The Vision flutters in the door," which is crossed out and "Eternity, I'm coming" substituted. In this version there is no anticipated marriage with God (or, possibly, a god-substitute); instead, there is the recurrent vision.

Now, in the marriage poems we have discussed, "vision" in "the daily own of love/ Depreciate the vision" refers primarily to the life envisioned; in "Ourselves were wed" marriage and vision were identified. In the cancelled line of this poem could she have meant Vision? Mrs. Stowe relates that the whole of Uncle Tom's Cabin came to her in a series of visions, the first being of the death of Uncle Tom while sitting at the communion-table in the little church in Brunswick, ME.[20] Mrs. Stowe's husband "saw visions, strange appearances he had learned to take for granted, a man and woman, sometimes a boy, sometimes vague cloudy shapes. He was also visited by clairvoyant intuitions about death and the dead." Similarly, the narrator of *Oldtown Folks* as a boy had had visions, and particularly one fairly constant one: "This was the form of a young boy of about my own age, who for a year past had frequently come to me at night, who seemed to look lovingly upon me, and with whom I used to have a sort of social communion, without words. . . ." This is something other than daydreaming, fantasy, or imagination in the ordinary sense; it has a supernatural quality, and carries with it the persuasion of actuality. To continue: he was "surrounded by a species of vision or apparition so clear and distinct that I often found great difficulty in distinguishing between the forms of real life and these shifting shapes, that had every appearance of reality, except that they dissolved at the touch."[21]

Dickinson deals with the problem and its association with religion in a cramped and curious poem. The speaker is male. He says, My bride's sweet weight had scarcely deigned to lie on my heart a night when, stirring—whether he or she isn't clear—, she slipped away. If it was a dream made solid just to confirm "the Heaven," or if I was dreamed by her, let the power to presume an answer remain with Him, that is, God, who gave to me as to all

> A fiction superseding faith
> By so much as 'twas real. (#518)

An astonishing conclusion. The Vision, the dream made solid, has a reality that supersedes religious faith, and it is given by God.

Some such visionary life is claimed in another poem:

> Alone I cannot be,
> The hosts do visit me,
> Recordless company
> Who baffle key.

I live in a populous spirit world whose figures, unlike those in a novel with a key, have no names or addresses:

551

They have no robes nor names,
No almanacs nor climes,
But general homes
Like gnomes.

Their coming may be known
By couriers within;
Their going is not,
For they're never gone. (#298)

Perhaps these texts account for the three letters addressed to "Master," particularly two of them, those unsent biographical puzzles of human anguish, which may never have been intended to be sent—how do you address a letter to a general home? And may have no key. Or if there is a key, the addressee may be dead, hence also spectral. "What would you do with me," she writes, "if I came 'in white?'"—With quotes around "in white." We read in Revelations (19:7-8), to choose one text of many, "Let us be glad and rejoice, and give honor to him: for the marriage of the Lamb is come, and his wife hath made herself ready. And to her was granted that she should be arrayed in fine linen, clean and white." And one more text: "they shall walk with me in white: for they are worthy." (3:4) The passage quoted above continues, "Have you the little chest to put the Alive in?" And the letter concludes: "I did'nt think to tell you, you did'nt come to me 'in white,' nor ever told me why."[22]

I will conclude with a poem that is explicit. The opening stanzas are neither good nor bad, but the last four have poetic authority:

I think to live may be a bliss
For those who dare to try,
Beyond my limit to conceive,
My lip to testify.

I think the heart I former wore
Could widen till to me
The other like the little bank
Appear unto the sea.

I think the days could every one
In ordination stand,
And majesty be easier
Than an inferior kind.

No numb alarm lest difference come,
No goblin on the bloom,
No start in apprehension's ear,
No bankruptcy, no doom,

But certainties of sun,
Midsummer in the mind,
A steadfast south upon the soul,
Her polar time behind.

The vision pondered long
So plausible becomes
That I esteem the fiction real,
The real fictitious seems.

How bountiful the dream,
What plenty it would be,
Had all my life been but mistake
Just rectified in thee. (#646)

The intrepid Springfield detective cited in the previous lecture conjectured that Dickinson's way of life was the consequence of a) a religious experience, b) a cherishing the dead, "mourning for a friend," or c) "come decree of fate," the predestined person. In this group of poems all three, though sometimes in special forms, are involved, and some understanding of those forms is needed to enter into her poetic life. But the forms are not private; they are the forms of her time, place, and tradition, including Vision:

The Vision pondered long
So plausible becomes
That I esteem the fiction real,
The real fictitious seems.

EDWIN ARLINGTON ROBINSON

A Brief Biography

Robinson was a man almost without biography who became a legend to his friends. He was decent, reticent, likable, and contrary—he himself called it selfish. He was not going to work for a living. He would do nothing but write poetry, except at times prose fiction or drama for their economic potentialities. But in this he failed; prose was not his language. And unsuccessful prose he ultimately transmuted to poetry. The prose sketch of 1894, "in a lighter vein," "of a philosophic tramp . . . looking for rest" becomes in a few years *Captain Craig*.

To think of oneself as a poet has serious consequences, even if one's dignity precludes the dionysiac role of a Hart Crane. The professed poet must keep writing, "scrivening to the end against his fate," for it is the justification of his life. So he wrote too much, and when written out he could not swear off. Again, the role is jealous of all other roles. Without an independent income and a secure place in society loneliness, dispossession, chronic indigence follow. Finally, the role is vatic; the poet must intuit and communicate a meaning in the universe. So he kept asking the inadmissable question, What is it all about? especially considering the pain. That it was unanswerable he thought guaranteed the question. He spoke again and again of the Light, which was now the Grail, now a woman, now "The light behind the stars" and always something that blurs "man's finite vision with misty glimmerings of the infinite." He believed in love and in belief with "a kind of optimistic desperation."

Tobacco, alcohol, and Wagner were his passions and his stay. The first he occasionally, but never seriously, gave up. The second, apparently under the persuasion of friends, he did for long periods, which is remarkable, for he drank whisky straight by the tumblerful. The last he never wearied of.

At twelve or thirteen he came under the influence of a local osteopath who had forsaken all else to write sonnets and the French forms. Now, metrical speech is a language which, like any language, must be learned young or never. And as a language it must have an audience; this the doctor and a cultivated local poetic circle provided so that in his later career he never faltered in meter, and at his most involved and obscure is still speaking to an audience.

At twenty-one, after three years of helping around the home place and doggedly writing, he entered Harvard College, "the object of almost the only patriotism I possess," as a special student. It was the making of the poet; for there is an educated ease with ideas and experience and a breadth that is denied to the self-tutored. It is interesting that later in the decade Frost and Stevens were also special students at Harvard.

After two years he returned home, the family dead, dying, or physical and spiritual wrecks. Four years later, at twenty-seven, he left home, finally settling in New York. The dissipation of the family fortune—he had tacitly expected to live on a modest patrimony—and a stubborn worldly incompetence reduced him at the age of thirty to absolute poverty, a life of cadging, and ten months' employment as a timekeeper on a construction job. The job finished, he was supported until his fiftieth year by public and private patronage: by a sinecure at the New York Customs House, arranged by President Theodore Roosevelt, by the contributions of his friends, ultimately made systematic, and by summer residence at the MacDowell Colony. At fifty-one, when the *Collected Poems* was awarded the first of his three Pulitzer prizes, he could finally live on what his poetry made, and with the extraordinary success of *Tristram* in 1927 he was able to repay many of his debts and remain financially secure. Thereafter he wrote long poems, one a year until his death, which were bought primarily by public libraries and gave him a steady income. The principal other event of these years was the First World War and the destruction of the world he had known, which he translated into the Arthurian legend, "And there was darkness over Camelot."

He lived during his mature life among the moderately wealthy and cultured and with the outcast and miscast. He belonged to the former by breeding, to the latter by experience, imagination, and compassion. And he wrote of both. Yet little that he wrote was a direct transcription of experience. He had a life of fantasy in which Tilbury Town was and was not Gardiner, Maine, and those who come no more to Calverly's had their own existence, transpositions or opposites of himself and his friends. Though celibate he wrote with insight and some tedium of sexual passion. And he knew we do not really know about others; we do not know about him.

Toward the end of his life he concluded: "As lives go, my own life would be called, and properly, a rather fortunate one." Most commentators have not thought so, but it seems true. He died of cancer at sixty-five.[1]

Though he wrote too much, he wrote much that was distinctive and good, and even in the dull wastes there are fragments. He commanded from the beginning the full range of late Victorian styles, from the flat naturalistic prose line (and his own special roundabout pentameter) through incantatory jingle and the tightly rhymed stanzas of the light verse tradition to the full diapason of Romantic rhetoric: "Something of ships and sunlight, streets and singing, / Troy falling, and the ages coming back, /

And ages coming forward." He had a gift for simile, "The stillness of October gold / Went out like beauty from a face," and especially for the abstract simile: the recurrent cadger "Familiar as an old mistake, / And futile as regret." He could secure the commonplace with the right epithet: "At someone's tinkling afternoon at home." He could manage unobtrusive profundity: "Love builds of what Time takes away, / Till Death itself is less than Change," and mark the quiet defeat of a life:

> nor was there anything
> To make a daily meaning for her life
> But the blank taste of time.[2]

THE STYLES & PROCEDURES
OF WALLACE STEVENS

Shortly before the last war it became apparent that Wallace Stevens was about to displace T. S. Eliot as the exemplar of American poetry, as the object of devotion, of imitation and explication by younger poets, critics, and academics. His own comments at that time on his predecessor in prestige will set our problem:

> I don't know what there is any longer to say about Eliot. His prodigious reputation is a great difficulty.
>
> While that sort of thing: more or less complete acceptance of it, helps to create the poetry of any poet, it also help to destroy it.[1]

I should like to rescue the poetry of Wallace Stevens from himself and from his friends. I feel it is worth rescuing, and I am sure it needs it. I speak, then, for the estate of poetry, of which I am the impersonal, and by definition, imperfect, spokesman. The situation is this: there are over twelve thousand lines of poetry, almost four hundred separate titles, and much of this is junk, and most is repetitious. There is, furthermore, an immense body of commentary which is, with some notable exceptions, scandalously wrong, irrelevant, and confusing, much of it consisting of centos of phrases from the poetry. The problem, then, is to sort out the poetry of Wallace Stevens, and to understand it. But, first, to understand it.

Anyone who reads through this mass of material will feel as one does who reads through the *Complete Poems* of Emily

Dickinson and the attendant commentary, that he has gotten his hands inextricably involved in the taffy—oversaturated, bewildered, unable to tell the good from the bad, snatching at this poem and that, this passage and that, to save something from the confusion. And, I think, for much the same reasons. They were both amateurs in poetry in all but one sense. Now, an amateur does things for his own sake, for the sake of doing them. A professional does things for the thing's sake.[2] The professional poet as a writer of poems may not like to write—he may, as Thomas Mann said, be a man who finds writing more difficult than most people do—but once engaged in a poem his single aim is to perfect the poem. The amateur, on the other hand, likes to write poems, and may perfect them or not. He doesn't mind botching the job. Stevens in one of his best poems begins a stanza with a parable, "A red bird flies across the golden floor," but after four lines, interesting in themselves, he discovers he has been carried away; he doesn't really know what the parable is about, and so muses, "Shall I uncrumple this much crumpled thing?"

Instead, he begins again, precisely and magnificently:

> I am a man of fortune greeting heirs;
> For it has come that thus I greet the spring.
> These choirs of welcome choir for me farewell. (13)[3]

and he leaves the unsuccessful attempt standing in the text. It is still there.

Again, not only was he an amateur in the writing of poetry, he was not in his public life professionally a poet; he was an insurance executive, as Dickinson was, professionally, a New England spinster, a maiden aunt. Only in his very private life, as Dickinson in hers, did he see himself as a poet, and this cherished fantasy was not to the good; it had to be validated again and again by the production of poems of whatever quality. For he needed to see himself as a poet, as poetry itself, not only because he was a man possessed by a genius for a prodigality of phrasing that was not to be denied, but also just to keep alive within the commonplaceness, the horror, the wantingness of American business civilization:

> Am I a man that is dead
>
> At a table on which the food is cold?
> Is my thought a memory, not alive?
>
> Is the spot on the floor, there, wine or blood
> And whichever it may be, is it mine? (173)

He was a man who must get up and go back to work on Monday morning, "in Monday's dirty light," where employer and employee contend while the pheasant sleeps late. "There is no place, / Here, for the lark fixed in the mind," for an absolute or imaginative conception of nature; the cock will serve only to waken them for work. "Morning is not sun, / It is this posture of the nerves" in which a poet blunted by business civilization holds tight to the nuances of poetry: "It must be this rhapsody or none." And so, in the winter of 1936-37, as the Depression dragged on:

> Here is the bread of time to come,
>
> Here is its actual stone. The bread
> Will be our bread, the stone will be

561

> Our bed and we shall sleep by night.
> We shall forget by day, except
>
> The moments when we choose to play
> The imagined pine, the imagined jay. (182-84)

The moments are preserved in the collected poems. He might have taken to drink; he took to poems, instead, to too many rot-gut poems.

Finally, he had, like Dickinson, only a few subjects, a group of rather simpleminded ideas and procedures, repetitive ways of getting started with a poem, and getting on with it. These have never been adequately discriminated and described, and it will be the novelty of this essay that they are discriminated and described. For a somewhat clearer understanding of them than Stevens had himself, as witnessed by his prose, is necessary to the understanding and evaluation of his work.

Let us begin with his recurrent concerns. There is, first of all, the loss of an implicit belief in the Christian God, or in any God—"The death of one god is the death of all" (381)—and hence of any belief in personal immortality, or, indeed in any structuring of the universe or of experience:

> This structure of ideas, these ghostly sequences
> Of the mind, result only in disaster. (326)

or, again:

> There is order in neither sea nor sun. (122)

But he had not lost the need to believe, to believe as one's grand-father had believed:

Is it ideas that I believe?
Good air, my only friend, believe,

Believe would be a brother full
Of love, believe would be a friend,

Friendlier than my only friend,
Good air . . .

He argues, if the old traditions are untrue, then they are ficti-
tious, myths, and we as poets can construct our own myths: "A
substitute for all the gods." (175-76) And we are driven to this
because whatever we are, whatever we attain—say a "complete
simplicity" that

Stripped one of all his torments, concealed
The evilly compounded, vital I
And made it fresh in a world of white,
A world of clear water, brilliant-edged,
Still one would want more, one would need more...

There would still remain the never-resting mind,
So that one would want to escape.

But not only to escape, also to

come back
To what had been so long composed.
The imperfect is our paradise.

And so he is driven from pole to pole of experience, and in this
process, delight is in the writing of poems:

> Note that, in this bitterness, delight,
> Since the imperfect is so hot in us,
> Lies in flawed words and stubborn sounds. (193-94)

Yet there is also a desire for rest, for stasis, for fulfilling peace:

> Is it I then that keep saying there is an hour
> Filled with expressible bliss, in which I have
>
> No need, am happy, forget need's golden hand,
> Am satisfied without solacing majesty,
> And if there is an hour there is a day,
>
> There is a month, a year, there is a time
> In which majesty is a mirror of the self:
> I have not but I am and as I am, I am. (404-05)

Allied to these concerns, which may be thought of as theological, is a preoccupation with philosophizing. Now, perhaps the most elementary thing one can think of in a philosophical way is that there is oneself and there is something other than oneself, and that the other exists for us insofar as we are aware of it, and that what we are aware of conditions our awareness. Subjective and objective. The terms can be distinguished and can be identified, and in this elementary occupation of distinguishing and identifying Stevens spent much of this mature life. One is his environment, his environment is him: "Nota: man is the intelligence of his soil" (27) and later: "his soil is man's intelligence." (36) The procedure is dialectical; a position is stated and then its opposite or contradictory; sometimes there intervenes a resolution, and then the terms or positions are again set free. These are the transformations of a Hartford Hegel. It is the residue of the teaching of Royce, William James, and Santayana, of Harvard College in the late 1890s, as his original style we will see is not to be distinguished from that of his immediate predecessors there, Robinson in his romantic mode, Trumbull Stickney, and Cabot Lodge.

The poles of subjective and objective are treated by Stevens under the rubrics of imagination and reality, sometimes distinguished, sometimes identified by the axiom that opposites are one, and the conjugation of these terms forms a meditation, or a system of meditation, which he sometimes feels is an imitation of, or a part of, or identified with, the essential meditation of the universe in its transformations from day to night, winter to summer. But we will never understand Stevens' poetry until we perceive that these ideas, except when he is being routine, are not ideas as such but rather specific kinds of experiences, just as in his better poetry what are sometimes thought of as the symbols of sun and moon, winter and summer, are really sun and moon, winter and summer, and their appropriate sun and winter experiences. Furthermore, the rubrics of imagination and reality refer now to one kind of experience and now to another, and hence we must describe and discriminate the quite different areas of experience alluded to by these terms.

We may distinguish under the rubrics of imagination at least six areas. First, it is the romantic as opposed to the realistic, in the ordinary high school sense of those terms—James Branch Cabell as opposed to Theodore Dreiser:

> O thin men of Haddam
> Why do you imagine golden birds?
> Do you not see how the blackbird
> Walks around the feet
> Of the women about you? (93)

Second, it is the kind of fantasy associated in Stevens with a high-spirited nonsense, by which one imagines "At night an Arabian in my room, / With his damned hoobla-hoobla-hoobla-how." (383), or by which "an old sailor, / Drunk and asleep in his boots, / Catches tigers / In red weather." (66) Something no proper housewife in a white nightgown would think of, and so in that way related to the first. Third, it is the distortion of feeling, the affective elements qualifying plain fact, the Imagistic enterprise:

> He rode over Connecticut
> In a glass coach.
> Once, a fear pierced him,
> In that he mistook
> The shadow of his equipage
> For blackbirds. (94)

I suspect, by the way, that the glass coach was in plain fact not Cinderella's equipage but the New York, New Haven, and Hartford Railroad. Fourth, it is the perception of resemblances, a perception between diverse phenomena by which we may intuit a oneness in the universe in which the intuiter may partake. It is an instrument of the monistic experience:

> The river is moving.
> The blackbird must be flying. (94)

The procedure can be consciously induced and pursued. One looks at a pineapple on the table and imagines:

> 1. The hut stands by itself beneath the palms.
> 2. Out of their bottle the green genii come. (*NA* 86)

It is "Not that which is but that which is apprehended," so that a mirror becomes "a lake of reflections in a room," and then "A glassy ocean lying at the door." (468) Fifth, it is a process of abstraction, a furious negative exclusion of all associations with the object, especially those of Christianity, but also of the trite and cliché, in order to intuit an inherent, a bare reality. To perceive "The inconceivable idea of the sun"

> You must become an ignorant man again
> And see the sun again with an ignorant eye
> And see it clearly in the idea of it.

> Never suppose an inventing mind as source
> Of this idea nor for that mind compose
> A voluminous master folded in his fire . . .

> The sun
> Must bear no name, gold flourisher, but be
> In the difficulty of what it is to be. (380-81)

But it is a reality of which ultimately nothing can be said, hence we must find it to be nothingness, or body it forth. And so, sixth, imagination is the act of constructing and projecting a myth, analogous to the Christian myth, that will represent the intuited reality. The myth may be of two sorts, a) grandiose, "a hero's head" (165), a giant, an immense rock or mountain, the bedrock of reality, the analogue of Mt. Olympus, or b) whimsical, trivial, ordinary, and antihero, the modern successor and parody of the heroic age: "The major abstraction is the idea of man / And major man is its exponent . . . "

Who is it?
What rabbi, grown furious with human wish . . .

Does not see these separate figures one by one,
And yet see only one, in his old coat,
His slouching pantaloons, beyond the town,

Looking for what was where it used to be?
Cloudless the morning. It is he. The man
In that old coat, those sagging pantaloons . . . (388-89)

But it is a fiction in which we do not believe; it isn't there. So we come full circle, we come back to plain fact, to reality.

Reality itself is also manifold. It is, first of all, things as we ordinarily see and describe them, external reality:

The eye's plain version is a thing apart,
The vulgate of experience. (465)

Of this there are two subdivisions, a) plain fact, and b) the fuller exact descriptive statement but without intrusion of feeling or illusion. It is, secondly, the humdrum of ordinary life in this civilization, to which one may be adjusted or not. The Canon Aspirin's sister in *Notes Toward a Supreme Fiction* is completely adjusted. She lived in her house in a sensible ecstasy, dressed her children in the poverty that became them:

She held
Them closelier to her by rejecting dreams.

The words they spoke were voices that she heard.
She looked at them and saw them as they were
And what she felt fought off the barest phrase. (402)

It is a life without imagination, and hence to the unadjusted an alien life, a life of horror and boredom, in which "The time of year has grown indifferent" (96), in which "A little less returned for him each spring":

Only last year he said that the naked moon
Was not the moon he used to see, to feel

(In the pale coherences of moon and mood
When he was young), naked and alien,
More leanly shining from a lankier sky. (148-49)

It is defined by the absence of imagination. But there is also real reality, ultimate reality, beyond or behind appearance, significance defeating boredom, to be attained by the procedures of imagination, monism at the heart of things. And finally, there is the discovery that there is no reality behind appearance, no significance in triviality; reality is nothingness. Such, then, is the machinery of much of Stevens' poetry.

How does it work out in the poems? A good deal that Stevens wrote, especially in his later years, was in the form of sequences of short poems. These are sometimes only a miscellany of items, numbered consecutively, and headed by an irrelevant title. (252-59) At other times they are a group of poems, more or less related to each other, especially at the beginning and end, but also intermittently in between. Of such sort, of course, are *Sunday Morning* and the monocle poem, but the sequences I have in mind now differ from those in that they make a more explicit, a more systematic though not finally systematic, use of the procedures I have enumerated under the rubrics of imagination and reality, which are at their extremes solipsism and monism. The skeleton of the method can be seen in an early poem, *Metaphors of a Magnifico:*

> Twenty men crossing a bridge,
> Into a village,
> Are twenty men crossing twenty bridges,
> Into twenty villages,

That is, each consciousness creates a separate world; it is solipsism:

> Or one man
> Crossing a single bridge into a village.

Or all participate in a central consciousness, a single world; it is monism. Then follows an arpeggio, an affective comment, a deviation on the principle: "The acquisitions of poetry are fortuitous; *trouvailles,* (Hence its disorder.)" (*OP* 169), though this is a very mild instance:

> This is old song
> That will not declare itself.

Then:

> Twenty men crossing a bridge,
> Into a village,
> Are twenty men crossing a bridge
> Into a village.

Or, it is just a fact:

> That will not declare itself
> Yet is certain as meaning . . .
> The boots of the men clump
> On the boards of the bridge.
> The first white wall of the village
> Rises through fruit-trees.

As fact it is subject to more extended description. And now follows a third arpeggio, and the repetition of part of the preceding two lines as a kind of dying cadence:

> Of what was it I was thinking?
> So the meaning escapes.

> The first white wall of the village . . .
> The fruit-trees. (19)

It is not much of a poem, but it shows in brief the procedures, the movement from one position to the next, the irrelevancies to the argument, the final messing it up. And the subjects are solipsism, monism, plain fact. Another early poem, *Thirteen Ways of Looking at a Blackbird*—had it been twelve or fourteen, would the poem have so caught the fancy of readers?—displays, along with a few purely imagistic sections, in a wholly unsystematic form the same procedures; in fact, I have already quoted three of the sections in illustration of the different aspects of imagination and reality, and now add one more:

A man and a woman
Are one
A man and a woman and a blackbird
Are one. (93)

There are two propositions: opposites involve each other; reality is monistic.

Let us look, now, briefly at some of the later and longer sequences. *The Man with the Blue Guitar* begins by posing explicitly the problem of imagination and reality and its relationship to writing poetry:

The man bent over his guitar,
A shearsman of sorts. The day was green.

They said, "You have a blue guitar,
You do not play things as they are."

The man replied, "Things as they are
Are changed upon the blue guitar."

And they said then, "But play, you must,
A tune beyond us, yet ourselves,

A tune upon the blue guitar
Of things exactly as they are." (165)

The day, of course, was green by the natural association of sunlight and greenery, and is rendered falsely in the blue of illusion. The problem is to get it exactly and at the same time to strike through to the reality beyond reality. In the next section the poet cannot quite strike through to an idea of man that would yet be a man; in the third section, Ah, if he could; in the fourth, attempting to get "A million people on one string," mankind and man at once, feeling suddenly breaks through

> The feelings crazily, craftily call,
> Like a buzzing of flies in autumn air. (166)

the distortion of feeling. So far, and for the next two, the sections pretty much develop out of each other, but soon they become somewhat more miscellaneous. This is an improvisatory poetry, but improvisation for the most part within the unsystematic system I have analyzed, yet permitting those intrusions from the mood and fact of the depression that were quoted at the beginning of this essay. And the sequence ends with a return to ordinary reality and the escapist imagination:

> The bread
> Will be our bread, the stone will be
>
> Our bed and we shall sleep by night.
> We shall forget by day, except
>
> The moments when we choose to play
> The imagined pine, the imagined jay. (184)

Notes Toward a Supreme Fiction, which many now say is Stevens' greatest poem, and which I regard as a failure, on the whole a mess with intermittent successful passages, employs the same general method. It, too, begins with an injunction: to perceive the idea of the world, as, for example, of the sun, the reality behind reality, to perceive it by a process of furious abstraction, by becoming "an ignorant man again," by negating traditional theological, mythological associations. (380-81) And at the end of the sequence we come back to ordinary reality, to the "Fat girl"—no doubt, one's wife—whom one thinks of "as strong or tired, / Bent over work, anxious, content, alone," and yet who also remains "the more than natural figure," "the soft-footed phantom, the irrational / Distortion," "The fiction that results from feeling." (406) Humdrum reality and the something more.

It is clear, then, that Stevens had a homemade machine for the endless production of poems. And so he could never come to a final belief about experience or the universe, for

> If ever the search for a tranquil belief should end,
> The future might stop emerging out of the past ... (151)

there would be no more poems. But he could never come to a final belief for a deeper reason: because he did not believe, and because he terribly wanted to believe; this kept him trying, that destroyed each attempt.

And now to sort out the poems. They are in one of four styles, and sometimes in a mixture of styles. The first is the imagistic style, whose characteristic instrument is the cadenced meter of the late 1910s. The coach passage I have quoted from the blackbird poem will illustrate the style. It is not a style of much interest, though some nice little things have been done in it.

The second is the mannered style. I observe in passing, since it is worth observation, how much of the literature of prestige in our time is mannered in the extreme: the prose of Gertrude Stein and *Finnegans Wake,* the *Cantos* of Ezra Pound, the poetry of Hart Crane and Dylan Thomas, surely there has not been such a collection of artificial languages in esteem since the latter days of the Roman Empire, and this among readers who believe they believe in the absolute virtue of the accents of real speech. But to return: Stevens' mannerism consists of a whole system of what I call hijinks: nonsense cries, exotic names of persons and places, extraordinarily rare words, ostentatious alliteration, and vulgarity in internal rhyming. It is the style of a man with no taste at all, of a man who regards poetry simply, in the words of Eliot's preface to *The Sacred Wood,* as "superior amusement," and by superior is also meant that the poet is being superior. The poems, or parts of poems, in this style are occasionally amusing, but usually merely tiresome. Yet occasionally amusing, as in *Bantams in Pine-Woods,* in which, curiously enough, both the banty cock and the poet are being superior. As the banty struts it is obvious he feels he is a ten-foot-tall poet, cock of the universe, and the poet an inchling. The poet replies, we both live in our own solipsistic grandeur. And the poet struts back, himself now taller than the pines:

> Chieftain Iffucan of Azcan in caftan
> Of tan with henna hackles, halt!
>
> Damned universal cock, as if the sun
> Was blackamoor to bear your blazing tail.
>
> Fat! Fat! Fat! Fat! I am the personal.
> Your world is you. I am my world.
>
> You ten-foot poet among inchlings.
> Fat! Begone! An inchling bristles in these pines,
>
> Bristles, and points their Appalachian tangs,
> And fears not portly Azcan nor his hoos. (75-76)

He is a chieftain If-you-can in a world where one lives as-can. And the style is a conglomerate of mannerisms. We have the nonsense cries, the "hoos," the vulgar internal rhyming, the flaunting alliteration, the apparently exotic names, and the extremely rare word *tang,* "projection," for the height of the pines. Yet there is gusto to it, and fun, control, a brilliant conceit ("As if the sun / Was blackamoor to bear your blazing tail"), and strut for strut is a human reaction. It is a good little poem. But, at the best, you can do no more than little things in this manner.

The third style is another matter. This is the nineteenth century rhetorical style of *Sunday Morning,* the style of Wordsworth's *Prelude,* Keats's *Ode to Autumn,* Tennyson's *Ulysses*; it was the style, as I indicated earlier, of his near contemporaries at Harvard, and of his own undergraduate verse, though now more sinewy. It is the style that his early education made available to him, as it is not available to a young man now. It is associated in his practice with the Christianity of his youth and with an erotic sentimentality. He corrupts it with the superiority of mannerism in the address *A High-Toned Old Christian Woman*; he alternates it with mannerism in *The Comedian as the Letter C*; and keeps a little distance between himself and its implicated feelings by touches of mannerism in the great poems of the style—a little in *Sunday Morning,* a good deal more in the monocle poem. When he uses it without protection, he writes with an almost persuasive badness, as in the idealistic sentimentality of *To One of Fictive Music,* or, with a less sustained rhetoric, the adolescent vision of the Nanzia Nunzio section of *Notes Toward a Supreme Fiction.*

Sunday Morning is the triumph of the style, and one of the great poems in the language. However, I have dealt with it at length elsewhere, and have nothing new to say. I shall illustrate the style, then, by a poem in the *Sunday Morning* stanza, and written apparently out of the same impulse, *Of Heaven Considered as a Tomb,* in which the very metaphor of heaven as a tomb signals the loss of belief in Christian, or any, immortality:

> What word have you, interpreters, of men
> Who in the tomb of heaven walk by night,
> The darkened ghosts of our old comedy?
> Do they believe they range the gusty cold,
> With lanterns borne aloft to light the way,
> Freemen of death, about and still about
> To find whatever it is they seek? Or does
> That burial, pillared up each day as porte
> And spiritous passage into nothingness,
> Foretell each night the one abysmal night,
> When the host shall no more wander, nor the light
> Of the steadfast lanterns creep across the dark?
> Make hue among the dark comedians,
> Halloo them in the topmost distances
> For answer from their icy Elysée. (56)

This is the eloquent style, his native inheritance.

But in some of the earlier poems, and in most of the later poems, he writes in a plain style, a style at its best unflavored by mannerisms or rhetoric, except for the rhetoric of simple repetition, as in *The Death of a Soldier:*

> Death is absolute and without memorial
> As in a season of autumn
> When the wind stops,
> When the wind stops and, over the heavens,
> The clouds go, nevertheless,
> In their direction. (97)

It is characteristic of the plain style that it is difficult to describe, for it is describable chiefly by negation. Styles are noticeable or unnoticeable, and what does one say of the unnoticeable? The mannerism of *Bantams in Pine-Woods* is obvious and obtrusive; it is more immediately noticeable than what is said in the poem. The rhetoric of *Sunday Morning,* though neither obvious nor obtrusive, it is yet noticeable; there is a sustained and elevated eloquence that is in itself striking. But a poem in the plain style has no such effect, it is scrupulously unmannered, and studiously uneloquent. It may be flat, humdrum, and dull; it may be relaxed, somewhat careless, undistinguished; or, as in the best of Stevens, apart from the great poems in the rhetorical style, it may be noticeably unnoticeable, a quietness so apt it is heard. One of the triumphs in this style, in what I may call the quiet plain style, is *The House was Quiet and the World was Calm* another in what one might call the cold plain style is *The Snow Man:*

> One must have a mind of winter
> To regard the frost and the boughs
> Of the pine-trees crusted with snow;
>
> And have been cold a long time
> To behold the junipers shagged with ice,
> The spruces rough in the distant glitter
>
> Of the January sun; and not to think
> Of any misery in the sound of the wind,
> In the sound of a few leaves,
>
> Which is the sound of the land
> Full of the same wind
> That is blowing in the same bare place

For the listener, who listens in the snow,
And, nothing himself, beholds
Nothing that is not there and the nothing that is. (9-10)

It is a poem of bleak acceptance of rejections. It takes a special kind of mind, a winter mind—and, clearly, this is the experience of becoming one's environment—to look coldly on a winter landscape, and to reject the ascription of anthropomorphic feeling or monistic intimation to the sound of the wind and a few leaves. Become depersonalized, one perceives only appearance, and that there is no reality behind appearance. Yet winter in this poem is not just a symbol, though it is the natural symbol for the experience; it is initially a New England winter, and Stevens took his winters hard, as I do.

Toward the end of his life he rewrote the poem at least twice: once in *The Course of a Particular* developing the theme of the "Nothing that is not there and the nothing that is":

Today the leaves cry, hanging on branches swept by wind,
Yet the nothingness of winter becomes a little less.
It is still full of icy shades and shapen snow.

The leaves cry . . . One holds off and merely hears the cry.
It is a busy cry, concerning someone else.
And though one says that one is part of everything,

There is a conflict, there is a resistance involved;
And being part is an exertion that declines:
One feels the life of that which gives life as it is.

The leaves cry. It is not a cry of divine attention,
Nor the smoke-drift of puffed-out heroes, nor human cry.
It is the cry of leaves that do not transcend themselves,

In the absence of fantasia, without meaning more
Than they are in the final finding of the ear,[4] in the thing
Itself, until, at last, the cry concerns no one at all.

(OP 96-97)

The poem, in a relaxed plain style, depicts not only the acceptance of rejections, but something of the process of acceptance. The cry of the leaves seeks for the moment to diminish the nothingness of winter, but winter persists, and one merely hears the cry as not concerning him. For though one tries to believe one is part of a universal monistic whole, it is an effort, and one gradually gives up. There is only that that gives things as they are, without divine solicitude or human, without imagination, meaning only what it is, a sound, in the final finding of the ear, of concern to no one at all.

The third version of this poem, written some ten years earlier, is on the theme of "nothing himself." It is now not January but early April, at the end of winter, when one is just beginning, if only in anticipation, to come back. It is written in what I would call a prose plain style:

On an early Sunday in April, a feeble day,
He felt curious about the winter hills
And wondered about the water in the lake.
It had been cold since December. Snow fell, first,
At New Year and, from then until April, lay

On everything. Now it had melted, leaving
The gray grass like a pallet, closely pressed;
And dirt. The wind blew in the empty place.
The winter wind blew in an empty place—
There was that difference between the and an,
The difference between himself and no man,
No man that heard a wind in an empty place.
It was time to be himself again, to see
If the place, in spite of its witheredness, was still
Within the difference. He felt curious
Whether the water was black and lashed about
Or whether the ice still covered the lake. There was still
Snow under the trees and on the northern rocks,
The dead rocks, not the green rocks, the live rocks. If,
When he looked, the water ran up the air or grew white
Against the edge of the ice, the abstraction would
Be broken and winter would be broken and done,
And being would be being himself again,
Being, becoming seeing and feeling and self,
Black water breaking into reality. (254-55)

And with spring and the spring sun comes hope, hope, for exam-
ple, that Ulysses will finally come to Penelope:

But was it Ulysses? Or was it only the warmth of the sun
On her pillow? The thought kept beating in her like her heart.
The two kept beating together. It was only day.
It was Ulysses and it was not. Yet they had met,
Friend and dear friend and a planet's encouragement
The barbarous strength within her would never fail.

(521)

And though he never comes, yet there is something, something that gives meaning, though not a personal, not a consoling meaning. It is, whatever it is, "the life of that which gives life as it is." (*OP* 96) Call it, if you will, *The River of Rivers in Connecticut,* "The river that flows nowhere, like a sea," the river this side of the river Styx. (533)

T. S. ELIOT ON POETRY & POETS

T. S. Eliot's short pieces of criticism, *On Poetry and Poets*,[1] supplements the earlier *Selected Essays*. The pieces are for the most part written for delivery on a public occasion and for delivery by a poet of recognized distinction. They are the utterances of a public figure and have on the whole the ease and authority that this circumstance permits. He speaks of the social function of poetry, of Vergil, Dr. Johnson, Byron, and one feels that what is said is what should have been said. To read this volume is to know that poetry is worthwhile, and to know it without demonstration.

It is, then, an impressive book, and yet it is a troubling one, troubling in an accumulation of small and gradually larger ways. For ease and authority sometimes mislead the author, and may mislead his audience. I give for the moment a small instance, an instance in which the imprecision of an amateur scholarship is given the appearance of care and precision. Mr. Eliot speaks in one sentence of George Herbert and "certain other poets his contemporaries—Donne, Vaughan and Traherne" and two sentences later discriminates between Herbert and a poet "a little senior to him," Herrick. This seems harmless enough, seems even to display a scholarly conscientiousness, yet Herrick was only a year or two older than Herbert, while Donne was over twenty years his senior, Vaughan about twenty-five years his junior, and Traherne was unborn at Herbert's death. A small instance, no doubt, though not perhaps to one interested in the history of English poetry. But if small, yet troubling, for it raises the suspicion that the speaker is more persuasive than is desirable.

The persuasiveness is soundly founded in rhetoric, in the employment of commonplaces and in the character of the speaker.

These pieces rehearse with a dry restatement the rubrics of modern criticism. We are, for instance, again and again tantalized with the common distinction between poetry and verse, and feel at home in the difficulties it provokes. If the speaker at one point confesses with respect to this distinction that "the critical tools we are accustomed to use in analysing and criticising poetry do not seem to work," we are won by the unassuming honesty of the declaration. For the speaker is not merely a public figure with a dignity imputed to him by his reputation. He is a carefully delineated personality, solidly placed in the literary history of his time, and with many engaging traits. He has even his fleeting moment of vanity, remarking of a translated work, "when I read it in French." But he is most engaging, and most conciliating, in the many statements of disavowal and recantation. Some are personal, as in the disavowal of "a few notorious phrases which have had a truly embarrassing success in the world," or in the account of the ingenuous origin of the notes to *The Waste Land*. Others are disavowals for his generation and tradition: of *Finnegans Wake* we may say "one book like this is enough." Such statements will be of great consolation to the common reader, and will relieve him of a burden of irritable guilt.

But the most valuable parts of the book, and the most convincing in delineating the character of the speaker, are the many passages of literary autobiography, some brief and in passing, some fairly extensive. These passages are peculiarly appropriate to the form of public address, and could not have been done better. There is no lapse of taste. But more than this. From these passages one could realize, one could relive if he had not lived it himself, the experience of the literary revolution of our times. This is what it is to have been in the center of literary achievement. And so the voice of the speaker is located in circumstance.

It is a voice of dry charm, distinguished, attractive, human, agile. It is the voice of an elderly revolutionary, of an usurper whose forces have long since conquered the kingdom of letters. He speaks now with the assurance of a de facto legitimacy. He sees no need for further revolution. Our task is to consolidate the position, to develop and exploit the tradition which he and his peers established: "If the poetry of the rest of this century takes the line of development which seems to me, reviewing the progress of poetry through the last three centuries, the right course, it will discover new and more elaborate patterns of a diction now established."

This is the issue. Can the tradition be developed, and should it? I do not myself believe that Mr. Eliot understands the nature of the revolution he was engaged in. He depicts it as a return to the colloquial and the particular, and this is both too general and surely untrue of a good deal even of his own work. But taking the tradition as we have it, what can we do with it? A tradition is a collection of models for imitation and an associated set of principles for the production of works. It is the task of criticism to provide the principles. Are Mr. Eliot's fruitful?

The principle he most commonly recurs to, and the only one he exemplifies at length, is what he calls the principle of musical structure. He is, of course, quite aware of the dangers of analogy, and protects himself and the reader from any illegitimate confusion of poetry and music. But he does feel we can speak legitimately of "the musical pattern of emotional overtones," of "a rhythm of fluctuating emotion essential to the musical structure of the whole," and he shows us in some detail how such structure operates by an analysis of the opening lines of *Hamlet*. I quote the passage entire, excising only the denomination of particular characters and actions and the extensive quotations: "From the short, brusque ejaculations at the beginning . . . the verse glides into a slower movement . . . and the movement changes again . . . into the solemn and sonorous. . . . . There is an abrupt change to staccato . . . this rhythm changes again. . . . The scene reaches a resolution with the words. . . . There emerges, when we analyse it, a kind of musical design."

The method consists in characterizing successive passages by appropriate adjectives, and in asserting that change and resolution occur. With this paradigm one could analyze the whole of recorded literature, needing only a store of adjectives and, for variety, synonyms for "change." By this method whatever one wrote himself in whatever sequence could be shown to have structure, "and structure," Mr. Eliot affirms,"I hold to be an important element of poetic composition."

We need a counter-revolution.

V

THE QUEST OF THE OPAL

A Commentary on *The Helmsman*

There is little to say of the imaginative figure to whom I ascribe these jottings except that he was a frequenter of small coffee shops where for a nickel or a dime one used to be able to sit undisturbed for as much as half an hour. There, particularly on a dark or rainy day, he would pen these notes, originally in verse and now in prose, on old sheets of paper or backs of envelopes amid shopping lists, algebraic formulae, and odd quotations from detective stories. They were what one could do in that time and under those conditions, but the circumstances should not be thought of merely as hindrances since they became like most hindrances a method. The notes were at first a way of saving some fragments from his ruminations, but in time his ruminations became a way of achieving notes. Consequence and implication, order and outline, the devices by which insight is aggravated into sufficient bulk and extended to the decent solemnity of prose became at last only ways of prospecting or what otherwise would have lain hidden. Hence, if he anticipated a time and place for coffee, he would fall into a meditative melancholy out of which when the occasion arrived he would begin to write as if he had not intended to. His notes were no longer memoranda for a work; the essays he spoke to himself in meditation were rather memoranda for notes. He became an epigrammatist.

What he then wrote in verse he later put in prose, for verse is obscure of its very nature since few are persuaded it can mean what it says, and sometimes what his verse said was itself obscure. Not that he claimed for himself the privileges of vatic exaltation;

he had trifled with this attitude once under the pressure of the modern tradition in poetry and from a desire not to be found wanting in the dark pretensions of his early associates who were almost without exception congenital romantics, however classical their creed; but this was accidental. Substantially, he viewed himself rather as a professional writer, however laconic, one to whom poetry was verse.

For the generally received distinction between poetry and verse, he said in *For My Contemporaries,*[1] derives from a widely and deeply felt discrimination not merely between the products of writing but also between the attitudes with which the act of writing is approached and between the kinds of life which surround and supplement it. Verse is a professional activity, social and objective, and its methods and standards are those of craftsmanship. It is a concern of the ordinary human self, and is on the whole within a man's power to do well or not. Its virtues are the civic virtues. If it lacks much, what it does have is ascertainable and can be judged. But poetry is amateurish, religious, and eminently unsociable. It dwells in the spiritual life, in the private haunts of theology or voodoo. It is passive to the powers it cannot evoke. It is the accidental issue, the plain bastard, of grace and inspiration, or of the demons of anxiety—even of somatic irritation, for indigestion may be your angel. In that region the elected of God and the elected of themselves are scarcely distinguishable, and if the true oracle is nonsense to sense, so nonsense is often taken for oracle.

But the earlier verses in his book were nothing but constructions that offered to the reader certain schemes of experience, certain progressions of thought and feeling from the first line to the last. The later ones were direct statements of something he had to say, given form and definitiveness by the technique of verse. But what he had to say was often in the legitimate sense of that term original, and the common expectation of the reader is that the idea of a poem should be commonplace or given, its expression original. Hence the reader is often baffled since his expectation is foiled, and a man will sooner change anything than his expectations.

Again, the lyric especially—that is, the short poem—is commonly thought to be of general application. It should be such that the reader can appropriate it as his own, can regard himself as speaking in his own circumstances the words of the poet. He usually intended to disappoint the reader in this expectation also. He wanted him to know that this was his poem, not yours; these were his circumstances, not yours; and these were the structures of thought by which he had penetrated them. He attempted to enforce this by a recurring exactitude of qualification. If the reader persists in regarding the poem as of general application—that is, as an utterance of the indiscriminate I who is anyone—the recurrent qualifications can only perplex him. The poem is impenetrable since he has missed the point of penetration. The author, in fact, was only satisfied with a poem when qualification complicated qualification and yet the whole contrivance seemed to achieve stability and absoluteness by a coincidence with some given and simple external form.

To these sources of difficulty or obscurity must be added some of less dignity: the use, especially in the earlier poems, of special learning and uncommon reference, certain failures in expression, and a few miserably ingenious turns or conceits which can only be characterized as mistakes. There were many more of these in poems excluded from *The Helmsman* or discarded completely; what remained were kept for the virtues of the rest of the poem and they were such as seemed ineradicable in revision without destroying the whole.

The poems in *The Helmsman* were arranged roughly in chronological order, and hence there was in the successive poems of the book a story; but it was not any reader's story, and it was not the conventional novel that some knowledge of the external events might prompt the reader to reconstruct. It could be told as well in technical terms as in dramatic; it could be regarded as the history of a style.

His native style was dry, abstract, tightly formal. It derived its texture from a chastity of diction and a crispness of technique, and its inner structure from some odd turn and complication of thought. It was a style without softness, downright, somewhat angular, more assured than it should have been. It was a style that, though capable of poetic effects, was essentially in the current sense unpoetic and certainly unlyrical. It got its drive from a white passion for exactitude of statement, and filled its lines with the residues of a mind that was too nimble—not, he hoped, tangled and confused, but crisscrossed and webbed with subtlety and distinctions and fragments of special learning.

Hence the history of the style in general was the history of an endeavor to attain, on the one hand, what may be called a poetic surface, with its attendant mastery of imagery, of human irrationality, of associative rhetoric, and of the full line in which sound and the choice of diction implicate feeling. This was the pursuit of what was then called sensibility. To this end he contrived poems that were schemes of experience. On the other hand, it was the history of the pursuit of simplicity. But the simplicity sought was not that which comes from an ignorance or rejection of the prolific complexity of thought or of thought's duty to approximate the wrinkled lineaments of experience and truth. It was a simplicity that would fix with an air of easiness and a lack of strain all the qualifications and hesitations that shade the vulgar outline of thought into a simulacrum of honesty and life. It was an attempt by this or that slight translation of the axes of reference, by some sharp attack from an untraditional center, though with all the appearance of tradition—for only thus does simplicity seem to be simple—to define the nimble and compounded lattice of qualification and distinction and the inescapable novelty of point of view to which time and logic had driven him. He returned at last to direct statement.

Perhaps the clearest example in this book of his native style and of the special difficulties inherent in it was *Lector Aere Perennior*. It was angular, dry, fairly lacking in poetic grace or adornment. What the poem says was somewhat original, and the gadgets used to say it were dependent on technical terms and not too common learning. The title referred to the famous ode in which Horace claimed that in his poems he had built a monument more enduring than bronze, a variant of the classical commonplace that furnished the first line: "Poets survive in fame." The poem was developed by means of the scholastic concepts of substance, matter, and form, a philological pun on breath, spirit, and inspiration, the theological notion of imputation, and by the metaphorical use of the Pythagorean doctrine of the transmigration or metamorphosis of souls. Yet, however gadgety, it was all statement.

One could hardly blame a reader for finding the poem difficult or obscure. Yet in this case the difficulty was perhaps legitimate. The special terms and knowledge employed were sufficiently commonplace to those few readers who had studied the Latin tradition so that there was a real, though small, audience to whom the poem was directly addressed. Furthermore, none of the details was used simply for its own sake or for ornamental or extraneous reasons. And finally, the poem though difficult was figurable; explanation will add nothing to the poem that is not implicit in the text.

The sense of the Latin epigraph (*Perire constat auctores, ruere monumenta, lectorem manere aere perenniorem*) was: "The writer dies, his bust crumbles on the shelf, the reader only remains."

The poem said: We are told that the immortality of a writer consists in the fact that his name lives. Yet this is no immortality that relates to him, for he was as a man an integrated substance of body and spirit and his work as a writer was a similarly integrated substance of text and meaning, whereas a reputation is a mere name. Insofar as he continues in a recurrent existence he lives as the text of his writings. This is the inert clay which a sympathetic reader can inform with the breath of existence if he has the irrational trick of assuming the spirit of the author, of inviting a kind of transmigration of soul. The text only is constant, but in this reader or that it may come to life again with the soul of its original meaning. Hence a writer's immortality as such lies in the possibility of his work's being realized again by some reader or other. The author dies; his text is inert; the reader is his life.

But the earliest poems in the book, *The Wandering Scholar's Prayer to St. Catherine of Egypt* and *The Dogdays,* were ones in which his native style was breaking down of itself, the unsimplified elements becoming refractory to plain statement, and in which, at the same time, it was being somewhat deliberately shattered and reformed in pursuit of modern feeling, of shadows and blunted light. Hence the alteration of tradition which in *The Dogdays* predicated "unachieved intent" of the full light of noon. He was becoming a little lost in the post-romantic chiaroscuro. He had said in an earlier poem (*Distinctions at Dusk*): Reason is light which distinguishes reality into shapes and shadows, but there are times and conditions in which all is shaded or light so diffused that nothing is distinguishable. Such are the obscure regions of spiritual pride where the sharp edge of reason cannot penetrate, yet such regions can in their own terms and by their own methods be mapped and charted. Similarly the dusk in a later poem (*Coffee*) represented the same area of engrossing irrational experience, one that did not respect the distinction between subjective and objective ("That no glass can oppose"), and hence was similar to the pantheistic experience, though different in quality. You cannot take these by the throat and throttle them, for there is nothing to get your hands on; you must outwait and outwit them; you must distract yourself and them by some odd device or other. Yet there were values there, curious accessions of insight and energy, intimations beyond the routine, and an ordering of all by an adjustment to the consistent grayness of a mood. But there was also waste and the perception of waste.

The Dogdays, then, was the first issue of what he called privately the quest of the opal: the attempt to court and possess, and at the same time disinterestedly to understand, roughly what was then called sensibility: the province of modern art, the deep well of creativity, the secret and sacred recesses of personality, the Gothic chamber of modern psychology, and the fall of light among the teacups. But an opal, particularly the deep fire opal, derives its color and attraction from flaws in the stone. If this were all, the flaws would be virtues. But any accidental sharp knock, as on the side of a basin while one is washing his hands, may cause the stone to crack; and though it remain in its setting for a while, in some unguarded moment the pieces will fall out, and one will have the ring without the jewel, the promise without the fulfillment. Yet he was not wholly at the mercy of magic and chance; he had his own sources, his unornamented being, and could return to them enriched by what he had lost. Hence it was a quest in which he succeeded for his own purposes and failed to all appearances, and need no longer feel any need of.

The whole course of this quest, so far at least as it was implicated in personal relationships, was clearly anticipated in *The Dogdays,* though it preceded by nine and a half years the conclusion. Yet it may be regarded not only as anticipatory of the undetermined future, but almost as an epilogue, a summary after the event, detailing the plot. So one may reflect that if there be an element of determinism in human personality, other than the mechanical determinism of flesh and nerve or the impingement of external event, of necessity and chance, this determinism may very well reside in that awareness in the individual which from the beginning supplies the lines of approach and of action, and which will, as it were quite unnoticed, demand the fulfillment in event, the artistic resolution in the real world, of its early perception. One's awareness conditions him, and conditions the response of others. That which he saw must be coped with will actualize itself because he saw it, and hence in the obvious sense cannot be coped with. We are determined by awareness, and we live only to accept and to adjust ourselves to the brutal fulfillment in the outer world of our insight. Premonition is destiny. Such at least will be the case when the attitude toward the situation is from the beginning adjusted to its necessary issue, though the full predication of necessity can only unfold in time.

The poems which followed in this sequence were not written after the event to illustrate a story or to develop a judgment, but were contrived from time to time out of the context of circumstance and idea. *All Choice is Error,* though it was overdecorated in the first half, contained in the middle an outrageous conceit, and was in fact the forced yoking together of two attempts, originally addressed to two quite different young women, nevertheless

596

stated in the latter half an idea of the greatest importance, if not generally, at least for the author. It was not an idea that would have come to him, as we say, naturally, from his training and his associates, nor was it one that intrigued him and that he found pleasant to play with. In fact, he did not know how it came or how it developed, except that it issued from the frame of experience: it was impersonal in that he could not evade it. It was the notion of particularity and of choice, and especially the formula which has shocked everyone that ever stopped to look at it, as it shocked him: "All choice is error." For choice implies exclusion, rejection, restriction, limitation. To choose *this* is not only to prefer one thing to something else, but rather to prefer it to everything else.

The doctrine was developed in a later poem, *Haecceity.* The subject of that poem was metaphysical evil, evil as a defect of being. Any realized particular, anything which is this and not that and that, is by the very fact evil. For to be this is to exclude not only any other alternative but to exclude all else in the universe. Perfection is in possibility, in the idea, but that which is realized, specific, determined, has no possibilities. It is precisely this and nothing else at all. It is lacking in all the being of the universe other than its own particularity. The more realized a thing is the greater its defect of being; hence any particular choice is as such evil though morally it may be the best choice.

It follows that the fundamental compulsion of one's life (*Epigram 36*) is not love, lust, gregariousness, the will to live, or any of the emotions or instincts assigned to man. It is that to live is at every moment to be and to do some particularity: in this respect *what* does not matter, only it must be something. The void must be specified. Loneliness is an intimation of the void which we attempt to defeat by some more notable specification.

Haecceity, or thisness, is the primal and ultimate compulsion of one's life; it is the principle of insufficient reason. But there is considerable human danger in too sharp an awareness of this truth. For if choice is purely arbitrary, as essentially it is, there is no reason we should not be purely arbitrary in choosing. Hence one's choices may have in them a good deal of the precipitancy and doggedness of despair.

The problem is certainly central, and very likely insoluble. For it is not merely philosophy but one's life. If he accepts the classic solution in which choice is thought of as the inevitable result in action of reasoned and considered judgment, then choice is completely determined in such fashion that the moral agent may be assured he has inescapably moved toward the best. Hence what he moves toward will be best, hence reasonable, and appetite is confounded with judgment. It is true that in classical ethics the rightness of right reason is considered to be constantly imperiled by passion, against which one must be unremittingly and warily on guard. But the consequence of this position is to enforce an absolute dualism of reason and passion, unmanageable except, perhaps, by religious and ritual means. And when such means must be invoked they tend insensibly to take primacy over reason, until through the dualism of reason and passion they come ultimately to be identified with passion, and with a passion that now, under the pseudo-authority of its impersonal source, delivers the personality to the absolute dictates of passion: called God, or that parody of God in the courtly tradition, Love.

He attempted to outwit this problem by the nature of his choice and the way in which he construed it. Hence, the central poem in this series was *The Beacon,* which seemed to be but was not at all Platonic. Its theme was commonplace. It was the problem of identity and difference in the special context of love. We identify ourselves with the object insofar as it is our own construction to which we can impute our own feelings; we distinguish it as object insofar as it is distinct from us, and as such it is ground for reflection and judgment. But this is commonplace in the sense of being ordinary only if the distinction does not in our special circumstances strike us, only if the problem is not a problem.

The point here is one of more general application. A good many arguments are over whether to take a proposition as an organizing insight into experience or as a truism. It is a question of concern: the subsidence of concern about an idea is its reduction to a truism. In this case the problem was really a problem: the distinction proved in time to be an ineradicable difficulty.

The poem said, in brief: Men give their hearts away but cannot pass judgment on this act so long as they construct the object of love according to their desires, for the will takes pleasure in begetting its own image. I on the contrary choose an object other and distant, a cold landmark toward which contemplation looks. The object remains apart, but let us hope that in time it may be possessed.

Or again, at greater length: The allegiances of the heart are absolute—our early loyalties are given and the later ones of reverence, of friendship, or of love are as emotional commitments unavoidable, and as such beyond our control. But if we give allegiance merely to allegiance, if the object is regarded merely as the shape of our needs or as the arbitrary name we give to our emotional life, there is no room for reason, reflection, or judgment. There is no otherness involved, for the will is delighted to beget itself. Hence we must reserve prestige for the external and the distant, the distinct and the remote. By this contrivance the will is deceived—its allegiance is no less committed but the impossibility of identifying itself with the object leaves the judgment free to contemplate and to assess. Yet this is a desperate situation and certainly not to be enjoyed for itself. Let us hope that before death revokes the possibility of fulfillment we may possess the object in its immediacy without sacrificing the distinctions of judgment. The desire to accomplish this in this life removes the poem from a Platonic or a Christian context.

But once allegiance has been assigned (*Choice*) and its irrevocability sealed in the Absolute, once it has been as possessed as things are in this world, how shall one live? Only by protecting himself against the consequences of his extravagance in the daily routine of society. That such a program did not in this instance work out too well, or that its working out entailed a disproportionate cost, may be conjectured from the lethargic resignation of *Summer Idyll,* the rather terrible inertia of a late June afternoon when the ripe apricots fall in the sullen orchard with a foreboding sound. In the poem the scenery of the immediate occasion, the Santa Clara valley in California, is transposed into imagery derived from his early life on the Montana plains. Though for many years he had scarcely recalled, and certainly never meditated on, any image or experience of his early life, he found that the patterns of his deepest feelings were most often clothed in the landscapes of that time.

By "ecstacy" in the first line of the original version of this poem he meant that standing apart from oneself, so that the personality, separate, retired, remote, and apparently inert, ripens and comes to fulfillment in its own internal term, a fulfillment of so absolute a value that it need never be manifested—the apparent unconsciousness of ripening may pass without a sigh into the unconsciousness of death. It is not precisely that "emotional maturity" which we use so handily on others, but rather an inner ripening through whatever quiet or hectic experiences, from which issues in time of trial, certainly not mastery or wisdom or insensibility, but a central poise arising from a boredom almost with one's own most primary concerns.

The poems that conclude this series were written almost on successive days. *August Hail, This Tower of Sun,* and *Autumn.* The first issued from a context similar to that of *Summer Idyll.* Its subject was the sudden incidence of passion, which comes like an impersonal force and apparently from the outside; and it had a moral: "Who shall revenge unreason?" though it destroy all. The meter of the poem was accentual: four, three, four, and two accents a line.

But what shall one do with passion? He wrote at this time a poem on the subject (*Passion*) in which he developed a pun on the word, on passion in the ordinary sense as an aspect of love and passion as the philosophic complement of act. The pun is taken as implying reality. Passion in the ordinary sense is here said to involve all that is unrealized in any particular act of love. By definition, then, it is unrealizable in terms of act. But in its own terms, as involving all the potentialities of love, surmised or rejected, it is latent in each act, surrounds it and gives resonance to it. The act is the tone of which passion is all the overtones. By this device he found a place for all those possible experiences that haunted his appetite and for which circumstance or morality afforded no actual place.

In *This Tower of Sun* he represented a decision on the alternatives suggested by the incidence of passion. The romantic experience of stillness and light, occurring in some solitary natural surrounding, with its quasi-mystical intimation of a vague absolute beyond, other than, or above the realized entelechy, he said, is an illusory experience. As illusion, of course, it has a certain existence, for an illusion is a reality which we prefer to disregard or to disvalue. It is a discriminated part of reality, marked off from what we normally call the real by applying the ancient distinction between Appearance and Reality, though both are real.

But to return to the poem: The quiet of this glade into which he suddenly emerges is merely relative; the illusion of absolute quiet is imported into the scene by the willful inattention of the observer. And the sudden almost palpable sunlight which strikes him as he comes out into such a clearing in the woods reveals at the same time the surrounding trees which are the instruments of the illusion. The feeling of absolute light derives from the contrasting shade which the light itself makes clearly visible.

The experience of romantic love is analogous, and its phantom object is contrived as willfully as the romantic object of such quasi-mystical experiences. But only a realized particular embodies the concept of love, the true ideal. What might be conjectured from such an experience as this—a romantic, higher, unrealized love—is precisely the absence of the Absolute; it is the undifferentiated many, realizable in no particular one, for if realized it would no longer have its characteristic property of being unspecific. This is a later application of the doctrine of choice, and represents in manner a return to the abstract and dry, to a poetry of statement.

The series was concluded in *Autumn,* a poem just short of successful, in which the whole manner of the quest was devoted to acquiescence in what amounted to its abandonment. Here experience has ripened for the harvest, the time of falling leaves, the time of acceptance—even of indifference—when grief is subdued to the resignation of the season. For the mellowing of the heart and the parallel dispersal of hope—like leaves flying in an autumn storm—is only what should be expected from the passing of time, and it should be accepted without rebellion. This is, if you will, a manifestation of tiredness of spirit, an embracing of fatigue. And so you may object that no sound moralist should retire and live sufficient to himself, seeking, as it were, a cloistered virtue. He answered that this is but the necessary act of the man of experience, the tried. He cannot keep the occasions of adventure or of hope far *from* his heart—he is not so much *The Scarecrow*—but he may and will keep them hidden far *in* his heart. He is acquainted with the occasions of adventure whose symbol is the passing train, but he will not heed their persuasions for he knows there is in them no abiding rest.

This in effect concluded the quest. Beyond this there was only the unraveling, the protracted dissipation of anger, and the return to himself and the lean winds of his own country. On the publication of his book he revived that final crisis in memory, and recorded the vision in an epigram (*Epigram 17*) that wore a deliberate air of obscurity, having a dark elevation consonant with its tone. But only the air of obscurity made it seem obscure. He interrogated an image of experience as if he would fix it by name and dispel the fears of spirit that came with its apparition. But he knew very well who it was and what were the fears. It was a ghost he had laid and, as a man will, had conjured again, whose values were an envisaged, though rejected, way of life, still happily unstayed by the voice of desire, still escaping though called, and escaping because dismayed by the intrinsic fears for which it had been previously rejected. The ghost was not the person—no ghost is—but the experience the person evoked: the temptation to the continued pursuit of the quest but transposed now into the vagrant way of life of *The Wandering Scholar*.

For concurrent with this series of poems was another, the poems that deal with those early experiences out of which his aptitude for the abstract and dry had been formed and corrupted. The earliest of this series, *The Wandering Scholar,* in which the passing train first occurs, attempts like the earliest and latest of the other, *The Dogdays* and *Autumn,* to apprehend and order those experiences by one of the recurrent schemes of irrationality in modern poetry: This is the scheme in which a scene is presented by details which implicate a personal situation and a mood, out of which a comment is struck that narrows the application of the scene, and then the poem curves oft like the curve of an hyperbola into some more general image of, perhaps, sunset or light, and leaves the reader, if he cooperates in the journey, soaring off into the vast or the remote. But this scheme was not native to him, who lived rather with the consecutive propositions of thought: it pressed on him with the urgency of experience demanding notice and evasion.

The details of *The Wandering Scholar* were in part realistic details from his year of wandering during the depression, apprehended as poetic lines through the structure of a rather irresponsible wit ("Clicking their heels"), through a Hart Crane-ish violence of epithet ("the ravelled faces of the park" are unshaven), and especially through that forced association, though it seemed natural at the time, of fragments of special learning with quite other aspects of life and feeling which it is now fashionable to call metaphysical. There was certainly a good deal of similarity between the kind of detail in this poem and in the dedicatory poem, but the material was more personal, the references less integrated in consecutive syntax, and the feeling not so subdued to the firmness of thought. The structure of the poem was in part a device for alluding to jagged bits of experience, and only in part itself a structure of experience. Yet on the far edge of one's nerves the poem held together.

For, if a man goes down at night to see the freight trains rumble into an unspecified distance, and if he is homeless and desperate, with tags of Latin learning and an inherited tradition of Catholicism that is as homeless as he is himself, he may well conceive that Catherine, the patron saint of scholars who was martyred by being racked on a wheel, is racked on these. At least at that age and in those circumstances the conceit will serve the purpose of stiffening some discordant experience into a few lines of verse. But the subject of the poem is the loss or betrayal of all one's early loyalties; hence the central comment, "Not unabsolved do they grow rude," for though one is never absolved by his associates, he is so absolutely.

The range of experiences which this poem refers to were handled again in *The Helmsman: An Ode, A Moral Poem,* and *Montana Pastoral.* The last was a curt autobiography, written seven years after the others, in which the details of fear, thirst, hunger, and the desperation of this huddled chill were hardly a just summary of his first twenty years but rather an epigrammatic presentation of the salient motives those years communicated to his later life.

The Helmsman: An Ode was more ambitious in dealing with the same material. It was in the first place an attempt to imitate the Horatian ode, in external form and in internal structure. The meter of the poem was intended to achieve in English the effect of the Alcaic strophe. It consisted of four lines, each of a different metrical pattern, so that the strophe stood out as a unit without the use of rhyme, though rhyme was admitted here and there as a figure of diction. The line consisted, to use the ordinary terminology, of a combination of disyllabic and trisyllabic feet, with the unaccented syllable at the end of the first two lines combining with the unaccented syllable at the beginning of the following line to give a further suggestion of trisyllabic feet. But the trisyllables were so arranged that whenever they began to gallop off with the poem they were pulled up short with disyllabics. The lines, however, admitted the ordinary substitutions and variations of standard meter, except that extra syllables were not admitted. The pattern, then, differed essentially from the ordinary patterns of standard meter in that the various feet occur at predetermined places and not as free variations. The *Elegy for a Cricket* employed the same kind of meter, in this case an imitation of the Catullan hendescasyllabics.

There were three other examples of metrical experiment in his book: the accentual meter of *August Hail,* and of *Fancy* in which the principle was that each line should have four accents and that there should be no regular pattern of feet; and the syllabic meter of *A Moral Poem,* in which the principle was that each line should consist of five syllables and that there should be no regular pattern of feet.

Helmsman was also an imitation of Horace in its method. The qualities he then saw in the Horatian ode were conceived of in contrast with the medieval Latin lyric, with which he identified, not wholly correctly, his native style. The latter he found uncompromisingly rational and logical in structure and detail. In the former he discerned a unity of sensibility which exhibited the vagaries and unpredictability of experience and resisted an abstract, logical, or classificatory form. Its unity resided in the unformulable feeling that, as the poem unfolded, its length and the arrangement of parts were proper and inevitable: "that just now is said what just now ought to be said." He found that the progression from detail to detail was by a kind of imagic shift or transformation image which, like a train through a tunnel, brings one to a new prospect on the other side of the divide. Under this persuasion he tried the wasp in *The Dogdays* and especially the outrageous root of the tree in *All Choice is Error*. But as he read on in Horace he came to see that the point of the method lay in the transitions from concrete detail to detail: that the transitions were not elliptical in the sense that the poet had merely omitted a chain of thought which the reader was to supply, and that the details themselves did not imply an abstraction that connected them. The meaning lay in the transitions themselves, in a certain balance of sensibility, a nice adjustment between imagery and statement which met the insoluble problems of life with a controlled use of distraction and irrelevance.

He analyzed the famous Soracte ode (1. 9) which begins with an extended description of a midwinter scene and closes with an extended, but in no way parallel, description of a summer love scene. By a relative clause, and in an unemphatic manner, a description of the equinoctial storms is worked in. The sequence of images gives by implication, but by implication only, the theme: that season follows season, and that time is fleeting. The transitions from image to image are effected by generalized statements that are related to but never state the central theme, so that the point of the poem is qualified by images, whole and concrete in themselves, which cannot be said to illustrate the point. They are not subsumed under it as examples; they are rather digressions that prove to be developments.

He attempted to order the experience of his tradition by this method, and wrote his own ode. The poem said: The normal course of a man's life, we are told, is through experience to maturity—to poise, assurance, mastery. The traditional term is wisdom. But such mastery, if in fact it visits us, is only accidental to the process of living, and is at the best casual, fitful, and dependent upon some source of illumination external to the inner personality. Furthermore, it presupposes normal, comfortable, easy circumstances; it is a consequence of good weather. But time may fail us, the loves that render such accomplishment possible may die or disappoint us, so that the very idea of fulfillment is only a childhood memory. There is a certain degree of want and loss, varying with circumstance, that destroys a man's self-respect. So he goes his own way, though the vision of what might have been intrudes from time to time like an importunate panhandler. He cuts free of the past—Ajax and the Grecian isles—putting out his last reserves for a special dinner and a pint of bootleg, and sets forth on his travels. If ever he should feel secure, he will drowse and fall from the wheel like Aeneas' helmsman, Palinurus, whose unburied bones will finally wash up on some unknown shore.

The latter half of the poem was stolen from Horace, *Odes* 1. 7. 21-32, and the *Aeneid* 5. 870-71.

A good deal of the experiences that lay behind these particular poems were bound up with his family, and much that bewildered him was sanctioned by family legend and, though disapproved of, had been ascribed to various of his direct and collateral ancestors. The tradition that surrounded him and formed much of the texture of his early years was the tradition of Irish Catholics along the railroads of the West. To this he finally bade such farewell as one can to his past in *A Moral Poem*. So far as a man's traditions are himself they cannot be altered but they need not be exploited. He who is inured to the past is at liberty to be what he becomes.

He dealt with the specific problem of his religious inheritance in *Timor Dei*. He was a Catholic by tradition, training, and deep feeling, but the Absolute is greedy, as pervasive and as destructively absorbent as sensation or passion or sympathy. Hence his own identity he fenced off, and though it formed part of the terrain it had its property lines. Yet he could look back to the smoke of burning leaves and grass, of the swinging censers, and of breath in the chill northern air of his boyhood and almost acquiesce: for though he would not regret the loss of what he would not have, the traditional patterns of feeling still had power to dominate him.

In brief, by one process or another, through experiences of the kind alluded to in these poems, he had lost almost all his loyalties, though loyalty was his predominant passion. But there still remained the structures of experience which those had satisfied, names calling for an object. In this very formulation of the problem he found the way to solution. He returned to himself, to his own talent for the abstract and dry; he decided he was not a man of sensibility and gave up the quest. He undertook the pursuit of simplicity. He said (in *L'Esprit*). So far as I am—and perhaps it is a matter of temperament—I am the idea that informs my experience; it is the Idea by whose evil eye I am held as men were by the legendary basilisk. He found himself maintaining that the devices of discourse, such notions as identity and diversity, essence and accident, out of which the traditional Absolute had been inferred into existence and dowered with all that its definition denied, so that its light supported all the realms of darkness and the plentitude of its being overflowed into the defect of being—all these were fictions though no less real than the specific which could not become real until apprehended in the form of such fictions.

He applied his doctrine to the quest, and dealt with the problem of universals in *The Metaphysical Amorist*. The idea was there regarded as method, having its own reality as method and having a guarded applicability to social phenomena. There is, for instance, the idea of Love and the situation one finds himself in. These are separate and distinct orders of reality, and yet relatable to each other, as the man who sees is distinct from what he sees and yet his way of seeing determines what it is he sees. The attempt to regard Idea as Phenomenon (Platonic realism), or Phenomenon as Idea (pragmatic nominalism), or to hold a mid-position between these terms (conceptualism) is a mistake. The terms are distinct. The Idea is the method by which we apprehend and order phenomena, yet the phenomena are amenable to various methods. One may have beer bottles and a method for counting them, yet the bottles are distinct from the method and the method from the bottles, and there are different methods.

He expounded his doctrine again in an expository poem, *Reason and Nature,* written a few days after the concluding poems of the other series. The subject was again the relation of method and material, thought and sensation, reason and nature. He said: The pool in a pure frame is the projection of reason in which reason can only see its own construction, and one's notion of his identity is such a construction. The unchanging, unalterable pool, therefore, is a fiction, a device of method. But what we call the real pool, the pool of sensation and experience where we may find a willow or two, is not unrippled. Though the alterations in its surface be as minute as the slight waves caused by skimming flies, these results of chaos and change will exemplify no given rule, will be the realization of no definable method. Nor will any isolatable part of change be a microcosm containing implicitly the whole, nor will it be a calculable curve from which the whole may be inferred. Our experience does not validate induction, just as our postulates have as such no reference.

In brief, he characterized the Idealist as one whose Ideals reflect merely their postulation. He now characterized the Sensationalist as a Narcissus who cannot possibly see his identity on the irrational surface of experience. But if he cannot find it in appearance he can even less find it in the annihilation of immediacy, for an engrossed fusion with experience destroys that distance by which alone any predication can be affirmed.

He asserted that he was both Sensationalist and Idealist, both change and constancy, both material and method. He knew both what he saw and what he thought, confusion and clarity, and though these were distinct and separate the one was applicable to the other, method to material, and applicable only because they were distinct. In this he developed the doctrine of *The Beacon,* but generalized and abstracted it from the special circumstances of that poem. He argued that to say one thing is another (A is A) is to affirm that they are different and yet that their identity is valid and constructible. A man is distinct from his experience or he could not speak of it, yet he is his experience or it would not be his. He must be both disinterested and engrossed.

He saw now that the pursuit of sensibility had been the pursuit of an engrossment in immediacy of experience, but immediacy by definition cannot be talked about, cannot yield a line of verse. Perhaps one sees himself immediately, which is as much as to say that the self is the self. But from this point of view, from the point of view of the concentrated duration of consciousness, all one's thoughts and actions are in an ultimate sense unreal. They are mistakes, if you will, since they are objectifications of the self and as such are other than the self; hence they have not the self's immediate validity except insofar as this is imputed to them by the customary psychic sleight of hand.

The appeal to immediacy of experience is always a recourse. It is always an apology and a defense of some thoughts and actions, for these are objectifications of the self, and only these need apology. On the level of immediacy, of the purely subjective (if it exist), no one needs apology or can offer it. What is is, and even this is to say too much. But one's thoughts and actions must either be sufficiently integrated in themselves so that for the most part they form a satisfactory structure of personality; or this failing, either because of the refractory nature of the materials or because of some failure in persistency and comprehensiveness of insight, the objectifications must be confused with the self by a desperate or innocent ambiguity so that these may then draw validity from the unassailable validity of the immediate.

Thus whenever one speaks in a critical situation of the immediate and the unique, whenever one invokes the primary self as an ultimate source of appeal, this is only a device, and sometimes a dodge, for denying the existing, available, obtruding categories of integration for the purpose of discovering or substituting others. The appeal to the self is obviously an objectification in the sense defined and not an immediacy, for on the level of immediacy no one acts or thinks; there everything is absolute simply because it undifferentiatedly is. In fine, immediacy is a methodological fiction, but a fiction is an Idea and not an immediacy. Hence the applicability of method to material, reason to nature, Idea to immediacy, is the necessary and irreducible postulate, and neither term can be sacrificed to the other.

Finally he observed that judgment and sympathy were terms of the same order and he wrote another book in which this was the theme.

THE JOURNAL OF JOHN CARDAN

I

When I began writing some years ago I had a shocking amount of assurance. I knew right and wrong, truth and error, and it all formed much of a system—what holes there were in it I knew could be worked out. But I feel quite differently now. It isn't that I've become anything so innocent as a sceptic or so crude as disillusioned; it is that I am left with limited insights, the plain implications of experience but restricted in generality, and cold assumptions whose systematic development unfolds as one lives them. These you might say constitute a group of points of whose location I am fairly assured; the curve that embraces them and the equation that generates the curve I trust are figurable. But there is all that paper that the curve will not enclose, if it be a closed curve, all those propositions that I used to make or that I now read in others' books but can make no sense of, can find nothing to refer them to. So perhaps the fragmentary form of these notes is not merely the result of exigency but rather proper to the form of my thought and experience.

II

To what extent does scandal reside in the dissemination of specific circumstances, of realistic detail, which invite the hearer to reenact the scene and at the same time offer to his attention those items of commonness and vulgarity which qualify the generalities of passion, evil, or social mischance that were the basis of scandal? In these latter some dignity is to be found, at least in the generality of application to others, and in private surmise to the hearer's self. But realistic detail impedes this effect, localizes the general in the particular places, times, and persons concerned, and makes it difficult for one to conceive that this could happen to him who is not those persons nor was in those times and places. So the foundation for sympathy is displaced and there is left chiefly the malice of discomfort at this disturbance of one's social security; the threat to oneself, being suppressed, grows malignant, and the arrogance of spiritual superiority is given full scope.

III

Where the issue of our commitments denies even a reasonable fulfillment to our desires we must act in accordance with the commitment, even to the extent of effectively pretending that we enjoy what cannot be altered. We can do this without in the least denying the existence, or the validity, or even the power of desire. So we save ourselves from the sentimental death of the heart, and at the same time protect ourselves from engrossment in our wayward wishes. For a man must live divided against himself: only the selfishly insane can integrate experience to the heart's desire, and only the emotionally sterile would not wish to.

IV

The current attitude toward love usually ignores the element of want or need, for it spreads from the protected children of the middle class who have never seen want face to face and whose needs wander among the luxuries, since they are provided with the necessities, of life. But need is more important than sentiment, for it simply is while the latter comes and goes and enjoys its own ambiguities. Hence another's need lays obligations upon us which we cannot reject without moral damage to ourselves, while another's sentiment is merely an invitation to share in the exploitation of his leisure.

V

No one will deny, what is overwhelmingly obvious, the immediacy and absoluteness in itself of one's primary experience. But this is by definition self-sealed, isolated, and incommunicable, whether this be its glory or its defect. To speak or to think or to write is to go beyond this, and even to risk—to put to the wager— this. For to write is to confront one's primary experience with the externally objective: first, with the facts of experience and with the norms of possibility and probability of experience; secondly, with the objective commonality of language and literary forms. To be successful in this enterprise is to integrate the subjectively primary, the immediate, with the objectively communicable, the mediate, to the alteration of both by their conformation to each other, by their connexity with and their immanence in each other. It is the conquest of solipsism, the dramatic conflict of self with, on the one hand, reality in all its objectivity and potentiality, and, on the other, with philology in its old and general sense: or, with private and with public history.

VI

No dignity, except in silence; no virtue, except in sinuous exacting speech. So a scrupulosity toward experience promotes scandal, and a scrupulosity toward scandal invites inertia, or dignity devoid of quickness and virtue.

VII

I have been reflecting on the common notions about intellectualism. I have observed that the intellectual, unless it be a fraud, derives its content and its vitality from emotion and experience. An intellectual distinction is both an emotional experience in itself, in the perception of it, and a realignment of the emotional experiences which are the content of the distinction. Hence the history of a man's thought is memoir as well as the history of his emotional life; and each of these, together with the other elements that could be distinguished, furnishes content and form to the other.

VIII

Contradictions are not to be put down side by side and gaily dismissed, as if this testified to a profundity that embraced the complexity of human nature. Nor are they to be admitted as a debater's device, to show how broadminded, even how humble, one is, for this is really to be so confident of one's conclusions that he can dispose of all difficulties by cheerfully admitting them. But this is not to say that contradictions are to be resolved by some dialectical agility: they are rather where the problem lies, and a sign that one's methods are unapt.

IX

The operations of logic, at least as far as regards the mind in its effort to grasp a logical method or distinction, are not so much subtle as massive. When we reflect on the process involved we feel that it cannot be expressed by the figures of thrusting and penetrating, of cutting and biting: what seems perhaps to others to be in effect a fine distinction has to the mind that achieved it no quality of thinness or edge. For logical apprehension seems rather to involve the moving of large blocks until—it may be suddenly—they settle deeply into place. We know they are in place because they settle, and though we test them they will not move.

X

In connection with Rilke one might develop, among other ideas that now occur to me: 1) the hierophantic style which issues from the concept of the poet-priest, an elevated obscurity whose most notable stylistic device is the rhetorical question; and 2), the Rilkean ideal involved in his notion of love, of death, of angels, and all the religious apparatus of surrender and goblin-chasing—an ideal whose pragmatic basis seems to be that state of feeling, that disturbed somatic exaltation which characterizes a woman in love, together with her active desire for passivity and surrender. But it is the state of feeling as such which is held valuable, and the effort is bent toward sustaining and prolonging that state by a skillful romantic excitation while denying to it any release either in the gross physical discharge of some sexual act, in the integration of that feeling into the social world by associating it with some person, or by directing its reference toward a theological structure of some definite content. It remains in Rilke both erotic and religious, but the eroticism is directed toward nubile and shadowy objects, and the theological structure is consciously emptied of as much content as possible, what is left being deliberately rendered ambiguous and confused.

XI

One recognizes with the misgivings of experience the imminence of the state of passion, of engrossed choice of an object to love. But the state of passion is an emanation of the indeterminable sources of personal identity, the void region of possibilities where dwells the promise of multiple and unrestricted fulfillments. The realm of history, personal or public, where particular acts occur in particular times and places is something else again. Hence love, the allegiance of passion to a given external object, betrays this inner void whose principle of being is to be neither this nor that, to be pregnant with every possible future, because not committed to any particular one. But choice turns the unconditioned idea into a conditioned process, into a succession of acts whose ultimate intention gives structure to each as it happens, while the feeling that surrounds each act hurries it on to its successor. So intimation falls away into fact.

XII

The premises of a logical or nonhistorical system are: 1) the causes determine the effect; 2) the fact, which is an effect, is an instance of the general, and hence the effect as a realized fact involves no element of radical novelty; and usually 3), the process is reversible, that is, nontemporal. The principles of order are therefore causal result and subsumption of instance under rule. But the premises of historical systems, on the other hand, are: 1) the effect determines the causes, or the principle of *post hoc, ergo propter hoc,* as qualified by some particular doctrine of relevance; 2) the specific fact is something other than an instance of the general, and in truth the general is only a methodological device for distinguishing those aspects of the specific which relate to the particular doctrine of relevance entertained. Hence, 3) the historical process is irreversible in time, since the subsequent effect alters the nature and relationship of the precedent effects which are its cause. But the premises of a historical system are inherently contradictory, since the doctrine of relevance which must be invoked if there is to be any order at all implies the premises of a nonhistorical system. The problem is yet to be solved.

Briefly, then: in nonhistorical systems the cause determines the effect; in historical systems the effect determines the cause.

Balboa and Palo Alto
1942-44

SEVERAL KINDS OF SHORT POEM

Poetry may be thought of in various ways, and the way one habitually thinks of it will qualify the poetry he writes. For definition is not subsequent to action but precedes it; it is not gathered from the result but shapes the result. I do not, for example, ordinarily think of poetry as vision, although I know it sometimes is, and so I have no vision. I have no intuition into the heart of things; I have no special way of seeing. I think of poetry as a way of speaking, a special way of speaking. As a poet I speak in meter, and sometimes in rhyme; I speak in lines. It follows naturally that I am a formalist and that anything that can be said in metrical lines is subject for poetry, even vision, and that anything worth saying should sometime be said. This last adds a principle of value, the principle of what is worth saying as distinguished from what is not. And to this, formalism adds another principle of value, for the aim of the formal is the definitive. A poem, then, on this view is metrical speech, and a good poem is the definitive statement in meter of something worth saying.

Such a view of poetry, if we do not take it too loosely, will somewhat narrow the kinds of poetry one writes. Some poems, for instance, are not in any ordinary sense of the term statements. They are constructs, fiction, things made up. I have written a few such—one, for example, on that mythical bird, *The Phoenix:*

> More than the ash stays you from nothingness!
> Nor here nor there is a consuming pyre!
> Your essence is in infinite regress
> That burns with varying consistent fire,
> Mythical bird that bears in burying!

I have not found you in exhausted breath
That carves its image on the Northern air,
I have not found you on the glass of death
Though I am told that I shall find you there,
Imperturbable in the final cold,

There where the North wind shapes white cenotaphs,
There where snowdrifts cover the fathers' mound,
Unmarked but for these wintry epitaphs,
Still are you singing there without sound,
Your mute voice on the crystal embers flinging.

But this is not my characteristic mode. Of such a poem one does not say that it is definitive or not, but that it is just right or it is not.

Other poems aim at recording a real or imagined personal experience; they are memoir. In such poems, if one has a partiality toward the definitive, the attitude is directed not so much toward the statement as toward the experience. The aim becomes not so much definitive statement as the asseveration under oath that this is exactly the way it was, in fact and feeling. The poems toward the end of this essay illustrate this aim, if not its accomplishment.

The characteristic poem motivated by a concern for definitive statement, however, will be the poem that explains—an expository poem, a statement in the ordinary sense of that word. And it will be short, for the concern for definitiveness is a prejudice for brevity. If one has said something definitively he will not be impelled to amplify, to say it again undefinitively. So the poet who holds this view becomes an epigrammatist. He writes:

When I shall be without regret
And shall mortality forget,
When I shall die who lived for this,
I shall not miss the things I miss.
And you who notice where I lie
Ask not my name. It is not I.

or:

In whose will is our peace? Thou happiness,
Thou ghostly promise, to thee I confess
Neither in thine nor love's nor in that form
Disquiet hints at have I yet been warm;
And if I rest not till I rest in thee
Cold as thy grace, whose hand shall comfort me?

or:

And what is love? Misunderstanding, pain,
Delusion, or retreat? It is in truth
Like an old brandy after a long rain,
Distinguished, and familiar, and aloof.

But the short poem in isolation has the defect of brevity; it comes naked to the reader without a locating context. It cannot build its own world, as *The Faerie Queene* and *The Prelude* do. And so one thinks, if he is committed by temperament and habit to the shorter poem, how he can make it longer.

There are two ways—perhaps there are more, but two I shall speak of here—by which a group of shorter poems can be aggrandized into a work of greater length. Length, however, is only a means; what one wants is a situation in which the several items can lend each other context, reference, and resonance, in which this short poem will be something more than it would be in isolation by belonging to a whole. The first method is an ancient one, invented, we are told, in Rome at the time of Vergil: one sets the poems in a matrix of relevant prose. The most famous, and most influential, work exemplifying this method is Boethius' *The Consolation of Philosophy.* It is the method of Dante's *The New Life.* And in both these works the poems gain stature from the surrounding prose. And, indeed, it is a matter of common observation that the poem we encounter in the course of reading a novel or an essay is more likely to stay in our memory than one read among other poems, for we come to it in a relevant context. Some fifteen to twenty years ago I used this method myself in a little work called *The Quest of the Opal.* There I surrounded a group of my early poems with prose commentary and paraphrase.

There is, however, a problem in the marriage of prose and verse that arises from an ambiguity of attitude on the part of audiences. On the one hand, the audience for poetry is willing, and sometimes eager, to hear the poet speak of his own work, as I am doing now, especially if he can adjoin to the work some anecdotal richness or give some hints of insight into the creative process. Yet the same audience on another occasion will feel, and sometimes strongly, that the poem should not need prose, that it should stand by itself unexplained, that the intrusion of commentary is a confession of failure. There is, then, both an appetite for commentary and a superiority to it, and what at one time is gratefully welcomed, at another is regarded with embarrassment.

There is an alternative way of aggrandizing a group of shorter poems into a work of greater length, and that is the poetic sequence. The sequence is a series of short poems in whose succession there is an implicit structure—in the case I have in mind, a narrative structure. The ancient precedent for the poetic sequence is the *Cynthia* of Propertius, a contemporary of Vergil. It consists of twenty-two or so elegies, what the Germans have called subjective erotic elegies, but though there are narrative elements in that sequence there is no story-line; the several poems are merely related to an established narrative context, and this is also the case with such a Renaissance sonnet sequence as Sir Philip Sidney's *Astrophil and Stella.* The particular form of sequence I have here in mind was invented, I believe, by Tennyson. It is likely that he discovered the form in the process of composing *In Memoriam,* for that sequence began apparently as a series of journal entries, acts of memoir, and was then developed within a structure of ideas and an implicit narrative structure, the Christmas poems marking off the years. Subsequently, he wrote *Maud,* a fictional narrative with primary attention to the emotional aspects, in which the narrative is implicit in the sequence of lyrics. It is an interesting form, though *Maud* is a bad poem.

An interest in a form is an invitation to attempt to realize it. I had entertained the general notion of such a sequence for many years and had designated the areas of experience that would be involved. The poems would deal with the American West, that vast spiritual region from Great Falls, Montana, to El Paso, Texas; from Fort Riley, Kansas, to the sinks of Nevada; and with the California Coast, another and perhaps less spiritual region. And the poems would relate some sort of illicit and finally terminated love affair. And there would be a fusion of the feeling in the personal relationship and the feeling for the West and the Coast. But nothing happened for eight or nine years until a few years ago, driving west through the Dakotas to Sheridan, Wyoming, I composed in memory these four lines:

I drive Westward. Tumble and loco weed
Persist. And in the vacancies of need,
The leisure of desire, whirlwinds a face
As luminous as love, lost as this place.

This was clearly the beginning of the sequence.

I turn now to the sequence in its final form, and say no more of the accidents of composition. It is entitled *To What Strangers, What Welcome,* and consists of an epigraph and fifteen poems. They are of various sorts, in the tradition of *Maud:* epigram, lyric, discourse; construct, memoir or purported memoir, and statement. They are in various formal patterns, some traditional and some as untraditional as octosyllabic blank verse and syllabic meters. Consequently, the unity of the sequence, if it has unity, will not depend on a formal consistency, as in a sonnet sequence, but on the story that is implied. It is, as it must be, a simple story, so common that any audience can supply what must be said between one poem and the next. A traveler drives west; he falls in love; he comes home. The conclusion is anticipated by the epigraph, which consists of some lines from Edwin Arlington Robinson's long Arthurian poem, *Merlin.* It is one of Robinson's finest passages. Merlin is speaking, having just returned to Camelot after three years in Broceliande with the Lady Vivian; he says if he does not go back to her the Lady Vivian will remember him, and say:

"I knew him when his heart was young,
Though I have lost him now. Time called him home,
And that was as it was. . . ."

The sequence proper opens with "I drive Westward," with its intimation of a face "As luminous as love, lost as this place."

There follows:

> On either side of the white line
> The emblems of a life appear
> In turn: purpose like lodgepole pine
> Competitive and thin, and fear
>
> Agile as aspen in a storm.
> And then the twilit harboring
> In a small park. The room is warm.
> And by the ache of traveling
>
> Removed from all immediacy,
> From all time, I as time grows late
> Sense in disordered fantasy
> The sound and smell of love and hate.

And then an unsent letter, meditated at midnight, to no one at all, of which this is the central stanza:

> I'll not summon you, or feel
> In the alert dream the give
> And stay of flesh, the tactile
> Conspiracy.
>   The snow falls
> With its inveterate meaning,
> And I follow the barbed wire
> To trough, to barn, to the house,
> To what strangers, what welcome
> In the late blizzard of time.

After certain unrewarding adventures, a pick-up at one time, at
another a stripper in Las Vegas, the traveler comes to the Pacific:

> the surf breaking,
> Repetitive and varied as love
> Enacted, and inevitably
> The last rim of sunset on the sea.

He has an apartment on the beach:

> The night is still. The unfailing surf
> In passion and subsidence moves
> As at a distance. The glass walls,
> And redwood, are my utmost being.
> And is there there in the last shadow,
> There in the final privacies
> Of unaccosted grace,—is there,
> Gracing the tedium to death,
> An intimation? Something much
> Like love, like loneliness adrowse
> In states more primitive than peace,
> In the warm wonder of winter sun.

The intimation becomes reality:

> A half hour for coffee, and at night
> An hour or so of unspoken speech,
> Hemming a summer dress as the tide
> Turns at the right time.
>   Must it be sin
> This consummation of who knows what?

This sharp cry at entrance, once, and twice?
This unfulfilled fulfillment?
                              Something
That happens because it must happen.
We live in the given. Consequence,
And lack of consequence, both fail us.
Good is what we can do with evil.

At this point "Time called him home, And that was as it was":

I drive Eastward. The ethics of return,
Like the night sound of coyotes on a hill
Heard in eroded canyons of concern,
Disposes what has happened, and what will.

There is the long drive back across the continent, over the high
desert, through the central plains, to the stone walls of New
England:

Absence, my angel, presence at my side,
I know you as an article of faith
By desert, prairie, and this stonewalled road—
As much my own as is the thought of death.

There in the last warmth of a New England autumn the story
comes to an end, and the traveler addresses himself:

Identity, that spectator
Of what he calls himself, that net
And aggregate of energies
In transient combination—some

So marginal are they mine? Or is
There mine? I sit in the last warmth
Of a New England fall, and I?
A premise of identity
Where the lost hurries to be lost,
Both in its own best interests
And in the interests of life.

TECHNOLOGY & POETRY

Over the past ten years I have been told by eight persons on eight occasions at cocktail parties, and I go very seldom to cocktail parties, that they had photocopied my first book in Iowa City. 1 have been told also of unauthorized broadcasts of taped poetry readings. Technology has made one's property freely available, with payment only to Xerox and Wollensak. But such mundane, practical matters are not here the object of concern. I will comment only that with the invention and diffusion of sound recording, we have not only an oral poetry and a written poetry, but also a written oral poetry, not written down from dictation but reproducible as spoken.

But the concern here is rather with those figures of our imagination, the epic heroes of our despair, Technological Man in his Technocratic Society, whether already realized or about to come into being. What will they do to the arts? What will the arts do with them?

Certainly there are relations between what we call the arts and what we call society. I am in one of my roles a historian. I observe that in *Midsummer Night's Dream* the head of state speaks in weighty blank verse, the highborn lovers in blank verse and rhymed couplets, the otherworldly characters may use lyric measures, and Bottom and company speak prose. In *As You Like It* what we would call romantic love is appropriate only to the high born; in them it may be amusing, but in the low born it is ridiculous. The class structure of society is a principle of order in the plays, even in the style.

But there is not only a sociology of the literary work, there is also a sociology of literary men. All the great figures of Elizabethan literature were related directly to the Court. Sir Thomas More and Sir Francis Bacon were Lords Chancellor of England, the highest office of state in precedence if not in power. Sir Philip Sidney was the nephew of two earls, the brother of a countess, and Governor of Flushing. Jonson had a state pension, and Shakespeare was servant to the Lord Chamberlain, later to the King, and on one attested State occasion wore the King's livery.

There are also relationships between my poetry, myself as poet, and the society in which I live and which in part structures my experience. But is that society a technological one? My role and its product, certainly, is premised on print, and on an education in which print is important. But this is too factual for the spirit of this occasion.

For the Idea of Technological Society has nothing to do with fact, much to do with feeling and with fears. It is an invention of rhetoric. It is instant history in the service of other causes. It expresses the fears of a managed society on the part of those who would manage society themselves, who speak of propaganda as if rhetoric and lying were new arts. It is the anti-image of the pastoral myth, or the mad scientist's dream of utopia. In one's name computerized, one's identity an assemblage of bits, is symbolized the rage of the unimportant that they are in fact unimportant. Indeed, the importance of the unimportant is immanent in much modern literature, as in Chekhov or in Williams: "so much depends / upon a red wheelbarrow / full of rainwater / beside the white chickens." So much depends. And, above all, the Technological Society comes with the light of Never Before, *Novus ordo saeculorum*. But new orders, new dispensations, new testaments are quite old. There is a history of Apocalypse: "and, lo, there was a great earthquake, and the sun became black as sackcloth of hair, and the moon became as blood, and the stars of heaven fell unto the earth. . . . For the great day of his wrath is come, and who shall be able to stand." It is apocalyptic vision in the service of that recurrent American phenomenon, Revivalism, which recently possessed the educated classes—a revivalism, however, without Christianity, without established places to put and to structure our irrationalities, that range from astrology and witchcraft to the science-fiction revelation of Technology. This vision has affected some poems but none I know of merit.

But there have been changes in society that do deeply affect poetry. The role of poet as professor or poet as dropout was not available to me when I was young; had they been, my life and poetry would have been different. Indeed, a few years earlier the role itself would not have been available. The class I grew up in, the upper lower class, did not write poetry. The art of compliment, which motivated so many love lyrics, has been lost; and sight-reading has something to do with the breakdown of meter. But let me conclude with two extraordinary changes and their effect on the art of poetry.

Consider the social act of death. This has so changed in my lifetime that any competent anthropologist would be forced to conclude that a whole society had been destroyed and replaced by invaders. Death is no longer ritualized. Men no longer train themselves to die a good death. We have no *Ars Bene Moriendi.* And when did you last see the black armband, the purple wreath? Formal mourning is out of style. This with the dissipation of Christianity, also in my lifetime, has profoundly affected poetry. One may come to the consequence sparely as in this epitaph for oneself:

When I shall be without regret
And shall mortality forget,
When I shall die who lived for this,
I shall not miss the things I miss.
And you who notice where I lie
Ask not my name. It is not I.

One may come to it through the traditional eloquence of blank verse, as in this modern consolation, *Consolatio Nova,* on the death of my friend and publisher Alan Swallow:

To speak of death is to deny it, is
To give unpredicated substance phrase
And being. So the discontinuous,
The present instant absent finally
Without future or past, is yet in time
For we are time, monads of purposes
Beyond ourselves that are not purposes,
A causeless all of momentary somes.
And in such fiction we can think of death.

One may come to it through the casualness of syllabic meter, as in *Think:*

Let us forget praise and blame,
Speak only of quietness
And survival. Mad toadstools
Grow in the dampness, englobed
Enormities, inherited
Treachery of all our pasts.
Forget. What was day is night.

In curtained sufficiency
Rest in the living silence,
Rest in arrogant sleep. Think
What houseflies have died in time.

But one must come to it somehow. Technology has not yet repealed death, and, if it did, who could live with the horror of immortality.

SHAKESPEARE: THREE TEXTUAL NOTES

I wish to propose two emendations in *Othello* and one in *Twelfth Night*.

   A. Othello, 5.1.41-42: Read

>   *Rod.* O wretched villain!   (*Two or three groans*)
>   *Lod.*   'Tis a heavy night:

Quarto 1 (1622) reads, "*Lod.* Two or three grones, it is a heavy"; Folio (1623), "*Lod.* Two or three groane. Tis heavy". An interpolated stage direction, the removal of which gives a divided metrical line.

   B. There is an instance similar to A in *Twelfth Night*, 4.2.12. Folio reads:

>   *Clo.* . . . but to be said an honest man and a good
>   housekeeper goes as fairely, as to say, a carefull man,
>   & a great scholler. The Competitors enter.
>   *Enter Toby.*

The Competitors enter is not text but stage direction, and probably the original direction. I would conjecture that *Enter Toby* is later and editorial.

   C. Othello, 5.2.101-2: Read

Should yawn at alteration.
Emil. [*Within*]   Good my lord,
I do beseech you I may speak with you.

Quarto 1 reads, "alteration. / *Em.* I doe beseech you I may speake
with you,—good my Lord. /"; Folio, "Alteration. / *mil.* I do be-
seech you / That I may speake with you. Oh good my Lord. /"
Good my lord normally precedes a speech (*MM*, 3. 2. 202; *2H4*,
2. 1. 69; *Ham*, 5. 2. 109; *Tmp*, 4.1. 204; contra, *Tim*, 4. 3. 494).
The dash in Quarto 1 may be a clue to, as it is certainly a fre-
quent symptom of, the mislineation (see Quarto *Oth*, 1. 3. 17-18;
1. 3. 171-72; 1. 3. 407-8; et passim). Folio seems an obvious so-
phistication of Quarto 1 to patch the meter and to regularize the
elliptical construction (see Quarto and Folio *Oth*, 1. 3. 220). The
emended lineation gives accurate meter.

A FEW REMARKS ON TRANSLATING

A translation is not the original. Yet, though it must be a poem of its own time and place, it should also be of the time and place of the original. Otherwise, the original is simply a point of departure, an incentive to write one's own poem, comparable to an arresting incident, a compelling idea, or the itch to write.

To succeed in translation is, of course, a matter of relevant knowledge; of motive—in this case I am writing a tiny book on Sappho—; of concern for aspects of the text other than those of literal transcription; and of luck. And one is more likely to be lucky in a short piece than in an extended one, as at the track.

The aspects of the text other than those of literal transcription are those of form, forms of experience and the linguistic forms of speaking in verse. The form of experience in the quatrain attributed to Sappho, is common to many, perhaps to all, ages and peoples. It is found in the old folk, and in the contemporary popular song, and hence the ancient experience is immediately accessible to us.

The principal linguistic form that marks off speaking in verse from speaking in prose is lineation. A poem is phrased not only in the units of syntax but also, and simultaneously, in units of lines which have their own internal linguistic principles. In fact, the quatrain translated is preserved in an ancient handbook on Greek meters, as an example of one of them. The translation, too, is an example of one of our English meters: the lines are each of six syllables, and unobtrusively iambic. And the lineation of the translation reflects, with one unavoidable exception, that of the original, for metrical form is part of the ancient experience.

Finally, translation is fun, and relieves us of the responsibility of being A Poet. We can leave that to the original.

deduke men a selanna

The moon has set now, and
The Pleiades. It is
Midnight, the hours go by,
And I lie here alone.

Commonly attributed to Sappho (ca. 600 B.C.)

Translation by J. V. Cunningham

INTRODUCTION TO A BOOK
OF COMMON VERSE

This is a book of verse, that dying technique, a book to be spoken, to be heard, if only in the mind's ear.

To begin with the obvious: most of the selections in this book are rhymed, as are most of the texts from which they have been selected. Most, not all of course, of the lines end with a completed grammatical pattern: sentence, clause, or phrase. Finally, most of the lines consist of eight or ten syllables in one or other of several patterns of stressed and unstressed syllables. Iambic is the usual form. As in the previous sentence, or in this. Seldom will you find trochaic. Yet at times, as in this sentence. The triple meters, I add—as in Dryden's Song: "Sylvia the Fair"—are rare and special. In brief, the selections are in large part marked by repetitive regularity.

It is said that repetition is monotonous and boring, and it may be. But it is also natural—I can bear with the repetitiveness of breathing—pleasing, reassuring (you know where you are), sometimes unavoidable. It is unifying, has an element of finality, and is an aid to memory. Aristotle in discussing a certain kind of artistic prose which employed some of the features of verse says: "The style has countable elements. That is why anyone can remember verses better than pell-mell prose: verses have number to measure them."

A book of verse, then, with toward the end a scattering of other than traditional verse forms, what is called free verse—which may indeed indicate that verse is a dying technique. But is it a common book?

There are, of course, and have been texts common to groups, societies, generations: the works of Lenin, the sayings of Chairman Mao. For the Baker Street Irregulars the Sherlock Holmes Stories. Harriet Beecher Stowe has described the common books of a young woman in rural New England, several miles outside of Newport, in the 1790s:

> A small table under the looking glass, bore the library of a well-taught young woman of those times. *The Spectator*, *Paradise Lost*, Shakespeare, and *Robinson Crusoe* stood for the admitted secular literature, and beside them the Bible and the works then published of Mr. Jonathan Edwards. Laid a little to one side, as if of doubtful reputation, was the only novel which the stricter people in those days allowed for the reading of their daughters: that seven-volumed, trailing, tedious, delightful old bore, Sir Charles Grandison.

And historians have observed how the school readers of the later Nineteenth Century in America, and indeed of my youth, gave a sense of unity to peoples without a common past: "As for me, give me liberty or give me death;" "We hold these truths to be self-evident . . ." And from poems, memorized, not merely read: "Here once the embattled farmers stood / And fired the shot heard round the world." The experience was social, not private, and hence political. A shared experience, belongingness, the recognition of allusions, a sense of heritage.

But the book you have here, though not without social and political context, is a transformed book. It is the Book of the Best, not morally, not politically, but aesthetically. And in the transformation there is loss. The belongingness of the shared text, and its truth, though not irrelevant, are not of primary concern. The appreciative experience is. Indeed, the Bible itself has undergone this transformation in the university; it is read as literature and not as revelation.

The archetypal common book of shorter poems in this tradition is *The Golden Treasury: Selected from the Best Songs and Lyrical Poems in the English Language* by Francis T. Palgrave (1861). The common books of Mrs. Stowe's heroine were not chosen by her after some years of browsing; they were given by tradition, the common books of that tight little society. In contrast, Palgrave selected his texts, in part, of course, attested to by prior judgements, in part suggested or corroborated by friends whose judgement he trusted, but, as he says, "for the final choice the Editor is alone responsible." In brief, tradition is individualized.

It is also in Palgrave and his successors narrowed. The Idea of Poetry as the lyrical, as occupied with the Sense of Beauty, excludes from its domain the greater part of human experience. It will admit, perhaps, Pope on the Good life (*Ode on Solitude*) but not Prior's *An Epitaph* on two who led that for them vacant life. It has no place for Greville's Scoggin or Swift's *Clever Tom Clinch Going to be Hanged.* For by Palgrave's time prose, especially the novel, had taken over much that had formerly been assigned to verse. A poem was what was left when all the novels had been written. In our own century, however, poets have sought to reclaim their ancient territory, as in Robinson's "The Clerks" or Frost's "Directive." Indeed, the vogue of free verse, in the form of lineated prose, is part of this attempt—as in Robert Lowell's "Memories of West Street and Lepke".

Finally, in Palgrave the principle of historical sequence is introduced, though in aesthetic terms. For the young woman in Mrs. Stowe's novel, Job, Shakespeare, and Sir Charles Grandison were contemporaries, and equally available to her. For Palgrave, and for us, this is no longer possible: "The English mind has passed through phases of thought and cultivation so various and so opposed during these three centuries of Poetry, that a rapid passage between old and new . . . will always be wearisome and hurtful to the Sense of Beauty." Hence he distributes his selections into four books. "They might be called the Books of Shakespeare Milton, Gray, and Wordsworth."

But it is hurtful to more than the Sense of Beauty; it is hurtful to the sense of the poem. For times change, and with them not only linguistic forms but also forms of experience. The wondering acceptance of the fact of the Incarnation in the anonymous "A God, and Yet a Man," and the act of perfect contrition addressed to the Triune God in Jonson's "To Heaven" become in Stevens' "Sunday Morning":

> The tomb in Palestine
> Is not the porch of spirits lingering.
> It is the grave of Jesus, where he lay.

or to Larkin, as he meditates in an empty church:

> Superstition, like belief, must die,
> And what remains when disbelief has gone?
> Grass, weedy pavement, brambles, buttress, sky . . .

But the latter experiences assume and include the former. It is in this sense, in the fulness of tradition, that this is a common book. May it also in the other sense become a common book.

INTERVIEW WITH J. V. CUNNINGHAM:
TIMOTHY STEELE

The following interview took place during the afternoons of September 12th, 13th, and 14th of 1983, in the basement study of J. V. Cunningham's home in Sudbury, Massachusetts. Though Cunningham had expressed doubts about being interviewed, he approached the occasion cordially. At one point in earlier correspondence, he had suggested: "The session—or sessions—should be planned, but still should have an oral context—like Homeric epic—to compare big things with little." Following this suggestion, I sent in advance a roster of questions, and these provided the basis of discussion. Once the interview began, however, it ranged independently over many topics concerning Cunningham's writing and career.

Anyone who meets Cunningham and who has read his poetry cannot help but be struck by the extraordinary—one might say almost physiognomic-resemblance between the man and his work. Lean and acute, Cunningham conveys an impression of great intelligence and scrupulosity. He is no more given to wasting words in conversation than to wasting them in poems, and when he says something one feels in the utterance a weight of care and reflection. At the same time, his speech and personality possess a quiet sympathy which makes him an engaging as well as an enlightening conversationalist. As the tapes wound from spool to spool on the low table between us, he spoke with precision yet without any indication of constraint.

J. V. Cunningham was born in Cumberland, Maryland, on August 23, 1911. As he remarks in the interview, his family moved west when he was young, and he grew up mainly in Billings,

Montana, and Denver. After his graduation from high school and a semester at St. Mary's College in Kansas, Cunningham worked in Denver and traveled for a while in the Southwest, doing freelance writing for the trade journals. Eventually, he entered Stanford University, where he received a B.A. in Classics and a Ph.D. in English. He subsequently taught at a variety of universities, including Hawaii, Chicago, and Virginia. In 1953 he joined the English Department at Brandeis, where he served until his retirement in 1980. As many readers know, he died on March 28, 1985, before this interview could be printed.

If twentieth-century literature has been distinguished by a number of notable poet/critics, Cunningham is arguably in a class by himself as a poet/scholar. In addition to publishing his remarkable poems, he has produced scholarship impressive equally for its range of interests and for its rigor of historical and philological analysis. He has written a landmark monograph on Shakespeare's tragedies, *Woe or Wonder,* an important study of Emily Dickinson, *Lyric and Legend: Dickinson* and seminal essays on, among other subjects, the Roman poet Statius, the Prologue to *The Canterbury Tales,* and Wallace Stevens' verse.

Yet it is as a poet that he is best known. At the age of twenty, he began publishing poems in magazines like *Poetry* and *Commonweal,* and now his poetic output, though comparatively compressed (his *Collected Poems and Epigrams* runs to only 142 pages), represents the steady achievement of over half a century of work. Of the work itself, commentators have frequently and rightly praised its agility and wit and, less frequently but no less rightly, its considerable emotional power. These characteristics are clearly displayed in Cunningham's epigrams, a form which, popular in Antiquity and the Renaissance, he has almost singlehandedly revived in this century. Overall, Cunningham's poetry exhibits a style which is lively and lucid and free of rhetorical eccentricities. This style has classical antecedents, but Cunningham's subject matter and approach have always been contemporary and fresh. In this sense, his poetry is a happy blend of traditional technique and original vision, and he richly deserves his place as one of the most moving and skillful poets in American literature.

—*T. S.*

TS: Could you tell us a little about your family background and your youth?

JVC: I was born in Cumberland, Maryland. Now my mother's family was an old Irish-Catholic family in western Maryland and around Zanesville, Ohio. Her uncle was editor/publisher of *The Cumberland Times,* but I know very little about my mother's family because we moved west when I was quite young.

My father was a steam shovel runner, and his family were all construction people and railroaders. His parents were immigrants from Ireland. The family legend was that Grandfather Cunningham got on a boat for America after he hit a man at a horse fair and didn't want to wait and see what happened. My father was born in Council Bluffs, Iowa—in other words, at one of the main junctions of the railroads. The oldest of the family, Uncle Dick, was a powder-man. My Uncle Jerry was a switchman on the Northern Pacific. My Aunt Kate's first husband was a steam shovel runner, as was her son, Morris Sisk, both of whom, I believe, died in industrial accidents. And when my Aunt Nell and her husband Uncle Bart took the train to California out of Ogden, she said, "Here's where we built thirty miles of the lake," referring to the rebuilding of the main line of the Union Pacific out of Ogden on landfill from Promontory Point.

My father's family settled down largely in Billings, Montana. My father was working on building something for the Western Maryland Railroad when I was born. When my older brother, two years before, had been born it was in upper New York State, where my father was working on the first building of the New York Aqueduct. My younger brother, two years younger, was born near Scranton, Pennsylvania, and I'm not sure what job my father was on at the time. But before my mother was married, her younger sister, who had been a Dominican novitiate, had contracted tuberculosis, and the sisters had sent her home, and she had died of TB. The fear of tuberculosis was apparently the motive that brought my mother and father west to join his family in Montana.

TS: How old were you when your family settled in Billings?

JVC: Probably four. We lived in several places, but all on the south side of town, the wrong side of the tracks, so to speak. And my father got a job, which to him was demeaning and a comedown, as a crane operator at the Great Western Sugar Company at the far south side of Billings: you see, as a steam shovel runner he was a skilled workman. I went through, as did my older and younger brother, St. Vincent's Parochial School, across the tracks, and all of us skipped two grades in the process. A most important part of our lives was the summers we spent—and we went out every summer—on a dry-land ranch, thirty-six miles from Billings, over the rimrock in the Wheat Basin country. This was through Tom Menamin, my father's former fireman (a steam shovel crew consisted of the operator and fireman); his Uncle Jim Wilson had homesteaded out there.

TS: Is the landscape of "Montana Pastoral" derived from those summers and the ranch?

JVC: It is exactly that, but, at the end of that poem, there is the incident of driving through blizzards and "this huddled chill," which refers to an experience of many years later. On the other hand, the poem "Montana Fifty Years Ago" is an attempt to summarize not so much my own experience, but to put into form the kind of situation out at the ranch.

TS: At what point did your family move to Denver?

JVC: It was in early 1923. The date I could find out exactly with a little research, because I remember vividly the headlines of the paper the day we came into the Denver station were about the Denver Mint robbery, which was one of the great robberies of those times. My father had quit the job as a crane operator and gone back to being a steam shovel operator, and I believe my mother's condition was that we get out of Billings and move to where the children could get a better education. To my mother, as to, I'm sure, innumerable mothers of various classes at that time, the dominant idea was that the children should be higher in the social world, in the real world, than their parents had been.

I finished the eighth grade at St. Elizabeth's School in North Denver on Tennyson Street. The next fall, I entered, as did my older brother, Regis High School, the Jesuit high school, on the northwest boundary of town. There I got the traditional and even, I think, at that time somewhat old-fashioned education: four years of Christian doctrine, four years of English, four years of Latin, two years of Greek, three and a half years of mathematics, three years of laboratory science—biology, chemistry, physics. And, of course, history. It was thorough, and I didn't find it oppressive.

TS: It was while you were living in Denver that your father died, wasn't it?

JVC: Yes. My father, as a steam shovel operator, worked wherever there was a job, worked away from home. He worked, for instance, on the initial building of the Moffat Tunnel through the Rockies and on the redoing of the pass through the Sierras at Truckee. Well, he had a job down in San Pedro Harbor, had been away from home for at least nine months and was due to come back in several weeks when, on the 28th of January, 1926, after Mass on a Sunday morning, in his Sunday clothes, he went out to move the shovel to the place where it should be to begin work on Monday morning. Apparently there was an incline, and, for some reason, the shovel ran away. He dropped the dipper—that was the normal practice to break a runaway—and the dipper apparently caught on an outcrop, and the shovel went completely over. He didn't live too much longer. I have his gold cufflinks, one quite smashed and the other perfectly all right.

TS: What happened after your father died?

JVC: Well, California had, just before the death of my father, introduced the first, I understand, of Workmen's Compensation Acts, so that there was a rather large sum of money for people in our circumstances. My mother invested in an apartment house opposite the Cathedral and a few blocks from the Capitol in Denver, and we moved there. I graduated from high school in

'27 and worked that fall as an office boy for *The Mountain States Telephone and Telegraph.* Then my mother, I imagine with the charity of the Jesuits, sent my younger brother and me for the second semester to St. Mary's College in Kansas. Curiously, one of my friends there was Kermit Kilmer, the son of Joyce Kilmer. And there was also a young man who later had some career in musical composition, Remi Gassmann. So my brother and I went through that semester and then came home. I think my brother went back for another year.

TS: Was there any particular reason you didn't go back?

JVC: Money, I think. Then my mother, through some friend or other, heard of a job, and I got it, as a copyboy on *The Denver Morning Post.* My basic ambition at the time was to become a newspaperman, so this was lovely. I began probably in August of 1928. I went to work, if I remember correctly, at five in the afternoon and got off at two in the morning. I edited fillers, learned to write headlines, and so on. And, unless my memory is wrong, the paper's star reporter at that time was H. Allen Smith.

Now *The Denver Morning Post* had been established by *The Denver Post*–it was the major paper and an evening paper. They had established *The Morning Post* to drive out the evening paper of the competition. That was *The Rocky Mountain News,* which was the major morning paper, and they had *The Denver Times* competing with the evening paper. However, *The Denver Post* and *The Rocky Mountain News* composed their differences by cancelling *The Denver Times* and *The Denver Morning Post,* which was announced on the evening of the Smith-Hoover election. I remember the election very well, because my job was to carry the results from the teletype out to the front of *The Denver Post,* where the street was packed with people watching the returns up on the board. That was the end of my newspaper career, and, strangely, I'm not sure how, it was the end of my ambition to go on as a newspaper person.

Anyway, within a short time, I got a job with what was the largest brokerage house in Denver, Otis and Company. It dominated the Denver market and was an operation of Cyrus Eaton, the Cleveland-Canadian financier. They had the one board room in town and occupied a large part of the ground floor and the floor above it of the Equitable Building on Seventeenth Street. I was called a runner, an office boy. Mostly we carried orders to the wire room, things to various banks, picked up bonds, and so forth, and then waited until something else came up.

TS: You were working for Otis and Company when the Market crashed in 1929. What was that like?

JVC: That perhaps has been the dominant experience of my life. I had been ill. I ran across a colleague, another runner, on the street. He told me things were bad, I'd better get back. I came back. The next week was black Thursday, then black Tuesday.

I recall, a few years ago, when the fiftieth anniversary of the Market Crash was being memorialized, going to one of the few cocktail parties I have gone to in recent years and coming up to a group of people who were discussing the crash. They were younger than I, and this woman said, quite firmly and positively, "I understand that very few people, much fewer than has ever been realized, lost their lives as a consequence of the Stock Market Crash." I looked at her and said, "I don't know what the statistics are; I only actually saw two." Which as a matter of fact I did. One in the large lobby of the Equitable Building, filled with people. I'd come back from a run, paused a moment before going into the office, and casually looked across the lobby, all the way across. A man put a gun to his temple, and you heard the shot. Perhaps a day or two later, I was in the corridor, waiting for a call, when a body landed on the skylight within ten or fifteen feet of where I was standing.

Things went on until, the following March, they fired about half of us. I then got a job with The International Trust Company, working in a safe deposit vault, which was a curious life: except for lunch, you were in the vault all day long.

TS: Was it at this period that you began seriously studying modern poetry?

JVC: Yes, and it would be nice if I could give you a clear account of this. I, of course, read poetry, was taught poetry, in grade school and high school. I was active in establishing a newspaper in the Jesuit High School. I acted in Schwartz's Shakespeare Company, which played four or five blocks from our house in Denver and about which I found many years later an article in the Sunday *New York Times Magazine.* I played small roles: Lorenzo in *The Merchant of Venice,* the Douglas in the Edwin Booth version of both first and second *Henry IV.* But after high school, in some way I got independently interested in poetry. I was active at St. Mary's in inventing a literary magazine that had one or two issues, and I wrote one or two poems for it. And there was a bookstore in Denver, The Bookery, on Walton Place between Sixteenth and Seventeenth Streets, that carried almost all the little magazines. That and the Denver Public Library became my life away from the brokerage house.

I don't know how to put it, because the truth is that people become interested in stamp collecting, in all sorts of things (I as a matter of fact was briefly interested in stamp collecting), and

I just got hooked and followed my nose; for more recent poetry, through the anthologies of Jesse Rittenhouse and Margaret Widdemer, through John Hall Wheelock, Vachel Lindsay, Carl Sandburg, through the very early Untermeyer anthologies, and so on, to, in effect, the modern movement, what was then called the advance guard.

I have been interested, over the years, in noticing in the accounts of people of my generation how they came on the movement. What was involved was very well put by Red Warren in an interview such as we are involved in, in *The Southern Review* about a year or so ago. When he went to Berkeley from Vanderbilt, where he had, of course, been associated with Tate and Ransom, he found that the people at Berkeley were not aware of Eliot, Pound, and so on. He said, "They hadn't got the Word."

Now the curious thing is that I got the Word, so to speak, alone. I really pursued it. In this sort of thing, you need documentation to support your memory, because memory is the mother of mythology. But I have, for instance, a copy of Stevens' *Harmonium,* and, in my own handwriting of the time, I have my signature and the date, December 26th, 1929. With dates about that time, I have copies of Williams' *Spring and All* and Mina Loy's *Lunar Baedeker.* I also typed out—we didn't have xerox machines—Stanley Kunitz's *Intellectual Things* from the Denver Public Library and James Agee's *Permit Me Voyage.* I read through *The Dial* from its refounding in 1920. I read through the book pages of *The New Republic.* I read through *Poetry.* On all these I made notes, so much so that, some years later, without really going back, I wrote an article on the history of *Poetry* out of the notes I took at this time. I was, in other words, committed.

At the same time, I was also reading—I really am astonished at how much I read; how much I understood is a different matter—the ante-Nicene Fathers in translation and Swift's poems in the old edition.

TS: Was there anyone with whom you shared all this?

JVC: I did run into two men who were interested, in general, in modern art. One had all the Proust that was available in translation and had planned year after year to read it on his vacation. I don't know if he ever did.

TS: What about the owner of The Bookery?

JVC: Morris Rosenfeld. Yes, he was an extraordinary man, an old-fashioned American communist, an IWW communist. I remember, for instance, that he had a copy of *Ulysses,* which he rented out to be read in the rear room and which he let me take home, as I came home from the brokerage office when he was closing up shop. Since the Stock Market in Denver opened at eight in the morning, I had it back to him by then. And I read *Ulysses* in this way. During the Sixties at one of those student agitation affairs about the English program, I mentioned this, and a very bright young graduate student said, "That's strange; we all read Ulysses in senior high school." But I'm afraid it wasn't in The Modern Library at the time.

Not many years ago, a girl at Brandeis, who had taken a number of courses and done a certain amount of independent work with me, just before graduation came to me and said, "Do you remember Morris Rosenfeld?" And I said, "The only man I know of by that name had a bookstore in Denver." She said, "Yes, he's my uncle."

TS: How long did you stay on working in Denver?

JVC: Until September, 1930. Then my older brother started freelancing through John Bartlett in Boulder and wanted to go on a trip picking up stories for business magazines. My mother wanted me to go with him, as a chaperon, I would almost say.

Now Bartlett, who, as people may remember, was Robert Frost's favorite student in his days of teaching in New Hampshire, was a literary agent, specializing in selling items to what were called the trade journals, that is, business magazines. Perhaps the best-paying of them was *Dry Goods Economist*. I also remember *The American Lumberman* and *The American Tobacconist* and innumerable others. Tom wanted to go through the Southwest—there was a woman in Phoenix who was a kind of ultimate quest—so I quit my job at The International Trust and in an old Studebaker, with my books and notes taking up a good part of the back seat, we set off south to Trinidad, and then drove down to Santa Fe. It was this occasion I alluded to earlier. We ran into a sudden blizzard and stayed for some days at a little cabin just short of the top of Raton Pass, just north of the New Mexico border. That experience was responsible for "the huddled chill" in "Montana Pastoral."

TS: I understand it was in Albuquerque that you assembled an anthology of what was then the new American poetry. How did that come about?

JVC: I knew that Norman Macleod, the poet and editor of a little magazine, lived in Albuquerque. I found his number and address in the phone book and called. He was not in Albuquerque, but his wife and their young baby were and a graduate student at the University of New Mexico, Duke Hendon, who took quite a liking to me and I to him. He had gotten a professor at the university—a very nice man named St. Clair—to schedule a graduate seminar in modern American poetry for the second semester of that year, and he suggested to me making an anthology of texts that would not be available in whatever anthology they were going to use. He supplied the legal-size stencils for mimeographing, and, in two weeks or so, I typed up from my notes and books and what was available in the Albuquerque libraries an anthology of modern American poetry, excluding authors that were widely available and recognized, such as Robinson and Frost, together with introductions, mostly from my notes—R. P. Blackmur in *Hound and Horn,* Allen Tate—and then at the end notes, partly my own, partly from other sources, like Zukofsky on Williams. The stencils were not run off until after I'd left Albuquerque, and I imagine Duke Hendon sent me copies. I may remark that he was a remarkable man, suffering from something like polio. A year later, he had a job at Gunnison, at Western State College of Colorado, and died within a year.

The anthology I thought was completely lost. Then I heard that a man in Michigan had one and that there was one in Albuquerque. I found one complete copy and an incomplete copy somewhere in my papers fifteen or eighteen years ago. [More recently, a copy turned up for sale for $3,250.00 in the catalogue of a book dealer in Berkeley.] It made perfectly clear what I'd thought was so: that I had by the age of nineteen pretty completely entered into the modern poetic tradition. I had read it. I had selected it. I had appreciated it. I had not necessarily imitated it. I had in those notes and texts the sorts of materials that later were put together to form that movement in criticism that John Crowe Ransom sort of accidentally called The New Criticism. The anthology is dated the beginning of February, 1931—that is, the beginning of the second semester at the university, but it was completed before we left Albuquerque.

TS: When exactly did you leave Albuquerque, and where did you go afterwards?

JVC: We left Albuquerque, I think, Christmas night, not Christmas Eve—I remember stopping for midnight Mass at Isleta Pueblo—and then drove west to Phoenix. From Phoenix we went to Tucson, where we lived back of a house on South Third Street, if I remember, in what was called a TB cottage: it was paneled halfway up and then screened. People who do not know the area do not realize that, even in the warm days of winter, it gets pretty cold in Tucson at night. It gets down toward freezing. And I remember—and it is the turning point of my life—one early February night—I don't know how long I had thought about it or how it came to me—I sat down and wrote a letter to the only man I knew of, and had had a couple of exchanges with, who was associated with an American university, and asked him if it was possible to go to college and stay alive. This was Yvor Winters.

I had written him a year or so earlier as a result of seeing in a footnote in an article by Allen Tate in *The Sewanee Review,* a reference to the little magazine, Gyroscope, and a post office box in Palo Alto where it was available. I had written for copies. Winters answered immediately. I didn't have the money, though it wasn't much, when I got the answer, and waited a while. He then independently sent copies, and asked if I wrote anything. I remember answering, sending a poem or two. One, I think, was the one—later in a two instead of a three-stanza version—entitled "Noon." And a short prose piece, dealing mainly with Lawrence, but, as I recall, first trying out the idea of the difference between a rational and, so to speak, an irrational sequence in a work. Winters told me later that his reply had been returned—we had left Denver—"Address Unknown." So that was, up to that point, my association with the man.

Now it is an extraordinary fact that, to that short one-paragraph letter I wrote, probably at one o'clock in the morning, he instantly replied, got his friends and students to write to me, and got his next-door neighbor to allow him to fix up a shed behind his house where I could stay. As a consequence, the following December I worked my way out to San Francisco, called Winters, and he told me what train to take to Palo Alto and said he would be standing on the station platform by the mailbox, wearing a long white scarf. I got off the train, and there the man was. He took me to his house and to the little shed, a very nice little shed, prepared for my occupancy. I was to do the dishes. Otherwise, they fed and housed me. In brief, Winters was a man of great generosity.

At the same time, of course, he was a dominant personality, and so, in my early days, was I; and I would imagine that we got along well for eight or ten days. Of course, I had been on the road, really a good deal of starving involved, we weren't making much with John Bartlett and I was not really in good condition, psychically. So it wasn't idyllic. But I must say that Mrs. Winters, Janet Lewis, was not merely kind but human, and made perhaps all the difference.

I guess I should throw in, because it is important to me, that on coming back from the Southwest trip in the late spring or early summer of 1931, through the Bartletts I met several times Robert Frost's daughter, Marjorie, whom I liked very much. I lent her books; we had some brief correspondence. By a strange coincidence, she met a student at the University of Colorado from Billings, Montana, and married him. Many years later, in 1959, when I visited Billings I discovered that my grade school pal was mayor of the city and also a friend of Marjorie Frost's widower, who still had some of the books. As a matter of fact, an indirect offer was made to give them back, but, of course that would have been silly. There were several, but the two I remember were an India paper edition of the translation of *The Magic Mountain,* which was not the best reading for a woman in a sanatorium, and Eliot's monograph on Dante.

TS: Marjorie Frost had tuberculosis?

JVC: Yes. Then she married, and in 1934 she died in Billings as a consequence of complications after childbirth. She remains a very vivid picture in my mind. When Frost spoke to me at Brandeis not too many years ago, I thought of speaking to him of it, but it wasn't a situation in which you could talk.

TS: What did you study during your undergraduate years at Stanford?

JVC: When I went to Stanford, I planned to major in mathematics. But I found that doing real mathematics, reading Horace, writing a poem or an article in the same night was impossible, and for a reason people may not quite understand. Real mathematics takes over. It is as obsessive a state as, or even more so than, the most passionate love affair. You give your life to it; it takes you. And I had to give it up. Some years later, and this is analogous, I had to do the same thing with chess. When I found myself coming awake at three or four in the morning, moving the pawn to Queen's Eight, it was time to run. So I switched to Classics, partly because in Classics you didn't need to buy any books. There were plenty of texts, more texts than anyone could use, in the library. But also, obviously, I was concerned with and involved in the subject. I took, in the English Department, the

History of Criticism from W. D. Briggs, a course in the English novel from Briggs, a course in medieval literature, and so on. I never, by the way, took a creative writing course.

TS: In recent decades, creative writing courses have become increasingly prominent in English department curricula. What do you think of this development?

JVC: It might be observed that the idea implied, almost asserted, in the term "creative writing" is not so good. There is a kind of pretension about it. There is a spiritual claim, the creative versus the inert, the organic versus the inorganic, and all that sort of thing. Anyone who is committed to the discipline of English should be able to write well on something and preferably on a variety of somethings. That among these somethings can be the sort of thing which does not involve dealing with prior texts as such, which in effect is the traditional discipline, would seem obvious.

TS: A development related to the increase in creative writing courses in universities is the increase in courses dealing with contemporary literature. What is your feeling about this?

JVC: I will only say that there is a difference, a complete difference, between being involved in a teaching situation with what is regarded as the approved tradition of the elders—that is, teaching *Tom Jones* or Shakespeare—and the teaching of texts that are currently newsworthy and felt to be in immediate fashion. My own feeling is that the older world, in which the second took place in private living rooms, in coffee shops, or at a bar, and the first belonged to the schools, was more the right thing. Now

I may perhaps be prejudiced in this sense: in my own academic career, the only course I took in English, or in any language, that got beyond the later seventeenth century was the course in the English novel from Briggs, which ended, as I remember, with Conrad.

TS: Turning to your writing career, you've managed throughout it to combine poetry and scholarship. Have you ever felt, in your case, that the two disciplines were in conflict, or have they been in general mutually supportive?

JVC: My general feeling is that I write scholarship with the right hand and I write my poems with the left, with no depreciation of the poems, of course. The primary conflict I have discovered, as distinguished from what a good many people obviously feel, is a simple matter of energy. I have only so much energy. If you are doing this, you are not doing that.

There are other problems involved. There is the problem of what people expect of you, and you tend to act up to what people expect of you more than you wish you would. I have found that being thought of as a poet is at times not something I'm comfortable with. I also know that the idea of the poet, the role, has seemed to have had really devastating effects on the personalities and personal lives of too many people I have known.

TS: In your criticism, you've been skeptical of the Romantic notion of the poet and of the lofty role in which the poet is sometimes cast. Referring to Shelley's dictum, you've said that poets "are not 'the unacknowledged legislators of the world,' and a good thing it is that they aren't."

JVC: I think I simply regard writing a poem as a professional task, and hence in the same province as writing an article involving a textual emendation in Shakespeare.

TS: Tradition is a principal concern of your scholarship. To what extent do you feel that you belong to a particular line of poets and embody in your own way and time certain poetic traditions?

JVC: I do not think of myself as belonging to any particular line of poets or embodying any specific great tradition. At the same time, I am perfectly aware that there are relations between what I do and what has been done. I ran across a note I made some years ago, wondering about what were—and this is in answer to your question—the sources of the bare plain style I find congenial, though certainly do not try to write in all the time. In that, I noted a small poem of Robinson, not the typical Robinson, but a small straightforward poem, "An Old Story," some Landor, and the poetry of Swift.

TS: Your mention of Robinson suggests another topic. In your brief biography of him, you remark that "metrical speech is a language which, like any language, must be learned young or never." How and when did you learn to write in meter?

JVC: I simply do not know. But since the question of meter is fairly fundamental to the whole literary/poetic situation at the present time, let us deal with it. I think a large part of the problem of meter, and not just of writing in meter, comes from the development in the later nineteenth century of the teaching of the poetry of one's own language in the schools, so that there developed something that would be comparable to the study of prosody in Latin and Greek. Out of this situation, as well as out of the critical thought of the time and of ours, there came a feeling of artificiality about meter.

Now it is perfectly true that meter is artificial, if you mean by that that it is a matter of art. But so is speech. What you mean by meter is a certain organization of normal speech patterns, or, to put it more accurately, a selection of the admissible ones, in a particular system, out of the total number. I once published a lecture, pointing out that a good number of our phrases and sentences are perfect iambic octosyllables or decasyllables. There are all sorts of examples: "Some people do, some people don't." Or, one I rather like: "We ought to be in Cleveland in an hour." But, even more, I remember a friend telling me about an unhappy love affair and a long-distance conversation he had, and this stuck in his mind: the woman said, "How often shall I see you in a lifetime?" I didn't point out to him then that part of the memorability of that was that it was an iambic pentameter, absolutely regular.

The result is there's been a good deal of rather false teaching. Any linguist knows that English speech is not made up of syllables that are accented or unaccented. It is made up of syllables of various forms of accent, and only one strong accent in any complete articulation. Consequently, there is a necessary translation in scanning, a translation that, I think, is made fairly clear in the scanning exercises I recall from my early education, in which you pronounced the poetic line in a language completely different from any language one uses in life. "*This* is the *for*est prim*ev*al, the *mur*muring *pines* and the *hem*locks." If you tried to talk that way in any other situation, you would be thought to be posturing. Something of that perhaps came over into the feeling about meter.

TS: In other words, people looked on the translation, on the method of scansion, as the reality of metrical composition, and didn't understand that it was a particular convention of reading or scanning which they were objecting to, and mistook the convention for meter itself?

JVC: Yes. And this links up with the basic premise of the importance in meter of norm and variation. Once you get this idea in, then the variations are meaningful and regularity is meaningless. And you start to write a poem in which you try to be metrical and keep violating meter. Now that's playing chess and making up the rules from time to time to suit your convenience.

TS: You're probably best known for your epigrams. When, early in your career, you were trying out forms and techniques, what qualities of the epigram most attracted you to it?

JVC: I don't know. But I am, so to speak, a short-breathed man, and simply found that I had an almost unthought-out preference for brief definitiveness of statement, so that there was a traditional form just waiting for me to find it. That, at least, would be part of the answer.

I feel that in a sense brevity has been my flaw. I think I have made in scholarship a number of contributions in passing that never were seen, simply because they should have had a couple thousand words around them. And with my knowledge of and respect for the ancient rhetorical tradition, I think that what I've done is in that sense not the thing to have done.

TS: You mention the rhetorical tradition. You refer in several places in your prose to Cicero's Orator and his definition of the plain style. To what extent do you think the rhetorical tradition has influenced your work?

JVC: That interest, in the terms in which you put it, came later; that is, at a time at which influence, in the sense that one usually thinks of it, is not so likely to happen. What I do believe was probably important was this. In the Jesuit high school, we used in English courses a series of textbooks called *Model English.* What I remember of those is that they involved the old exercise of imitation. I can recall being asked to take a paragraph of Macaulay—the one of the New Zealander looking on the remains, some centuries later, of European civilization—and to write a paragraph on an analogous subject, keeping the same grammatical structure, the same complex or compound sentences, yet using totally different content.

Now it was, I think, or could have been, this sort of exercise that gave me that feeling for what puzzles people sometimes when I speak of the form of a poem, meaning the inner form, the structure you would imitate if you were given this exercise. Strict Chaucerians go out of their way to say very nicely to me that they don't believe my little essay on the Prologue to *The Canterbury Tales.* And they don't because Chaucer is supposed to have at this point broken through the literary conventions of his day. They see only the mere fact that he's dropped the idea of the dream vision; they don't see that he's kept the underlying scheme of the dream vision prologue, with its serial descriptions of characters. He's kept, that is, that sequence which, if I were writing an imitation of one of his dream vision prologues, with the stipulation that it be applied to describing members of contemporary society, would furnish me with the necessary succession of topics.

TS: In your commitment to meter and to exactitude of statement, you have been going against the temper of the times. Has this been difficult for you or have you sensed a community of readers and writers which has been sustaining?

JVC: One needs, when he starts to write, an audience. There comes a time when a felt audience is not necessary, except at intervals to reassure one that he is being heard and responded to at least somewhat within the terms that he thinks he is speaking. I have on the whole been fortunate enough to have had enough response, enough audience, to feel that I have been heard.

Now to the part of the question about the temper of the times. I think I dealt with that matter too briefly—I looked it up the other day—in the introduction to *The Collected Essays*, in which I say that, if my work is not of my time, it is part of the evidence of what the times were. But one really ought to go a little more deeply into it. The whole procedure of applying, to a contemporary situation, the kind of reconstruction one makes to understand that fragment of a previous society that has been preserved to us, and then of making this construction a kind of prescription as to what the modern or post-modern temper is, or should be, is really rather preposterous. You don't analyze the times. You get it. You can't avoid getting it. You belong. So that phrase, "The temper of the times," is essentially propagandistic.

TS: You've observed that one of modernity's features is an alienation from the past, especially the religious past. Several of your poems deal with or refer to the Catholicism of your youth. What are your religious beliefs?

JVC: My answer to that is, if I can trust my judgment, I have no religious beliefs. At the same time, religion was an integral part of my boyhood. I was an altar boy for years. I was neither reluctant nor pushy about it; it was just part of life. And this obviously lives with one. I can give you an incident which came back to my mind not too long ago. One evening, around 1950, I came back from visiting friends to our barracks apartment at the University of Chicago, opened the door of the apartment, hesitated briefly, and went in. Then it struck me as odd that I had made this brief hesitation. It puzzled me for a short while, and all of the sudden it came to me. When I was in high school the Jesuits had, each Lenten period, a three-day retreat for the student body, three days of fasting, abstinence, and complete silence, if you could manage it, together with various exercises and a number of talks by various priests. And I remember one afternoon this priest speaking to us; he spoke of our guardian angels. And he said, "Have you ever paused at the door to let your guardian angel precede you?" I thought, "My God, no, I never have." So for some time after, perhaps not too long, I made a practice of pausing and letting my guardian angel precede me; then, of course it dropped out. But it returned to me that evening in Chicago, though why? I thought of the events of the day and recent things and could find no prompting cause. At all events, if it is ever part of your life, it remains in some way part of your life.

TS: To continue with the subject of modernity, in one of your essays you observe in passing, with reference to Gertrude Stein, *Finnegans Wake,* Pound's *Cantos,* and the verse of Hart Crane and Dylan Thomas, "Surely there has not been such a collection of artificial languages in esteem since the latter days of the Roman Empire, and this among readers who believe they believe in the absolute virtue of the accents of real speech." Is there a way to explain the simultaneous elevation of the natural and the manneristic? How have these evidently contradictory beliefs or practices coincided with and reinforced one another?

JVC: Now let me ask you a question. Do you feel that that statement is accurate?

TS: Yes.

JVC: Yes. I don't know how to answer the question. I will make some observations. Going back to those days when I came from the brokerage house to find my way into the world of, let us say, the advance guard, I found it not a unified movement. It was not as if you were Robert Herrick coming into the world of Ben Jonson. People were going all sorts of different ways. They belonged together more or less, as the various ingredients in a Chinese dish. At that stage, the various ones were distinguishable in taste. Now what happened shortly after, with the advent of the New Criticism, and it occurred very, very quickly in the late Thirties, the triumph of modernity, was something like having what is left over of that Chinese dish warmed up the next day. The individual elements have now fused, and there is a kind of homogeneous Chinesity or modernity, which is something other than that originally diverse and merely associated-with-each-other experience. Is that clear?

TS: Yes. I was wondering, too, specifically about the question of real speech and mannerism. I'm thinking, for instance, of Eliot, who emphasized throughout his career the importance of real speech, and of the way that that emphasis ended up producing a poetry like his own, which often, I think most people would agree, is not particularly reflective of real speech.

JVC: The dialogue in the second part of *The Waste Land* would not represent even an edited transcript of a tape recording of what one heard on such an occasion. Even more extreme are long passages in Ezra Pound's *Cantos* in which he is writing a kind of Artemus Ward version of the vernacular. Nobody ever talked that way. The truth is the notion of real speech needs fumigation.

TS: Another paradoxical situation that you've observed is that, though many of the attitudes of modernity achieved orthodoxy in the Thirties, subsequent poets and critics have adopted them as new. Do you have any account for this phenomenon of recycled novelty?

JVC: No, but I was interested in your stating this. It is a very strange thing. I came into the modern movement in the late Twenties, and I was about the last in age to whom the modern movement was not public property. Then it triumphed—let us date it by Eliot's tenure of the Norton Professorship at Harvard in 1933-34. The tide came in. There came the war. The modern movement became part of the educational system, as is illustrated by the girl who said she had read *Ulysses* in senior high. Then the tide came in again. And the second time it came in, it came with a missionary feeling of discovery about something that had already been discovered and sold. Everybody belonged to a very special group to which everybody belonged. It was almost as if George Washington had brought the news that Columbus had discovered America.

TS: This suggests a comment I remember your making some years ago in conversation. You remarked that the canon of modern poetry hasn't changed much in the last fifty years and that modern literature in the sense that you understood it when you were twenty is still modern literature. Do you think that there will be a change in the canon?

JVC: We are probably due for a drastic revision of the judgments on the literature of the 1910s, the Twenties and Thirties. This does not mean that the judgments of a few years ago were wrong, and anyone's are right, because the new ones will go through in their day another revision. A clear case: it was just about the time of the last war that Eliot lost his preeminence. After that, he was a revered figure, but no longer The Poet. Stevens became one of the substitutes, as did, a few years later, and even more dominantly, Williams. So there are, and must be, alterations in the semi-official rating book.

TS: For many today, Pound is the preeminent figure of the modern movement. What is your estimate of him and of how his work will be viewed in the future?

JVC: Pound is a curious case. He was, as he apparently said at the end of his life, a complete failure. He was a strange, almost mythological character. One thing to be said is that Pound is not from the West. He happened to be born in Hailey, Idaho, when his father was there working for the United States Mint, and he did spend a few very early years with part of the family in Michigan. But he grew up in Philadelphia, and went to Hamilton College and the University of Pennsylvania. However, it is not wholly a mistake of outsiders to see him as a Westerner, for he went to England like Joaquin Miller or, indeed, like Buffalo Bill.

I haven't gone back to the *Cantos* very much over the years. I think they simply are dead. I even think that the few that some people pick out don't really stand up. There is a kind of remaining sentimental allegiance that keeps people hoping to say good things about Pound, though then you run into the difficulty of not giving in to the irrational opposition to his irrationality in politics. I think Pound is a footnote, and I say this as one who was once immersed in him.

TS: What happened after you graduated from Stanford?

671

JVC: When I graduated in March of 1934, my mother was in the hospital with terminal cancer. I returned to Denver and sat up with her in St. Luke's Hospital for a little over three months. I'd come to the hospital at nine or ten at night, dodge out for coffee—there was a shop a block or so up the street on Colfax—and stay until the nurses came on duty at five-thirty or six in the morning. Then, my memory is, the day after the funeral—it could perhaps have been two or three days—I got a letter in the mail from Briggs, chairman of the English Department at Stanford. Was I in a position to accept a full tuition scholarship for graduate work at Stanford and a teaching assistantship in English? I had a young brother and a much younger sister on my hands, a mortgaged house, and not the slightest idea of what I would do either with myself or with them. My younger brother had a job with Singer Sewing Machine, but it didn't pay much. People ask me why I went into teaching; it was from my point of view pure chance, and a godsend. It was obviously the thing for me to do.

I was able then to take my younger sister, with the aid of John Conley and his family, and have her placed in the Dominican school at San Rafael, California, and get my brother into the University of California, Berkeley. And with that, it seemed things had worked out.

TS: Speaking of schools and teaching, you've had a long and happy association with Brandeis University. I wonder if you could talk a bit about that.

JVC: Brandeis deserves much more than I can say. In 1953 I was at the University of Virginia, Charlottesville, as lovely a place to live as I can think of, or it was at that time. But I had already spent eight years as a full-time instructor at Stanford and seven years as an assistant professor at Hawaii and Chicago, so that, at the end of my first year at Virginia, that made sixteen years as Instructor and Assistant Professor. And Virginia promised five more years.

Then I got a telephone call one August afternoon—and this was another unsolicited, unthought-of chance—from a man with a notorious Jewish accent—people who know him know what I mean—Joseph Cheskis, at Brandeis University, as he said. I had heard vaguely of Brandeis, but just vaguely. He wanted to know if I was interested in a position. My wife and I drove up to Waltham, and talked to Abram Sachar, the President of Brandeis. They offered me fifty per cent more than I was making at Virginia, and I was to set up a new graduate program in what Max Lerner, an important character in Brandeis in the early years, always had put down in the catalogue as American and English Literature, which I always changed in proof to English and American Literature. It was one of our long battles.

The buildings that have come up since would obscure to any present visitor the paucity that was there when I came. We had a campus that was the remains of a failed veterinary school. They had just finished the fourth year and just graduated the first senior class. Brandeis was a gamble, not only for me; the whole institution was a gamble. There was a sense of risk, if you will, of adventure. And coming at the same time I did was Irving Howe, who, together with some of those who had already come, formed the nucleus for what could be a viable enterprise.

To round the story off, within about ten years, there was published—my memory says in *PMLA,* but at all events somewhere sufficiently official—a list of the leading graduate schools in English and American Literature, and Brandeis, though not at the top, of course, still was there in ninth or tenth position.

Whatever the merits of that or any survey are, nevertheless it did indicate that we had made it. I would find it difficult to write a novel that would convincingly, in realistic convention, show how one came from St. Vincent's Parochial School in Billings, Montana, to Brandeis University in Waltham, Massachusetts, but that's what happened.

TS: Though you did quite a bit of reviewing early in your career, it seems you subsequently turned almost entirely from criticism to scholarship. Was this a conscious decision?

JVC: It was. The tradition of scholarship was to me a kind of conversion, though I can't remember any blinding light on the road to anywhere. There were at Stanford what one, I think, could properly call great men in the academic tradition. Briggs, of course. Hardin Craig, for all that he and I didn't get along and for all he sometimes tended to go haywire a bit, nevertheless was a great scholar. Even the man in Middle English who much disliked me, Arthur Kennedy, was very good at his facts. In Classics, there was B. O. Foster, who was my principal teacher, Sonny Boy Harriman, who published little, if anything, but who introduced me, in the early 1930s, to the whole linguistic structuralism movement that has had such strange developments and has come out into almost the current counterpart of The New Criticism, with, of course, other elements and streams contributing to it. And in 1935 a refugee from Germany, Hermann Frankel. But quite independently of these, and not directly as a consequence of any desire to emulate a particular man, I was interested simply in scholarship as such.

TS: In view of what you say about scholarship, it's not surprising that you've often expressed distrust of critical methods for producing, independently of philological and historical analysis, interpretations of literary works, interpretations which may be interesting in and of themselves but which are essentially opinion and contribute no hard knowledge to our understanding of the texts they address.

JVC: I do not really care for the development of special forms of handling a text, the sort of thing that originally was associated with The New Criticism. My perhaps slightly-unfair-analogy for this is that you learn to construct a machine that looks something like a mimeograph machine. You slip in the text of the poem on this side, turn the wheel, and on the other side comes out a prose paragraph or two of explication.

TS: I gather The New Criticism influenced not only the study of literature, but the teaching of it, too.

JVC: I remember some of the courses in English at Stanford. Kennedy's was perhaps an extreme example. His course in Middle English consisted really mostly of his reciting bibliographies. I found this very useful because, in the first place, I was interested in the subject and in the bibliography and, in the second place, I did not want to know what Arthur Kennedy felt about the texts as works of literature. But we had that curious revolution as a result of which you had these courses in which you had to deal with the text, you had to fill up an hour with discussion on the text. You couldn't get rid of thirty minutes with biography and bibliography. You had to take the naked *Ode to a Nightingale* and fill the class hour up. You also were not supposed to, as I remember, recite it: that would have taken up some time. In brief, both the instructor and the student who had to write papers needed methods, needed, if you will, gimmicks to get through.

Now in the old tradition, you could take up a large part of the hour with difficulties in the language, with parsing, and so on. I had a marvelous course in Livy from Foster; he was the Loeb translator of Livy, and, though he died before completing the project, he did most of it. There were maybe six or eight of us, and the course consisted of us in turn reading aloud a paragraph in Latin. Then both from what he knew of the text itself and from the way you pronounced it, he asked you questions. He knew where you didn't miss the point, and so forth. We read Livy; it was a living experience. But we didn't analyze Livy. We didn't—well, I have a term for it—we didn't produce a substitute experience.

TS: Though the body of your work is compressed, your production of poems has been fairly steady, to judge from the appendix in Charles Gullans's bibliography, which lists the dates of composition of the poems in your four main collections. Have you pretty much followed, throughout your career, the same procedures in writing your poems?

JVC: When I began writing, I did a good deal not merely of rewriting, but of smashing an original version to pieces and doing it completely over, maybe several times. Since about 1940 what I write I tend to write almost straight off. The corrections, the redoing is in the process of writing it down, and then it's through. Now one must put in this footnote: what I write is short and, consequently, is compassable in a single experience of writing.

I often find that I have odd lines here and there that suggest something, and, of course, much that I write is suggested by a phrase in language, and then I find a kind of meaning that this phrase could assume. For instance, there's a little epigram which reads:

> Genius is born and made. This heel who mastered
> By infinite pains his trade was born a bastard.

I recall the genesis of that. I was sitting over coffee, just toying with the idea of finding a good rhyme for "bastard." Then I thought of "mastered," and then I thought of mastering an art. Then I thought of genius—is it born or made?—and of genius as the capacity for taking infinite pains. In brief, all these, so to speak, fossils in the language entered into it. When I had finished, I could think of a number of real situations, real persons, to whom it would refer.

TS: What are you working on at the moment?

JVC: Nothing big, just a little of this and that, some Sappho, some Shakespeare, *Hamlet* and Real Life, and so on.

TS: This brings us to the last question I have. You mentioned at the outset the family legend about your grandfather and the skirmish at the horse fair. You yourself have had a long-standing interest in horses and horse racing. Is it true that Brandeis presented you, as a retirement gift, a trip to Saratoga?

JVC: Yes, and that was one of the nicest things that has happened to me—the going-away gift of the university. This is usually a dinner and a plaque, or something like that, but was in my case a trip to Saratoga for my wife and me and the department chairman and his wife for the Travers. We had a really glorious time. We saw a pseudo-Elizabethan play one night and stayed at Lake George. And if you are going to be ushered out, that is as nice a way of doing it as can be done.

NOTES

Most Shakespeare citations throughout this book are from George Lyman Kittredge, ed., *The Complete Works of Shakespeare* (Boston, 1936). 1 have generally modernized texts.

I

WOE OR WONDER:

The Emotional Effect of Shakespearean Tragedy

Woe or Wonder was completed in 1945. I have since cut, rearranged, and rephrased parts of it but have made no substantial alterations.

Ripeness is All

1. G. B. Harrison, *Shakespeare: 23 Plays and the Sonnets* (New York, 1948), 3. Similarly O. J. Campbell, *The Living Shakespeare* (New York, 1949), 1: "In his plays we constantly meet our own experiences; in his poetry we constantly find our inmost thoughts and feelings expressed with an eloquence and a precision far beyond our reach."
2. T. S. Eliot, *Selected Essays* (New York, 1950), 231.
3. Robert Bechtold Heilman, *This Great Stage* (Baton Rouge, 1948), 112. The correct interpretation is given in passing by Alfred Harbage, *As They Liked It* (New York, 1947), 56.
4. Hugh Latimer, *Sermons* (Everyman's Library, London, 1906), 352-53.
5. Thomas Wilson, *Art of Rhetoric,* ed. G. H. Mair (Oxford, 1909), 83. *Cf.* John Bruce, ed., *Diary of John Manningham* (Camden Society Publication, XCIX, Westminster, 1868), 146, under March 24, 1602 [1603]: "This morning about three at clock her Majesty departed this life, mildly like a lamb, like a ripe apple from the tree."

1.   "De ratione studii," *Opera Omnia* (Leyden, 1703), I, 528C-D. There is a paraphrastic translation of the treatise in William Harrison Woodward, *Desiderius Erasmus concerning the Aim and Method of Education* (Cambridge, 1904), 162-78.

2.   *If This be not a Good Play, the Devil is in It* in *The Dramatic Works of Thomas Dekker* (London, 1873), III, 265.

3.   John Burnet, ed., *Platonis Opera* (Oxford, 1903), III

4.   Ingram Bywater, ed., tr., *Aristotle on the Art of Poetry* (Oxford, 1909), ad 1452a4, 60a11, 60a18.

5.   The classic formulation, cited from the index, *s.v., casus,* of the Vives edition (Paris, 1862 and 1861) of Thomas Aquinas, *Summa Theologica.* Hereafter referred to as *ST.*

6.   C. F. Tucker Brooke, ed., *The Shakespeare Apocrypha* (Oxford, 1908), 44.

7.   "tristitia namque tragoediae proprium." Diomedes, *Ars Grammatica* in Heinrich Keil, ed., *Grammatici Latini* (Leipzig, 1857), I, 488.

8.   Thomas Dekker, *The Magnificent Entertainment . . .* (London, 1604) in *Dramatic Works, op. cit.,* I, 269. Sir Philip Sidney, *Works,* ed. Albert Feuillerat (Cambridge, 1923), III, 23.

9.   Hardin Craig, *The Enchanted Glass* (New York, 1936), 27; Hardin Craig, *Shakespeare* (Chicago, 1932), 804.

10.   Richard Hooker, *Works,* ed. John Keble (7th ed., Oxford, 1888). Hereafter referred to as *EP.*

11.   However, for a generalized argument see John Marston's *Sophonisba.*

12.   Julius Caesar Scaliger, *Poetice,* 3. 97 in F. M. Padelford, tr., *Select Translations from Scaliger's Poetics* (New York, 1905), 57. John Jewel, *The Defence of the Apology* (Publications of the Parker Society, XXV, Cambridge, 1848), 249-50.

1. The material in the following pages is vulgate: Wilhelm Cloetta, *Beitrage zur Litteraturgeschichte des Mittelalters und der Renaissance* (Halle, 1890-92); Joel E. Spingarn, A *History of Literary Criticism in the Renaissance* (2nd ed., New York, 1908); John W. Cunliffe, ed., *Early English Classical Tragedies* (Oxford, 1912); L. E. Kastner and H. B. Charlton, eds., *The Poetical Works of Sir William Alexander* (Manchester, 1921); A. Philip McMahon, "Seven Questions on Aristotelian Definitions of Tragedy and Comedy," *Harvard Studies in Classical Philology,* XL (1929), 97-198.

2. "Inter tragoediam autem et comoediam cum multa tum inprimis hoc distat, quod in comoedia mediocres fortunae hominum, parvi impetus periculorum, laetique sunt exitus actionum, at in tragoedia omnia contra, ingentes personae, magni timores, exitus funesti habentur; et illic prima turbulenta, tranquilla ultima, in tragoedia contrario ordine res aguntur; tum quod in tragoedia fugi- enda vita, in comoedia capessenda exprimitur; postremo quod omnis comoedia de fictis est argumentis, tragoedia saepe de historia fide petitur." Cited from McMahon, *op. cit.,* 128-29. The text is apparently by Evanthius, whose treatise on comedy is included in the Donatan commentary.

3. A Renaissance commonplace: see Justus Lipsius, *Two Bookes of Constancie,* tr. Sir John Stradling, ed. Rudolph Kirk (New Brunswick, NJ., 1939), 85-86.

4. Jacobus Zabarella, *Opera Logica* (Venice, 1586), 81: "Quod Rhetorica et Poetica solius civilis disciplinae instrumenta sint, et quomodo."

5. Sidney, *Works, op. cit.,* Ill, 23.

6. McMahon, *op. cit.;* A. Philip McMahon, "On the Second Book of Aristotle's Poetics and the Source of Theophrastus' Definition of Tragedy," *Harvard Studies in Classical Philology,* XXVIII (1917), 1-46.

7. "Tragoedia est heroicae fortunae in adversis conprehensio. a Theophrasto ita definite est, *tragoidia estin eroikes tuches peristasis.* . . . Comoedia est privatae civilisque fortunae sine periculo

vitae conprehensio, apud Graecos ita definita, *komoidia estin idiotikon pragmaton akindunos perioche* . . . in ea viculorum, id est humilium domuum, fortunae conprehendantur, non ut in tragoedia publicarum regiarumque . . . comoedia a tragoedia differt, quod in tragoedia introducuntur heroes duces reges, in comoedia humiles atque privatae personae; in ilia luctus exilia caedes, in hac amores, virginum raptus: deinde quod in illa frequenter et paene semper laetis rebus exitus tristes et liberorum fortunarumque priorum in peius adgnitio. quare varia definitione discrctae sunt, altera enim *akindunos perioche,* altera *tuches peristasis* dicta est. tristitia namque tragoediae proprium." Keil, *op. cit.*

8. Cited from Cunliffe, *op. cit.,* xvi*ff.*

9. Frederick S. Boas, ed., *The Works of Thomas Kyd* (Oxford, 1901), 164.

10. Richard Simpson, ed., *The School of Shakespeare* (London, 1878), II, 241*ff.*

11. Brooke, *op. cit.,* 35.

Wonder

1. Sidney, *Works, op. cit.,* III, 23.

2. For fuller discussion and citation with respect to the history of wonder as an aesthetic term, sec my unpublished Ph.D. dissertation, "Tragic Effect and Tragic Process . . ." (Stanford, 1945); Richard Heinze, *Virgils Epische Technik* (Leipzig, 1903), 454*ff*; Manin Herrick, "Some Neglected Sources of *Admiratio,*" *Modern Language Notes,* LXII (1947), 222-26. The historians of Renaissance criticism, until Herrick's note, had regarded the concept as introduced in the middle of the sixteenth century by Minturno and without effective influence on the drama until Corneille: Gregory Smith, *Elizabethan Critical Essays* (Oxford, 1904), I, 392; Spingarn, *op. cit.,* 52-53, 72, 78-79, 285; René Bray, *La Formation de la Doctrine Classique en France* (Paris, 1927), 213*ff.* and 319; Allan H. Gilbert, *Literary Criticism: Plato to Dryden* (New York, 1940), 461 and index, s.v., "admiration."

3. Bywater, *op. cit.* For the relationship of wonder (*to thaumaston*) and astonishment (*ekplexis*), see Aristotle, *Topics,* 4. 5. 126bl3*ff.*

4. Gorgias, *Helena,* 9, ed. Otto Immisch (Berlin, 1927), though the text seems untrustworthy; E. E. Sikes, *The Greek View of Poetry* (London, 1931); Max Pohlenz, "Die Anfänge der griechischen Poetik," *Nachr. d. Gott. Ges. d. Wiss.* (1920), 167*ff.*

5. Gilbert, *op. cit.,* 15.

6. Leonhard Spengel, ed., *Rhetores Graeci* (Leipzig, 1853-56), II, 455.

7. Plotinus, *Enneades,* ed. Emile Bréhier (Collection Bude, Paris, 1924); translation revised from Stephen McKenna, *The Ethical Treatises* (London, 1926).

8. Horace Leonard Jones, ed., tr., *The Geography of Strabo* (Loeb Library, London, 1917), I, 23.

9. Polybius, *The Histories,* ed., tr. W. R. Paton (Loeb Library, London, 1922), 1, 377, 379.

10. Plutarch, *Moralia,* ed., tr. Frank Cole Babbitt (Loeb Library, London, 1927), 1.

11. Cited by Sikes, *op. cit.,* 112.

12. Aristotle, *Rhetorica,* tr. W. Rhys Roberts in W. D. Ross, ed., *The Works of Aristotle* (Oxford, 1946), XI. I have revised the second sentence.

13. Cited and translated by G. L. Hendrickson, "The Origin and Meaning of the Ancient Characters of Style," *American Journal of Philology,* XXVI (1905), 255-56. I have substituted "astonished" for "moved" toward the end of the next-to-last sentence. Text, Augustus Mayer, ed., *Theophrasti Peri Lexeos Libri Fragmenta* (Leipzig, 1910), 14-15.

14. T. H. Moxon, tr., *Aristotle's Poetics, Demetrius on Style* (London, 1934); I have made some revisions. Text, W. Rhys Roberts, ed. (Cambridge, 1902).

15. [Longinus,] *On the Sublime,* ed., tr. W. Rhys Roberts (Cambridge, 1907). There is an excellent translation by Benedict Einarson (Chicago, 1945).

16. Cicero, *De Oratore . . . De Partitions Oratoria,* ed. H. Rackham (Loeb Library, London, 1942), II, 329, 337, 355, 365.

17. Quintilian, *Institutes of Oratory,* tr. John Selby Watson (London, 1909-10), II, 78, 87. I have substituted "wonder" for "admiration" in the last two sentences. L. Rademacher, ed. (Leipzig, 1935).

18. *Patrologia Latina,* XLII, 90.

19. *Opera Omnia,* ed. Augustus Borgnet (Paris, 1890), VI, 30a-31a. My translation.

20. My translation.

21. The relevant passages are reprinted and translated by Ruth Kelso, "Girolamo Fracastoro, *Naugerius sive De Poetica Dialogus,*" *University of Illinois Studies in Language and Literature,* IX (1924), *75ff.*

22. *Ibid.,* 58-59.

23. My translation. The texts are cited in Bernard Weinberg, "The Poetic Theories of Minturno," *Studies in Honor of Frederick W. Shipley* (St. Louis, 1942), 104*n*6(l), 110*n*l7.

24. E. K. Chambers, *William Shakespeare* (Oxford, 1930), I, 412 and II, 188.

25. Brooke, *op. cit.*

26. J. Churton Collins, ed., *The Plays and Poems of Robert Greene* (Oxford, 1905), I, 264.

27. Henry Harvey Wood, ed., *The Plays of John Marston* (Edinburgh, 1934-39), I.

28. Brooke, *op. cit.*

29. Ben Jonson, *Works,* ed. C. H. Herford, Percy Simpson, and Evelyn Simpson (Oxford, 1925-52), IV.

30. A. H. Bullen, ed., *The Works of Thomas Middleton* (Boston, 1885-86), VI, 370-71.

Reason Panders Will

For the interpretation of Hamlet's phrase, "reason panders will," I am deeply indebted to Lily B. Campbell, *Shakespeare's Tragic Heroes* (Cambridge, 1930), 146.

1. "Definitio . . . est imitatio actionis illustris, voluntarie perfectae, cui inest vis universalis circa res praestantiores, non autem particularis de singula re praestanti: qua quidem imitatione animi recta afficiuntur affectione per'mise- ricordiam atque terrorem in eis orta." *Voluntarie* can also be construed as an adjective without significant change of meaning. "Paraphrasis in librum Poeticae Aristotelis," tr. Jacobus Mantinus, ed. Fridericus Heidenhain, *Jahrbiicher fur classische Philologie,* 17th Supplementband (1890), 359. For Renaissance editions see Lane Cooper and Alfred Gudeman. *A Bibliography of the Poetics of Aristotle* (Cornell Studies in English, XI, New Haven, 1928), s.n. Averroes.

2. A medieval commonplace: see Alexander of Hales, *Summa,* 1. 1. 1. ad 1 and ad 2 (Quaracchi, 1924), I.

3. Charles R. S. Harris, *Duns Scotus* (Oxford, 1927), II, 28*ff.*; see also Arthur C. McGiffert, *History of Christian Thought* (New York, 1932-35), II, *299ff.;* D. E. Sharp, *Franciscan Philosophy at Oxford* (Oxford, 1930), 336-41. *ST,* 1-2, 8. 1. For St. Thomas' doctrine, see Michael Wittmann, *Die Ethik des Hl. Thomas von Aquin* (Munich, 1933); Etienne Gilson, *Moral Values and the Moral Life,* tr. Leo R. Ward (London, 1931).

4. *Phaedra, 177ff.; Metamorphoses,* 7. 20-21. These passages are cited by Melanch- thon in his refutation of Stoic fatalism, *Corpus Reformatorm* XVI, 42-50 189-201, 336-46.

5. Craig, *Enchanted Glass, op. cit.,* 116.

6. Ludwig Schutz, *Thomas-Lexicon* (Paderborn, 1895), *s.vv.*

7. C. F. Tucker Brooke and Nathaniel Burton Paradise, eds., *English Drama: 1580-1642* (Boston, 1933).

8. A. W. Verity, ed., *Thomas Heywood* (London, n.d.).

9. The punctuation is from Q1.

10. G. W. Kitchin, ed., *Bacon's "Advancement of Learning"* (Everyman's Library, London, 1930), 132.

11. Lancelot Andrewes, *Lectures* (London, 1657), 256.

12. Elmer E. Stoll, *Othello* (Minneapolis, 1915); Elmer E Stoll, *Art and Artifice in Shakespeare* (Cambridge, 1933), *6ff.;* Craig, *Shakespeare, op. cit.,* 715-16.

13. Jewel, *op. cit.,* 70.

14. In the following analysis I obviously owe a good deal to Walter Clyde Curry's *Shakespeare's Philosophical Patterns* (Baton Rouge, 1937).

15. Kitchin, *op. cit.,* 146.

16. Simpson, *op. cit.*

Appendix I
The Ancient Quarrel Between History & Poetry

1. Curry, *op. cit.,* xi-xii.

II

TRADITION & POETIC STRUCTURE

Poetry, Structure, and Tradition

1. Archibald MacLeish, *Collected Poems: 1917-1952* (Boston, 1952), 41.

2. *Shorter Oxford English Dictionary* (Oxford, 1933), s.v. See also James Craig La Driere, "Poetry and Prose" in Joseph T. Shipley, ed., *Dictionary of World Literature* (New York, 1943).

3. Aristotle, *Poetics,* 1. See Gerald Else, *Aristotle's Poetics: The Argument* (Cambridge, Mass., 1957), *ad loc.*

4. St. Petersburg, April 21, 1914.

5. The theory and point of view here developed closely parallels that of Wellek in René Wellek and Austin Warren, *Theory of Literature* (New York, 1949), Chapter 12.

6. St. Augustine, *Confessions,* tr. E. B. Pusey (Everyman's Library, London, 1907), 274-75.

1. Statius, *Silvae,* 5. 4, ed. Henri Frere, tr. H. H. Izaac (Paris, 1944), 205.

2. J. W. Mackail, *Latin Literature* (New York, 1895), 189-90.

3. Robert Yelverton Tyrrell, *Anthology of Latin Poetry* (London, 1901), 302-03; D. A. Slater, *The Silvae of Statius* (Oxford, 1908), 22-23; H. W. Garrod, ed., *The Oxford Book of Latin Verse* (Oxford, 1912), 495-500; E. E. Sikes, *Roman Poetry* (London, 1923), 86-88; J. H. Mozley, ed., tr., *Statius* (London, New York,1928), xii; J. Wight Duff, *Literary History of Rome in the Silver Age* (London, 1927), 492; Philip Schuyler Allen, *The Romanesque Lyric* (Chapel Hill, 1928), 76-77. In this last the Latin text is printed in an appendix (321) with the Argus passage excised.

4. H. W. Garrod, ed., *The Poetical Works of John Keats* (Oxford, 1939), 460, 533.

5. John W. Cunliffe, ed., *The Complete Works of George Gascoigne* (Cambridge, 1907-10), II, 143; Frank Allen Patterson, ed., *The Student's Milton* (New York, 1931), 160.

6. This is deliberate with Gascoigne: "Certayne notes of Instruction," *Works,* I, 465#.

7. Patterson, *op. cit.,* 159.

8. Whether there is any such playing of accent against quantity in classical Latin is still under dispute.

9. W. H. Fyfe, in fact, reduces the four lines to one—"But my sad eyes their nightly vigil keep"—and expands the second line into two in order to achieve a sonnet. Garrod, *The Oxford Book of Latin Verse,* 495. Slater, *op. cit.,* 23.

10. E. de Selincourt and Helen Darbshire, eds., *Works* (Oxford, 1946), III, 8-9.

11. *Silvae,* 5. 1. 34-35; Ovid, *Metamorphoses,* 14. 708.

12. Friedrich Vollmer, ed., *Silvae* (Leipzig, 1898), 10; *Silvae,* 3. 5. 37-42.

1. Richard von Mises, *Positivism* (Cambridge, Mass., 1951), 289.

2. Harold R. Walley and J. Harold Wilson, *The Anatomy of Literature* (New York, 1934), 143, 144.

3. Scholiast cited in Otto Bird, "The Seven Liberal Arts" in Shipley, *op. cit.*, 55; Joel E. Spingarn, *A History of literary Criticism in the Renaissance* (2nd ed., New York, 1908), 24-27; David Hume, *Philosophical Works* (Boston, Edinburgh, 1854), III, 264; von Mises, *op. cit.*

4. H. M. Margouliouth, cd., *The Poems and Letters* (Oxford, 1927), II.

5. T. S. Eliot, *Selected Essays* (new ed., New York, 1950), 254; Helen C. White, Ruth C. Wallerstein, and Ricardo Quintana, eds., *Seventeenth Century Verse and Prose* (New York, 1951), I, 454.

6. Eliot, *op. cit.*, 253-54, 255.

7. John M. Berdan, ed., *The Poems of John Cleveland* (New Haven, 1911), 80-81.

8. Wright Thomas and Stuart Gerry Brown, eds., *Reading Poems* (New York, 1941), 702; Douglas Bush, *English Literature in the Earlier Seventeenth Century* (Oxford, 1945), 163.

9. My translation, except for "the brief sum of life forbids our opening a long account with hope," which is Gildersleeve's; see Paul Shorey and Gordon J. Lang, eds., *Horace: Odes and Epodes* (rev. ed., Chicago, 1910), *ad loc.*

10. W. Mackay Mackenzie, ed., *The Poems of William Dunbar* (Edinburgh, 1932), 20-23.

11. Ronald B. McKerrow, ed., *The Works of Thomas Nashe* (London, 1904-10), III, 283.

12. *Contra Gentiles*, 3. 27, 29-31, 36, 48, in *Opera Omnia* (Rome, 1882-1948), XIV; Anton C. Pegis, ed., *Basic Writings of Saint Thomas Aquinas* (New York, 1945), II.

13. James Joyce, A *Portrait of the Artist as a Young Man* (Modern Library, New York, 1928), 273-75.

14. McKerrow, *op. cit.*, IV, 440.

15.	This essay has been refuted by Frank Towne, "Logic, Lyric, and Drama," *Modern Philology,* LI (1953-54), 265-68.

Convention as Structure

1.	Fred N. Robinson, ed., *The Complete Works of Geoffrey Chaucer* (Boston 1933), 2; John Livingston Lowes, *Geoffrey Chaucer* (Boston, 1934), 198; Robert Dudley French, *A Chaucer Handbook* (2nd ed., New York 1947) 203.

2.	French, *op. cit.,* 203.

3.	Robinson, *op. cit.,* 2-3.

4.	William Witherle Lawrence, *Chaucer and the Canterbury Tales* (New York, 1950), 38.

5.	Robert Armstrong Pratt and Karl Young, "The Literary Framework of the Canterbury Tales" in W. F. Bryan and Germaine Dempster, eds., *Sources and Analogues of Chaucer's "Canterbury Tales"* (Chicago, 1941), 2.

6.	George Lyman Kittredge, *Chaucer and His Poetry* (Cambridge, Mass., 1915), 149: "There is not one chance in a hundred that he had not gone on a Canterbury pilgrimage himself."

7.	Robinson, *op. cit.,* 663.

8.	*Ibid.,* 315.

9.	4. 1245*ff.* G. C. Macaulay, ed., *The Complete Works of John Gower* (Oxford, 1901), II. 335*ff.*

10.	Suggested by Emile Legouis, *Geoffrey Chaucer,* tr. L. Lailavoix (London, 1928), 85-86.

11.	Howard R. Patch, "Characters in Medieval Literature," *Modern Language Notes,* XL (1925), 1-14.

12.	Lines 812-16 in the Middle English version; 796-800 in the original. Ernest Langlois, ed., *Le Roman de la Rose* (Société des Anciens Textes Français, CXII, Paris, 1920), II.

13.	M.E., 160-61, original, 150-51; M.E., 220-21, original, 208-09.

14.	Kittredge, *Chaucer,* 166; Lawrence, *op. cit.,* 30.

1. William Oldys and Thomas Birch, eds., *The Works of Sir Walter Ralegh* (Oxford,   1829), II, xlvi.

2. Richard Hooker, *Laws of Ecclesiastical Polity* in *Works,* ed. John Keble (7th ed., Oxford, 1888), II, 247-48.

3. St. Thomas Aquinas, *Summa Theologica* in *Opera Omnia* (Leonine ed., Rome, 1882-1948). Hereafter *ST.*

4. Some details of the following interpretations have been anticipated by other scholars, particularly by the Indian scholar, Ranjee. See William Shakespeare, *The Poems,* ed. Hyder Edward Rollins (The New Variorum, Philadelphia, 1938), 323-31, 559-83.

5. Alexander B. Grosart, ed., *Robert Chester's "Loves Martyr"* (London, 1878), 169 (top pagination).

6. John Gerard, *The Autobiography of an Elizabethan,* tr. Philip Caraman (London, 1951), 48: "I must not forget to mention a certain lady and her husband (they were gentlefolk) who made a vow of chastity. . . . I kept in touch with them for many years afterward and I can say that during all that time they remained faithful to their vow." See also on Mrs. Line: ". . . she made a vow of chastity, a virtue she practiced in her married life." (86) Father Gerard was a noted Jesuit; the events described occurred in the 1590s.

    The only testimony relating to the circumstances of this poem, if it does relate to this poem, is the remark made in passing by Fr. Henry More, SJ. (1660) about Ann, Lady Stourton: "a daughter of Edward, Earl of Derby, and sister to the Stanley whose epitaph Shakespeare wrote." (Rollins, *op. cit.,* 578) There were five sisters (John Seacome, *The History of the House of Stanley* [Preston, 1793], 130-31), but none of them seems to fit the apparent specifications of the poem. Sir John Sainsbury's wife, of course, was a natural daughter of the fourth Earl of Derby, and hence a niece of Lady Stourton's, as was Dorothy Halsall, her sister, with whom Sir John seems to have been in love. (Carleton Brown, ed., *Poems by Sir John Salisbury and Robert Chester*

[E.E.T.S., e.s. cxiii: London, 1914], xxxviii*ff.*). I add, for the fun of it, that Sainsbury's motto, "posse et nolle nobile" (Brown, xxix) is the theme of Shakespeare's Sonnet 94.

7.   Grosart, *op, cit.,* 177, 181-86 (top pagination).

8.   The last line of the *Epode* appears in *England's Parnassus* (1600).

9.   A. J. Denomy, "An Inquiry into the Origins of Courtly Love," *Medieval Studies,* Pontifical Institute of Medieval Studies, Toronto, VI (1944), 175-260, especially 209.

10. Robert Ellrodt in *Shakespeare Survey* 15 (1962) offers new material on the Phoenix tradition. However, further investigation of that tradition is unlikely to yield useful results. The symbolism of *The Phoenix and Turtle,* except for the bare idea of the Phoenix, is sufficiently explicated in the poem, as it is in the following epigram on Queen Jane and Edward VI:

> Phaenix Jana jacet nate Phaenice: dolendum est
> Saecula Phaenices nulla tulesse duas.

The Phoenix as Phoenix offers no problem.

But there are problems to be investigated. 1) We need a history of married chastity, particularly in the decade before 1601. It involved a mutual vow to cohabit without intercourse, as in the case of the Virgin Mary. (*ST,* 3. 28. 4) According to Father Gerard it was practiced by at least two couples in this decade. 2) We need a few paragraphs on the customary order of funerals. 3) We need to classify the poem. It is hyperbolical compliment of a conventional sort: the lovers are the Ideas. 4) We would like to know the occasion of the poem. What are the referents, real or supposititious? And what occasioned Shakespeare to write of them? The latter question can be partially answered from context. The "new compositions" appended to *Loves Martyr* were commissioned (see Jonson's *Praeludium*), and Shakespeare's poem was available to Marston and hence may have been the starting point for the others. But Marston's poem has different referents, for his birds have issue. As for the identity of the birds,

I have been unable to find any gold in the only clue I know, the statement that Shakespeare wrote an epitaph for a daughter of Edward, Earl of Derby (*supra,* note 6). Finally, there are the two important problems 5) of the stylistic tradition and 6) of the value of the poem.

Plots & Errors

1. A. C. Bradley, *Shakespearean Tragedy* (London, 1912), 89; Allardyce Nicoll, *Studies in Shakespeare* (London, 1927), 43.

2. E. M. Forster, *Aspects of the Novel* (New York, 1927), 144: "The plot, then, is the novel in its logical intellectual aspect."

3. Henry James, *The Ambassadors* (New York, 1909), II, 200-01 (Bk. X, ch. 3).

4. Mark Twain, *The Adventures of Huckleberry Finn,* introductory Notice; André Gide, *Journal of "The Counterfeiters"* (New York, 1951), July 11, 1919 entry; Forster, *op. cit.,* 152; Sherwood Anderson in Robert E. Spiller, et. al., eds., *Literary History of the United States* (New York, 1948), II, 1230-31; Elizabeth Bowen, *Collected Impressions* (London, 1950), 249; Edwin Muir, *The Structure of the Novel* (London, 1928), 38, 39, 40, 43, 47-48.

5. Ben Jonson, *Masque of Blackness,* line 6 in *Works,* ed. C. H. Hereford Percy Simpson, and Evelyn Simpson (Oxford, 1925-52).

6. *Discoveries,* 2747-49: "For the episodes and digressions in a fable are the same that household stuff and other furniture are in a house."

7. Samuel T. Coleridge, *Lectures and Notes on Shakespeare* (London, 1897), 472.

8. T. W. Baldwin, *Shakespeare's Five-Act Structure* (Urbana, 1947); Marvin Theodore Herrick, *Comic Theory in the Sixteenth Century* (Urbana, 1950); Madeleine Doran, *Endeavors of Art* (Madison, 1954).

9. Kittredge, *ad loc.*

10. Iodocus Willichius, ed. (Cologne, 1567), on *Andria,* 1. L; "Quod autem actus fabularum partimur in scenas, aliamque primam, aliam secundam, et sic deinceps dicimus, quam perite et intelligenter id

fiat, quaerendum puto. Equidem libere ut dicam, grammaticorum hanc, non poetarum, esse partitionem arbitror." *Orationes, Epistolae, et Poemata* (Leipzig, 1698), 696: "omnino autem illam inutilem et supervacaneam, et a stultis literatoribus excogitatum actuum in scenas divisionem, quaeso te, ut tollas." Baldwin, *op. cit.,* cites these passages and the Jonson. (277)

11. Quintilian, 3. 5. 5.
12. Allan H. Gilbert, *Literary Criticism: Plato to Dryden* (New York, 1940), 511.
13. Baldwin, *op. cit.,* ch. 2; text, ed. Paul Wessner (Leipzig, 1902), 2 vols.
14. 5. 4. 255-56.
15. *Discoveries,* 2625.
16. Giraldi Cinthio in Gilbert, *op. cit.,* 254.
17. Gilbert, 528-29.

Tradition & Modernity

1. References to Stevens' *Collected Poems* (New York, 1954) are by page number in parentheses.
2. *The Necessary Angel* (New York, 1951), 26.
3. *Prelude,* 1. 337-44.
4. Lines 126-33 and 800-08.
5. *Life on a Battleship* in *Opus Posthumus,* ed. Samuel French Morse (New York, 1957), 79.
6. *The Necessary Angel,* 86.

III

The Problem of Form

1. William A. Ringler, Jr., ed., *The Poems of Sir Philip Sidney* (Oxford, 1962), 105, lines, 67-68.

The Problem of Style

1. Hart Crane, *Atlantis.*
2. Emily Dickinson, *There's a certain slant of light* (258).
3. There have been many attempts to describe the rhythms of English prose, and how successful they have been becomes clear when we notice that scarcely anyone builds on the work of his predecessors. Yet, the ancients write clearly and securely about prose rhythm, and there is much evidence that not only did speakers consciously employ certain rhythms but also that their audiences explicitly recognized them. Such an open employment of recognizable rhythmical patterns is not in our tradition, certainly not in prose, and it is becoming somewhat rare in poetry. This discrepancy between ancient and contemporary experience calls for explanation.
4. Diodorus Siculus, 12. 53. 2-4, tr. C. H. Oldfather (London, 1950).

How Shall the Poem be Written?

1. John Donne, *Elegy,* 10. 14.
2. Sir Philip Sidney, *Astrophil and Stella,* 91. 13.
3. *The Collected Poems and Epigrams of J. V. Cunningham* (Chicago, 1971), 84.
4. *Ibid.,* Epigram 90.
5. *Ibid.,* Epigram 83.
6. *Ibid.,* "To What Strangers, What Welcome," Poem 8 (sometimes entitled *Miramar Beach*).
7. This paragraph and several sentences on page 267 are from my essay "The Problem of Form."

IV

Ideal Fiction

1. *Ars Poetica,* 128-35.
2. Chaucer, *The Knight's Tale,* 1668-69.
3. Aristotle, *Rhetoric,* 2. 24. 1402a.
4. Cicero, *Rhetorica ad Herennium,* 1. 8. 13.

The Renaissance in England

1. Thomas Campian, *Observations in the Art of English Poesy.*
2. Francis Bacon, *Of the Advancement of Learning,* I.
3. *The Life of the Renowned Sir Philip Sidney,* cited from Mona Wilson, *Sir Philip Sidney* (New York, 1932), 100.
4. *Evil May Day* is the anthology title for the scene in *The Book of Sir Thomas More,* often ascribed to Shakespeare.
5. Wilson, *op. cit.,* 100-01.
6. *The Autobiography of Thomas Whythorne,* ed. James M. Osborn (London, 1962), 80, 82.
7. See my essay "The Problem of Form," 249.
8. For the relationship of Campion and Donne to the Latin elegiac tradition, see my "Campion and Propertius," *Philological Quarterly* XXXI (January 1951), 96; Donne's *Canonization* has the same internal form.

Lyric Style in the 1590s

1. The character is called Lorenzo, Jr. in the 1601 edition of the play (produced 1598), Edward Knowell in the revised 1616 edition.
2. C. S. Lewis, *English Literature in the Sixteenth Century* (Oxford, 1954), 64-65.
3. Cicero, *Orator,* 42.

4. Thomas Kyd, *The Spanish Tragedy*, 3. 2. 1-4.

5. I owe this date to Professor Walter R. Davis of the University of Notre Dame.

6. Cicero, *Orator*, 76.

With That Facility

1. *Love's Labour's Lost, 1598.* Shakespeare Quarto Facsimiles, No. 10 (Oxford, 1957). All quotations are from this text.

2. R. B. McKerrow, "Booksellers, Printers, and the Stationers' Trade" in *Shakespeare's England: An Account of the Life & Manners of His Age* (Oxford, 1932), H, 231. Percival Vivian, ed., *Campion's Works* (Oxford, 1909), 34.

3. E. K. Chambers, *The Elizabethan Stage* (Oxford, 1923), III, 461; IV, 48; III, 483, 485.

4. E. K. Chambers, *William Shakespeare: A Study of Facts and Problems* (Oxford 1930), II, 188.

5. "Preface to R. Greene's 'Menaphon'" in Ronald B. McKerrow, ed., *The Works of Thomas Nashe* (Oxford, 1958), III, 312.

6. *The Collected Poems of Joseph Hall,* ed. A. Davenport (Liverpool, 1949), 16.

7. Chambers, *Shakespeare*, II, 189, 195, 194.

8. *The Arte of English Poesie* (London, 1589; Kent, Ohio, 1970, facsimile ed.) 3. 2,p. 115; 3.1, p. 114-15; 1. 22, p. 36.

9. Capell in Variorum (Philadelphia, n.d.), 4th impression, ad 4. 3. 317-22 and 330-38, p. 193.

10. *The Two Gentlemen of Verona*, 3. 1. 283.

11. McKerrow, *Works of Nashe*, III, 312.

12. Louise Brown Osborn, *The Life, Letters, and Writings of John Hoskyns* (New Haven, 1937), 125.

13. Ben Jonson, *Works,* ed. C. H. Herford, Percy Simpson, and Evelyn Simpson (Oxford, 1925-52), VIII, 584.

1. Fulke Greville, *Poems and Dramas,* ed. Geoffrey Bullough (Oxford, 1945), I, 161.

2. Joseph Quincy Adams, ed., *Hamlet* (Boston, 1929), *ad loc.*

3. A. C. Bradley, *Shakespearean Tragedy* (New York, 1955), 79.

4. Harley Granville-Barker, *Prefaces to Shakespeare: Hamlet* (Princeton, 1946), 258.

5. Maynard Mack, "The World of Hamlet," *Yale Review* XLI (1952), 506, 522.

6. Saxo Grammaticus, *Danish History* in Joseph Satin, ed., *Shakespeare and His Sources* (Boston, 1966), 387.

7. Francois de Belleforest, *Tragic Stories* in Satin, *ibid.,* 399.

8. Pelican and Signet editions, *ad loc.* Maynard Mack says of *Lear* that "it is peculiarly the play of [Shakespeare's] that speaks with urgency to our time." "'We Came Crying Hither': An Essay on Some Characteristics of *King Lear"* in Gerald W. Chapman, ed., *Essays on Shakespeare* (Princeton, 1965), 138.

9. *Hamlet,* 1. 4. 37 reads in Quarto "of a doubt," but a pronoun is needed, either "it" or "'em."

10. St. Thomas Aquinas, *Summa Theologica,* 2-2. 43.

11. Richard Hooker, *Of the Laws of Ecclesiastical Polity,* 4. 12. 2 (Everyman's Library, London, 1907), I, 406.

Sorting Out

1. The poem numbers in parentheses are those in Thomas H. Johnson, ed., *The Poems of Emily Dickinson* (Cambridge, Mass., 1955). Texts have been normalized.

2. *L,* followed by volume and page, refers to Thomas H. Johnson, ed., *The Letters of Emily Dickinson* (Cambridge, Mass., 1958).

3. George W. Noyes, comp., *The Religious Experience of John Humphrey Noyes* (New York, 1923), 138-40, 143, 353.

"I Had a Terror Since September"

1. William Dean Howells, *Literary Friends and Acquaintances,* ed. David F. Hiatt and Edwin H. Cady (Bloomington, Ind., 1968), p. 10.

2. Albert J. Gelpi, *The Poet in America: 1650 to the Present* (Lexington, Mass., 1973), p. 298.

3. Jay Leyda, *The Years and Hours of Emily Dickinson* (1970; reprint of New Haven, 1960), II, 38. Hereafter *Leyda*. The note is dated late 1861.

4. *The Letters of Emily Dickinson,* ed. Thomas H. Johnson (Cambridge, Mass., 1965), II, 404. Hereafter *Letters,* cited by volume and page.

5. Thomas H. Johnson, *Emily Dickinson: An Interpretive Biography* (New York, 1967), p. 81. Hereafter *Johnson.*

6. *The Poems of Emily Dickinson,* ed. Thomas H. Johnson (Cambridge, Mass., 1963). Quotations from the poems are identified in the text by the number of the poem in this edition. Texts have been normalized in spelling, punctuation, and lineation: see *Poems,* I, p. lxvii.

7. *Letters,* II, 436 and I, 113 (see also p. 149).

8. "Letter to a Young Contributor," *Atlantic Monthly,* vol. IX, No. LIV (April 1862). No page numbers.

9. *Letters,* II, 408.

10. *Johnson,* p. 203.

11. Harriet Beecher Stowe, *Oldtown Folks* (Cambridge, Mass., 1966), pp. 79-80. (chapter 4). First edition: Boston, 1869.

12. *The Heart of Hawthorne's Journals,* ed. Newton Arvin (1967), p. 4.

13. *Letters,* I. 32.

14. E. M. Forster, "De Senectudine," *London Magazine* (Nov. 1957). Cited from Kenneth Marsden, *The Poems of Thomas Hardy* (New York, 1969), 62.

15. George S. Merriam, *The Life and Times of Samuel Bowles* (New York, 1885), II, 413; see also p. 436.

16. *The Journal of Richard Henry Dana, Jr.,* ed. Robert F. Lucid (Cambridge, Mass., 1968), I, 173: "Aunt Martha" on the death of Washington Allston: "Her only painful thought was that she was not with him at the moment. There might have been a word or a look of recognition."

17. Letters, III, 711. H. Humphrey, *Memoir of Rev. Nathan W. Fiske* (Amherst, 1850), p.69.

18. *Letters,* I, 282-83. Leyda, I, 264.

19. *Oldtown Folks,* p. 115 (chapter 6), and p. 454 (chapter 33).

20. T. W. Higginson, "An Open Portfolio," *Christian Union,* 42 (Sept. 25, 1890), 392-3; Blake, Caesar R. and Carlton F. Wells, eds., *The Recognition of Emily Dickinson* (Ann Arbor, 1964), 3-10.

21. Bernard Weisberger, *They Gathered at the River* (Boston, 1958), 27.

22. *Letters,* I. 27-8.

23. *Letters,* I, 305-6.

24. Part 2, section 13.

25. William James, *Varieties of Religious Experience* (The Modern Library), pp. 218 (Lecture 9) and 280 (Lectures 11, 12, and 13).

26. p. 284.

27. *Oldtown Folks,* p. 353 (chap. 26).

"He Never Saw Me in This Life"

1. *Letters,* II, 408.

2. *Letters,* II, 460.

3. *Johnson,* 85.

4. Alexis de Tocqueville, *Democracy in America, ed.* Phillips Bradley (New York, Vintage Press, n.d.), II, 500 (Appendix III).

5. *Letters,* I, 36.

6. Johnson, *The Poems,* I, xviii.

7. *Leyda,* II, 34, 68, 76, 77. *Letters,* III, 784-5.

8. Richard B. Sewall, ed. "The Lyman Letters," *Massachusetts Review* (Autumn, 1965), 761, 731, 763.

9. *Leyda,* II, 472.

10. *Leyda,* II, 76.

11. *Letters*, III, 730.

12. *Letters*, II, 450.

13. Daniel J. Boorstein, *The Americans: The National Experience* (New York, n.d.), 348.

14. John Evangelist Walsh, *The Hidden Life of Emily Dickinson* (New York, 1971), 140.

15. *Letters*, II, 409.

16. Introduction (by T. W. Higginson) to Emily Dickinson, *Poems* (Boston, 1890), [iii].

17. pp. 82 and 152 (Chapters 5 and 9).

18. *Leyda*, 167-9; *Poems*: #3.

19. *Leyda*, II, 43, 48, 46.

20. *Letters*, II, 408, 563.

21. *Letters*, II, 460, 461.

22. *Leyda*, II, 472.

23. *Springfield Daily Republican*, May 18, 1886. *Leyda*, II, 473, omitting the last sentence of the quotation. Martha Dickinson Bianchi, *Emily Dickinson Face to Face* (Boston and New York, 1932), 104-5 (complete).

24. *Leyda*, II, 296.

25. *Leyda*, II, 297.

26. *Leyda*, II, 357, 377. Charles Dickens, *Great Expectations*, Chapter 8.

27. *Letters*, II, 412.

28. George Frisbie Whicher, *This Was a Poet* (Ann Arbor, 1957 p.b.), 96.

29. Thomas Wentworth Higginson, "Emily Dickinson's Letters," *Atlantic Monthly*, 68 (Oct. 1891), 452.

30. p. 235 (Chapter 18).

"The Vision Pondered Long"

1. Ruth Miller, *The Poetry of Emily Dickinson* (Middletown, Conn., 1968), 80-81.

2. de Tocqueville, *Democracy in America*, II, 202, 209, 212, 213.

3. *Johnson*, 40-41.

4. *Century Dictionary*, s.v., "sign" 8b.

5. *My Wife and I* (New York, 1871: AMS Press, reprint Riverside ed., New York, 1967), 50-51, 131 (Chapters 4 and 11).

6. Edgar Johnson, *Charles Dickens* (New York, 1952), I, 37g.

7. *Oldtown Folks,* 208 (Chapter 16).

8. J. G. Holland, *The Complete Poetical Writings* (New York, 1907), 153. *Kathrina* (New York, 1867), 31.

9. John Humphrey Noyes, *Strange Cults and Utopias of 19th Century America* (New York, 1966), a reprint of Noyes, *History of American Socialisms* (Philadelphia, 1870), 592 (Chapter 44).

10. Arvin, *Hawthorne's Journals,* 4.

11. *Oldtown Folks,* 482 (Chapter 35).

12. *The King of Folly Island and Other People* (Boston, 1888), reprinted in *Tales of New England* (Boston and New York, 1895), 266-68.

13. *Letters,* I, 277. *Oldtown Folks,* 583 (Chapter 47), II Kings, 2:11.

14. *Leyda,* II, 17.

15. [Helen Hunt Jackson], *Mercy Philbrick's Choice* (Boston, 1876), p. 286 (Chapter 13).

16. John Greenleaf Whittier, *The Complete Poetical Works* (Cam-bridge Edition: Boston and New York, 1894), 101.

17. John Hyde, Jun., *Mormonism: Its Leaders and Designs* (New York, 1857), 84, 85.

18. Noyes, p. 620. *Letters,* I, 104.

19. *Letters,* II, 377.

20. "Introduction" (1878).

21. *Oldtown Folks,* Introduction, 30-31; 216, 214 (Chapter 17).

22. *Letters,* II, 375.

Edwin Arlington Robinson

1. The poem numbers in parentheses are those in Thomas H. Johnson, ed., *The* York, 1940), 101; hereafter *SL. Untriangulated Stars,* ed. Denham Sutcliffe (Cambridge, Mass., 1947), 150; hereafter *US. SL,* 90. *US,* 124. *Collected Poems* (New York, 1928), 24; hereafter *CP. SL,* 75. *CP,* 177, 178. *Selections from the Letters of Thomas Sergeant Perry,* ed.

E. A. Robinson (New York, 1929), 6. *US,* 155, 244, 246. *SL,* 137, 75. *US,* 216, 24 (September 13, 1891). *CP,* 314. *SL,* 32, 103. *US,* 119, 161. *SL,* 163 (September 18, 1931).

2.   *CP,* 178, 52, 56, 544, 17, 188.

The Styles & Procedures of Wallace Stevens

1.   *The Harvard Advocate,* CXXV (Dec. 1938), 41-42, cited from Daniel Fuchs, *The Comic Spirit of Wallace Stevens* (Durham, N.C., 1963), 26-27*n*20.
2.   "It was William James, I think, who defined the difference between the professional and the amateur by saying that the latter interests himself especially in the result obtained, the former in the way in which he obtains it." Henri Bergson, *Mind-Energy: Lectures and Essays* (New York, 1920), 78.
3.   References to Stevens' *Collected Poems* (New York, 1954) are by page number in parentheses, to *The Necessary Angel* (New York, 1951) by page number preceded by *NA,* to *Opus Posthumous* (New York, 1957) by page number preceded by *OP.*
4.   In *The Course of a Particular* I read, with Yvor Winters, "ear" for "air," as originally printed in the *Hudson Review,* Spring 1951.

T. S. Eliot on Poetry & Poets

1.   T. S. Eliot, *On Poetry and Poets* (New York, 1957).

V

The Quest of the Opal

1.   The poems referred to in this essay can be found in *The Collected Poems and Epigrams of J. V. Cunningham* (Chicago, 1971).

INDEX

Eliot, T. S., xiii, xxviii, xxxv–xxxvii, xli, 3, 152, 225–231, 249, 283, 341, 354, 356–357, 559, 575, 583–586, 654, 660, 669–671. *See also titles of works*

Elizabethan age, liv, lxxi, 14, 16, 24, 54–55, 87, 108, 112, 142, 248, 271, 410, 436, 438, 446, 451,; class distinctions, 377–384; knowledge and learning, 385–389; literary innovations, 399–401; religion, 391–394; theatrical traditions, 287–291; Elizabethan literature, 22, 30–31, 397–398, 632; stage, xxxii, 41, 43, 64–65, 110, 115, 120, 129–130, 428, 678

Elyot, Sir Thomas, 375, 377, 378, 380, 401

Epigram (Campian), 391

Epigram 8 (Cunningham), 623

Epigram 17 (Cunningham), 603

Epigram 19 (Cunningham), 623, 634

Epigram 30, (Cunningham), x

Epigram 36 (Cunningham), 597

Epigram 54 (Cunningham), 623

Epigram 83 (Cunningham), 348

Epigram 90 (Cunningham), 347

Epigrams (Davies), 420

Erasmus, Desiderius, 13, 371, 373, 374

Eratosthenes, 77–78, 80, 85

Esprit, L' (Cunningham), 609

Essential oils are wrung (Dickinson), 478

Every Man in His Humour (Jonson), 410, 415

Every Man Out of His Humour (Jonson), 288, 290

Evil May Day, 375, 377

Experience of literature, 176–180, 449–452

Extracts from Addresses to the Academy of Fine Ideas (Stevens), 569, 580–581

Faerie Queene (Spenser), 98–102, 397, 623

Faithful Shepherdess (Fletcher), 64

Faith is a fine invention (Dickinson), 476

Fancy (Cunningham), 606

Meres, Francis, 428, 430

Merlin (Robinson), 626–627

Merry Wives of Windsor (Shakespeare), 291–292

Metamorphoses (Apuleius), 76

Metaphors of a Magnifico (Stevens), 570–571

Metaphysical Amorist, The (Cunningham), 609–610

Meter, liv, lvi, 109, 167–168, 173-175, 186–189, 197, 240, 314, 322, 330–331, 339–357, 397–401, 467–472, 605–606, 638, 663–667; classical, 345–346; Dickinson, 466–474; in everyday speech, 328, 350–353, 575, 669–670; parasitic, liv, 253–256, 339, 346, 348, 353–356; Traditional, 314, 322, 341, 344–352, 400–401, 467–468, 516, 626, 634, 641, 665

Middleton, Thomas, 122

Midsummer's Night Dream, A (Shakespeare), 62, 104–105, 114, 382, 631

Milton, John, 98, 128, 185–187, 197, 307, 357, 644

Mine by the right of the white election (Dickinson), 480

Minturno, Antonio, 97

Miramar Beach (Cunningham), 349, 628

Missing all prevented me, The (Dickinson), 487

Monday Morning (Cunningham), 344–345

Monocle de Mon Oncle, Le (Stevens), 305, 560, 570, 576

Montana Pastoral (Cunningham), 605, 649, 656

Moral choice, in tragedy, 28, 125–150

Moral poem, 412–413

Moral Poem, A (Cunningham), 605, 606, 608

More, Sir Thomas, 365, 369–371, 374, 377, 379, 632. *See also titles of works*

Mucedorus, 55, 117

Much Ado About Nothing (Shakespeare), 107, 113–114, 292, 363

Muir, Edwin, 286

My life closed twice (Dickinson), 473–474

My life had stood a loaded gun (Dickinson), 478

My period had come for prayer (Dickinson), 477

Mystery, in Shakespeare, 453–461

289, 291; tragicomedy, 291–292; tragedy, 3–11, 13–38, 42–43, 125, 135, 284–286, 291, 294; mystery, 453–461; process of moral choice, 28, 125–150; wonder, 13–38, 69–122, 457. *See also titles of works*

Sidney, Sir Philip, l, liii, 21, 43, 69, 97, 115, 183, 184, 216, 299, 329, 330, 344, 366, 370, 376, 378–381, 385, 392–393, 402, 414, 416, 423, 424, 625, 632. *See also titles of works*

Skelton, John, 205, 380, 387

Sledd, James, 335

Sleep (Statius), 181–197

Snow Man, The (Stevens), 312, 578–579

Soliman and Perseda (Kyd), 64

Some keep the Sabbath going to church (Dickinson), 477

Sonnet, 181–184, 187–188, 189–192, 196–197, 328

Sonnet LXIV (Shakespeare), 305

Sonnet LXVI (Shakespeare), 383

Sonnet LXXVI (Shakespeare), 431–432

Sonnet CXXXVIII (Shakespeare), 421–422

Sonnet sequence, 392–393, 396, 625, 626

Soul has bandaged moments, The (Dickinson), 464

Soul selects her own society, The (Dickinson), 477

Soul that hath a guest, The (Dickinson), 476

Soul, wilt thou toss again? (Dickinson), 479

Southwell, Robert, 412

Spanish Tragedy, The (Kyd), 50, 55, 110, 152–153, 161, 399

Spenser, Edmund, 97, 370, 381–382, 391, 394, 402, 410, 419, 428

Statius, Publius Papinius, lvii, 181–197, 221, 646

Steele Glas, The (Gascoigne), 185–186, 399

Stein, Gertrude, 574, 668

Stevens, Wallace, lxvi, 301–323, 342–343, 355–356, 556, 559–582, 644; poems, lxvi, 301, 304–305, 306, 307–318, 321–323; styles, 355–356, 559–582; subjects, 562–569. *See also titles of poems*

Stevenson, Robert Louis, 334

ACKNOWLEDGMENTS

The following notes include the original Acknowledgments included in *The Collected Essays of J. V. Cunningham*.

I

My Ph.D. dissertation, "Tragic Effect and Tragic Process . . . ." (Stanford University, 1945), was cut and revised and published as *Woe or Wonder* in 1951 by the University of Denver Press; by Alan Swallow, Denver, in 1960; Appendix I was published in *Poetry*, September 1949; and Appendix II in *Tradition and Poetic Structure*, 1960.

II

Tradition and Poetic Structure was published by Alan Swallow, Denver, in 1960. These essays, except for the ones on Statius and Stevens, were public lectures at the University of Chicago, Spring 1952. The Statius in earlier form was read at the Stanford Philological Society about 1938, and published in *Philological Quarterly*, October 1948; the Stevens was a public lecture at the University of Michigan, Spring 1949, and published in *Poetry*, December 1949. "My Fires & Fears Are Met: Sappho, Longinus, & the Rhetorical Tradition," third and last of the Evening Lectures given at UCLA in the Spring of 1973; also appeared in *Antaeus Magazine*. "Logic and Lyric," *Modern Philology*, August 1953. "Convention as Structure," *Modem Philology*, February 1952. "Idea as Structure," *ELH*, December 1952.

III

"The Problem of Form," read at Library of Congress, October 24, 1962; *Shenandoah,* Winter 1963. "The Problem of Style," Introduction to *The Problem of Style,* Fawcett, New York, 1966. "How Shall the Poem be Written?" read at University of Denver, November 17, 1966; *Denver Quarterly,* Spring 1967. "Graduate Training in English," *Carleton Miscellany,* Winter 1964.

IV

"Ideal Fiction," read at MLA, Chicago, 1967; *Shenandoah,* Winter 1968. "The Renaissance in England," Introduction to *The Renaissance in England,* Harcourt, Brace and World, New York, 1966. "Lyric Style in the 1590s," read in earlier form at Brandeis University, 1961; read in present form at English Institute, 1965; *Folio,* Brandeis, Spring 1966. "With That Facility," read at University of Denver Spring 1964; in present form in *Essays on Shakespeare,* ed. Gerald W. Chapman Princeton University Press, 1965; in shorter form in *Love's Labour's Lost,* Dell, New York, 1965. "In Shakespeare's Day," Introduction to *In Shakespeare's Day,* Fawcett, New York, 1970. "The Heart of His Mystery," read at MLA, Chicago, 1973 "Sorting Out," read at Mt. Holyoke College, November 14, 1967; at University of California, Berkeley, January 17, 1968; *The Southern Review,* Spring 1969; *Emily Dickinson: Lyric and Legend* (Sylvester & Orphanos, Los Angeles: 1980). "Edwin Arlington Robinson," *Denver Quarterly,* Spring 1968; in *Atlantic Brief Lives,* ed. Louis Kronenberger, Little, Brown, Boston, 1971. "The Styles and Procedures of Wallace Stevens," read in earlier form at University of Virginia, March 4, 1964; in present form at Bennington College, March 17, 1965, and at University of Denver, April 7, 1966; *Denver Quarterly,* Spring 1966. "T. S. Eliot on Poetry and Poets," *Virginia Quarterly,* Winter 1958.

The Quest of the Opal, Alan Swallow, Denver, 1950. "The Journal of John Cardan," *Sequoia,* Stanford, Winter 1961; in *The Journal of John Cardan,* Alan Swallow, Denver, 1964. "Several Kinds of Short Poem," read on Voice of America broadcast, September 21 and 24,1964; in *Poets on Poetry,* ed. Howard Nemerov, Basic Books, New York, 1966. "Technology and Poetry," read at Seton Hall University, April 16,1970; *Modern Occasions,* Spring 1972. "Shakespeare: Three Textual Notes": *Brandeis Essays in Literature,* ed. John Hazel Smith (Brandeis University: Waltham, MA: 1983). "A Few Remarks on Translating": *Inscape* 81, vol 36. "An Introduction to a Book of Common Verse," was to have been a brief introduction to an anthology of short poems in English that was never published. "An Interview with J. V. Cunningham": *The Iowa Review*, Fall 1985, vol 15, no 3.

ABOUT J. V. CUNNINGHAM

J. V. Cunningham was an American poet, critic, and teacher. Born in 1911 in Cumberland, Maryland, to Irish Catholic parents, he grew up in Billings, Montana. After high school, he worked as a messenger boy at the Denver Stock Exchange. The Great Crash of 1929 threw him out of work and reduced him to homelessness and penurious wandering in the Southwest, but he eventually enrolled in Stanford University, thanks to the encouragement of Yvor Winters. Cunningham later taught English and writing at several universities, including Harvard and Brandeis. The author of eighteen books, including ten of poetry, he was awarded two Guggenheim fellowships, the Academy of American Poets Fellowship, and grants from the National Institute of Arts and Letters and the National Endowment for the Arts. He died in Waltham, Massachusetts, in 1985.

www.ingramcontent.com/pod-product-compliance
Lightning Source LLC
Chambersburg PA
CBHW061128120626
46546CB00005B/1705